D.HALLOCK **HELL**
HEALING AND
RESISTANCE
VETERANS SPEAK

FOREWORD BY THICH NHAT HANH
PREFACE BY PHILIP BERRIGAN

THE PLOUGH PUBLISHING HOUSE

©1998 by The Plough Publishing House
of the Bruderhof Foundation
Farmington PA 15437 USA
Robertsbridge, E. Sussex TN32 5DR UK

"Let America Be America Again" is from *Collected
Poems* by Langston Hughes.
Copyright © 1994 by the Estate of Langston Hughes.
Reprinted by permission of Alfred A. Knopf Inc.

Jacket photograph, "jungle burning after napalm
airstrikes," by Kyoichi Sawada. Private Collection.
Used with permission of Horst Faas / Indochina
Photo Requiem Project, Inc.
Inset by Marcus Mommsen, Woodcrest Bruderhof

A catalog record for this book is available
from the British Library.

Library of Congress Cataloging-in-Publication Data

Hallock, Daniel William.
    Hell, healing, and resistance : veterans speak /
Daniel William Hallock ; foreword by Thich Nhat
Hanh.
        p. cm.
    Includes bibliographical references (p.).
    ISBN 0-87486-959-5
    1. War--Moral and ethical aspects. 2. War--
Psychological aspects. 3. Veterans--United States--
Interviews. I. Title.
U22.H35 1998
172´.42--dc21   98-29729
                                             CIP

ISBN pbk: 0-87486-962-5

Printed in the USA

D.HALLOCK**HELL
HEALING**AND
RESISTANCE
VETERANS SPEAK

FOREWORD BY THICH NHAT HANH
PREFACE BY PHILIP BERRIGAN

To the conscience of a nation...

Contents

Foreword

Thich Nhat Hanh

During an historic peace mission to the United States at the height of the Vietnam War, in 1966, Buddhist monk Thich Nhat Hanh traveled from his native Vietnam to meet with Secretary of Defense Robert McNamara, Catholic mystic Thomas Merton, and Martin Luther King, Jr., among others. A year later, he was nominated for the Nobel Peace Prize by King. Though still banned from his homeland, Thich Nhat Hanh continues to teach peacemaking in Europe, Asia, and North America. The author of eighty-two books, he has taught at Columbia University and the Sorbonne. He is also the spiritual leader of Plum Village, a Buddhist community in France, whose members include monks and nuns from Vietnam and many other countries.

In the 1960s and 1970s, the Buddhist struggle for peace in Vietnam arose from great suffering. Blood and fire ravaged the countryside, and people everywhere were uprooted. Yet few understood that we only wanted peace, not a "victory" by either side.

When I came to the United States in 1966, I was exiled from my own country because the voice of the Vietnamese people, asking for peace, was being heard. The teachings and practices of Vietnamese Buddhists have always sought to heal the deep wounds of society; to transform the suffering, hatred, and anger of all wars so that people will be able to accept, love, and embrace each other.

I have come to believe that men kill in war because they do not know their real enemy and because they are pushed into a position where they must kill. We are taught to think that we need a foreign enemy. Governments work hard to get us to be afraid and to hate so we will rally behind them. If we do not have an enemy, they will invent one in order to mobilize us. Yet they are also victims.

When soldiers return from war, they cry because they are alive. Their parents, wives, husbands, children, and friends cry for joy. But when the parades end, what do we have? What do the wives, husbands, children, brothers, and sisters of soldiers receive when their loved ones return from war after so much fear, hatred, and killing? Soon the war wells up from within their deepest consciousness. Their families and the whole of society endures their pain for a long time. For whom is this a victory?

We must look deeply into the souls of the soldiers who have returned from war so we can see the real suffering that war causes, not only to soldiers, but to everyone. When we train young people every day to kill, the damage is deep. They have known anger, frustration, and the fear of being killed. If they survive, they bear scars for many years. These kinds of wounds last for a long time and are transmitted to future generations. We cannot imagine the long-term effects of watering so many seeds of war.

Even so, we cannot divide reality into two camps – the violent and the non-violent – and stand in one camp while attacking the other. We cannot blame and condemn those we feel are responsible for wars and social injustice, without recognizing violence in ourselves. It is not correct to believe that the world's situation is in the hands of the government and that, if the President would only have the correct policies, there would be peace. It is our daily lives that have the most to do with war.

If we look deeply into the weapons of war, we will see our own minds, our own prejudices, fears, and ignorance. To work for peace is to uproot war from ourselves and from the hearts of men and women. To do this, we must learn to listen in a way that helps us to understand the suffering of others, to see the real losses, the real casualties of war. Just by listening deeply, we can already alleviate a great deal of pain. This is the beginning of healing.

If veterans can achieve awareness, transformation, understanding, and peace, they can share with the rest of society the realities of war. We who have experienced war directly have a responsibility to share our insights and experiences concerning the truth of war. For if people do not know what war is, they will not be able to appreciate peace and will destroy the peace that is available. This is a very hard fact for those of us who have come out of a war and know exactly what it is. And so we must share the truth, not out of anger, but out of love. Our people need us to do it.

We do not have time to embrace our pain in private anymore. We have to reveal ourselves so that we will be able to avoid starting another war in the future. We have to open the door for young people to come and touch the war, the bomb that is ready to explode everywhere. We have to show the young the hell and suffering that is war. Then they will be able to identify, appreciate, and protect peace. To make the world a peaceful place, to ensure for our children and grandchildren a life worth living, we need a transformation.

The veterans in this book are the light at the tip of the candle, illuminating the way for the whole nation. When the nation comes to understand the true nature of war, loving-kindness will begin to surface, and healing will begin. Then a force for change will be released.

Village des Pruniers, France
February 1998

Preface

Philip Berrigan

Once upon a time, I rode off to a crusade and rode home again the proud victor. The year was 1943, and I was a drafted into the service with three older brothers from our Irish Catholic family. I was in a field artillery unit which swept into Normandy and fired on German submarine emplacements at Lorient and Brittany. Later we moved across Northern France and into the low countries toward Germany, always fearful of their 88-millimeter guns and the Luftwaffe.

I was a very good young killer, a superior marksman, I knew how to handle an M-1, a bayonet, and my Browning Automatic Rifle. I was eager to get into combat because my brothers had paid so much and because so many of my friends were in combat. It was my job to take care of Hitler and win the war. I killed in order to prove the immorality of killing. I massacred in order to demonstrate the illegality of mass murder. I laid waste to show that laying waste is unjust.

Near the end of the war, I was reassigned to the Eighth Infantry Division. We did maneuvers near the Danish border before being shipped back to the States to prepare for the invasion of Japan. And then we dropped the Bomb on Hiroshima and Nagasaki. While on a thirty-day leave, I visited my brother Daniel at a theologiate outside of Baltimore, and we had a victory celebration. It was my last hour of slumber.

With demobilization under Eisenhower, I was discharged from the service, purposeless, and basking in a false and fading glory. I had a lot of healing to do. But it was my years as a Josephite priest, teaching at a Catholic high school in the Deep South, which started the process of awakening.

Before the war, I had passed by Georgia sharecroppers, standing quietly as horses in their humble yards. According to the law, these people were free to move into the future. Yet violence and discrimination chained them to the past. Economic Servitude, their sweet-talking master, grinned and tightened their shackles. I had tucked the faces and plights of those sharecroppers into the recesses of my mind as I sailed for the killing fields of Europe. But when I returned, the students of St. Augustine in New Orleans gave me my first real education, gently, but firmly, healing my blindness. And the more I learned from my African-American students and friends, the more outrage I felt. Outrage and a deep sense of betrayal.

I was brought up to respect authority. When my country told me to go to war, I went. When the army ordered me to kill, I killed. My black parishioners showed me what it means to be an African-American in a racist society. They weren't vindictive. They didn't want to kill their tormentors. Three hundred years earlier, their ancestors had been chained head to foot, starved, beaten, raped, and thrown to the sharks, and still, my parishioners sang about love, not revenge. My skin was white, the color of oppression, but they accepted me. Their hearts refused to turn to stone. I came to the realization that we were one of the most racist people in the world, and learned that Hitler nurtured his sick, Aryan philosophy by studying American racism.

The Cuban Missile Crisis of 1962 was another corner turned. If Kennedy and Krushchev could threaten the people that I had fought for and tried to serve, then anything was possible. They were playing God with my life and with people around the globe. If it had come to the crunch, millions of Americans would have died, and we would have retaliated by slaughtering the Soviet Union in return.

Slowly, I was led to reflect on my war experiences and to come to a position against the war brewing in Vietnam. In 1965, I worked at an African-American parish in Baltimore's West Side. Young men were coming home dead from overseas, and we were burying them in tin boxes. They were mercenaries without being aware of it; fighting the empire's wars when they had no rights as citizens back home.

Vietnam was the first, and most definitely the last, television war. Never again would the war-makers allow journalists to crawl through the muck with American troops, recording their dying moans, capturing their fear, their rage, and their despair on film. War had always been ugly, but before Vietnam, Hollywood could spin the killing into a pageant or ballet, with beautiful women, heart-warming songs, and a cuddly happy-ever-after ending. Vietnam put the mud and the blood on stage. By 1966, I had come to the conclusion that anything short of direct personal action was unavailing, untruthful, and unjust.

Today I write from federal prison as a result of three decades' protest against the Bomb and against interventionary force. I have no illusions about the military state. Congressmen and women won't visit me in jail; the Pentagon isn't going to invite me over for a chat; the President will never call to ascertain my motives for boarding a Naval Destroyer, hammering at her controls and pouring my own blood in proclamation of the sin of mass destruction.

My brother Daniel and I have spent years in prison because we believe that true Christianity and nonviolent revolution are synonymous. We have never advocated an attempt to reform or overthrow the government. We don't care who sits in the White House, or who walks the hallowed halls of Congress. As Daniel once said, we have simply set about the task of confronting the "spiritually insane" – not with mere words, but through symbols. Our blood confronts the irrational, makes megadeath concrete, summons the war-makers to their senses. The authorities react to us with apprehension, even hatred. We fill them with fear and dread, as though we carry a plague. We are locked up. But the killing will never be in our name. We leave it up to others to measure our success or failure.

Prison is designed to silence dissent. But it has strengthened my commitment to peace and social justice. It has made me more determined to live in a loving community, and more committed to resisting militarism, even if that means spending more years behind bars.

In our American culture, fear speaks to us, attempting to beguile us with the many rewards of silence. And the silence is deafening. Just acquiesce, says fear, and things will be fine. Don't rock the boat. Don't upset the apple cart. Play it safe. Accept a life of quiet desperation. But we can't deny our fears, any more than we can ignore the poverty in our neighborhood. Indeed, weapons of mass destruction express a deep human terror; a desperate, failed effort to conquer human fear.

As we approach the new millennium, war has been transformed into a video game or a sci-fi adventure. We edit out the napalm, booby traps, and saturation bombing. We never show search-and-destroy missions. We censor atrocity. We place a clean set of cross-hairs on the screen; quiet little puffs to show where the bombs hit; and smile-face generals bubbling about target-rich environments. But we continue to live under the insanity of the Bomb.

The pages that follow are a scalding indictment of our empire's wars – World War I, World War II, Korea, Vietnam, Central America, the Gulf War. Hallock has compiled an undeniable testimony to the fact that the tragedy of the United States is the tragedy of its wars. It is a hell of a book, which I endorse without qualification.

Herein lies a riddle: How can a people so gifted by God become so seduced by naked power, so greedy for money, so addicted to violence, so slavish before mediocre and treacherous leadership, so paranoid, deluded, lunatic?

Hallock's answer is the Bomb and war, our number-one business, our social idolatry, our cause as a people, our pact with the devil, our national shame. War is a fork in the road – it will either destroy us or convert us to God and human-kind. This book challenges us to transcend our fears, to embrace the pain of war, to side with the poor, to challenge injustice.

Healing is always a two-way street, and the veterans in this book have made a wonderful response. God does not give up, even if a battered veteran like my-self sometimes may. We all have a position to work out if war is ever going to end. We've got better things to do in our war-sick nation. We have a role; we have a mission; we have a truth to tell. For those who are open to it, this book will have a profound relevance.

Dire as is the state of the world, God writes straight with crooked lines. We must believe this. And we must believe that our fellow countrymen will yet wake up and heed their God, their victims, their poor, their imprisoned peacemakers, and their sometime soldiers. For it is these more than any others who can lead us to a renaissance – to a life of nonviolence, justice, and peace.

Petersburg, Virginia
July 1998

To the Reader

Daniel Hallock

This book is not mine alone. Rather, it is a collective effort – the work of countless veterans and friends who poured their hearts and minds into its pages. It has been five years in the making, with fits and starts, and with much soul-searching. It is a project that will never really be finished, because I hear new stories every day...

It all began when I met a combat veteran who'd held local police at bay in a twenty-hour standoff, perched atop the roof of his glass-and-cedar home with a .22 caliber rifle. He had made no demands but had taunted the officers and shouted at himself. In the end, his son had driven up from the city and managed to entice his father out onto the porch. That gave police an opening; he was subdued and taken away.

Now I was standing in front of him, in the Ulster County Jail, searching for an opening of my own. He stared back at me through the bars, his eyes radiating a kind of wild intensity. A guard motioned for me to stand back, away from the cell, adding with a knowing wink, "We've got a 'live' one here." I let him size me up and felt weak as his gaze burned a hole right through me, far beyond the confines of the filthy corridor.

"Where are you from?" I asked. "Where are *you* from?" he shot back. I tried to relax, leaned back against the wall. "Long Island," I said. "East End." He knew the area like the back of his hand. But he was hardly rational, and his train of thought jumped erratically from one topic to the next. Our conversation was unpredictable and tense.

John rolled his eyes at a nearby correctional officer: "These men have no respect for uniforms!" I told him I'd worn one myself and had been through boot camp in the Marines. "Where?" "Little Creek." "Not good enough!" he said. His eyes were now more wild than at first, his gaze rock-solid. I asked if he'd ever been in the military. "Nam," he said. "What difference does it make?"

We steered away from the subject and talked about farming sod on Long Island. We talked about helicopters. John claimed he could fly anything that moves, and knew his military-class aircraft extremely well. We talked about everything under the sun. He had lost a firm grip on reality, yet he was brilliant, even poetic – a very spicy character. There were moments when he became downright belligerent, yet when he realized that someone was willing just to stand there and talk with him, listen to him, he became more relaxed and thoughtful.

As I left, John mumbled on behind the wall: "Running across a rice paddy... black guy from Tennessee in one arm and a white kid from Jersey in the other." "Monsters," I said to another inmate. "Do you hear that man? He's still living in 1969."

The local papers had portrayed his arrest as a victory. "Patience Pays Off," the paper reported. Most of the people interviewed said he had a history of terrorizing the community. Many had filed for restraining orders; no one on Carney Road had anything nice to say about the man. Allegedly, he had recently sawed down a neighbor's tree.

John is a man who served his country with everything he had and lost his mind in the process. His life after Vietnam has been one long cry for help, yet our response has been cold, unfeeling, uncaring. He is the spent cartridge of a man thrown aside to rust and molder. And the loss of a tree looms more important than the soul of a man...

Have we lost all appreciation for the horrors of war? Are we unable to muster some measure of understanding for the memories that haunt him day and night? I wish I might have better understood the language John spoke. Perhaps I would have been able to point him to healing, to stability, to a new start.

That wish inspired this book. It caused me, outside a dark cell in the Ulster County Jail, to think deeply about the legacy of the military experience, including my own. And it sparked a journey that challenges our common perceptions of war and war-making, even as it opens the door to understanding and hope. It was a journey of unforgettable encounters in unexpected places – from a humble cabin in Massachusetts to an elegant apartment complex in Washington; from a Jesuit hospice in Manhattan to the home of a Black Panther in New Haven; from Pennsylvania's death row to a Buddhist retreat in the Catskills; from a county jail in Portland, Maine to the quiet kitchen of a friend in Woodstock, New York.

In all, I conducted over forty personal interviews and collected close to one hundred written accounts from veterans of nearly every American war in this century. Here are their stories: from World War I to the Persian Gulf; from Hitler to Saddam Hussein; from clandestine skirmishes in Central America to the steamy jungles of Vietnam — the stories not only of the men who fought and died, but also the stories of their mothers, their wives, their nurses, and their children. The people who share their lives in this book represent many races, nationalities, and religions, yet we speak as one voice. Together, we will tell you a story you can never forget. It is not easy to tell, but we share it hoping that it might change your life, even as it has changed ours.

To the reader who might question my patriotism, I can say only this: true patriotism is love of country, and real love is more than blind allegiance. If we love a person, we will look out for him and help him to understand when he is doing something wrong, just as we want him to do for us. The same is true for love of a nation, its leaders, and its people. This is always painful, but without such honest self-examination we will never become a better nation, and we will find no healing from our tortured past. If we face our past squarely, however, and make an attempt to alter our present course, the future is bright.

This book is not an exhaustive or scholarly treatise on war. Rather, it is an attempt to understand the truth about war and the military – and the social, economic, and political injustices which make it inevitable – through the personal stories of the men and women who have "been there."

Unless otherwise noted, the quotations used in this text are taken from field notes and tape recordings of interviews with veterans and their families, or letters written to me. To protect their privacy, I have in some instances omitted or changed names.

Rifton, New York
May 1998

CHAPTER 1

Lee

A true war story is never moral. It does not instruct, nor encourage virtue, nor suggest models of proper human behavior, nor restrain men from doing the things men have always done. If a story seems moral, do not believe it. If at the end of a war story you feel uplifted, or if you feel that some small bit of rectitude has been salvaged from the larger waste, then you have been made the victim of a very old and terrible lie. There is no rectitude whatsoever. There is no virtue. As a first rule of thumb, therefore, you can tell a true war story by its absolute and uncompromising allegiance to obscenity and evil...You can tell a true war story if it embarrasses you. If you don't care for obscenity, you don't care for the truth...You can tell a true war story by the way it never seems to end...And in the end, really, there's nothing much to say about a true war story except maybe "Oh." True war stories do not generalize. They do not indulge in abstraction or analysis. For example: "War is hell." As a moral declaration the old truism seems perfectly true, and yet because it abstracts, because it generalizes, I can't believe it in my stomach. Nothing turns inside. It comes down to gut instinct. A true war story, if truly told, makes the stomach believe.

Tim O'Brien, The Things They Carried

On the surface, Lee looks like any hired laborer. His face and hands are tanned and weather-beaten, and his trademark flannel shirt and dangling cigarette identify him unmistakably. He is a quiet man who loves horses but more often than not shies away from people. And if you take the time to listen, he can tell you why:

May 15, 1969, was the day that would change the rest of my life. I had joined the Army in August 1968 and asked to be sent to Vietnam. On May 18 I was on my way. I left from Fort Lewis, Washington, an army base where we had last-minute training. We flew on a civilian airline, and it took us eighteen hours to get there — a very long flight. None of us on the flight knew anyone else.

We landed at Cam Ranh Bay air base and were sent right away to a replacement battalion where we stayed until it was time to go to our new units. It was 118 degrees when we got to Nam…

I was sent to a construction company in Don Duong, a tiny village beneath a huge dam built by the Japanese during World War II. There were four hundred of us stationed at the base of the dam, just a mile away from the village. There were no other Americans within forty miles.

My first job was to build the living and working areas. This was a brand new unit, and so at first we lived in large drain pipes, dug half-underground with tons of sandbags on top to stop mortars and rockets.

Within a few weeks our hooches (living/fighting bunkers) were done, and I joined a unit driving tractor trailers. Our job was to build roads from the central highlands to the outlying villages south and west. I trucked all day, six days a week. We had Sunday afternoons off.

Nam is a beautiful and amazing country, and I saw a lot of it over the next two years: the white sand beaches, the jungles, the mountains; monks and monasteries; a gold Buddha on a hilltop; animals I had never heard of before. I also saw truly ugly things: death.

On my Sunday afternoons off I would either go swimming at the dam, or go to the village for pot. You could buy a "key" (kilo) for $40 and do a lot of partying, with a lot of people, for a long time. There was always a place to buy pot. Most villages had a barn where you could go and sample different kinds before buying.

One day I met a girl on the road near the village. She knew a bit of English and we talked awhile. Her name was Chi. We liked each other from the start, and it wasn't long before she began to move around with me when our trucks were on the road for more than a few days. I even began to sneak out of the compound just to see her. That was very difficult: I had to crawl through barbed wire many times, and I remember getting stoned by a group of boys as I left one village. I had some bruises after that night, but I never got caught.

I had a lot of fun with Chi. I learned a lot about the Vietnamese people from her — their ways and customs, even a bit of their language.

Our trucks came under fire many times as we moved through the country, and so did our compound. Charlie (the Vietcong) hit us a lot, just to let us know he was there. He would blow up a couple of trucks, or throw in a few mortar rounds and blow up a few buildings, but I think he liked us being there, because we built roads that they still use today…

Once, when our convoy was hauling equipment to a road-building site, we came upon an accident. Everyone in front of me drove around it and kept right on going, but I stopped to see what was going on, so everyone behind me stopped too. An officer in one of the jeeps ahead of me flew back to see what the holdup was. He was mad when he saw me standing over a girl lying on the side of the road: "We cannot stop a whole convoy because of a gook," he shouted. "We can't leave her here," I shouted back. I picked her up and put her on the back of his jeep. He was ranting and raving; he wanted me to get her off and leave her — but I couldn't. Her leg was really messed up. She had been on the back of a motorcycle, and the young man who'd been driving her was dead.

I finally convinced the second lieutenant to help me. He ordered a driver to take over my truck; we took her up the road to a village to see if anyone knew her. Someone did and took us to her home. They were Montagnards: they lived in the hills outside the village. They are like Vietnamese hillbillies, a very tough people. Before long a crowd had gathered, and then a doctor came. The second lieutenant was in a hurry to leave, but I wanted to see if she was all right, as she was going in and out of consciousness. Her papa-san came and thanked me over and over. He wanted us to stay, but the lieutenant insisted that we go, so we did. I don't know what ever happened to her. I was reprimanded for putting the convoy in danger by stopping, but I didn't care. Spending half an hour with the Montagnards on their home ground and seeing the thankfulness in their faces had made it worth it.

Six months after I got to Nam I was transferred to a transportation company sixty miles away. But an officer going through the hooches found a huge bag of pot outside my window, so I was sent on. I became a convoy driver, and I was sent anywhere at any time. I loved being in a truck, driving around the country. I saw so much. I had made a lot of friends with the guys in my first unit, but I knew no one in my new company, and I decided to keep it that way. Chi moved to a village a mile away, and we continued to see each other whenever we could.

I traveled on just about every road in Vietnam, and some that weren't even roads yet. I remember driving to a firebase that had just been built: I had to take a ten-ton tractor with a loaded forty-foot flatbed trailer up a footpath! Mountain on one side and a cliff on the other. My trailer wheels hung in mid-air around some of the turns. I was sent first, before any of the other big trucks — I guess it was getting around that I was crazy, because it seemed I was put on all the dangerous convoys. Or maybe they liked the way I drove, high all the time...

When I came to the village to see Chi one night, she told me she was pregnant. I was stunned. Me – the father of a child – in a country 10,000 miles from home! Wow, what do I do?

We kept seeing each other as much as possible. She grew bigger and bigger. I was going to be a dad, and I started to think about what to do. I paid less attention to the other drivers, and spent more time getting high and thinking. I made very few friends from then on. On my way out of one base a guy ran up to me and asked me for a lift. He jumped in, and I just drove on. I paid no attention to him, but I could tell he was a new arrival. About fifteen miles later we were driving on a road through the rice paddies when all of a sudden I was lying in a ditch, looking up at my tractor. It was totally engulfed in flames, and my passenger was still sitting in it. He was screaming, screaming like I had never heard anyone scream before. The smell, the heat, the noise – I was confused for just a second. Then I realized we had been hit by rockets. I had been blown out of the truck. It burned as I lay in the water-filled ditch. And so did he, a soldier whose name I had never asked.

I became even harder toward people – all people – except Chi. I remember my commanding officer dragging me into his office after that, to make me write a letter home. I had become so hard inside that I hadn't written for almost two months. I wrote Mom a letter, but I didn't say much about what was going on in my head. Why was he killed, and not me? Why hadn't I at least asked him his name? This truly haunted me, but I never said a word about it to Chi. She knew something had happened, that I was somehow different, but she never asked. Why did he die, and not me?

Chi was getting bigger and bigger. I was on the road more and more. I volunteered for every convoy I could. Convoys don't move after dark much, it's too dangerous. But every time a truck had to go out at night I made sure I was there. I just wanted to be out of the compound; I hated sitting around. No one wanted to ride with me once they knew me. I didn't talk; I just drove and got high, which left the shotgun talking to himself...

Once I was sent out to retrieve two trucks that another convoy had left behind with mechanical troubles. We were going to tow them back. It was just before dark when we left – two wreckers and a jeep. I was driving a wrecker. We had to stop for an ARVN (Army of the Republic of Vietnam) checkpoint. They had pulled barbed wire across the road when they saw us coming. We stopped, and they told us the road was closed. We tried to explain that two trucks and two drivers were out there and that we *had* to get them. An argument broke out, and one of the ARVNs pointed his M-16 at the jeep. All of a sudden a dozen bullets hit him and his partner. We blew the whole place apart, and then went on our way. It was after dark when we found the two trucks. We checked them for booby traps, hooked them up, and took them away. When we passed the ARVN checkpoint again, it was just as we left it, but we kept going. A fool pointing his rifle the wrong way cost two lives, but that was the way things seemed to go. Stupid people (me included) did stupid things that cost human lives.

We were losing more trucks – and soldiers – to Charlie. Most of the time you never saw where the shells came from. Many of us were going crazy because we didn't know where to fire back. It's hard fighting an enemy you can't see. Sometimes they would shoot just one GI, and other times they would blow up a whole convoy. One day we came upon the site of a Vietcong ambush of an American convoy. The trucks were still burning, and the drivers had been crucified and were still hanging on crosses at the side of the road. I was scared all the time that I would die like that, and I began to hate every Vietnamese person I saw.

We were coming out of a village one day and an old man was riding a bike toward us. As he got close, I took off my helmet and bashed him on the head. He fell under my trailer and I ran him over. Every truck behind me ran him over, on purpose. Payback was ours – even though he had done nothing to us. We killed him (actually I killed him) to make up for those who had died. It was wrong of us to do this, but it felt good. He died in place of the gooks that we could not see.

Chi and I got married, by a Vietnamese village chief. There wasn't much of a ceremony. First he asked me some questions (mostly through Chi – I couldn't understand much of what he was saying). Then I gave him my dog tags so he could write my name and "New York/America" on the paper. Chi gave him her "papers" for proof of who she was. We went into a small stone building and he spoke and waved his hands, looking at both of us. There was a small Buddha in there with incense burning all over the place. When the priest smiled at us both and joined our hands I knew we were married. Just Chi and I were there – her family was in Saigon. Her mom was a prostitute, and she had a brother a year older than her, and a sister two years younger. She had no father.

My daughter was born in September of 1970. I was on a convoy when she was born, so she was three days old when I first saw her. She was beautiful! Chi wanted to name her after me, but I took one 'e' out. Le was her name. I loved her so much.

I began making arrangements to bring Chi and my baby back to the United States. Deep in my heart I knew that if I couldn't, Chi would become a prostitute. Women with mixed-blood children were the lowest of the low in the eyes of the Vietnamese people, because they want to keep their blood lines as pure as possible. So I don't think she would have had a chance doing anything besides selling herself. Her mom had sold her twelve-year-old sister to an American officer for $400 for one night. When I asked how she could do this to a young girl, her own daughter, so young, her response was something to the effect of: look what you are doing to my other young daughter, and I am not even getting any money from you! So I didn't like her mom at all. But I guess survival came first in Vietnam, no matter what.

I had to extend my tour of duty again. A year is a normal tour. I had already extended my tour by six months, and I wanted to extend it another six months. That way I would get out of the Army five months ahead of schedule. I went to see my commanding officer about extending my tour, and when I did, I told him I was married and had a new daughter. That is when all hell broke loose. He told me that he would not extend my tour because he thought I was going over the edge, mentally.

Also, he wanted to see my Vietnamese wedding and birth papers. I gave him our marriage papers, but I had no birth paper for Le because she wasn't born in a hospital. I was sent to see all kinds of other officers. Somehow, my marriage papers were "lost" and I was told I was not married anymore. I was told that the Army would not have recognized my marriage anyway, because they hadn't married us. I went through hell. I talked to more officers than I had ever seen before. In spite of all the bullshit, I did get my extension through. I guess someone liked my driving ability or something. So I had more time to work on bringing Chi and Le home.

Life was very strange now. I was full of hatred, but also full of love for Chi. I was going nuts. I didn't want anything to do with Americans anymore, but I had to keep trying to get the official papers to bring my family home. Whenever I went to a large army base I would talk to the highest ranking officers I could find. They gave me all kinds of excuses and stories but did nothing for me. I got more and more depressed. I even talked to the highest army chaplain on the base. He said he would look into my situation, but nothing happened.

Months passed quickly. Chi and Le couldn't move around much now, so I saw them less. And I was on the road even more. I guess the officers figured that if they kept me away I would cause fewer headaches for them. I was so angry that for the first time I wanted to kill American officers. I was hurting very badly. I didn't know what to do. My mind was in bad shape.

I tried to get work as a civilian in Vietnam. There were a number of companies there working for the American government. But each time I filled out an application, I was turned down: when they did the background check, my CO would tell them I was nuts.

About two weeks before I was to leave Nam, I was called into the CO's office. He told me to forget about bringing Chi and Le home. Apparently the chaplain I had talked to had contacted him and asked what could be done, but the Army had checked up on Chi and found that she had a shady past, that her brother was a suspected Vietcong. The boy was sixteen years old and hadn't joined the Vietnamese Army, so he was suspected of being a Vietcong. What a joke.

It was made very clear to me then that I had two choices: to leave them behind or desert the Army. I had been told all my life that the worst thing a soldier can do is to desert. Where would I go in Vietnam? As long as the Americans were there they would be looking for me. When they left, the Vietnamese government, communist or not, would get me. What was I to do? Get high. Nothing meant anything to me now – except Chi and Le.

Everything I had done in Vietnam was now catching up with me. Chi and I met one last time before I was supposed to leave. We both cried our eyes out. It was so bad, so much pain. We trembled in each other's arms. I left her and went back to my unit. Then she sent me a note saying to meet her at a cliff above the South China Sea, a very beautiful place where we had gone a lot. I went. I was leaving tomorrow, so I had to see her today. I took an officer's jeep and drove to the cliff. There they were, waiting, crying. We didn't talk, we just held each other, with Le in between us. We cried so much. I reached into my pocket and took out my pistol, put it to Chi's head and pulled the trigger. There was a splatter – then her blood gushed out – all over me. I held her tightly – with Le screaming still between us. I held her as long as I could – then let her go – over the cliff and into the sea they both fell. I pounded the earth as hard as I could – I screamed till I had no voice. I had nothing left inside me when I drove back. I should have died in Vietnam instead of living the thousands of deaths that I have.

Back at the hooch no one said a word to me. I had walked in covered with blood and looked pretty bad – no one said a word. I left Vietnam the next day. When the plane took off, everyone screamed with happiness – all but me. I didn't sleep, from the morning of the day I pulled the trigger till I got to Fort Lewis, Washington. We got to Fort Lewis at 2:00 A.M. I hadn't said a word to anyone for two days. I lay down and dozed off. Everyone got up at 6:00, went to chow, then started processing out of the Army. This took until early afternoon. I processed out of the Army without saying a word to anyone.

We were loaded onto a bus and taken to the Seattle-Tacoma airport where we boarded our planes to go home. After we took off for New York, a stewardess came to sit down with me. She started talking to me – I must have looked pretty bad – and she asked if I had just come from Vietnam. She wanted to know if there was anything she could do for me. I said, "Yes, please give me a needle and thread, so I can sew my stuff (ribbons and patches) on my army jacket." She took the coat and sewed everything on it for me. She treated me nice – the only one to treat me nice for two years. I fell asleep. And she woke me and gave me my jacket when we got to New York City.

I came home a very different person than when I left. My mind, heart, and soul were gone. I had sent some pot home from Nam in my baggage, so I stayed high all the time. I got a car, and within a few months married my high school girlfriend.

She was a high school senior when we snuck away and got married, on June 1, 1971. She had lived in five foster homes and wanted to get out on her own. I needed something, anything, to keep me from totally going over the edge. We married, but we didn't really love each other. It was more a marriage of convenience to us both. We didn't tell our parents right away, because we didn't want trouble for her with the child-welfare people who were responsible for her. Some weeks later she told me she was pregnant. She was working as a nurse, and I was unemployable.

Eight months later our daughter was born. Faith was born in April of 1972. She would become my life for the next sixteen years. Everything I had left in me went to her. She was my little girl. The one to make right the wrongs I had done.

I hated myself. I didn't care about myself, I hurt so much. I couldn't stop thinking, dreaming, about what I had done. I died every time I shut my eyes. Chi and Le were there, covered with blood, inside my mind, in my thoughts. I started to have nightmares. I was a husband and father again, but how can this be – for the second time, a husband and father, again? I loved my daughter, but I still loved Chi so much that there was nothing for my wife. Can I ever forgive myself for what I have done? No.

I got a job just two weeks before Faith was born, at a water-filter plant. The town wanted a Vietnam vet to work at their plant, so I got the job. I worked a different shift each week, so my body never caught up. On the evening and night shifts there was five minutes' work each hour, and fifty-five minutes to think. I worked this job two years, and then I couldn't take it any more. I was numb in mind and body. Faith was my only reason for living. I did everything she asked me, except to stop smoking pot. I couldn't – it was all that kept me from death. I got high all the time. Pot was the only thing that kept my mind from burning out. That's the only thing she asked me to do that I couldn't. And I can't forgive myself.

My wife was in college most of our marriage. Working, studying, going to school, and sleeping was all she did. I was not very nice to her sometimes. I never hit her, but I did push her down, and I threw a plate of spaghetti at her once. I was mentally cruel to her, though. We argued whenever we were together. We would go to her friends' parties, and I would sit outside all night while she drank, talked, and danced. I hated to be around people, and she was a people-person. I guess I embarrassed her by not participating in her social events.

I didn't sleep much; I had bad thoughts on my mind. I was nasty, so I stayed away from people. There were a few I thought were friends, but in the end one of them even slept with my wife. I tried to trust her, but couldn't. As the years went on, I found out about some of the others she had been seeing. I really can't blame her, though. My wife was not a bad person; she had a rough life to live. She put up with more than most, living with me.

Once, during an argument, she hurt me very badly without even knowing it. She knew that Faith's middle name, Le, was the name of a child of mine in Nam, so she screamed out, "What's going to happen? Is some little gook kid going to come knocking at our door someday, hollering Daddy, Daddy?" That set me back years – I was without words. I just walked out, drove around for hours getting high. I had never told anyone about what I had done to Chi and Le, so she didn't know what I was going through. Things were never the same after that, and I went further and further downhill.

We had a son, Charles, seven years after Faith was born, and as my children grew, I had to spend more time around people. I didn't like that. Faith was a girl scout, so I had to take her to meetings and be around other parents. I didn't talk to them much. Then Charlie wanted to join the cub scouts. I took him to sign him up, and the scout leader said, "This is not the place to take a kid for baby-sitting; you have to actively participate with us." So Charlie never joined the cub scouts – I just could not participate with them. Faith did join a drum-and-bugle corps, and I would take her every week to practice at the local firehouse. I sat in my van waiting for her, three hours at a time, for two years – winter, spring, summer, fall. I could not be with the other parents waiting for their children.

As Faith grew, we were together all the time. Her mom went to college, worked, slept, and studied. Faith and I did the rest. I worked my jobs around Faith's schedule and my wife's schedule. Faith and I did all the cooking, cleaning, shopping, laundry – everything. We were family – her mom wasn't. In seventeen years of marriage, my wife worked night shift a dozen or more years, so I raised our kids and worked at whatever I could. I could never hold a job for more than two years. I wasn't a very pleasant person. I worked by myself or with small companies with few employees so I wouldn't have to be around people. Twice I ran my own tractor-trailers. I didn't make much money, but it felt good.

This came to an end one day. As I was driving down a mountain, a tractor trailer in front of me slammed into the mountainside and caught fire. I stopped, and as I walked closer I smelled the smell of death. It took me back — back to the guy burning to death in my cab, the guy whose name I never asked. I drove my rig home, parked it, and I have never driven one since. But I still smell the smell.

When Faith was twelve, I bought her a horse. As soon as she learned to ride, she wanted to start showing her horse. She was a very good rider. I bought her a western-style show saddle for Christmas and she was ready. Early spring came, and we were off to the horse shows. Faith and her horse were probably the best thing that could have happened to me. I had to take her and the horse to all the shows, every weekend from April to November, so I *had* to be around other people. I would be there all day, and eventually people would come over and talk to me.

Soon Charlie started coming to the shows, riding lead line with Faith's horse. He had a little western outfit he wore. When I realized he liked his riding, I got him a pony. With both of them showing, I had to be around people. I met a lot of horse-show parents, horse traders, and tack-shop owners, nice people for the most part. I would talk to them, but I wouldn't befriend them.

Being at horse shows was good for me. I liked the horses and I think they liked me too. I would go down to the field and talk to them quite often. They listened to me, didn't pass judgment, and hung out with me just because they wanted to. When they were tired of me, they just walked away, without lying or making excuses. I would rather be with horses than people...

As the years went by, my problems got harder and harder to handle. My wife didn't like horses, so she didn't come to the shows. I think she was upset because we would be at a show every weekend and never did anything with her. I had bad dreams, couldn't sleep, and was working full-time as well as raising my family and doing all the indoor and outdoor household chores. I was tired of it all.

I couldn't trust anyone, so I never talked about my problems with anyone, and that cost me a lot. All my feelings built up inside of me, and finally something threw me over the edge. I fell hard, and in one second's time I lost everything. I was arrested and sent to jail. When I was released, I was ordered by the court to stay away from my family.

After a few days, I checked into the VA (Veterans Administration) mental hospital. I was numb in mind and body. I was on suicide watch twenty-four hours a day. Something happened in my mind that just wiped out much of my memory. I was awaiting trial from August 1988 to July 1989. During those months, the state police picked me up twice more and took me to the VA hospital where I was put on the psychiatric intensive-care ward. This is a place where there is a line of rubber beds on both sides of the room, and a table and chairs in the middle. Nothing else. No books, no radio, no TV, nothing. Their intensive care was to leave you sitting, doing nothing, twenty-four hours a day. For one hour a day you would sit in front of a whole panel of doctors, psychiatrists, and other strange people, all asking you questions. Then you would go back and sit in the ward for another twenty-three hours. What a joke. You wore pajamas with no pockets, no shorts or T-shirt. You were watched twenty-four hours a day by the nurses, even when you had to go to the bathroom or shower. This was psychiatric intensive care.

Just before Christmas of '88 I got a letter saying I was now divorced. I had gotten a letter earlier saying that my wife had filed for divorce, that I should notify her attorney of my intentions. I had called her attorney and told her I would fight the divorce when I got money for an attorney. But a month and a half later, here were the final papers. I couldn't understand this. If it took two of us to get married, why didn't it take two of us to get divorced?

I was never invited to the hearing. So my wife got total custody of both children and all of our possessions, which included my birth certificate and social security card. Everything was gone. Never to see my children again. I called the judge who granted the divorce, and he told me there was nothing I could do about it.

There *was* nothing I could do. My mind was in a real bad way. And I had brought all this on myself by my actions in Vietnam. I got out of the hospital to go to jail for eight months, never to see my children again. This was July 1989. I was on twenty-four-hour suicide watch for eight months. I was given pills by the jail nurse to keep me down, and I had to talk to a counselor each week. But I had no will to live. The guards knew it and I knew it. Those eight months in jail were much longer than two years in Nam…

My problems are not the worst problems in the world, but they affect me as well as everyone around me. This is not just a story – it is a part of my life. And I don't know if I can ever forgive myself for my wrongs. I live from day to day and I am tired all the time – tired. Will it ever end? I don't see how. It's been with me over twenty-five years now.

■ ■ ■ ■ ■ ■ ■

Lee was there when two hundred of us gathered under the trees on a warm summer evening in Woodcrest.* I had invited a group of eight veterans to speak to our community – men who had seen war in Germany, Japan, Korea, and

* Woodcrest Bruderhof in Rifton, New York. See Appendix 2, "The Bruderhof."

Vietnam. They had agreed to tell us — though it would hurt — what it was like for them, why they went, and what it means to "survive." They had come to help our young people understand what glitters falsely, what pulls and what pushes with almost irresistible force, what passes for courage and what masks cowardice, what it means to be horribly and irrevocably "conned."

Fred Louis, a member of the local chapter of Veterans for Peace, was the first to speak. He donned his glasses, shuffled some papers uneasily near the microphone, and opened another window into Vietnam:

> I was less than a month in-country, very green. We were on patrol in a free-fire zone. As we walked along a ridge, we spotted a few people in black pajamas and coolie hats walking on a trail in the valley below us. The whole company, over a hundred men, lined up and started shooting. My weapon was an M-79 grenade launcher, so they were well beyond my range. I stood and watched, stunned, bewildered, afraid, and fascinated by this somewhat bizarre shooting gallery. A buddy offered to let me shoot his rifle. I said, "No, that's okay." A small patrol went down and found a young boy with a belly wound. They left him. Our captain called in three VC kills to headquarters. A bitter taste of my year to come.
>
> Later on I watched my squad leader check the papers of a wrinkled Vietnamese man walking with his granddaughter. His head was bowed in fear, eyes darting. My sergeant handed the papers back and said, "Go." We watched him walk away in relief and apprehension. Then my squad leader raised his rifle and shot the man in the head. You must understand something about M-16 rifles: they are small caliber, just slightly bigger than a .22, but the muzzle velocity is extremely high and the barrel rifling is specially designed. This causes the bullet to strike a human body with enormous impact and to tumble around once inside. So the man's head exploded like a watermelon hit with a sledge hammer. Small chunks of brain, white with flecks of blood, landed on the toe of my boot. I remember gently brushing away those pieces with the back of my fingers. That's all I remember. I shut down some more. Must survive.
>
> I have taken over twenty-eight years to cry for the old man, for his granddaughter, for my sergeant, for me. I did nothing. That's what you did. Nothing. SOP, Standard Operating Procedure. You depended on your comrades for your very life. They carried loaded weapons and much anger. Little My Lai's — little massacres — happened hundreds of times a day in Vietnam. You must remember that it does not take monsters to commit monstrous acts. My squad leader returned home a decorated hero, a Bronze Star and a Purple Heart on his chest. You may know him. He may deliver your mail or wait on you in the hardware store or teach your children. Or he may be stalking the

jungles of Hawaii or some other forest with other men unable to return home. Or he may be one of the 100,000 suicides since the end of the war.

I must apologize. I gave you wrong facts. I don't remember if my sergeant used a rifle or a pistol. I don't know if the old man and the young girl were related. I brushed someone's brains off my boot, although I don't know if it was that day. But what I have said is still absolutely true.

I come here to open my throat, to spread my arms, to awaken my heart, to reclaim my life. The people and space here help me to remember what it's like to feel full and not empty, and to trust that feeling.

Next, Fred read a piece by Bruce Cole, a friend who had been a Marine Company Commander in '66 or '67:

One of his hands had just fallen right off, burned off. Now his charred wrist bone was sticking out from under the poncho we'd wrapped him in to drag him here. We had to use a second poncho to cover where the first one had melted, he was burned so hot.

PFC Wall died today. Burned to death in the service of his country. A blond, fair-haired kid whom everyone loved. Didn't even shave yet. The other men would tease him: "Hey, Wall, let me borrow your razor, ha-ha-ha." Now, sitting here, everything is very still. Sunset, orange sky, red clouds moving slowly. Water buffalo knee-deep in the pink-orange water, grazing on tender green marsh grass along the shore. Fishermen's sampans anchored out in the lagoon. Fish cooking, smoke rising, no wind. Everything calm, so serene. How do they go on living day to day like this, with the war going on all around?

Now I can hear birds singing all around. Dark-green mountain forest reflected in the mirror lagoon. PFC Wall's cooked body is cooling off. The sick-sweet smell is going away. Now it's too late to fly his body out. His charred, contorted body is lying here next to me. He's a "routine medevac." That means we don't send the dead out before the wounded. The wounded have higher priority. It makes grim sense in this insanity. Too many wounded today. His body stays with me tonight, burned black, cooked meat.

Now the fishermen's fires seem brighter. The sun is gone, the birds have stopped singing. Darkness comes. Swoosh! Crack! Incoming! Fuck! Rockets from uphill. Blinding flashes, shrapnel cracking, men screaming. "Doc, doc, where the fuck is doc?" Doc's hit. The first rocket hit his position. Crack! Crack! Now I hear mortar tubes thumping out there. Rockets and mortars. Can't do a fucking thing but lie here, face down, caught in the open. Hear shrapnel cracking into trees, smell the broken trees. Each explosion comes closer. Fuck. They're walking the mortars across our position. Each one closer, each one louder. The ground jumps higher, dirt and rocks fall on my head. Hot shrapnel. No helmet. Shit. The next one's coming up my ass. Jesus Christ, I'll kill those fuckers. Just let the next round pass me. Come on! Come on! Come on! Crack! They miss me. I breathe the delicious smoke and dust.

I am lying with the top of my head in PFC Wall's armpit. The meat is falling off the bones. It's stuck in my hair. I wonder if his body took any shrapnel from me. I don't want to know. I cover him up. A man is crying for his mother. Gurgled coughing. Muffled sobbing in the quiet of the night. Too quiet. Assault coming soon. I can feel it. I know it. Too quiet. Got to get our shit together. Perimeter defense. Redistribute ammunition. I will never again remember the cooked flesh stuck in my hair. I never want to. I never will.

I remember now, twenty-six years later, that…that…I shaved my head.

There is a long, still moment of quiet. Fred takes off his glasses, slowly, and says, "Thanks for listening. Those of you who are in high school or about to go to high school: know that what is in your history texts is baloney. History books are written so that they don't cause any trouble anywhere. They contain just generalizations and facts, but nothing of what's in the stomach…You know, the thing that made me cry the most in Tim O'Brien's book was when he said, 'I survived, but it's not a happy ending. I was a coward. I went to the war.'"[1]

CHAPTER 2

The Sell

When I was young, it seemed that life was so wonderful,
　　a miracle, oh it was beautiful, magical.
And all the birds in the trees, well they'd be singing so happily,
　　joyfully, playfully watching me.
But then they sent me away to teach me how to be sensible,
　　logical, responsible, practical.
And they showed me a world where I could be so dependable,
　　clinical, intellectual, cynical.

There are times when all the world's asleep,
the questions run too deep
　　for such a simple man.
Won't you please, please tell me what we've learned
I know it sounds absurd
but please tell me who I am.

Now watch what you say or they'll be calling you a radical,
　　liberal, fanatical, criminal.
Won't you sign up your name, we'd like to feel you're
　　acceptable, respectable, presentable, a vegetable!

At night, when all the world's asleep,
the questions run so deep
　　for such a simple man.
Won't you please, please tell me what we've learned
I know it sounds absurd
but please tell me who I am.

Supertramp, "The Logical Song"

Supertramp's "Logical Song" meant a lot to me back in the summer of 1979, when it first came out. It matched the thoughts running around in my head so perfectly that I felt as if I had written the words myself. I was on active duty aboard the USS *Shreveport* at the mammoth naval base in Norfolk, Virginia, confused and bewildered by the fast track to the unknown that had become my life. I couldn't figure out what was happening to me, and couldn't pinpoint the emotions roiling my heart and mind. I was young, only nineteen.

My world of security was shattered on my first trip home from college for the Thanksgiving holidays, when I found out my father was abandoning our family for another woman. Everything went black. I tried to comfort my mother – a strong woman who held all six of us kids together in the end – as she sat in the darkness on the basement steps, weeping and numbing the agony with bottles of rum.

I looked at her, and I saw all that she had gone through in her life: her teenage years spent caring for her mentally ill mother, trying to hold the family together while her father worked himself to the bone in a navy shipyard during World War II and then as a sign maker. She and my dad had eked out a wonderful childhood for us, but I had made her grow old when I almost died in a car accident at the age of seventeen. She had been there that whole night long in the emergency room, watching me writhe and scream in blood and agony as my nose was reconstructed. She was there to see me transported to a hospital further west on Long Island; there to see my blackened, unrecognizable face for months afterward; there to see the doctors re-break my top jaw and reset it in the right place. Her son. For me, it was pure hell, but for her it was worse, far worse. And now this.

"Isn't it a kick in the head?" she'd asked me, with tears, when I first heard the news of Dad's adultery. I put my arms around her, but it felt so strange. I loved her so much, but she had always comforted me. Now I was supposed to comfort her from the void within myself. I had nothing to give. I looked at her and I cried. "Damn," I thought, "she's seen so much." Many years later, she told me what Dad had said about us kids as he went packing: "They'll survive." I need to believe that he couldn't know just how barely.

Inside, I was sinking fast. The drug and alcohol habits I picked up in high school became a way of life, and I could no longer live without the anesthetic. I saw very little worth living for.

I had wanted to be a veterinarian. Enamored early on with the writings of James Herriot, I had envisioned a deeply satisfying life caring for animals among green, rolling hills and familiar barnyards. I had grown up caring for cows and goats and horses, and had always loved animals. But that dream, like many of the dreams of childhood, was not to be. Veterinary training was long and expensive, and the demise of the small farmer made thriving practices increasingly scarce. I excelled in math, and the market for engineers was booming, so I found myself prudently nudged in this new direction.

Things unfolded rather quickly during my senior year in high school, but it all seemed to make sense. I was accepted at a top-notch Ivy League university and needed a scholarship to foot the bill. I knew nothing about Reserve Officers' Training Corps, but my dad had been in the National Guard, and the promise of four years of free tuition seemed too good to pass up. I could have gone to a cheaper school, but I was ambitious: an honor-society member and A-student in the toughest technical courses in high school, I wanted to rocket myself into an exciting and impressive career.

ROTC seemed the perfect stepping stone. I would endure it, and get out of it whatever I needed to get through Cornell. I would do the four years of active duty and kiss it goodbye. Very soon, however, I was to regret that impulse. I began to realize that I had paid a powerful piper, one that wouldn't let me so easily go and didn't care about who I had wanted to become.

■ ■ ■ ■ ■ ■ ■

The art of military recruiting is an ancient one. Militaries throughout history have used the darker side of human nature to their advantage and have long understood that "the passions that are to be kindled in war must already be inherent in the people."[1]

In time of war, those passions are more base, more immediate. Young men are driven by hate and fear, not only of the "enemy," but of the reactions of friends and family and society, should they fail to conform. Many would rather die than risk disapproval and loss of respect; would rather have their blood ebb away on distant sands than turn against the tide of common emotion and expectation. As Vietnam veteran and author Tim O'Brien observed, "the soldier's greatest fear [is the] fear of blushing. Men killed, and died, because they were embarrassed not to...They were too frightened to be cowards."[2]

In times of so-called peace, these "inherent passions" are less immediate but can be exploited nonetheless. Ambition, pride, elitism, and wanderlust; the quest for physical prowess, power, and control – all these are engendered by the familiar army slogan, "Be all you can be."

The military entices youth with all sorts of promises: higher education, travel, excitement, camaraderie, purpose, and honor. But the truth is that most of these promises never materialize. Young people – especially those looking for a ticket out of poverty, family strife, inferior education, and disenfranchisement from middle-class opportunities – are very often disappointed. In the end, the military sets them back instead of ahead. Jim Murphy, a Vietnam veteran and dean at West Side High School in Manhattan, explains:

It's an American tradition that the military is viewed as a career option for our kids. My kids are especially susceptible to this. The high school where I teach is about 50 percent Latino and 50 percent African-American. Most of my kids come from Washington Heights and Kings Bridge, or Harlem. Ninety-six percent of the kids in my high school are eligible for the free-lunch program. That's a very clear economic indicator; it says that they are living in borderline poverty. Last year I lost three students, killed during the summer. The year before that I lost six kids; the year before that there was one. Every year I walk back into school in September, and someone's been shot. That's the environment in which a lot of my kids live, day in and day out.

There was a very interesting study done on the demographics of my kids' neighborhoods as compared to Westchester County. They asked kids from Harlem if they'd borrow $10,000 to go to school and about 80 percent said no, they wouldn't borrow that much money. Then they asked the same number of kids in Westchester if they'd borrow $100,000 to go to school and 75 percent said yes, they would. So my kids don't have a sense of success in their future. And when a recruiter comes to school and says, "We can work out a deal where you're going to earn $40,000 for college," that's really a dream.

He's offering a career, he's offering money for college, yet when my kids go into the military they have a failure rate that's pretty high. A lot of them just aren't going to accept a racist comment from a drill instructor. They are going to react to it. And the military itself, the basic training, is based on breaking people down. I would imagine the average drill instructor probably insults everyone about equally, but my kids aren't going to take that. So they leave, and they don't get the $40,000, and because they've "dropped out," now they are going to have a difficult time getting even a simple civil-service job.

Military advertising, such as a U.S. Marine Corps letter to seniors, is only bluffing when it encourages young people to "get all the information you can, from as many sources as possible." Though they clearly have access to it, they would never make available the vast majority of the material in this book. And they would never tell the story of Vietnam Veterans of America founder Bobby Muller, who said:

I went into the Student Union Building, and there was a Marine officer...He looked very sharp: he had his dress blues on, and he had the old crimson stripe down the side of his trousers. I said, "That looks good! I'm going to be a Marine."

Right there, in that sentence, is really the tragedy of my life, as I view it. The tragedy of my life was not being shot in Vietnam; the tragedy in my life is one that has been shared by all too many Americans, and is still being shared today. For me, knowledge of the fact that my government had seen fit to involve us militarily in Vietnam was sufficient for me. *I never asked the reason why.* I just took it on blind faith that my government knew a hell of a lot more than I ever could, and that they must be right. My opinion has changed since then.[3]

Nor would they tell the story of Ron Kovic, perhaps the most famous Vietnam veteran, who remembers the day he was paralyzed in a firefight in Vietnam and was carried away from the battle amidst screaming human wreckage:

"Oh God get me out of here!" "Please help!"…Oh Jesus, like little children now, not like marines, not like the posters, not like that day in the high school, this is for real…"Oh I don't want to die!" screams a young boy cupping his intestines with his hands. "Oh please, oh no, oh God, oh help! Mother!" he screams again…[4]

Not surprisingly, the whole subject of war is neatly excised from military advertising. Instead, a USMC home-page advertisement focuses on flattering images and the mysterious wonders of boot camp:

From the very first haircut to the last drill evaluation, we take each step of boot camp with one thing in mind: pride. We want you to walk away proud to wear the title United States Marine.

Sure, we demand a lot of you, from tough physical training to long hours in the classroom studying Marine Corps history and traditions. You'll learn the applications of strategy, tactics, and how to handle the challenges only The Few can.

With every exercise you'll become stronger. Because we want you to be the best there is. We want you to develop that spirit of "nothing's impossible." The unwavering self-confidence that comes from being one of the best.

We're inspiring you, motivating you, while you show us you've got the heart and smarts it takes to become a Marine.

There are times you'll wonder why you're doing it, but you won't wonder for long. Because twelve short weeks later comes Graduation Day. The day you realize very few people can accomplish what you have.

After you receive your basic uniform issue and finish your physical examination and administrative processing, you'll meet the individual who's going to make these next twelve weeks worth every ounce of sweat and determination you put into it. He's your drill instructor, better known as your D.I.

Even though there are times you'll wonder whose side he's on, you'll learn he's the one man you'll want by your side. He'll teach you everything you need to know. And he'll never demand anything of you he wouldn't demand of himself.

He'll show you how to fire a rifle. How to conquer the obstacle course. How to get yourself in shape and stay that way. How to build mental and physical confidence. How to respond to orders.

Throughout boot camp he'll be there. Pushing you and giving you the discipline you need to be your best.

But more importantly, he'll show you what it means to be a team player. To make a group of men function as one. In short, he'll teach you what it means to be part of one of the most elite military organizations ever created, the United States Marine Corps.

On the highway not far from my home in upstate New York is a large billboard with a picture of a U.S. Marine in full uniform, standing ramrod straight and at attention, with a firmly grasped sword lightly touching the brim of his gold-braided hat. A caption reads simply: "The Change Is Forever." Having gone through boot camp in the Marines myself, I can attest to the truth of that statement, though not in the sense intended by the advertiser. Rather, I must side with Vietnam veteran Gerald McCarthy, now a professor at St. Thomas Aquinas College, who says:

> Going to boot camp *will* change you forever. I wouldn't let my son go to boot camp. Forget going to war – I wouldn't even let him go to boot camp. I wouldn't go back to boot camp for all the money you could give me. And it's not because I'm afraid of dying in boot camp, but because I think it can change you psychologically forever. Why would you want to lose your youth? There are so many ways to spend it.

Perhaps one of the most tragic aspects of military advertising is the way in which it appeals to those young men and women whose lives have been shattered by dysfunctional families and communities. Such advertisements go to great lengths to replace the natural yearning for family with hopes for camaraderie and acceptance in the military. For example, the letter to high school seniors asks, "Who will give me a sense of belonging?" It then promises to make them part of a team, a "group of men who function as one."

David Harvey, a British Special-Ops veteran, served in Italy, Egypt, Germany, China, Kenya, and Hong Kong. He was an orphan when he enlisted at age sixteen, and he joined the military in search of a better life.

The reason I joined was that I didn't have a family. I'd left school at thirteen, and I had a number of mundane jobs that were going nowhere. The country was at war, and there were a lot of military personnel about. I guess I had the idea that maybe I'd be okay in the services. I didn't look at it as a career. I looked at it as a way out. There was nothing for me in civilian life, not at this stage anyway.

In the service, we lived quite a good life. We had plenty of spare time, plenty of sports, and I couldn't see anything wrong with it at all. I had a wage, I had food, I had clothing, and I had comradeship, which was very much encouraged in the services. I thought it was a good life.

Now, at age seventy, he reflects on the years that led to his retirement from the British military at the age of thirty:

I looked back on my life in the service and realized it had done me no favors whatsoever. I had no guidance. I didn't have parents who were able to warn me of pitfalls. And I guess I was something of a mess when I first came out...

It was all a grave mistake. I don't have anything to look back on, apart from the comradeship and the fellowship of similar servicemen. The rest, the things that I was asked to do and did willingly – had I known what I know today, had I been a wiser person at the time, I would never, ever have done them.

If ever a young person said to me, "You were in the service – what do you think?" my advice would have to be, "Don't go." There's no reward, or at least there hasn't been any for me. In fact, it's been the complete opposite. It was very much a waste of time, a waste of life, heading in the wrong direction. Looking back on it, I feel pretty badly.

I knew that what I was doing wasn't right already before I left. I didn't actually have to wait until my time in the service was over to come to that realization. But of course, as you get older, you reflect more deeply on your life, and your regrets become stronger. It isn't something that fades away. You just keep saying to yourself, "I wish I hadn't." But I have. I was young and naïve, and now I'm older and wiser.

■ ■ ■ ■ ■ ■ ■

The money and manpower poured into the military's sell are enormous. The Nonviolent Action Community of Cascadia, an affiliate of the War Resisters League, recently described a new army campaign aided by a "Cinema Van": a tractor-trailer equipped with nine slide projectors and three screens, eight portable cinema pods; and an "Adventure Van," which features a simulated tank, a helicopter, and a "weaponeer" – an M-16.[5] According to the Army, these "vans" visited 2,000 schools across the country in 1995, reaching 380,000 "recruitable" high school students.

Why such a strenuous effort? College advisors assert that most teenagers aspire to civilian occupations: flying planes, building bridges, and operating computers. But because they are unaware of their options, including the nearly universal availability of adequate financial aid, they dismiss the idea of college from the outset and enter the military — usually for no other reason than to escape home.

Few realize that the average army training consists of only fifty-six days of "skills training," compared to courses lasting anywhere from twelve to eighteen months in civilian-sector trade schools. True, they may provide "advanced training" in a very limited field of expertise, but even at their best, they can never provide students with the kind of general skills that can be applied elsewhere down the road.

Despite this reality, the Department of Defense has in recent years pursued a goal of doubling the number of Junior Reserve Officers Training Corps (JROTC) units around the country, and is attempting to set special precedents in the nation's capital. Four public schools in the District of Columbia — three high schools and one junior high — now *mandate* a year of participation in the JROTC program. Fourteen-year-olds are required to wear military uniforms, practice military drills, and submit to the orders of retired military officials. Physical abuse is not uncommon: one young woman reported being whipped severely with a belt. Incoming freshmen are enrolled automatically, and only a scant few have been granted religious exemption; the units must maintain a minimum number of cadets in order to receive continued funding.

The seventeen JROTC programs now in place have cost the District $571,285, and although the Pentagon has contributed another $465,979, teachers are being laid off and school buildings have been ordered closed for lack of repairs. Recently, a new superintendent hired by the school board was dismissed and replaced with a retired army general.[6]

Vietnam veteran Dr. Leo Sandy, a professor of education and a psychologist, says that JROTC specifically targets children of indigent and minority backgrounds, and he raises serious questions about the overall philosophy of the program:

> The curriculum JROTC uses mentions, among other things, the military success of pushing the Indians farther west and then wiping them out. JROTC texts present military solutions as inevitable and desirable. War is seen as a technical endeavor, while its morality and human costs go unmentioned. The promotional literature also implies that cadets are more patriotic than other citizens, suggesting that militarism is equated to patriotism and that those

who exercise their rights of free speech may be less patriotic and even subversive…JROTC is a major recruiting tool, although this is vehemently denied by its proponents. The rate at which its cadets go into the military – 45 percent – is much larger than that of the general population. [7]

Retired Navy Rear Admiral Eugene Carroll made similar observations in a 1993 editorial for *The New York Times:*

> In his State of the Union Address, [President Clinton] said America can "responsibly reduce our defense budget" in the post-cold-war world. Why then does he now support the Pentagon's effort to more than double the size of its Junior Reserve Officers' Training Corps program for high school students?
>
> I was astonished in the 1970s when I learned such a program existed: military training for 14-year-olds?…
>
> The Pentagon claims these units are "not intended to teach military combat skills or military missions." Then why do they stress close-order drill, marksmanship, military history, and missions of the armed services? Why does the program feature opportunities for the cadets to spend time each summer at such bases as Fort Devens, Massachusetts and Fort Benning, Georgia, where they practice their skills and learn what the military does in the field?
>
> If you swallow the party line, the Pentagon's motive is not to create a stockpile of future candidates for military service – nothing so crass. The sales pitch is that training has great social value. Gen. Colin L. Powell, chairman of the Joint Chiefs of Staff, praises the program as "the best opportunity for the Department of Defense to make a positive impact on the nation's youth."
>
> The Pentagon, justifying expansion of the program, says it is valuable for youths "at risk" in cities, because the training will counter the dangers of drugs, crime, and gang involvement and prevent school dropouts. The retired military instructors, it says, will become role models for the cadets, thus helping reverse undesirable trends in rough neighborhoods.
>
> It is appalling that the Pentagon is selling a military training program as a remedy for intractable social and economic problems in inner cities. Surely, its real motive is to inculcate a positive attitude toward military service at a very early age, thus creating a storehouse of potential recruits.
>
> To be certain they get the message, cadets who complete at least two years of training receive advanced standing in certain active-duty programs. There is great satisfaction in the Pentagon that about a third of the cadets enter military service – active duty, National Guard, or reserve – after graduation.
>
> If the administration's true goal is to educate productive, law-abiding citizens, these hundreds of millions of dollars could be spent far more effectively on core educational activities. [8]

In November of 1997, I had the opportunity to meet Admiral Carroll in person at the Center for Defense Information in Washington, DC, where he serves as deputy director. A man of impeccable credentials who is well-qualified to pass judgment on the institution he has served for over forty years (he served on destroyers in the Pacific and in Vietnam, and in Cold War Europe with General Haig), Carroll makes no attempts to hide his dislike for JROTC. When asked what he would say to an idealistic young person contemplating a career in the military to make the world a better place, he responded:

> First, I'd disabuse him of the notion that the military makes anything better. The military exists to kill and destroy. Now you can rationalize it, and you can justify it on the grounds that, well, there's great evil out there that we must redress, but that involves killing and destroying. And everybody is the loser, humanity is the loser. So I would certainly disabuse him of any idea that we're going to be a force for uplifting people and the quality of life in this world. I would tell him to get busy learning about energy, to become a leader in developing new alternative energy sources that don't pollute the earth, to be a leader in agriculture and help nations that are starving to grow food that will improve their lot. There are all sorts of practical and very needful ways to help improve life, and the military isn't one of them.

At the end of our interview, he reflected on our national defense policy and the meaning of true patriotism:

> There's terrible waste in the military elements of our economic process — disgraceful, obscene waste — and our economy can function very well without those elements. It would function better, in my estimation. There are plenty of statistics showing that military production and activity using public funds produces a relatively small number of jobs. For example, a billion dollars of public funds can create, for a year, about 15,000 to 20,000 jobs. If you spend that same billion dollars on education, you get 50,000 jobs. Healthcare gives you 50,000; building housing, 35,000 to 40,000 jobs. So the notion that military spending is good for the economy is just a falsehood. It is not good for the economy. And we have to educate people, because everybody just accepts at face value what they're told by their members of Congress.
>
> I don't know how we break that cycle. We certainly can't out-advertise them. We can't take out TV commercials. I see TV commercials here in this town every day, virtually touting military systems. They're really put on for the benefit of Congress to say Martin Marietta is doing this, or Boeing is doing that, and urging them to vote for big appropriations. There's no way in the world we can compete with that. It's going to have to be people like you and other such organizations.

I would say, in desperation – that's too strong a word, in exasperation – that there's a hell of a lot more interest in this town right now in the basketball team and the hockey team than there is in the 270 billion dollars that are going into the military budget. Bread and circuses is what society dwells on, and it's awfully hard to break.

Now you take a horrible depression, people begging on street corners (they already are, but I'm talking now about a third of our population unemployed and desperate), then there would be some recognition. We couldn't afford to pump this money into the military. But I don't want to get rid of the problem that way. I want to get rid of the problem by rational thought, not in a crisis...

True patriotism is allegiance to the founding concept of this nation, which is that individuals have rights and dignity, and that their government will reflect the will of the majority of the informed citizens and will make it a better country. That's true patriotism. If you're working to improve this country, whether it be through education, through agriculture – that's patriotism.

JROTC is an abomination. It is just absolutely unconscionable to start teaching thirteen- and fourteen-year-olds about military science, how to handle a gun, that wearing a uniform with an insignia on it makes you an important person, and so on. It is the inculcation of immature people, immature personalities. And that training affects you for the rest of your life. And that's why JROTC is an abomination and unconscionable. It's absolutely immoral. But it's true: they come out with a knowledge of firearms and with some sense of organizational discipline. They can put together a drug gang and arm it and operate it more effectively. I'm not saying the military trains them to do that, but they can apply that training. The whole idea of trying to teach a child that wearing a uniform and shooting a gun is patriotic – that this makes you a patriot, to kill somebody – is obscene.

Retired Vice-Admiral Jack Shanahan is director of the Center for Defense Information. He enlisted in the Navy prior to World War II, served in the Pacific off the coast of Korea, and commanded a number of tours in the Tonkin Gulf during Vietnam. He also spent a year in-country as Commander of the Coastal Surveillance and Interdiction Force headquartered in Cam Ranh Bay. Shanahan once commanded the U.S. Second Fleet and NATO Strike Fleet Atlantic, the guided missile destroyer *Cochrane* and the destroyer escort *Evans,* and six other destroyers and missile ships. Though he upholds his belief in a strong national defense, he is committed to exposing gross waste, senselessness, and mismanagement of military matériel and personnel. He, too, offered some remarkable insights into the long-term consequences of military training:

Now that we've created a professional military force, we expect people to be signing up for a career. In other words, they should know when they're going in that this is what they're going to do. Instead of being a lawyer or doctor or writer, they're going to be a soldier or sailor or a Marine. And they're probably going to do that for twenty-five years. And then they're going to leave the service. And, quite frankly, there isn't a lot of gainful employment out there after a guy has spent twenty-five or thirty years in the military. What is he qualified to do on the outside? Not very much, and that is a significant problem.

To young people contemplating a military career, I'd say, "Dig. Make sure." Because if you're going to go down that path, you ought to know exactly where you're going, and not just accept the word of the guy who's trying to get your name on the bottom line. You want to make sure that you look under all the rocks.

People need to know that the needs of the service will come first. So if the needs of the service change, even after you've signed, all bets are off. You want to make sure that you look very carefully at what you're talking about, because nothing is certain. Go to other people, to other sources. And I don't mean other military sources: talk to your peers, to your teachers, to your guidance counselors.

In a video on military enlistment called "Signing Up: It's Your Choice," a recruiter says, "We don't make 'em join the Army. We just give 'em an option. They want to better themselves, and we try to help them out." But the most important, and least discussed, aspect of a military career is left to a high school guidance counselor, who adds:

> They make students believe that they can join the military, that they can go to exotic places. But they don't bring home the reality that you can die very easily, that you can be killed.

Such denial has played a heavy role in the life of Joseph Hughes, a Vietnam veteran whom I interviewed in the Borden Avenue Homeless Shelter in Brooklyn. Hughes grew up in a white, middle-class family in New Jersey and entered Seton Hall University in 1963. Back then, ROTC was mandatory:

> In '67, two ROTC graduates from my school got killed in Nam. They got killed within three months of one another, and it hit that campus all of a sudden that it was reality. This is a shootin' war, you know. And everybody started scramblin': what are *they* going to do? And most of the guys did not want to go in.

I was in a lot of turmoil. Should I, shouldn't I? Cousin Billy came home, Billy Hughes. He was an infantry soldier in the Delta, 9th Division. Saw a lot of stuff, went through hell, looked like an old man when he came back. And he told me what it was like. But I didn't know what to do…

Patriotism. You know, patriotism. So I went. Plus I had this goofy idea in my head that because I was a mechanic, nothing can happen, I can't really get hurt. I can skin my knuckles fixing a machine or maybe get run over by a truck or something, but as far as combat, it's not going to happen. But things were different when I got to the Nam…

A World War II veteran friend of mine put this most succinctly when he said, "The Army can't make you fight, but it can bring you to where the fighting is going on and leave you there."

Another friend, Bill Wiser, experienced this firsthand when he journeyed to the Persian Gulf between December 28, 1990, and January 6, 1991. He was taken aback by the disbelief, among enlisted soldiers, that they would ever have to see live action. On the trip over, a security guard at John F. Kennedy International Airport said to him, "I don't want war, but I may be called. And I don't want to fight, but I'll do what I have to do. I'm in the reserves. I made a choice, and sometimes you choose to destroy yourself."

In Saudi Arabia, Bill talked with a serviceman from Georgia:

I don't have anything against serving my country, but this is something more than that. We were told we'd be given thirty days notice if we left the country. We were given two hours. I have two boys in school, and I didn't even get a chance to say good-bye. We were told we'd get home shortly and now it's been five months. My wife tells me she's trying to be Mom *and* Dad…If this thing happens there's going to be a lot of bloodshed, and the closer it gets the more scared I get.

After meeting with many more American soldiers, Bill wrote:

The troops are the least keen to fight. Again and again I was told, "I don't want war. I don't want to see action. I don't want to fight." What do they want? They want to get home to their wives and kids. If there is war, they will fight. Why? They have no love of the country that is hosting them. They have no love of the country they may be liberating. They simply signed a contract, and they will fulfill their obligation to the end.

In January of 1991, he received a phone call from the mother of an American serviceman stationed in Saudi Arabia. She was part of a network of parents of Gulf War soldiers, and she told him:

Nobody wants to see war break out. We don't know anyone who wants to
fight…The leaders seem to think this is a computer game, but it is our sons
and daughters. My son comes from a working-class family, white. He wanted
to better himself, to get a good education and a good job. What has happened
was part of the risk he took, but none of us thought of the reality of actual
conflict. With the end of the Cold War we thought we were looking at peace.

My kid is just a child. Sure, he's twenty years old, but he's still just a
grown-up kid. He doesn't know if he's more scared of getting killed than of
killing someone. The whole thing is so awful…

Later, Bill heard from the mother of another soldier, one who had seen action
during the ground war in Kuwait. Between bouts of tears, she related:

He's having a real struggle with what he is seeing there. He was just sobbing – beyond sobbing. Young kid from Iraq. They had killed him. "He
looked just like my brother Brad when he was younger. There he lay, dead,
with his eyes staring up at us." It makes me sick. How will he handle this
when he gets home?

I love Mike…I dread it every time I hear a car. Will this be the Army coming to tell me he's dead? A part of me would die if he gets killed.

Manuel Carvalho, a veteran at the Bruderhof, learned these same lessons the
hard way. He was sent to Vietnam early in the war to set up the air base at Da
Nang. At an evening gathering in our community he remembered:

What eighteen-year-old knows what democracy is? Or what picking up a gun
and shooting someone is like? They don't tell you that side. They tell you that
they're "looking for a few good men," that you're going to get a nice uniform,
that you'll look pretty for the girls. But they don't tell you the reality.

And the reality comes in many ways. I enlisted in a time when there was
no war, in 1963. I thought it was a good time: I'd get it done, get it over with,
and put it in the past. And then I found myself in boot camp, and then in
Okinawa, and suddenly I'm on the shores of Vietnam right after this Gulf of
Tonkin business.

Well, to make a long story short, I wound up in a firefight in 1965 and
got my legs smashed up by some rounds, and lay in a hospital back in St.
Albans, in Queens, New York, reading about the war I just left, and I
couldn't believe it. The stories, the misinformation! Only then did I start to
believe that I was being conned. I was conned to get out of the military
with a disability, but they weren't about to give it to me. I served, I got shot
up, I got purple hearts, bronze stars, got paraded by Mayor John Lindsey in
New York City and hey, hey, hey. Yeah, hey, hey, hey…

I had a run-in with one of my neighbors after getting out of the military. Met this commander who was a recruiter, a naval commander, right in Brooklyn, and he asked me, "Well, how was your time?" I said, "Pretty tough, but I hear you are a recruiter. And you know what? We are on opposite sides." "What?" "We're on opposite sides. I'll do anything I can to stop anybody from signing their life away."

Because that's exactly what it was, signing your life away. But you don't realize it. You're eighteen, you've got the world by the tail, and you have no worries...

I think we need to educate people. Go into the schools, go into the colleges, be almost forceful, tell them that we shouldn't allow anyone to come in and try to convince us to kill someone. If we educate the people there won't be anyone to fight the wars, and they'll have to do it themselves, and they are not going to do it themselves, because they'll get killed.

■ ■ ■ ■ ■ ■ ■

And so we return to the thoughtful silence of that summer evening under the trees in Woodcrest. Fred Louis is done reading, and shuffles his papers in finality. The soft crackle seems somehow appropriate. "I survived, but it's not a happy ending. I was a coward. I went to the war," he quotes. There is a pause and then Jay Wenk, a World War II veteran and member of Veterans for Peace from Woodstock, rises to speak:

My recruiters were in the newspapers, in the magazines, in the films, on the radio, billboards, everywhere. Growing up in that milieu, I was, like all my friends, all of them, dying to get into it. Couldn't wait until I was old enough to get into it. I started to change my mind as I got closer to the sound of the guns. But nevertheless, I was there, I went. I was very scared, I was very shy, I was very naïve, I was very insecure. That's a hell of a place to be carrying a rifle. I carried that rifle in World War II in Germany and chased the Germans from one end of Czechoslovakia to the other. When I went into the Army I was not quite eighteen. When I went to war, I went to defend democracy. What I knew of democracy was "Oh, beautiful...for amber waves of grain..." I knew the Boy Scout motto, and that was about it. I knew what some of the symbols of a purported democracy were, but I did not know what democracy was.

Before I went into the Army in 1941, Pearl Harbor was attacked. Every billboard along the roads, every publication like *Life* magazine, was loaded, absolutely loaded with propaganda. All you have to do is dig up any publication from those times, those years, and you'll see what I mean. There were pictures of dead Americans lying on beaches in the South Pacific. There were signs that had been put up on the beach next to these bodies. The signs said, "Kill the bastards," referring to the Japanese, of course, or whoever it was.

Sure, we can understand the anger and the heartbreak that people feel when their friends have been killed. But we also have to understand the profound and crazily insidious propaganda effected by that kind of thing when it's repeated over and over and over and over and over a thousand times a day, day after day, year after year: kill the bastards. Immediately when hostilities break out, we are the good guys, whatever country it is, and they are the bad guys, and they deserve to die. We learn this. When I say "we" I'm talking about all of us, because we cannot separate ourselves from anyone else in the world.

On his last day in office Eisenhower said, "Beware of the military-industrial complex." My point is that people on the top of the chain of command lie. They lie for whatever reasons. And that's the irony. And the poor schnooks of us who are on the line deal with heroism in one degree or another, depending on what's happening. But those people at the top lie. And they lie shamelessly and endlessly, and I don't care what President you want to name, they lie. The generals and admirals in their wardrooms, they lie. They lie, they lie, they lie. And it's very hard for me to make a distinction between this country, where I was born and raised, and the leaders of this country. It's a difficult distinction to make.

I'd rather see people burn the flag in anger than to follow the flag blindly into some ill-advised and corrupt process, of which we've had plenty of examples. We usually don't know that we're being propagandized when we are. I hope that, whoever has to face the choice of going into the military in order to get an education, realizes that they may get an education different from what they are looking for.

Certainly education from without is crucial: reading, talking, taking in everything you can. But that's only one piece of it. The rest of it, and I think the most important part of it, is internal. How do you know when you're being conned? When somebody is offering you something that looks very nice at a very low price. What I like to do is to go back inside myself and be in touch with that part of me that wants something for nothing. That's one way of knowing that you're being conned.

There are better ways to serve our country than in the military. There are organizations that people can put their energy into and get something worthwhile out of it. I can't stress enough the importance of finding alternative ways of serving yourselves and serving the greater ideals of what this country and others stand for.

Pete Murphy, a World War II vet and member of the local VFW dying from cancer, sat in the circle of veterans with hands folded and eyes fixed on the floor. He had been quiet all evening, even during supper, and I couldn't guess what was going on inside him. After Jay spoke, Pete felt it was time to say his piece in a few simple but powerful words:

> I joined the Marine Corps when I was twenty years old and had a wife and two children. I went to Parris Island and, as this gentleman said, they lied to me all the way. I hated everybody. Then one day I killed a soldier. He was Japanese. His wallet came out of his jacket, and I opened it up and I looked at it. And there was a picture of him, his wife, and his three children. And I said, "What the hell am I doing here? Here's a guy that's never done a thing to me, and yet I had to kill him because his boss said "go to war" and my boss said "go to war." And they lie and they lie and they are still lying to us. And they are ruining this country. Your son goes, and do you think they care if he comes back? No they don't. I've seen it with my own eyes.

Jim Murphy of New York City's West Side High added the Vietnam angle to what Jay and Pete expressed:

> It's hard for me to describe the conditioning process I went through at the time. It was almost like we were raised to fight that war. I mean, it's strange, and I know it sounds strange put in that context, but I think my generation was simply raised to fight the Vietnam War.
>
> We started off life in kindergarten pledging allegiance to the flag, and then we joined the Cub Scouts where they gave us a little uniform and taught us nifty little salutes, and then we went into Boy Scouts, and then high school football where everything was team-oriented and you had to obey the coach. Then we got drafted, and by that time we'd already had lots of the conditioning necessary not to question.
>
> When I got my draft notice, I enlisted. I was afraid that if I was drafted I would automatically be sent to Vietnam for two years. So I did the smart thing: I enlisted for four years. And they sent me to Vietnam.
>
> But I was ready. We all just jumped right into the boat. It was like something that we had been taught; it was our duty and our obligation and we just accepted it. We didn't know that Ho Chi Minh returned downed Air Force flyers during the Second World War and that the French had supported the Japanese in order to maintain their economic stronghold in Vietnam. We didn't know that Ho Chi Minh was an ally, because that was never in any of our books. We never knew that the Vietnamese just wanted to be left alone by European powers; it wasn't part of the history we were taught. What we were told was that the communists – this little room filled with commu-

nists — was going to take over Southeast Asia, and the domino theory and all that. Which gets back to those textbooks again. I strongly recommend that you question the textbooks.

Gerald McCarthy was next to speak:

I have some things to say to you people who are in high school, but I don't think you want to hear what I have to say, because it's really disturbing. I was tricked and fooled. I relied on my misconceptions, on my uncertainties. And I think that's something that's really dangerous. It's what gets guys to enlist...

The recruiters had a field day during Vietnam. People were enlisting, and they were good Christian guys. They weren't anarchists. But they were people who were unsure about their feelings, about themselves in one way or another.

Ben Chitty served with the Navy in the Gulf of Tonkin during Vietnam. During a stop in San Diego in April of 1968, as the country was rocked by the assassination of Martin Luther King, Jr., Ben was given a .45 and sent to "keep the peace" amid the tension and rioting on the West Coast. When he realized he was just as upset as the people he was supposed to be controlling, he began to resist actively within the military. Upon his discharge, he became an outspoken member of Vietnam Veterans Against the War. Ben complemented Gerald's comments with an important observation about veterans and their children in time of war:

Veterans, I think, are in a very peculiar position because a lot of people who are not veterans would like to be veterans — and why not? You go to the movies, you watch television, you read books, war heroism is looked up to, war is presented as a glorious experience. I was raised on stories of Cowboys and Indians, and the Cowboys always wore white hats and they always won, and of course you would want to be one of those good guys, one of those heroes, one of those people that won. And yet a veteran — particularly a veteran of combat — knows that it's not such a good thing.

One way that you can tell if somebody is really a veteran is to ask him, "Do you really want your son to do what you did?" Most veterans would say no. They don't have any choice about themselves anymore, but they do have choices for their children.

Although they number far fewer than their male counterparts, women in the military face the same kind of deception as do men. Carol Picou, who served in the Middle East during the Gulf War, now suffers from what is probably the combined effects of toxic medications and radiation from depleted uranium:

risks about which she was never warned, and which the Pentagon still tries to hide. She doubts that the Pentagon will ever be brought to task for its systematic deception, but she wishes she could be allowed to place her own advertisement alongside the recruitment billboards.

I would love to make a commercial now. When I joined the Army it was, "Be all you can be."

So take us and show us in basic training, firing our weapons, climbing mountains, rappelling, doing all these wonderful things the Army teaches you to do, and then show us now, with our crippled bones, our incontinence, take all of us in our wheelchairs, missing our arms and legs, and dying of cancer and brain tumors, take our graves, and put *that* on a commercial.

"Be all you can be!" Now, what *can* we be? Would they let that be aired? Of course not. And who would make my commercial? Nobody.

■ ■ ■ ■ ■ ■ ■

The boys fight the wars of men.

Herman Melville

CHAPTER 3

You're in the Army Now

Rape the town and kill the people, that's the thing we love to do!
Rape the town and kill the people, that's the only thing to do!
Watch the kiddies scream and shout, rape the town and kill the
people, that's the thing we love to do!

Boot camp chant, U.S. Marine Corps

I got sick the day of my induction. Threw up in the bathroom at the hotel near campus, overwhelmed with a familiar dread. I knew it well, had experienced it before every wrestling match for five years in junior high and high school. It had a lot to do with forcing myself to become something I feared.

I remember my wrestling coach telling us to become animals, to imagine killing our opponent to attain the drive to win. In the late 1970s, there was an outstanding American Olympic wrestler who said that he won so consistently because he imagined his opponent to be the man who had raped his sister. Our coach pointed to this attitude as an ideal frame of mind. I feared coach so much that I didn't have the guts to tell him I wanted off the wrestling team until my senior year. He was a fierce recruiter, and hard to refuse.

I'd had reservations about going into the military, but ROTC looked too good to pass up. It offered free tuition, adventure, a building of one's character, leadership, interesting jobs in technical fields. During the school year, I would train to be an officer. We would dress up in uniform, do a lot of drilling and marching, and go to classes on military expertise, rules, and regulations. Summers were to be spent on active duty in the Navy and Marines.

Now I feel the old familiar tightening of my stomach, the trepidation. Once again I find myself doing something I really don't want to do, becoming something I really don't want to become, because I somehow feel pressured into it. I have heard stories about military indoctrination and hazing and want to get it over with.

In a daze, I scurry through the rigors of the first day, pawing through uniforms and sea bags, standing in formation, taking oaths transferring my person to the property of the U.S. Government, snapping to attention at the first jarring screams of drill sergeants, trying to absorb new schedules, strict rules, and codes of appearance and behavior. The presence of my mother and grandfather somewhere outside doesn't help much. They have accompanied me to see me off, but my lifeline to sanity is tenuous and vanishing fast. By mid afternoon they are gone...

We are sitting in a training class in the dilapidated old gym. The ROTC headquarters is little more than a series of bunkers built onto the inside wall of a turn-of-the-century physical education hall. At the front of the room is Major C. I cannot remember him without the old fear welling up inside of me. He is not a fearsome man to look at, wiry and of medium height, but with a look of emotionless steel, aside from a rare outbreak of military humor. Every day I have to stand rigidly for inspection before him, unable to move a muscle as his eyes absorb every detail of polish and uniform and bearing – every detail except the fact that it is a human being standing there before him. His insensitivity to violence, indeed his avid support of the necessity for violence, frightens me, perhaps today like at no other time.

Now he has digressed from the lecture and is telling foxhole stories from his tour in Vietnam. He is, unbelievably, laughing. He is telling how funny it is when two Marines are diving for the same hole under mortar fire and they cannot both fit. He is asked if he has ever killed anyone. He says, "Yeah, I had to kill some people," and then goes on with the story.

I watch some of my classmates. Now they are laughing, too. They are beginning to become comfortable with the class, with everything. They are being groomed, and it is clear, from the looks and smiles and nods, that they are progressing very well. I listen uncomfortably from the back of the room.

Inside, part of me is screaming for humanity, for reality to break in. But another part of me wants to be accepted by them all, to be this definition of a man, to see it all as necessary and virtuous so that my inner torment will end...

I am running along the piers at Norfolk Naval Base during my first summer in the Navy. Today I take a new route and find myself cut off by a fenced-in helicopter landing area, with no way back to my ship except to cross the area. I fail to see the security signs on the chain-link gate and work my way through a gap in the fencing. I am most of the way across when I hear screams from two military police near a hangar on the far side of the tarmac. One of them has a gun strapped to his side. Making a split-second decision, I race the rest of the way across the asphalt, bound the fence, and sprint along the piers. The MPs spurt after me in a jeep, and I know it is only a matter of time before they will reach me. There is perhaps a mile between me and the ship and it is no use running, but I try to think fast, my heart pounding with adrenaline. I look quickly to my right at the frothing ocean, and decide in an instant. I jump into the freezing waves, my hands groping for the large rocks fringing the pier. I dive into a crack between two boulders, and surface in a small air space hidden from view, neck-deep in the slapping water. Above me, the jeep comes to a screeching halt at the pier's edge. The MPs are cursing, and I can just see their boots pacing back and forth along the lip of the tarmac. They think I am under the water and wait for me to surface, but see nothing. After ten minutes they decide to give up, and I hear them driving away. Ever so slowly, I swim out from under the rocks and climb to the edge of the pier, dripping and trembling. I shake off the water and jog back to the ship, make my way to the midshipman's quarters puffing and squishing. My bunk mates stare, but nobody asks any questions.

I am standing on the quay alongside my ship in my bright midshipman's dress-whites. A group of enlisted men surrounds me. They are cursing. They are telling me, in colorful language, that I am nothing, that I am a privileged pain, a good-for-nothing, snot-nosed little momma's boy. Their faces contort with disgust, hatred, resentment. I come to a new realization: this is an organization of intense hierarchy. You take orders. Some people give orders. The ones who take orders don't much like the ones who give orders, especially green young boys training to give orders. So much for camaraderie.

The drinking club on the base becomes my refuge. Alcohol and marijuana (plentiful in the military) anesthetize me, make the nagging questions go away. There are strip dancers at the club every night. Their lewd smiles and movements disgust even me, despite the fact that I keep coming back, night after night, to escape the tension and frustration of military life. I ignore them, downing my rum-and-cokes, mentally scoffing the enlisted men who leer and laugh beneath the stage.

Two lifers notice my midshipman's bars and stroll up to my stool. They are very drunk. They want to play pool, so I humor them. We go into an adjoining room, but it's empty and there are no pool tables. I look at the enlisted men and they smirk in return. "You ever fuck a black girl?" one of them asks. "No," I reply, beginning to get apprehensive. "You got to fuck a black girl then," he says. He calls out her name, loud. "No!" I shout, trying to make myself clear. "Fucking middy!" laughs the other, and calls her name again. "Yeah, you gonna fuck a blacky!" One of them puts his hand on my shoulder. "No!" I shout again. I jerk myself free and walk quickly back into the room full of people and smoke. They follow me, but I am out the door and running, and they are too drunk to give chase.

After that incident, I never go back to the club but spend the rest of my tour smoking pot alone under the dark sky each night. My bunk mates, most of them middies too, are hardly friendly. They're confused like me, suspicious, resentful, and I spend as much time away from them as possible.

I meet my first friend that summer, an enlisted guy in electronics. I think he is the coolest person I have ever met in the Navy. He wants to get out real bad. We talk about philosophy a lot — anything but the Navy. During a week at sea, we take apart an entire radar console, even though he doesn't have a clue how to put it back together again. He said you've got to make work for yourself in this joint so you don't die of boredom. He likes to hang out in a small room filled with instruments, and record the electronic signals they emit. He gets high a lot, biding his time and dreaming of what he's going to do when this is all over...

It's a new school year, and we are standing in formation, becoming rigid for inspection, still dropping comments out of earshot of the gunnies. "Check it out. McKenna." One of my fellow middies flips his eyes sideways, toward a female midshipman emerging from the bunker door. "I'll bet she's tight." "Uh-uh, military pussy. Don't touch that shit." "You serious?" "She's an ugly bitch anyway." I ignore their bantering, but not because I'm any better. I've had enough of these guys and their brown-nosing. Spit and polish on the outside, when you need to look good. Dirty deeds out of uniform. I turn my eyes and watch McKenna. She wants to be a Marine, she says. "Damn," I think to myself. "What are girls doing in this man's Navy anyway? There's gotta be something wrong in her head."

It is my second summer of active duty, and I am aboard the SSBN-class nuclear submarine USS *Daniel Boone*. We've been under a week, and the endless darkness and boredom are beginning to take their toll. They step up the training and show some mildly pornographic films in the mess to keep us occupied. At night it is blacker than black, and quieter than the grave. My eyes strain, open wide, for some glimmer of light to offer a sense of direction, but it is useless. I lie on my bunk awake, deprived of my senses, trying to think pleasant thoughts.

One day we are trained in the control room. They show us the reactor, glowing eerily behind a thick, translucent panel. They say we have sixteen nuclear missiles aboard, each with sixteen MIRVs (multiple, independently-targetable warheads), each MIRV one hundred times the megatonnage of the bomb dropped on Hiroshima. Dimly, my mind tries to comprehend the awesome fire-power; the fact that the vessel we ride, floating through the Atlantic deep, is capable of destroying an entire continent. The thought hits me, dangles for a second, and is gone...

I am at Little Creek, Virginia, in the first week of boot camp in the Marines. We are awakened at 4:00 A.M. by the crash of metal garbage cans against the doors of our barracks and the screams of gunnery sergeants: "Up ladies! Get the fuck up, now!" We have five minutes to make our beds, dress, and be down on the tarmac in formation, or there will be hell to pay. A gunnery sergeant, whose face I only remember as fierce and angry, is screaming at me as our platoon stands at attention in the cold darkness of early morning. I have done something wrong again. He reaches out, grabs some stray whiskers I missed while shaving, and rips them out of my neck.

We are jogging. The gunnery sergeant starts to chant to the rhythm of clomping boots and yells at us to join in. It is obscene. It is about our mothers — my mother, whom I love. We have to sing it. Next comes the familiar mantra: "Kill." Left, right. "Kill." Left, right. "Kill the motherfuckers." Left, right. We hit the dunes by 6:00 A.M. There are huge machine guns in pits. We are ordered to jump in and begin firing at tires along a far bank in the distance. We are told: "Fill the bastards with lead. That's the enemy, boys!" I see the tires catch on fire from the friction of so many bullets. I wonder...and wonder some more.

Some poor freshman in boot camp left his socks on his bed before inspection. They screamed at him for a long time. Now he is just a heap on the floor, sob-bing, crying like a baby. He will have to go home to his mommy and daddy, we are told. They do a lot of screaming here. We are told it is to make a man out of us. After a while you become numb. The yelling seems to come from far away, and your thoughts run round in circles. You don't listen, because nothing is re-ally being said. It is just loud noise. Maybe that is what they want. Become numb. Don't ask anything. Don't say anything. Just do it. When the screaming begins, you cannot even move your eyes. You are automata.

I am leaving boot camp early because of an injury sustained during the obstacle course. I ham it up in front of the gunny, wincing in pain amid the chaos of training jeeps and track-wheeled vehicles careening all over the place in the sand. It works. I am sent to a nearby naval clinic, my leg swathed in Ace ban-dages by a medic who knows I am partly faking but takes pity on me.

I have returned to the base and am called into the gunny's darkened office. All the others are still out at the dunes, preparing for a helicopter jump with full packs and weapons. The fierce-faced sergeant looks up at me from his desk. The room is dead quiet. "You gonna stick with it, son?" "Can't, sir. I'm injured." Suddenly, unexpectedly, the gunny is changed. For a passing second he is just a man, and for the first time I see a small, weak human being like me, with questions and uncertainty and even a little fear. "Son, you know there's a rhyme and a reason to all of this, don't you?" I feel unable to answer him. It is a simple question, which demands a simple, thoughtless confirmation, yet in his tone and in his face I see and hear a plea of desperation. After a long moment, I croak: "No, sir. I don't." And then I walk away. They let me go. Get a bus, get high, board a plane, come home.

My girlfriend is the only anchor left. That is what I believe, but she is sixteen – only sixteen – and couldn't know or understand. I have to hand it to her: she took the stream of pain and confusion head-on and wanted so much to help, but the waves were too high and too strong. I destroyed something in her as I groped for love out of desperation – I was lost in an abyss, and took her with me...

I am back for my junior year at Cornell, and the shock of boot camp has dulled a bit with time. I try to forget about it. "That's the Marines," I say to myself. "They're fucked in the head." I brace myself for the decision, and really believe I am ready to sign the papers that will commit me to two more years of ROTC at Cornell followed by four years of active duty in the U.S. Navy. It's hard to see any other way to do it. The papers are due to come in on Friday, but get lost in the mail. I would have signed them but over the weekend something happens to me inside. I don't know what it is, but a voice within grows louder and louder: "Get the hell out! This isn't you. It isn't you!"

I obey that voice, call my mom and tell her what I'm thinking. Battle-scarred, she wants her son to have a good foundation; she fights, gets mad that I'm throwing it all away. We have it out, but she gives in.

That voice inside me is fermenting into certainty. I take the fork in the road. On Monday the papers arrive, but I walk into the ROTC bunker in Barton Hall and tell the officers I want out. The past merges with the present, and my head swims: "I did it again, coach! See me? I'm telling you, I want out!" There is a stunned silence. Faces change in a heartbeat. I see something new in the eyes of the gunnies, majors, and midshipmen that day, something beyond suspicion and misunderstanding. There is dark condescension, cold isolation. A single sentence has cut me off forever. I am no longer one of them.

Mechanically, I go through the motions of my discharge in the electric silence, hand in my uniforms and other military paraphernalia, avoiding eye contact. My mind still races with fear; I cannot yet believe it is all true, that I am really free. With the final token handed in and the last stroke of the pen, I

walk – float – out of the door. I am giddy, wonderfully uncertain about the future. What the hell happens now? I don't know, and I don't care. I stop in the
late-summer air outside. The world looks somehow different now. I take a
breath and step into it.

■ ■ ■ ■ ■ ■ ■

Anna Simons, an anthropologist at UCLA, observes that young recruits shed
much more than pounds during boot camp. She notes that drill instructors place
paramount emphasis on stripping away critical and independent thought, and
end up recalibrating graduates to a dangerous level of group think. She recounts
statements by drill instructors such as: "Before we leave my island, we will be
thinking and breathing exactly alike," and "Nobody's an individual, understand?" This drive for conformity and homogeneity goes to such excessive
lengths that sentences beginning with the first person "I" are strictly forbidden.
Surprisingly, she concludes that such indoctrination might be beneficial for dis-
solute youth, and endorses a program of compulsory national service which in-
cludes the discipline of boot camp.[1]

For those of us unfortunate enough to have been beyond the "presentable
edge" of boot camp, such a prospect is frightening. It is crucial to understand
that, while the military makes much of team cohesion and plays heavily on the
human desire to belong, its ultimate purpose is the calculated killing of other
human beings. Buried under the lofty goals of self-sacrifice and self-denial for
the good of the whole, the noble end of training is nothing other than death.

We make much of cults whose leaders deceive naïve followers and lead them
down paths of death and destruction; national ire is kindled at the very mention
of Jonestown, Waco, and Heaven's Gate. But what would we say if we were to
learn of an organization that entices hundreds of thousands of teenagers into its
ranks each year, offering money and adventure, a new family, a new identity,
and a promise for membership in "one of the most elite organizations ever created"? And what if we heard that this organization makes it illegal to leave, and
imprisons or shoots members who try? What if we were told that the leaders of
this organization systematically corrupt the morals of its new converts, teach
them the dehumanization of whole nations and classes of people, take them to
foreign countries, put weapons in their hands, and force them to kill? And what
if the new converts were forced to chant: "To kill, to kill, to kill with no mercy!
Blood, blood makes the grass grow! Ready to kill, ready to die but never will!
Blood makes the grass grow!"[2] Isn't that the kind of thing we put Charles
Manson away for? And wouldn't such an organization be perceived as one of

the biggest cults of all time? Welcome to the U.S. Marine Corps, Army, Navy, and Air Force.

"The 55 men who have run West Point since 1802 have all grappled with the same problem: how to produce officer-warriors vicious enough to kill and sensitive enough to inspire the troops of a democratic nation to follow," mused Michael Winerip in a recent article in *The New York Times Magazine*.[3] Our friend, British veteran David Harvey, ponders the same contradictions in typically understated fashion:

> If I had been there solely for the purpose of comradeship, that would have been absolutely great by me. But, you know, that isn't why they have armies. You're in there to do a job...When the American troops were in Vietnam they had great comradeship with each other. But they weren't sent to Vietnam to indulge in their love and comradeship for each other, were they? As part of the British colonial forces, I also remember the friendship and the sharing and the strong bonds we had for each other, but that wasn't what I was paid for.

Paul Pappas, a Bruderhof member who is also a World War II veteran of the U.S. Marines, recently shared with me his reflections on boot camp indoctrination and the "fruits" of his training:

> In spite of not wanting to get killed, I chose to serve in the most dangerous branch of the forces, the Marine Corps. Movies depicting the South Pacific had emphasized only the glory of fighting the wicked Japanese...During boot camp the base commander spoke to us: "Everything in your training has a purpose." How true his words were I did not grasp until later.
>
> Not being an athletic person, I found the physical training strenuous, and it was not easy to keep up. But what was most devastating was the psychological manipulation aimed at making me what I was not and did not want to be – a killer.
>
> I didn't realize this fully until right before the invasion of Okinawa. They did everything they could to make us hate. The caste system of rank was rigidly enforced, and we were constantly kept on edge with spot inspections and forced marches in the middle of the night – whatever could be done to aggravate and anger us. It got so bad that someone blew up the NCO's privy.
>
> The control over us was relentless; there was no room to breathe or relax. All we did was to react – inwardly, not outwardly. Anger, frustration, and hatred built up inside of me; tenderness and compassion were destroyed, and we became beasts, killing machines. There came a point where they had to draw the line, because somebody was going to get killed and it wasn't going to be the enemy.

We were pawns, and we were controlled by powers over which we had no control. The world was going to hell and we could do nothing about it. But it was years before I was able to sort out my feelings or even speak about them...

In times of war, governments and armies work hand in hand to engage the general public in their campaigns, heightening the sense of obligation and duty to a feverish pitch. Clearly, something far beyond human influence is at work when countless families fall in line and enthusiastically support the sacrifice of sons and daughters to "the cause." Defying sanity and reason, these forces compel society, along with its soldiers, to plunge forward into a mission that can only be described as suicidal.

In December of 1937, Japanese soldiers killed an estimated 260,000 to 350,000 people in the newly established capital of the Republic of China. Chinese-American author Iris Chang reports that during the atrocity, which was to become known as the Rape of Nanking:

Between 20,000 and 80,000 Chinese women were raped – and many soldiers went beyond rape to disembowel women, slice off their breasts, nail them alive to walls. So brutal were the Japanese in Nanking that even the Nazis in the city were shocked. John Rabe, a German businessman who led the local Nazi party, joined other foreigners in working tirelessly to save the innocent from slaughter by creating a safety zone where some 250,000 civilians found shelter.

Once again, we must recognize that atrocities on the scale of the Rape of Nanking did not happen overnight. As Chang explains:

In trying to understand the actions of the Japanese, we must begin with a little history. To prepare for what it viewed as an inevitable war with China, Japan had spent decades training its men. The molding of young men to serve in the Japanese military began early: in the 1930s, toy shops became virtual shrines to war, selling arsenals of toy soldiers, tanks, rifles, anti-aircraft guns, bugles, and howitzers. Japanese schools operated like miniature military units. Indeed, some of the teachers were military officers, who lectured students on their duty to help Japan fulfill its divine destiny of conquering Asia and being able to stand up to the world's nations as a people second to none. They taught young boys how to handle wooden models of guns, and older boys how to handle real ones. Textbooks became vehicles for military propaganda. Teachers also instilled in boys hatred and contempt for the Chinese people, preparing them psychologically for a future invasion of the Chinese mainland. One historian tells the story of a squeamish Japanese schoolboy in the 1930s who burst into tears when told to dissect a frog. His teacher slammed his knuckles against the boy's head and yelled, "Why are you crying about one lousy frog? When you grow up you'll have to kill one hundred, two hundred chinks!" [4]

Whether we are prepared to admit it or not, all of us have, at one time or another, given ourselves over to the zeitgeist, which created the monsters of Nanking and My Lai, Oradour and Lidice, Auschwitz and Bosnia. We have been good salesmen whenever we have aroused passions with words of prejudice, division, and hatred, or flattered with appeals to justice, morality, and self-sacrifice. And we will be willing customers as long as we allow our governments to seduce us with a false bill of goods, to sell us short on empty promises of freedom and democracy.

CHAPTER 4

Bloody Century

Once upon a time, it matters little when, and in stalwart England, it matters little where, a fierce battle was fought...The painted butterfly took blood into the air upon the edges of its wings. The stream ran red. The trodden ground became a quagmire, whence, from sullen pools collected in the prints of human feet and horses' hoofs, the one prevailing hue still lowered and glimmered at the sun.

Heaven keep us from a knowledge of the sights the moon beheld upon that field, when, coming up above the black line of distant rising ground, softened and blurred at the edge by trees, she rose into the sky and looked upon the plain, strewn with upturned faces that had once at mothers' breasts sought mothers' eyes, or slumbered happily. Heaven keep us from a knowledge of the secrets whispered afterwards upon the tainted wind that blew across the scene of that day's work and that night's death and suffering! Many a lonely moon was bright upon the battleground, and many a star kept mournful watch upon it, and many a wind from every quarter of the earth blew over it, before the traces of the fight were worn away.

Charles Dickens, "The Battle of Life"

Dickens' story indicates that medieval England was no less bloody than Vietnam; a cursory examination of the Old Testament will likewise reveal carnage on nearly every page. A look at the wars of this century alone reveals a constant, universal evil, irrespective of time and place.

World War I

High school history books tell us that World War I, the "Great War," began with the assassination of the heir to the Austrian throne by a Serbian nationalist. We are taught that this was the spark that ignited the tinderbox, as though war were inevitable; it seems as though the assassin, a tubercular high school student by the name of Gavrilo Prinzip, was only playing to history's demands.

The war began triumphantly, ending a period of great faith and hope in man's accomplishments and in the inherent goodness and integrity of the Western world. As Dalton Trumbo suggests, however, the Age of Enlightenment seems to have had little lasting effect:

> World War I began like a summer festival – all billowing skirts and golden epaulets. Millions upon millions cheered from the sidewalks while plumed imperial highnesses, serenities, field marshals and other such fools paraded through the capital cities of Europe at the head of their shining legions.
>
> It was a season of generosity; a time for boasts, bands, poems, songs, innocent prayers. It was an August made palpitant and breathless by the prenuptial nights of young gentlemen-officers and the girls they left permanently behind them...
>
> Nine million corpses later, when the bands stopped and the serenities started running, the wail of bagpipes would never again sound quite the same. It was the last of the romantic wars...[1]

Woodrow Wilson was only one in a long series of U.S. presidents to deceive the American people and win reelection with promises about keeping America out of war. On August 19, 1914, Wilson cited the 1901 Declaration of London, stating that the United States would not take sides in the European dispute. He called on the American people "to be neutral in fact as well as in name... impartial in thought as well as in deed."[2]

The sinking of the British Cunard liner *Lusitania* by a German U-boat on May 7, 1915, began to turn the tide; among the 1200 who drowned were one hundred and twenty-eight American citizens. The torpedoing of the largest passenger ship in the world was portrayed as an act of unprovoked aggression, under which Wilson was "forced" to reconsider U.S. neutrality. In fact, the German government had published a formal warning to American citizens traveling on "belligerent passenger ships" a week before, indicating the *Lusitania* by name.[3] At the time, British and American leaders feigned horror that a passenger ship should be so targeted, but it is now known that the ship was heavily armed and carried thousands of cases of ammunition.[4]

The year 1916 was the most prosperous year in all of previous American history. Following a severe recession in 1914, war orders from the European Allies had stimulated the economy and precipitated the sale of more than $2 billion in matériel. When Secretary of State Robert Lansing announced the likelihood of American involvement in the war, stock market prices soared to a 15-year high. Foreign trade soared to a record $8 billion, while domestic output peaked at $45 billion. America was fast becoming banker to the world, and its new status brought both power and arrogance. As historian Howard Zinn writes, "governments flourished, patriotism bloomed, class struggle was stilled, and young men died in frightful numbers on the battlefields."[5]

Randolph Bourne later observed that "war is the health of the state." War was good business, but it was bloody, too, and the full extent of its bloodiness had to be kept from the public view if economies were to continue to thrive. In the first Battle of the Marne, 1,000,000 British, French, and German soldiers died. When the Germans tried to break through at Verdun, the Allies lost 600,000 men. Britain alone lost 20,000 men on the first *day* of the Battle of the Somme in 1916, as grim-faced generals flung ever greater numbers of human bodies over the trenches at a gain of mere yards. Altogether more than a million men, an entire generation, died in this one battle alone.[6]

That such carnage was kept well hidden back home is evidenced in remarks by British Prime Minister David Lloyd George himself, who attended a dinner party for the respected journalist Philip Gibbs late in 1917. Gibbs had just returned from the front, and his reports clearly shocked the British leader.

> Even an audience of hardened politicians and journalists was strongly affected. If people really knew, the war would be stopped tomorrow. But of course they don't know and can't know...The thing is horrible beyond human nature to bear, and I feel I can't go on with the bloody business: I would rather resign.[7]

Why the people of England couldn't know is left unsaid, and one can only wonder what they might have done if they had known.

President Wilson began to quell antiwar sentiment as early as 1916, and already in his inaugural address he warned that "no faction of disloyal intrigue break the harmony or embarrass the spirit of our people."[8] "Rough Rider" Teddy Roosevelt used fewer words than the collegiate Wilson: "The man who believes in peace at any price...should instantly move to China. If he stays here, then more manly men will have to defend him, and he is not worth defending."[9]

In 1918, Congress added the Sedition Act to its Sabotage and Espionage Acts, mandating imprisonment for those who would "willfully cause or attempt to cause insubordination, disloyalty, mutiny, or refusal of duty in the military or naval forces of the United States, or…willfully obstruct the recruiting or enlistment service of the U.S."[10] An American Defense Society replete with Vigilante Patrols was formed to put an end to "seditious street oratory," and dissenters faced jail time for "criticizing the flag, government, draft, or arms production." Such laws were needed, it was said, to protect these institutions from "profane, violent, scurrilous, contemptuous, slurring, or abusive language." [11]

As Wilson announced a declaration of war against Germany in 1917, he waxed eloquent:

> It is a fearful thing to lead this great, peaceful people into war, the most terrible of wars. But the right is more precious than the peace, and we shall fight for the things that we have always carried nearest our hearts…for democracy…for the rights and liberties of small nations, for a universal dominion of right by such a concert of free peoples as shall bring peace and safety to all nations and make the world itself at last free.[12]

British Foreign Affairs Secretary Sir Edward Grey was less enthusiastic, and envisioned not peace or safety but impending catastrophe: "The lamps are going out all over Europe; we shall not see them lit again in our lifetime."[13]

■ ■ ■ ■ ■ ■ ■

Among the many men and women who joined our Bruderhof movement in its early years, in the 1920s and 1930s, several had fought as soldiers in the war. Others had suffered as children or wives, those innocents who "couldn't know" then, but later did. Their stories give human faces to mind-numbing statistics and help us to understand the awful realities of the "war to end all wars."

Arthur Woolston, an 83-year-old member of the Bruderhof, recently showed me a sheaf of yellowed letters sent home by his father from the front toward the end of the war. Arthur Sr. was called up in 1917 and trained at Blandford, Dorset, England; from there he was sent on to France, where he fought in the trenches until he was killed by a shell on March 25, 1918. His wife was not forgotten by the British government, and at the end of the war she received a large bronze medal inscribed with the words, "He died to save civilization." But Arthur's letters, written in simple, local dialect, show no such grandiose delusions:

Dear Evelyn and the boy,   July 1917
Again I send a few lines just to let you know how I am. Well I am putting up

with it the best I can. My word you have to go through it with inoculation. I can't lift my arm up. We are supposed to have 48 hours off but we have been marching about after kit. This morning we went filling beds with straw ready for recruits. They keep coming as fast as they can...

Sept 10, 1917

Some started learning Louis guns this morning, others rifle grenades, so that makes me think that we shall get a fortnight at it. You say you don't think Artie had better have any cartridges, they are only empties they would do to play with. As for being a soldier, I shall do all in my power to keep him from a lot like this. I hope he will learn a trade that will keep him from it. A chap in our tent only said yesterday he will see none of his children comes in it...

My dear wife and Artie,   Oct 20, 1917
We set off again yesterday for another train journey. We marched down to the station and it did weigh. I can tell you it's enough to break our backs. We had rounds of ammunition to carry as well. It's a job to lift it on our backs. We started from the station about dinner time and got to the station where we were to get out at seven o'clock. We had to march about eight miles or more to get to the place where we were putting up at. I don't know how we got there. It's the worst go I have had. I were beat by the time we got there. We never seemed to get any nearer. Everyone we asked kept saying the same so we didn't seem to get any nearer. We had to rest four or five times so you can tell we were glad to drop down anywhere...

We arrived here about twelve. They put us in barns. There are about forty or fifty in this one, we had no blanket or anything and we were starved. We are experiencing something now. We can hear the bombardment from here, some of our chaps got left behind and the rations too. We have had only two biscuits and bully beef all day today. I had four packets of cigarettes given since I have been out here. I give most of them away. They are twice as cheap out here...

You are all in my mind, after all our hardships I look on the other side of seeing you again shortly when this is over...

Dear Grandad and everybody and Evelyn and the *children*,   Dec 5, 1917
I were very pleased to hear from you and to hear that Evelyn is over the stile now. I am pleased to hear both are doing well and I do hope they will, fancy a boy. I daresay Evelyn would have liked a little girl and I wouldn't have minded. I should never like to think little Artie and the youngster would ever become a soldier, they never will if I can rule...Let Evelyn have all she

needs, never mind about money. She knows where there is plenty and she can have as much as she wants...I should have loved to have been at home and it was my place. It's a downright shame that we should have to be away. I shall look forward to the time of coming home more and more...

Jan 11, 1918

We have had a rough time since we have been here. I think it had been a bit quiet until we got here. My word we did get a shelling on the 30th. I shall never forget it. I shall have plenty to tell you when I come home. We lost about half the battalion. I think they were bent on making a big advance but they didn't succeed. I think we can get through anything after that, it's enough to wreck anyone's nerves.

We are having terrible weather for the trenches, my word it's freezing, fancy being out all night in this weather, don't know what to do with our feet. I am pleased we have come down for a day or two it's time we had a rest but we are still in reach of shell fire. We have such a job to walk after being so cold, just as we are getting warm it takes effect...

I am longing for the time when I shall be with you all again...I hope the leave I get will be to stay, and may it soon come. I shall do my part after this and I don't think I were bad before always at work but this will alter many a man. Some will be worse but I kept straight through it and mean to. I shall prosper in the end...It is about over shoe tops in mud and water today. God help them in the trenches...

Jan 12, 1918

We hear all sorts of rumors about peace and such like and when we shall be relieved but it's no use taking it in. We have to wait. Nothing certain in the army...

My word we have [to] do things here that we should carry on about in civil life, such donkey work. All we can do is grumble and do it. It makes you feel that you don't care for anything, it does fetch it out of you. When I read the letters and think of you all it touches me. I could have a good time, but I do hope it will soon be over. I am longing to be home again. I don't wonder the war costing so much, there is so much wasted, some things you could well do with. I have a rare cold. I hope you will send the gloves as soon as possible, my coat is thick in mud. I can't get it off but we are expected to keep clean. It is over shoe tops in mud today.

Jan 24, 1918

The first day we had in supports, well when we got there there were no where to get shelter and the trenches were terrible with mud...We walked right to the trenches on the top so you can see, fancy that they say they are Saxons in the front we were in and they don't want to fight. It were impossible to think about fighting under such conditions. We had to lunge on the side of the trench all night it did seem a long night. The next morning when it were light Fritz were walking about on top just as if there were no war on. He shouts out good morning boys, he were not more than twenty yards from us in his trench...

Later on several of Fritz's came and sat in our trench against us and started talking and giving us souvenirs. They looked very bad. They are fed up with it, they love to get hold of a piece of our bread. They don't like theirs much according to what they said. We said German bread good, they said no, and patted their stomachs. They gave me a cigarette and a mark in German which I am sending home for you to keep. Have a look and see what a mark is worth. The same morning I told you three of us went up the front line, well the other that were left in the place that we made got killed that morning. A piece of shrapnel went right through the zinc and hit him in the thigh. We were all very sorry. He were a good chap, a Welsh, and he had only just come from hospital...

March 11, 1918

I thought of you yesterday being Sunday. I fancied myself with you and the boys going for a walk as we used to. I thought what a shame it were to be throwing the time away in this manner...I hear Rumania has signed peace no wonder I think Russia has let her in I don't know what will become of it all. They will leave us in it to finish it yet. It's time someone looked into it and settled it. They haven't sent so many on leave the last three weeks but I hope they will start again so our turn will come quicker.

My dear wife and little Sunbeams,   March 20, 1918

...We had fair weather lately but yesterday it broke it poured of rain and we were about up neck in mud again it's a terror it makes us tired out hardly lift our feet up. We had some experience at dodging minny werfers this time. I think they are the most deadly shells I have seen. We had warning by the Hoods that were there they had two blown to pieces the day before and that were the place we had to be, they happened to be inside a bivvy. You can see them coming in the air and we had to scuffle if they were coming toward us, the hole they made would bury a horse and cart.

I hope we shall get a rest after this time up so if we do you can stop parcel for a week or two, we may be able to get things if they have us back and I know you can do with it. I must thank you for the parcel it were all right and thank Fred and Elsie for what they sent and Julia it were all right, the fruit were very nice and the pudding extra. I have received a photo of our family and it is very good. I don't know if I shall be able to send this but I hope so. I remain with best love from your loving husband, Arthur.

Five days later, on March 25, 1918, Arthur was killed by an exploding shell.

■ ■ ■ ■ ■ ■ ■

Perhaps there is no more fitting tribute to the desolation of World War I – indeed to all wars everywhere – than the closing chapters of *Johnny Got His Gun*. Published on September 3, 1939, two days after the start of the next great conflagration, Dalton Trumbo's novel about soldier Joe Bonham has been eerily prophetic of carnage yet to come; take away the date, and many modern readers would set the scene in Vietnam. Minus four limbs and his face blown away by a shell, Joe is deaf, dumb, and blind, and must lift and drop his head against a hospital pillow to tap out (in Morse code) his scathing message to all of mankind. He asks that the wretched trunk of his body be placed in a glass case and taken around the world on display:

> Take me into the schoolhouses all the schoolhouses in the world. Suffer little children to come unto me isn't that right? They may scream at first and have nightmares at night but they'll get used to it because they've got to get used to it and it's best to start them young. Gather them around my case and say here little girl here little boy come and take a look at your daddy. Come and look at yourself. You'll be like that when you grow up to be great big strong men and women. You'll have a chance to die for your country. And you may not die you may come back like this. Not everybody dies little kiddies.
>
> Closer please…Come on youngsters take a nice look and then we'll go into our nursery rhymes. New nursery rhymes for new times. Hickory dickory dock my daddy's nuts from shellshock. Humpty dumpty thought he was wise till gas came along and burned out his eyes. A dillar a dollar a ten o'clock scholar blow off his legs and then watch him holler. Rockabye baby in the treetop don't stop a bomb or you'll probably flop. Now I lay me down to sleep my bombproof cellar's good and deep but if I'm killed before I wake remember god it's for your sake amen.
>
> Take me into the colleges and universities and academies and convents. Call the girls together all the healthy beautiful young girls. Point down to me and say here girls is your father. Here is that boy who was strong last night. Here is your little son your baby son the fruit of your love the hope of your future. Look down on him girls so you won't forget him. See that red gash there with mucus hanging to it? That was his face girls. Here girls touch it

don't be afraid. Bend down and kiss it. You'll have to wipe your lips afterward because they will have a strange rotten stuff on them but that's all right because a lover is a lover and here is your lover.

Call all the young men together and say here is your brother here is your best friend here you are young men. This is a very interesting case young men because we know there is a mind buried down there...there you are young gentlemen breathing and thinking and dead like a frog under chloroform with its stomach laid open so that its heartbeat may be seen so quiet so helpless but yet alive. There is your future and your sweet wild dreams there is the thing your sweethearts loved and there is the thing your leaders urged it to be. Think well young gentlemen. Think sharply young gentlemen...

Take me wherever there are parliaments and diets and congresses and chambers of statesmen. I want to be there when they talk about honor and justice and making the world safe for democracy and fourteen points and the self determination of peoples...Put my glass case upon the speaker's desk and every time the gavel descends let me feel its vibration through my little jewel case. Then let them speak of trade policies and embargoes and new colonies and old grudges...Let them talk more munitions and airplanes and battleships and tanks and gases why of course we've got to have them we can't get along without them how in the world could we protect the peace if we didn't have them?...

Take me into your churches your great towering cathedrals that have to be rebuilt every fifty years because they are destroyed by war. Carry me in my glass box down the aisles where kings and priests and brides and children at their confirmation have gone so many times before to kiss a splinter of wood from a true cross on which was nailed the body of a man who was lucky enough to die. Set me high on your altars and call on god to look down upon his murderous little children his dearly beloved little children. Wave over me the incense I can't smell. Swill down the sacramental wine I can't taste. Drone out the prayers I can't hear. Go through the old holy gestures for which I have no legs and no arms. Chorus out the hallelujas I can't sing. Bring them out loud and strong for me your hallelujas all of them for me because I know the truth and you don't you fools. You fools you fools you fools...

He was the future he was a perfect picture of the future and they were afraid to let anyone see what the future was like. Already they were looking ahead they were figuring the future and somewhere in the future they saw war. To fight that war they would need men and if men saw the future they wouldn't fight. So they were masking the future they were keeping the future a soft quiet deadly secret. They knew that if all the little people all the little guys saw the future they would begin to ask questions and they would find answers and they would say to the guys who wanted them to fight they would say you lying thieving sons-of-bitches we won't fight we won't be dead we will live we are the world we are the future and we will not let you butcher us no matter what you say no matter what speeches you make no matter what slogans you write...

Remember this. Remember this well you people who plan for war. Remember this you patriots you fierce ones you spawners of hate you inventors of slogans. Remember this as you have never remembered anything else in your lives.[14]

World War II

As in the Great War, American involvement in the "Good War" was about power and money. Twelve years had passed since Wall Street's Black Tuesday, and the nation remained mired in economic depression. War was the inevitable way out, and fascism abroad was a ready reason. Once again, truth was an early casualty.

History books offer a benignant version of the grandfatherly FDR. Yet consider that Roosevelt, in his own diary, complained of the "difficulty in inveigling the Japanese into attacking us first."[15] Consider also that Roosevelt turned away more than one ship of Jewish refugees from American harbors, and that Washington knew of Hitler's concentration camps as early as 1933...The "Good War" soon loses some of its luster.

For Leonard Dietz, World War II is not a happy memory. Now a recently retired nuclear physicist, he enlisted in the Army Air Corps in the fall of 1943 and received his silver pilot's wings at age twenty-one. Mustangs were his favorite, and soon flying was as natural as breathing. After graduation, he was transferred to the 506th Fighter Group and shipped to Guam. A few weeks later, his group flew to Tinian.

His first view of Iwo Jima shocked him. The raw earth beneath his wings looked like a lunar landscape, pockmarked everywhere by shellfire. He could see no trace of anything green or living. On the ground, it was even more depressing: the stench of death was everywhere and could not be avoided. It persisted for many weeks and became especially bad after the earth was bulldozed or after a heavy rain, when body parts washed out of the hillsides. Twenty thousand Japanese defenders and 6800 American Marines had died there, and twenty-two thousand more Marines were wounded in the ghastly battle.

Waiting in line on the tarmac before his first bombing run, the six 50-caliber machine guns on his wings armed and loaded, he realized he'd reached a turning point in his life. "Until this moment flying had been fun," he recalls. "Now it was time to pay the piper." In the air, his squadron intercepted two Japanese fighters. The Tojos dropped their external fuel tanks, rolled onto their backs, and began diving toward the ground. Then they split apart, going in opposite directions. Leonard and his element leader rolled into a very steep dive, closing on the Japanese pilots at well over 500 miles per hour. As he passed within range of one of the Tojos, Leonard fired a burst from his machine guns. A ball of flame billowed from under the fuselage of the Japanese fighter, and he watched as the pilot rolled back his canopy and tried to push his head and shoulders above the windshield into the slipstream. He was less than a hundred yards away. But the Tojo was in a shallow dive and began to spiral out of control. The pilot struggled for two or three seconds against the tremendous force of the wind, but could not bail out. In Leonard's words:

> Horrified, I watched him collapse back into his seat; moments later his airplane crashed into a hillside and exploded. I was breathing hard and my heart was pounding, even though I had my oxygen mask on. My eyes burned, and I was aware that my mouth was extremely dry and my tongue was sticking to its roof. I looked back at the thin column of black smoke marking the Japanese pilot's funeral pyre and felt remorse for shooting him down in such a cold-blooded fashion.

For Leonard and his fellow pilots, participation in the war became a bad dream that wouldn't go away. The atomic bombs were dropped on August 6 and August 9, but bombing missions over Japan continued until August 15, when Emperor Hirohito spoke to the Japanese people by radio for the first time, urging them to accept the Allied terms of surrender. Leonard recalled:

> On August 10th, the day after the Nagasaki bombing, I took my last daylight mission to Tokyo to strike the Tokyo arsenal. There were three waves of B-29s, twenty bombers each. I remember looking down — we were at 23,000 feet — and we could see nothing of the city of Tokyo because it was leveled. It was like a giant hand had come out of the sky and mashed everything to the ground. It looked like it was hit by an atomic bomb.
>
> The intensity of the air war in Japan was horrendous. The American public has not really ever been aware of the extent of the damage. It may have been reported in the press, but it didn't get much attention. More people were killed by fire bombs than were killed by the atomic bombs. Far more. This went on right until the 14th and 15th of August. The day of the 14th, there were

a thousand airplanes over Japan, about two hundred fighters and eight hundred bombers. They struck targets all over Japan, whole islands, all through the morning of the 15th of August.

Years later, Leonard reflected at a Veterans Day service:

> I learned that war is not glorious but is about suffering and dying. It is a vile and evil business that blights everything it touches, robs people of their lives and futures, and forces many good people to do bad things against their better natures. The whole thing was so bad, no matter how you look at it, that we can't ever let anything like this ever happen again.[16]

■ ■ ■ ■ ■ ■ ■

While Leonard Dietz chased Tojos in the South Pacific, Siegfried Ellwanger was halfway around the world, fighting the Russians. Born in Germany on August 7, 1924, Siegfried and his generation sought to avenge the wrongs of the past and embraced the new National Socialism with hope and fervor. Yet, like for generations of idealistic youth before them, their dreams were soon to be shattered. In an account of that time, he writes:

> *Germany in the early 1930s:* A hopeless time of economic decline with all its consequences – unemployment, hunger, need and suffering in the families, alcoholism, crime, clashes of political opinions – Communists, National Socialists, and many other parties…
>
> Smear campaigns against the so-called "enslavement of the German people" as a consequence of losing the First World War…And in the midst of this national chaos, a youth without a future, without any prospects.

> *Then, in 1933, Hitler's rise to power:* Finally the "new time," promised for years, would become reality! Rousing battle songs of the Hitler Youth rang through the streets of the town, accompanied by fanfares, drums, and flags.

> > With the flag of youth for freedom and bread…
> > our flag flies ahead of us,
> > our flag leads us into eternity,
> > our flag is more than death.

One year later I finally was old enough to join the march, like nearly all of my classmates. Who can imagine what went on in my ten-year-old heart, when for the first time in my life I experienced "community"? When I heard from all sides: you are called to great things! With you we will rule over the world! Together we are strong!

Proudly we wore our uniforms. We could hardly wait to go to camp during vacation, and often on weekends, too. It was an experience of camaraderie and community. This sense of togetherness enthused us:

Long hikes, through the day and night, orientation with the help of a compass, or determining our direction by the sun...

In scouting games we fought "brown" against "red" and took "prisoners"...

Then, late into the night: campfires, setting up tents, singing, reading heroic stories. At six o'clock in the morning the blast of a trumpet, lining up in shorts, with our wash things, and jogging to the nearby stream. Then flag-raising, breakfast together, sitting in a circle, the beginning of a new day, full of expectation. Yes, we were the pride of the nation – and I was part of it!

And then: "The enemy is lurking at our borders, with nothing else in mind than to humiliate this proud nation..." Our holy fatherland, in danger! Who wouldn't want to be a hero, to defend this fatherland with all he had – even to stake his life for it?

End of August 1939: Headlines splashed across the newspapers and announcements on the radio: "Polish troops have crossed the German border!"

It was announced that on the first day of September we would all hear a most important speech by Adolf Hitler to the German nation. Everyone who lived in our house gathered in one of the big living rooms and heard Hitler shouting: "Since 4:45 this morning we have been shooting back!"

There was a disconcerted silence amongst the older people, and so we younger ones couldn't just shout with enthusiasm. I was fifteen years old and thought: "Why are they so silent?" Somebody whispered: "This is the end of Germany."

Early 1940: Within weeks Poland was defeated, Denmark and Norway occupied, France quickly overcome. Daily we heard of the victories, even on the eastern front in the fight against the Russians. Were Hitler's promises really coming true: a "German kingdom of honor, of power and justice – amen"?

When our youth leaders came home on leave – some of them already highly decorated, wearing medals for bravery – they told us, full of enthusiasm, about their experiences at the front. We younger ones began to envy them. When would it be our turn, my turn? Or will the war be over by then?

Sure enough, in 1942 my draft card was in the mailbox. I had just turned eighteen, old enough to be one of the fighters for the fatherland.

After a short training as a recruit in the south of France, our whole artillery company boarded a train in Marseilles, together with cannons, horses, and other soldiers. In the early morning of a cold day in December the train started rolling...

We passed through France, Germany, Poland, and on into the boundless plains of Russia. 1000 – 2000 – 3000 kilometers. After three long weeks – often interrupted by long waits – our train finally stopped beside the ruins of an old railway station. Darkness was falling. Suddenly we heard commands: "Get ready to unload!" Far off we heard the roar of the artillery. We had just reached the outskirts of the surrounded city of Stalingrad.

As we started marching to the front line, an ice-cold east wind hit our faces. The horses managed only with supreme effort to drag the guns through ice and knee-deep snow. The temperature was minus 35 degrees centigrade, and soon the first comrades had to be taken back because of frostbitten hands and feet.

Suddenly we passed a gully strewn with dead Russian soldiers – signs of a battle that had happened not long ago. Depressed, thoughtful, and speechless, we stood there for a short while. Why did these men have to die? Most of them were no older than we and would have had all of life before them. The first gnawing thoughts arose in me: what have they done to me? Why am I here at all – so many thousands of kilometers away from home?

In the midst of a vast field we set up our guns. No tree, no bush to be seen. We were far away from the next village. There were old abandoned houses where we sheltered our horses. We put up small tents for ourselves; a thin layer of straw covered the rock-hard, frozen ground.

Now and then we got a letter from home. They wrote about the "fight of the heroes in Stalingrad," where many hundreds of thousands of soldiers lost their lives. They also wrote about the merciless bombing of the German cities, where mostly women and children were killed.

Eventually we marched back to the Donets River, where we stayed for most of the summer. Our front was interrupted only by artillery fire. Then, at the beginning of fall 1943, in the middle of the night – after we had fired all our remaining ammunition at the Russians, as a pretended warning of attack – we were ordered to retreat. The reason given was that the front had to be "shortened." In actual fact, the last big summer offensive of the Soviets had begun, which finally caused the breakdown of Germany's whole eastern front.

For me and for all the others, the high spirits quickly turned to deadly seriousness. During the nights we marched, hard-pressed by the Russian troops, often wading through mud and dirt. During the days both sides usually halted. And when night fell we went on – with our last ounce of strength. And still we hadn't seen the enemy. But that soon would change.

Fall 1943: We lay alongside a road with our guns, hiding under bushes. Our infantry had already retreated. Our group of twenty soldiers had been ordered to stay until evening to fend off any Russian attacks. In the late afternoon we suddenly heard shooting from the distance. Then shouting, louder and louder: "Uraaah! Uraaah!" In a cornfield across from us we saw Russian soldiers in brown uniforms storming toward us. We only had a few grenades left, which we shot into the air to scare them off. Our situation was hopeless...Suddenly, about 100 meters away from us, they raised their arms and came running towards us. Was that a trick? No. They had no weapons and were surrendering. We took them prisoner and brought them back behind our lines. They were 38 men!

But here let me tell what we experienced when we now saw them face to face: Were these the so-called "gangsters," as it had been drilled into us? No! They were human beings like us, full of fear, sighing with relief and thankfulness that their lives were saved. And when we asked them to empty their rucksacks, we were flabbergasted: Chesterfield and Philip Morris cigarettes, cans with ham and eggs – American brand – and other things we never had seen before. Our officer proposed that we share these treasures with them...

Another experience: We had gone into a small Russian village in firing position, shooting now and then to hold up the Russians, to irritate them. We stood around in small groups talking about letters from home, wondering when the war would ever end. With a good friend you could even sometimes talk about the senselessness of this war...

Suddenly we heard the sound of enemy artillery, hissing and roaring. Only seconds later we were in the center of a tremendous barrage. Within a short time sixty, eighty, a hundred grenades had landed among us. Then it was over, and from all sides came the terrible groans, the shouts, the stifled cries for help. The sight around us was terrible. The crying and groaning gradually stopped. Many were dead, many wounded. Why? For what? For whom? Some couldn't even be recognized anymore. And a few minutes ago we had been standing together, talking about the senselessness and hoping for a happy ending...

Just shortly before this inferno I had actually prayed that God might save my life, as I often did in difficult situations. But why? I could no longer imagine a future without suffering and war.

Numerous similar experiences followed, and I asked myself again and again: why are we here in this country? What did these people do, that we should wage war against their sons, husbands, and fathers?

Summer 1944: Typhoid fever helped me out of all this. In my delirium I saw them storming on us again and again. There they lay, friend beside enemy. When I came to, I was lying in a hospital train, rolling back toward the West from Romania. We traveled all night, and there was no morning without a stop to carry out the dead.

Then we heard the news: the English and Americans have invaded France. They were advancing toward Germany. As soon as I could walk, I had to march again: "Continue fighting! The enemy is at the border."

In the meantime I had been promoted. Now I was in command of more than forty soldiers. In December 1944 we got orders to join the attack at the Belgian-French border. How many years had passed since we set off with such enthusiasm?

A wave of propaganda accompanied this final stand. Placards hung from the houses: "Victory or Siberia!" – while in the East, by early 1945, the Red Army was already on German soil.

April 1945: One day we had to defend a small village in the middle of Germany. Where were the people who had once lived in these houses? Where were the flowers that had once blossomed between these houses? Where were the fathers, the sons, the mothers with their children?

Many of these half-timbered houses were burning. We sought shelter in the basement of an old farmhouse. The shooting of the American artillery stopped, and then we heard machine guns and rifles. We peeped through a crack in the door. There they came running! "Americans," we whispered. The basement door flew open. "Hands up!" With rifles leveled, they led us toward a wood and into an abandoned quarry. "Shirts and shoes off! Faces to the wall! Arms up!"

The war was over, at least for us. We waited for the shots. But why did they examine us? Suddenly we understood: they were looking for that telltale, unmistakable sign. Each member of the SS had his blood type tattooed under the arm...

Finally we were allowed to turn around. We were still alive! In open trucks we were transported to France. On the way, we could scarcely recognize our country, which had once been so beautiful. Every town and village destroyed, bombed, scattered. Old women, sitting in the rubble, waving to us with tearful eyes. Everything broken, also inwardly, in our hearts.

1948: After three years as a prisoner, I finally came back home to Germany. In 1946, the Americans had handed me over to the French. And now I heard the terrible reality: millions of Jews had been murdered, killed in concentration camps, tortured and tormented. Thousands of Germans had lost their lives, too – those few that had recognized the devilish regime long ago and had tried to rise up against it long before the war.

I looked back at the many events of the past fifteen years. Where had my youth gone? And what did my life mean, now that it had been saved? I was only twenty-four, a student with no occupation...

Siegfried's search was to last another four decades. In 1986, at the age of sixty-two, he and his wife Renate joined our Bruderhof in England, where they dedicated themselves unconditionally to the cause of peace. All the same, he cannot forget his part in Hitler's *Reich;* he knows that history cannot be undone.

The Vietnam War

I've been to Washington's Vietnam Veterans Memorial more than once, but after having worked on this book for over a year, I was eager to see it again. Perhaps "eager" isn't the right word – there is nothing pleasurable about contemplating 58,000 unnecessary deaths – but at the very least I would see The Wall with new eyes. On a recent trip, I parked on Constitution Avenue and braved the damp chill of November to walk along the Reflecting Pool toward the memorial, which looks like a polished, black gash in the earth. It was two days after Veterans Day, and brightly colored wreaths still lined the walkway along the monument. A few letters and memorabilia were scattered at the base of the wall itself.

Once again I was overwhelmed by the senselessness and the magnitude of this loss of life. The lines of names go on and on, from Dale R. Buis in 1959 to Richard Vande Geer in 1975 – fifty-eight thousand names. Mostly they are all-American names, like Richard and John and Robert – but I noted a disproportionate number of Hispanic names, too, names destined to be on that Wall because they were born at the wrong time or in the wrong place.

I listened to people as they passed by, tightening their coats against the cold, soft-spoken and respectful, but for the most part seemingly unmoved. A fashionably dressed young couple seemed more intent on the wreaths of flowers than on the panels themselves, and an older man wondered, rather superficially, why the panels had omitted any mention of rank. An old woman sighed to her companion, "All these men. For what?" A child wondered innocently and persistently why "they" had to die, but was hushed by her mother, who snapped, "You're disturbing everybody."

Yet these questions must be answered if we are ever to close the door on one of the ugliest chapters in American history, and they remain largely unanswered after more than thirty years.

The entire war was, of course, built on deception. Statesmen and generals alike, our leaders lied about Vietnam from beginning to end, from Lyndon Johnson's fabricated "incident" in the Gulf of Tonkin in 1964 to Kissinger's cease-fire agreement in Paris in January 1973. None other than Johnson had proclaimed, while still a senator in 1954, that he was "against sending American GIs into the mud and muck of Indochina on a bloodletting spree to perpetuate colonialism and white man's exploitation in Asia."[17] Ten years later, as President, he had affirmed once again that he was "not about to send American boys nine or ten thousand miles from home to do what Asian boys ought to be doing for themselves."[18]

But as Benjamin Spock found out, Johnson could not be trusted to keep his word. Like Wilson before him, Johnson had campaigned on a platform of cautious nonintervention, but plunged headfirst into the chaos as soon as he entered office. Spock, already then famous as "America's baby doctor," had campaigned for Johnson in 1964 because he was alarmed by Senator Goldwater's "belligerent proposals in regard to Vietnam." Johnson had even called Spock personally after the election to thank him, hoping that he might prove "worthy of...trust." Within three months, however, Spock was awaiting trial, accused of having conspired to counsel young men to resist the draft. Spock was outraged at the about-face, and redoubled his efforts for peace.[19]

Johnson, of course, was following a script written for him years earlier – a policy stated perhaps most truthfully by President Eisenhower in 1953, at a conference of U.S. governors:

> Now let us assume that we lost Indochina...The tin and tungsten that we greatly value from that area would cease coming...So when the United States votes 400 million dollars to help that war, we are not voting a give-away program. We are voting for the cheapest way...to prevent the occurrence of something that would be of the most terrible significance to the United States of America...[the loss of] our power and ability to get certain things we need from the riches of the Indochinese territory and from Southeast Asia.

Certainly Johnson was more than just a pawn, however. His quest for control was insatiable and diabolical, evidenced by an Oval Office press meeting during which he opened his pants, placed his member on the desk, and said, "That, boys, is *power!*"[20] His disdain for the anti-war movement at home was legendary, and he once commented that he loved nothing more than peace, but hated nothing more than surrender.[21] As the following quote from a recent book on his presidency shows, he was much more concerned about his public image than the fact that thousands of Americans – and Vietnamese – were dying needlessly:

> In Johnson's wartime lexicon, "principled opposition" was an oxymoron. When Congressman Tip O'Neill split with the administration on Vietnam – relatively late, in September 1967 – Johnson dressed him down in the Oval

Office. "Tip, what kind of son-of-a-bitch are you?" Johnson shouted. As O'Neill justified himself, unburdening a conscience weary and troubled by the war, Johnson was almost baffled by the congressman's sincerity. "Is that what you think?" Johnson asked. "I thought you did this for political reasons." It was a revelation for the President: "You're doing this," he repeated, seemingly awestruck, "because you really believe it." If LBJ appeared more forgiving, it was because he and O'Neill were friendly and, more important, O'Neill agreed to keep quiet on the war.[22]

Before his resignation in 1968, Secretary of Defense Robert McNamara had glowed with pretentiousness: "We can stand a five-year war, a ten-year war, or a twenty-year war! I speak for two and three-quarter million men who are in the armed forces today who I guarantee can stand it, and I think the 180 million who stand behind them can stand it."[23] Guarantees about public support aside, it wasn't long before Johnson could not appear publicly without encountering youthful demonstrators chanting, "LBJ, LBJ, how many kids did you kill today?" In the spring of 1968, Johnson announced he would not seek re-election.

Richard Nixon was elected in the fall of 1968 and also pledged to get the United States out of Vietnam. Secretly, however, he had plans to expand the war. When he began to withdraw American troops, he was ending only its most unpopular aspect, the use of American troops to "defend" the soil of a faraway country. By 1970, he had launched a secret invasion of Cambodia, after months of air strikes that were never disclosed to the public. The invasion was a disastrous failure and led not only to widespread domestic protest but to a congressional action that barred Nixon from further independent action in the region.[24]

■ ■ ■ ■ ■ ■ ■

Don, an inmate on Pennsylvania's death row, was changed forever by Vietnam. I met him in August of 1997 at the State Correctional Institution in Greene County, a sprawling complex laced with razor wire. SCI Greene is squeaky clean; the gleaming tiled floors and wooden furniture look almost posh, but hard. I was not allowed to bring anything in past the visitors' desk. I placed my identification, pen and paper in a locker outside, and after being given a slip with Don's name and ID, I was shown to an area filled with rows of heavy chairs. Receptionists and prison guards joked good-naturedly, and I noticed a glass case filled with sports trophies along one wall. The whole character of the place was saccharine and artificial in light of its ultimate purpose: to warehouse and kill human beings.

Don's name was finally called, and I was directed to "go back" to the visiting area. Only then, as I followed an endless gleaming corridor, my own footfalls the only sound, did I realize the deliberateness of the minimalist decor. It was Pink Floyd's "Welcome to the Machine," a scene from the bureaucratic hell in the film *Brazil*. I reached a set of heavy steel sliding doors and waited while an electronic eye acknowledged me and opened the door with a heavy clunk. The effect was stark, dehumanizing. The guard at the console, silent behind thick-paned protective glass, pointed to a dimly-lit cubicle at the back of the room. When I entered, Don was already standing there, separated from me by a heavy barrier of plexiglass. For an instant, Don looked apprehensive, but then pretended to shake hands with me through the glass.

We couldn't swap stories for long without talking about Vietnam. Like so many others of his generation, Don had gone to the war thinking he was going to help people. But by the early 1970s, he was going to meetings of the Vietnam Veterans Against the War in Pittsburgh. Among the other veterans who attended, some were so traumatized they could hardly speak about what they'd seen and done. Don, however, wrote down a few of the experiences that haunted him, and his initiative sparked an entire collection of Vietnam journals, many of which are still preserved in a veterans' center in Monroeville. Don recalls one vet who never spoke at all, but who, after reading an account in one of the diaries, suddenly piped up, "Hey, that happened to me, too."

Don copied several pages from his collection and sent them to me. I was skeptical that he could possibly add anything unique to the plethora of stories already in print; by that time, I was near to overdosing on Vietnam. But on reading his pages of handwritten cursive interspersed with neatly-pasted magazine and newspaper clippings, I was shaken — not by the blood and the gore and the obscenity, but by the sheer emotional impact. The vignettes I pored over seemed to encapsulate the entire experience of the war — the insanity and boredom and terror and bone-weariness — into the space of a single, powerful moment. These were far more than war stories. They rang so true — and with such intensity — that I felt as if I were there, in Vietnam, in the midst of them.

On August 19th a young soldier arrived at the Bien Hoa Airbase in South Vietnam. Memories of Woodstock only a few days earlier tranquilized him as the big military transport rolled to a halt. The ramp opened, and the young soldier was greeted by a wave of oppressive heat and a sickening stench of rot and decay. In time the stench would soak into his skin, eat into his clothing, mingle with his food, and become normal — but never quite unnoticeable — nor forgettable.

Undaunted, he hoisted his pack and seabag onto his shoulder and walked down the ramp. He was destined for his assigned fate somewhere in the jungles and he was eager to face that challenge, to follow his illusions. Ready to serve his beliefs, beliefs for which his small-town patriotism was as much to blame as his youth. With his pack and seabag he carried a conviction that he was an honorable soldier, that his country needed him, that he was doing something noble and good. He kept the pack and seabag throughout his tour in Southeast Asia. The conviction, he lost – left behind with his youth, his ambition, and his soul.

Third day in-country I reached my assignment at Can Tho in the Mekong Delta. The Can Tho army airfield – bigger than a bread box, smaller than a city block. An oval-shaped perimeter of barbed wire, water-filled trenches and craters, claymore mines, and sandbag bunkers – surrounded by thick jungle swamp and wide, muddy rivers. A real vacation spot. Narrow PSP walkways connected the shacks, hooches, and sandbag bunkers – metal side-walks. I stepped off and immediately sank up to my knees in mud. My new assignment was with the "Loach" Scout Team Air Crew of the 271st Assault Helicopter Group, which was attached to the Search-and-Destroy Battalion.

The 271st consisted of about 130 men and 16 armed helicopters – Loaches, Cobras, Huey Gunships, Huey Slicks, Chinooks, and a Kiowa. It had 14 combat air crews, each assigned to its own helicopter. Its headquarters and support staff stayed at Can Tho. The air crews and helicopters stayed in the field, living at different camps around the Delta, moving where they were needed, returning to Can Tho only for periodic maintenance inspections. Forty-five men with no base – no permanent home – working in bunches of threes or fours here and there, eating C-rations, living in their clothes, sleeping wherever they could. A pretty tight-knit bunch – by necessity.

I had never been stoned before in my life. Didn't even know what marijuana smelled like. I had finished my three weeks of orientation and scout training. They taught me how to stay alive in a Loach: always fly low and fast, never hover. They gave me my own Loach and crew and sent us to Fire Base Grant with two other Loach teams. We had been there a couple of days. Hadn't seen any action – just spotting for artillery.

One night I was in the team bunker, and my gunner said he wanted to bring a couple other gunners over and get stoned – did I mind? I said why not – I've been to California.

You hear about people who don't get high the first time they smoke. Whoa! Not true. They passed a pipe around, and I woke up the next morning with my feet down in the bunker and just laid out straight back. They had taken my brain out the night before and passed it around and played with it –

they had fun with me. They were my flight team and it was the first time we got to know each other. It made a big difference, becoming part of the team.

They certainly initiated me.

The Siege of Cao Lam

We were at Cao Lam, a mud-hole outpost on the border. The camp was triangle-shaped, about the size of a football field, maybe slightly bigger – a wide mud wall for a perimeter – fighting holes dug along this wall and mud bunkers at the three corners. It was home to an ARVN company with American advisors. We were there to scout the border – two Loaches and a Slick – ten men.

I was lying on the wall in about an inch of water, bone tired – half sleeping, half watching the mist float on the river. We'd heard reports of enemy movement: NVA regulars just across the border in Cambodia – a few hundred well-trained, battle-tested enemy. We had lost Varnado and his crew that day – in a ball of fire on the side of a mountain. Lying there, a song Varnie always sang kept running over and over in my mind, a song about aviators in World War II – we live in the air and die by fire...da da da...

Suddenly there was a loud, cracking sound, like lightning, and the wall shook. The wall was really just a built-up mud embankment, and I sort of instinctively rolled over into the hole I'd picked out for myself. I don't know why – I didn't know what was going on but I had a feeling it wasn't good.

A few seconds later there was a whistling sound, like a high-pitched scream, and the wall shuddered again – harder and more violently. Then mud and debris started falling on me, and I heard someone yell: INNNCOMMMING!

And then it began – a furious concentration – the fiendish wail and screeching of short artillery and mortar rounds dropping into the camp. A diabolical howling of torment. An enormous and continuous roar that went on for a full five minutes – it was a lifetime. With each explosive impact the ground bounced me – actually slammed against me and bounced me in the air. I could hear hot shrapnel zinging – pinging – wooshing – over my head. I flattened myself out in the hole, pushing myself deeper into the mud, trying to become a part of it. Movies on TV hadn't prepared me for the reality. I grabbed handfuls of mud in a feeble and pathetic attempt to hold onto the earth – a fool's anchor. I was afraid of being bounced out of my hole up into the murderous space above.

A few moments of silence, and then again the savage wailing salvo – tormented demons – and the intense roar. Blast stung my side – heat singed my hair – the ground slammed violently up against me and I bounced at least six inches straight up. I heard someone let out a cry — the pitiful cry of a frightened child — and then I realized I was alone in the hole.

The siege continued for eleven days.

In the first minutes of the siege our helicopters went up in flames, bright orange balls that lit up the night. Sappers had snuck in and tossed satchel charges. We never saw them.

Helicopter Assault

How does one explain a helicopter assault — flying straight into an enemy position at 100 mph, 10 feet off the ground — all your guns blazing at him, all his guns blazing at you. There's a lot of excitement in it the first time, a strange excitement. After that it becomes extremely unpleasant. When engaging the enemy on the ground you have some control over your destiny, or at least an illusion of it. But in a helicopter you don't even have that.

The noise, the speed, the enclosed space, the sense of helplessness — total helplessness. These emotional pressures are so intense you clamp your teeth until they hurt. You are pulled and shoved in so many different directions all at once by an incredible range of extreme, conflicting sensations — the indifferent forces of gravity, the jarring twists and thuds of ballistics, the screaming machinery. In the cramped cockpit claustrophobia claws at you. You're trapped and powerless, and you can't breathe. It's absolutely unbearable. Yet you have to bear it. Pull out too soon, and you expose your underside to the enemy guns, before you can kill him — and you die instead.

Your mind screams to be through the run and out the other side — to do it quickly — but that desire is twisted by the danger that's waiting there for you. Still you are attracted by the danger — drawn to it — because you know it's the only way out. That's all you want, so you hold the approach — coming closer and closer. You see the enemy guns flashing — licks of red-orange flames directly in front of you, red and green tracers arching toward you — hunting for you. You slump in the seat, instinctively pulling in your elbows and knees, hoping it will make you a smaller target. And the screaming increases. You know you are now screaming out loud, at the top of your lungs. You don't hear it with your ears. You just feel it. It's the fear inside you screaming to escape — to flee. A fear so deep and so basic it makes you cold and you shiver in the 100 degree heat. An absolute terror so overwhelming that your body separates from your mind. It takes over, reacting instinctively. Your stomach tightens — bile burns your throat — your mouth is too dry to swallow — your vision tunnels — you lose control of your bladder. And with it comes an uncontrollable rage deep inside you, a blind fury toward that force which makes you powerless: the enemy. You can see him now. You can see the fear on his face. You recognize the look. It's the same fear. He knows what you know – in a matter of a few seconds one of you will be dead. There's no other choice. No other way. Later, if you live, he'll revisit you – a slow motion movie in your mind. He may have been a good person, maybe someone's father or brother. He may have been a beloved teacher or gentleman farmer. In another place and time you might even have been friends. But at the moment you have to take his life – or he will take yours. Even if he doesn't want to. And when he visits later you will feel a heavy sadness, wondering who really is the loser – him or you.

The rage builds inside you, becoming a beast unleashed. And it focuses on the enemy, on his fear, and it becomes a fierce resolve to fight – to kick, gouge, hit, claw, bite – until the danger is gone. Until you have killed a human you did not hate, a gentleman farmer who could have been your friend. They call that courage and award it with medals, but it can never be separated from the fear that aroused it, or from the madness that accompanies it.

All of these emotions are so intense and so painful you can't handle it very long. All you can think about is ending your anguish. You don't care about rights and wrongs. You don't consider life and death. You give no thought to the chances of victory or defeat, or to the battle's purpose or lack of purpose. All that matters is the final critical instant when you release yourself into that violent catharsis you both seek and dread – and fly out the other side.

Now jam all this into twelve seconds – the average time of a typical helicopter gun-run.

Windows into Vietnam

I saw my first dead person, my first dead human being. I watched him die – saw the life go out of his eyes. He was running past my hole. A mortar round went off and he dropped right there, right in front of me, no more than two feet away. He looked at me and asked if I would help him. It was all very calm. No sense of urgency. I said sure, I'd help him – he'd be fine. And then he just died – very calmly, very quietly. And I guess I felt something inside me die with him.

His name was Billy Boy. He was nineteen years old. From the waist down he had no body left. Barely enough for his family to bury.

When I'm doing nothing – like sitting or trying to sleep but can't – it all comes back. Over and over. I could always picture myself as a casualty. I'd think, will I get it tomorrow? Will a piece of metal tear me apart, too?

Water was our biggest problem – there wasn't any. A camp enclosed by a slimy mud embankment, pools of stagnant run-off everywhere you crawled, surrounded by swamp and rivers – and we had no water. Pure irony. We took water from the pools, boiled it on hobo fires, and dumped in lots of C-ration instant coffee to mask the taste and smell — to conceal anything in the water. During the brief lulls we brushed our teeth and washed our feet with cold swamp-water coffee.

They tried to resupply us. Big C-130s would roar over and drop parachuted packages. Two guys were killed — crushed to death in their hole when a supply pallet dropped on them.

I remember I had ringworm and sores all over my legs. There was no hot food, no tents or cots, no clean clothes. Leeches were all over me. I gave up trying to burn them off. They'd just get fat and swollen. When they were full they'd drop off. I rolled around in my own filth and forgot how bad I smelled. It got so it was natural.

We didn't eat — we didn't have time. Just shoot, duck, stuff some C-rats in your mouth, and shoot. It was fighting day and night and the NVA tried every trick in the book: they hit us with artillery, mortar, machine-gun fire, rifle fire, B-40s, recoilless barrages, everything — and it was all point-blank. They even set the jungle on fire. We let it burn over the top of us because they were right behind it — just got down in our holes and let it burn, then got back up and started shooting again.

Sometimes they would come at a dead run — right at us — hollering and screaming, blowing horns. Other times they came in well-organized assaults. They were NVA — professionals — the best. But there was no way out for us, so we just kept shooting.

There were a couple of days that I don't have any memory of. I guess I sort of went berserk. That's what they told me anyway. They said I was throwing rocks at the NVA. I don't know. I have no memory of it.

Drugs were everywhere in Vietnam — everywhere, and just about anything you wanted. At the bigger base camps they would just suddenly pop up whenever anyone went looking. At the small camps and distant outposts they were brought in by Air America. That was a small civilian flight service which turned out to be a CIA company operation. At Chau Doc I went to an opium den — the real thing. It was off limits to everyone except officers.

I see politicians preaching and campaigning about the evils of drugs — pointing fingers and claiming the other guy is soft on drug crimes — saying they will change the laws and send all the drug dealers to prison.

Well, who do the politicians think they were when they funded CIA Air America operations and issued congressional warrants for officers to visit opium dens? Isn't that being a drug dealer? Of course, what should we expect: they're the same politicians who sent nineteen-year-old kids to die in a war no one wanted — no one except the big corporations who were raking in enormous profits on the war. The same corporations who funded the politicians' political careers.

Am I the only one who sees this...?

Once, I was sent to MAC-V Headquarters to attend an awards ceremony put on for the press. I was to receive the Vietnam Cross of Gallantry.

As I stood there in my dusty nomex, mud still in my ears, and in desperate need of sleep, I listened to the brigade commander's words of glory and praise and how war is hell but necessary. And I began to hate that fat little shit standing in front of me in his clean, fresh uniform and his neat haircut. I hated him because he sent young boys into steamy jungles to die while he relaxed in the comfort of his plush, air-conditioned office. Who the hell was he to speak of brave men and their total dedication fighting for a free Vietnam!

So, I pretty much expressed my feelings by pissing on the back of his leg. He turned and looked at me in shock — not anger, just shock — and there I was, eyes straight ahead, at a perfect stance of attention, pissing over his feet. The press people were having a field day. When I finished, I gave him a smart military salute, turned, and marched away. No one said STOP. No one said a word. The only sound heard over the clicking of cameras was a cheer from a company of grunts who had been made to stand the formation. And I just marched away.

I walked to the flight-line, climbed into the first helicopter and simply flew away — no crew, no clearance, no flight gear, no Gallantry Cross.

When I got back to Can Tho, I started to cry — and I couldn't stop. For two days I wept continuously, never stopping. All I could think about were the people I had killed, about the good men I saw die, about my buddy — and I kept crying until our company doctor sedated me. I was taken to 3rd Surg where I told a doctor everything I had seen and done in the past nineteen months. All he did was put me on 60 mg of valium a day and lock me in a room for two weeks...

One time at Chau Doc a soldier stepped on a mine. It blew off his leg below the knee, as well as his other foot. We watched from the perimeter. His buddy panicked and started screaming MEDIC — MEDIC — all the while drawing sniper fire from the tree-line. The other guy, the one whose legs were gone, was in shock. He kept trying to get up and walk away...

One day Chau Doc was hit hard. All hell broke loose on the perimeter. Tracers flying everywhere, guns roaring and popping all along the line. Everybody yelling and screaming. A couple of VC sappers were shot trying to blow the wire — their lifeless bodies hung over the posts. And it was raining the whole time, coming down in solid sheets.

Then suddenly the rain stopped, and there in the sky was this beautiful rainbow — the most beautiful thing I'd ever seen. And at that moment I began to hate what we were doing in Vietnam — began to hate myself for believing in it, for being a part of it.

I heard someone in the bunker say out loud, "Hey God, you trying to tell us sumpthin?"

People back home had forgotten us. They considered us murderers, animals, misfits. They didn't want anything to do with us, just left us to live or die — whatever — so long as they weren't involved. They didn't think about the fact that they had sent us there. We were to blame — not them.

But in Vietnam we helped each other, cared about each other. And we respected each other. We were all we had. We didn't fight for any ideology or higher purpose. We fought simply to survive — nothing more. And we looked out for each other. Men who fought together in Vietnam loved each other, without ever saying it. We were brothers in the truest sense.

My friend died in Vietnam. He was murdered. Pieces of hot jagged metal ripped his body to shreds — and I don't know who to blame. I escorted him home for burial. A big gray casket. I sat with it the whole way, touching it every now and then to see if it was real — hoping it wasn't. I worried about what I would say to his family, hoping it would be positive, something they would remember and pass on. But they wouldn't talk to me — didn't want to see me. They sent a minister to tell me not to attend the funeral. They didn't want me there. I didn't blame them.

I wish I could remember what it was *you* said…It wasn't important or anything, but it haunts me. And if I could remember, I'd write it down on this page, and maybe make you seem as alive to others as you still seem to me.

An old Vietnamese farmer at Tay Ninh offered to plant marijuana for us. He also offered us his daughters. There was no degradation attached to it. Such things were accepted, it was the way of his culture. He believed that was what Americans wanted, and he was just trying to be friendly, to be accepted by the Americans. I thought it was disgusting, and I slapped him. His smiling family and other villagers were standing there in support of the offer — and I slapped him across the face with my open hand. To a Vietnamese there is no worse possible insult. But I was an American, so there was nothing he could do about it. He knew that and I knew that. So he just hung his head and shuffled away.

I didn't hit him, or beat him, or kill him. I did something much worse. All he had in this world was his dignity, and in front of his family and his villagers I took that from him and left him alive – to live with the shame.

Still today that old man visits me from time to time. Each time I tell him I'm sorry. I hope he hears me.

I got a postcard from my gunner, Kush. He got hit while we were flying in Cambodia. He was writing from an army hospital in Japan:

> Dear Pilot – Divide up my gear among the other gunners in our team and send all my mail to this address. Let me know who gets killed or wounded. They had to cut off my foot. Later, Kush

I remember Jimmy "Boo" – nice little guy from Ohio. He came to Nam scared stiff, trembled so much he made the plane rattle on the way over. That's why we called him "Boo" – scared to death.

Anyway, one night we got mortared. The hooch I was in took a direct hit, and I was so paralyzed with fear I couldn't move. Boo crawled up to me – this would never be funny to anyone else – he had on baggy green drawers, combat boots, and a helmet that was way too big for him. He looked like a comic-strip character. But he crawled up to me, slapped me on the back of my head, and said, "C'mon, man! They're writing U.S. ARMY in the sky! Let's move!" He had it together and I didn't.

One of the new guys was trapped under the rubble. We couldn't get to him. We listened to him scream and cry until he died – for nearly two hours.

Every man reacts differently to living with combat. Some went insane – just completely bonkers. Everyone snapped over that line once in a while and no one cared. Others retreated into cynicism or despair. The nineteen-year-old male is the most destructive and aggressive creature on earth. When circumstances permit, such as in Vietnam, he can and will kill another human being without hesitation or thought – man, woman, or child – no matter what his moral or religious feelings might be.

One day I was just sort of hanging around the command bunker at Cao Lam, watching a group of new recruits. They had just arrived in Vietnam. They were all joking, smoking, playing grab-ass – it was pretty loose.

All of a sudden, four helicopters came swooping in – not even touching the ground. They just started dumping bags from about five feet off the ground. One of the bags broke open when it hit the ground, and what came out was hardly recognizable as a human being.

The new guys stopped laughing. Nobody was saying anything. Reality had suddenly gone beyond words. A couple of guys were shaking, some started throwing up, and one guy got down and started to pray.

And I said to myself, "Welcome to Vietnam, guys."

Newsweek Jan. 1970:

> Sealed Off. The destruction of Ben Suc, a Saigon River village complex that supported the Viet Cong, was typical. It took only a minute and a half for 60 helicopters to descend on the village with a battalion of the U.S. 1st Division. While loudspeakers warned residents to stay in their homes, infantrymen quickly sealed off the town, catching many of its Viet Cong defenders by surprise. The villagers were assembled and the men between 15 and 45 led off for questioning. Within three days, Ben Suc was deserted, its people and their possessions loaded aboard boats and shipped twelve miles downriver to a refugee camp until they can be permanently relocated. Shortly after they left, torches were put to their homes. After Operation Cedar Falls ends, it will be a long time before the Viet Cong, or anyone else, will be able to use the Iron Triangle again.

I remember looking down between my feet and seeing the embers of desolation not more than 20 feet below the helicopter. Smoldering craters, human bodies, and burning skeletons of hooches – of homes. And I remember a guilt pressing down on me so heavily I could hardly breathe. I was sick of it all – sick of war, of what it was doing to us, but mostly I was sick of myself.

It wasn't just the senseless obliteration of Ben Suc Village that bothered me. It was the dark, destructive emotions I felt during the assault, from the moment we slipped in over the treetops through the morning mist lifting off the sleeping village – urges to kill and destroy that seemed to rise furiously from the fear of being destroyed myself.

I had enjoyed killing the three Vietcong who ran from the tree line near the village. Feeling like a glorious bird of prey swooping down, I watched the mini-gun rounds splash through the paddy toward the running men, then ripping and tearing their bodies to lifelessness.

I remember the strange sensation of seeing myself as in a movie – one part of me doing something while the other part watched from a distance, shocked by what it saw, powerless to stop it.

I was awarded an air medal for my actions that day.

For heroism, they said.

How absurd, I remember thinking.

I can analyze myself all I want, relive the horrors of Ben Suc Village for a million years, as I feel destined to do, but that won't make a new village rise from those ashes. It won't answer the questions that still burn in my mind. Nor will it lighten the burden of my guilt.

Doi sau...

Two American jets had just napalmed a grazing cow and the three of us in the Loach laughed. Then the jets zoomed in again, dropping more napalm. They made one low pass and we cheered. An hour later we landed for a pickup, and I got to see the survivors. They were carrying their belongings and they had no place to go. It was like a parade across the rice paddy — a string of 75 or 100 peasants carrying burned and screaming babies, women, old men, some badly cut up with shrapnel wounds. When I got back to camp I got drunk for the first time in my life.

Time Dec. 1969:

> Assigning top priority to making Saigon secure, the U.S. last month committed three combat battalions to Operation Rang Dong, a long-range, large-scale drive that sent 2500 U.S. troops against Viet Cong forces operating in the three provincial districts south and east of the city. Last week, to clear the communists out of the area to Saigon's north, American forces launched the largest offensive of the war to date, sending 28 battalions and 34 batteries of artillery into the 25 sq. mi. wedge known as the Iron Triangle, a notorious communist stronghold ever since the days of the French.
>
> Composed of jungle, paddy fields, and a network of concrete bunkers just 20 miles northwest of Saigon, the Iron Triangle also conceals scores of Viet Cong military base camps, supply depots and field hospitals, all connected by miles of underground tunnels. Intelligence reports indicated that it was the headquarters of the Viet Cong's Fourth Military Region, which commands communist activities in and around Saigon and had placed practically all hamlets in the area under communist control. The U.S. has bombed the place repeatedly in the past 18 months, but the only previous venture of U.S. troops into the area in force was frustrated when the Viet Cong simply faded into the jungle.

Word quietly comes down that a Christmas cease-fire has gone into effect. From the darkness of the perimeter you hear "Ain't Christmas fun out here in the mud and the rain and the shit!"

There's a loud roar and a hard, hot slap of air, great pressure, and something slams you viciously in the back. You go facedown in the mud, ears ringing, a familiar sensation of having your mouth stuffed with cotton. You hear a carbine rattle off a few automatic bursts, and someone screams: "Medic, Medic!" It all sounds so far away.

A few yards behind you is a scorched, smoking crater of earth. Lying beside it is a soldier. He slowly gets up on his feet and then falls when one leg collapses under him. He lies there flopping one arm back and forth saying, "Boom, boom…"

Beside you is another soldier, still down in the mud, mumbling. There's blood oozing from holes in the back of his head, and you numbly try to hold a compress over them. Your hands turn red with his blood.

Lying closer to the crater is another wounded soldier – his face peppered with shrapnel. A mass of raspberry red. His partner fans him and cries, "He keeps goin' out, man! Medic!! He's gonna go out for good, man!"

And then you see your own partner lying on the other side of the crater – the Doc over him. And you realize with gut-twisting horror that he has been hit. In your blind run to his side you notice gauze and compresses covering his chest and stomach. The compress over a hole torn in his chest is soaked with blood. Every time he breathes, pink bubbles form around the hole and burst. He makes a wheezing sound and tries to talk but can't – his windpipe fills with blood. But it's his eyes that frighten you most – the hurt, dumb eyes of a child who has been severely beaten and doesn't know why.

You feel the separation in his eyes and you know he's alone in another world – isolated by a pain you can't share with him and by a terror of the darkness that's swallowing him. His eyes and his silence, and the foamy blood and the wheezing gurgle in his chest, arouse in you a sorrow so deep and a rage so powerful you can't distinguish between the two.

You sit there helpless, hurting, the rain falling on you all the time. You watch your friend fall into unconsciousness. And you almost envy him…

Merry Christmas, Brother.

Today I see things the way nobody else sees them. I look at people and at kids especially, and it scares me. Because they're babies, and babies are alive and they're beautiful and they're perfect and they have arms and legs and feet and toes and their mind is like an empty bowl that hasn't had all these things poured into it. And I think, "If you ever saw what I've seen…"

On the night of April 26, 1970, five helicopters of the 271st airlifted a company of the 44th ARVN Rangers into the village of Prasant in the Parrot's Beak of Cambodia. I flew gun cover for the assault. The real killings of the Cambodia invasion began that night – four days before the actual invasion – but the government never told of those deaths.

The Rangers swarmed into the village and simply shot everyone. Afterwards, at daybreak, they threw the bodies into the river. Then we assaulted the village of Changwar. Again the villagers were all shot, their hands tied behind their backs, and the bodies were thrown into the Mekong.

We followed this pattern of destroying villages for the next three days, and by the time the invasion was initiated on April 30, 1970, the Mekong River was clogged with swollen bodies floating downstream. The water was the color of rust.

For the second day of the invasion my flight group was called out to the village of Takeo. Heavy fighting was expected and the ground troops wanted gunship support just in case...

As we put down in the village, I saw pools of coagulating blood everywhere and millions of flies buzzing around. Dozens of wounded villagers were on the ground, gasping and squirming in the heat. I remember one old man lying on his back in a pool of his own blood – he had stuffed his clothes into his gaping stomach.

A few yards away the soldiers were lounging in the shade. And about a hundred yards away was a hospital, but no one was giving any help to the wounded villagers. Everyone simply ignored them – even me.

Sooner or later it got to be too much for all of us. I saw men deliberately try to get wounded. I saw one man casually stand up during a fire fight and get it through the head. Another stood up too, and only got it in the arm and leg. He was sent to a hospital in Japan, and everyone thought he was the luckiest guy in the world because he was safe and free again.

I was always nervous – in fact, I can't remember ever not being afraid. For one thing, in combat you never know what's going on. Especially at night. Everybody screaming or moaning or calling out for help. I always saw myself dying – my legs blown off, my brains splattered all over, shivering in shock, talking madly. That was reality for me. I used to say, anyone wanting to send eighteen- and nineteen-year-old kids to fight a war should try it on himself or his own sons first...

I remember one gunner – a young PFC from Michigan. We were going out to fly an assault mission and this gunner climbed into the Loach, strung his ammo belts, braced himself with his M-60, and never said a word. But he was trembling – from start to finish of the mission, all day long he trembled. I kept quiet. We didn't laugh at him. We didn't dare. It was "there, but for the grace of God, go I."

It was his last combat mission before going home, and he was in absolute terror.

I actually came to enjoy combat. It seemed only heavy combat and killing could make me feel so alive. I would fly into situations others thought were insane — certain deathtraps. And slowly I came to understand that I didn't enjoy it, I'd only convinced myself that I did — to justify killing other humans. It was a way of denying the guilt I felt — that I hated myself for what I was doing. I eagerly went into those death-trap situations because I was trying to kill myself — to end the anguish. Others saw it and refused to fly with me.

They took me off the Loach Team roster — said it was almost time to go home, said I'd be safer hauling troops and supplies — no more gun-runs. So they put me on the Chinook Team roster.

I had certainly been down the road. I had fought in some nasty battles — U Minh, Iron Triangle, Parrot's Beak, Cambodia, Cao Lam...I had flown gun for the 1st Infantry, 9th Infantry, 25th Infantry, 5th and 7th ARVNs, 44th ARVN Rangers, and some unidentified cloak-and-dagger outfit of some kind — black ops, they called it. I had flown combat assault, gun cover, hunter-killer, scout, recon, river patrol, and once I even flew armed escort for the Miss America show which toured the Delta. I slept in all kinds of places — Can Tho, Dong Tam, My Tho, Chau Doc, Cao Lam, Di-An, the Plantation, Fire Base Grant, Tay Ninh, the Iron Triangle, Outpost Spider, Black Virgin Mountains, Cambodia, and a few places that didn't even have names. Over 2000 combat flight hours. I felt like an old, old man. I was twenty.

Finally I fell apart — complete emotional collapse — and they sent me home. Not because I fell apart, but because I had nothing left. I was of no use to them anymore. They had sucked everything out of me — all I had — my strength, my humanity, my youth — I had nothing left, so they sent me home. Okay, we're done with you — you can go now. So they sedated me and took me to 3rd Field Surg in Saigon. A doctor wrote in the record: suffering physical and emotional exhaustion, malaria, and drug addiction; subject weighs a mere 118 pounds; recommend release from combat status. So they sent me home. They didn't fix me or help me or anything — they just pumped me full of valium and dumped me in the middle of Main Street, USA.

I thought, "Wow. Unbelievable. I'm home, really back home." But then people started yelling at us. Someone spit at me. They were calling us murderers, trying to pin the whole thing on us as if we were personally responsible for the war. I just couldn't take that kind of a reception, and so I hopped right back onto the next plane for Nam. I knew there were guys who understood me back there. We understood one another...

Welcome Home
You visited hell and survived
A lifetime of experiences crammed into a year
You saw the heights and depths of human behavior
Violence and horrors so inconceivable
They raised more fascination than disgust
And now you are home
Back in the world
But gone now is your ambition
Gone is your optimism
You have no more hopes and no more dreams
You know only alienation
And a desire to sleep
You have curious feelings
Of being much older than twenty
And an old man's conviction
That the future holds no more surprises
You are unable to concentrate
Unable to cope with loud noises
You have a childlike fear of the dark
And chronic nightmares
You have shifting moods of depression and rage
That come from nowhere
For no reason
Seems everything you had was committed
To that battle for emotional survival
Back when you visited hell
Now you have nothing left for other struggles
Welcome home

After reading through one of Don's journals, I wrote back to encourage him. In the ensuing correspondence, he wrote:

When mentioning my notes about Vietnam you said that the "same darkness is in all of us." But Vietnam veterans have always felt they are different because of the things they did in Vietnam...

To this day, every Vietnam veteran on this planet feels an overwhelming sense of alienation. After all, what sane person would commit the acts we committed? We *did*, so there must be something in us that makes us different —

and whatever it is, no one except those of us who went will ever understand it...But those few words break through that, and you are the first person I've known to see it. Thank you. We're *not* different. Thank you for seeing that.

The Gulf War

One night in mid-January of 1991, while visiting inmates at the local county jail, my attention was drawn to the television blaring away in the center of the long corridor in front of the cells. All eyes were riveted to what appeared to be a highly realistic video game, with jets screaming in and out of view, bombs exploding in tidy, white puffs, and an excited commentator providing a blow-by-blow account of the action.

It took me several seconds to realize that I was watching the launching of Desert Storm, the U.S. air war against Iraq. What struck me more than anything else was the commentator's tone, which was one of excitement and pride in our nation's technical prowess. The names of the aircraft and bombs used in the attack were described in glittering detail, like a roll call of U.S. military accomplishments. But there were no explanations of the bombs' effects, no images of what was happening down there beneath the tidy, white puffs. And there was no discussion whatsoever on the cause of the war itself.

On the surface, it seemed to be about oil and the urgent need to stop a brutal dictator. But there was more: a kind of panic had set in at the collapse of the Soviet Union and the abrupt end of the Cold War. No one denied that the last serious threat to American national security had been removed, but the military budget was still enormous, and the defense industry seriously bloated. To begin to dismantle it all would mean the loss of hundreds of thousands of jobs.

There were, of course, political ends as well. In October of 1990, the *Washington Post* had reported: "Some observers in [Bush's] own party worry that the President will be forced to initiate combat to prevent further erosion of his support at home." Elizabeth Drew, writing for the *New Yorker*, quoted Bush's aide John Sununu, who said that a "short successful war would be pure political gold for the President and would guarantee his reelection."

Finally, there was what Bush himself had dubbed the "Vietnam syndrome," an American boil which had to be lanced. The invasion of Panama had been too small and too inconclusive to weaken the public's abhorrence, since Vietnam, of foreign military interventions. And yet a war against Iraq could not drag on indefinitely; it had to be brief enough to preclude the development of a significant antiwar movement.

Bush's war worked. The punishing air strikes against Iraq brought about an immediate surge in Bush's popularity, and the defense industry was satisfied. A cheering crowd of executives at the opening of the Fifth Annual Defense Contracting Workshop chorused, "Thank you, Saddam Hussein!" And as the bombing drew to a close, a beaming Bush reflected, "The specter of Vietnam has been buried forever."

The Pentagon, it seems, had learned the lessons of Vietnam well. If Studs Terkel dubbed his oral history of World War II the "Good War," then the attack on Iraq could aptly be called the "Clean War." Restricted press coverage of the war on the ground helped create the perception of a quick, decisive victory at low cost to human life. Air strikes hit their targets with "surgical" precision, and sophisticated, laser-guided "smart bombs" added a mystique of high-tech thrill and cool vanity. U.S. casualties were minimal.

During the Persian Gulf War, America was entertained in the spirit of ancient Rome's gladiatorial games. Vietnam veteran Bill Pelke noted a chilling parallel between the sensationalism of the war and our attitude to capital punishment:

> Knowing that the bombs were landing and innocent people were being killed; knowing that American people were cheering and talking about how good we are, that we can make this bomb do this and that, made me really sick. We were cheering about the deaths of people. It was the popular thing to do. But you know, it reminded me of the vigils I've held at executions. I was at convicted murderer John Gacy's execution. There were about 2200 people there that night. About 150 were against the death penalty. The other 2000-plus were for it. They were just cheering, just roaring because somebody was killed. I can't understand that.

Though the war failed to win reelection for President Bush, he retired gracefully. In the 1996 television interview with the BBC's David Frost, he reflected, "The mission was to end the aggression...I don't think war is immoral...I think history will say we did the right thing." But what really happened in Iraq is a story without an ending. And it is one that only the Iraqi people and veterans of the Persian Gulf War can truly tell.

Paul Sullivan, director of the National Gulf War Resource Center and combat veteran of the ground war in Iraq, shared his insights with me last September. His description of the infamous "highway to hell" outside Baghdad is far removed from the glistening fighter jets and little white puffs of CNN:

When you see the battlefield littered with dead bodies as far as you can see and there's smoke swirling around, and the smell from the dead bodies, the ammunition, the fuel, the explosions, it's very overpowering. It's very sickening. You're offered very, very little opportunity during wartime for any type of introspection. You are so geared toward killing and surviving that any other type of emotion, as well as any type of reaction to what you're seeing, is deeply suppressed. I think some of that comes about as a result of the training. In the military you are focused on "the mission," as they say...

You see it with the soldiers. They'll set their lips, tighten their eyes, grimace, and just keep looking forward. They can drive through miles and miles and miles of charred trucks, tanks, blown-up buildings, pieces of arms, pieces of legs every which way. Folks may remember what they called the "highway of death" that led from Kuwait up to Basra. That had to be one of the most hideous, grotesque, disgusting abominations that I've ever witnessed in my entire life. And it's a result of the lies. It starts when people say, "That's mine. You can't have it," or, "I'm better than you." That's where it starts...

In the Gulf War, we were the world's largest, fastest, most well-trained and well-equipped firing squad that ever existed. We systematically cut off Iraq's water, electricity, telephones, you name it, and completely immobilized the whole country. It was like a boxing match in which you blindfold your opponent first and then tie his hands behind his back and then turn out the lights. They couldn't see us and we just sat there and pummeled them for thirty days. And then we came in with the thousands upon thousands of tanks, all lined up side by side, across hundreds of miles of desert, every tank within eyesight of the next tank, and swept across the desert like fire ants, killing, blowing up, destroying, crushing, demolishing, and blasting every single thing in front of us. It was a "scorched earth" campaign, and when we were done there was nothing left except the charred remains: tanks, cars, bodies and body parts strewn all over the desert. That was the Gulf War. It's not like some smart bomb just went down Highway 1 and hung left at the stoplight and went down Highway 5 and then went smoothly down a smokestack to destroy some evil Arabs who were plotting to destroy American women and children. That's just not true...

Even as I write this chapter in February of 1998, news reports roll in about the latest showdown between U.S. weapons inspectors and Saddam Hussein. President Clinton is threatening Iraq with military action once again, and radio announcers wonder how the financial markets will be affected by the saber-rattling. Such vacuous commentary serves only to reinforce the fact that America is slumbering on in a state of denial. As Vietnam veteran Gerald McCarthy says, we are rotting from within because of our "will to myth."

Perhaps Wendell Berry, a man who has written passionately about the demise of American culture for nearly four decades, says it best:

> [The Gulf War] was said to be "about peace." So have they all been said to be...But peace is not the result of war, any more than love is the result of hate or generosity the result of greed...
>
> This was a war to bring about a "new world order."...In fact, this war produced not order but disorder probably greater than the disorder with which it began. We have by no means shown that disorder can be put in order by means of suffering, death, and destruction.[25]

U.S. Intervention in Central America

I met Doug at a veterans' retreat in Rhinebeck, New York. He was young, only twenty-nine, but his brooding face, far older than its years, was one I could not forget. "I'm obviously not a Vietnam vet," he said, and mumbled a few more reluctant words about recent treatment at a VA hospital. He sat in the dark, away from the circle of light that brightened the center of the room.

Over the next few days, I watched as he slowly opened up to the members of our group. And I saw him shake, his lips trembling uncontrollably, as he released a few small pieces of shrapnel from deep within. They were blurry: shots fired, gasoline, a dead woman, a dead friend. "Did we volunteer for all this shit? Did we volunteer for the hurt, the anger, the shame, the guilt? Would we still have volunteered?...I want you to breathe again, I want you to walk by my side again," he cried.

In the hazy light which filtered through the windows that afternoon, the faces of Vietnam vets around me were fixed in pain. They knew. And they let the tears come, flowing freely down their cheeks. The silence was power. It swirled within each of us. Nothing could be said; it was "the truth," universal and frozen in time. All debate ceased, and the heart of war was revealed — throbbing, glistening; hideous, insistent.

In the months since that week in October, Doug and I have kept in touch. Though hesitant to stir his memories to the surface, I was also determined to learn his story. For Doug was a veteran of a hidden war, a modern warrior who knew the jungles of Guatemala and El Salvador and the streets of Panama like the lines on his hand. He had been trained at the School of Americas in Fort Benning, Georgia, as a sniper, a "pathfinder." He had studied the art of killing at Fort Bragg, and had apparently learned well.

I was unprepared for the envelope that appeared early in 1998, containing Doug's story and a very brief note: "I hope the holidays have treated you well. Here is my story. I don't know if you will be able to use it. It was very hard for me to write. I felt that I needed to share my life so that people could understand war better. I also needed to write this down, so even if you don't use it, I want to thank you for asking me to write. Peace, Doug."

It's two o'clock in the morning, and I find myself at the top of the stairs drenched in sweat, crying. The nightmares have come back. This is the first time that this has happened in a long time. I wish Abby was here with me. But like most things in my life, she is gone too. I feel so alone in this world we call life...

It all started eighteen years ago, when I was about ten years old. I learned my first lesson about being a hunter. It was how to walk and move quietly through the forest. I learned this lesson from my father, a man whom I admired very much. He taught me different skills that I would later use in my own survival. I wish I could tell him thank-you today.

There are many events in my life that I don't wish to go into here...You would probably be bored to death, because it would take many more pages to tell you how I ended up where I did. I've also purposefully left out exact dates, because most of the missions I took part in are considered never to have happened. I am writing not to bring attention to myself, but to bring healing to my own life...

I served as a sniper in the U.S. Army, in Delta Force, the covert military group responsible for "antiterrorism." They are "the best of the best." My job took me to all the hot spots in the world, but mainly to Central America. There, I was baptized into hell...

My main job was to wreak havoc upon the National Guatemalan Revolutionary Unity, the sworn enemies of the CIA-backed Guatemalan Army. My first kill was a man who was a local leader of the Revolutionary Unity. At the moment I pulled the trigger, my life changed forever. The time leading up to that point and immediately after was filled with pure adrenaline. It was very powerful. My next five kills had the same effect. We had other engagements with the drug armies, but the kills there were justified, because they had a fighting chance. The sniper kills never knew what happened to them. One minute they were talking to their friends or family, and the next minute they were dead.

After the sixth kill, I was sent to Germany for further training. This was at the time of the conflict with Panama...

Throughout my entire time in the military I was separated from regular soldiers. I liked it a lot, but it was also very lonely. I could talk to only one person, and that was my scout, Michael. He was responsible for watching my back, for determining wind direction and speed, and estimating the range of the target.

One thing you need to understand is that we were inserted into position at night. This took anywhere from a couple of hours to several days. We took down our targets from 600 to 1000 yards away...

Snipers are probably one of the worst agents of destruction there are in a conventional war. Three of the people that I shot were with their family at the time they were taken down. Drug lords. At the time, I had to remind myself that they were the scum of the earth, responsible for the drugs on our streets and the horrible conditions of their own countries. They deserved to die.

At the end of my training I was sent back to the "Ranch," Fort Bragg. At this point I was pretty dead emotionally, and looking back, I can see that I died a little bit with every mission.

At Fort Bragg, I was ordered to go on a mission against a group of people I had never dreamed of – our own soldiers. I was assembled along with Michael and four other men whom I never had met before. We were among the few soldiers in the U.S. Army at the time with combat experience, with confirmed sniper kills; we were also the best of the best.

The thinking at the Pentagon was that to get the soldiers stationed in Panama to fight, they had to have very good reasons. We're talking here about soldiers who have never experienced combat before. And the best way to get them riled up was to attack them. When Michael asked what the other four men in our mission were doing, we were told it was none of our business...

You see, American soldiers, especially infantry soldiers, stick together. If one of them gets into a predicament in a bar – I mean a fight – the others don't walk away, they join in. You don't fight one of them, you fight all of them. Their training has taught them to be a team; they depend on each other, and it doesn't matter if it's a barroom brawl or not. They depend on each other to get home. So what better way to get them all worked up than to take pot shots at them? We were told that we would be saving lives by doing this. For weeks leading up to the invasion of Panama, Michael and I took pot shots at soldiers during the night...

During the invasion, we were to provide support fire for Task Force White, a Seal team that would take patrol boats out of Balboa and secure the Paitilla Airfield. There were a lot of casualties that day. I had never seen so much death and destruction before.

As we were moving back into Balboa, we were attacked by a small group of the PDF and supporters. As we came around a street corner they were lying in ambush for us, and Michael was shot in the left arm by a woman who was maybe twenty or twenty-one years old. Seeing him fall to the ground, wounded, unleashed within me a rage of anger that I had never before experienced. I went crazy. After about thirty minutes we secured the area. I then proceeded to do something that I never envisioned in my life. The woman who shot Michael in the arm was lying in a doorway, screaming for her friends to help. I walked over to her as she was yelling at me, and I slit her throat. It was out-and-out murder.

And it was what we had been taught. It was an attitude of defiance, a way of saying, "You will not fuck with my friends. If you do, I will kill you." And I did. I killed her over a flesh wound. But it was more than that, emotionally. She had tried to kill the only friend that I ever had.

Several weeks later, my life started flashing before my eyes. That was when the flashbacks started. I realized who I was: nothing but a killer. No better than the people I killed, just luckier. I really started analyzing myself at this point in time, and I knew it would not be very long before either Michael or I would be killed.

Although we can try to hide our emotions, inside we are all human. Humans feel. Michael and I were sent to Fort Benning, Georgia, to the School of Americas, to teach Latin American soldiers sniper skills in a jungle environment. It was considered downtime for us. You work from 7:00 A.M. to 5:00 P.M., eat and sleep and have fun. After about six weeks we were told to get ready to leave; we would be heading out in the morning.

Something you need to know is that we were never told more than what was considered relevant. And where you were going was never "relevant." It did not matter. I lived within a world of secrets. I never guessed that twenty-four hours later I would be back in Central America and that this would be our last mission together.

As we were getting ready to leave, Michael was reading the newspaper. He showed me an article. The headline said, "The Pentagon denies allegations that American soldiers are involved in the drug wars of Central America." We shared a short laugh.

We were flown into Panama and given our OP orders by a spook (CIA). Our mission was to take out a Salvadoran ex-soldier who was responsible for guarding drug caches waiting to be shipped to the United States. One of the reasons he was a target was that he had killed several Americans in Guatemala and El Salvador. And the other reason was that he was a graduate of the School of Americas.

This mission was very dangerous. We were going to be choppered in to an LZ (landing zone) about twenty klicks (kilometers) away, which I felt would surely alert everyone in the area. On previous missions we had moved in either by foot or by parachute "halo" (high-altitude low-opening) in the night; we'd been picked up by choppers ten to fifteen klicks away. Going in you always had the upper hand, because they never knew you were coming. Going out, you knew it was going to be hot. On this mission, we were going in hot and coming out hot. It gave us a very bad feeling.

We finally decided on two different LZs. If it was too hot at the first LZ, we would move on to the second LZ, which was about forty klicks away from the first LZ. We would have to move about sixty klicks in four days, which, through the jungle, is very strenuous even under the most favorable conditions – and we were being hunted by people who knew the area better than we. We moved into the area with no problem. It was a very quick insertion. We rappelled into a small clearing around 9:00 P.M. We then moved on until daylight and holed up on a ridgeline until the afternoon. Then we moved out, taking the last ten klicks very slowly. We moved into position on another ridge overlooking a small village. Our intended target was to be in this village sometime during the day. As the morning moved on, we could hear more and more movement all around us. We figured "he" had to be coming soon, because of the increasing patrols around us. Around 2:30 P.M. he finally showed up.

It had been a very long forty hours, with little catnaps here and there. For some reason I was very tired. I had no adrenaline running, but rather fear, which had always been there before, but not like on that day. I was done. This was it. When we got out and got home, I was finished. I was not going to do this anymore. And I told this to Michael. He told me I was just scared, and so was he, and what would I do anyway but work at McDonald's? I would feel dead...I told him I was already dead – it couldn't get any worse. I didn't know at the time that it would...

I had been having flashbacks for a while, mostly when I was asleep. Although I couldn't remember the dreams, I would wake up screaming or crying, drenched in my sweat and blood. In my sleep, I had dug at my arms till they bled. I think Michael knew that I was going through this, although he never came out and told me. But he would hint at it. He would say we have done things that we are not proud of, but we had to do what we had to do to survive...

Our target finally arrived, but there was a small problem. It looked like he was with his family. All that went through my head was, I can't kill this man with his family watching. Michael knew this. I was the leader. Everything had to be perfect before I took the shot. I could call this off at any point. The problem was, everything was perfect. There was no reason why I couldn't take the shot.

They started to kick a soccer ball around, and that was when we decided to take the shot. I remember Michael calling the distance and wind off to me. I will never forget that: "550 meters, two klicks to the right." The man's head came into my scope. I pulled the trigger and watched his head explode. I closed my eyes and started crying. I was in my own world. All I could see was that woman lying in the doorway...

I remember Michael telling me to move. "Let's go! Get moving!" I picked up my weapon and put my ruck on my back and we started moving toward the LZ.

The jungle around us came alive with men looking for us. I decided that we would not even go to the primary LZ; we would move on to the secondary LZ. We would be safer that way. If we kept moving, putting distance between us, we would be better off. I have never been so wrong in my life as I was in that decision. We moved on into the night, avoiding the patrols. We stopped around 9:00 P.M. to rest until around 1:00 A.M., when we would move on until daylight and try and hole up for a while. The countdown would then begin, and we would have twenty-four hours to make the LZ and get the hell out.

The area around us was still pretty hot. At dawn we started into a hollow which seemed to be a good spot to hole up. All of a sudden, I had the urge to go to the bathroom. We settled in about fifteen yards apart so we could watch each other. I moved off to do my business. I had to go; I couldn't wait any longer. All I kept thinking was, "Someone is going to smell this. They are going to find us." When I finished, I couldn't see Michael from where I was. I started to crawl back into my position when I heard gunfire erupting from his position. As I came up on my knees I could see two Indians. They had Michael pinned down. I took the first one out. At that time I don't think they knew we were both there. Michael was able to move back toward me. We were about five feet apart. I lost sight of the other Indian.

We both knew what to do. We had to take him out very quickly, before the others came. It was quiet for a moment or two, and then all of sudden Michael just stood up and started firing at the spot where he thought the Indian was. I started yelling, "Get down! Get down! What are you doing?!" Michael got down. It was too late. I heard the shot and saw the muzzle blast from a small bush. All of sudden I was wet. It was blood and body parts. It was Michael. He was lying in front of me, and he wasn't moving.

The next couple of minutes were just a blur to me. I could hear a man whimpering and breathing very hard. He was hit. I just stood up; I didn't care if I died or not. Nothing mattered anymore. Michael's killer was lying on the ground, out of ammo. I climbed on top of him and just starting stabbing him in the chest with my bayonet. I don't know how long this went on...

Michael and I had made a promise a long time ago: no matter what, we would never leave the other to rot somewhere. So I picked up his body and started to head for the LZ. I made it there without any problems. I sat and held him for the next ten to twelve hours. I couldn't move. I couldn't let him go.

Finally I heard the chopper coming. I moved into the edge of the clearing. Once the chopper landed, I picked Michael up and started for it. We were going home.

The chopper and the ride back to Fort Bragg is a blur to me. I was debriefed at the Ranch and I stayed drunk for several days. Something happened to me. I died in the jungle that day. Nothing mattered anymore.

I pulled light duty from that point on. Basically, I reported in during the morning, and at night I was not allowed to leave the Ranch. My enlistment in the Army would be ending in another six months. I knew that I couldn't reenlist; that was not an option.

I was paid a visit by two spooks (CIA), who told me that I had a job with "the company" if I wanted. At this point, I was a complete wreck. Losing Michael was like losing my brother. And on top of it all, I felt, and still feel, completely responsible for his death. I told my commanding officer I wanted out. I didn't care if it was a dishonorable discharge or not. If he didn't get me out, I would probably be going AWOL. He told me he would find out for me what my "options" were.

A couple of days later he came back and told me the paperwork was started, although I would have to go through several weeks of debriefing. At this time, I didn't care about anything in the world. I just wanted to go home.

I was deemed psychologically fit to be released. I signed a lot of different papers, and I was told that nothing we did ever happened. Point-blank. I was processed out with an empty personnel folder. My DD214 is completely blank. I never existed.

Once out, I realized I couldn't go home. I couldn't face the people I loved. I moved in with some people I knew, but it didn't last very long. I was soon homeless and addicted to coke. It was the only way I could numb my emotions. I stayed this way for approximately three years, in and out of contact with my family. Every time I would get close to sharing with them, I would leave town.

During this time, I was completely whacked-out. Somehow I had managed to get married, but the relationship ended after only four months. I moved in with my parents, but that didn't work either. So I took off one morning and moved into a state forest, living as I had in the jungle. I think I was in flashback twenty-four hours a day for about three months. Close to winter, I decided it was time to go back to society.

I walked out to a small town and called my cousin and my uncle, who was a Vietnam vet. They came and picked me up. We decided that what I needed was a good drink, and we proceeded to get drunk in a local bar. Sometime during the drinking, I walked out of the bar, went to a liquor store, bought a case of beer, and went to get drunk by myself. No one understood me, not even my uncle. I somehow managed to call my mother and told her to come pick me up. I needed to go to a hospital. She took me there, but it was very hard for her to see me hurting so much and unable to talk. I stayed in the hospital for several weeks before going into a private rehab center. Then I moved into a halfway house about four hours away, where I was able to stay clean for about six months.

Then I relapsed and spent the next few months drunk and high. I found myself mixed in again with the wrong people, and I found work running drugs and guns. I was so addicted to coke that I was actually completely worthless except as a user. The only thing that saved me was that I knew how people operated.

It wasn't long before I started robbing the dealers hard. Within a month, I was on the run, living in an abandoned factory during the day and hitting the dealers at night. My adrenaline was back. I was at home. I was safe and secure, always one step ahead of everyone else.

It all ended very quickly.

I went to a farm where I had worked at the halfway house. I stole a pickup truck and headed back toward western Maryland where my family lives. Once back in my hometown, I needed gas for the truck, so I stole it. I broke into several garages looking for gasoline. Somehow, during one of the break-ins, someone saw me and called the police. They found the pickup truck, which had my coat and other belongings in it. I was now on the run from the police, but again I was one step ahead of them. I circled my parents' house, which was surrounded by the police. My father was on the porch. He didn't have a clue as to what was going on. They hadn't seen or heard from me for months.

I proceeded to head for the railroad tracks, hoping to hop a train and be gone. But something happened within me. I knew that I couldn't keep running. I was tired of running. I wanted everything to stop: the dreams, the flashbacks, the memories.

I saw a police car. They were looking for me. So I moved out into the street and lay down spread-eagled in the middle of the road.

My life changed from that point on. I did a year in jail. When I was released, I moved into a halfway house in Baltimore, where I met two men who were working on the street, serving breakfast to homeless people. I started going out with them in the mornings. It was a very healthy experience. The nightmares stopped. We started a small nonprofit group, serving homeless men and women breakfast and going around to different churches, talking to people about homelessness. It was during this time that I met Abby, and we became friends over the next year.

But the peace I had found was slowly leaving me. I found myself needing to be in dangerous situations just so that I could "feel" again. I started going out at night, hoping that someone would try to rob me or kill me, so I could kill them. I needed that release, that challenge.

The people I was working with knew something was wrong with me. They thought it would be good for me to move into the shelter again. I did, and once there, one of the counselors, who had been a chopper pilot in Vietnam, talked me into going to the hospital. I checked into the psych ward of Perry Point, VA...

When I was finally released I went to a halfway house right outside the hospital grounds. I enrolled in a hospital work program. The nightmares were gone, and so was Michael, but only for a little while. Soon I moved in with Abby. But after a couple of months, the anger at myself started showing in different ways. The dreams came back. I was always angry at Abby for some ridiculous reason. I was flipping out again. I could feel it coming on.

Abby and I talked. I checked myself back into the hospital. I came very close to hurting a fellow patient on the psych ward, and ended up in restraints, drugged up in the "quiet room." I was very explosive then...Michael was in my head every moment of the day, and I couldn't share anything with anyone. I couldn't tell anyone my hurt. I slowly started to talk in group session, but I still couldn't talk with Abby.

After my release, Abby and I were married. I knew that she really loved me for who I was – nothing else, just Doug. But my anger was still present, and we rode the waves. It was like being on a roller coaster, although you didn't know how high you were going or how fast you would go down. And it came to an end in June of '97. By September, Abby had moved out into a safe place. I did not know where.

Before she left, she had signed us up for a Buddhist retreat in New York State. Part of it was a veterans' retreat, and she also signed me up for that. I was not happy about it, but I knew that if I didn't go, I would lose my family and myself.

I found a lot of healing during this retreat. I was finally able to talk about my experiences, and even though I still held some of them back, I was able to put my feelings into writing.

Dan asked me if I would like to contribute to this book, and I told him I would...

My thoughts on war and combat are that everyone loses. In some ways, my experience is different from that of Vietnam vets. But in a lot of ways it is the same. One of the ways it is different is that I was never drafted like a lot of them were. I volunteered for everything that I did. But I didn't really volunteer for the emotions and the life afterwards...

In the military, everyone is expendable. It doesn't matter who you are or what you are capable of. They will bring the primal beast out from everyone, and they will train you how to kill another human being. What they don't teach you, though, is how to deal with the emotions afterward. They just spit you out and find someone else to take your place. You do not matter.

The one question that I keep asking myself – and I think more people need to ask it, too – is this: who ever gave our government the right to decide which side is right and which is wrong? Who says that we are on the right side in Croatia? In the Gulf War, were we really there to help the people of Kuwait, or to protect the oil companies of the world?

I think that the only way we are going to find peace is through our children...As one of the most powerful countries on the planet, we need to start finding peace within ourselves. And we need to take drastic measures. We need to ban nuclear and biological and chemical weapons altogether. And the CIA needs to be dissolved completely...

I don't think world peace is something that will be achieved in my lifetime, but we need to start teaching our children that even if people all over the world are different we all have things in common. Instead of teaching about the Vietnam War, why not teach about the people of Vietnam and what a beautiful country they have? Or how about teaching respect for all people, no matter what they believe in?

The Hitlers and Saddams of the world will always be with us as long as we believe that only the rich and powerful are good, that they are the only ones worthy of living. We teach this in different ways. For example, we have nuclear fallout shelters for the leaders of our country but for no one else. To me, that says we are all expendable.

I hope that you can see the true hell I live through every day. My experience has left me a very lonely person. I have no real friends, and I don't think I ever will until I find peace within myself. The true hell of war doesn't start until you come home. You are a different person altogether. You become dead. What killing does is to slowly eat away at you until you are dead emo-

tionally. That is the only way that I can describe it. To this day, my experience is still with me. I still wake up in the middle of the night...War is not
worth the price.

I hope that some day I will be able to forgive myself...

■ ■ ■ ■ ■ ■ ■

The trouble with much familiar talk about the lyric glory of war is
that it comes from people who never saw any soldiers except the
American troops, fresh, resilient, who had time to go over the
parapet about once...Did you look, as I have looked, into the
faces of young men who had been over the top...four, five, six
times? Never talk to a man who has seen that about the lyric
glory of war...Did Sir Walter Scott, Macaulay, or Tennyson ever
see war? I should say not. That is where the glory of war comes
from. We have heard very little about it from the real soldiers...[26]

Harry Emerson Fosdick, "The Unknown Soldier," 1933

CHAPTER 5

The Change Is Forever

One guy I'll never forget would come to work with a canvas bag full of kittens. He would go out back and fill up a pail of water and put those kittens in the water, and then he'd come around and open the window next to his desk so he could hear them cry. That was the type of thing that was going on inside of him...

I remember another guy who'd been on a PT boat in Nam, and he had these terrible pictures of heads on poles and bodies, obviously tortured, of the Vietcong. And we just laughed at them. That's how encrusted your heart becomes.

John Risser, U.S. Navy veteran

In an age rife with images of holocausts in Poland and Germany, Bosnia, Rwanda, East Timor, Tibet, and many other places in the world – an age in which we measure the carnage on television by the number of violent deaths per hour – it may be harder than ever to imagine people so affected by traumatic experiences that they can no longer function normally. But we delude ourselves if we think such people do not exist.

I met Billy last October, at a retreat in Rhinebeck, New York. His story is one of those war stories that hit me in the stomach, one to which author and Vietnam veteran Tim O'Brien would have said, "Oh." It's the description of a friendly-fire incident in which his Navy gun-crew killed nine American GIs, and it shows how just one man – out of the millions that served in Vietnam – was changed forever.

For years and years, I ran around, unable to admit I was a vet. There were about eight thousand reasons, but one of them was that I didn't see myself as being on the same level as an in-country combat veteran. I was in the Navy.

Gunfire support. We ran rampant off the coast of Vietnam from the DMZ to Da Nang. Wherever anybody needed support, we fired our heavy artillery from two miles out and sent things over the mountains and onto the beach. That's what I did. Until they deemed I was a bad boy and stuck me on a river boat for a while. But that isn't what this is about. I want to read you a poem; it's called "Too Soon."

sticks turn to steel stones to lead
magically King of the Hill becomes real
and a mother's distant cries of concern
become muffled by the ordered blurbs
of some khaki bastard crone
in the middle of a good-night kiss
too soon
we became our own heroes

10:00 P.M. DMZ, gunfire mission completed, fifty-some odd rounds flying into the darkness, by our five-inch pea shooter. Where do they go? What happens when they reach their destination? Who gives a fuck. Roll that bone and fire it up, huh. What's taking you so goddamn long, you need help? Hey man, you know my fingers are all full of grease and powder. If you think you can do better, be my guest, jerk off. After all the amenities and anecdotes are given, the sacred bone is passed reverently from one greasy hand to another in silence. Three fire missions today. We're all really beat. We haven't had a shower in over a week. The compartment reeks of the sweet and sour odors of Aqua Velva, BO, grease, and gunpowder. As the last poke is pulled, I'm already making my move to my rack, which is hanging directly in front of the forward gun hatchway. I'm way too tired to pull the racks down to set up, so I grab my pillow and curl up on the deck. I yank at my crotch in a vain attempt to dislodge my four-day-old skivvies from my butt. Squirming around on the greasy tiles I think, what a shitty life, man. I'd be better off in the bush. At least I'd only have mud in my butt instead of grease. Whatever happened to the clean sheets, the good food, the simple regimen of six to three? Man, I want a fucking Hershey bar. Ah, the hell with it. The reefer is working its magic. My head nestles into the pillow and I think I'm asleep. The boatswain's whistle blows, a bell sounds, the horn blows. Battle stations! Battle stations! All hands to forward, gun mount. Battle stations. Huh? Gallager's mallet smashes the watermelon. No time to expound on thought. Lurch for the hole. Where the hell is Davy? Boy, I got just enough time to down a few hits of speed. Hey, what time is it anyhow? Aw, man, it's three o'clock. Are we still on the DMZ? Fuck it, who cares. It's 3:00 A.M. and it's too much noise. Don't you people ever want to go to bed? Take this egg and shove it up the hole, will ya? I accept the shell, cradle it in my arms as a Vietnamese mother might cradle her young one. The breach is wide open, hungrily, yet patiently awaiting its 100-pound meal. Obediently I present my beast with its repast. I hear its mantra: Feed me. Feed me. Feed me. I reply with hypnotic deafness and precision. The breach closes. My job is done for a short five seconds when the sequence is run thirty, maybe forty more times, feeding, swallowing, belching. Powder smoke fills the compartment. The guys in the powder room are taking a smoke break and pass me a hit of one in between feedings. I work like a well-programmed robot. Shell, cradle, present, nudge, push, move away. Kind of reminds me of football practice: repeat, repeat, repeat till you can do it in your sleep. A winner never quits, a quitter never wins. Don't do as I do, do as I say. Yes, coach. Yes, coach. Yes sir, yes sir, yes sir. 5:00 A.M. the boatswain mate pipes, "Stand down." Religiously, the sacred bone appears again, passing from one greasy paw to another. The mission is now officially complete. Last poke and head for the tiles. And into fetal position and muse, sleep.

6:05 the boatswain pipes, "All gun-mount hands to the mess decks." I'd like to take that pipe and cram it so far up the guy's butt that it becomes part of his brain. "Hey, Billy, what's up?" "I don't know, man. All I know is, it better be good or some fuckers are gonna be missing their shoes tomorrow while I'm on duty watch." Thirty or forty guys flop into the mess-decks area, some setting on benches, some on the tables, some lying on the floors. We come to the conclusion that we're gonna get popped for breaking into the officers' mess two nights before, for swiping their five-pound can of potato chips. It's amazing what we'll chance when a tough case of the munchies sticks in. No big deal. Anyway, what are you gonna do? Send me to Vietnam? Fuck them officers, eating ham and eggs, doing single shifts, clean uniforms and sheets. They give us any shit, we'll heave 'em over the side and let the sea snakes choke on 'em. We all sneer in agreement. Morbid humor is the only thing that can crack through the angst right now. "Attention on deck!" No one even flinches. As I raise my eyebrow, there he is, planted under the ventilator, tall, erect, handsome, cover squared, uniform tucked and creased. It's six o'clock in the fucking morning. You know? What did this guy do while we were pounding out our shit? Guy's a goddamn clone. That's it. All of the officers are clones. There are two or three of them, each all dressed the same, being programmed by the executive officer to break our balls. Lieutenant Maldoon peruses us with those icy steel-blue eyes, clears his throat. "Men, our last mission was tarnished by an incident of improper communication. The 3rd Marine Division, who we had lent our support to, is now minus nine, due to a case of friendly fire. Blah blah, blah blah, blah blah." Maldoon's voice fades away. I lean towards Lain and say, "Friendly fire? What the hell is that?" All of a sudden the volume's turned up as old steely-eyes, who has not changed his demeanor, answers for him. "Friendly fire is a scenario of blah blah blah blah blah." Hey, lieutenant, you mean we killed our own guys? "Well, yes, that's what it boils down to." What the hell is so friendly about that? My head felt like somebody unscrewed it. I couldn't breathe. "Hey, Billy, are you okay?"

I bolt for the forward hatchway and head for my compartment, pick up my bag of reefers, crawl up the ladder to the main deck forward. The day greets me, but I flip it the bird and settle down under the forward gun-mount, roll me one bone, and start to cry like a repenting convicted murderer on his way to the chair. Friendly fire. Nine fucking guys. That ain't supposed to happen. Who were they? Where did they come from? Well if they were there, they probably deserved it. I try to blow it off. What if they had kids? I wonder if I killed any gooks. How the hell do I explain this? Nine fucking guys. Ask me for help, and I blew 'em all away. I blew 'em all over the place.

That's my only reference point to Vietnam. When I go into schools to speak, young kids ask me if I killed anybody...The only thing that raised my consciousness about that war was when I killed the nine guys. I knew what they looked like. It took me a long time to deal with these guys, because I could have been them. I live for those nine guys every day of my life...

■ ■ ■ ■ ■ ■ ■

Charlie lived with us in Woodcrest for three years. A Vietnam veteran originally from California, he stumbled across the Bruderhof and stayed when he felt he'd found a little bit of that nameless something which had been missing from his own life for a very long time. He never became a committed member, but he lived happily in an out-of-the-way apartment where he could come and go in his van. The children loved Charlie and soon nicknamed him the Candy Man in honor of his clockwork appearance with a bag of treats every Wednesday afternoon. Charlie came to our communal meals and meetings and contributed to those gatherings in a way that endeared him to all of us.

Last year, Charlie left for the West Coast. He had some important personal decisions to make, and he wanted to try to regain his health, which had deteriorated from smoking, obesity, and diabetes. His greatest battle, however, has to do with the defining experience of his life: even after thirty long years, Vietnam grips his heart in a stranglehold that won't let go.

In his letters, Charlie pours out the anger and hurt still boiling inside. It's not a steady barrage, but it's there, and it comes out in sudden fits and spurts. He

went to Vietnam to sacrifice his life for his country. The first American to see
him home called him a murderer. She was a flight attendant, and at first he
thought he had heard wrong. He hadn't. Those words touched off an ongoing
journey to try to understand just what it was that had happened to his life.

Many of Charlie's relatives were killed in the Holocaust. In a recent letter, he
pondered, "I'm not pro-war. But who is going to protect today's Jews?" A good
question, which I felt inadequate to answer. But who are "today's Jews" after all,
and what does protecting them really mean?

Charlie's emotions grew thick a few lines later: "The American people blamed
us for the war. They should be the ones asking our forgiveness. They should get
down on their knees and ask us to forgive them." Somehow, I felt that Charlie
was right.

While Charlie was with us, he went through a month-long program for Vietnam
veterans at the VA hospital in Montrose, New York. Near the end of it, he invited a few of us down for the Watch Fire barbecue. We didn't quite understand
what it was all about, but we learned something that night.

The Franklin Delano Roosevelt VA Hospital sprawls along the eastern banks
of the Hudson River in the town of Montrose. The picnic grounds are at the
water's edge and are very beautiful. They would have been more so drenched in
sunshine, but the day was windy and gray with a fine drizzle. When we arrived,
there wasn't a soul around, and we began to wonder if we'd come on the wrong
date. We noticed a massive pile of wood in the center of the broad peninsula –
huge logs and tree roots, pallets, broken picnic tables, doors and framing – about
twenty feet high and forty feet in diameter.

Suddenly, the group began to arrive and, after a few false starts, the barbecue
was in full swing. We felt warm acceptance from this group of combat veterans,
but it was clear that deep inside they were carrying something outside of our
experience. It was written on their faces and bodies: the enormous burdens they
had shouldered for so many years, the struggle to cope with horror and despair.

One veteran, lank and wasted with strain, wore a jacket from his Marine battalion in Vietnam. It was covered from top to bottom with medals. He said he
had jumped out of helicopters into hot LZs forty-five times; when he was told
he would get the "big medal" if he made it to fifty, he had "told them to go to
hell." He talked as though it were only a small thing, but it was obvious that
those jumps haunt him still.

We were having such a good time mingling among the crowd and enjoying
the food that we almost forgot about the fire. The Watch Fire is surrounded by
tradition. Legend has it that George Washington used to light watch fires all up
and down the Hudson, to call back lost patrols and to help them navigate in the

dark. For the Vietnam veterans of FDR, its meaning has become symbolic. The fires are lighted to "call back" the hosts of war dead: the multitude of lives cut short by a senseless and stupid war, the thousands of MIAs and POWs still unaccounted for. I had thought the lighting of the Watch Fire would be a solemn, ceremonious ritual, but it happened when one of the vets looked up from his hamburger and called out: "Whaddya think? Should we light it up?"

I don't think I have ever seen a fire that huge and that hot. When it was fully ablaze you couldn't stand within fifty feet of it. One vet told me it would burn for three days. As it burned, smaller fires began to appear on the opposite shore in the gathering darkness. There must have been twenty or so in Montrose alone. I looked around at the faces of the men once the novelty of the lighting was over. This was the solemn time, and it was clear that the Watch Fire was not merely superficial, but an experience that stirred deep.

One veteran whispered to me that the guy with the Marine jacket used to burn whole villages with a flamethrower, sometimes killing women and children and animals. Some bowed their heads. Others covered their faces with their hands. Still others looked deep into the flames, lost in a place and time from which they are unable to escape. Time has stopped for many of these men. Inside, the clock is frozen in the year 1969 (or is it 1967, or 1971?). And they wait for a hand to set it going again, to give answer to man's inhumanity to man.

■ ■ ■ ■ ■ ■ ■

Despite false images of cool, collected Rambos and *Miami Vice* cops braving mortal danger to kill in the line of duty, it is clear that there is something about the *real* experience of war that has the power to permanently cripple the human psyche. In 1990, a congressionally-mandated landmark study concluded that over half of Vietnam combat vets suffered from significant psychological and emotional problems. These problems, collectively termed post-traumatic stress disorder or PTSD, include depression, alienation, isolation, anxiety, rage-reactions, intrusive thoughts, problems with intimacy, psychic numbing, emotional constriction, and self-defeating and self-deceiving behavior. The study also revealed that ninety percent of these afflicted men and women (8000 of them nurses) had never been near a VA hospital or sought therapeutic help of any kind.[1]

PTSD has also been linked to physical illness. Compared to Vietnam veterans who saw little combat, those with PTSD are much more likely to have circulatory, digestive, musculoskeletal, respiratory, and infectious problems, up to twenty years after military service.[2]

PTSD is not unique to the Vietnam veteran. It is common among people who have been through events considered to be beyond the bounds of "normal" human experience, and it certainly isn't new among veterans, although its name has changed from war to war. In the Civil War, it was called "soldier's heart"; in World War I, it was "shell shock"; in World War II, "combat neurosis."

In his documentary video *Beyond Vietnam*, Steve Bentley (former chair of the Vietnam Veterans of America Post Traumatic Stress Disorder and Substance Abuse Committee) details a government study of returning World War II veterans that revealed such uncomfortable facts about the long-term effects of war that its findings were suppressed. The study revealed that at least 300,000 of the 800,000 U.S. ground soldiers who saw combat in World War II were psychiatrically discharged.

> There was a movie made in 1947, commissioned by the military. It was made by the famous director John Houston, and it was titled *Let There Be Light*. What the military asked him to do was to go into the VA hospitals in 1947 with his cameras. He did such a good job of capturing the kind of inner turmoil and horror that these men were going through – the survivor guilt, the suicidal thoughts, the flashbacks, the nightmares, the depression, the anxiety, the fear – that the military suppressed the film until 1982. They wanted to silence the evidence which showed that an abnormal response to an abnormal situation is normal behavior. In other words, if some things don't make you crazy, you aren't very sane to begin with. One of those things is war…Given enough time and enough exposure to combat, all normal human beings will eventually break down.

PTSD is an aftereffect of all war, independent of time or place. But there were a number of peculiarities to the Vietnam War, which created an especially acute epidemic of PTSD among its veterans. Psychologist Jim Goodwin, himself a Marine Corps veteran, explains why:

> Military planners [of the Vietnam War] looked to previous war experiences to help alleviate the problem of psychological disorder in combat. By then it was an understood fact that those combatants with the most combat exposure suffered the highest incidence of breakdown.* In Korea, this knowledge resulted in use, to some extent, of a "point system." After accumulating so many points, an individual was rotated home, regardless of the progress of the war. This was further refined in Vietnam, the outcome being the DEROS (date of expected return from overseas) system. Every individual serving in Vietnam, except

---

* One World War II infantry scout in Italy remembered that "we felt simply that we had been left to die. Men in our division gave up all hope of being relieved. They thought the Army intended to keep them in action until everybody was killed…All the men have hope of getting back, but most of the hope is that you'll get hit someplace that won't kill you. That's all they talk about" (Roger J. Spiller, "My Guns: A Memoir of the Second World War," *American Heritage Supplement, World War II Chronicles*, 1996, 9).

general officers, knew before leaving the United States when he or she was scheduled to return. The tour lasted 12 months for everyone except the Marines who, known for their one-upmanship, did a 13-month tour...

The disadvantages of DEROS were not clear, and some time elapsed before they were noticed. DEROS was a very personal thing; each individual was rotated on his own with his own specific date. This meant that tours in Vietnam were solitary, individual episodes...Bourne said it best: "The war becomes a highly individualized and encapsulated event for each man. His war begins the day he arrives in the country, and ends the day he leaves...He feels no continuity with those who precede or follow him: He even feels apart from those who are with him but rotating on a different schedule."...

Those motivators that kept the combatant fighting – unit *esprit de corps,* small group solidarity, and an ideological belief that this was the good fight – were not present in Vietnam. Unit *esprit* was effectively slashed by the DEROS system...Veterans who had finally reached a level of proficiency had also reached their DEROS date and were rotated. Green troops or "fucking new guys" with almost no experience in combat were thrown into their places. These FNGs were essentially avoided by the unit, at least until after a few months of experience; "short-timers" did not want to get themselves killed by relying on inexperienced replacements...

Another factor unique to the Vietnam War was that the ideological basis for the war was very difficult to grasp...The enemy was rarely uniformed, and American troops were often forced to kill women and children combatants...Most American forces had been trained to fight in conventional warfare, in which other human beings are confronted and a block of land is either acquired or lost in the fray. However, in Vietnam, surprise firing devices such as booby traps accounted for a large number of casualties with the human foe rarely sighted...It was an endless war with rarely seen foes and no ground gains, just a constant flow of troops in and out of the country. The only observable outcome was an interminable production of maimed, crippled bodies and countless corpses. Some were so disfigured it was hard to tell if they were Vietnamese or American, but they were all dead...Rather than a war with a just ideological basis, Vietnam became a private war of survival for every American individual involved...

Veterans of World War II spent weeks or months with their units returning on ships from all over the world. During the long trip home, these men had the closeness and emotional support of one another to rework the especially traumatic episodes they had experienced together. The epitaph for the Vietnam veteran, however, was a solitary plane ride home with complete strangers and a head full of grief, conflict, confusion, and joy...Many made the transition from rice paddy to Southern California in less than 36 hours.

Goodwin goes on to catalogue the common experiences and emotions of veterans suffering from PTSD. Again, it must be emphasized that while these feelings are in no way unique to veterans of Vietnam, they afflict its survivors in disproportionate numbers and must therefore be examined in the context of that particular conflict. The list is endless: depression, helplessness, isolation. Feelings of betrayal. Alienation from "normal" society. Rage. Guilt of survival. Overwhelming anxiety.

> Many veterans find it extremely uncomfortable to feel love and compassion for others. To do this, they would have to thaw their numb reactions to the death and horror that surrounded them in Vietnam. Some veterans we interviewed actually believe that if they once again allowed themselves to feel, they might never stop crying or might completely lose control of themselves. Therefore, many of these veterans go through life with an impaired capacity to love and care for others. They have no feeling of direction or purpose in life. They are not sure why they even exist.[3]

■ ■ ■ ■ ■ ■ ■

Joseph Hughes* is only one of the thousands of veterans with PTSD who continue to suffer deeply from a war that ended more than a quarter-century ago. When I first interviewed him at a shelter in New York City, I was surprised by his relaxed demeanor. His eyes were alert and attentive, and the hint of a smile played on his lips. He looked every bit the average, middle-aged Irish-Catholic, and I thought to myself, "They've got this one pegged wrong. This guy is well-adjusted."

Joseph seemed almost happy to tell his story, though he spoke in staccato phrases, clipping off articles and pronouns like some kind of radio commentator. His memory was incredible, and he never hesitated as he spoke. But I soon realized that behind the mask was a deeply hurting man whose heart and mind had been irreparably damaged by Vietnam. His cynicism, distrust, and professed absence of humanity were almost frightening, yet at times I could sense something of a tiny spark within — a flicker of soul in a man still crying desperately after thirty long years. Joseph told me how it all began:

> We were told to avoid civilian casualties and stuff like that. That was the official line. Then you get in-country and you listen to the guys who've been through it already, who've got six months, or maybe a year. And you don't trust any of them. You don't trust any Vietnamese. I don't care if you're in

---

* 124th Signal Battalion, 4th Infantry Division, Pleiku Base Camp.

town, in a whorehouse, out in the field, on a convoy, or later on in the PX (postal exchange). And I was still kind of a boy scout, you know, Peace Corps volunteer, did some work in Honduras in '64. I still had that crazy idea in my head that you had to differentiate. But I got straightened out on that real quick, by the senior guys.

One time when I was new with the company I rode shotgun on a water truck to the other side of the air force base, to get 5,000 gallons of water for the base camp showers. And I caught a little kid. My buddy was in the bushes with a Madam K, you know, one of the truck-stop hookers. I'm a new guy. I have my rifle loaded up, and I'm outside the truck. And I catch this ten or eleven-year-old kid putting a hand grenade in the gas tank with scotch tape around the handle. Gas eats away the tape. I couldn't believe it, I was brand new. I grabbed him. He had the grenade in one hand, the pin down, and I got the kid. These women were screaming and yelling, and I dropped him. I panicked. Locked and loaded, and I shot at the kid. But I missed him on purpose. I could have killed him easy, but I didn't. And that's always bothered me. I've told this to a few VA psychiatrists, and they say, "Well, it's good you didn't, because you'd feel guilty." But I feel guilty that I didn't kill the kid, because he was a combatant. Just as willing and able to kill me or any other GI. And so that's tough shit for him. I should have killed that little bastard. Bothers me to this day.

We had a commando patrol about a month later. Walking down this road, and three guys step out of the tree line. And everybody opened up. It's a miracle we didn't shoot each other, because the way we were staggered, bullets flying past my ear, I'm shooting past this other guy ahead of me. One of the slopes went down. He rolled into a ditch, and I remember running up to him. He had a head wound, brain tissue coming out, and this medic comes up from out of nowhere and starts putting an IV into his arm. And a tall, lanky infantryman kicks the gook right in the face. He says, "Get the fuck out of here! You save that for us." Any kind of medical care you get, you don't waste on the enemy. So he kicked the slope in the face, and shit went flying, blood and brain tissue. That's when I started to get hard. 'Cause the E7 was right, I mean, fuck the gook. He's the enemy. I don't care if it's man, woman, or child. They're the enemy. That's it. They die. And no thinking about it. You can't feel sorry for the enemy in a time of war.

Vietnam was, I think the fancy word is "superlative." Any emotion was maxed out, totally maximum. If you were scared, it was the most scared you'll ever be. If you were bored, it was the most intensely boring time you've ever gone through. If you hated somebody, it was the most intense hatred you'd ever felt. So it was a lot of boredom, punctuated by extreme excitement, extreme rushes. Some of the guys were very special soldiers. I mean, they volunteered again and again. They'd get high on war. And I experienced some of that. I can't put myself in their class; I don't have that honor. But I experienced some of that same high.

It's still there. I always thought the war was righteous, and I still do. And it really galls me, it infuriates me that we lost 58,000 men and maimed 300,000 for life, and it was for nothing. Because the big shots screwed up bad. Kennedy, Johnson, I liked them, but they were losers. McNamara, look at him with his new book! All those men died for nothing, because the big shots screwed up.

I wasn't home a couple of weeks when I stepped off the deep end with the drinking. I wasn't home two weeks when I looked like my Uncle Joe, a heavy-duty alky...And then the girls I had been dating before Nam: Gabbi Wiser, she says, "Who the hell are you? I don't even know you anymore." Mary Brennan said the same thing after a couple dates. Well, fuck them. Plenty of women around. Who needs them? And things have been downhill ever since.

I've been homeless most of the time. Very depressed. My life's been a mess. Put my wife and my mother through nothing but torture. It's almost impossible for me to make a decision, stay with anything. 'Cause the Army doesn't believe in that. That's your camouflage, the haircuts and uniforms. And you hide in there. Guys who tried to maintain their individuality, they got the shit knocked out of them. It's all group think.

Been mostly unemployed. Twenty-eight years. My anniversary's coming up, September 19, when I came back. That's a lot of years, and I've been unemployed more than half of that time. A lot of drinking, a lot of pot smoking. You know, last six, seven years been all drinking, out of work all the time. Divorced. Like I said, I have this big conflict. I would do Nam again. I don't know. It sounds crazy. Makes me sound like heroic. It's just unfinished business.

When I got back from the Nam I just didn't belong. Odd man out. I'm still standing on the outside, like I tell my psychiatrist over here. Twenty-five years and I feel like I'm on the outside of civilian society, and I'm starving to death, and everybody's getting invited to a sit-down Christmas dinner with all the trimmings. And I'm starving. And I can see it. I can see everybody sitting down. I go around and get in line. When they open the door I can smell the aromas. And as soon as I go in, the civilians just close the door and say, "Not you. Step aside. Throw this bum out."

So fuck the civilian world. Fuck it. I like to borrow something from what the Marines say: no such thing as an ex-Marine. And it's true. No such thing as an ex-serviceman. No such thing. So fuck the civilian world. Excuse my language, but fuck it.

■ ■ ■ ■ ■ ■ ■

Without a doubt, PTSD is most acute in veterans who have seen or participated in the killing of defenseless people, especially women and children. Though such killing is a war crime by definition, it happened over and over at the hands of Americans in Vietnam and elsewhere. Incidents like the My Lai massacre in 1968 remain white-hot with controversy because the guilt lies somewhere between the soldiers involved and the factors which drove the war: the reality of woman and child combatants, the VC's use of villages for protection and hiding, the booby traps, mines, and snipers, the pressure for "body counts" and "kills," and the dehumanization of the Vietnamese people as "gooks" and "dinks." In the final analysis, lives were ruined on all sides – the villagers of My Lai, the young men pushed to the brink and scarred to the depths of their souls, and a little bit of each one of us. As a GI mother later cried, "I gave them a good boy, and they made him a murderer."[4]

Many Vietnam veterans will confirm that My Lai was not an isolated incident but happened again and again. That this is probably true does nothing to mitigate its horror; rather, it suggests that what happened to the men of Charlie Company in the wake of the atrocity can be extended to thousands of others.

In a shaking account of the massacre and its aftereffects, authors Michael Bilton and Kevin Sim relate an interview with My Lai GI Varnado Simpson. It is a glimpse into a private and unimaginable hell.

> At the end of April 1982, a 34-year-old black "Vietnam era" veteran was admitted to a Veterans Administration hospital in Jackson, Mississippi. His name was Varnado Simpson. He was of average height, around 140 pounds, well dressed, and well groomed. Although he possessed above-average intelligence and a good vocabulary, it was observed that he was nervous as he spoke, smoking continuously and making wringing movements with his hands. He always sat with his back to the wall and would never allow anyone to get behind him.
>
> According to their notes, Varnado Simpson told doctors at the hospital that he had entered military service in 1967 and had been posted the following year to Vietnam. There his company had attacked the village of "Milai" and were "apparently" ordered "not to leave anyone alive." He himself had killed women and children in the village and described "other very traumatic events occurring during this action."
>
> When he returned home from the war, Simpson started work in a bank. But in 1969, with the revelations of what had happened at My Lai, followed by the trial of Lt. Calley, he had left his job. People in the street called him "child-killer" and "baby-killer," and he felt that customers were withdrawing their money from the bank because he worked there. Since then, he had become reclusive, extremely fearful, and "somewhat paranoid." Nightmares had become

so frequent that he was afraid to go to sleep. The people he had killed in Vietnam, he said, were not really dead and were going to come back and kill him.

In 1977, Varnado Simpson's 10-year-old son was playing in the front yard of his home on the northern edge of Jackson. Teenagers across the road began arguing and one of them pulled a gun. A wild shot hit his little boy in the head.

> I was in the house. And I came out and picked him up. But he was already dead...he was dying. He died in my arms. And when I looked at him, his face was like the same face of the child that I had killed. And I said: this is the punishment for me killing the people that I killed.

Doctors could do very little for Varnado Simpson. They described his condition as post-traumatic stress disorder, "chronic and very severe." In the year he remained in the hospital they had the greatest difficulty in trying to get him to talk about his experiences. Any discussion or activation of his memories from Vietnam created such extreme discomfort that he simply could not tolerate it. "Mr. Simpson has been one of the most uncomfortable people that I have ever seen," his doctor wrote. His prognosis was considered "very guarded and very poor."

In July 1983, with his doctors' agreement, Varnado Simpson went to live by himself in a small house on the same street where his son had died. He barred the windows and put a battery of locks on the doors. In his own house, he felt better able to control his own fate.

Six years later, in the summer of 1989, he still lived alone in the same house. There were more bars on the windows now, and more locks on the doors. The curtains were always drawn. Not much of the bright, hot Mississippi summer filtered indoors.

Inside, the living room was gloomy. Varnado Simpson's hands were still shaking wildly. He tried in vain to rest them on his legs, but his legs shook too. His whole body shuddered in distress. There was the same thin moustache he wore in the twenty-year-old photograph taken during the war, though his face was rounder, almost swollen, and there was a puffiness under the eyes as if he had been crying, or was about to cry. He sat in an old armchair, his head a little to one side, with a look of utter resignation on his face and his back to the wall. And he began to talk about what happened in Vietnam.

"That day in My Lai, I was personally responsible for killing about 25 people. Personally. Men, women. From shooting them, to cutting their throats, scalping them, to...cutting off their hands and cutting out their tongue. I did it."

Why did he do all that? Why did he kill them and do that?

"I just went. My mind just went. And I wasn't the only one that did it. A lot of other people did it. I just killed. Once I started, the...the training, the whole programming part of killing, it just came out."

But your training didn't tell you to scalp people or cut ears off.

"No. But a lot of people were doing it. So I just followed suit. I just lost all sense of direction, of purpose. I just started killing any kinda way I could kill. It just came. I didn't know I had it in me.

"But like I say, after I killed the child, my whole mind just went. It just went. And once you start, it's very easy to keep on. Once you start. The hardest — the part that's hard is to kill, but once you kill, that becomes easier, to kill the next person and the next one and the next one. Because I had no feelings or no emotions or no nothing. No direction. I just killed. It can happen to anyone. Because, see, I wasn't the only one that did it. Hung 'em, you know — all type of ways. Any type of way you could kill someone, that's what they did. And it can happen."

"It can happen." It did happen. One hundred and five GIs from Charlie Company went into the village of My Lai. Almost all of them are still alive, living quietly all over America. Each of them must have their own way of dealing with the things they have seen and the deeds they have committed. But it is in Varnado Simpson's sunless room that the poison of the memory of My Lai seems to survive in its most concentrated form.

"I can't remember — you know. I can't remember everything. I don't want to remember," he says. But the truth is that he never forgets. Remembering has become a compulsion. Suddenly, without warning, he jumps up and pulls a large brown book out of a cupboard. A scrapbook of My Lai. Twenty-year-old photographs and news clippings are neatly preserved in an old photo album.

Why has he kept it?

"This is my life," he answers without hesitation. "This is my past. This is my present, and this is my future. And I keep it to remind me. But it's always there. This is my life. This is everything. This is the way I am. This is what made me this way.

"I have an image of it in my mind every night, every day. I have nightmares. I constantly have nightmares of the children or someone. I can see the people. I can go somewhere and see a face that reminds me of the people that I killed. I can see that vividly, just like it's happened today, right now."

Varnado Simpson remains caught in a trap sprung twenty years ago in Vietnam. He wants to be put out of his misery. He has attempted suicide three times and does not know if he will still be here "the next time you come around." On a table, there are dozens of bottles containing the pills which he takes throughout the day and night. One jar is labeled simply: "For Pain." Nothing prescribed by his physicians seems to have much effect or even relevance to his case. He is stretched out somewhere between life and death, scared of both, convinced that on Judgment Day his will be a hopeless case.

For there is little doubt that Varnado Simpson sees himself as a man who has already been damned.

"How can you forgive?" he asks. "You know, I can't forgive myself for the things I did. How can I forget that – or forgive? There's a part of me that's kind and gentle. There's another part of me that's evil and destructive. There's more destructiveness in my mind than goodness. There's more wanting to kill or to hurt than to love or to care. I don't let anyone get close to me. The loving feeling and the caring feeling is not there.

"That was caused by My Lai, the war. My feelings and the way I feel and the way my life is.

"Yes, I'm ashamed, I'm sorry, I'm guilty. But I did it, you know. What else could I tell you? It happened. It can happen if you go to war. Those are the type of things that will happen and can happen to anyone..."[5]

In late 1997, just a few months shy of the thirtieth anniversary of the My Lai massacre, Varnardo Simpson took his life.

■ ■ ■ ■ ■ ■ ■

All too often, the anxiety and self-destructive behavior of veterans suffering severe PTSD ends in suicide. Though controversy swirls around the actual numbers – ranging from as low as 10,000 to as high as 120,000 – the Vietnam War continues to exact a heavy toll back home. If a study published in 1987 in the New England Journal of Medicine is near the mark, then the number of Vietnam veterans who died at their own hands after the war equals the number killed during the war. As widow Deborah Cook writes, even one suicide – and the awful wake of pain and anguish it leaves behind – is one too many.

> During my only visit to the Vietnam Memorial in Washington, DC, I was determined not to make this my catharsis but just visit. As I walked slowly and quietly down the walk my eyes caught a letter almost waving to me in the mild breeze.
>
> I picked up the letter and as I read, all of my personal emotion welled up and the sadness, anger, and bitterness was right there, right there at the foot of all those names of the Vietnam dead. The letter was from a woman writing to her lost love. It said something to the effect: "If you had lived, we would have been married, had children, but you didn't come back." I wanted to find her and tell her my story because my love did come back...
>
> Larry and I met when I was fourteen and he was sixteen. High school sweethearts, we became engaged when I was sixteen, just before he left for

Vietnam. I wrote a letter to him each day, sometimes more. He was shot in the leg in the twelfth month of his thirteen-month assignment. He came home, and during his convalescent leave we were married. Ten months later our daughter Laura was born while Larry was in the Mediterranean. He left the Marine Corps shortly after his return.

His problems started shortly after the birth of our son Kevin, two years later. I won't go into all of the detail of the hell we lived through. I will tell you that the last year of his life was torture for both of us. Vietnam came back to him in bits and pieces till, in those last days, he was sure people from Vietnam were in the grocery store, at the gas station, or wherever we went. He became paranoid. He attempted suicide perhaps three times before he was successful. I saw it. He shot himself in the head as I walked through the front door (yes, he was under the care of a doctor).

I was a twenty-four-year-old widow with two babies. I would like to tell the woman who left the letter what it is like to be twenty-four years old and see your husband blow his brains out. I would like to tell her what it's like to tell your kids a thousand times what happened but you can't tell them why.

How did Vietnam change my life? It has been almost twenty years since that day in July. I have lived with it every day. I have cried and screamed so many times it feels like that is who I am sometimes. My kids grew up without a dad. My daughter was married last year; we both cried because her dad wasn't there to give her away. She recently gave birth to our grandson. Weeks before he was born, Laura cried and cried because Larry wouldn't see his grandson. God, I hope he can see him – my joy, my respite in this struggle.

My husband's name is not on the Vietnam Wall, but he is as much a fallen soldier as any. Vietnam will live for a long time in the lives of those whose loved ones fell, both there and here.[6]

Admiral Jack Shanahan, of the Center for Defense Information in Washington, DC, said, "In the military we train people to break things, to kill and to destroy. So if you suddenly put these people in a humanitarian area, they don't know how to deal with it…You kind of don't expect them to return to the private sector of civilian society." I thought that a powerful, albeit reserved, statement about the crippling nature of military indoctrination and combat experience, one that explains why veterans like Joseph Hughes have never really "returned" to the civilian world. Lt. Col. David A. Grossman says it most succinctly: "War is an environment that will psychologically debilitate 98 percent of all who participate in it for any length of time."[7]

■ ■ ■ ■ ■ ■ ■

James Burks entered the Air Force in 1969 and spent his tour in Vietnam cleaning up human refuse after rocket attacks and attempting to kill "sappers,"
Vietcong who made their way through the wire fencing around the perimeter of
the base. For an entire year, he lived in fear of sudden death. And the pieces of
flesh which were once his buddies still crowd his thoughts each day.

I met James at the Borden Avenue Homeless Shelter in Queens. He was a
quiet man, so soft-spoken it was almost hard to hear what he was saying at times.
His eyes had a look that was all too familiar — a world of pain swimming in the
recesses of his mind, waiting and hoping to spill over and drain away. He was
somewhat matter of fact in his tone as he told me about the struggle of his life,
but I realized quickly how much he needed to hide his emotions in order to
speak about them. His words revealed again the private pain carried by so many
in the aftermath of war.

When I first got to Nam, it was the first time that I'd ever been out of the
United States. The people reminded me so much of my own culture...an oppressed people.

Then immediately we started to get bombarded. Rockets, shrapnel, killing
people. And this started to wear on my nerves. I lived in constant fright, so I
turned to alcohol. I started doing things that I would never have done
before...Alcohol hid my fears and brought me out of myself. It was like living a double identity.

We had sappers coming through the fence line. My job was to finish them
off...In combat, I was a squad leader, and you had to make decisions rapidly
and you had to be accurate. You didn't have time to sit and think about it.
Maybe that's why I'm impulsive today. I just do things impulsively and hope
that I've made the right decision. But sometimes you're not that fortunate.

In Vietnam, things came out of me that I didn't even know I possessed.
The hardness and the coldness, how you could just do things and have no
remorse, no feelings...You take a chicken and wring its neck and you have no
remorse whatsoever. But when you look at humans in the same way, you're a
psychopath. You have no concern for human life...

I did what I had to do in Vietnam because I was a soldier. I did what I did
because I was scared and I didn't want to die. And I did it because I was ordered to do it, not because I liked doing it.

Some of my friends didn't make it back, and sometimes I feel like they
were the lucky ones. Because since I've been back I've been living a life in
hell. I haven't been able to find myself. I don't have an identity. I've just been
one drink after another, one drug after another, just living in a circle that has
no ending. It just keeps revolving.

I've been married three times, and I have six kids. But I never gave them anything but material things. I never gave myself because I didn't have a self to give. I don't have a person to give them. What they have is a shell of a person.

I have things to make amends for, especially to my previous wives. Because I did everything to destroy their world. I'm pretty sure that they have Vietnam stories that they could tell, and they were never there...

I take a lot of drugs to keep my mind together, but it's a struggle. I've been in and out of hospitals for the last seven years...When I got out of the military they gave me a debriefing. And once the debriefing was over, I was supposed to be a civilian and be happy for the rest of my life, don't worry about it. But Vietnam changed my life so drastically that now I can't adjust to civilian life...

Ninety percent of the people in this shelter are veterans. Most of them, I can relate to. They have some inkling as to what I'm talking about. But trying to relate to normal people out there in the streets? They really can't understand what I'm talking about...

■ ■ ■ ■ ■ ■ ■

Steve Bentley has written extensively about PTSD since the early 1980s. In his video *Beyond Vietnam* he stresses the point that no normal person can pass through a combat situation and remain unaffected, adding that those who are unaffected are psychotic to begin with. Steve ought to know. He was a Rome Plow operator in the jungles of Vietnam, clearing the field in areas of heavy enemy contact, booby traps, landmines, or mortar and rocket attacks. "You can't tiptoe through the jungle in a twenty-five-ton bulldozer," he said. "They know where you are."

Steve has tirelessly advocated the cause of fellow Vietnam veterans suffering from PTSD, a work all the more remarkable for his long personal struggle toward wholeness through a tragic family background, drug and alcohol addiction, and a series of hospitalizations after the war. It was clear, when I met Steve at a Buddhist retreat for Vietnam veterans in October of '97, that he is still working on the "healing end" of his experience (he said he felt he was meant to be there, in that time and place, with that group of fellow veterans), but his gift for articulating the pain and struggle, the cry from the depths among so many Vietnam vets, has helped others immeasurably. Steve has "been there." The following is excerpted from his writings and articles on PTSD:

1984: Dana Bradford is a Vietnam veteran who was recently ordered by U.S. District Judge Gene Carter to be taken from the Togus, Maine, VA hospital to Augusta Mental Health Institute for evaluation after he allegedly threatened President Reagan's life. According to a fellow veteran on his ward at Togus, Bradford said that he would shoot the President "if he turned El Salvador into another Vietnam." Overhearing this, a male nurse felt it was his duty to call in the Secret Service, and they subsequently felt it was theirs to transfer Bradford, in shackles, from Togus to AMHI.

Talk about a sad state of affairs.

Here we have a man already in a psychiatric ward. He's filled with psychotropic chemicals and tranquilizing drugs. He's acknowledged by the VA to be 100-percent disabled with post-traumatic stress disorder (PTSD) which is marked by, among other things, suicidal feelings and thoughts, fantasies of retaliation and destruction, cynicism and distrust of government and authority, extreme anger and fits of rage as well as self-deceiving and self-punishing behavior, in short, all the behavior and emotions that Bradford was displaying. When a man has a wound, you should expect him to bleed...

I have been in a group situation with Bradford for a number of months now. I feel I know him very well...Bradford's threat was simply the cry of a man who suffers daily from the madness that was Vietnam.

The faces of the dead wash over him constantly, and he is haunted by his sense of the meaninglessness of it all. He is only saying that it should not happen again. That others should not have to live with the ghosts he lives with.

But not everyone understands him. And not everyone really hears him. And so the Secret Service comes in the night.[8]

1989: There will be much said in the name of the dead this Memorial Day. But what about the living? The way to honor our ideals is not by projecting them onto the dead. It's by practicing them among those still alive – by providing adequate care to those who fought and served beside those who died.[9]

1991: While the Gulf buildup and battle were wrapped in ribbons and bows, and as the flags fly in jubilation over the victory, Vietnam vets have been showing up at vet centers and VA hospitals in record numbers...

It is war itself that makes men mad, and all the parades in the world won't heal those Persian Gulf vets who have looked into the abyss.[10]

1992: Four months ago, in late November, Vietnam veteran Robert Daigneau left the Togus Veterans Administration Hospital after a 28-day stay on the post-traumatic stress treatment unit. He immediately drove to Kentucky where he shot five people to death, including himself.

A week later, 20-year veteran Bruce Allen returned to Limestone after a 2-week stay at the Togus facility. The night he returned he shot himself in the head with a .357 magnum and died. On January 12, Vietnam veteran Dave

Garland jumped to his death from an abandoned mill in Old Town. Less than a week later, Vietnam veteran Michael "Mickey" Obrin returned from Togus and shot himself to death in his Portland apartment. On March 17, Vietnam veteran William Harrington returned from one of many visits to Togus and held at least a dozen police officers at bay for an hour while threatening to kill himself with a hunting knife.

One might ask at this point just what the hell it is that the Togus VA facility is doing to these people that allows for such behavior right after discharge. A letter sent to Maine's congressional delegation by wounded Vietnam combat veteran Frank Muchie on March 20 would appear to provide part of the answer. According to Frank, what the hospital is doing to these people is nothing, absolutely nothing. Frank reports that during his 22-day stay there were days at a time when he had nothing to do but worry and wonder and wander the halls...

All the major studies have warned that as the majority of Vietnam veterans enter midlife crisis, dragging along the unfinished business of Vietnam, their problems will intensify...We must add to that...the effect the Persian Gulf War had on these men.

There are vet centers. However, they are overloaded and understaffed. And while they should be expanding, some Republicans are pushing to phase them out...Denying these problems won't make them go away.

How can it be that a nation has hundreds of billions of dollars to spend destroying human beings and yet not nearly enough to heal them, and what values were we defending in Europe, Asia, and the Gulf if we have money to send children to war, but none to heal men? If those who spill their blood and sear their souls in service to our country can't get justice from our country, then who in God's name can?[11]

Steve's last question is the central issue in the whole tragedy of PTSD. We – the people, our government, our military – use men as if they were artillery. We cast them back like spent cartridges, into an uncomprehending society, hoping that the sands of time will cover their pain and anguish from our view. But, like a used shell on a battlefield, it does not go away; it surfaces again and again, rustier, uglier, and ever more compelling.

Vietnamese Buddhist monk Thich Nhat Hanh once said that "veterans are the light at the tip of the candle, illuminating the way for the whole nation. If veterans can achieve awareness, transformation, understanding, and peace, they can share with the rest of society the realities of war. And they can teach us how to make peace with ourselves and each other..."[12]

Veterans need to look deeply into their past and find redemption from deeds and actions which their consciences tell them were wrong and evil. But the stories they tell must be lessons for all of us. Every one of us needs to look deeply into the war that lurks within our own hearts and minds, to shatter our perceptions of ourselves and of others; to share our guilt with others; to ask forgiveness. As many veterans have testified, this is the road to rebirth, to true freedom.

We need to create "spaces" in which to share their pain. We need to listen and to understand; most of all, we need to believe them when they cry, "No more war, ever again!" This is something all of us can do. Sadly, there are so many veterans with PTSD that everyone who reads this book will know at least one. That's a good place to start.

■ ■ ■ ■ ■ ■ ■

The story that follows was sent to me by Moni Loewenthal, a woman who lives not far from me in upstate New York. It is a story that exemplifies the need for love and forgiveness not only in her community, but in society as a whole:

Crazy Bob lives alone on the outskirts of our remote town in the Catskill Mountains, avoiding – and avoided by – his neighbors. His two dogs, Chin-Chin and Cola, are his only family. Strange stories are told about him. He is said to have broken into a house to steal a pair of new boots, leaving his worn-out shoes in their place. Another time, he appeared at a social event, filled a cup with honey, and then slurped it down with his fingers. "He's out of it," they say. "He's on drugs."

Everyone "knows" that he grows weed behind his house. "I wouldn't trust him," says a neighbor. "You never know what he'll do next." Yes, Bob is crazy. The bumper stickers on his pickup read: "I brake for butterflies" and "God is coming and she is pissed."

Bob is very tall and lean. In spite of his hunchback, he still stands over six feet tall. Rumor has it that in the war he was hit in the back by a helicopter rotor. When he returned from Vietnam he took to the road, travelling for ten years, knapsack on his back, until he settled here. His face is creased, his chin stubbled with a three-days' growth of beard. The lines on his face tell of long suffering, and when he smiles you can see that he is missing his front teeth. He doesn't smile often, though. He coughs a lot…

Vesna arrived last winter, from Yugoslavia. Her baby was due in December, and she hoped to give him a good start in the "land of opportunity." She stayed first at a crowded and filthy shelter in New York City, but was hospitalized with dehydration after only two weeks in the country. Would her baby live? She was discharged from the hospital after three days, alone in a foreign city with nowhere to go. But a Yugoslav woman who immigrated fifteen years ago rescued her – brought her here, to a trailer in the mountains.

Vesna needed regular checkups at the clinic. Who would help her? Crazy Bob offered to take her to the doctor. The villagers snickered, but none of them offered to help. First every two weeks, then weekly, then twice a week, Bob drove to the clinic an hour away, down the mountain and then back up again. What was his motive? The neighbors assumed the worst. But there was a whisper that he'd been touched by the helplessness of this woman and wanted in some way to atone for the horror he'd been a part of in Vietnam.

The baby was born on Christmas Eve. No heralding angels, for sure, but Vesna was radiant with her little son. Bob called the hospital to find out how she was doing. He visited. He brought gifts for the baby. He took pictures. He helped. This was Christmas, after all, wasn't it?

All of us have shut Crazy Bob out of our lives. We would rather not see him, rather not let him upset our decent and orderly lives. But what did we do to help Bob adjust when he came home from Vietnam – or to keep him out of the war in the first place? We want to forget, to push aside and hide the ugliness. Isn't Crazy Bob ours? Isn't he us?

■ ■ ■ ■ ■ ■ ■

What happened to us, what we did, is stuff that most people don't want to hear. And the people that particularly don't want to hear it are the people that sent us over. The only people who really understand what I am talking about – who even care to hear what I am talking about; who care to share war stories that are immoral, obscene, stories that really nobody should have to listen to but that we tell each other for some reason – are other veterans. The only people in America who took the war as seriously as we did were the people in the antiwar movement. Most other people in the United States didn't care. And it wasn't that they were bad people or unkind or stupid or couldn't see what was going on, it was because they were busy. They were busy working, they were busy being parents, they were busy at their jobs, they were busy going to school, they were busy going to the movies, busy going to McDonalds, busy going to Burger King, they were too busy to pay attention to the half-million Americans over in Vietnam, the 58,000 being killed. They were just too busy.

Ben Chitty, U.S. Navy, 1965–69

CHAPTER 6

The Silenced Majority

O, let my land be a land where Liberty
Is crowned with no false patriotic wreath,
But opportunity is real, and life is free,
Equality is in the air we breathe.

(There's never been equality for me,
Nor freedom in this "homeland of the free.")

"Say who are you that mumbles in the dark?
And who are you that draws your veil across the stars?"

I am the poor white, fooled and pushed apart,
I am the Negro bearing slavery's scars.
I am the red man driven from the land,
I am the immigrant clutching the hope I seek –
And finding only the same old stupid plan
Of dog eat dog, of mighty crush the weak...

Sure, call me any ugly name you choose –
The steel of freedom does not stain.
From those who live like leeches on the people's lives,
We must take back our land again,
America!

O, yes,
I say it plain,
America never was America to me...

Langston Hughes, from "Let America be America Again"

From the Civil War on, countless soldiers have placed their hope in the military as the great equalizer, the one system whereby the demands of war strip away all distinction between race and class. In the First World War, new immigrants to America filled the ranks of the United States Army, and the military was trumpeted as the "point of entry into the American mainstream." Hoping to stave off prejudice and persecution, some minority groups even sought to "legitimize" themselves through military service. One such example is the large number of Japanese Americans who joined the Army during World War II, desperate to prove their loyalty to a nation that was interning their wives and children as "enemy aliens."[1]

But if the military has taken its toll on lower- and middle-class whites, it has been a crushing deception for minorities. Those who enlist to break free of inequality and stigmatization soon find that the military is no safe haven from racism. Instead, it mirrors the injustices of society at large.

Jesuit and thirty-year activist Daniel Berrigan tells of a Veterans Day parade he watched from a city apartment building window. When the parade ended and the veterans began to disperse, he saw how white and minority veterans parted ways: the blacks and Hispanics into the ghettoes, and the whites uptown. As Daniel later reflected, he was treated that day to a powerful symbol of the facade of equality and camaraderie in the military which is only uniform-deep. In truth, as the following stories will show, the racial tensions and injustices permeating the military-industrial complex are perhaps stronger than anywhere else.

In terms of the historical context of such injustices, it is hard to find a more concise summary than that provided by Malcolm X early in the Vietnam War: "Here lies a YM, killed by a BM, fighting for the WM, who killed all the RM." Alex Haley, then interviewing Malcolm for his biography, decoded this message, which the black leader had scrawled on a napkin: "Here lies a yellow man, killed by a black man, fighting for the white man, who killed all the red men." Haley wrote in the epilogue to Malcolm's biography: "Decoding that wasn't difficult, knowing Malcolm X." Native American veteran Tom Holm comments, "The note obviously points out that Malcolm X was convinced that black people, the victims of racism in America, were being used by whites to oppress other people of color...Little wonder that many minority veterans looked upon their period of service in the war as time and effort wasted. It had gained them neither greater acceptance nor financial security."[2]

Holm's observation applies just as much to minority veterans across the board — women, Native Americans, Chicanos, Puerto Ricans, and others — as it does to blacks. In the wealth of literature on the Vietnam War, for example, each minority group provides ample evidence not only of exploitation but also of carefully planned marginalization, even to the point of "invisibility." Yet the experience of minorities who served in Vietnam is universal, and extends from far in the past to the very present. Collectively, these minority veterans comprise the "silenced majority," voices that have been stilled by the extraordinary burden of war, compounded by discrimination and injustice on the front lines as well as back home.

■ ■ ■ ■ ■ ■ ■

On March 13, 1997, a BBC broadcast called "Chocolate Soldier from the USA" took an in-depth look at racial injustices suffered by soldiers in the European Theater during World War II.[3] The centerpiece of the program was the case of Henry Leroy, a black supply technician in the U.S. Army, who was convicted of raping a British white woman on the night of May 5, 1944, and sentenced to death. According to Leroy, his confession was obtained by force:

> When they took me over to the station, it was about 4:00. They put me down in a room there. I lay down and went to sleep and waked up later. They were peering through a cut place in the door, peeping through. And a few minutes later they came on in. This CID that had the brown coat on had two long sheets of paper and they were sitting over on the bunk across from me and had me standing up, asking me questions. A few questions I answered and some I did not, because all that stuff was not true. And anyway, he just wrote what he wanted to write down, and I never did know what was on the paper, and as far as I know he never did read it off to me.
>
> And while he was sitting there trying to get a statement a blind flash went over me and I fell all at once. After that something booted me from behind while I was laying down on the floor, and they picked me up and shook me and tried to make me stand at attention. They sat me on the bed and asked me questions about that paper and went on and filled the paper out. And they asked me was I going to sign it, and I said no. He said, Goddamn it, I would sign it, and if I knew what was good I had better sign. I was out of my head, but I never heard him read it to me. He called this captain down, and he told me I had better sign it. I did put my name on one or two sheets, and I never did know what was on the paper.

Professor Robert Lily of North Kentucky University, who researched Leroy Henry's case extensively, noted that the trial transcript revealed that ten witnesses were called for the prosecution, but not a single witness for the defense. BBC producer Marc Jobst says, "Leroy Henry's trial marks a notorious chapter in the history of the American military, the British Parliament, and the sovereignty of both countries during the Second World War. It's a case that brings into question the notion of fundamental justice for black soldiers at the time."

Indeed, Lily's research unearthed some damning statistics. Prior to the arrival of American "Negroes" in Britain during World War II, rape had not been a capital offense in Britain for more than eighty years. Of the seventy people officially executed by the military in the European Theater, 80 percent were African-Americans — who represented only 10 percent of the American troops. Incredibly, *all* of the people executed for rape in England during the war were either African-American or Latino.

The BBC broadcast cited an incident in which a white soldier was convicted of raping a sixteen-year-old girl who was a "camp follower." The man was articulate and had a good defense, and his commanding officer said he could not afford to lose him. In the end, discipline was administered by the commander, who simply gave this white soldier thirty days.

Britain was desperate for military assistance and turned to the United States for aid. President Roosevelt wanted to step in but had to placate opposition in Congress as well, so he outlined certain terms of agreement which were met by the Visiting Forces Act of 1942. These were hastily drawn up by the British government and forced rapidly through the houses of Parliament. According to Lily, the act "gave the Americans carte blanche to import not just their troops, but also their system of racial segregation and military justice." He cites a telling statement by General J. C. Lee in 1945:

> The colored soldiers are akin to well-meaning but irresponsible children. As such, they have to be given the best possible care by their officers and at the same time be subjected to rigid discipline. Generally they cannot be trusted to tell the truth, to execute complicated orders, or to act on their own initiative, except in certain individual circumstances. Among the peculiar characteristics of the colored race, influences such as excitement, fear, religion, dope, liquor, or the accomplishment of something without their usual sphere, they individually or collectively can change form with amazing rapidity from a timid or bashful individual to brazen boldness or madness or become hysterical.

The BBC program provides a revealing overview of American and British attitudes toward the black soldiers of World War II; it also indicates that those executed were convicted as much by their social circumstances as by the crimes they committed:

> Not only was [Leroy Henry] accused of rape but, almost more incriminatingly, of raping a white woman. This violated a fundamental code of behavior for Americans at the time, that there should be no co-mingling of races.

By contrast, there was a much more open and curious attitude to black people in Britain. So, when segregated American troops arrived in an inquisitive and welcoming Britain, there was a substantial clash of attitudes. This seriously threatened the status of white GIs. Anticipating this reaction, the British government tried to discourage the U.S. from sending black troops. Foreign Secretary Anthony Eden rather mysteriously told the American ambassador, "Our climate is badly suited to Negroes." Nonetheless, by D day 1944 more than 130,000 black troops were on duty in Britain. They had money in their pockets, were different, exciting, and were noted for their courteousness. Inevitably then, black boy kept meeting white girl...

Leroy Henry, like most of the black U.S. troops serving in the European theater of operations, was involved in service-related activities. Black soldiers were mostly required to do heavy manual work, little different to that expected of them back home. The general perception of the time was that black soldiers were not suitable for fighting, and that perception emanated from the top. U.S. Secretary of War Stimson had stated, "Leadership is not embedded in the Negro race," and this view was echoed by other military leaders.

David Smith, a company clerk, recalls a chilling moment when he and several other GIs were forced to witness the execution, by hanging, of a fellow black soldier. Having volunteered for an unknown assignment, he and six other men were driven to a deserted field outside of Cherbourg, France, where they were paraded in front of a Frenchwoman who had apparently been violated; one of the unlucky volunteers was promptly "identified" by a pointing finger. The cavalier manner in which the accused was subsequently convicted is explained by Professor Lily, who notes that such executions served as much more than a very obvious deterrent against sexual assault:

> It has nothing to do with justice at all. But it has to do with maintaining discipline. The U.S. Army was very concerned that black soldiers, particularly, would not learn to act differently when they were away from home. Rape was one way in which they could be reminded of their place. It was a part of the fear of black sexual prowess, and it was a fear of co-mingling of races. The Army had a very serious PR problem in the United States, first of all taking troops abroad, but also the Army did not want to see a picture of a U.S. Army soldier in uniform walking through Picadilly with a white woman on his arm if he was black. That wouldn't look good in the pictures of the Southern newspapers...

If within the U.S. military itself change, albeit small, is occurring in terms of the role played by black soldiers in the Second World War, there is scant recognition. It wasn't until President Clinton's second-term inauguration address, more than fifty years after the war, that seven medals of honor, the highest accolade, were awarded to black soldiers. But, it has to be said, six of them posthumously.

■ ■ ■ ■ ■ ■ ■

Though organized black opposition to World War II was suppressed by fear, there was plenty of bitterness about the absurdity of fighting against fascism abroad in the face of so much racism at home. One black journalist wrote: "The Negro…is angry, resentful, and utterly apathetic about the war. 'Fight for what?' he is asking. 'This war doesn't mean a thing to me. If we win, I lose, so what?'" At an all-black college, a student told his teacher: "The Army jim-crows us. The Navy lets us serve only as mess men. The Red Cross refuses our blood. Employers and labor unions shut us out. Lynchings continue. We are dis-enfranchised, jim-crowed, spat upon. What more could Hitler do than that?"[4]

Despite the Civil Rights Movement of the fifties and sixties, little in the military changed. The burgeoning conflict in Southeast Asia heralded the first "fully integrated" American war, but the fact that black and white men fought side by side seems to have amplified racial tensions more than it helped to overcome them. Blacks fought and died in Vietnam in disproportionately high numbers. From 1965 to 1967, blacks represented only one-tenth of the U.S. population but roughly one-quarter of its combat casualties.[5] Those who survived came home to levels of hatred and discrimination even greater than those they had faced in the Civil Rights era.

Only a few months before his assassination, in late 1967, Martin Luther King, Jr., gave a series of five talks through the Canadian Broadcasting Corporation. These talks culminated in a "sermon on peace" delivered from the pulpit of the Ebenezer Church in Atlanta, Georgia, on Christmas Eve. In a scathing indictment of the Vietnam War, Dr. King elucidated the struggles of men dying for a cause that was not their own:

> I was increasingly compelled to see the [Vietnam] war not only as a moral outrage but also as an enemy of the poor, and to attack it as such.
>
> Perhaps a more tragic recognition of reality took place when it became clear to me that the war was doing far more than devastating the hopes of the poor at home. It was sending their sons and their brothers and their husbands to fight and to die in extraordinarily higher proportions relative to the rest of the population. We were taking the black young men who had been crippled by our society and sending them eight thousand miles away to guarantee liberties in Southeast Asia which they had not found in southwest Georgia and

East Harlem. And so we have been repeatedly faced with the cruel irony of watching Negro and white boys on TV screens as they kill and die together for a nation that has been unable to seat them together in the same schools. We watch them in brutal solidarity burning the huts of a poor village, but we realize that they would never live on the same block in Detroit. I could not be silent in the face of such cruel manipulation of the poor...[6]

When Martin Luther King, Jr., equated "poor" with "black" in his statement on Vietnam, he was speaking accurately of a military that had systematically ruined the lives of poor minority soldiers. More than that, he had brought the movement for civil rights to a whole new level, that of protest against a very "white" war. The formation of this coalition between civil-rights and antiwar forces was too much for the establishment to bear, and it was to cost King his life only five months later.

Writing of PTSD in the wake of the Vietnam War, Tom Holm observed that the higher levels of stress seen in nonwhite veterans were as much about class as they were about race. Poorer Americans were twice as likely to be assigned to nontechnical military occupations as were members of the upper classes. Because of their lower educational levels, minorities were also more apt to enter military service in the first place, and therefore to participate in combat.[7]

This fact was brought home to me personally and powerfully when I first visited New York City's Borden Avenue Homeless Shelter. As I sat in the train on my way down to the city, I prepared myself for an ordeal. The friend who had suggested I visit there had warned me that these men were at the bottom rung as far as processing their experiences was concerned, and I wasn't exactly sure what I should expect to find.

The shelter is an inconspicuous, single-level brick building in Queens, with a small "Salvation Army" sign out front. George Jones, the director, met us at the security desk and took us to his office, where he explained his organization's background. In the years following Vietnam, the vast numbers of veterans on the streets became painfully visible, and the city was pressured into building a shelter. Of course, nobody wanted veterans in their backyard; they were now "baby killers and murderers," though in another time and place they would have been received as heroes. As a result, the project floundered; the Salvation Army finally stepped forward to take it on. Today, it receives funding from both charities and the city; it is still run by the Salvation Army.

George explained that they like to keep a low profile because of a general anti-veteran sentiment, and that most people in the city don't even know that the shelter exists. Aside from the minimal counseling and medical care provided by the Veterans Administration, the men spend time cleaning up the neighborhood and involving themselves in other tasks of community service.

The shelter houses 410 veterans from every modern "conflict" the U.S. has known: World War II, Korea, Vietnam, Grenada, Panama, Somalia, and the Persian Gulf War. A labyrinth of administrative offices divided into random temporary cubicles opens up into a sprawling residential area, filled with lockers and simple metal-frame beds in neat rows. Each narrow bed and locker is "home" for the veteran who occupies it. Pictures, clothes, and personal memorabilia identify each bunk. I was led into the "program room," a small, cafeteria-like cubicle where I was to hold interviews with veterans who had volunteered to meet with me.

I had asked to meet with a cross section of combat veterans, and of the five I interviewed that day, four were black. All had served in Vietnam. All were suffering under some manifestation of post-traumatic stress disorder. The stories I heard moved me very deeply; they penetrated far beyond the experience of the war itself to touch on the institutionalized racism that permeates our society and exploits the poor and the disenfranchised. In a very real sense, Vietnam, for black soldiers who survived, was a microcosm of their entire life experience, another heavy "brick in the wall." As Philip Berrigan, World War II veteran and Catholic peace activist, wrote in his autobiography:

> I discovered that blacks represented ten percent of the American population, but made up one-third of the combat troops in Vietnam. Poor young kids from the bayous and ghettos of America were joining combat units for the extra pay, which they sent home to their poverty-stricken families. Black men who couldn't vote, couldn't get an education, and couldn't get a job in America, were being sent off to fight, they thought, for peace and social justice in Vietnam. This was more than cruel irony. The United States government wasn't lynching African-Americans; it was convincing them to lynch themselves...[8]

For me, the visit to Borden Avenue was another important mile along a journey that began several years ago, when I first started providing spiritual advice and support to young men incarcerated in our local county jail. Most of these young men are black, and although we meet for little more than a few hours each week, I get to know many of them well. These relationships have been some of the most eye-opening experiences of my life: I have learned about a world I did not know existed, a world of stark realities, ceaseless trauma and violence, one that never touches the white middle class.

One of these young men was raised not far from here, in the Brownsville section of Brooklyn, one of the most dangerous, violent, and drug-infested neighborhoods in New York City. He went to school at Thomas Jefferson High in East

New York, at the time the "deadliest high school in the nation" in terms of homicide. His home was Brownsville's infamous projects (a place he referred to as the "brown monster"), a hellish, crowded cluster of dilapidated apartment buildings, rife with sexual immorality, drug abuse, and gunfire. The law of Brownsville's streets is brutal and unrelenting – a law of instant retaliation for "disrespect," of reputation and power built on fear, and complete disregard for the value of human life. For the "sons" of Brownsville emerging into adulthood, life is hell, and they place little value on it. This young man told me that they have no fear; their lives are nothing but a slow death, eased and anesthetized by the escape of crack addiction, and they welcome the chance to look down the barrel of a gun. I tried to imagine a world where young men *want* to die.

The more our relationships develop, the more I learn of an existence where violent confrontation and death is not a shocking aberration but a way of life. Crack-war executions mingle with automatic weapon fire in the projects to create a familiar din. At three years old, children can tell the difference between firecrackers, the backfiring of automobiles, and gunshots. When I think of places like Brownsville and East New York now, I wonder about America's deep concern and involvement in the war-torn nations of Bosnia, Rwanda, Burundi, and Somalia. The horrors of Bosnia are on display in our own backyard...

As I traveled down to Borden Avenue, I was struck by the bitter irony of sending such young black men to fight "white man's wars." From the Civil War to the Persian Gulf, blacks have been used as ammunition in a crusade to protect a lifestyle they rarely enjoy or benefit from. Muhammad Ali crisply framed the injustice of black men being drafted to fight in Vietnam when he said, "No Vietcong ever called me a 'nigger.'"[9] And Phil Berrigan said to me, "These guys were mercenaries without being aware of it, fighting the empire's wars, and they had no full rights as citizens back home."

One Black Panther recalled: "For me the thought of being killed in the Black Panther Party by the police and the thought of being killed by Vietnamese was just a qualitative difference. I had left one war and came back and got into another one. Most of the Panthers then were veterans. We figured if we had been over in Vietnam fighting for our country, which at that point wasn't serving us properly, it was only proper that we had to go out and fight for our own cause. We had already fought for the white man in Vietnam. It was clearly his war."[10]

The ruining of young black men for a counterfeit cause only increased their trauma and created a vast reserve of black veterans who have simply dropped off the edge of society and stayed there. Because their existence today challenges the socio-economic machine that abused them, we try to hide the evidence, tucking them away to suffer silently in inner-city shelters and other haunts of anonymity.

What follows is a testament, not only to the black experience of the Vietnam War, but to the black experience of America at the lowest rung. My respect for these men runs deep, and my heart overflows.

■ ■ ■ ■ ■ ■ ■

Nathaniel Goodwin was born in Alabama in a time when black childhood was almost universally bitter, dominated by racism and poverty. He moved north to Jamaica, New York, while he was still young, volunteered, and ended up in Vietnam in the 4th Infantry Division. In an unlikely conversation with his Vietcong "enemies," he learned the truth about the war:

> I was born in Alabama, in a little town called Mentol. My father made like two, three dollars a day. And we needed more money, so we moved to New York. I had asthma frequently, and so we moved out to Queens.
>
> At that time, 1958, it was bad: my mother would always tell me to ride the back of the bus; the front is for the other people. I went through a lot during that time of my life. I was slow in school...When I was seventeen things started picking up a little bit; I thought I was a man now and I can take care of myself. That's what I told my father. And I didn't really want to stay home anymore.
>
> This Vietnam thing was going around, and I knew that I was going to get drafted, so I figured I'll just volunteer. I don't know why, but I thought I could get back home safely. So I volunteered to go to Vietnam. I was twenty-two.
>
> My first day was hard for me, because we arrived at 12:00 midnight. The temperature was 115°. It was a shocker to me. The heat was unbearable. And that first night we got mortared. I was out there all alone, and I was scared. The fear hit you, just like this. I didn't want to die, man, I really didn't want to die...
>
> Then I started getting sick. My asthma started coming on. I had seen a lot of dudes getting it out there, you know – I picked up arms and legs and put 'em in bags. That was affecting me, smelling death in the air. It really bothered me a whole lot.
>
> Now, when I came back to base camp, everybody was getting high. They were shooting themselves up with morphine, smoking weed, drinking liquor, and I started doing the same thing. I started to buy liquor to put in my water bottles. I had four or five. And smoking that weed, because you needed that to confront your fears. You couldn't just go out there and confront Charlie straight up.
>
> They sent me back out in the field, made me walk point man for the 4th Infantry Division. And one day I walk into this Vietcong. I grab his weapon, and

we're struggling. My company all comes running and so we chase him and put about seven clips of magazines in him. He stayed alive for a long time...

I felt like John Wayne. I said, "Wow, I can take it now." I was high. I had medicated myself with drugs. Maybe I shouldn't have been feeling so good, but it was my first kill, you know, and it felt good.

Another time my company got hit, overran, and I was lost out there. We found ourselves with a couple of guys from a Green Beret outfit, and they had a prisoner. And one of their guys cut the prisoner's arm off, you know, like an initiation. Then they gave me the machete, and it was kinda like, this is what I have to do, to show them I'm on their side. And I'm not gonna punk out, you know. So I cut his arm off. Then one of the Green Beret's cut his head off...A lot of things were running through my mind when I saw that. What if that was me?

We worked out of Pleiku, and we did a lot of ridiculous stuff, really crazy. We armed water buffaloes to run into a convoy. We tied grenades around monkeys. Like John Wayne, you know.

I went to the city one day to see this young lady, you know, money for love, and suddenly she tells me the Vietcong are there. So they come in, and I start acting like a clown. I can speak Vietnamese pretty well, used to translate. And they said, "Well, you really know Vietnamese!" To save my life I had to act like an idiot, so I said, "Let's talk a while." They asked me why I was fighting and I told them: "Because I'm fighting for my life. I don't want to kill nobody, but I don't want to get killed, either. I just want to get back to the States alive."

And they said, "You're stupid, man, we're fighting for the same thing you're fighting for back in the States. We don't want to fight you, man. We got a beef with the white guy."

It's all about freedom...It's all about giving us a break. It's just like white against black in 1955. And we want our freedom, you know. We deserve it, bad.

■ ■ ■ ■ ■ ■ ■

Walter Wells is a stocky, dark-skinned man who grew up in the South Bronx and served as a helicopter door gunner in Vietnam. He walked into the room quietly while I was interviewing another vet and stood at the end of the table, looking at us intensely. He was dressed neatly in a dark-blue suit and nice shoes. His close-cropped black hair was interrupted only by a small, braided ponytail. A long scar disfigured the left cheek of his wide face. But it was his eyes that riveted me. They were windows into tragedy — a long, sad story I already knew.

Walter has been "missing in action" from the age of twelve onward: first in the Bronx, then in Vietnam, and then in prison. He has never really come home. Tears flowed from his eyes as he told his story; he was not there as he told it, but lost in the story itself. I was moved beyond words to see a man so powerful in outward appearance bare his soul and his tears.

Vietnam was not an aberration in his life, but a stop along the way. His mother would tell him as a child, "There's no such thing as hell, underground, with fire and all that, as people say. You're already *living* in hell." I could only listen, and try to understand.

He told me that he entered the military at seventeen simply to escape his environment – the drug scene and the gangs of the South Bronx. But when his boot-camp sergeant made him lie down on the road, and ordered the entire platoon to walk over him, Walter realized he hadn't found what he was looking for.

I had no feeling for my country. I just didn't want my brother to get drafted. They were saying they would send only one family member over, and my brother wouldn't have made it. He was hit by a bus and wasn't mentally there. He would have been the sole surviving son if I were to die...

But then again, I didn't really care. I was just tired of living here and going through the trials and tribulations of childhood. But I guess I jumped out of the frying pan into the fire, because when I got there it was so very ugly. The cruelty, the racism was unbelievable. Towards blacks, and Asians.

I mean, they used us very, very badly. They used us in the front lines. They made us do things they would never do. They gave me a court-martial for wearing a Black Unity band on my wrist. Now, the military code of justice states you cannot wear anything but drab olive green. But they wore their gold jewelry, rings and stuff, and I chose to wear a black boot-lace bracelet on my wrist. That's me. Got a court-martial for that. They called it disobeying a direct order. I lost money, I lost rank. They made me sleep on the floor for thirty days in the orderly room, like a dog.

You know, that's one of the stories that nobody focuses on, the racism that was in Vietnam. It came from sophisticated whites, Southern whites. But whites from New York, from California, they got along with blacks and they hung out with us. They knew that we all had to stick together...

I don't think I would have survived Vietnam if I hadn't used drugs, man. Heroin was so plentiful over there, marijuana was so plentiful over there. And I strongly believe that CIA shit, what came out in the *New York Times* about the drugs. Because they really didn't do anything, and they knew that a lot of us were messed up on drugs. At the end when you came home they gave you a urine test, but you could beat that. Even thirty years later, I medicate myself...

Within thirty days of coming home from Vietnam I was in prison. I was carrying a gun. I mean, how can you take a person out of combat and expect him to act differently, without having any type of resocialization program? They had no deprogramming when we came home. They just said, "Washington – New York – Good-bye." From that day on I've spent close to twenty years in the penitentiary, in and out of prison. I've been to Attica. I've been to Sing-Sing. I've been to Napanoch, I've been to Collins Correctional Facility, Elmira, Wallkill, Downstate, Peekskill, Clinton. The big ones. I came home in 1971; 1990 was the last time I was in prison.

I cry about it sometimes, wish I never came back. It's hard for me to talk about my feelings, about what I've been through, and living here in the shelter, losing my family because of drugs, not really getting any help...You know, nobody's really reaching out to help or to do anything for us. I mean, we can go to the VA; we can sit and talk about what we've seen in Vietnam, but nobody really understands: how you can take a young man out of the ghetto, set him into a situation like that, and then bring him back home where people spit at him and call him a baby-killer and shit like that. Then you have Desert Storm, and everybody's a fucking hero. War is no good for nobody, man.

I have a lot of pain inside. I like walking in the rain by myself, in a storm. I like to be alone. And that's when things are real dangerous with me, when I'm alone, because I'm with my own mind. I dream...I pray a lot, and that helps; God's been good to me lately. But I'm still in a lot of fucking pain.

I've seen all the movies about Vietnam. But I don't see any movies that talk about the real person: what the military took out of that person, and what they put back in. You know, they made some really vicious individuals over there. And they didn't ever have SWAT teams until you got a lot of Vietnam vets that had come back...They were easy to use.

I guess my message to the younger guys is: before you sign up, know what you're signing up for. Oh, man. I just hope those kids think about what they're doing before they go in. They can throw all the beautiful fringe benefits in your face, but when it comes time to pay up, forget about it.

Toward the end of our interview, Walter's intensity waned, his voice softened, and he looked very tired. I will never forget that distant look, his thoughts a thousand miles away, stranded somewhere in the bygone years of a hellish life, as he repeated, ever so gently: "War ain't good for nobody, man...War ain't good for nobody."

On the subway back to Grand Central, I sat numbed. So many people, so many lives; so many misled by what is man-made, artificial, transient. So many unknowing, unseeing, in the face of what I had experienced that day. And life goes on…I arrived home late, with a very tired body and a very full heart.

■ ■ ■ ■ ■ ■ ■

Sergeant Major Edgar Huff served in the 1st Military Police Battalion from 1967 to 1968 and then in the Third Marine Amphibious Force in Da Nang from 1970 to 1971. His story is one of out-and-out racism, and it is particularly galling when one considers that his greatest act of bravery in Vietnam was saving a white comrade. But the racism began long before he left for Asia.

I got on the bus, and when it pulled into Atlanta, I got off and went in the station. It was two Marine MPs. They walked up to me. One said, "Hey, boy. C'mere." I started out with my little bag. "What you doing with that uniform on?" I say, "I'm a Marine." They say, "There ain't no damn nigger Marines. You going to jail." I give them my furlough papers. They tore 'em up right in my damn face. Said I was impersonating a Marine…I was in jail on my first Christmas in the Marine Corps. When the Navy chaplain came in for Christmas prayers, he wouldn't even talk to me…

At the outbreak of the Tet Offensive in January of 1968, Edgar experienced the most horrifying fire fight of his life, during which he courageously rescued a white radio operator:

Rick…was hit and pinned down out there, maybe 50 yards. They saw him out there in this field, and they were trying to finish him off. They was shooting with automatic fire, you know. And every time Rick'd move a little, they would fire out after him…Rick was hollering, "Mother. Mother." I could stand it no more. I started out. And the colonel said, "No. No. Just wait." I said, "Sorry, Colonel." This wasn't a black boy. He was a white boy. I knew I might get killed saving a white boy. But he was my man. That's what mattered. And I took off…

They was firing from the tree line. And I got maybe 20 yards, and I was hit on the head…And it spin me around, knocked me down. And I got up and started again. And another round hit on the side of the helmet and knocked me down again. And I started crawling…Then I got to him. Then they opened up everything they had right there into that position. And I fell on top of him to keep him from getting hit again, and this fragmentation grenade hit us and ripped my flak jacket all into pieces. And it got me in the shoulder and arm…

It was with such memories in mind that Edgar recalled a shattering incident which happened many years later, three weeks after his retirement party. "I kinda wished that boy could've been there," he said.

> We were having some friends over for dinner, and we were out on the patio...At this time, a car drove up. And four white Marines started throwing hand grenades. They were white phosphorus. Threw one right through my station wagon...And they threw another one into the house. And another one hit the Marine emblem on my gate. And everything was lit up like Christmas around here...The Marine Corps never did nothin' to them at all. Three of them got transferred or discharged...I've fought for 30 years for the Marine Corps...[Later, they told a Naval investigator that] they didn't understand how a nigger could be living this way, sitting out there eating on a nice lawn, under that American flag...[11]

Robert Holcolmb, an infantryman and "specialist" who served at An Khe in 1970, started out as an antiwar activist at Tennessee State University. He went to the war after being approached by the FBI, who pressured him to join them in the exploitation of his people or else face stiff penalties for months of draft evasion:

> The FBI offered me an option. I could work for them as a plant, an informant, or I could go to the service...They wanted to plant me within various black or radical groups, like the Black Panthers, the Student Nonviolent Coordinating Committee, and the Symbionese Liberation Army...For each person that I helped them capture on an outstanding warrant, they would pay me from $1000 to $3000...[12]

Lest racism within the military be perceived as a thing of the past, an incident that occurred during the United Nations mission in Somalia in 1993 should serve to set the record straight. An article appearing in that year's *World Press Review* bemoaned the demise of a Canadian peacekeeping division stationed in Somalia, describing with the aid of vivid photographs how a group of elite soldiers tortured a teenage Somali intruder to death. The boy had reportedly wandered into the camp by mistake, and it was later determined that white supremacists in the regiment's commando unit were responsible for the killing. Other photographs surfaced later on, including one of a corporal making a Nazi salute and a lone black serviceman being led around on all fours by a makeshift leash, with "I love the KKK" written on his back in excrement. A journalist concluded that such footage might shock civilian readers, but should come as "no surprise to anyone familiar with military life."

■ ■ ■ ■ ■ ■ ■

Despite glitzy television ads portraying Army women as well-adjusted and respected members of the "team," females who join the ranks of the armed services face harassment and abuse on a scale no less challenging than that faced by people of color. Although the overwhelming majority of these women have been nurses, they have seen and experienced as much as any man. The discrimination they suffer is perhaps different in many ways, yet their stories are no less compelling. And like other minorities, their role in wartime has been understated, unknown, and misunderstood.

In the 1960s, the military recruited heavily at nursing schools. The prospect of assisting at emergency surgeries in a far-off jungle sounded glamorous; for a student nurse from a working class background, the Army's monthly check also meant free tuition and "all expenses paid."[13] But the realities of Vietnam soon overwhelmed young women beyond their wildest imagination.

In *Nurses in Vietnam*, Jacqueline Rhoads tells of her "first real exposure to the war" after only five days in-country:

> It was at Phu Bai. We received 25 body bags in on this giant Chinook helicopter...One of the nurses' responsibilities was to look inside these body bags to determine cause of death. Of course, they couldn't release the doctors for such trivial work. What you had to do was open the bag, look inside and see what possibly could have killed this person, and then write down on the tag what you felt the cause of death was. It was so obvious most of the time. That's something I still have flashbacks about – unzipping those bags. It was my first exposure to maggots, something I had never seen before in my life...
>
> But to have to go looking for the dog tags, to find the dog tags on a person, that bothered me. I remember the first time I looked in a body bag I shook so badly. One of the doctors was kind enough to help me through it, saying, "Come on, it's your duty and you're going to have to do this. It's just something that I'm going to help you through. It's just a dead person."[14]

Nurse Lorraine Boudreau, who also served in Vietnam, remembers that caring for sick or wounded soldiers wasn't that easy:

> With wounded guys, especially the 19- and 20-year-olds, you were many things. You represented their girlfriends, their wives, their mothers. But, on the other hand, there was a sense of helplessness. You just couldn't do anything for the soldier with his brains pouring out, or a malaria patient who dies in your arms. It becomes overwhelming, so you try to depersonalize it. But no matter what you do, you can never shut it out altogether.[15]

In October of 1997 I met Heidi Baruch, a nurse who had done two tours in Vietnam. As we talked, Heidi shared something of her personal story:

I was a nurse in Vietnam for two years. I went for the first time at the age of twenty-one. I grew up in a town of three hundred people and had never really left home until I went into the military.

I came home after the first year and I didn't fit in anymore...I couldn't bear the thought of all those people dying back there, either, without the support of their countrymen back home. So I went back for a second tour. I worked primarily in the emergency room and in intensive care.

I wrote this letter, this whatever it is...I guess if I were to give it a title, it'd be "I only remember five":

I don't remember being with many people when they died, but I know I was. I remember a number of more than a dozen in one night shift, and I only remember five specific deaths. But they have never held a name or a face, just a haunting memory. The first was in the ER when I didn't know how to triage yet. I tried to resuscitate a man when his brains fell out in my hands. I don't remember his face, but I remember going through his wallet, and then I saw he was a son, he was a father, he was a husband.

Then the next was the intensive care unit. That stupid doctor wouldn't let him die, but he was dead. His legs smelled of rotten tissue, so we kept putting blankets on him so the smell would be reduced. We would take turns sitting with him. When his blood pressure dropped we had to call the doctor, so he would make us give more medicine to raise his blood pressure and keep him breathing. And he wouldn't let him die. I finally remember screaming at the doctor to let him die. And I felt the guilt for having to have an argument at his side. I hope he knew I was on his side. I wanted him to have peace.

Then I remember the three. They burned up in a tank. The stupid government built those damn tanks so the guys had to crawl out over the gas tank when they exploded. They got out, but they were charred. We didn't know if they were white or black. They did not have an inch where we could even put an IV. They had no pain, except the pain of lying there waiting to die. And they died one at a time. And they would ask, "Am I going to die?" I couldn't say no. I could only be there.

It was always important for me to be there and not let someone die alone. I don't know why. That's all I had to offer. There was a time I started to write letters to families just to say, "I want you to know your loved one did not die alone." I guess death was so scary to me that I did not want them to be so scared when they died.

I didn't know how to deal with death, and I didn't know how to deal with it because my stupid religion didn't offer me any support. Nobody offered me support, because everyone else was in the same awful place. We only knew how to support each other by the stupid jokes, the alcohol, the sex. How could the government think so many mixed-up people could do anything with any effect?

The whole stupid war was a mess, and it seemed no one cared. That's why I had to go back, too, because no one cared. So I had to go, and I had to care. But how stupid I was, because I don't think I knew how to care.

Author Kathryn Marshall further relates the unique pain faced by women veterans of Vietnam:

The need to talk was perhaps the single overwhelming need of the men and women who had gone to the Vietnam War. But if talking was hard for the men, it was harder for the women. Because their numbers were smaller and because they had worked for such a variety of organizations, the women were more isolated from each other than the men were...

In the popular imagination, Vietnam remained a zone where no woman had been. Perhaps it was inconceivable that women had gone to such a dirty, confused war, a war America had lost, a war that bore no resemblance to World War II movies; or perhaps no one wanted to confront the possibility that women, too, might have come back changed...[16]

Nurse Jill Mishkel returned from Vietnam a deeply changed person. Like Heidi, she was haunted by the knowledge that young men were still dying over there. As Jill says, her military training made it harder for her to "let go," and harder still to face the misunderstanding at home:

I got home and was just freaked out. The first, maybe the second, night back, I went out to a bar with my girlfriends. I told them not to tell anybody that I'd just come back from Nam, so of course they went around and told everyone in the bar. People came up to me, screamed stupid things like "Medic!" Asked stupid questions, like "did you kill anyone over there?" What they didn't know is I could have killed them right then...

I also remember going shopping with my two sisters and being really freaked out. It was summertime and everybody was...laughing and having fun and shopping and buying things. And I'm thinking, "God, I'm more at home in Vietnam." Yeah, I was in Sears, I was buying underwear. My two sisters said something like, "we'll be right back," and I'm handing this woman money for underwear and I start crying. They didn't know why I was crying, didn't know what was going on. I didn't either. All I knew was, guys were fighting a war over there, and here everybody was having a great time at this mall, buying things they didn't need...

After I got out of the Army I only told a few people I was a veteran. At Hartford Hospital I worked in the intensive care unit, but I wasn't friends with the people I worked with. I remember people thinking I was really weird. When I told people, they just looked at me and walked away. Or they asked, "Why did you go? Why did you want to do something like that?" Or they'd be talking about the war and not want to hear anything I had to say about it. Finally I stopped telling people. I think that happened when one woman told me to just forget about it and it would go away. I started scream- ing, "I don't want to forget about it! It's a year of my life, what do you mean forget about it!" But I did. I buried it really deeply.[17]

Leslie McClusky was in Washington, DC, visiting the Vietnam Veterans Memo- rial, when she realized how much she had buried:

I was afraid [to go up to the Wall] because I knew the dam was trying to burst. But I went over to the Wall…I sat down and looked at all the names. And suddenly I couldn't stop crying. I was crying so hard I couldn't get up – every time I tried to get up I'd start crying again. It was as though I was never going to be able to stop. And I'd always had this thing about self-control and nobody seeing me cry.

So I was sitting there, trying to get up, when this big black guy came over and put his hand on my shoulder. "It's OK," he said. I looked up at him and couldn't talk. He backed away then – backed away but stood next to me. Finally, when I was able to stand up, I went over to him and saw tears in his eyes and he put his arms around me and I was hugging him. I couldn't believe it. And this was just the beginning.[18]

Laura Palmer tells the story of a nurse named "Dusty" who left a letter at the Viet- nam Veterans Memorial dedicated to the eight women nurses who died in Vietnam.[19] In an interview, Dusty shared the personal toll exacted from a survivor:

Vietnam cost me a great deal: a marriage, two babies, the ability to bear healthy children, the ability to practice my life's chosen profession, my physical health, and at times, my emotional stability. After the weight of my postwar trauma reached a critical mass, I changed my name, my profession, my residence, and my past. Silence and isolation allowed me to rebuild a life…

Palmer goes on to describe the moral obligations nurses like Dusty placed upon themselves:

Dusty went to Vietnam in 1966 because she hated the war. "If I went out into the streets, I would simply add one more body to the mob. It wouldn't do any good. The only way I knew how to stop killing and dying was to use the skill I was trained in. That's why I went." When she came home, in 1968, she found that the hostility that greeted the soldiers was there for her, too. But there was an additional twist for women – the lewd comments from casual acquaintances and strangers. Sure, nurses on duty were saviors. But off duty, they were sluts. Everyone, it seemed, knew that.

Those who protested the war at home felt that women who went, even as nurses, were part of the war machine. But very few bothered to find out how they felt.

Hello, David — my name is Dusty.
I'm your night nurse.
I will stay with you.
I will check your vitals
    every 15 minutes.
I will document
    inevitability.
I will hang more blood
    and give you something
    for your pain.
I will stay with you
    and I will touch your face.

Yes, of course,
    I will write your mother
    and tell her you were brave.
I will write your mother
    and tell her how much you loved her.
I will write your mother
    and tell her to give your bratty kid sister
    a big kiss and hug.
What I will not tell her
    is that you were wasted.
I will stay with you
    and I will hold your hand.
I will stay with you
    and watch your life
    flow through my fingers
    into my soul.
I will stay with you
    until you stay with me.

Good-bye, David — my name is Dusty.
I'm the last person
    you will see.
I'm the last person
    you will touch.

I'm the last person
   who will love you.

So long, David — my name is Dusty.
David — who will give me something
   for my pain?

■ ■ ■ ■ ■ ■ ■

In October of 1997, I spent the afternoon with Carol Picou, a veteran suffering from Gulf War illnesses. Aside from the saga of her betrayal by the U.S. Army, Carol experienced the added burdens that come with being a woman in a male-dominated military. Before she joined, Carol had done her homework, demanding a recruiter "that was not going to lie to me" and traveling down to Fort Dix to observe new recruits in basic training. But she was still unprepared for her first assignments.

I was sent to Fort Lewis, Washington, and I wasn't working in my MOS (military occupational specialty). The commander there felt all the women should be around him, and the only way you were going to get promoted was to go out with him. It was plain sexual harassment. I couldn't deal with this man. So I wrote my congressman; I was good friends with my congressman because I had put our little town on the map, and when I left for the military he had said, "If you ever need anything, just write."

So I did. I wrote and asked him why the army would spend $15,000 to train me in a field I wasn't allowed to work in. This commander had me typing; I was his secretary. I had no typing skills, but because he wanted me by his side, I had to do it.

Things got worse. My commander exposed himself to me. All the women were getting promoted over the males because they were going to bed with him...

I couldn't avoid this man. He kept me there, wanted me to be his driver — and I can't even drive a stick-shift. He even sent me down to the motor pool, and they said, "Oh, with a little practice you'll be fine." But I refused to learn and so I failed the written part of the exam. Then they threatened me that if I didn't pass, I would lose a stripe, that I'd be court-martialed because I couldn't fulfill the obligations of the military to get a driver's license. I finally did pass, but then I pretended I didn't know how to back up a jeep, and that was it. I never had to drive for him again. But still, he never let me out of his oily room. I had to do all his typing.

The sexual harassment from men in the army was unreal. We women couldn't even walk down the street without being called. Even on the lunch line, men would hit on the women: "Hey, Mama! Let's get naked and do things." It was just so degrading. So I went to our commander and said, "Look, sir, why don't you do something about these men? When we walk to the mess hall it is so horrible. We don't even want to eat there, but we have no choice." He didn't do anything about it, and then, one day, I finally had enough. I walked into the mess hall and this soldier said to me, "Hey, Mama, let's get naked and do something!"

I got so mad I took my tray and I threw it across the table. I grabbed him by the shirt and twisted it up against his throat and I said, "How can you call me your Mama? I don't think you'd even give your Mama any respect. Look at my name tag. My name is nothing like yours. I'm not your Mama. Until you can show a little more respect, don't even talk to me..." To make a long story short, I told the mess sergeant I'd pay for whatever damage I'd done. But he said, "This one is on me; they deserved it."

Later, when my commander found out, I was sent down to the motor pool to grease vans...

When Carol found herself on the front lines of the Persian Gulf War years later, she was to experience a new strain of exploitation, which ultimately led to the ongoing physical suffering she endures today.

You could hear the bombing. It went on for something like thirty-seven days, and you just wondered how anybody could survive it. And when they briefed us about the area into which we would be going, eight of the men refused to go. These eight men were friends with the master sergeant, and they came and asked me if I would recruit myself with seven other women, to go to the front instead of them.

So we went. We just felt we were doing our jobs. I felt that I had to go; I needed to be there. If I could hold even one person's hand as he was dying, I'd have done my job. The next day, I got a letter from my husband: "Don't go to the front. Don't be a hero. Just come home." And I cried.

■ ■ ■ ■ ■ ■ ■

The legacy of Hispanic Americans in the U.S. military is not at all unlike that of blacks. San Francisco poet and writer Victor Martinez asserts: "The adage that the poor make more resolute and [compliant] soldiers is verified when applied to Chicanos...Chicanos were often the easiest and most malleable resource the U.S. had for achieving its quota for combat soldiers. And to those

ends, they were used generously...Most were victims of an economic exploitation and pernicious cultural suppression at home that made the military a step up
in stature."[20]

In his oral history of the Vietnam War, *Soldados*, Charley Trujillo makes a
familiar case for the deliberate invisibility of yet another minority military
population that suffered disproportionately during the war. He notes that while
Hispanics made up more than a quarter of all combat deaths in Vietnam, they
are not even mentioned in two of the leading best-sellers on the Vietnam War.

The stories of Chicano veterans in Trujillo's *Soldados*, all from the small
farming community of Corcoran in the San Joaquin Valley, California, paint an
impressive picture of a struggling community whose men were used as human
ammunition in an alien war.

Miguel Lemus tells of picking cotton, dropping out of school and working as
a garbageman to support his family before being drafted in 1967. "We can't do
nothing about it, either you go to Vietnam or go to jail," his mother told him.
"Do the best you can and pray to God you'll be back." Miguel took her advice;
he survived but later reflected that America had become as much a jungle as
Vietnam.[21]

Miguel Gastelo's father was from Mexico. He had moved to Delano in the
1920s, forced to leave Mexico because he and his brothers had fought under
Pancho Villa. When Miguel ended up in Vietnam, he found that the Chicanos
and Puerto Ricans were made to do "all the point walking and carrying the M-
60. Whenever we got into contact with the enemy, they were the first ones up
front. The gabachos (whites) would go along, but they'd let the Chicanos and
Puerto Ricans go to the front and they'd follow."[22]

Manuel Marin joined the service as "payback." Having once been an illegal
alien, he felt indebted to the country that had allowed him to "live...and go to
school." Even though his adopted country showed him no such gratitude,
Manuel thinks he "made a good trade." He remembers the time when a young
Vietnamese man walked up to him and pointed at his arm because it was the
same color as his own, and feels it was symbolic of an unspoken understanding
between himself and the Vietnamese. Years later, he said, "I understand a little
more now and I'm hoping, against the odds, that we will never go to war again. I
think it's futile. It is very difficult to understand how 58,000 people died and to
see that nothing good came of it."[23]

Guillermo Alvidrez had an uncle and a cousin who served in World War II.
Three of his brothers were in the Korean War, and he ended up in Vietnam.
When he got there in 1967, he found that 60 percent of the troops in his unit
were black, Puerto Rican, or Chicano. Larry Holguin, who served in the 3rd Marine Division from 1968 to 1969, also found that his "platoon was about 60 per-

cent minority – Chicanos, blacks, Puerto Ricans, and Indians." Mike Soliz, who
served as an infantryman from 1968–1971, claimed that the units "out in the
field" were 80 percent minorities: blacks, Chicanos, Indians, and Puerto Ricans:

> It seemed like it was the minorities who were always the infantry guys and
> the other people (whites) who had the rear jobs, maintenance, clerks, and
> desk jobs...I got to meet a lot of Chicanos over there. They were from all
> over, but the majority of them were from Texas, California, New Mexico,
> and Arizona. My whole squad was made up of Chicanos. I also met some
> Indians. Most of them were from the Dakotas and Minnesota. They even
> spoke Indian amongst themselves.[24]

Trujillo himself offers a poignant vignette of the racism in Vietnam, which he
remembers from the aftermath of a deadly firefight: "Martinelli was shot in the
chest with a dead black medic on him. It is ironic that he died as the black medic
was giving him mouth-to-mouth because Martinelli hated blacks. He used to
say, 'I hate niggers,' and here he died with a 'nigger' giving him mouth-to-
mouth."[25]

Like blacks, Hispanic soldiers in Vietnam often found themselves at war with
their white American counterparts, which gave their experience of war a
"double impact." Richard Holguin, for example, voluntarily stayed in the
jungles until the day he left Vietnam, for fear of the hassles in the rear.

Among the tribulations of Hispanic GIs, the story of Mike Soliz is perhaps
the most incredible. Having survived a hellish first tour and several serious injuries, he returned home in 1969 ecstatic to be alive. "I was glad to be one of the
fortunate ones who made it," he said. "A lot of guys got killed over there." He
still had seven months left but was happy to be offered a four-thousand-dollar
reenlistment bonus and a job at Travis Air Force Base. Since Travis was only a
short distance from his home town of Corcoran, the job sounded like a good
career opportunity. His mother was wary and advised him to finish his seven
months and quit. But Mike reassured her that things would be okay; after talking
it over with his wife, he accepted.

Nothing, however, could have prepared him for the news he received upon
reporting for duty: he was informed that "they" needed the "experienced guys"
back in Vietnam, and that he was slated to go. According to the sergeant, "too
many" new soldiers were getting killed.

Mike was incredulous and his wife was crushed. She cried for days. When
Mike went back to see his reenlistment officer, he was told, "Soliz, you got the
shaft. There isn't anything I can do."

En route to Vietnam he was surprised to meet his brother Ruben in Oakland
and was talking with him in the mess hall when a fellow soldier pointed out that,

according to draft policy, two brothers were not supposed to serve in Vietnam at the same time. The day before Mike was slated to leave, the brothers were called into the office and told that there'd been a "mistake": only one of them had to go. Ruben wanted to spare his brother another tour, but Mike wasn't about to let such a greenhorn go. He returned to Vietnam.

Mike thought that his first tour would give him seniority, and that he would be assigned to the rear, but as soon as he reported to his new company, the captain told him, "Sergeant Soliz, you're here just in time. You're going to be in charge of the first rifle platoon."

Mike thought he would die for sure this time. Of the "second hell," he recalls:

One day we had to go on a company-size mission. That's when I got wounded again. A sniper hit me in the leg. When I was hit I couldn't move. There were a couple of Chicanos who I thought were my friends and they didn't help me. It was a black guy that picked me up in a fireman's carry and carried me to safety...

[Then] I got wounded for the last time. I got shot maybe thirteen days before I was to go on R&R. It was a sniper again. This time I was sent to the hospital in Saigon. When I got there, a black female lieutenant colonel doctor looked at my medical records, and she said, "Your war days are over for you boy, it's over, you're going home. They can't expect you to win the war by yourself. You've been wounded too many times..."

Mike was sent home for a convalescence leave, and told to wait at home for orders telling him where to report next. The orders never came. He slowly recovered and got a job on a farm. His mother told him he should probably go to Fort Ord and report, but Mike didn't feel there was any reason to do so.

Three years later, an FBI officer came to Mike's house and informed him that he was AWOL. The officer gave him two days to report. Mike's wife was hysterical, and told the FBI, "You aren't going to do it to him again!" But Mike was subjected to a general court-martial and threatened with punishment; only when he threatened legal recourse did the military finally decide to drop the matter.[26]

■ ■ ■ ■ ■ ■ ■

Of the exploitation of minorities, the history of the near-extermination and systematic disenfranchisement of Native American peoples ranks second to none. Popular books like Dee Brown's *Bury My Heart at Wounded Knee* and Peter Mathhiessen's *In the Spirit of Crazy Horse* chronicle well this long and tragic saga.

In terms of exploitation by the armed forces, Native Americans were especially vulnerable during the years of the Vietnam War. Veteran Tom Holm explains:

The factors of low economic and educational levels (some reservations have reported unemployment rates as high as 80 percent and education averaging at the eighth-grade level) as well as a very youthful population (the average age of Native Americans in the period of the Vietnam War was between 19 and 21) virtually assured that most Indian males would be primary candidates for military service. These factors also meant that, once in the armed forces, Indians would be assigned nontechnical military occupations. Thus, they were very likely to become infantrymen and experience combat in Vietnam.

And so they did. According to one source, more than 42,000 Native Americans served in Southeast Asia either as advisors or as combat troops between 1960 and 1973...

The problem that still plagues many Native American veterans is that virtually no one save their own people knows of their sacrifices in the war, much less that they had fought in numbers exceeding their proportional population. American Indians...made up more than 2 percent of all troops who served in Vietnam. Since Native Americans comprise less than 1 percent of the entire U.S. population, their proportional numbers in combat more than doubled their number in the general population. While the issue of minorities bearing a disproportionate share of the war was discussed in the nation's press during the period, Indians were not specifically mentioned in a single article...

Whites still tend to think of minority "problems" in terms of the larger minority groups. And if today's Native American population of 1.9 million individuals is conspicuous by its absence in the contemporary American mind, the Indian veterans who fought in an unpopular war are even more so. To non-Indians, they are a subcategory of a subcategory – a shadow of a shadow.[27]

Despite their long and harrowing history of oppression, many Native Americans have been subjugated to the point of silence or even indifference. As I sought to collect stories of Native American veterans for this book, I found a wall of silence, acquiescence, and even patriotic support for the same military machinery which had once aimed its withering fire at the Indians themselves. With time, I began to see this contradiction as just another, if more unsettling, form of victimization.

In November of 1997, I visited World War II veteran Roy Black Bear at his little shop in the nearby town of Esopus. Roy is a full-blooded Native American who grew up dirt-poor and under heavy prejudice. He remembers putting cardboard in his shoes each day to cover gaping holes; he wore the same pair of pants every day for four straight years of high school. By graduation they had become so threadbare that his legs were visible in several places, and he had to hold his books against his legs to hide them.

Roy's father warned him again and again to keep his Native American ancestry a secret. "If anyone asks, just say you're American," he advised. The family moved around a lot, and Roy had to change schools often. For a time, he got beat up by the school bully every time the family moved to a new location. Finally Roy's father told him to seek out the toughest kid in school on the first day, and when they met, to punch him as hard as he could. That would keep people away and make them afraid to mess with him...

As I stood at the counter in his cold little trinket shop one morning only a few days before Thanksgiving, he related a remarkable story, filled with conflicting loyalties and tragic ironies, of a Native American at war with a foreign America:

I grew up in the Depression. And it was rough. My dad was mostly out of work, like most people were. Most of the time we lived out in the country. We grew almost everything that we ate. We had some chickens. The man next door raised hogs and I used to help him slaughter them, so we'd always get some pork. Anyway, it wasn't easy, growing up. But I think in the long run it was probably a good thing for me. A terrible experience to go through, but a good one at the end.

Both my parents were Native Americans. My father was Mohawk, and my mother was Delaware and Wampanoag – a fact that was not advertised at that particular time. It was not a good thing to be an Indian. We were looked on worse than the blacks ever were, and we still are. The things we did in our house were not the things we did outside. Those were private, personal things, and they were kept that way. My dad always told me that when people asked what my ancestry was, I should just tell them "American." "If they ask any more, I'll be glad to go up and talk to them," he said.

I finally got a job jerking sodas at twenty cents an hour. I worked thirty-five hours a week and got seven dollars, which of course went into the house. It wasn't for me. While I was in high school I talked about being a sailor, and my father was horrified, because all our ancestors had been in the Army. We always fought, since the Revolution. My people fought with the British, against the colonials around Plymouth. My father was horrified to think I wanted to be a sailor, because all they did was get drunk and chase girls. You know, they're a bunch of bums. I was convinced the opposite was true. I thought sailors were great people. So I enlisted in the Coast Guard.

When I was seventeen, Roosevelt organized a national guard and got 'em into active duty. Whether he knew we were going to get into a war, or whether it was to help the economy, I have no idea. But a lot of my friends in high school were in the National Guard.

Now, I never felt that I would be fighting for this government. We fight for the land, for our homes, for our people. Not for the country of the United States. Not for the country. Definitely not for the government, because the government has always abused Native Americans and has a history of doing so and always will. I'm not enamored of the U.S. government, and right now, I don't think anybody is.

So I had a cause that I fought for. I didn't realize, of course, that we were going to be in a war, because I enlisted the day after I graduated from high school in 1940. Nobody was even thinking about a war. They knew there was a war in Europe, and England was having a hard time, but I don't believe people thought we'd be involved in it. I certainly didn't.

I went down to New York City and got my physical two days after graduation. That was it, and away we go.

I think one of the best experiences of my life was boot camp. For one thing, I never saw that much food in my whole life. Never. Many times before I'd gone to bed hungry. It's just a fact. I couldn't understand all these guys complaining about the food. It was better food than I ever had in my whole life.

So I got through boot camp and I loved it. The structure was very important to me, the discipline. I couldn't understand why people were complaining. A lot of them moaned and groaned about everything, but I thought it was wonderful. I learned all kinds of new things...

And then, didn't I land up on Guadalcanal. I was in the first wave, the only boat in the whole first wave that was fired on by the Japs. I was on a landing craft that carried thirty-six troops, and there was a heavy Japanese machine gun way out on the beach. That son of a gun opened fire on me.

Everybody was down low. It was a very rude awakening for me. Very rude. Because I'm thinking, "There's somebody shooting at me, obviously trying to kill me or put me out of commission one way or another. And he doesn't even know me. Why would he want to kill me if he doesn't know me?" I just couldn't get it through my head, you know.

As far as I was concerned — and most Native Americans I've talked with feel the same way — the Japanese were threatening to take over this country. If they took over this country, then our families were in peril, you know. So you gotta fight to protect your homes and families. The Indians have been badly criticized for defending their homes and families. And that's why I say most American Indian people don't fight for the government. You don't fight for the established country. You fight for your homes and your families and your land, which doesn't belong to us anyway, but it's where we reside. This is what we have to protect. This is our duty.

When you see a seventeen-year-old Marine tied to a palm tree with a couple hundred bayonet wounds in his body, his private parts cut off and stuffed in his mouth, both eyes put out, tongue cut off, it generates a real bad feeling against people. It does. And that ain't prejudice. That's a learned feeling.

What Europeans did to my people was even worse. I know that. There was a Methodist minister, Colonel Chemington, and all he wanted to do is kill Indians. He made tobacco pouches out of women's breasts, bayoneted little infants, pregnant women, then shot the women too. The most inhuman people in the world, as far as I'm concerned, are the people we allowed into this country. Terrible, horrible people. And they haven't changed much, most of them.

The hour I'd planned to spend in Roy's shop turned into two and then three hours. I was mesmerized by his tales of childhood and the stories of his encounters with people from many different cultural and religious backgrounds. Roy told me that during the years when his family lived on a reservation, he noticed that all of the Indians who became power-hungry and greedy were the ones who had converted to Christianity. His father used to watch Protestant churchgoers through his window across the street and giggle at their obsession with clothes and fashion. "Now they'll all go on in there and pretend they love one another," he'd say, "but all the time they're comparing each others' hats and dresses."

Though Roy must have grown up with a deep caution toward white people and their religion, I felt from him only a friendly warmth, and perhaps a little loneliness. Somehow, the experiences of his life — the military included — were part of an unspoken quest for acceptance among those of us who had so deeply humiliated his people and dominated American culture for centuries. I was both shamed and moved by our time together.

■ ■ ■ ■ ■ ■ ■

The white people have to surrender their arms to the Great Spirit. This purification is coming real soon, and all the guns and gold will melt. The holy spirit, the atom, the power of god, will melt those guns and tanks and poison gases they create...They will be standing by themselves...When the time comes, there won't be no amnesty. We're going back to the beginning of time...I have no fear, I have no slightest fear whatsoever. Even if I have to face death like Chief Big Foot, it's very beautiful. We hold the key to eternity, where it is beautiful and it is everlasting for everyone. That's where we're going. We're going home. And finally, we will be back in the Great Spirit's hands again — Grandmother's arms again. She'll cradle us in her arms again.[28]

Wallace Black Elk (Lakota)

CHAPTER 7

Worth the Price?

*It is a difficult decision to make, but we think
the price is worth it.*

*U.N. ambassador Madeleine Albright, on the deaths of 500,000 Iraqi
children due to economic sanctions after the Gulf War*

One of the most damning aspects of war is that it is never confined to the legions of young men who spill their blood in battle. Invariably it boils over to affect civilians caught between the hammer and the anvil. Even modern technology is powerless to erase this awful fact. "Smart bombs" did nothing to save the 1,200 innocent women and children incinerated in the Al-Amariyah Shelter during the 1991 bombing of Baghdad. And the 100 million landmines currently scattered over 62 nations worldwide have killed more people in times of peace than they did in the wars during which they were deployed.[1]

In fact, technology has become warring mankind's own worst enemy; more, rather than fewer, civilians are killed with each successive generation. One-fifth of those killed in World War I were civilians; in World War II, this figure rose to one-half. In the wars of the past few decades, it has been 90 percent.[2] The modern economic sanction is perhaps even more cruel; it is a form of warfare in which one hundred percent of the casualties are civilian.

At the present time, entire populations live under the threat of biological, chemical, and nuclear warfare and its long-term effects. The resources required to manufacture this threat sap the lifeblood of nations and rob their citizens of food, health care, and education. President Clinton's proposed budget for the year 1998, for example, allocates $265 billion to the military, vastly eclipsing money allocated to education ($31 billion), health ($25 billion), justice ($24 billion), veterans benefits and services ($19 billion), and training, employment, and social services ($15 billion). The cost of one Seawolf submarine equals all the money allocated to the Head Start program for young children. The cost of one Patriot missile system almost equals all the grants to prevent violence against women. The price tag on one nuclear aircraft carrier would fund the National Cancer Institute for three years. And one V-22 Osprey aircraft costs as much as the entire national home-heating program for low-income families.[3]

But murder is more compelling, and more wrenching, than assault and robbery. From the ancient slaughter of whole cities and peoples recorded in the Old Testament to the deaths of hundreds of thousands of Iraqi children under UN sanctions, war has exacted a horrific toll on civilians.

Between 1898 and 1910, U.S. forces killed 600,000 Filipinos while seizing their country from Spain.[4] When the Japanese launched a massive attack on the Republic of China's newly established capital in 1937, 300,000 Chinese were massacred and 50,000 women raped and mutilated.[5]

In the war to follow (1939–1945), 6 million Chinese civilians were left dead; Japan lost 2 million. The Soviets suffered the loss of more than 7 million civilians; Poland lost 3 million; 6 million more, all Jews, died in Hitler's extermination camps.[6]

The occupied nations of Western Europe fared not much better. More than 1.5 million Yugoslavs died under German occupation; in Greece, a total of 380,600 civilians died from privation and hunger and execution by occupying forces.[7] France lost 108,000, Belgium 101,000, and the Netherlands 242,000. Great Britain, which was never occupied but suffered prolonged bombing, lost 61,000.[8]

Civilians under the Axis powers were no more fortunate. When the British Royal Air Force raided Dresden on February 13, 1945, with phosphorus and high-explosive bombs, they created a firestorm that killed an estimated 135,000 civilians in one night.[9] Altogether, the Germans calculated 3,600,000 civilians dead.[10] And when more than 100 U.S. bombers raided the city of Tokyo with incendiary bombs on the night of March 9, 1945, they killed more than 124,000 civilians.[11] In Hiroshima, an estimated 100,000 people died the day of the atomic bombing; another 100,000 died soon thereafter from burns, injuries, and radiation.[12]

Of those national or ethnic groups that suffered the loss of a million dead or more, the total dead is in excess of 46 million.[13] Despite attempts to estimate civilian dead, however, the number of those who died in the Second World War will never be known with precision. Millions of men, women, and children were killed without record of their names, or when and how they died.[14]

During the "American War," Vietnam was poisoned with 18 million gallons of herbicides and devastated by more than 15 million tons of explosives, twice the amount used by the U.S. in all of Europe and Asia in World War II. The war left

3 million dead and millions traumatized, disfigured, handicapped, orphaned, childless, and displaced.[15] Between 1969 and 1975, an additional 2 million neighboring Cambodians died as the result of bombing, starvation, and political chaos.[16]

During the Persian Gulf War, nearly 200,000 people were killed in the invasions of Iraq and Kuwait;[17] the Pentagon exposed another million from the U.S.-led alliance and 3 million Iraqis to radioactive aerosols from depleted-uranium weapons.[18] The economic embargo that followed Iraq's collapse in early 1991 resulted in a five-fold increase in child mortality, and more than 500,000 children under the age of five have succumbed in the past seven years.[19] Armed conflict has led to unmitigated suffering in Bosnia, Sudan, Somalia, Angola, and the former Soviet republics. In the past decade 2 million children have been killed, and three times as many have been permanently disabled or seriously injured.[20]

It is impossible for the human mind and heart to comprehend such statistics or to take in the magnitude of such suffering. We cannot embrace its impact. Numbers on the scale of millions escape our imagination, leaving us numbed and overloaded. But the legacy of civilian suffering in wartime is a true war story in itself: in the words of Tim O'Brien, it is not moral, it does not instruct, nor does it restrain men from doing the things men have always done.[21] Nevertheless, the stories of civilians who have suffered innocently in times of war can shake us into realization, and change our perceptions and lives.

Lowell LeBlanc, a World War II veteran now living at the Bruderhof, served under false identity in the Counterintelligence Corps in England. Stationed in the rear, he saw very little of the war's horror until the fighting was over. Recently he told me of the one experience that changed his attitude toward war forever and ultimately led him to brotherhood and community:

> I was drafted into the Army April 1942 at the age of twenty-two, with more or less everyone's blessing and acquiescence. Much like the typical draftee of that time, I was not all that sure or that eager to go. At a medical examination before entering the military, a psychologist asked me how I felt about the Army. I told him, "I'm in, so what's to feel?" Much later I realized that he was right to imply that one should be either for or against it.
>
> Shortly after V-E day, our airfield was used as a landing place to repatriate 1,500 people from a concentration camp in Czechoslovakia. I was asked by the owner of a local cafe to go down to the courthouse with him to get thirty stretchers, and when we then drove out to the center of the field, we saw thirty men whom I can only describe as being a few breaths away from death. Some could move, and one or two could talk, but for the rest the only sign of life was an occasional flicker of the eyes.

Death was right there, lying on the ground. They were that close. These men were helpless, and they had no means of altering their situation. It was a turning point for me, as I finally saw with my own eyes the result of man's inhumanity to man.

After what I had experienced, I felt that I could not continue to serve the military. I had initially worked for Boeing, but could no longer be a part of an industry that was hand-in-glove with the military. So I found another job, although the pay was about a third less.

My minister warned me about my responsibility to my wife and three children, but Norma and I felt we should take this step in faith, for conscience' sake, and that God would take care of the rest. And so it was that we eventually came into contact with the Bruderhof, where people shared everything like the first Christians, sought actively for unity, and lived a life dedicated to brotherly love and nonviolence.

■ ■ ■ ■ ■ ■ ■

Le Ly Hayslip was a young Vietnamese girl caught in the maelstrom of the "American War." The legacy of her people's suffering, which began long before the first Americans arrived, plunged many of her compatriots into despair and resignation. But for Le Ly it gradually gave birth to personal transformation and profound insights on the nature of war. She writes:

[We are the ones] who did not fight – but suffered, wept, raged, bled, and died just the same. We all did what we had to do. By mingling our blood and tears on the earth, god has made us brothers and sisters.

If you were an American GI, I ask you to…look into the heart of one you once called enemy. I have witnessed, firsthand, all that you went through. I will try to tell you who your enemy was and why almost everyone in the country you tried to help resented, feared, and misunderstood you. It was not your fault. It could not have been otherwise. Long before you arrived, my country had yielded to the terrible logic of war. What for you was normal – a life of peace and plenty – was for us a hazy dream known only in our legends.

Because we had to appease the allied forces by day and were terrorized by Viet Cong at night, we slept as little as you did. We obeyed both sides and wound up pleasing neither. We were people in the middle. We were what the war was all about…Children and soldiers have always known it to be terrible…[22]

Before he died, Le Ly's father reminded her that she had not been born to hate, and that her main battle in life was to raise her small son.

> I decided I should draw the strength of compassion, not the weakness of bitterness, from this most important lesson – from the lessons I had learned from every American that fate or luck or god had sent to be my teacher... Hating people who had wronged me only kept me in their power. Forgiving them and thanking them for the lesson they had taught me, on the other hand, set me free to continue on my way...

> Vietnam already had too many people who were ready to die for their beliefs. What it needed was men and women – brothers and sisters – who refused to accept either death or death-dealing as a solution to their problems. If you keep compassion in your heart, I discovered, you never long for death yourself. Death and suffering, not people, become your enemy; and anything that lives is your ally. It was as if, by realizing this, an enormous burden had been lifted from my young shoulders...

> My task, I was beginning to see, was to find life in the midst of death and nourish it like a flower – a lonely flower in the graveyard my country had become...

> Houses could be rebuilt and damaged dikes repaired – but the loss of our temples and shrines meant the death of our culture itself. It meant that a generation of children would grow up without fathers to teach them about their ancestors or the rituals of worship. Families would lose records of their lineage and with them the umbilicals to the very root of our society – not just old buildings and books, but *people* who once lived and loved like them. Our ties to our past were being severed, setting us adrift on a sea of borrowed Western materialism, disrespect for the elderly, and selfishness. The war no longer seemed like a fight to see which view would prevail. Instead, it had become a fight to see just how much and how far the Vietnam of my ancestors would be transformed. It was as if I was standing by the cradle of a dying child and speculating with its aunts and uncles on what the doomed baby would have looked like had it grown up. By tugging on their baby so brutally, both parents had wound up killing it. Even worse, the war now attacked Mother Earth – the seedbed of us all. This, to me, was the highest crime – the frenzied suicide of cannibals. How shall one mourn a lifeless planet?...

> It was as if life's cycle was no longer birth, growth, and death but only endless dying brought about by endless war. I realized that I, along with so many of my countrymen, had been born into war and that my soul knew nothing else. I tried to imagine people somewhere who knew only peace – what paradise!

...Perhaps such a place was America, although American wives and mothers, too, were losing husbands and sons every day in the evil vortex between heaven and hell that my country had become...[23]

■ ■ ■ ■ ■ ■ ■

In the summer of 1997, I drove out to Woodstock to the home of Jay Wenk, a World War II veteran and local member of Veterans for Peace. Jay had participated in our veterans' evening in Woodcrest that August, and I was impressed by the depth of insight he had offered on wartime recruiting and propaganda.

It didn't take long for us to get down to the business of the interview, and we were soon in his wood-paneled kitchen, discussing the background to the war, pacifism, patriotism, and psychopathology. Playing devil's advocate, I questioned his assertion that World War II was more about money than fascism: didn't Hitler need to be stopped? His response was short and to the point: "Of course he did. But so did Wilson and Roosevelt and Truman and McNamara and Johnson and Reagan."

Though Jay has seen his share of firefights, they are not among the memories that have left him the most scarred. I was caught off guard when, about halfway through our interview, he shared his "most horrific" war story with us, one he had never told anyone else in nearly fifty years:

> I wanted to share with you my own most horrific story. It's quite different from what the others were. It's at least part of the reason why I feel that young men and women shouldn't go into the services.
>
> Towards the tail end of the war we were almost out of Germany and approaching Czechoslovakia. We captured a town not far from Schweinfurt, where they were making ball bearings and bombs. There was another factory making radios for the *Wehrmacht*. And there was a small camp full of displaced people or prisoners who worked at the factory. Like many of these labor camps, it was operated by a private firm. My patrol was going out to the eastern edge of town. We took up a spot at the very end of the village.
>
> There was a little cottage where my patrol was domiciled overnight. Every once in a while one of us was supposed to get up and stand guard duty. After it got dark the patrol leader came back. He had gone away some place and came back to our cottage with five or six women. He had given them cigarettes or chocolate or whatever, black-market stuff. And they were brought there to have sex with us.
>
> I got into bed with one of those women and had intercourse with her. It was the first time in my life. The first time in my life, under conditions like

that. I don't know how to describe the horror of it. It didn't hit me till later. At the time, you know, you got into this cot and bang, bang, bang, that was it. But later...

Early the next morning the man who was on guard outside rousted us all out of bed. He had seen a German squad up in the woods on a hill right next to us. We went running up the hill and there was a little bit of a firefight. The Germans took off pretty quickly, but there was shooting going on both ways. Nobody was hurt on our side, and I don't think any of the Germans were hit either. In any event, coming back down the hill, going towards the cottage, we saw the faces of these women looking out the window.

We had just been chasing, looking to kill, their husbands, their brothers, their uncles. There they were, looking at us – not with hatred in their faces, but with a kind of curious inquiry of some sort that I can't describe. I still see them looking at me, at us. I felt guilty and embarrassed and tried to justify doing what we had to do. It was a horrible evening, a horrible night, a horrible morning.

I could tell you other kinds of war stories, but that was the most horrific. To use women like that, to go anywhere near that kind of thing, there's a poison there which can infect. Even in so-called peace time. I've never told that story before...

The day before we crossed the Rhine we were in the city of Mainz. I was rummaging around, walking around in the basement of this apartment building. There were chicken-wired cubicles, with people's furniture and God knows what. Locks on the doors. Walking around, I heard a woman cry out. It was nearby. I followed the sound. There was a young woman – I guess she was in her late teens or early twenties – a German woman, and she was holding what looked like a big loaf of pumpernickel. My squad leader was trying to pull it away from her. I said to him, "You can't do that." He gave me a look of disgust and said, "She's German." I said, "She's a civilian, she's a woman, she's hungry. We have plenty of food. We're not starving."

We did have plenty of food. The look of disgust, I won't forget. He turned and left. The next day I was sent to the heavy-weapons platoon, meaning I was loaded down with cans and cans of 50-caliber ammunition. It was painful. The whole incident touched a guilt button. One of my guilt buttons went off, and I remembered that story from "my basement."

Ilse von Köller, a member of our Bruderhof communities who died in 1995, grew up in a villa on the outskirts of Leipzig. In the early years of World War II she met her husband-to-be Ulrich, and they were married in January of 1942. By the time their daughter Martina was born in October, Ulrich was already fighting on the Russian front. Ilse was left with her child and her twin sister in Eisenach, worrying from day to day whether her husband would be killed in action.

She couldn't have known then that before the war was over she would have to fight her own war, and that as a German mother "caught in the middle" she would see plenty of action. She was on the other side of Jay Wenk's war; a German woman looking back at him through the window. Yet she did not look back with "curious inquiry" but with a compassion and understanding not unlike that of Le Ly Hayslip twenty years later. Only a few years before her death, Ilse remembered:

> The war went on and the bombing of the cities got worse and worse. One morning on the radio we heard of a bombardment on Leipzig the night before — 400 American bombers had dropped incendiary, high-explosive, and demolition bombs on the city between 11 P.M. and 7 A.M. One third of the city was destroyed.
>
> My mother lived alone in Leipzig at that time, so I immediately went to find her. I traveled by truck, by train, and also a long time on foot to look for her, to find out if she had survived. When I arrived in the city, a ghostly, still, uncanny atmosphere surrounded me. The smell from the conflagration was terrible, and gray smoke lay heavily over the city. Everywhere there were men from the Survival Service with their long probes, searching for survivors, for a sign of life under the fallen houses. The dead, covered with rags, were lying at the sides of the street. The people had empty faces — sad, confused, hopeless, frightened.
>
> The steeples of the churches were still burning; houses were still smoldering. Some of the streets were completely impassable. The houses, some more than six floors high, were now only a heap of rubble. Under them, people were buried alive. The temperature was -22 degrees C. There was only frozen water, no electricity, no gas.
>
> My mother's apartment was seriously damaged and empty. Where was my dear mother now? A man told me he had seen her running out of the house, raving, confused. I searched desperately from one *Auffangplatz* (a place where survivors could register, get something to drink and eat, and be given a place to sleep) to the next. At last I found my mother, after thirty-six hours of searching.
>
> She was not at all pleased to see me: "Go back, oh, please go back to your child! What will happen to you when the bombers come again tonight?" She

didn't want to come with me to Eisenach, so I left her with a friend. It was
hard to leave her, but she pleaded with me to go and wouldn't relax until I
said good-bye.

Then the bombing got worse in Eisenach, too. I took my Martina and
went to my mother-in-law in East Pomerania, in the country. There we were
finally able to sleep through the night without running to the cellar when the
sirens wailed.

Toward the end of the summer we began to see refugees from East Prussia
in kilometer-long lines walking on the highroads – mothers with babies and
children and old people carrying all their belongings on their backs, or on top
of their prams, or pulling handcarts. The weather turned bad and it rained a
lot. The refugees could hardly move forward on the muddy highroads. All
these people had lost their homes in the east and were on their way to the
west. On top of all their misery, they were often attacked by low-level flyers
who shot at the people with their machine-guns. Often there wasn't enough
time to run for the ditches, and they were wounded or even killed.

The noise from the Russian cannons grew louder and louder. Day and
night the shooting came nearer and the front line rapidly approached. The
temperature plummeted below zero. I had to flee to the west with Martina.

A truck drove us mothers with babies and little children a few kilometers
westward. There we were herded into a stock-car. We were thirty-five
women, lying on straw side by side in the dark. The cracks in the wooden
walls afforded little daylight but a lot of draft. Our furniture consisted of an
iron stove for heat and for melting snow, a bowl, and a box. A bucket standing in the corner served as a toilet. The heavy sliding door was locked from
outside.

Our car was part of a military train carrying the survivors of an air-force
fighter wing. They had just returned from an air base in Russia and like us
were being forced back to the West. Whenever the train stopped the airmen
brought us wood or charcoal for the stove, snow to melt for water, and food
from their own rations. We traveled for many days, and because the tracks
and bridges were often destroyed, we had to make long detours.

One evening we had stopped on a siding near the city Güstrow, next to
two long trains. We were already asleep when the sliding door was pushed
open. "Raus! Raus! Come out, come out!" the airmen shouted. The air-raid
alarm wailed. We threw our still-sleeping children down into the out-
stretched arms of the airmen, and they ran swiftly with them into a nearby
field. They sat down with our children in the snow. At first I couldn't find
Martina, because an officer had her under his big winter coat to keep her
warm.

In the sky overhead, American fighters swarmed over the city. First they launched colorful balls, yellow, green, and red, which hung suspended in the air to tell the flyers where to drop their bombs. The sky was strangely beautiful, like a decorated Christmas tree with colorful burning candles. Then German planes flew up to fight them, and at the same time the antiaircraft guns and artillery started up, sweeping their powerful searchlights across the sky. Desperately the planes tried to escape from being seen and shot. To be illuminated meant great danger; the wings and tails of some planes were already burning. One exploded into burning pieces, which dropped down to the earth. The German airmen next to us watched the fight with binoculars and explained to us women which planes were hit – German or American. I saw seven planes burning, and from one of them, two parachutists sprang out. Where and how would they land?

Then the bombers came – always twelve bombers together. They flew in an arrow, an exact V, like wild geese. One wave after another arrived. They flew very high and then, above the city, they came in very low and dropped their bombs. With great speed they took to the air again and vanished. They dropped more then 10,000 bombs – incendiary bombs, high-explosive bombs – all over the houses, factories, churches, schools, hospitals, ammunition and oil depots.

There was fire everywhere – blue, red, black, and orange. When a spirits depot was hit, we saw the conflagration rise hundreds of meters high. The whole city was a sea of flames. To see that was more than a human heart could take in, to think of the helpless children, women, and old people. Why did they have to suffer so much misery and distress? Where was God's mercy?

The terror, the chaos, the senselessness took away any human feeling. What remained in people's hearts was dullness, apathy, bitterness, or else thoughts of revenge and hatred. The cry to God, begging for mercy and help, thanking him for sparing us, was missing. We thought only of how we could save ourselves.

Suddenly the air-force officer sitting close to me stood up, gave me my child and his coat, and whispered to another flyer. Then he crawled to the next field, toward some undergrowth. We heard two shots. Then he came back to us and said, *"Erledigt* (settled)."

I asked him, "What is settled?"

He replied, "The spy is dead; I shot him."

"Why didn't you take him captive first?"

"A spy caught red-handed must be shot immediately," he said.

Behind the undergrowth several flares had been sent up to the bombers in the sky, advising the enemy of the four military trains that stood only a few hundred meters away.

The officer continued with great seriousness in his voice: "You didn't know that two of the trains are hospital trains, full of seriously wounded soldiers with their nurses and doctors, returning from the front. Should they be bombed, too?"

I wasn't able to reply. I didn't know myself what was right to do. The bombing of Güstrow continued till morning. Two-thirds of the city was destroyed, and two thousand deaths were mourned that night.

We traveled on by train. One morning we awoke to find the sliding door ajar, and looking out, we saw that we had been abandoned. Our car had been left on a sidetrack. The military train was gone. After many difficulties Martina and I managed to find lodging with the burgomaster of Cracow. This family showed us much love, and soon we lived like a real family together.

The Russians conquered more and more German towns. Many institutions and establishments had to be evacuated. We lived on a busy street and saw everything that passed by the house. Once, more than a thousand Russian prisoners were marched down our street on their way to camps further to the West. They were worn and tired, and obviously in need of nourishment, but we were forbidden to give any food or drink to a prisoner. All the same, an old woman from a house directly across the street threw a sandwich out of the window. In no time the men were fighting, and finally some lay on the ground. The long train of prisoners was out of order, and the escort soldiers got furious. They beat the men on the ground cruelly with their rifle-butts. Three of them were unable to get up and were left lying on the side of the street until they were thrown into an open cart at the rear of the train.

Two days later a very different procession passed by, once again heading West. This time, however, those marching were thoroughbred horses: five-hundred beautiful horses, mares and stallions, colts and fillies, all beautifully brushed and certainly well fed. They were traveling from Stolp, a town in East Germany that had a world-famous stud farm. These horses couldn't be used to pull a carriage; they were saddle horses, trained for the races. Their coats shone brightly in the sunshine. During the war they had suffered nothing, no bombing, no hunger, no strafing by low-level flyers. All arrived safely at their destination, where they were confiscated and flown under protection to England...

When the Russian front line stopped at the River Oder, my twin sister Ruth came from Eisenach to fetch us. She was fearful that the Russian army

would soon be in Cracow and was quite sure it would be better to be conquered by the Americans than by the brutal Russians. But I couldn't believe
that the Russian army would cross the Oder. I had finally found my own
lodging, and I wanted to wait until the war was over. Eisenach was hardly
habitable and was still being bombed by the Americans. So with a very sad
and heavy heart, my sister left us.

It was only weeks before the Russians arrived. The shooting came nearer
and nearer, and we looked for a place to hide. Together with the wives of the
burgomaster and school principal, we rowed to an island on one of Cracow's
many lakes. Martina was two and a half years old. Although the shack had
neither windows nor a door, we were grateful for a roof. But it was only
days before we were betrayed, and one day twenty Russian soldiers raided
the island.

The leader barked and an interpreter translated: "You hid yourselves here
because you didn't want to remain in Cracow. You are partisans in the
Hitlerpartei, and worst of all, you have high functions in it. I am commanded
to shoot you...You!" he pointed at me. "Your name, and where is your
husband?"

"Ilse von Köller, refugee from East Pomerania. My husband is in the war
in Russia," I replied.

"Yes, you spoke the truth. I'm informed about you all."

To be German was bad enough, but the aristocratic "von" was even
worse. In 1918 the nobility had been shot in Russia...

We had to stand in a line against the shack. Five soldiers stood in front of
us with their rifles in hand. The leader counted and the rifles were pointed at
us. My only thought was, "What will become of my child Martina when I am
dead? Abandoned, left alone in the hands of these brutal soldiers?" I saw her
in my thoughts, unhappy, desperately crying, *"Mutti, Mutti!"* Then, still in
my thoughts, she was going slowly to the shore, and she fell into the lake. I
saw her little body lying on the bottom of the lake. That would be more than
terrible. I took her in my arms; she had to be killed with me. I pressed her
firmly to my heart. Then I calmly looked the leader straight in the eye. Without hate or fear, not asking for pity, I whispered, "I am ready. Do what is your
duty."

The leader watched me and Martina. His expression changed from one of
strict determination to one of love and kindness. Was this not the same warm
look I had seen in Ulrich when he left me for the war? The thought of Ulrich
overwhelmed me. Wasn't that tall leader with the gentle blue eyes Ulrich saying good-bye to wife and child?...The leader spoke some words to the soldiers, and they lowered their rifles and turned aside. He came to us with the
interpreter and said, "The child saved your life."

I broke down. My knees collapsed, I was trembling from head to foot, and my teeth were chattering. I couldn't stop it, I was unable to speak. I felt completely empty. The leader tried to calm me down and offered me a cigarette, but I wasn't able to take it — my hands were shaking too much. So he took his burning cigarette out of his mouth and put it in my hand. Without thinking, I crushed it in my hand. When I felt the sudden searing pain in my palm, I became immediately calm and stopped shaking. The soldiers began to loot our belongings, but the leader stopped their plundering and commanded them to leave. We were told to return to Cracow the next morning. Greatly relieved, we saw them rowing away.

Back in town we heard about the terrible things the soldiers had done to our neighbors. The brutality and cruelty suffered by the young women and girls is not to be described in words. As conquerors, they had been encouraged to do what they liked with us women to take revenge. And they were merciless. It is true that the Russians suffered terribly under the Germans, though, and for that they hated us very much.

In the next days, weeks, and months I encountered many dangers to life and soul. But the grace of God often came to me in unexpected and inconceivable ways. Against my human nature, against my wish to repay all the evil done to me, I could not hate or curse. In my deepest heart I felt compassion for these men who were no longer human beings.

Once, I was forcefully pulled down to the ground by a drunken soldier. I shoved him away with all my might. His face, so near to mine, was coarse and full of lust, and I was overwhelmed with horror and disgust. I wanted so very much to hate him, to curse him, but suddenly I saw in him the suffering of all mankind. A deep feeling of great pity overpowered me, a feeling I had never known before. I couldn't hate or curse him. Was he not also a victim of this dreadful and merciless war? My resistance vanished. I was calm, and a peace, not of this world, came into my heart. The soldier was astonished. His arms, which were holding me as tight as iron wires, loosened a bit. In that second I was able to free myself and I dashed away. Furiously he shouted, *"Frau komm! Frau komm!"* (Every Russian soldier knew that much German.) He shot after me, and although the bullets hissed around me, I was able to escape.

I ran into a nearby forest, where I met five women. We all hid, and when we came out from behind the trees I was sure they would welcome me, glad that I had escaped. But what a shock to see how angry and furious they were! With faces full of hatred, their fists threatening, they surrounded me. "Why did you run away? Why did you not stay with him? Those bullets flew at us, too. How easily we could all have been shot!"

I wanted to shout back, but again I felt something different flood over my heart. I was sorry, really sorry, for these women. I could understand their anger. They only wanted to live, wanted nothing else but to be alive. So I looked calmly back into their faces and replied not a word. Shouting and scolding, they went away. Only then my knees collapsed, and shaking from head to foot, I was able to pray...

On another occasion a soldier forced his way into my room at night. As I cried, "No, no, no!" I suddenly heard a man's voice behind me. He was another refugee, who lived next door with his young wife. He took the soldier by the arm and finally managed to persuade him to leave. The next morning when I thanked him, he said, "You helped my wife once, too. Now it was my turn to help."

Then I remembered how his wife had come running upstairs, trembling with fear. She had seen the soldiers coming into our house, and her husband wasn't there. With all my might I had pushed her under a very low sofa standing against the wall, and I squeezed under it, too. A Russian entered the room, and in spite of the fact that the sofa was shaking visibly, he left again almost immediately. This poor woman was so afraid that she had completely lost control over herself. She was very embarrassed about that, but I calmed her down and said, "Weren't we lucky!" And we laughed together.

Later, her husband told me where he had taken my night-time intruder: to a woman who sold herself to earn food for her children. I knew that woman – a mother of six girls. She looked out of the window and waved to the soldiers as they passed by. Everyone gossiped about her because of that. But when someone told me what a bad mother she was, I said straight away: "Why do you blame her? Give her food for her children." She was a refugee and she possessed nothing, only six children – and those children needed to eat every day.

That wasn't the last of my frightening experiences. One day a young Russian soldier was furious with me because I had left the queue, and he put his pistol up against my right temple and pushed me forward with it. Silently, without any resistance, I let myself be pushed. I felt the cold, round rim of the pistol on my temple. Suddenly he shot twice in the air, and then ran off, laughing at me devilishly. Even a long time afterward, whenever I thought of that event, I felt the cold pressure on my temple...

Some months later Ulrich came home. He had been released from captivity early because he was an agriculturist, and Germany was in great need of skilled men. On his way, searching for us, he had seen and heard all that had happened to the women. He became more and more fearful as he approached Cracow. How thankful and glad he was to find that his wife and child had survived, and that both of them were healthy in body and soul. After two days of rest in Cracow, we journeyed many days on foot back to Eisenach.

All the bridges over the rivers were destroyed, and we could cross only by ferryboat. For that we needed permission from the Russians.

They said they would give us permission only if a young woman would come first into their hut. The Russians were drunk and slept all day long in that warm hut. We sat day and night on the bank in the cold rain. After twenty-four hours the young daughter of an old, ill mother went into the hut. She thought her mother would die if she had to wait one night longer in the cold and rain. She went out of love for her ill mother. Who can judge if she did the right thing?

Ilse's story was not yet over; she and most other Germans continued to suffer long after the war ended in May 1945. Yet even the few episodes she has shared here are a powerful reminder that everyone suffers in time of war, that the battle rages far beyond the battlefield — and that fight goes on long after the cease-fire has been signed.

■ ■ ■ ■ ■ ■ ■

I was reminded of this again when I met Jane Leary at a Buddhist Veterans' Retreat in Rhinebeck, New York. Jane never saw war firsthand, but she remains scarred thirty years after the death of her brother John Dennis. As her story shows, there is a long "tail" to the death of even one soldier: a sister, a brother, a wife, parents, children.

Forty of us were gathered that first night in a cabin on the edge of a field; most were Vietnam veterans, but spouses and friends were there, too. The room was lit from the center of the ceiling, and Jane sat silently on the carpet in the half-darkness behind the circle. We went around and briefly introduced ourselves. When it was Jane's turn, she said she'd come because her brother had been killed in Vietnam, and she was seeking some healing for that. Her voice was laden with emotion, and I was struck by the freshness of her pain. "Time heals," we tell one another when bad things happen — but it wasn't true for Jane.

For months I'd been meeting with veterans and trying to take in their special brand of suffering, but Jane's story moved me in a particular way. Not because it was unique — there are 58,000 families who've suffered such loss through Vietnam — but because of the way Jane loved her brother, so strongly that time was powerless to make her grief fade. Perhaps it was the stupidity and senselessness of her brother's sudden death. Or that there were so many missed opportunities in his short life, so many things left unsaid by a father who died of lung cancer shortly before the war. Things which might have made a difference and saved her brother...

A few days later, when one of the veterans at the retreat sang a song he'd written about Vietnam, I watched Jane's tears flow and began to grasp something of the timelessness of her wound. I spoke with her again a few weeks after the retreat. She was grateful to stay in touch because she had wanted to keep the experience of the retreat alive. Jane said a number of times that when others listen to her story and share her pain, however briefly, it validates her brother. "Validate?" I wondered. What kind of society have we become, that people like Jane must seek endlessly to validate loved ones who've been senselessly wrenched from their lives?

A close friend who provided much-needed support throughout the writing of this book said to me, "Your stories help me to grasp the awful suffering and torment caused by war. It couldn't have happened without great numbers of unloving, uncaring people. I feel myself judged; my own coldness and indifference appalls me."

If we really listened to the voices of survivors like Jane, perhaps there would never be another war.

> In the sixties I was a hippie. I got pregnant and I wasn't married. I decided I didn't want to be with the father, because he was doing drugs. So I gave the baby away for adoption and came home to a father who was dying of lung cancer. I didn't have time to grieve the loss of my child when I lost my father. Then my brother was drafted. He graduated from high school in 1967 and went in April of '68. And because my father was a veteran of the Marines, he joined them.
>
> I was really upset with him, because if you were in the Marines you were guaranteed to go to Vietnam. If you were in another part of the service you might get lucky…But he joined, and my father's death had a lot to do with it, because he felt he had to be like his father. If Dad had been alive he might have tried — I'm sure he would have tried to talk him out of it.
>
> My brother went to Parris Island and then Lejeune, and then home for thirty days, and then Pendleton. I drove him to the airport. It was me and my younger brother — my mother didn't want to go. The car was quiet on the way over. Nobody talked much.
>
> I was a secretary then, and I used to write to him every day. He went to boot camp in April, and he left for Vietnam on September 5, 1968. He called home right before he left. My mother wasn't there. I could just hear the despair in his voice. He didn't complain, but it turns out — which I didn't know at the time — that he had called some of his friends the same day and said that he didn't think he'd be back.
>
> One weekend in April I drove up to the home of a friend in New York. His cousin was getting married and he asked me to go to the wedding with him. It

was on a Sunday, April 27, and little did I know that it was the day my brother was killed. I stayed overnight in New York and drove home on Monday. I was in a strange mood. I'd had a nice weekend, but I just couldn't figure out what was wrong. I went to work the next day, and I couldn't concentrate. I must have been acting differently, because I remember having lunch with two of the girls I worked with, and they kept saying, "What's the matter with you? You're awfully quiet. Didn't you have a good time?" And I said, "Yeah, everything's okay." And then I can remember trying to think I would write him a letter, and then I thought, "No, I better get my work done first, since I missed Monday."

Well, we came back from lunch and I'm sitting at the typewriter. It was just inside the door, in the reception area. My boss came in and threw his hat on the chair and he went back towards the lab instead of going to his office. I remember thinking, "That's weird." Then the next thing you know, I'm looking up from my typewriter and one of my father's best friends and one of my mother's best friends are standing there. So I know that something has happened – but I really didn't think he was dead.

I remember I was so upset. Adolf was holding me, and he couldn't even talk. I kept saying, "What happened? What happened?" And Mrs. Powers was facing me, and she just said, "He's dead." Then the doctor came in and shoved a needle in my arm...

It was two weeks before I returned to work. There were all these people at the house. My brother had been an outstanding athlete; he had gotten the Brooks Irvine award at the high school, which is the highest honor you can get, and he was voted best-looking in his class. He had been a punter for the Colonial Conference Champion Football team, undefeated. He had gone all the way to the state wrestling championship. He just was really very well liked. The street we lived on went right through town, and on every block there were three or four flags flying at half mast.

Jim came down from New York for the funeral. He'd been shot down in Vietnam, and he'd lost his arm and had badly injured both legs. But he was able to walk in casts. He sang at my brother's funeral, and I don't think there was a dry eye in the church. Sister Wilhelmina, who was the second-grade teacher from the parish church, had all the second-graders out lining the street along the curb. When the hearse went by they saluted. We were lucky enough to get one of the Marine pall bearers, and so they did a gun salute at the cemetery. I still have one of the shells. It seems like I'll never forget him...O God, I was close to Denny!

Jane has helped me to understand that war never ends. The "Vietnam syndrome" will never be over, despite what presidents and politicians would like to think.

At the very least, this should give us pause. We cannot move on from one war to the next, recovering and sacrificing and recovering again. Sooner or later, the pain and the death and the unanswered questions will destroy our nation's soul.

■ ■ ■ ■ ■ ■ ■

Alexander Rivas visited our community in 1992. He was sixteen, from El Salvador, and we stayed up till the wee hours of the morning listening to stories of a country torn by war for twelve long years. His comrade José Peña, a serious young man and a powerful singer, told of the terrible atrocities inflicted upon his fellow peasants, and of his vision for "one country" of peace for all nations and races.

When the revolution began, Alexander was only a small child and lived in an agrarian commune formed by the peasants in response to the growing economic and social crisis. In these "base communities," individual needs could be carried by many and the tide of U.S.-sponsored military oppression faced together. But the communities were soon perceived as a threat to the government and endured a reign of terror. Soldiers continually confiscated food and supplies, harassed and beat the peasants, and shot them when they opposed.

Alexander's mother died in childbirth due to inadequate medical care, and he told us of countless others who had died from impossible living conditions, or who had simply "disappeared" after being apprehended by soldiers. One afternoon, just days after another round of interrogations and pillaging, Alex went out into the fields to tend to the community's crops. As he bent down to dig in the dirt, he was blinded by a brilliant flash as a violent explosion hurled his body into the air. Both of his arms were blown off above the elbows and one of his eyes was irreparably damaged. The soldiers had planted mines in the peasants' fields before they left in order to "teach them a lesson."

When I met with Alex in 1992, he was wearing an artificial eye that had to be taken out at night. He needed help to eat and bathe, but he was able to hold a phone or rub his eye, which seemed to irritate him continually. I was moved by his attitude to life, which was cheerful and enthusiastic. A bit of a jokester, he was nearly always smiling, nudging his companions with his shoulder or the stump of his arm, and laughing.

One cannot meet a person like Alex Rivas without being angry, despite his cheerful demeanor, at the reckless and callous manufacture of "anti-personnel devices." The United Nations estimates that there are more than a 100 million mines deployed in 63 nations worldwide. Every week, approximately 500 people, nearly all civilians, are killed or maimed by these "devices." They have killed or maimed more people than all nuclear, biological, and chemical weapons combined. It is estimated that it would cost from 20 to 30 billion dollars to disarm all the landmines currently deployed, and even then there are an additional 100 million more stockpiled around the world.[24]

At the time of this writing, landmines continue to be manufactured by the United States and several other countries in defiance of both the 1949 Geneva Conventions and an International Campaign to Ban Landmines, which is endorsed and supported by forty-one countries.

The United States has offered plenty of rhetorical support for the ban, but delays and obstacles continue to arise. A recent UN conference was deadlocked partly because the U.S. wanted to explore conversion to "smart" mines which could deactivate themselves, and President Clinton's much-touted call for the elimination of all "dumb" mines by 1999 is a meaningless political ploy: companies stopped making such mines years ago, and existing stocks were already scheduled to be destroyed."[25]

A statement issued by the Center for Defense Information in July of 1996 concludes: "The President's decision to take no meaningful steps stands in stark contrast to the recent actions of other nations...In announcing his policy President Clinton is failing to fulfill his September 1994 pledge to eliminate landmines. He is yielding to the wishes of his most hawkish military advisers."[26]

■ ■ ■ ■ ■ ■ ■

That children suffer terribly in time of war is no surprise, and yet I was astounded to uncover a newsletter put out by Washington's Center for Defense Information that detailed the particularly gruesome plight of child soldiers. As many as a quarter of a million children worldwide have been conscripted to serve in armed conflicts; some of them are as young as five. In Mozambique, recruiters have hardened children by forcing them to kill people from their home villages. In Peru, the rebel group Shining Path has forced young children to eat the body parts of those they have killed. Such abominations remain largely invisible because they occur in remote areas, far removed from media scrutiny. And although one could argue that the phenomenon is not new, there are reasons for its recent escalation.

> Involving children as soldiers has been made easier by the proliferation of inexpensive light weapons. As recently as a generation ago, battlefield weapons were still heavy and bulky, generally limiting children's participation to

support-roles. But modern guns are so light that children can easily use them, and so simple that they can be stripped and reassembled by a child of 10...

The very high proportion of children in the armed forces of El Salvador during the 1980–1992 civil war suggests this was a routine occurrence. Of the approximately 60,000 personnel in the Salvadoran military, ex-soldiers estimate that about 80 percent, or 48,000, were under 18 years of age.

Quite often child "recruits" are arbitrarily seized from the streets or even from schools and orphanages. Press-gang tactics were prevalent in Ethiopia in the 1980s, when armed militias, police, or army cadres would roam the streets picking up anyone they encountered. Children from the poorer sectors of society are particularly vulnerable to this tactic...In Burma, whole groups of children from 15 to 17 years old have been surrounded in their schools and forcibly conscripted. Children are also recruited from refugee camps and forced to join armed opposition groups in their country of origin or the armed forces of the country providing asylum.

In addition to being forcibly recruited, children also voluntarily present themselves for service. It is misleading, however, to consider this "voluntary." They may be driven by cultural, social, political or, more often, economic pressures. Hunger and poverty often drive parents to offer their children for service. In some cases, armies pay a minor's wage directly to the family. Children themselves may volunteer if they believe that this is the only way to obtain regular meals, clothing, or medical attention. Some parents encourage their daughters to become soldiers if their marriage prospects are poor.

Some are persuaded to join by propaganda and religious fervor. For example, the marching chant of a column of 15,000 Iranian children on their way to the front during the war with Iraq was, "Come on, come on, plunge on. Those who step on mines will go to paradise." It is said those children were sent across minefields ahead of more valuable, trained adult soldiers...

Once recruited as soldiers, children generally receive much the same treatment as adults, including often brutal induction ceremonies...Even those who start out in "support" functions cannot escape exposure to the risks and hardships most often associated with combat roles. Children often serve as porters, carrying heavy loads up to 132 pounds. Children who are too weak to carry their loads may be savagely beaten or even shot. Children are also used extensively as messengers and lookouts...In Latin America, government forces reportedly have deliberately killed even the youngest children in peasant communities on the grounds that they, too, could be "dangerous."[27]

Why are most Americans unaware of this international horror? One would think that a nation truly committed to the defense of human rights would make brutalized children its top priority. Retired Admiral Carroll, interviewed at Washington's Center for Defense Information, maintains that the Pentagon has a very strong reason to hide the truth: interest in military service in the United States peaks at sixteen and seventeen years of age.

> They have all these high school programs, JROTC, all the advertising, little angels flying around, all the war films, and it's exciting, you know: bang-bang, lasers, and so on. That's when they're vulnerable to the enlistment pitch. If they were to stop these programs they would lose probably five or ten percent of their recruits, and they don't want to do that. Now to be fair about it, maybe overly fair, we have administrative procedures so that some-one under eighteen years of age doesn't go to a combat situation, is not ex-posed to active violence. But that's too late to solve the problem. You've already got the thirteen-year-old kid in uniform, and you're teaching him to shoot and kill and so on.

Le Ly Hayslip, who survived Vietnam, said it best: "Children and soldiers have always known war to be terrible..."

CHAPTER 8

Hush

Let us put up a monument to the lie.

Joseph Brodsky

I have often marveled, in the course of meeting with veterans and learning about the wars of this century, at the selective silence that blankets so much of what has transpired. Selective, because there are certain things we are allowed to see and to know. We know all about the impudence of Pearl Harbor and the valor of Iwo Jima. We have seen countless images of the concentration camps: the bulldozers unearthing mass graves, the chimneys of Auschwitz. The Wall, with its 58,000 names, has become a household word. And in recent times we have been treated generously to images of burning Kuwaiti oils wells and acts of Arab terrorism on the six o'clock news. Why is it, then, that we haven't heard the other side?

Why have we rarely seen photos of the Japanese internment camps in the U.S. during World War II, the cities of Dresden or Tokyo after they were carpet-bombed, or the city of Hiroshima in the first hours and days following the detonation of "Little Boy?" Where is our "wall" for the Vietnamese?* Why have we never heard of the "smart-bombing" of the Al-Amariyah Shelter, which incinerated hundreds of Iraqi women and children?

Perhaps it's just human nature, plain and simple. We prefer to broadcast our accomplishments rather than our failures and trumpet the injustices done to us while downplaying our own wrongdoing. We hope that covering up the dark parts of the past will help us feel better about our future, and we shy away from the truth, because it hurts.

■ ■ ■ ■ ■ ■ ■

---

* A monument in Okinawa displays the names of American and European soldiers killed along with the names of Japanese and Korean war dead.

Abraham Lincoln has been called "honest." At the very least, he publicly recognized that Americans do a disservice to themselves when they fail to face up to individual and national wrongdoing. On April 30, 1863, he proclaimed a "national day of fasting, humiliation, and prayer":

> We have been the recipients of the choicest bounties of heaven; we have been preserved these many years in peace and prosperity; we have grown in numbers, wealth, and power as no other nation has ever grown. But we have forgotten God...We have vainly imagined, in the deceitfulness of our hearts, that all these blessings were produced by some superior wisdom and virtue of our own. Intoxicated with unbroken success, we have become too self-sufficient to feel the necessity of redeeming and preserving grace, too proud to pray to the God that made us. It behooves us, then, to humble ourselves before the offended Power, to confess our national sins, and to pray for clemency and forgiveness...[1]

Was "Honest Abe" right? If America has always been the "land of the free and the brave," if she, as "Liberty enlightening the world," has always opened her arms in compassion to the "huddled masses yearning to be free," if we have always "kept the world safe for democracy" and have only done what is good and just and prudent — then why have we gone to such great lengths to hide the truth surrounding these good deeds?

The trouble with trying to appear good and right all the time is that the strain of the effort invariably leaves a flank exposed. Somewhere, somehow, the outward curtain will fall away, and we will be seen for what we really are. If only we, as individuals and as a nation, would understand that honesty brings true freedom! Then we would become the people and the nation we were meant to be — the "land of the free, and the home of the brave" — in deed as well as in song.

■ ■ ■ ■ ■ ■ ■

This was the stuff that filled my mind during a visit to Washington, DC, one raw, rainy day in November. As I walked away from the Vietnam Veterans Memorial, it struck me that an entire "wall" of children die every *day* in the world from hunger-related diseases, many because of cruel U.S. embargoes and sanctions. Somehow this ongoing tragedy does not strike us in the same way as the tragedy of American war-dead in Vietnam. It occurred to me that we are a very inward-looking people, concerned with our own suffering but not with that of others.

Nowhere was this more evident than at the controversial *Enola Gay* exhibit in the Smithsonian's Air and Space Museum. The exhibit was originally intended to be a comprehensive exploration of the dropping of the atomic bombs on Hiroshima and Nagasaki, but the first draft of the guide was so honest that it was pulled by the Senate Rules and Administration Committee in response to the outcry of organizations like the Veterans of Foreign Wars and the American Legion, who wanted "anti-American" material expunged.

Senator Ted Stevens of Alaska, who chaired the committee, framed the directive to the Smithsonian most succinctly: "I don't think you have any authority to display an exhibit questioning U.S. use of the atomic bomb…"[2]

The committee got its way. What I saw at the *Enola Gay* exhibit was history sanitized beyond belief. The first thing that confronts the eye is the huge vertical stabilizer and rudder of the restored B-52, gleaming silver, adorned with a large black "R" inside a perfect circle. After reading an exhaustive history of the development of the B-52 and the construction of the *Enola Gay*, visitors follow a corridor through displays of propellers, engine cowlings, and piping.

The focal point of the display is a large space containing the entire forward fuselage of the aircraft. It looks so pristine; the shining silver of the riveted plating and the polished black of the interior controls give no hint of atrocity, no evidence of the monstrous devastation once unleashed upon mankind through the yawning bomb-bay doors. As the visitor walks around the nose of the bomber, a glass casing beneath its belly comes into view. Inside is a replica of "Little Boy" itself: a nine-foot cylinder with square fins, painted a flat army green.

The superficiality of the exhibit is at once sinister and ridiculous: museum-goers are reassured that the restoration materials are "authentic," and that the replica of the bomb itself poses no risk of radiation. A small plaque states only that the bomb casing inside the glass is a dummy used for "training."

The tour ends in a small movie theater, where members of the American bombing crews are interviewed on film before and after the destruction of Hiroshima. The reel is short and to the point: over footage of American preparations on the morning of August 6, 1945, we hear a chaplain calling on God to protect the men of *Enola Gay* as they "make the world safe for peace and for democracy – in the name of Jesus Christ, Amen." One member of the *Enola Gay* crew reflects, almost unbelievably, "We succeeded in bringing the carnage to an end."

Visitors never see the hell which was Hiroshima on the day of the bombing, nor are they told that initial footage of the bomb's effects was systematically confiscated and destroyed. They do not hear of the typhoon that further battered the city only two weeks later, washing bloated bodies out to sea. No one will know that the widely reproduced "lunar landscape" of the city was taken in late September nearly two months after the bombing. And no one is informed that the United States had broken Japanese codes long before Pearl Harbor, and that American intelligence knew of Japanese efforts to surrender even as the Potsdam summit approached.[3]

Those who doubt may read Truman's own diary, which clearly records Emperor Hirohito's efforts to surrender before August 6. They need look no further than the Pentagon publications comparing the Japanese to lice, stating that "before a complete cure may be affected...the breeding grounds around the Tokyo area must be completely annihilated." And they should be reminded of how Hollywood depicted the Japanese: "Stinking little savages."[4]

Leaving the museum, I couldn't help thinking of Claude Eatherly, the commander of the reconnaissance plane that had cleared the way for *Enola Gay*. I'd seen his name flash by on a roster of airmen back inside, but the film had focused on other crew members such as Paul Tibbets. And I knew why.

At 7:15 in the morning of August 6, 1945, Claude Eatherly, commander of the lead reconnaissance plane *Straight Flush,* was seated in the cockpit. His mission was to reach the target of Hiroshima, ascertain the weather situation and the possibility of receiving enemy fire from air or ground, and radio back. Scattered stratocumulus clouds floated toward the city of Hiroshima at an altitude of 12,000 to 15,000 feet, but the bridge on the outskirts of the city was clear. The weather seemed ideal. At 7:30 A.M., according to the official history of the United States Airforce, Claude Eatherly radioed back a coded weather report which sealed the city's fate and forever etched the word "Hiroshima" into the consciousness of human history. Uncoded, the report said "Bomb primary [target]."[5]

At 8:15 A.M. Japanese time, the *Enola Gay* released its terrifying cargo over the city. Among the messages scrawled on the bomb was one that read: "Greetings to the Emperor from the men of the *Indianapolis.*"* Captain Robert Lewis, the aircraft commander, saw the massive, blinding flash of the explosion and called out: "My God, look at that son-of-a-bitch go!" In that instant, 80,000 people were killed, and more than 35,000 injured. Jacob Beser, one of the crewmen, commented, "It's pretty terrific. What a relief it worked."[6]

---

* Eleven days earlier, on July 26, the American cruiser *Indianapolis* had arrived at Tinian Island with the atomic bomb on board. On July 29, the ship was torpedoed at midnight between Tinian and Guam. Approximately 350 of the crew of 1,196 were killed in the explosion or drowned. More than 800 men floundered in the sea, only to be driven mad by salt water ingestion or eaten by sharks in the following days. In all, 883 men died in the *Indianapolis* disaster, the greatest loss at sea in the history of the United States Navy, and the last major warship to be lost at sea in the Second World War (Gilbert, 709).

News of the *Enola Gay*'s success arrived as President Truman was eating lunch aboard the cruiser *Augusta,* on his way back from the Potsdam Conference. Grasping the hand of the map room officer who brought him the radiogram, Truman said, "Captain Graham, this is the greatest thing in history." The President tapped his glass with a spoon and announced the news to his dining companions. While they cheered, Truman spread word about this incredible bomb to others on the ship. "We won the gamble," he said, smiling broadly.[7]

On the ground beneath the blast, a frantic Japanese MP raved and ranted at American POWs being held at Hiroshima Castle: "Look what you have done! One bomb! One bomb! Look there: that blue light is women burning. It is babies burning. Is it wonderful to see the babies burning?"[8]

A group of twenty soldiers huddled in a clump of bushes inside the city, motionless, dying. One called out for something to drink. "Their faces were wholly burned; their eye sockets were hollow, the fluid from their melted eyes had run down their cheeks." Perhaps they were anti-aircraft personnel, and had turned their faces upward as the bomb went off. Their mouths were swollen wounds which could not stretch enough to drink from a cup. So a kindly priest found a large piece of grass, drew out the stem to make a straw, and gave the men water.[9]

The force of the explosion was unlike anything ever seen. Birds shriveled in midair. People died in nightmarish ways: their skin peeled off, their brains, eyes, and intestines burst, or they burnt to cinders while still standing. A Jesuit priest reported: "In the Hakushima district, naked, burnt cadavers are particularly numerous. Frightfully injured forms beckon to us and then collapse."[10] Victims who could still walk made their way to one of the seven rivers in the city to slake their consuming thirst. Thousands, burned and irradiated, with skin sloughing off, died there, choking the rivers with corpses.

When Major Eatherly returned to the island base of Tinian to await his demobilization, he spoke to no one for days on end. The members of his bomber group acquired instant worldwide notoriety, and they basked in the glow of Hiroshima. Eatherly's moroseness wasn't taken seriously. "Battle fatigue," they called it. After all, he had succumbed to a nervous breakdown two years earlier, following thirteen months of continuous patrol duty over the South Pacific.

The rest of the crew went on as usual, joking and cursing, slapping each other's backs, and reliving the high points of the big day. But Eatherly's battle fatigue wouldn't go away.

In the months to follow, crew members played to an adoring press. Colonel Paul Tibbets, the "decent, patriotic, and efficient" pilot, said he would do it all over again for the cause of democracy. In an article for the *New Yorker,* he reflected, "People keep asking me these days whether I wasn't shaken by the importance of our atomic bomb work. Myself, I found that I was just as anxious as ever to finish up and get back to that steak dinner and 'Terry and the Pirates.'"[11] Eatherly remained the black sheep, the sole member of the bomber group who refused to be enshrined as a hero of war.

Twelve years later, he was arrested and tried in Abilene, Texas, for breaking into two U.S. post offices at night. His defense revealed an interesting summary: apparently, Eatherly felt responsible for the deaths of the Japanese at Hiroshima, and "wanted punishment." In the years following the war, he had also run guns for a Central American revolution, forged checks, held up grocery stores, and been in and out of mental hospitals. According to his psychiatrist, he was so tormented by dreams of Hiroshima that he had begun to involve himself in criminal activity, hoping to bring about punishment on himself. The chasm between the voice of conscience and the accolades of society was so great that he was driven to desperation in an attempt to bridge the gap.

In 1959, Claude Eatherly's illegal exploits mysteriously came to an end, and he began to speak out against the horrors of nuclear war. Until this point he had been considered "safe" enough for voluntary hospitalization; now, a Texas jury suddenly found him to be deranged, and he was committed indefinitely, and against his will, to a mental hospital. Obviously concerned that Eatherly's outspokenness might disturb America's postwar contentment, the federal government collaborated with the Eatherly family to ensure that his ravings would be confined to the corridors of an institution.

Vienna philosopher Günther Anders maintained an active correspondence with the captive Eatherly, and later published most of the letters in his chronicle, *Burning Conscience.* In the book's preface, Bertrand Russell writes:

> The case of Claude Eatherly is not only one of appalling and prolonged injustice to an individual, but is also symbolic of the suicidal madness of our time. No unbiased person, after reading Eatherly's letters, can honestly doubt his sanity, and I find it very difficult to believe that the doctors who pronounced him insane were persuaded of the accuracy of their own testimony. He has been punished solely because he repented of his comparatively innocent participation in a wanton act of mass murder. The steps that he took to awaken men's consciences to our present insanity were, perhaps, not always the wisest that could have been taken, but they were actuated by motives which deserve the admiration of all who are capable of feelings of humanity. The world was prepared to honour him for his part in the massacre, but, when he repented, it turned against him, seeing in his act of repentance its own condemnation...[12]

Robert Oppenheimer, director of the Manhattan Project, is said to have reflected on the prophetic words of the Bhagavad Gita as he watched the first test explosion in the New Mexico desert on July 16, 1945: "If the radiance of a thousand suns were to burst into the sky, that would be like the splendor of the Mighty One...I am become death, destroyer of worlds."[13] But in the aftermath of Hiroshima, which good American really felt he had?

Popular sentiment celebrated with Churchill and Truman: the bomb had supposedly saved a million American lives and brought a quick end to the war. "Up to this moment," Churchill later recalled, "we had shaped our ideas towards an assault upon the homeland of Japan by terrific air bombing and by the invasion of very large armies." The British prime minister waxed eloquent as he envisioned an end to the nightmare in "one or two violent shocks." And he went so far as to suggest that the Japanese would be grateful for the sparing of further calamity, should these "shocks" be successful.[14]

Truman privately balked at the thought of having to kill "all those kids" in a second bombing, this time of Nagasaki, but he was effervescent in public. He spoke of guarding the new secret to ensure that its power would be an "overwhelming influence toward world peace." And he thanked God that it had come "to us, instead of to our enemies; and we pray that he may guide us to use it in his ways and for his purposes." He confided further to his diary that it was "certainly a good thing for the world that Hitler's crowd or Stalin's did not discover this atomic bomb. It seems to be the most terrible thing ever discovered, but it can be made the most useful."[15]

Against the backdrop of such feverish self-justification and manufactured Providence, Claude Eatherly's voice was unacceptable and had to be silenced. After escaping from his involuntary incarceration in a Waco, Texas, VA hospital he wrote to Anders: "This country is much like many other countries. It is nearly impossible to go against the military."[16] In another letter, he reflected:

One has only one life, and if the experiences of my life can be used for the benefit of the human race, then that is the way it will be used; not for money nor fame, but because of the responsibility I owe everyone. In that way I will receive a great benefit and feel relief of my guilt. If I were to receive the money for any other purpose, it would only remind me of the 30 pieces of silver Judas Iscariot received for his betrayal. Although it has always seemed to me that the *real* culprit responsible for the judicial murder of Christ was the High Priest, Caiaphas — the representative of the pious and the respectable, the "conventional good people" of all ages including our own. These people, while not blameworthy in the same sense as Judas, are yet guilty in a more subtle but also more profound sense than he. This is the reason why I have been having such difficulty in getting society to recognize the fact of my guilt, which I have long since realized. The truth is that society simply *cannot* accept the fact of my guilt without at the same time recognizing its own far deeper guilt. But it is, of course, highly desirable that society should recognize this, which is why *my* and *our* story is of such vital importance. Now I accept the fact that I am unlikely to bring about that recognition by getting into scrapes with the law, that I have been doing in my determination to shatter the "hero image" of me, by which society has sought to perpetuate its own complacency.[17]

Newsweek magazine attempted to squash rumors about the "mad bomber" with evenhanded rationalizations: Eatherly was simply suicidal, and Hiroshima in itself could not adequately explain his behavior; further therapy would surely uncover the real reasons for his disposition.[18] While the establishment explained him away, Eatherly was busy writing, mailing off letters and essays on war and peace to supporters in Europe and Asia. Some of his statements appeared in Tokyo newspapers in 1957, and in 1959 the leaders of Yuwa Kai, the Japanese Fellowship of Reconciliation, wrote back:

> We believe that you were acting either under the orders of your superiors, which you could not disobey, or under impulses of war psychology into which men and women are driven in wartime in any country and engage in horrible, inhuman actions without realizing what consequences they entail...We regard you as a victim of war in much the same way as those who were injured in the war and are praying for your complete recovery.[19]

In further letters to Anders, Eatherly poured out his feelings of guilt. He was unable to forget his act and now felt that war was "wild and inhuman." And while he found no understanding among his fellow Americans, he received comfort from the most unexpected quarter of all: a group of thirty young Japanese women, all victims of Hiroshima:

> Dear Sir,   July 24, 1959
> We, the undersigned girls of Hiroshima, send you our warm greetings. We are all girls who escaped death fortunately but received injuries in our faces, limbs, and/or bodies from the atomic bomb that was dropped on Hiroshima City in the last war. We have scars or traces of the injury in our faces and limbs, and we do wish that that horrible thing called "war" shall never happen again either for us or for anybody living in this world. Now, we heard recently that you have been tormented by a sense of guilt after the Hiroshima incident and that because of it, you have been hospitalized for mental treatment.
>   This letter comes to you to convey our sincere sympathy with you and to assure you that we now do not harbour any sense of enmity to you personally.

You were perhaps ordered to do what you did, or thought it would help people by ending the war. But you know that bombs do not end wars on this earth. We have been treated with great kindness by the Christian people (Quakers) in America. We have learned to feel towards you a fellow-feeling, thinking that you are also a victim of war like us.

We wish that you will recover soon completely and decide to join those people who are engaged in the good work to abolish this barbarous thing called "war" with the spirit of brotherhood.[20]

A letter from the Japanese XY Society brought him similar encouragement:

We are continuing to pray for your complete recovery and entry into a new life. This letter we hope will reach you on or around the historic Hiroshima Day. It is a day dedicated to the cause of reconciliation among the nations, a day with a memory, which hereafter must serve to deliver mankind from mutual suspicion, enmity, and war, but to live instead in mutual trust and with brotherly love.[21]

"Whatever may happen in the future," Eatherly wrote, looking back, "I know that I have learned...things which will remain forever convictions of my heart and mind. Life, even the hardest life, is the most beautiful, wonderful, and miraculous treasure in the world...Cruelty, hatred, violence, and injustice never can and never will be able to create a mental, moral, and material millennium. The only road to it is the all-giving creative love, trust, and brotherhood, not only preached but consistently practised."[22]

On July 7, 1978, the *New York Times* reported:

Claude Robert Eatherly, who, as a young Army Air Corps pilot, picked a hole through the clouds over Japan on the morning of August 6, 1945 and radioed the B-29 *Enola Gay* to drop its atomic bomb on Hiroshima, died of cancer last Saturday in Houston. He was 57 years old...

In 1962, he was [one] of four persons at a demonstration in New York, including Pablo Casals, given "Hiroshima Awards" for "outstanding contributions to world peace."...After his funeral, Mr. Eatherly's brother James, of Midland, Tex., told reporters: "I can remember him waking up night after night. He said his brain was on fire. He said he could feel those people burning."[23]

■ ■ ■ ■ ■ ■ ■

Vietnam veteran Steve Bentley has fought long and hard to reveal another cover-up: the exposure of thousands of Vietnam veterans to a toxic chemical defoliant, Agent Orange. The former chair of the Vietnam Veterans of America PTSD and Substance Abuse Committee has worked tirelessly to pierce the barrier of silence that surrounded the Pentagon's use of such chemicals for decades. Steve writes:

> Nationally, 220,000 Vietnam veterans have requested physical examinations from the Veterans Administration because of suspicion that their health problems are caused by exposure to the 12 million gallons of herbicide that was sprayed on Vietnam...
>
> [Recently, chemical companies agreed to a] $180 million settlement...in order to keep [them] from going to court...In order to receive any part of that money, the veteran must prove he was exposed to Agent Orange in Vietnam, has been suffering from long-term disability, and is 100-percent disabled by Social Security standards. This last requirement obviously leaves out the vast majority of Vietnam vets who work despite health problems, and it leaves out all those whose children have suffered birth defects and cancer.
>
> The chemical companies seem to be saying that, while they don't really believe these problems exist at all, it is absolutely necessary for us to be totally disabled by these non-existent problems in order to be compensated even a little bit. If you meet these requirements, the average expected payment is $5700. That is, unless you were unfortunate enough to have these imaginary problems kill you; then the maximum death benefit is $3400. To those families most affected, even inadequate compensation is better than nothing. However, the attitude this settlement reinforces in many Vietnam vets is summed up in the bumper sticker "Sprayed and Betrayed"...

Steve goes on to note that the very government which sent him to Vietnam has concluded, via its Centers for Disease Control, that it will not bother even to look into such health problems because they are "statistically insignificant."

> Ironically, these statistically insignificant soldiers who were heavily exposed to dioxin also turn out to be those who were most involved in combat by virtue of the fact we were the ones in the jungle. This fact makes further mockery of the VA's much-touted slogan, "To care for those who have borne the battle."[24]

Steve is incensed by a government that "panders to veterans about the symbols of justice while real live human beings stumble from one alley to another." Spurred by the hype following Operation Desert Storm in 1991, he put his thoughts to paper in an article entitled "In the Name of Freedom":

In the name of freedom for the people, the leaders of the U.S. government spent $170 billion and 60,000 American lives in Vietnam. Now, 20 years later, the administration continues to drag out the MIA/POW issue, thereby blocking diplomatic relations with Vietnam. The ultimate result is continued economic devastation for Vietnam and ongoing untold suffering for the very people we professed to care about.

Again, in the name of freedom for the people, the U.S. leadership spent well over $500 million on many forms of lethal aid in hopes of facilitating the overthrow of Nicaragua's Sandinista government. When the people of Nicaragua voted out the Sandinistas, the hard-liners were quick to take credit and justify the expenditure in the name of freedom for the people.

Now, after years of war and U.S.-backed embargo, most Nicaraguans live in such conditions of squalor that a cholera epidemic threatens to kill tens of thousands of them. It's estimated that $20 million of medicines would quell this epidemic. The United States is able to come up with less than $2 million for the people.

In the name of freedom for the people, the United States government helped to create and nourish a madman in Iraq and then, when he acted as madmen do, our leaders spent billions of dollars and hundreds of American lives blowing at least 100,000 Iraq people to smithereens. Meanwhile, we left the madman in power.

Recently, a Harvard team of health experts returned from Iraq to inform us that 200,000 Iraq children are destined to die if we continue sanctions. We're told, however, that we must continue sanctions so we can get the madman out of power in the name of freedom for the people.

In the midst of all this, President Bush wants to give "most favored nation status" to a bunch of power-hungry old men who slaughtered their children in the town square.*

Who's kidding whom? This government doesn't give a damn about freedom for the people. It has nothing to do with freedom. It's about power, it's about money, it's about racism and elitism and greed. It's about pride and stupidity and ugly, insidious forms of paranoia, projection, and delusion, but it has nothing to do with a commitment to freedom for the people [and] even less to do with their well-being.

To make matters worse, it appears the majority of the citizens that make up this nation buy into this nationalistic babble like so many freshly caught carp. Which all serves to remind me of the words of Thomas Jefferson, "I tremble for my country when I reflect that God is just."[25]

---

* Reference to the June 4, 1989, massacre at Tiananmen Square, Beijing, China.

Like Claude Eatherly, former Marine Smedley Butler chose loyalty to his conscience over the adoration of a mindless populace. Butler joined the Marine Corps during the Spanish-American War of 1898, earned a medal during the Boxer Rebellion in China, and was promoted to major general in France during World War I. Following the capture of Fort Riviere in Haiti in 1915, he won the Medal of Honor.

As a recent letter to the editor of the New York *Daily News* shows, Butler is still venerated as a shining example of the "few and the proud":

> Our reputation as "the first to fight" and as the world's finest fighting force was built on extreme personalities such as Smedley Butler...Ask any enemy who has had the misfortune to face Marines in battle, if they lived to talk about it, and they will agree...We are *Semper Fidelis* and even our Marine's hymn claims that "the streets of heaven are guarded by United States Marines"...

The effusive manner in which the writer of this letter praises the Marine Corps is hardly shared by Butler himself, however. Despite two congressional Medals of Honor and decades of distinguished "service," Butler later spoke out plainly against the realities of American armed intervention into foreign affairs:

> I spent 33 years and 4 months in active military service as a member of our country's most agile military force – the Marine Corps. I served in all commissioned ranks, from second lieutenant to major general. And during that period I spent most of my time being a high-class muscle man for Big Business, for Wall Street, and for the bankers. In short, I was a racketeer, a gangster for capitalism.
>
> I suspected I was just part of a racket at the time. Now I am sure of it. Like all members of the military profession, I never had a single original thought until I left the service. My mental faculties remained in suspended animation while I obeyed the orders of the higher-ups. This is typical of everyone in the military service.
>
> Thus I helped make Mexico, and especially Tampico, safe for American oil interests in 1914. I helped make Haiti and Cuba a decent place for the National City Bank boys to collect revenues in. I helped in the raping of half a dozen Central American republics for the benefit of Wall Street. The record of racketeering is long. I helped purify Nicaragua for the international banking house of Brown Brothers in 1909–12. I brought light into the Dominican Republic for American sugar interests in 1916. In China in 1927 I helped to see to it that Standard Oil went its way unmolested.
>
> During those years, I had, as the boys in the back room would say, "a swell racket." I was rewarded with honors, medals, and promotion. Looking back on

it, I feel that I might have given Al Capone a few hints. The best he could do was operate his racket in three city districts. I operated on three continents.[26]

George F. Kennan, architect and commentator on U.S. foreign policy for almost fifty years, summarized Butler's "American approach" in 1948. As head of the State Department's policy planning staff, he wrote in a now-famous memorandum:

> We have about 50 percent of the world's wealth but only 6.3 percent of its population...In this situation, we cannot fail to be the object of envy and resentment. Our real task in the coming period is to devise a pattern of relationships which will permit us to maintain this position of disparity...To do so, we will have to dispense with all sentimentality and day-dreaming...We should cease to talk about vague and...unreal objectives such as human rights, the raising of the living-standards, and democratization. The day is not far off when we are going to have to deal in straight power concepts. The less we are then hampered by idealistic slogans, the better.[27]

Half a century later, Kennan's policy of greed and exploitation is alive and well. And it is a policy that remains shrouded in a fog of deception and willful ambiguity.

In August of 1990, while the U.S. military was winding down its most visible spate of exploits in Central America, and the U.S. government was laying the groundwork for the Persian Gulf War, Senator Daniel Patrick Moynihan observed: "The secrecy system protects intelligence errors, it protects officials from criticism. Even with the best of intentions the lack of public information tends to produce errors; the natural correctives – public debate, academic criticism – are missing."[28]

A 1993 issue of *The Defense Monitor* similarly concurred: "We must...lift the veils of secrecy and get the public involved in decision-making if our democracy is to operate effectively in the post-cold war world. The spending of the Central Intelligence Agency...[is] still not buried in the 'black' part of the budget."[29]

Where, exactly, has all this money been going? Even the mainstream media concedes that much of it flows to Central America and other areas of the so-called Third World, where the CIA has worked for decades to destabilize local political structures and provide unlimited access for American business interests. While the CIA adamantly denies wrongdoing, a trove of in-house documents recently obtained by the National Security Archives suggests a rather sinister *modus operandi*. Take, for example, the memo entitled "A Study of Assassination," which offers options for the disposal of "dangerous" opposing interests:

...It should be assumed that [assassination] will never be ordered or autho-
rized by any U.S. Headquarters, though the latter may in rare instances agree
to its execution by members of an associated foreign service. This reticence is
partly due to the necessity of committing communications to paper. No assassination instructions should ever be written or recorded. Consequently,
the decision to employ this technique must nearly always be reached in the
field, at the area where the act will take place.

...Assassination of persons responsible for atrocities or reprisals may be regarded as just punishment. Killing a political leader whose burgeoning career is
a clear and present danger to the cause of freedom may be held necessary.

But assassination can seldom be employed with a clear conscience. Persons who are morally squeamish should not attempt it.

The essential point of assassination is the death of the subject. A human
being may be killed in many ways but sureness is often overlooked by those
who may be emotionally unstrung by the seriousness of this act they intend
to commit. The specific techniques employed will depend upon a large number of variables, but should be constant in one point: death must be absolutely certain...

The pamphlet goes on to detail the various means by which assassinations can be
carried out, noting that accidents, blunt weapons, and bare hands all constitute a
useful arsenal:

It is possible to kill a man with bare hands, but very few are skillful enough to
do it well. Even a highly trained Judo expert will hesitate to risk killing by
hand unless he has absolutely no alternative. However, the simplest local
tools are often much the most efficient means of assassination. A hammer,
axe, wrench, screw driver, fire poker, kitchen knife, lamp stand, or anything
hard, heavy, and handy will suffice. A length of rope or wire or a belt will do
if the assassin is strong and agile. All such improvised weapons have the advantage of availability and apparent innocence. The obviously lethal machine gun failed to kill Trotsky where an item of sporting goods
succeeded...[30]

The absence of public outcry in the face of such horrifying memoranda is a
clear indication of our national apathy. We cower in silent acquiescence, unable
to deal with the ugly reality of what is no longer an American Dream but a gar-
ish nightmare. And our leaders blather on. When asked about the CIA's involvement in Chile, in his 1973 Senate confirmation hearings for U.S. Secretary
of State, a shameless Henry Kissinger replied, "The CIA had nothing to do
with the coup, to the best of my knowledge and belief, and I only put in that

qualification in case some madman appears down there who, without instruction, talked to somebody."[31]

When lying is this transparent, it would seem that the public might start to take notice. But James Loewen argues that men like Kissinger will continue to lie with impunity as long as the establishment that protects and supports them lies, too. In his radical *Lies My Teacher Told Me*, which examines the well-entrenched myths of high school history textbooks, he concludes:

> Educators...seem to want to inculcate in the next generation blind allegiance to our country...Textbooks merely assume that the government tried to do the right thing. Citizens who embrace the textbook view would presumably support *any* intervention, armed or otherwise, and *any* policy, protective of our legitimate national interests or not, because they would be persuaded that all our policies and interventions are on behalf of humanitarian aims. They could never credit our enemies with equal humanity.[32]

Loewen goes on to bemoan a 1925 directive from the American Legion, which announces that the textbooks used in American schools "must inspire the children with patriotism...must be careful to tell the truth optimistically...must dwell on failure only for its value as a moral lesson, must speak chiefly of success...must give each State and Section full space and value for the achievements of each.[33] The Prussian general and military strategist Carl von Clausewitz was right: war *is* a remarkable trinity of the people, the army, and the government.

■ ■ ■ ■ ■ ■ ■

One cannot speak of war and its attendant dishonesty without thinking of the massacre at My Lai, recounted earlier; its systematic cover-up remains one of the greatest fiascoes in modern history. Although the Army knew about the murderous rampage almost immediately, news of the "incident," as it was quickly renamed, appeared in the American press only two years later. As angry journalists mobbed the Pentagon, the Army's general counsel, Robert Jordan, told them:

> Some of you enterprising members of the press have been poking and digging around the last few days and you have identified some people that are identified in this and you've found out where they are and you've gone out and interviewed them. We don't consider it within our purview to order everybody who is in the Army not to talk to you...[34]
>
> Look, let's be realistic about this. Enough information has come out about this case...that any question about the Army protecting itself is really kind

of silly, you know, the fat is in the fire. If you're talking about trying to cover up, we aren't trying to cover up and we haven't been trying to cover up.[35]

But Jordan's defensive assurances were at odds with Army policy that had been in effect ever since the beginning of the war. This policy had been underscored in October 1967, as General Westmoreland sought to stem the flow of increasingly harrowing reports and photographs to the American media.

In a confidential letter to his deputy, General Bruce Palmer, Westmoreland had called for restraint, warning that "the war in Vietnam is being degraded by a growing segment of the press and public at large." He demanded that any activity "reflecting unfavorably on the military image" be eliminated, and specifically listed prostitution, excessive drinking, and violations of the Geneva Conventions and the Law of Land Warfare. In a closing line that lays bare the true underpinnings of the democratic process, he reminded Palmer that the "tensions of the forthcoming election year will focus to a major extent on virtually every aspect of our effort here."[36]

When the internal Army investigation into the My Lai "incident" was disbanded on April 8, 1968, only three weeks after the killings, Brigade Commander Henderson congratulated the men of "Charlie Company" himself: "The praiseworthy role of units of the 11th Infantry Brigade directly reflects your expert guidance, leadership, and devotion to duty...The quick response and professionalism displayed during this action has again enhanced the Brigade's image in the eyes of higher commands."[37] The message to the murderers was clear. There was no need to worry about further investigations, and the truth would be quietly buried.

The Americal Division's commander, Major General Samuel Koster, was forced to resign his newly appointed position as superintendent of West Point when it was found that he had deliberately withheld reports indicating that a massacre was in progress. He was hardly repentant. From the balcony overlooking the dining hall, he announced to the academy's cadets that he was "requesting reassignment to save the academy from further publicity." He spoke of the cherished principles of West Point ("duty, honor, and country") as the guide for his military career and added, emotionally, "I shall continue to follow these principles as long as I live. Every one of you can have a wonderful experience in the military profession. To serve one's country true and faithfully is one of the highest callings...Don't let the bastards grind you down!"[38] Koster never identified who the "bastards" were.

As the truth about My Lai unfolded, a newly promoted Alexander Haig kept the White House appraised of developments in the case. Henry Kissinger, in turn, passed the information to Haldeman and Nixon. "Now the cat is out of the bag," he wrote the chief of staff only days before Calley was formally charged with a capital offense. "I recommend keeping the President and the White House out of the matter entirely."[39]

An exasperated Richard Nixon was less delicate, and as public reaction to the news became more hostile, he blamed the "dirty rotten Jews from New York" — ostensibly, the editorial management of the *Times*. When college students scheduled a nation-wide antiwar protest for October 15, he turned angrily to Chief of Staff Bob Haldeman: "It is absolutely essential that we react insurmountably and powerfully to blunt this attack." He was talking not of the NVA, but of American citizens, marching unarmed through ivied campuses.[40]

British investigators Bilton and Sim provide a rare view into the world of the Vietnam-era White House, and their portrayal of deceit at the highest levels of government lends new weight to the concept of media control:

> Nixon's tactic, true to form, was to go on the attack, to turn the stories about My Lai on their head...At a meeting with Haldeman on December 1, the President secretly ordered that the campaign against media bias be kept boiling and that a covert offensive should be mounted on My Lai. Haldeman's personal notes of the meeting, which remain among Nixon's White House files in the National Archives, reveal the President's bidding: "Dirty tricks — not too high a level; discredit one witness, get out facts on Hue; admin line — may have to use a senator or two, so don't go off in different directions; keep working on the problem." Nixon condemned the atrocity in public. But one night, according to a White House assistant, Alexander Butterfield, he spent two hours attacking the press for the My Lai publicity.[41]

Daniel Patrick Moynihan, then councilor to the President, wrote a personal memo to Nixon, expressing his fears:

> It is clear that something hideous happened at My Lai...I would doubt the war effort can now be the same, nor the position of the military...I fear the answer of too many Americans will simply be that this is a hideous, corrupt society. I fear and dread what this will do to our society unless we try to understand it... I think it would be a grave error for the Presidency to be silent while the Army and the press pass judgment. For it is America that is being judged."[42]

The memo fell on deaf ears, and as time would tell, Moynihan was only partly right. The antiwar movement was certainly galvanized, but the position of the military remained, predictably, unchanged. Public outcry gave way to the myth of moral superiority; like famine and the plague, war crimes were the property of uncivilized foreigners.[43]

The cover-up of My Lai continues to this day. Until 1998 few had heard the story of Hugh Thompson, a helicopter pilot who accidentally came upon the massacre, in progress, as he flew over the jungle on a scouting mission. Thompson set his chopper down between a group of frightened civilians and the advancing American soldiers, and threatened to open fire on his own men should they kill any more civilians. He managed to rescue a three-year-old boy and ten other Vietnamese who had hidden in a bunker. At the time, the Pentagon's official report hailed Thompson as a hero; the Army offered him a Distinguished Flying Cross in 1969.[44]

More recently, in 1996, Thompson's name came up again – he was recommended for the prestigious Soldier's Medal, for bravery. But an internal Pentagon memo from an anonymous major advised Army Secretary Sara Lister to hold off: "We would be putting an ugly, controversial, and horrible story on the media's table," it said. "...I recommend sitting on this until clear of the election." In November 1997, the Army tried to play down Thompson's role once again: this time, they suggested giving Thompson the medal in a "private ceremony."[45] In March of 1998, as publicity surrounding the thirtieth anniversary of My Lai built, he finally received the prestigious Soldier's Medal in a ceremony at the Vietnam Veterans Memorial in Washington, DC.

The 1937 Rape of Nanking dwarfs the My Lai massacre in sheer numbers, if not in cruelty. Despite its magnitude, however, it remained largely hidden in the annals of World War II history until recently.

> The broad details of the rape are, except among the Japanese, not in dispute. In November 1937, after their successful invasion of Shanghai, the Japanese launched a massive attack on the newly established capital of the Republic of China. When the city fell on December 13, 1937, Japanese soldiers began an orgy of cruelty seldom if ever matched in world history. Tens of thousands of young men were rounded up and herded to the outer areas of the city, where they were mowed down by machine guns, used for bayonet practice, or soaked with gasoline and burned alive. By the end of the massacre an estimated 260,000 to 350,000 Chinese had been killed. Between 20,000 and 80,000 Chinese women were raped – and many soldiers went beyond rape to disembowel women, slice off their breasts, nail them alive to walls.

Why has this abomination remained so obscure? The number of deaths far exceeds that of Hiroshima and Nagasaki combined, and yet the horror of Nanking remains virtually unknown outside of Asia.

> The Rape of Nanking did not penetrate the world consciousness in the same manner as the Jewish Holocaust or Hiroshima, because the victims themselves remained silent. The custodian of the curtain of silence was politics.

The People's Republic of China, Taiwan, and even the United States, all contributed to the historical neglect of this event for reasons deeply rooted in the Cold War. After the 1949 Communist revolution in China, neither the People's Republic of China nor Taiwan demanded wartime reparations from Japan (as Israel had from Germany), because the two governments were competing for Japanese trade and political recognition. And even the United States, faced with the threat of communism in the Soviet Union and main-land China, sought to ensure the friendship and loyalty of its former enemy Japan. In this manner, Cold War tensions permitted Japan to escape much of the intense critical examination that its wartime ally was forced to undergo.[46]

The cover-up of Nanking is typical of the selective silence and propaganda of the "Good War." And it is by no means the only incident that was sidelined willfully. Recently, *U.S. News and World Report* admitted that the righteous Allies themselves were hardly immune to Hitler's greed:

Europe's past keeps sending awful bonbons to its present. In recent months, we have learned that Swiss banks piled up millions of dollars in assets stolen from Jewish victims of the Nazis. Portugal, Turkey, Spain, and Sweden also traded in Nazi loot. The French, who pride themselves on their resistance movement, in reality produced more collaborators – like Maurice Papon, who is on trial for his role in deporting Jews in World War II – than heroes. And now we discover that the United States and Britain knowingly melted the belongings of Holocaust victims into gold bars and distributed them to central banks in Europe as reparations. Everyone has been implicated in a crime once attributed to a single nation: Germany...European countries, no-tably Switzerland and France, enjoyed decades of silence about their wartime history while Germany did penance...[47]

■ ■ ■ ■ ■ ■ ■

When I invited a group of veterans to speak at our Woodcrest community one evening last summer, I read out a statement by Dwight D. Eisenhower that I hoped would kick off our discussion:

Every gun that is made, every warship launched, every rocket fired signifies, in the final sense, a theft from those who hunger and are not fed, those who are cold and are not clothed. This world in arms is not spending money alone. It is spending the sweat of its laborers, the genius of its scientists, the hopes of its children. This is not a way of life at all, in any true sense. Under the cloud of threatening war it is humanity hanging from a cross of iron.[48]

Coming from an American general, 34th President of the United States, and supreme commander of the Allied force that launched the invasion of Normandy and oversaw the final defeat of Germany, I thought this a remarkable statement. I also quoted a shocker from General Douglas MacArthur: "The next great advance in the evolution of civilization cannot take place until war is abolished."

Among the group I'd invited was World War II veteran Jay Wenk. I'll never forget his words that evening:

> These kinds of quotes, where people like Eisenhower describe what the world loses in humanitarianism, peace, and real issues, what we lose to war supplies, are a lot of baloney. Dwight Eisenhower also said on his last day in office, "Beware of the military-industrial complex." My point is that politicians, which include military people, will say whatever is useful. General Sherman said during the Civil War that war is hell, but it did not stop him from going on to massacre the Indians out West after the Civil War ended. None of these people have ever lifted a finger to do anything about war when they realized that it is horrible.
>
> Someone here said, at the beginning, that we are now at peace. With respect, I beg to differ. We are not at peace. When I was six or seven or eight years old and I first became aware of the world outside of myself and my family and my neighborhood, the Japanese were invading Manchuria. The Spanish Civil War was going on. It wasn't going on in Boston, where I lived at the time, but it was going on. War has been going on all my life and all of your lives. We are not at peace. Nobody is shooting at us right now, but we are enjoying the benefits, the absolute benefits, of the blood and screams and horrors that are being shed in other parts of the world. Absolutely. We are not at peace. We certainly can't be at peace with ourselves.

Several veterans of Vietnam chimed in to agree, and Gerald McCarthy, a professor at St. Thomas Aquinas College, poet, and member of Vietnam Veterans Against the War, elaborated:

> I was asked to go to the dedication services for the Vietnam Veterans Memorial, tricked into it. There's a quote from Joseph Brodsky, the Russian poet: "Let us put up a monument to the lie." I'm not against the design of the Memorial. But I don't think that monument truly does justice to the numbers of people who were killed in Vietnam. I'm not talking about the Americans but the Vietnamese. I don't think it gives us a reason why we were there. It's not the design I'm objecting to, but the fact that there are no words there that tell us why we fought, who sent us, what was going on — which again attests to this history book thing…

When I went to graduate school, people told me not to write about Vietnam. And one of the people I taught with later, at the college, told me my students didn't need to know anything about Malcolm X anymore...I went to the Writers' Workshop at the University of Iowa, which is pretty elite; I didn't realize how elite at the time. But one of the things I was instructed was, "Why not write about earth, fire, water, air?" Obviously I had something else that I had to do first.

Daryll Byrne, a medic in the Persian Gulf ground war, went on to speak about the control of information during Desert Storm and Desert Shield:

We've talked about the press and how they deal with war. In the Persian Gulf, at least where I was stationed, there were no TV cameras, no reporters. So the picture was painted by people who weren't there. What you saw back here was mostly military footage.

When I came back, I was amazed at the videos, the television programs, the magazines with the detailed accounts of everything that had occurred. I learned more about the Persian Gulf War after I came back than when I was there fighting it. When you're at war, you don't get this information. What you get comes from the military, and that information is always tainted.

Philip Caputo, a war correspondent who later became a best-selling novelist, supported the Gulf War but complained nonetheless about what he perceived to be excessive control of the media. Clearly, the military had learned well the lessons of Vietnam, at least as far as "bad press" was concerned: "The Pentagon...censor[ed] the press beyond reasonable need," he wrote. "We see only what it wants us to see, which is a war weirdly sanitized of the pain, fear, and death that are the essence of war."[49]

Retired Army Colonel David Hackworth, the nation's most-decorated living veteran, covered the Gulf War for *Newsweek*. He, too, was displeased and berated his former colleagues for their "paranoia and their thought-police who control the press":

Although I managed to go out on my own, we didn't have the freedom of movement to make an independent assessment of what the military is all about. Everything was spoon-fed. We were like animals in a zoo, and the press officers were the zookeepers who threw us a piece of meat occasionally...I had more guns pointed at me by Americans and Saudis who were into controlling the press than in all my years of actual combat.[50]

Of course, there were plenty of things the Pentagon needed to hide. Not the least of these was the secret exposure of thousands of American troops to new and highly radioactive artillery which was used in the Gulf War for the first time. An extremely dense by-product of the higher-grade material used in nuclear bombs, depleted uranium (DU), soon caused the Gulf War veterans to fall ill by the thousands. Besides being exposed to DU, Gulf War soldiers were given experimental vaccines and drugs to counteract a variety of toxic agents developed for use in chemical warfare.

Paul Sullivan, director of the National Gulf War Resource Center, himself suffering from Gulf War illnesses, offered his perspective in an interview in September 1997:

> For the military to carry out its objective of killing people, it has to have secrets. It has to have secrets about its weapons, secrets about its plans, secrets about its training. And once you have a secret, then you start to lie, because you have to deny the existence of certain things. When people find out about that, then you have to lie again.
>
> We're seeing this very clearly with Gulf War illnesses. The secretary of Defense, the secretary of the Department of Veterans Affairs, and the secretary of the Department of Health and Human Services all lied in testimony in front of Congress and again in letters sent to the veterans. They said that they had conducted a thorough investigation and found that no one, at no time, was ever exposed to any chemicals during the Gulf War. Well, through painstaking research over several years, Gulf War veterans discovered the web of lies. We've found soldiers who received Purple Hearts for being exposed to chemicals during the Gulf War, and in order for them to be exposed, chemicals had to be present, and they had to be released. There is no other explanation. The whole web of lies comes crashing down.
>
> We've also discovered that the Pentagon knew before the war that the chemical detection and protection equipment they gave us was no good. They knew it, and they knowingly sent people into battle without the protection they needed in order to survive. Any reasonable person will conclude that the Pentagon intentionally sacrificed Gulf War veterans, knowingly sending them into a chemical battlefield to die.
>
> Approximately 155,000 veterans of the Gulf War are sick. And the Department of Veterans Affairs refuses to release the number of dead. That, in and of itself, heightens speculation, based on this history of lies. The Department of Veterans Affairs and the Department of Defense are still withholding their information on casualty count. So the war continues.
>
> The Pentagon is not talking; it's denying that anyone was ever exposed. But that's a big lie. They've already admitted (although they had to be dragged kicking and screaming) that during the Reagan and Bush administration, American chemical companies sent all manner of biological and chemical warfare agents, along with "delivery systems," to Iraq.

Paul's assessment is substantiated by thousands of other incidents, including the following letter submitted to the Department of Veterans Affairs by former Army doctor Asaf Durakovic:

Dear President Clinton: February 11, 1997
I am bringing to your attention the conspiracy against the Veterans of the United States.

In the Persian Gulf War some veterans were exposed to radioactive contamination with Depleted Uranium. I personally served in the Operation Desert Shield as a Unit Commander of 531 Army Medical Detachment. After the war I was in charge of Nuclear Medicine Service at Department of Veterans Affairs Medical Center in Wilmington, Delaware. A group of uranium contaminated US Veterans were referred to my attention as an expert in nuclear contamination. I properly referred them for the diagnostic tests to different Institutions dealing with transuranium elements. All of the records have been lost in this Hospital and in referring Institutions. Only a small part of information was recorded in Presidential Advisory Committee report on Gulf War Illnesses. Recently I received an order by the Chief of Staff of this Institution to start the veterans examinations again since all of the records have been lost.

Today I was informed in writing that my job was terminated as a reduction in force. I have been at this position for over eight years with an outstanding job performance and I am convinced with certainty that my elimination from the job is a direct result of my involvement in the management of Gulf War Veterans and discrimination for raising nuclear safety issues.

The lost records, lost laboratory specimens and retaliations which are well documented point to no less than conspiracy to terminate my efforts of proper management of Gulf War Veterans. I am sure that you will have an interest in this matter for the benefit of the veterans of The United States of America.

Most respectfully
(signed)
Asaf Durakovic, M.D., D.V.M., M.Sc., Ph.D., F.A.C.P
Professor of Radiology and Nuclear Medicine
Chief, Nuclear Medicine Service, VAMC Wilmington
Colonel, U.S. Army Medical Corps (R)

■ ■ ■ ■ ■ ■ ■

Of all the evidence of the "hush" enveloping the Persian Gulf War, I find Gulf War veteran Carol Picou's story most damning. Her saga of ongoing suffering is but a microcosm of the selective silence that surrounds every war; to hear and see her pain firsthand gives immediacy to a problem otherwise buried by statistics.

Carol speaks out with all her remaining strength, but there are many thousands like her who suffer quietly, waiting for someone, somehow, to shed light on the "misunderstanding." Carol knows better than to hope for apologies or recompense, but she isn't ready to die either. On a recent speaking tour, she stopped at our Woodcrest community to speak about the war she's still fighting:

> When we arrived in the Gulf, we were given pills, and we were ordered to take them three times a day, every eight hours. They told us it was to protect us in case of chemical warfare. So we took them, and within one hour my muscles started to ache and my eyes began to tear. Very soon my nose was running, and I was drooling and my muscles were twitching.
>
> "Guys," I said, "there's something wrong." But I was ignored. They told us to keep taking them, and each time I did, I had the same symptoms. Finally on the third day I secretly spit my dose into a Pepsi can. And the symptoms disappeared...
>
> Later, at a field hospital, we were told to stand in formation, and we had to take the pills again. By then many of the other soldiers were also complaining of muscle aches and cramps. I refused to take the pills, and when the platoon sergeant noticed, he pressured me, saying that I needed to take the pills "for my own protection."
>
> One hour later, my symptoms were back. I talked to the NBC officer, the nuclear-biological-chemical doctor. "Well," he said, "You just proved that it's peaking and that it's working on your nervous system. Just keep taking it."
>
> We were forced to take this drug for fifteen days, and by the time we finally got word to stop, the war was over. And the damage was already done.
>
> By the time I came back to the United States I was having more problems. I wasn't sweating anymore, I was hoarse, and I was having urinary difficulties. The Army reassured me: it was a change in my diet. I was back in the United States now, and all of this would straighten itself out. But it never did.
>
> Within a month of my return in July 1991 I was incontinent, and I had diarrhea. Then I started to lose my memory – I'd forget to pick up my son after work. In October I had an accident in the doctor's office, and they finally sent me to urology. By January 1992 I was wearing diapers. I wanted to know why. Why was I getting like this? Why was I having these problems? Nobody could answer my questions, so I went public: what's wrong with us soldiers?

It took off from there. I started to do research with a veteran who thought it was depleted uranium, and a researcher at the Library of Congress helped me to write a paper; I was called to testify before Congress the next spring.

I was actually the first active-duty soldier to testify in June of '93. But I didn't go in military uniform. I went on my own, because I didn't want any repercussions. I testified before Congress, and of course no one believed anything. The government said that all of this didn't happen...

Then I started getting phone calls: better be prepared for what's going to happen to you. Vietnam veterans would call and tell me I had no idea of what I was getting into. I got one phone call, and the caller was holding something by his voice to distort the sound: you don't know me, but they're watching you. They know what you're up to. And then he hung up.

The Army also threatened to destroy my career, and they told me I was going to lose my private health insurance and my life insurance. That happened. They discharged me, non-combat-related, with a $20,000 medical bill, and I was really stuck. The insurance people said it was combat-related, and the Army said it was not. And then my insurance company dropped me anyway. My husband lost his job fighting them...

Then we tried the VA hospital, and they said I should be able to get Social Security. But the people at Social Security said I was too young and too educated. I wasn't eligible. Of course I wasn't eligible for unemployment, either. They just pass the buck from one person to another.

My illness has destroyed my life. My son is afraid I'm going to die, because my friends are dying...We used to play ball and ride our bikes together, but I don't anymore, because I get too tired. I can't even go watch him play soccer anymore. I have no feeling from my waist down, and so I soil myself. Then my little boy says, "Mommy, we need to go home." He's been through a lot...

I obtained a document in 1994 that described everything we soldiers had been exposed to: weapons, insecticides, pesticides, anthrax, experimental vaccines, pills. Shortly after receiving the report, we were in conference, on the phone, with a whole network of ex-service people, uranium miners, and Native Americans, talking about what we could do to get this exposed. My husband read the report over the phone and said, "We'll get it in the mail to you on Monday."

I left the house with that report later the same day, and then forgot to bring the papers in from the car. And at 1:45 the next morning I awoke from a sound sleep. Something said, "Carol, wake up and look out the window." I did, and our car was totally engulfed in flames.

I've had the opportunity to go back into Iraq since the war; I spent nine days in the area where we fought. People came from the surrounding villages and brought me their children. I held a three-year-old child who was no bigger than my arm. I held babies that were lifeless...Then I was in Baghdad for three days, in and out of hospitals, meeting people who are affected by depleted uranium. Their babies and their children are dying; their soldiers are dying of strange cancers. That was very hard to see.

At first, I didn't hug those Iraqi children. I didn't embrace them like I would have liked to, because I felt responsible. I had helped to destroy these people. But at the same time I felt I had a responsibility to expose their suffering, to try and help these people.

In the United States we have soldiers dying, too. The brain tumors and the cancers are just amazing: young soldiers, twenty-three, twenty-four years old, with non-Hodgkin's lymphoma. Our babies are being born without arms or legs, missing eyes, missing ears, hearts on the wrong side.

But the Iraqi soldiers and children have identical problems, and they can't even get medicine. They don't have the means to provide even basic supportive care. And I ask myself, "Which is the more barbaric nation?"

An Iraqi colonel I met has the same symptoms I do: the neurological damage, the suppressed immune system, the bone and joint deterioration. He said that out of the twenty-six years that he has served in the Iraqi Army he's never seen a weapon so deadly. Certainly it was a different kind of war, unlike anything anyone's ever seen: the tanks were burned, and all the bodies in and around them were charred, or even melted onto their sides...

Their land is permanently contaminated. When I went back we took Geiger counters, and we climbed into some of the same vehicles that we had destroyed. They were highly radioactive, six years after war. Even animals are being born deformed. We have destroyed their land, their people, their future.

This is where I struggle, because when I joined the military I thought I was just serving my country. At one time I felt proud to be an American – I felt it patriotic to join the military. But the military teaches you to "search and destroy." It is not there to help, to build back up...

It took the Pentagon twenty-two years to listen to the problems of Vietnam veterans, forty-six years to admit to the mustard-agent problems of World War II. And we're in our sixth year with the Persian Gulf. So we just have to keep at it.

Little did Leonard Dietz know, when he came home a scarred veteran of World War II, that he was to become an advocate for veterans of another war nearly fifty years into the future. That chapter of his life would begin when "new" veterans like Carol Picou were still in grade school, learning about democracy and freedom and the "Good War." And, once again, it would be a chapter cloaked in propaganda, secrecy, and deception.

In the fall of 1979, Leonard worked as a nuclear physicist at the Knolls Atomic Power Laboratory in Schenectady, New York, which was operated by the General Electric Company for the Department of Energy. While troubleshooting a problem for GE's radiology group, he and his colleagues accidentally discovered depleted uranium aerosols in environmental air filters at the Knolls site. They traced the source of the uranium contamination to the National Lead Industries plant in Colonie, 10 miles east of the Knolls site, near Albany. At the time, National Lead was fabricating depleted uranium penetrators for 30-mm cannon rounds. Leonard's team also discovered depleted uranium at another site 26 miles north of the National Lead plant, suggesting that the radioactive aerosols were scattered over an area of 2000 square miles. The plant was subsequently shut down by state health officials, but for an unrelated incident: National Lead was exceeding the monthly DEC radioactivity limit, equivalent to only one and a half of the penetrators used in every 30-mm round.

More than a decade later, when word of the military's use of depleted uranium penetrators in the Gulf War began to leak out, Leonard was deeply alarmed. As a physicist, he knew why such deadly material was being used. Uranium metal, when alloyed with titanium, is extremely dense and hard, and the penetrators, which are thin rods of this alloy about two feet long, are pyrophoric. That is, they combust upon impact: Traveling at nearly a mile per second when they strike a tank, they ignite and burn, literally melting through otherwise impenetrable tank armor. The combustion also releases a deadly cloud of aerosolized uranium particles.

This airborne uranium can be taken into the lungs, where the tiny particles enter the bloodstream and migrate to the lymphatic system and virtually everywhere else in the body. And there they stay. Radioactive contamination from depleted uranium aerosols is permanent, and cells surrounding the particles are irradiated for a lifetime, causing cancers, birth defects, and other health problems.

Under the Freedom of Information Act, Leonard was able to obtain a copy of the technical report documenting his findings at GE in 1979 and testified before a House Sub-Committee on Human Resources, chaired by Christopher Shays, on June 26, 1997. In his introductory remarks, he stated:

During four days of ground fighting [in the Persian Gulf War], at least 300 tons of depleted uranium munitions were fired. An Army report describing research on hard target testing states that up to 70 percent of a depleted uranium penetrator can become aerosolized when it strikes a tank. Even if only 2 percent of the uranium burned up, then at least 6 tons of depleted uranium aerosol particles were generated – a huge amount – much of which would have become airborne over the battlefields. This amount in 4 days is more than 10,000 times greater than the maximum airborne emissions of depleted uranium allowed in the air over Albany in one month...

Unprotected U.S. service personnel inhaled and ingested quantities of depleted uranium particles into their lungs and bodies. They were never told about the health dangers of uranium particles and were given no means to protect themselves...After the war, many thousands of service personnel entered Iraqi tanks and armored vehicles that had been destroyed by depleted uranium penetrators, looking for souvenirs. They became contaminated... Twenty-seven soldiers of the 144th Army National Guard and Supply Company worked on and in 29 U.S. combat vehicles that had been hit by "friendly fire" and became contaminated with depleted uranium. They worked for 3 weeks without any protective gear before being informed that the vehicles were contaminated...U.S. troops were exposed to depleted uranium during [an ammunition storage area] fire and subsequent cleanup operations. They wore no protective clothing or masks during or after the fire. Approximately 3500 soldiers were based [there]...

This massive exposure to depleted uranium aerosol particles on the battlefield raises many questions about depleted uranium and how it might have caused at least some of the health problems now being experienced by Gulf War veterans...

It has been reported in *The Nation* that the Department of Veterans Affairs conducted a statewide survey of 251 Gulf War veterans' families in Mississippi. Of their children conceived and born since the war, an astonishing 67 percent have illnesses rated severe or have missing eyes, missing ears, blood infections, respiratory problems, and fused fingers. The causes of these birth defects should be investigated. The human cost of using depleted uranium munitions in conflicts is not worth any short-term advantage if it permanently contaminates the environment and results in irreparable damage to our service personnel and causes genetic defects in their offspring.

Speaking as a World War II veteran, I am troubled about the health of Gulf War veterans and the seeming lack of concern shown by the Department of Veterans Affairs and the Army. They have refused to investigate the role of depleted uranium as a possible cause of Gulf War syndrome.

Leonard visited Woodcrest twice in the fall of 1997. During a visit to our school in November, he gave a talk to the upper classes, telling of his experiences in World War II, providing a crash course in nuclear physics, and explaining the problem of depleted uranium and its probable connection to Gulf War illnesses. Of the latter, he reported:

> Thirty-six thousand Gulf War veterans are suffering from illnesses brought about during their service there, and nobody knows for sure what all the causes are. There's a possible connection with depleted uranium because depleted uranium metal was used in armor-piercing artillery. But the military refuses to acknowledge the dangers of the depleted uranium used in the Gulf.
>
> In June of this year, I was invited to testify before Congress in a discussion on chemical exposure and uranium exposure in the Gulf War. The symptoms that the Gulf War veterans are suffering include chronic fatigue, rashes that come and go for no apparent reason, joint and muscle pain, headaches, memory loss, depression, lack of concentration, stomach problems, and many other maladies. Gulf War syndrome probably results from a combination of exposures, including depleted uranium.
>
> The Committee on Government Reform and Oversight issued a report on the 7th of this month that was entered into the Congressional Record.[51] It's a devastating document, extremely critical of the Department of Defense, and contains the testimony of Gulf War veterans. And it has many more details that I've not seen elsewhere. It paints a totally different picture of what went on in the Gulf War. I genuinely think that the committee did everything it possibly could to bring the truth out on this issue in terms of the illnesses that Gulf War veterans have suffered, and it is a big step forward. It has confronted the highest levels of government for the very first time on this whole issue.

I sat with Leonard after his lecture, and he reflected at greater length on the use of depleted uranium and the ethical issues surrounding it:

> I was surprised to find out that the use of uranium metal in penetrators originated with the Nazis, in World War II. They were trying to develop an atomic weapon before us; they had access to uranium from the Belgian Congo, and they were trying to develop a centrifuge method for separating the isotopes. But they soon realized they were never going to beat us, because they had to keep moving their research sites around. They were being bombed out continually by the Allies. So they thought they might as well use the uranium in cannon projectiles and shoot them at our tanks...
>
> People aren't going to drop dead the day after they're exposed to this. And the military realized that there was no way they could protect the soldiers on

the battlefield; even today they refuse to admit that these particles can travel 26 miles. Fortunately I wrote that internal technical memorandum back in January of 1980, which documents the actual numbers we measured.

I think the military will continue to deny the problem all along. I don't think they're going to change their view. They said so right before Shays' committee. A colonel from the Radio-Biological Research Institute got up and said, "I want to go on record that it is our position that depleted uranium is not dangerous." And he sat down.

To some degree, this kind of deception has been present in all wars, because one of the things the military does not want to do is to make public what's going on in a war while it's actually happening. A lot of information got to the American public during the Vietnam War which the military did not want publicized. But the Gulf War was totally different from all preceding wars in that there was absolute and total censorship of the press, and no reporters were allowed to accompany troops into the field. First time in our history. As a result, the public has been fed a lot of serious misinformation, and it's had an enormous effect.

The Gulf War is not an issue to most people anymore. It's over with. They killed any curiosity early in the game and did not let people in on what was really happening. Otherwise, it would have been a different picture entirely.

I can't imagine a military commander ducking responsibility like the Gulf War commanders did. On an NBC program three years ago, General Calvin Waller, who reported to Schwarzkopf, claimed that neither he nor Schwarzkopf knew anything about the health dangers of depleted uranium. Nobody told them. I find that hard to believe. Waller was being challenged by an NBC reporter with a document from a book called *Uranium Battlefields Home and Abroad*, which said, in effect, "Don't go into tanks that have been hit by depleted uranium munitions. They're radioactive." It gave instructions to troops on how to handle radioactive material, and those instructions came from the Army Chemical Command. And they were deliberately withheld until after the war.

Anybody who goes near Gulf War battlefields from now on risks contamination. Slowly, it'll become integrated in the soil. The uranium particles have a propensity for becoming attached to mineral particles in the soil. But they can become resuspended. Look at the helicopters flying over the battlefield, resuspending all that dust...The military knew that there was no possible way to prevent or clean up contamination on the battlefield, and therefore they decided to do nothing about it.

It's been reported in Iraq that civilians there are showing the same symptoms as Gulf War veterans, and I understand the death rate among children is around five times what it was before the war...

There are many, many first-rate scientists in the government laboratories. But the research is always directed toward a particular objective. I've tried to imagine how it came about that we actually used this deadly stuff in the first place. And I suspect the answer lies in taking the safety issue, for example, and breaking it down into little bits. You look for information that will reinforce your idea, so that you can go ahead and use it. You give it to a scientist, and you limit what he can tell you. It's like a lawyer, exactly analogous to a lawyer in a courtroom, trying to limit what a witness can say regarding a particular case. You're not free to say anything you want to. You might even suspect what the big picture is, and you probably do, because if you didn't you aren't very bright. But you're only asked one very specific thing, and you have to respond to that question only, and that's it. Everything else is extraneous.

I think one of the great fears in the scientific community is that you're going to look foolish if you make a statement and you're later proven to be wrong. I agonized over going public a long time before deciding that I *had* to go public. This was before the war began, based on what I knew about the transport of uranium particles. I was an insider. Yet I wrote this unclassified report, which I was glad to see released under the Freedom of Information Act. It's a smoking gun. I knew that it was an important discovery at the time. What I didn't know exactly was how it fitted in...

People want to forget about the war. Every war is like that. I think it's very important for anybody who's contemplating a military career to look at what's happened to the veterans of past wars. I've been asked, "Which was worse, to drop the atomic bombs or to drop the firebombs?" And I've come to the conclusion that it's a meaningless question. The real question is: What about war itself? I've come to believe, as a person and as a scientist, that war is immoral and cannot be tolerated. We have to eliminate war. If we don't do it, the human race will not survive. That's my conclusion.

As shocking as the stories of Carol Picou and Leonard Dietz are, a much bigger question has yet to be asked: what were Americans doing in Iraq at all, in the first place? Like the travesty of depleted uranium and Gulf War illnesses, the awful answer to this question remains buried by glowing euphemisms and outright lies.

Immediately following the Gulf War, Washington incited the Kurds in the north of Iraq and the Shiites in the south to open rebellion. What is shocking to realize, however, is that President Bush never intended to topple Saddam Hussein's "evil" regime: he sought only to weaken Iraq to protect Western financial interests.[52]

Toward the end of the war, in repeated broadcasts over Saudi radio and the Voice of America, President Bush actively encouraged Iraqi units to revolt, promising U.S. support. But when the mutiny began, U.S. troops immediately withdrew, giving Hussein's elite Republican Guard free reign to crush the opposition. For a brief period, the American coalition stood by as the Guard unleashed helicopter gunships against its own people, killing thousands of Iraqis, including many innocent women and children. Many of those who survived fled to the Iranian border, where they sought asylum in refugee camps that the United Nations later said were worse than any others in the world, including those in Rwanda, Ethiopia, or Vietnam.[53]

■ ■ ■ ■ ■ ■ ■

That this sequence of events really happened can be confirmed by Hassan, a veteran of the Iraqi Army whom I interviewed for this book in December 1997. Hassan joined in the uprisings in 1991 and spent the next five years in Saudi concentration camps before finally emigrating to the United States with the help of UN officials.

> When Iraq entered Kuwait, I was a soldier...Almost all of the young people in my country were in the Army at that time, because we had been at war with Iran for eight years. Most of us never agreed with the invasion of Kuwait, but we were scared to protest. People were forced to fight or die; they didn't have a choice...
>
> I decided not to participate in this war because I felt that, either way, I would die. So in October of 1990, I escaped from the Army and I went to my city. Nearly half of our soldiers escaped and hid with their parents...I stayed with my cousins until six months after the war.
>
> I remember the first day of the bombing. It was January 16, 1991. The Americans attacked Iraq in the night. All you could see was smoke, and all you heard was the noise of the airplanes. First they started with airports, phone centers, media, and communications. My city is a hundred miles south of Baghdad, but the sound of the bombing was loud. Between my city and the capital, there is the biggest arms manufacturer in Iraq. They bombed these places, and it felt like an earthquake.
>
> They continued bombing for fourteen days or more. In two days Iraq lost everything. There was no rescue, no resistance from Iraq against the airplanes, no missiles. After three days, I had to go to the capital because my grandmother forgot her medicine, and I had to go to bring it to her. It was a risk, but I felt I had to do it. I went there, and I found too many missiles

around the capital. It is the truth, I saw them by my eyes. They looked like shining big airplanes or something. They fell on oil companies, and they burned for a whole week.

Everything stopped in my country: no electric, no water, nothing. People depended on what they saved. It's a custom in my country that we say thank God for giving us what we need. We save every month, as a custom. Not like here in the U.S. So people lived on what they saved in their houses.

The only news we could get was from Saudi Arabia. They reported that we were hiding weapons in the schools, so the schools became a target, and they didn't care. They bombed the schools, which are surrounded by houses. Too many houses-full of people were killed for this...

Then the uprising happened. People were very angry. They were dying anyway, so why not try to change the situation? I lived in hell with this government...

You might say the uprising happened by accident. There was no agreement about it beforehand. Everyone felt the same way, so we started to attack government centers. Then President Bush called on the Iraqi people to rebel, and he promised to support us. But then, when we made the uprising, the Americans let the government crush us. We were between two powers. The Americans said, "We support you," and nothing happened. All they did was support the government for no reason. They said they were enemies, but they looked very friendly in that time. They allowed our government to use helicopters, against the United Nations law, to crush the uprising. They said, "Now only helicopters can fly inside Iraq." They played games on the people...

Our government arrested thousands of people from the cities, even if they hadn't participated in the uprising. They took all the young people away in buses and took them to big camps outside the city. They executed them. And the Americans didn't want to help us. They said, "We are against Saddam," but the truth is that they are against the people of Iraq.

In time, Bush would speak of "mistakes" made in the armistice meeting on March 3, 1991, when General Schwarzkopf agreed to let Hussein fly armed helicopters anywhere within his borders, as long as they stayed clear of the American forces. And he would concede that these helicopters were used, along with the few tanks Hussein had left, to crush the rebelling Kurds and Shiites.[54]

But was Bush's silent acquiescence to Hussein's internal reign of terror really a "mistake"? When interviewed by the BBC in 1996, the former President said that capturing or eliminating Hussein was not an option he had ever been willing to contemplate. He claimed that he had stopped the coalition troops short of Baghdad because his main goal was to "end the aggression...[and not] to increase the body count by stacking up...another 50,000 fleeing soldiers, murderous though they had been in Kuwait." He had "miscalculated," and Hussein had "fooled" him; all the same, history would be on his side.

> In retrospect we could have done more...[but] the Allies were right to end the Gulf War when they did...There we would be, in downtown Baghdad, America occupying a foreign land, searching for this brutal dictator who had the best security in the world, involved in an urban guerrilla war. That is not a formula I wanted to contemplate.[55]

What was it, then, that Bush was contemplating? Prior to Operation Desert Storm, he had spent months demonizing Hussein in the media, convincing the American people that such a "brutal dictator" had to go, and railing against his record of human-rights abuses. The President failed to heed the wisdom of Kennedy advisor Arthur Schlesinger, who once remarked that "when lies must be told, they should be told by subordinate officials."[56]

The saga of Desert Storm is one of Orwellian control and deadening apathy, an indictment of the American mind and its willingness to accept anything and everything. As Kentucky farmer and radical political thinker Wendell Berry wrote: "We have made much of Saddam's tyranny, which logically would imply some sympathy for his people, who were the first victims of his tyranny. But we have shown them no sympathy at all."[57] How much truer that statement is today, when U.S. sanctions against Iraq have taken the lives of over one million people, nearly half of them children!

The only conclusion that can be drawn is that our lofty concern for human rights is pure facade. We have punished the people of Iraq for no other reason than to protect our economic interests. Even worse, we have used the Iraqi people as an experiment; we have turned their desert home into a sophisticated, deadly playground. And as Hassan's story suggests, it is a playground for the rich, for those who must play war games with their shiny new toys.

> I think the United States doesn't agree with Saddam Hussein, but they want to keep him in power because if the situation changed in Iraq, they would lose their influence...
>
> Iraq lost everything after the war. Saddam Hussein signed a blank check to give them everything they wanted, so why would they want to replace him? It's a political agenda. Because I would feel bad to treat some animals the way the Iraqi people have been treated. So if the United States is concerned about human rights, they would change what they are doing. Because they know exactly. They know that even if they keep the sanctions going for a long, long time, Saddam will not fall.

Who lost his money, the Iraqi people or Saddam Hussein? Who lost his food? People or Saddam Hussein? Saddam gets goods from Italy and Britain, the best furniture, the best things in the world. His wife is the richest woman in the world. They didn't lose anything. But the people, they lost. They lost before the Gulf War when they fought Iran. They lost after the Gulf War. Somehow I don't think there is anything to do with human rights in this. And the big people in the United States, they know the facts exactly. Do you think there is no light in Saddam's house?

I couldn't stay in Iraq. They took us to the border between Iraq and Saudi Arabia, and they put us in the desert. For six or seven months we were under United Nations jurisdiction. They put us in camps built for prisoners of war, in tents. It looked temporary. There are no cities around, no fresh water, nothing. No utilities. Then after eight months, the United States Army pulled out from Saudi Arabia, and the Saudi Army took us. They thought we were prisoners of war; that we had fought against them. They hated us. I don't know the expression for that kind of hate. And they wanted to kill us, that is the truth. Too many times they attacked us with weapons inside the camps. Some people lost their kidneys because they got shot. Some people got broken legs, hands. It happened too many times.

When the United States Army was still there, they took people from the uprising, who had been shot or injured with chemicals, into their hospitals. They treat us good, I don't deny this because it's the truth. I felt that they gave us the right to talk, to be safe. But then, when they left, people were thrown into the desert for no reason. That's where we lived for five years, and no one talked to us. No health care, no fresh water. People forgot about us…

It was like a fenced farm without trees or animals. They put us there without any utilities. They brought us salty water, which we couldn't drink. Most people had diarrhea for a long, long time from this. When we asked why, they said it's expensive and we are in the desert, so we can't bring these things.

Then, after two more years, the United Nations came to us. I came here, in October of 1995. There are still 4700 refugees of the uprising in the camps…

People here in the United States live very well. There are big problems in the rest of the world, but people here don't know really about them. They judge by their government's opinion or by the media's opinion. And they don't care. It's very busy, and most people try to relax after work. I mean, they just take care of their business.

■ ■ ■ ■ ■ ■ ■

In dealing with a madman, people of common sense try not to provoke him to greater acts of madness. How Saddam's acts of violence were to be satisfactorily limited or controlled by our own acts of greater violence has not been explained…[The Gulf War] was, as any war must be, in part a war against ourselves. Even in winning, we lost. Many of our young people were killed or hurt – though we look on this as a bargain price for the massive slaughter of our enemies. Our war industries are richer, but as a nation we are poorer…It was not just Saddam Hussein's world that we damaged; it was *our* world…

Wendell Berry, Sex, Economy, Freedom and Community

CHAPTER 9

God on Our Side

Here we were not only winning this war, but we were routing the enemy – absolutely routing the enemy – and yet our casualties were practically…nonexistent. You know, that kind of made you feel that God was on your side…

General Schwarzkopf,
commander of the U.S. forces during
the Persian Gulf War, March 1991

From the Crusades to the Gulf War, leaders of both church and state have used God's name to justify the most awful butcheries in world history. There is no more effective catalyst, no finer inspiration in battle, than an appeal to the very Maker of man. When a nation and its armies stand convinced that they are aligned with the divine cause, wavering is banished, and the bloodiest carnage can proceed unhindered.

The invocation of the jihad, the holy war, is a ritual that has been refined through the ages. The Bible's Old Testament is rife with wholesale slaughter in the name of a just and righteous God, carried out at the hands of a people with God on their side. Yet buried deep within the clamor is the disconcerting whisper of God, speaking to King David of all that has gone before: "You have killed too many men in great wars. You have reddened the ground before me with blood: so you are not to build my Temple."[1]

Down to the present day, leaders of church and state alike have ignored this whisper. It is as an aberration, a blip in the stream of consciousness that persistently aligns the Creator with man's destruction of creation. And the notion of killing for God has taken forms that are ever more subtle, more presentable, and perhaps more effective.

As the new year began in 1981, a newly elected President Ronald Reagan stirred the pious emotions of Americans with his first inaugural address:

...No weapon in the arsenals of the world is so formidable as the will and moral courage of free men and women. It is a weapon our adversaries in today's world do not have...Let that be understood by those who practice terrorism and prey upon their neighbors. I am told that tens of thousands of prayer meetings are being held on this day, and for that I am deeply grateful. We are a nation under God, and I believe God intended for us to be free. It would be fitting and good, I think, if each Inauguration Day in future years should be declared a day of prayer.

Just before Reagan took office, a revolution in Nicaragua led by Sandinistas had overthrown the corrupt, U.S.-supported Somoza dynasty. And as the Sandinistas worked to bring land, education, and health care to the country's poor, the Reagan administration manufactured a "communist threat" to justify an attack on the peasants who jeopardized U.S. control.

From bases in Honduras, CIA-backed contras initiated a reign of terror, raiding farms and villages and killing men, women, and children. A former contra, Edgar Chamorro, testified before the World Court that "civilians were killed in cold blood. Many others were tortured, mutilated, raped, robbed, or otherwise abused...When I agreed to join...I had hoped that it would be an organization of Nicaraguans...[It] turned out to be an instrument of the U.S. government..."[2]

In 1980, a technician overseeing U.S.-sponsored "agrarian reform" in El Salvador reported: "The troops came and told the peasants the land was theirs now. They could elect their own leaders and run it themselves. The peasants couldn't believe their ears, but they held elections that very night. The next morning the troops came back, and I watched as they shot every one of the elected leaders."[3]

In Central America and the Caribbean, U.S. invasions were justified on the basis of protecting citizens, but when four church women were killed by government-sponsored death squads in El Salvador in 1980, nothing happened. To the contrary, military aid to the government, including the training of death squads, went on unabated.[4]

When Salvadoran Archbishop Oscar Romero was assassinated only months after asking President Carter for a cessation of military aid to El Salvador, Congress was "sufficiently embarrassed...to require that before any more aid was given the President must certify that progress in human rights was taking place." Such legislation did nothing to stop Carter's successor, Reagan, who vetoed it as soon as it was passed.[5]

The incessant violence and destruction at the hands of the United States did not diminish Ronald Reagan's religious fervor. At the start of his second term, in his 1985 inaugural address, he once again whitewashed his administration's exploits in Central America with lavish appeals to God:

Today, we utter no prayer more fervently than the ancient prayer for peace on earth. Yet history has shown that peace will not come, nor will our freedom be preserved, by goodwill alone...We have made progress in restoring our defense capability. But much remains to be done. There must be no wavering by us, nor any doubts by others, that America will meet her responsibilities to remain free, secûre, and at peace...

We strive for peace and security, heartened by the changes all around us. Since the turn of the century, the number of democracies in the world has grown fourfold. Human freedom is on the march, and nowhere more so than in our own hemisphere. Freedom is one of the deepest and noblest aspirations of the human spirit...

Every blow we inflict against poverty will be a blow against its dark allies of oppression and war. Every victory for human freedom will be a victory for world peace...We think of those who traveled before us...and the song echoes out forever and fills the unknowing air. It is the American sound. It is hopeful, bighearted, idealistic, daring, decent, and fair. That's our heritage; that is our song. We sing it still. For all our problems, our differences, we are together as of old, as we raise our voices to the God who is the Author of this most tender music.

And may he continue to hold us close as we fill the world with our sound – sound in unity, affection, and love – one people under God, dedicated to the dream of freedom that he has placed in the human heart, called upon now to pass that dream on to a waiting and hopeful world. God bless you, and may God bless America.

Like Reagan before him, George Bush understood well the tremendous weight that "God-inspired" intervention carried with the American people. In his inaugural address in January of 1989, the ex-CIA head glowed piously:

My first act as President is a prayer. I ask you to bow your heads. Heavenly Father...write on our hearts these words: "Use power to help people." For we are given power not to advance our own purposes, nor to make a great show in the world, nor a name. There is but one just use of power, and it is to serve people. Help us to remember it, Lord. Amen...

America today is a proud, free nation, decent and civil, a place we cannot help but love. We know in our hearts, not loudly and proudly, but as a simple fact, that this country has meaning beyond what we see, and that our strength is a force for good...What do we want the men and women who work with us to say when we are no longer there? That we were more driven to succeed than anyone around us? Or that we stopped to ask if a sick child had gotten better, and stayed a moment there to trade a word of friendship?...America is never wholly herself unless she is engaged in high moral principle. We as a people have such a purpose today.

That such sentiments swayed the hearts of the religious establishment is certain; that Bush used his power to "help people" is not. I will never forget seeing the 1992 Academy Award-winning documentary, *The Panama Deception*, in a nineteenth-century movie house in the small town of Redhook, New York. I watched, unbelieving, as smuggled footage of the actual U.S. invasion of Panama was dubbed over glowing clips of U.S. government officials praising the "surgical" nature of Bush's crusade to capture Noriega.

Whole residential areas of Panama City were aflame. In a brutally enforced media blackout, a journalist was shot by U.S. forces when he stepped over the tape around the "no see" zone. U.S. Marines dragged screaming Panamanian citizens out of their houses, laid them face down in the street and shot them in cold blood. And in the aftermath of the invasion, which the U.S. government official claimed had taken the lives of only a very few civilians, Panamanian workers were shown uncovering mass graves of executed citizens. A number of corpses had holes burned through their bodies – caused, according to the testimony of eyewitnesses, by experimental laser weaponry.

It was impossible to watch such a documentary and not arrive at the conclusion that the highly publicized hunt for Noriega was nothing more than a smoke screen, a cover-up of a blow to the Panamanian Defense Forces protecting the canal* and an opportunity to exercise American troops with the latest military weaponry on innocent civilians.

Apparently troubled by his somewhat messy "victory" in Panama, Bush proceeded to lead America into yet another massacre – this time of hundreds of thousands of Iraqis in the Persian Gulf War. "This will not be another Vietnam," he assured the American people shortly before the attack. "Our troops will have the best possible support in the entire world. They will not be asked to fight with one hand tied behind their back." In other words, the U.S. military would be free to unleash its full firepower against a vastly inferior nation without political constraint; they would be free to "let the Iraqis have it." They did.

In October of 1992, George Bush sermonized once again on the divine sanction of American endeavors: "We believe in…the Judeo-Christian heritage that informs our culture…[We must] advocate the recitation of the Pledge of Allegiance as a reminder of the principles that sustain us as one nation under God."

---

* The Panamanian Defense Forces was one of the primary targets of the invasion. The Canal Treaty signed by President Carter and General Torrijos states that in order for the canal to return to Panama in 1999, Panama must have the means to protect it. Following the invasion, Panama amended its constitution to abolish the P.D.F.

As shocking as these words may seem, their spirit is not new. Every war in this century has been defended in no less scandalous a fashion, and with similar appeals to duty and moral conviction. Each time, thousands of young men have responded, many recognizing too late the hypocrisy that would be inherent in a God who blesses war.

■ ■ ■ ■ ■ ■ ■

Father George Zabelka, a Catholic chaplain with the U.S. Army Air Force, was stationed on Tinian Island in the South Pacific in August of 1945. Zabelka served as a priest for the airmen who dropped the atomic bombs on Hiroshima and Nagasaki, and his long and painful inward journey began when he counseled an airman who had flown a low-level reconnaissance flight over the city of Nagasaki shortly after the detonation of "Fat Man."

Not much could be seen from bombing altitude, but a low run directly above the city revealed a scene out of Dante's *Inferno*. Thousands of scorched, twisted bodies writhed on the ground in the final throes of death, while those still on their feet wandered aimlessly in shock — flesh seared, melted, and falling off — like the walking dead. The crewman's description raised a stifled cry from the depths of Zabelka's soul: "My God, what have we done?" And over the next twenty years, he gradually came to believe that he had been terribly wrong, that he had denied the very foundations of his faith by lending moral and religious support to the men who had wreaked such hellish destruction.

When asked if he had known that civilians were being destroyed by the thousands in air raids, long before the atomic bombing, he replied:

Oh, indeed I did know, and I knew with a clarity that few others could have had...

The destruction of civilians in war was always forbidden by the church, and if a soldier came to me and asked if he could put a bullet through a child's head, I would have told him, absolutely not. That would be mortally sinful. But in 1945 Tinian Island was the largest airfield in the world. Three planes a minute could take off from it around the clock. Many of these planes went to Japan with the express purpose of killing not one child or one civilian but of slaughtering hundreds and thousands and tens of thousands of children and civilians — and I said nothing...

I never preached a single sermon against killing civilians to the men who were doing it...I was brainwashed! It never entered my mind to protest publicly the consequences of these massive air raids. I was told it was necessary — told openly by the military and told implicitly by my church's leadership. To the best of my knowledge no American cardinals or bishops were opposing these mass air raids. Silence in such matters, especially by a public body like the American bishops, is a stamp of approval.[6]

How did Zabelka come to change his views so radically? At a 1985 Pax Christi conference, he told his story in words filled with urgency and power:

I worked with Martin Luther King, Jr. during the Civil Rights struggle in Flint, Michigan. His example and his words of nonviolent action, choosing love instead of hate, truth instead of lies, and nonviolence instead of violence stirred me deeply. This brought me face to face with pacifism...active non-violent resistance to evil. I recall his words after he was jailed in Montgomery, and this blew my mind. He said, "Blood may flow in the streets of Montgomery before we gain our freedom, but it must be our blood that flows, and not that of the white man. We must not harm a single hair on the head of our white brothers..." I struggled. I argued. But yes, there it was in the Sermon on the Mount, very clear: "Love your enemies. Return good for evil." I went through a crisis of faith – a crisis of faith, not a crisis of priesthood; that's simple! A crisis of faith. Either accept what Christ said, as unpassable and silly as it may seem, or deny him completely...

For the last 1700 years the church has not only been making war respectable: it has been inducing people to believe it is an honorable profession, an honorable *Christian* profession. This is not true. We have been brainwashed. This is a lie...

War is now, always has been, and always will be bad, bad news. I was there. I saw real war. Those who have seen real war will bear me out. I assure you, it is not of Christ. It is not Christ's way. There is no way to conduct real war in conformity with the teachings of Jesus. There is no way to train people for real war in conformity with the teachings of Jesus.

The morality of the balance of terrorism is a morality that Christ never taught. The ethics of mass butchery cannot be found in the teachings of Jesus. In Just War ethics, Jesus Christ, who is supposed to be all in the Christian life, is irrelevant. He might as well never have existed. In Just War ethics, no appeal is made to him or his teaching, because no appeal can be made to him or his teaching, for neither he nor his teaching gives standards for Christians to follow in order to determine what level of slaughter is acceptable.

So the world is watching today. Ethical hairsplitting over the morality of various types of instruments and structures of mass slaughter is not what the world needs from the church, although it is what the world has come to expect from the followers of Christ. What the world needs is a grouping of Christians that will stand up and pay up with Jesus Christ. What the world needs is Christians who, in language that the simplest soul could understand, will proclaim: the follower of Christ cannot participate in mass slaughter. He or she must love as Christ loved, live as Christ lived and, if necessary, die as Christ died, loving ones enemies…When Christ disarmed Peter he disarmed all Christians…[7]

Zabelka died in 1992, without many Americans ever hearing his extraordinary story. But in reflections confided to at least a few listening ears, he unmasked the moral and religious hypocrisy of the atomic bombings with unparalleled conviction. He spent his last years elaborating on the absolute incompatibility between the teachings of war and the teachings of Christ.

■ ■ ■ ■ ■ ■ ■

Richard McSorely, like George Zabelka, had his eyes opened after World War II, when he was first confronted by the problem of racism and its strong connection to war. A Jesuit priest and cofounder of the pacifist group Pax Christi USA, this 83-year-old Georgetown University professor clarified his position against war early on in his tenure at Georgetown, and the antiwar classes he organized were well attended, even if frowned on by university officials. Back then, they were an administrative embarrassment; now, they are a showpiece. McSorely knew the Kennedy family well and was a personal tutor of both John and Bobby's children. He watched movies in the White House with the President and recalls taking "John-John" for walks in Central Park after the President's 1963 assassination. During the Vietnam War, he rallied with the likes of historian Howard Zinn, and did jail time in the same cell as famed baby doctor Benjamin Spock.

But how did he arrive at his pacifist beliefs? As we sat together in a small living room at Georgetown's Jesuit community, he related his story:

> I was a prisoner of war during World War II for three years and three months. At the time, the evil of war didn't impress me very much. I was suffering, but I didn't see it in moral terms. When I came back to the States I was appointed pastor of a small parish in southern Maryland, about seventy-five miles south of Washington. It was really out in the country. And it was very racist. The blacks sat on a separate side of the church and received Holy Communion after the whites. Everything was segregated. I had never talked to a black person at all except in an elevator…
>
> It was a rather poor church and small too, with room for no more than fifty or sixty people. We had to heat it with a woodstove, and before the service one day a black man came up to me and said, "Father, I'll help you. I know how to

make a fire." So he made the fire, and I prepared for mass. After mass I called him back into the sacristy behind the church. I said, "Mr. Butler" — and I remember feeling very proud of myself for using the "mister" because black people down there were usually called "boy" or worse — "Thank you for making the fire. I wonder if you could help next Sunday." He said he would, and I offered to pay him if he would do it regularly. I said, "Well, how much do you make in your regular job?" He said, "I drives a truck for the Navy, and I makes 94 cents an hour." I said, "Well, suppose I pay you a dollar an hour." I thought I was being very generous. He said, "You can't pay me. I'se doin' this for Gawd." I felt like somebody had slapped me in the face. But then I asked myself, "Why am I treating him this way? I would never treat a white person this way!" I realized then that I was racist myself.

A little while later I was at the home of a white family. We were talking about the Indians. There was a local tribe that had just been celebrating their history, and I said, "You know, it seems to me that we treated the Indians the way we treat the Negroes today." The lady of the house said, "You better be careful, Father. You'll get the reputation of being a nigger lover." She put her hand over her mouth. I was annoyed by that, and I said, "Well, Mrs. McCoy, I don't deserve to be a nigger lover, because that's what Christ was." She looked at her husband, her husband looked back at her, silent. And I said, "Well, I guess we're running out of conversation. It's time to go." They walked me down the steps, and I got into my car. Then the man of the house came up to my open window and said, "Well, Father, just put it down to the fact that we're dumb Southerners. We don't know no more. Don't know no better." He wanted me to say, "Oh, forget about it." But I answered, "Okay, Fred, you're dumb Southerners and you don't know no better. Good night." I knew that this would spread all over town, because I was a new priest and they wanted to feel me out on the racial issue. I had taken a stand without even trying, and that was only the beginning.

Well, I was removed from that church because of my feelings about race and justice. I didn't know it that at the time, but I was removed by the bishop. But I knew there would be a price to pay for taking a stand. At the same time, Martin Luther King and Dan Berrigan and Phil Berrigan were getting arrested and risking their lives for their faith. And then in 1964, Martin Luther King said in New York that he opposed the Vietnam War. He gave a great talk about the relationship between war and racism — how they're blood brothers and work on the same theology, the same false reasoning. King said he couldn't oppose racism but then stop at the three-mile limit. So I thought, he represents people that are clearly the Christ-figures of our time. And I'd better be opposing this war too — at least, I have to look into it.

By that time I was teaching in Georgetown, and I gave my first talk against the war. Some of the students walked out, walked right out of the chapel. And they wrote something in the school paper about it. So I answered their letter, and we had quite a dialogue about it. I had begun to read Gandhi, and I found a book on the gospel and war that helped me, too. So I began to speak out clearly, and it brought all kinds of results, just as my stand on racism had.

Martin Luther King was a great example, because I knew from my own experience that he was going to lose support, lose money. His own followers told him not to take a stand against the war – he'd lose too much money and political support. But he said, "I can't be against something because it's wrong and then just stop because it's beyond the twelve-mile limit." So he lost a lot. He suffered a lot and was finally killed for his stand.

There were many offshoots. I started to counsel students who wanted to file for status as conscientious objectors, and I preached and I talked and I wrote three or four books. Once, they had a meeting here at the university of 225 Catholic chaplains, in uniform, and the bishop was the head of the military diocese. He gave a talk on the just-war theory. I don't remember exactly what all he said, but when he was done the floor was opened for questions. So I got up; I had my clerical dress on, and I said, "Now everybody in this auditorium is either a Catholic priest or a Catholic bishop. So I'm sure that Jesus is a very important person in your lives. So my question is: 'Was Jesus a pacifist?'" And they all just burst out laughing, on the stage and in the audience. A panel member on the stage said, "That's a very tough question." But they were going to let it just pass by. I had a friend there who had been a conscientious objector in World War II, and he got up and said, "Yes, Christ was a pacifist." He gave examples from the Bible, and things got very quiet. But nobody else was willing to say anything about Christ being a pacifist. And I'm convinced it is the gospel – Jesus *was* a pacifist.

Another time I was sitting at breakfast in the dining room and a priest, very friendly and much older than I, came over and said, "Dick, why do you oppose the military on campus?" I said, "Well, I oppose them because I think Christ would oppose them." He said, "You're saying that Christ was a pacifist?" I said, "I haven't been saying that, but he was." He threw up his hands: "You're impossible!" There just isn't a decent argument that can show Christ to be a militarist of any kind. So when you bring Christ into it, with a priest or anybody who is supposed to have a sense of who Christ was, there is no debate, no discussion.

The trouble is that the church gives a false image of Christ. The church never says that war is good and Christ is a war-maker. They never do that. But they don't say anything. What's behind it is that the church wants to benefit from the state – tax exemption is the bribe for silence. So you have a kind of dance of death going on between the church and the state. They don't step on each other's toes. The state wants background support from the churches: "God bless your wars. God be with you." It all started with the emperor of Rome giving buildings to the church in the third century under Constantine. The church has never recovered...

Once, I gave a talk on the primacy of conscience. I said that the conscience has to be followed; it is the voice of God speaking directly into the heart, and because it hasn't gone through the church or any other authority first – because it's direct to you – it's your obligation to follow it. A gentleman got up, and he said, "I came here thinking this was a Catholic group, and I find my own church being criticized." I said, "Your church isn't being criticized. Your church is being praised – the church has always taught the primacy of conscience. It just never respects it."

Unfortunately, history bears out this assertion. Not only has the institutional church buckled under pressure from the state in time of war, leaving warriors of conscience high and dry, but it has also changed colors like a chameleon, unwilling to stand firm on any point or honestly face its own past. Father McSorely, for example, received precious little support from his colleagues during Vietnam, but today he is famous on the Georgetown University campus, so much so that a large portrait of him hangs in the cafeteria.

■ ■ ■ ■ ■ ■ ■

The churches of America are not alone in this guilt. Maureen Burn, whose husband Matthew fought in World War I, remembers well how the British newspaper editors and clergy alike exhorted the masses to join in the "war to end war."

Matthew was an Anglican choirboy in 1914, but he ran away from school and enlisted. His parents went to fetch him because he was not yet of age, but were dissuaded by an officer who told them, "With your boy, this war is a holy crusade. He will just run away again."

Soon Matthew was in France, where he experienced the full horrors of trench warfare; he came home a changed and bitter man. Recently, Maureen told me:

> Matthew declared he was not going to do a thing for a rotten society, where even the clergy preached war to their young people. He said he would just be a tramp and wander from one poorhouse to another when it was too cold to sleep outdoors.

But his older sister, who was a dedicated nurse, told him, "You are a victim of this rotten society, but what good could you do for other victims of this rotten society if you were just a tramp? It would be quite a different thing if you would study to be a doctor." That convinced him. He went to Edinburgh University, and after finishing the basic course went on to study tropical medicine.

I remember a walk with Matthew that changed my outlook on life. He asked me about my father, and when I told him Father had been a clergyman and a missionary, he said, "The clergy are just parasites. They should do a hard day's work." I was shocked. I asked him why he said this, and he said that the clergy had conscripted all his friends and they had all been killed. Then he said the only time he had ever seen the Christian spirit was in the frontline trenches, when the crudest Tommy would give his last crust to a dying companion. "But," he added, "that spirit never lasted behind the lines, when the fellows got into safety."

I left the church when I realized that it went along with war. I wanted to join the Quakers, the only historical peace church in Britain, but Matthew said, "The Quakers are just the Red Cross behind the capitalist firing lines!" He explained that the Quakers were the first bankers, and their banks were heavily involved in big business and war. So I didn't join them, although I attended their meetings.

I threw myself into the peace movement, but Matthew, who was more of a realist than I was, was quite skeptical about it. He had always wanted to go to Germany and meet Germans who had been in the front line, but he knew no German. I had studied German in school, so we took a walking tour of the Black Forest, putting up in the little village inns where the local people came in for a drink of wine in the evenings. He could spot an ex-frontline man, and he would ask me to tell this or that man that he recognized him as such. Then he would offer him a drink. At first the German would be a bit taken aback, but then he would become friendly when he realized that Matthew had been through the same experience and hated war. They always ended up saying, *"Krieg ist Wahnsinn"* (war is madness).

On Armistice Day he always disappeared. I don't know where he went. He thought it an insult to the dead to have a big military parade at the cenotaph where the Unknown Soldier was buried…

■ ■ ■ ■ ■ ■ ■

Eberhard Arnold, a German pastor and theologian, also blessed his country's war efforts. A convinced young Christian from an intellectual, upper middle-class home, he received a doctoral degree in philosophy from Erlangen in 1909, and soon he defied his family's social and academic standing by immersing himself in social issues, such as the plight of the poor, and in saving souls for Christ. By 1920 he had become an avowed pacifist, unable to reconcile a soldier's duty with the demands of the gospel. But in 1914, when the war first broke out, he had reported eagerly for duty.

Though soon discharged for health reasons, Arnold felt that the war had a divine import: it was a call to a deeper Christianity. In 1915 he joined the Relief Action Committee for Prisoners of War, which provided encouraging literary material to prisoners of war and to wounded soldiers in military hospitals. In an article he wrote:

> We are living in a tremendous time, and we cannot be thankful enough for what God has brought about by enthusing men for the fatherland and by lifting men's hearts up to God. A love has arisen in our nation that does not move in sweetly sentimental ways, but rather gives itself essentially in strength. It is a love shown in action, ready to sacrifice itself where so much has been given, a love that lays down its life on the altar of the fatherland, for the emperor, for relatives, and compatriots...
>
> In this war, too, everything depends on love remaining in us, for it is love that impels us to give our lives for our brothers. The soldiers who know that Jesus died for them will show the greatest endurance. They will most confidently and serenely risk their lives for their brothers. There is no holier incentive for a soldier than this fact: Jesus died for me, therefore I owe it to give my life, too. Our nation will be victorious if the roots of our strength lie not in hatred but in love, if we have the impulse of love for our enemies.
>
> At present the soldiers have to overcome the lies with fire and the sword, but the driving power of our military action has to be the well-tried German love; more than that, it has to be the love of Jesus, which wants to include the love for England, for the peoples under England's yoke, and for all nations groaning for love...[8]

As the war dragged on, however, Arnold's convictions were increasingly challenged by the suffering he saw around him:

> If anyone had an eye for the suffering of the people in the city, how grieved his soul would be, seeing the terrible suffering caused by misled longing and exploited nostalgia! It is deplorable how many souls are stripped of their innocence, as when the bloom is brushed from a butterfly's wings. Oh, what sorrow grips us at the sight of such deluded yearning. But we can offer a hope to all men, even to those most deeply wounded, to every disappointed soul; the hope that all who have been disappointed by false love can find true love.[9]

By 1917, his tone had changed completely. No longer did he speak of a "well-tried German love," but rather of the evil that had wrought such protracted, senseless carnage:

> These years we are living in have shown more and more what power hatred has among men and in what a frightening way the love of men is destroyed by wickedness and lawlessness; how men's fury, goaded on by the lawless acts of some other faction, drives them to fanatical extremes of hatred. I will not recall how the nations work themselves up to strangle each other, and the classes within nations in turn work each other up to hate and murder one another; how lawlessness among the social classes keeps fanning the hatred to a blazing fire so that no one can tell how horrible the end will be. Yes, war reveals the evil of hatred and murder and lawlessness – the evil of love grown cold.[10]

The war finally over, Arnold went through a period of deep soul-searching to find what God really demanded of him as a Christian. His previous belief in a "personal" Christianity, focused on saving souls amidst the upheaval of world events, seemed empty, inadequate. He wrote:

> We saw the condition of the men who came home. One young officer came back with both his legs shot off. He came back to his fiancée, hoping to receive the loving care he needed so badly from her, and she informed him that she had become engaged to a man who had a healthy body.
>
> Then the time of hunger came to Berlin. People ate turnips morning, noon, and evening...I saw a horse fall in the street; the driver was knocked aside by the starving people who rushed in to cut pieces of the meat from the still warm and steaming body so that they would have something to take home to their wives and children...
>
> After such experiences and after the enormous revolutionary changes, which resulted in turning elegant apartments with parquet floors and huge reception rooms over to working-class families, I realized that the whole situation was unbearable. I was told...that a high state official demanded of me that I should be silent about the social problems, about the war, and about the suffering that cried out to heaven...[11]

By now convinced that war, in any form and for any reason, was utterly wrong, Arnold felt led to abandon not only war, but the whole social and economic order that brought it about:

> Jesus gives an absolute mandate never to resist the power of evil. Only thus can evil be turned to good. He prefers to be struck twice rather than to counter with even one blow...Love does not take the slightest part in hostilities, strife, or war, nor can it ever return curses and hate, hurt and enmity...Love is not influ-

enced by any hostile power. No change of circumstance can change the attitude of Jesus and his followers; he does nothing but love, make peace, wish and ask for good, and work good deeds. Where the peace of Jesus dwells, war dies out, weapons are melted down, and hostility vanishes. Love has become boundless in Jesus; it has achieved absolute sovereignty.[12]

■ ■ ■ ■ ■ ■ ■

Like Eberhard Arnold, Adolf Braun was called up for duty when the war broke out in 1914. The son of a Baptist minister, he had entered the military service in 1913 and was a member of the Prussian Garde Artillery Regiment in Spandau, Berlin. He was one of thousands of German soldiers gripped by a sense of "sacred duty to defend the fatherland," and he and his comrades left their hometowns amidst enthusiastic singing, the strewing of flowers, flag-waving by families and friends. Churchmen prayed for victory and for the safe return of soldiers. Adolf was ebullient: "With God, for king and fatherland!"

He fought on both fronts, in France and Russia, where he became known for his valor in jumping out of trenches to throw hand grenades at the enemy, which resulted in his being wounded several times. Then in July 1915 he was injured by shrapnel that entered his head behind the ear.

He was in critical condition for weeks and remained hospitalized for five months. But in February 1917 the Army was desperate for soldiers – even wounded ones – and Adolf was drafted a second time. He was sent again to France, for a final desperate effort in a war that was by then clearly lost.

It was in this last wrenching year that Adolf was profoundly affected by the insanity of it all. Once, when stationed with his men in the woods, he looked down through the fog and smoke to see a French observer in another tree, not far away. Bullets whistled around him in the cold rain, and he thought of home, where his bride and loved ones were surely praying for him. Then he looked over at the Frenchman and wondered, "Are his loved ones praying for him, too?" He was shaken by this thought and decided that if he ever got out alive, his life would be very different. The losses during this battle were particularly heavy, and when he came down from his post in the tree, he found that of his entire company he was the only one left alive.

One night his men were ordered to attack a company of French soldiers camped in a small grove of trees. It was to be a surprise attack, and in order not to wake the French, no shot was to be fired: they would engage only in hand-to-hand bayonet fighting. When it was over, the men were so exhausted that they fell asleep right next to the cannons. But Adolf and a comrade were awakened by moaning, and after following the sound they found a young French officer crying in pain. Adolf bent over to console him, but the Frenchman pointed weakly to his pack. In it was a bloodstained Bible and a photograph of his family.

As Adolf read to the dying man from the Bible, he was suddenly overcome by the madness of the whole situation: here he was, trying to comfort a man he had ordered his men to kill! Before dying, the enemy soldier gave Adolf his Bible and begged him to notify his wife of his death.

When Adolf returned home, he was unable to settle down into the comfortable existence of a "normal" life. He was offered promotion to officer's rank, an honor to be bestowed by the Kaiser himself, but he refused; had it not been for his good connections, that snubbing that could have cost him his life. The war left Adolf shattered. He was determined to see that there would never be war again. His war bride, Martha, felt as he did, and together they sought a way of life that would be completely different from the one that had led them and their countrymen to war.

Adolf and Martha began to reach out, helping to alleviate the tremendous need they saw all around them. Adolf began visiting men in prison, assisting their families with packages of food and clothing. He spoke out against the war with a candor grounded in his own experiences and argued that talk of a "hero's death for the fatherland" was meaningless and hypocritical. All this earned him more than a few enemies, and his friends worried for his safety and even his life.

Eventually, his search for peace and social justice led him toward Christian community as described in the Book of Acts: community devoid of rich and poor, where the needs of each member are cared for by all. Years later, after being driven from Germany by the Nazis and forced to emigrate to Paraguay, Adolf wrote to his family back home:

> You will perhaps recall how in 1914, as a young Christian patriot, I went into battle "with God for king and fatherland." But like hundreds of thousands of my compatriots, I had no inkling of the powers that dictate world events and manipulate things for their own interests; how the nations are played off, one against the other; how poets — surely in poetic blindness — make brutality appealing; how the representatives of almost every religion bless weapons with their false intercessions and their propaganda for a "Christian" state — something that cannot be; how on both sides soldiers are consecrated for a sacrifice that is completely misunderstood. And finally, how the holy sacrificial death of Jesus is compared – even equated – with the sacrifice of soldiers, although in reality none of them is ready to sacrifice *himself*, but only the life of the enemy...
>
> Your letter was the first sign of life after the dreadful time that should now lie behind us, if men only knew how to make true peace! But that is of course

impossible, as long as we do not courageously face up to the real motives that
lead to war; impossible, when even in times of so-called peace everyone is
battling everyone else; impossible, as long as stubbornness, selfishness, and
private property are protected and supported by Christian morality...[13]

■ ■ ■ ■ ■ ■ ■

Soldiers like Adolf were not the only ones to indict the church for its support
of the Great War – in fact, some of its sharpest condemners were found among
the clergy themselves. In this regard, few public addresses surpass that of Harry
Emerson Fosdick, an American military chaplain who on November 12, 1933,
delivered a sermon entitled "The Unknown Soldier," a speech later printed in
the U.S. Congressional Record:

> You may not say that I, being a Christian minister, did not know [the Un-
> known Soldier]. I knew him well. From the north of Scotland, where they
> planted the sea with mines, to the trenches of France, I lived with him and his
> fellows – British, Australian, New Zealander, French, American. The places
> where he fought, from Ypres through the Somme battlefield to the southern
> trenches, I saw while he still was there. I lived with him in dugouts, in the
> trenches, and on destroyers searching for submarines off the shores of
> France. Short of actual battle, from training camp to hospital, from fleet to
> no-man's-land, I, a Christian minister, saw the war. Moreover, I, a Christian
> minister, participated in it. I, too, was persuaded that it was a war to end war.
> I, too, was a gullible fool and thought that modern war could somehow make
> the world safe for democracy. They sent men like me to explain to the Army
> the high meanings of war and, by every argument we could command, to
> strengthen their morale. I wonder if I ever spoke to the Unknown Soldier.
>
> One night, in a ruined barn behind the lines, I spoke at sunset to a com-
> pany of hand-grenaders who were going out that night to raid the German
> trenches. They told me that on the average no more than half a company
> came back from such a raid, and I, a minister of Christ, tried to nerve them
> for their suicidal and murderous endeavor. I wonder if the Unknown Soldier
> was in that barn that night...
>
> You here this morning may listen to the rest of this sermon or not – as
> you please. It makes much less difference to me than usual what you do or
> think. I have an account to settle in this pulpit today between my soul and the
> Unknown Soldier.
>
> He is not so utterly unknown as we sometimes think. Of one thing we can
> be certain: he was sound of mind and body. We made sure of that. All primi-
> tive gods who demanded bloody sacrifices on their altars insisted that the

animals should be of the best, without mar or hurt. Turn to the Old Testament and you find it written there: "Whether male or female, he shall offer it without blemish before Jehovah." The god of war still maintains the old demand. These men to be sacrificed upon his altars were sound and strong. Once there might have been guessing about that. Not now. Now we have medical science, which tests the prospective soldier's body. Now we have psychiatry, which tests his mind. We used them both to make sure that these sacrifices for the god of war were without blemish. Of all insane and suicidal procedures, can you imagine anything madder than this, that all the nations should pick out their best, use their scientific skill to make certain that they are the best, and then in one mighty holocaust offer 10,000,000 of them on the battlefields of one war?

I have an account to settle between my soul and the Unknown Soldier. I deceived him. I deceived myself first, unwittingly, and then I deceived him, assuring him that good consequence could come out of that. As a matter of hard-headed, biological fact, what good can come out of that? Mad civilization, you cannot sacrifice on bloody altars the best of your breed and expect anything to compensate for that...

When you stand in Arlington before the tomb of the Unknown Soldier on some occasion, let us say, when the panoply of military glory decks it with music and color, are you thrilled? I am not – not anymore. I see there the memorial of one of the saddest things in American history – from the continued repetition of which may God deliver us! – the conscripted boy...

If I blame anybody about this matter, it is men like myself, who ought to have known better...

The glory of war comes from poets, preachers, orators, the writers of martial music, statesmen preparing flowery proclamations for the people, who dress up war for other men to fight. They do not go to the trenches. They do not go over the top again and again and again...

I will myself do the best I can to settle my account with the Unknown Soldier. I renounce war. I renounce war because of what it does to our own men. I have watched them coming gassed from the frontline trenches. I have seen the long, long hospital trains filled with their mutilated bodies. I have heard the cries of the crazed and the prayers of those who wanted to die and could not, and I remember the maimed and ruined men for whom the war is not yet over. I renounce war because of what it compels us to do to our enemies, bombing their mothers in villages, starving their children by blockades, laughing over our coffee cups about every damnable thing we have been able to do to them. I renounce war for its consequences, for the lies it lives on and propagates, for the undying hatreds it arouses, for the dictatorships it puts in the place of democracy, for the starvation that stalks after it. I renounce war, and never again, directly or indirectly, will I sanction or support another...[14]

■ ■ ■ ■ ■ ■ ■

The stand of American churches in regard to the Vietnam War was hauntingly familiar. As in the past, there were churches that protested the war, but for the most part, institutional religion once again repeated its practiced dance with governmental might, solemnly acceding to carnage in the name of democracy. Jerry Voll, a Bruderhof member who served as a minister in Lancaster, Pennsylvania, during the late 1960s, remembers:

> The Franklin and Marshall campus was a real seedbed for the protest movement. After a Sunday morning service, a young man from the college came up to me – he was probably around twenty-one – and said, "Reverend, does your church believe in war, or does your church take a stand against war?" I looked at him and I was speechless, but I knew what my answer had to be, and I didn't like it. I said, "No, the church does not take a stand against the war – you can believe whatever you want to believe." At that very moment, I knew this was wrong.
>
> That young man convinced me to do something about the war, and because I was on the local council of churches responsible for community action, I recommended at the next meeting that we support and recognize the young people who were doing such a good job making us aware of these issues. One minister after another said they couldn't, for one reason or another, and in the end I just got up and left. That was about the end of my career as a minister.

Author Gloria Emerson met more than just apathy in her interviews with Vietnam-era military chaplains. One, a certain Colonel Beaver, said, "[Jesus] was wrong. Greater love hath no man than when he lay down his life for a *stranger*...That is what the United States is doing in Vietnam." Another, Major Emlyn Jones of the Church of the Brethren, recalled his tour in Vietnam with vehemence: "It gave me sorrow," he said, "but most of all it gave me a tremendous hatred of communists. Man! I hated those spastics!"[15]

In the 1990s, as Reagan's reign of terror in Central America gave way to Bush's exploits in the Middle East, institutionalized religion responded, once again, with support or silence.

A student at Stanford University and a member of the Army reserves, Aimee Allison became a conscientious objector several months before her unit was activated, in December 1990, for the Persian Gulf War. But her moment of truth came long before, while training in the Red Desert of North Carolina:

I was raised in the Methodist church, and had assumed a sort of nonviolent message, but I hadn't thought about it on a conscious level. And there we were — 300 women, out there on the training field doing bayonet exercises. We had on fatigues, and we're holding these M-16s with bayonets attached at the ends. And the drill sergeants are standing on platforms with bullhorns, and they're yelling, "Attack position," and we all get into attack position, and scream.

And they say, "What makes the grass grow?" And we yell, "Blood, blood makes the grass grow!" We were practicing killing people. We were in columns facing one another, and the woman I was facing was crying because she was realizing that this was antithetical to everything she'd ever been taught and believed.

I looked off to the side of the field, and there was the military chaplain, just smiling and nodding, saying "good job." And I thought, "Wait a minute!"

That was confusing, but it was also a turning point in my life. It was the beginning of a consciousness of what the military was really about. It didn't seem right to me, and although I wasn't able to find the words exactly, I knew that it was wrong.

CHAPTER 10

America
the Redeemer

If we turn away and let the rationalizations crowd into our minds to protect us, we are degraded. We want to go on with our daily lives, and we may wonder, Why should my life be interrupted by this? Why should I take on this suffering on behalf of these victims? However much we may resist it, the choice has been made for us, irrevocably. Whether we manage to bear the grief or whether we freeze, the massacre enters into us and becomes a part of us. The massacre calls for self-examination and for action, but if we deny the call and try to go on as before, as though nothing had happened, our knowledge, which can never leave us once we have acquired it, will bring about an unnoticed but crucial alteration in us, numbing our most precious faculties and withering our souls. For if we learn to accept this, there is nothing we will not accept.

Jonathan Schell, on the massacre at My Lai,
The New Yorker, *December 20, 1969*

I **grew up** on the North Fork of Long Island, a serene, beautiful, and fertile finger of land only a few miles wide. The waters of the bays along the south, and Long Island Sound to the north, were my backyard. Our family business for many years was chartering a windjammer schooner in the waters around Shelter Island, Block Island, Martha's Vineyard, Nantucket, Mystic Seaport, and the Connecticut River, and we came to know these places like the backs of our hands. I felt — and still feel — the history of the land and the sea in my blood and bones.

My father's side of the family can be traced back nearly twenty generations, to one of thirteen Pilgrim Fathers who landed on the North Fork in 1640 to establish a "new heaven and earth." In fact, Peter Hallock was said to have founded the town of Southold, where I grew up and went to high school. The oral history of the land, and that recorded in the family genealogy, was to all appearances benign. Peter reportedly bought the entire eastern tip of the North Fork (what is now known as Orient Point) from the Corchaug Indians, but found that the land had been resold after he returned from a trip back to England, where he was married. The Indians didn't know what it meant to own land, and so had gratefully accepted English trinkets and the novel experience of signing a piece of paper. Peter is said to have taken the news in stride, and bought new land farther west.

In all the years of my growing up on Long Island, I was told very little about what had happened to the once vast population of Corchaugs, though I certainly pondered the "lost people" a great deal. You could hardly till the land anywhere on the North Fork without unearthing paint pots and arrowheads, and we had quite a collection from our years of sod farming. Early settlers had told of looking out across the bays that border the south of the island and seeing Indian fishing canoes dotting the water for miles. Today, there is only one small reservation of Shinnecock Indians left on the Island, and I do not remember ever visiting there.

Only in recent years did I learn that the last encampment of Corchaug Indians had dwindled to death on a small plot of land at the head of Richmond Creek. For many years I had lived on the banks of that creek. I fished there, I swam, I sailed its length, raked its bottom for clams, caught the eels and crabs teeming in it. But I never knew about the Corchaugs and their last stand – a people who had, no doubt, once rejoiced in the fruits of the land and water as much as I.

Only recently did I learn, too, about one of the most cold-blooded acts of genocide ever to occur on American soil. And the Pequot Wars happened in my own backyard.

Just before dawn on May 26, 1637, an army of English soldiers led by Captains John Mason and John Underhill, along with Mohegan-Pequots under Uncas and a contingent of Narragansetts and Eastern Niantics, assaulted the Pequots' eastern fort on the Mystic River. This attack, which occurred while most of the Pequot men were away, resulted in the deaths of between three hundred and seven hundred women, children, and old men. Many of the Indians were killed when Mason ordered the wigwams burned. The English and their allied Indians surrounded the village and cut down those trying to flee. During the massacre, which lasted less than an hour, all but seven

Pequots perished. Two Englishmen were killed and twenty wounded, while twenty Indian allies were also wounded. Captain Underhill later reflected on the events of that day:

> Captain Mason entering into a wigwam, brought out a firebrand, after he had wounded many in the house. Then he set fire on the west side, where he entered; myself set fire on the south end with a train of powder. The fires of both meeting in the centre of the fort, blazed most terribly, and burnt all in the space of half an hour. Many courageous fellows were unwilling to come out, and fought most desperately through the palisades, so as they were scorched and burnt with the very flame, and were deprived of their arms – in regard the fire burnt their very bowstrings – and so perished valiantly. Mercy did they deserve for their valor, could we have had the opportunity to have bestowed it. Many were burnt in the fort, both men, women, and children. Others forced out, and came in troops to the Indians, twenty and thirty at a time, which our soldiers received and entertained with the point of the sword. Down fell men, women, and children; those that scaped us, fell into the hands of the Indians that were in the rear of us. It is reported by themselves that there were about four hundred souls in this fort, and not above five of them escaped out of our hands. Great and doleful was the bloody sight to the view of young soldiers that never had been in war, to see so many souls lie gasping on the ground, so thick, in some places, that you could hardly pass along. It may be demanded, Why should you be so furious? (as some have said). Should not Christians have more mercy and compassion? But I would refer you to David's war. When a people is grown to such a height of blood, and sin against God and man, and all confederates in the action, there he hath no respect to persons, but harrows them, and saws them, and puts them to the sword, and the most terriblest death that may be. Sometimes the Scripture declareth women and children must perish with their parents. Sometimes the case alters; but we will not dispute it now. We had sufficient light from the word of God for our proceedings.[1]

William Bradford, who also witnessed the scene, wrote: "It was a fearful sight to see them thus frying in the fire...but the victory seemed a sweet sacrifice, and they gave praise thereof to God, who had wrought so wonderfully for them."[2]

The Pequot Wars officially ended in September 1638. Sachems for the remaining Pequots were forced to sign the Treaty of Hartford, also called the Tripartite Treaty, whereby the Pequot nation was declared to be dissolved. Colonial authorities in Connecticut and Massachusetts Bay even outlawed the use of the tribal name "Pequot," and a people viewed as "aggressive, bellicose, blasphemous, and even satanic" were practically exterminated. A Puritan account from 1643 reveals the thinking of the times – a horrid mixture, often repeated throughout the next three and a half centuries, of patriotism and religion:

In the war, which we made against [the Pequots], God's hand from heaven was so manifested that a very few of our men in a short time pursued through the wilderness, slew, and took prisoners about 1400 of them, even all they could find, to the great terror and amazement of all the Indians to this day; so that the name of the Pequots (as of Amalech) is blotted out from under heaven, there being not one that is, or (at least) dare call himself a Pequot.[3]

A cursory examination of the years following Columbus's first landfall shows that the extermination of the Pequots simply followed a well-established New World precedent. Columbus himself wrote in his log about the Arawak Indians living on islands in the Caribbean: "They do not bear arms...They have no iron. Their spears are made of cane...They would make fine servants...With fifty men we could subjugate them all and make them do whatever we want."[4]

He proceeded to do exactly that, emptying the islands of natives and selling them into slavery. Indians were forced to dig for nonexistent gold, and when they failed to deliver, their hands were chopped off and they were hunted down with dogs. Women and young girls were used as slaves for sex and labor. Columbus wrote to a friend in 1500: "A hundred *castellanos* are as easily obtained for a woman as for a farm, and it is very general and there are plenty of dealers who go about looking for girls; those from nine to ten are now in demand."[5]

Arawaks who tried to resist were hanged, shot, or burned to death. According to Ferdinand Columbus's biography of his father: "The soldiers mowed down dozens with point-blank volleys, loosed the dogs to rip open limbs and bellies, chased fleeing Indians into the bush to skewer them on sword and pike, and 'with God's aid soon gained a complete victory, killing many Indians and capturing others who were also killed.'"[6]

The population of native Haitians went from 250,000 down to 500 by the year 1550; by 1650, all of the original Arawaks had been exterminated. Throughout his escapades in the New World, Columbus was full of religious justification in reports to the royal court in Madrid: "Thus the eternal God, our Lord, gives victory to those who follow his way over apparent impossibilities...Let us in the name of the Holy Trinity go on sending all the slaves that can be sold."[7]

Such audacity lasted well beyond the fall of the Spanish conquistadores. Although more often cloaked in sweeping and magnanimous rhetoric, the nineteenth century concepts of exploration and expansion were no less evil. Take for example this statement by the members of the Big Horn Association of Cheyenne, Wyoming, issued in the *Daily Leader* on March 3, 1870:

The rich and beautiful valleys of Wyoming are destined for the occupancy and sustenance of the Anglo-Saxon race. The wealth that for untold ages has lain hidden beneath the snowcapped summits of our mountains has been placed there by Providence to reward the brave spirits whose lot it is to compose the advance guard of civilization. The Indians must stand aside or be overwhelmed by the ever-advancing and ever-increasing tide of emigration. The destiny of the aborigines is written in characters not to be mistaken. The same inscrutable Arbiter that decreed the downfall of Rome has pronounced the doom of extinction upon the red men of America.[8]

■ ■ ■ ■ ■ ■ ■

Throughout American history, we have viewed ourselves as a "global redeemer" of sorts. We believe in some inherent moral superiority which enables us to see the most clearly, which imbues us with the special power and authority to police the world. Nowhere is this reasoning more pronounced, and generally felt to be more indisputable, than in the history of America's response to the Third Reich. The development of National Socialism in the 1930s was a shocking and undeniable evil, and thus the Allied victory that cost thousands of American lives is rarely questioned as anything more than the triumph of democracy and goodwill.

Yet the United States has easily matched if not surpassed the Third Reich with regard to its stated goals of racial extermination. Native American people and culture were all but annihilated by the relentless application of belief in Manifest Destiny.

The term "Manifest Destiny" was coined in the 1840s to justify the westward expansion of Europeans across the American continent. A magazine article from 1852 sums up the prevalent attitude: "[the Anglo-Saxon race] will occupy the entire extent of America, the rich and fertile plains of Asia, together with the intermediate isles of the sea, in fulfillment of the great purpose of heaven, of the ultimate enlightenment of the whole earth, and the gradual elevation of man to the dignity and glory of the promised millennial day."[9] What is said less emphatically is that in order for Anglo-Saxons to accomplish this lofty goal, the indigenous populations would have to be eliminated.

This reality had not escaped General W. T. Sherman, and in 1866 he wrote to General Ulysses Grant: "We must act with vindictive earnestness against the Sioux, even to their extermination – men, women, and children. Nothing less will reach the root of the case"[10] — the "case," of course, being the full implementation of Manifest Destiny.

Actor John Wayne was an icon of the guts-and-glory mindset that propelled us into Vietnam. His musings on the Indian's plight may now appear to be patently shallow, but they are echoed repeatedly through the pages of American history: "I don't feel we did wrong in taking this great country away from them. Here were great numbers of people who needed new land, and the Indians were selfishly trying to keep it for themselves."

For the most part, America's "final solution" to the Indian problem was successful. The few Native Americans left are still reeling, and they continue to be savaged and marginalized by a society that has long ago buried the truth about who displaced whom. And despite repeated attempts to set the historical record straight, our government continues to suppress the real story.

For example, in November of 1997, two Native Americans dropped by our Woodcrest Bruderhof to tell us about an alarming incident that had occurred in Massachusetts the day before. They had with them a copy of a front-page article in the *Boston Herald*, detailing the beatings and arrests of American Indians during a peaceful Thanksgiving Day demonstration at Plymouth Rock. Photographs showed Indians knocked to the ground, their hair being yanked, their arms wrenched behind their backs, and their bodies carried in midair by arms strained tight in handcuffs.

Police sprayed pepper fluid in the faces of other demonstrators, then descended upon them. "My head was slammed to the ground. I was dazed," said John Perry Ryan of Provincetown. Marcher Peggy Lilienthal said police were "throwing people to the ground. They were very violent." The Indians carried banners; the only weapons they had were drums. "The police came very quickly and knocked me to the ground and started choking me," said another participant. "I was confused. I'm a pacifist..." Police denied any wrongdoing.

The Native Americans' crime apparently involved their belief that Thanksgiving did not happen the way it is traditionally depicted, with pious, generous Pilgrims sharing their bounty with the wretched natives. Rather, historical information points to a Pilgrim population dwindling under the effects of exposure and starvation, who only survived with the help of the very same people they plundered and abused.

One Plymouth resident said she felt bad about the way American Indians had been treated by European settlers, but didn't think that this should change anything today. "It happened everywhere," she said. "What about Africa?"

The pattern that began when the first Europeans set foot on American shores has changed only to suit new circumstances and to demonize new enemies. An honest and informed look at American history (a perspective most schools today refuse to offer) reveals a powerful, unspoken code. The thread running through each and every "conflict" is simply that we, the conquering power, are superior to the peoples we wish to subjugate and oppress. Our lives are worth more. We deserve to take. We are better. We are smarter. We are more good, more just, more civilized.

That is a lie, a myth handed down from generation to generation. And unraveling the myth of American superiority is crucial to understanding the truth about war and the military, because it is the unspoken consent to myth that has caused fearsome numbers of young American soldiers to die needlessly on the battlefield.

Retired Rear Admiral Eugene Carroll, the spicy ex-officer who once served on aircraft carriers in the Pacific, tackles this myth every day. When I interviewed him in his small office at Washington's Center for Defense Information, he minced no words. He is well qualified to criticize: in his lifetime, he commanded the USS *Midway* in Vietnam, directed Task Force 60 in the Mediterranean, and served on General Alexander Haig's staff in Europe from 1977 to 1979. He spent his last assignment on active duty in the Pentagon as Assistant Deputy Chief of Naval Operation for Plans, Policy, and Operations, in which capacity he was engaged in U.S. naval planning for conventional and nuclear war:

> We depend too much upon military power as our primary presence and representation around the world. We bill ourselves as the world's only superpower, with a quarter of a million young Americans ready to go to war, anywhere in the world, instantly. Quarter of a million Americans overseas, acting as a policeman on a global beat. This is madness, because no nation is wealthy enough to police the world. No empire has ever succeeded on that basis. Every nation, every empire has gone. And we will go too. We will bankrupt and destroy our own social, economic, and moral fiber if we try to keep it up.
>
> The American people will realize this in time, and they're going to back away from it. They're not going to support this wasteful and dangerous process. The rest of the world isn't going to stand for it either, and we're seeing this right now.
>
> Think how much more ready the world community would be to deal with someone like Saddam Hussein if the United States had put its strength and its support into the United Nations over the years. Then we would have the apparatus and a body of precedents so that the UN, not the United States, would deal with Saddam Hussein on behalf of the world community...But the United States has undercut, weakened the United Nations every step of the way. We have a group of chauvinists in Congress, and to a degree in the

White House, who say, "No, no, we are the power. We must be in charge." George Bush even talked about "calling the shots." We're trying to call the shots. It just doesn't work, won't work, can't work.

Such revolutionary thinking cost Admiral Carroll his job near the end of an illustrious military career.

In the late seventies, I worked for General Haig in Europe. As part of my duties I was responsible for the security, readiness, and control of the use of 7,000 nuclear weapons. I had all the plans. I came back just absolutely convinced that this is madness. I got a job in the Pentagon where I thought I was going to be able to do something about it, and the second I expressed any questions or reservations about moving further out on that scale, I was confronted. I said, "This is foolishness. We're spending national treasure on something we could never use." "Well, you're nutty," they said. "You're not part of the team." And I wasn't.

I put in my request and left the Navy to come here to the Center for Defense Information to at least be free to express these opinions and to try to communicate knowledge and understanding to the American public, the press, the Congress, from a professional point of view. And that's what CDI does: we attempt to educate people as to what is wrong with our military strategy, our programs, the waste and excesses and the dangers of what we are doing...

So that's where we are. Let's reduce our reliance on military power, let's reduce our waste of precious resources on military power, particularly those forms we can never use, and get about the business of strengthening our own country, our own society, solving the many problems we have, rather than being on guard in Indonesia and Somalia and Bosnia, and now once again in the Persian Gulf.

The nation's leadership is in a state of denial. And they exploit chauvinism, patriotism, pride – false pride – in our great strength, as the American military embodies that strength. You've seen it over the years. You're not patriotic if you don't support a big military that takes charge. The people themselves don't see the connection between this treasure that we're investing in the military and what that waste does to the other situations we should be addressing.

We need to make those connections. Go out and tell people: we've got our own problems. The environment, drugs, education, racism, you name it. We've got things we should be working on at home, and you need leadership and you need money to do that. Instead, we devote money and great leadership, potential leadership, to preparing for the next war.

The cloud of our will to ignorance must be pierced if we truly love our country; things will never change for the better unless we look at ourselves honestly. War is ultimately about greed, and it depends not only on myths that rationalize the destruction of people, but also on the presumption of moral and political rectitude. This attitude is borne out rather crassly by a publication of the United States Army, which states emphatically and unambiguously that American soldiers always do the right thing:

> ...U.S. Army commanders are expected to comply with the laws of land warfare, but they are not expected to be thwarted or even diverted from the successful accomplishment of their mission because of the complexity of international law. The Army trains its officers from the very beginning in the basic laws of land warfare and continues to incorporate instruction about the laws and expected ethical behavior at every subsequent level of training. The ideas of lawful land warfare and ethical behavior are so deeply woven into the fabric of Army training that they are seldom specifically included in lesson plans. The tactical commander does not need a lawyer standing next to him in the field. He rarely thinks about the law; he instinctively does what is right.[11]

■ ■ ■ ■ ■ ■ ■

The survivors of My Lai remember otherwise. On the morning of March 16, 1968, a group of American GIs called Charlie Company entered their sleeping hamlet in Quang Ngai Province on the coast of Central Vietnam and proceeded to murder more than four hundred old men, women, and children. In the course of four hours, they torched homes and pagodas, slaughtered water buffaloes and chickens, raped women and children at gunpoint, and filled irrigation ditches with more than four hundred brutally mutilated bodies.

When the story finally broke in 1969, the distinguished Protestant theologian Reinhold Niebuhr wrote: "I think there is a good deal of evidence that we thought all along that we were a redeemer nation. There was a lot of illusion in our national history. Now it is about to be shattered."[12]

British authors Michael Bilton and Kevin Sim, in their book *Four Hours in My Lai*, offer a similar conclusion:

> The massacre at My Lai and its subsequent cover-up stand in the history of the Vietnam War at the point where deception and self-deception converged. If the Tet Offensive of 1968 had mocked America's complacent expectation

of an imminent victory, My Lai's exposure late in 1969 poisoned the idea that the war was a moral enterprise. The implications were too clear to escape. The parallels with other infamous massacres were too telling and too painful. My Lai had been on the same scale as the World War II atrocities at Oradour in France, and Lidice in Czechoslovakia, outrages which had helped diabolize the Nazis. Reports now suggested that, if anything, the behavior of the American troops had been even worse. Americans, who at Nuremberg had played a great part in creating the judicial machinery which had brought the Nazi monsters to book, now had to deal with a monstrosity of their own making.[13]

Bilton and Sim go on to point out that "atrocity has been as much a part of the American experience of war as of any other nation...The circumstances may change from conflict to conflict, but the experience of atrocity is remarkably consistent."[14] To illustrate their point, the authors cite several examples from World War II:

> The May 22, 1944, edition of *Life* magazine published a full-page picture of a "conspicuously decent and middle-class" girl writing a thank-you letter to her sailor boyfriend who had thoughtfully sent her the Japanese skull resting on the desk before her.
>
> In April 1943, the *Baltimore Sun* ran a story about a local mother who had petitioned the authorities to permit her son to send her an ear he had cut off a Japanese soldier in the South Pacific.
>
> On August 9, 1944, President Roosevelt announced that he had declined to accept the gift, sent to him by a serviceman in the Pacific, of a letter opener fashioned from a Japanese thighbone.[15]

The truth is that we are no better than any other people or nation. We are guilty of the same atrocities, the same oppression, the same injustice. We are not the global redeemers we believe ourselves to be, and may be most in need of redemption among all the nations of the earth.

Our national arrogance has been heightened only further in recent decades. If we are to believe the 1989 inaugural address of former President George Bush, a nation that comprises only 5 percent of world population but hoards 40 percent of the natural resources is inherently good and courageous.

In this same address, Bush stated that "the final lesson of Vietnam is that no great nation can long afford to be sundered by a memory." To the contrary, it is not the memory which will divide us, but our willful inability to assimilate the truth. We are urged again and again to plunge the experiences of war into the sea of forgetfulness. But we will never become a "proud, free nation, decent and civil, a place we cannot help but love" unless we reject such false healing and seek the truth wholeheartedly. Only when we allow ourselves to take in the pain of our crimes against humanity, when we begin to see ourselves as we really are, will we ever become "decent and civil."

■ ■ ■ ■ ■ ■ ■

When the trial of Timothy McVeigh unfolded in the spring of 1997, American hearts and minds were once again filled with images and reflections surrounding the Oklahoma City bombing, of that particular place and time – the Alfred P. Murrah building, on April 19, 1995 – when 168 people lost their lives in the single largest mass murder in American history. It was wrenching, as Americans, to feel ourselves so violated. And for those who mourned the bombing's victims, there remained only unquenchable pain and anguish at the senseless, brutal loss of precious lives. It was a tragedy that will never be purged from the American memory.

There are other tragedies, however, which escape the notice of all but a few. Consider the following scene: Inside a sturdy building, women are caring for little children. A sudden, searing blast rips the morning air, annihilating hundreds of people, and leaving many injured beneath the concrete rubble. Long strands of reinforcing rod, once embedded in the walls and ceilings of the structure, splay outward from a gaping hole – exposed, gnarled, grotesque. Shock gives way to numbed disbelief. Sobs fill the air as rescue workers begin a frantic search for survivors and try to comfort friends and relatives of the dead. Inside, charred silhouettes have captured forever the last motions of children's hands. A ghastly tomb is all that remains of the building. Outside, a grieving father whispers in pain: "They were all so beautiful, so intelligent. But now..."[16]

This tragedy happened across the world from Oklahoma City, in a building called the Al-Amariyah Shelter, four years before anyone had ever heard of Timothy McVeigh. It was in the early morning hours of February 13, 1991, and the U.S. Desert Storm forces had unleashed a devastating air attack on the city of Baghdad. Hundreds of women and children living in the Swedish-made shelter huddled together against the terrifying thunder of explosions outside. During the strike, allegedly intended to destroy strategic military targets only, a spiral bomb struck the roof of the shelter dead-center, boring a hole through six feet of cement and multiple layers of steel rod. Inside, it was pandemonium as survivors rushed through one set of steel doors only to find the outer doors still locked. Then, four minutes after the first explosion, a second firebomb missile plunged through the opening made by the first, striking a water tank and incinerating 1200 women and children in a flash of heat and steam. Both bombs were made in Texas.

Timothy McVeigh was a Gulf War soldier. He was trained to kill Iraqis, and he was good at it. "He was a good soldier," said James Ives, a sergeant in McVeigh's Army infantry unit. "If he was given a mission and a target, it was gone."[17] Members of McVeigh's unit remember him hitting an Iraqi from 1100 yards with a 25-mm cannon: "His head was there one minute and it was gone the next." McVeigh reportedly took the carnage in stride and even photographed his dead victims. Some accounts say he actually buried Iraqi soldiers alive in trenches, using the Bradley fighting vehicle he manned.* When he got home, he told his aunt that "after the first time, it got easy."[18] Yet in an interview with *Spin* magazine, he later reflected: "We were falsely hyped up to kill Iraqi troops, and we get there and find out they are normal like me and you...War woke me up. War will open your eyes."

It has been said that the Army's hardest job is not to get new recruits to risk death, but rather to break down their reluctance to kill people they don't know and don't hate; the predictable result is a society in which millions of people must be taught to "cross the line." McVeigh's proficiency at killing in the Persian Gulf was duly rewarded — with a Bronze Star and the coveted Combat Infantry Badge. He was decorated as a hero because he "crossed the line"; he absorbed well the message that was fed to a new crop of young soldiers. But when he came home, his learning soured and, sickeningly, he turned his sights on a new enemy: the government and society that had molded him into a tool of destruction. The object of his indoctrination shifted from a people he didn't know and didn't hate to people he ought to have known and loved. He applied his training to a population it was never intended for.

But what of the population it *was* intended for? Why is it that perhaps only a handful of Americans know about the pain of Mohammad Ahmed Khader, a Palestinian professor at the University of Baghdad, who lost his wife and four daughters in the Al-Amariyah Shelter? And what about Raida, the mother who lost all nine of her children when she left them in the shelter to do her family's laundry? Are we aware that the equivalent of seven Hiroshima bombs showered down on the country of Iraq during the Gulf War, and that U.S. sanctions still in effect are directly responsible for the deaths of over a million Iraqis, most of them young children?

---

* See *Newsday*, September 12, 1991, which reported that thousands of Iraqi troops were buried alive in the first two days of the ground offensive. See also Clark, 51–52.

If we do not know such things, is it simply because they happened in a far-off country, halfway around the world, or is there something else, something far more serious at work? Is the suffering of innocent civilians in Iraq at the hands of America an isolated incident, or is it more chronic, more deeply ingrained in the history of American war-making?

For Timothy McVeigh and the many people who died at his hands, the recognition that the enemy is "normal like me and you" came too late. War "woke him up." War "opened his eyes." What will it take to open ours?

■ ■ ■ ■ ■ ■ ■

If we have to use force, it is because we are America!
We are the indispensable nation. We stand tall.
We see further into the future.

U.S. Secretary of State Madeleine Albright

CHAPTER 11

The Other Veterans

I shall die,
but that is all that
I shall do for Death.
I hear him leading his
horse out of the stall;
I hear the clatter on the barn floor.
He is in haste; he has business in Cuba,
business in the Balkans,
many calls to make this morning.
But I will not hold the bridle
while he cinches the girth.
And he may mount by himself:
I will not give him a leg up.
Though he flick my shoulders with his whip
I will not tell him which way the fox ran.
With his hoof on my breast, I will not tell him
where the black boy hides in the swamp.
I shall die, but that is all that I shall do for Death;
I am not on his payroll.
I will not tell him the whereabouts of my friends
nor of my enemies either.
Though he promise me much,
I will not map him the route to any man's door.
Am I a spy in the land of the living, that I should
deliver men to Death?
Brother, the passwords and the plans of our city
are safe with me;
never through me
shall you be overcome.

Edna St. Vincent Millay, "Conscientious Objector"

Franz Jägerstätter was born on May 20, 1907, in the small Upper Austrian village of St. Radegund. His father had been killed in World War I when he was still a child, and his mother had remarried. As a young man, he gained the reputation of a ruffian; his friends recalled that he was "a little wild in his ways and style of living," and always "ready for a fight." As a member of the village "gang," he was involved in a number of clashes, including a fight over a woodland boundary and a protracted feud over a girl. But most of the villagers of St. Radegund remember the remarkable change that came over Franz sometime around 1936, when he married, traveled with his bride to Rome for their honeymoon, and received a papal blessing.

The change was so sudden that it took the villagers by surprise. Some attributed it to his devout wife and others to the pope's blessing; in any event, Franz soon came to be considered a religious fanatic – perhaps even mentally deranged. He would be seen pausing in the midst of plowing his field to say the rosary, singing hymns while tending cows in the village pasture, or interrupting farm work to read from the Bible. He fasted frequently and reached out to the local poor, taking foodstuffs to them in his knapsack. He dedicated himself to working for the parish church and was soon appointed sexton.

It was at this point that Franz began openly to oppose the growing Nazi presence in his country. He returned the greeting *"Heil Hitler!"* with "Phooey Hitler!" – an extremely dangerous expression of opinion – and he refused to buy the National Socialist mixture of religion and politics. He made no contribution to Nazi fund drives, and rejected his government's benefits as well, including family assistance programs. Following Austria's voluntary surrender to Hitler on March 12, 1938, he berated the clergy for praising the Party instead of opposing the April 10 plebiscite: "I believe that what took place in the spring of 1938 was not much different from that Maundy Thursday nineteen-hundred years ago, when the Jewish crowd was given a free choice between the innocent Savior and the criminal Barabbas."[1]

All along, he made clear his intentions to resist military service, despite the fact that virtually all of his fellow townspeople, and the pastor himself, had tried to dissuade him from such a "hopeless" and futile course of action. But Franz was unshakable: the war was unjust, and he would have no part in it. In a letter to his pastor dated February 22, 1943, he stated:

> Everyone tells me, of course, that I should not do what I am doing because of the danger of death; but it seems to me that the others who do fight are not completely free of the same danger of death. People say that four or five men from St. Radegund were in the Stalingrad battle. May God reward these poor fellows in the hereafter for all that they have had to bear in soul and body –

234 HELL, HEALING, AND RESISTANCE

for, truly, as far as this world is concerned, it is generally taken for granted that their sacrifices were made in vain. If so many terrible things are permitted by this terrible gang, I believe it is better to sacrifice one's life right away than to place oneself in the grave danger of committing sin and then dying.

His induction order finally came in the spring of 1943, and though he reported obediently to the authorities at Enns, he made it clear that he could not serve in Hitler's Army. As was to be expected, he was placed under immediate arrest and taken to the military prison at Linz. Here he waited for what he thought would be a prompt execution.

Earlier, as he struggled over what position to take when faced with the prospect of conscription, he had sought advice from Bishop Fliesser of Linz. But the bishop tried to dissuade him from insubordination, and later recalled: "To no avail I spelled out for him the moral principles defining the degree of responsibility borne by citizens and private individuals for the acts of civil authority. I reminded him of his far greater responsibility for his own state of life, in particular for his family."

After having taken his decisive step, Franz received repeated urgent appeals to his familial obligations. A local police official offered to write to the military authorities on his behalf, requesting that he be assigned to noncombatant service; his wife, too, pleaded with him to change his mind. But Franz was resolute: the demands of faith stood above those of his family, and if death was the consequence, he was ready.

> If I had ten children, the greatest demand upon me is still the one I must make of myself...Again and again people stress the obligations of conscience as they concern my wife and children. Yet I cannot believe that, just because one has a wife and children, he is free to offend God by lying (not to mention all the other things he would be called upon to do).

Nonetheless, he sought to comfort his wife and children at every opportunity:

> Dear wife, you should not be sad because of my present situation...As long as a man has an untroubled conscience and knows that he is not really a criminal, he can live at peace even in prison...I think it is better for you to tell the children where their father is than to have to lie to them...I am always troubled by the fear that you have much to suffer on my account: forgive me everything if I bring injustice down upon you.

> And now to my little dear ones!...It makes me very happy that you pray for me so often and that, as I hope, you have also become better children...It would make me so happy if I could see you again – I would gather you all together so that you would soon learn not to fight among yourselves any-

more. Also, you must not lie, and at mealtime you should always be satisfied with what you get.

While still at Linz, Franz wrote to his wife: "When people ask you if you agree with my decision not to fight, just tell them how you honestly feel...For if I did not have such a great horror of lies and double-dealing, I would not be sitting here."

One of his fellow prisoners later recalled, in a letter to Franz's widow:

I was in the same cell with Franz for a long time, and I can only assure you that we found a good friend in Franz who, in the darkest moments, was always able to find a word of comfort and always managed to give us his last piece of bread from the meager morning and evening meals we took in the cell, while he satisfied himself with a little black coffee. His faith in God and justice was beyond measure...

Another cellmate remembered:

Jägerstätter was always very quiet...With me, both German and soldier against my will, he dropped some of his reserve. He confided to me that he refused to fight in a war that was senseless and doomed in advance...He loved Austria intensely, and he absolutely refused to serve the oppressor of his country. He always knew and said that he would be executed, but he preferred to die this way than to do evil to others and die anyway on the battle front.

On May 4, Franz was suddenly transferred to Berlin. There he was placed under the care of a chaplain by the name of Baldinger, who tried to convince him to recant. Baldinger assured him that, as a private citizen, he had no responsibility for the acts and policies of his government; by taking the oath and accepting military service, he would not be endorsing Nazi objectives, but would merely be obeying orders like millions of other good Catholics. Furthermore, Baldinger advised him that, as an ordinary peasant, he was limited in his "sphere of activity," and had "neither the facts nor the competence to pass a final judgment as to the justice or injustice of the war."

...When Feldmann [Jägerstätter's attorney]...point[ed] out that millions of other Catholics found it possible to do their duty to the nation – and he, like so many others, gave particular emphasis to the seminarians and priests, some of whom were actually engaged in combat – the peasant merely replied, "They have not been given the grace" to see things otherwise. Pursuing his line of argument further, the attorney had challenged Jägerstätter to cite a single instance in which a bishop – in a pastoral letter, a sermon, or anything else — had called upon Catholics not to support the war or to refuse military service. The prisoner admitted that he knew of no such instance, adding again that this proved nothing more than the fact that they had not been "given the grace" either.

Turning next to arguments of more theological substance, the attorney cited the familiar scriptural injunction to "give unto Caesar the things that are Caesar's," and he asked by what right the peasant thought he could take a position that was "more Catholic" than that taken by priests and bishops, who bore the responsibility for making theological judgments.

Such arguments had no impact on Franz's conviction. "What is there in all this world more lovely than peace?" he asked in a letter. "Let us pray to God...that a real and lasting peace may soon descend upon this world."

Franz's trial was held on July 6, 1943. The two high-ranking officers who served as his judges first lectured him sternly on his obligation to serve the fatherland and warned him that his persistent stubborn refusal meant certain death. Franz maintained that he was fully aware of this consequence, but that his conscience would not permit him to fight. Next, they pleaded with him not to "force" them to condemn him; they even promised that he would not have to bear arms if he would only withdraw his refusal to serve. But he rejected their offer, explaining that such a provision would only add falsehood to an already immoral compromise; from then on, the proceedings were brief and formal.

A few days before his death, Franz wrote:

Dearest wife and mother! I thank you once more from my heart for everything that you have done for me in my lifetime, for all the love and sacrifice that you have borne for me...It was not possible for me to free you from the pain that you must now suffer on my account...I thank...Jesus, too, that I am privileged to suffer and even die for Him...How painful life often is when one lives as a halfway Christian; it is more like vegetating than living...

The true Christian is to be recognized more in his works and deeds than in his speech. The surest mark of all is found in deeds showing love of neighbor. To do unto one's neighbor what one would desire for himself is more than merely not doing to others what one would not want done to himself. Let us love our enemies...

All my dear ones, the hour comes ever closer...I would have liked...to spare you...pain and sorrow...But you know we must love God even more than family, and we must lose everything dear and worthwhile on earth rather than commit even the slightest offense against God...

His wife was allowed to visit him once more in Berlin, and together with a priest, she begged him one last time to change his mind. On the eve of his execution, his confessor Father Jochmann offered him a final means of escape: he had only to sign a document consenting to military service, and his life would be spared. But Franz smiled, pushed the papers aside, and refused; his eyes shone with such joy and confidence that the priest was unable to forget his gaze.

On the evening of the following day, August 9, 1943, Franz walked calmly to the scaffold and was beheaded. His body was cremated and his ashes buried a week later. Once dead, Franz was praised for his conviction; in the company of Catholic sisters who retrieved his ashes after the war, Father Jochmann said, "I can only congratulate you on this countryman of yours who lived as a saint and has now died a hero. I say with certainty that this simple man is the only saint that I have ever met in my lifetime."

In recent years, the diocese of Linz has begun preparations to canonize Franz Jägerstätter, seeking his inclusion in the "register of officially recognized models of Christian life."[2] But one wonders if the church and country who once tried strenuously to stay his "insane course" have truly understood his message. Franz sought not recognition but the honesty and self-examination becoming those who call themselves followers of Christ. As he had written:

> The war which we Germans are already carrying on against almost all peoples of the world, [is not] something that broke upon us without warning – like a terrible hailstorm, perhaps, which one can only watch helplessly and, at most, pray that it will end soon without causing too much damage...Did Nazism fall down upon us out of a clear blue sky? I think we need not waste many words about that, for anyone who has not been sleeping through the past ten years knows perfectly well how and why things have come to be as they are...The...church let herself be taken prisoner, and ever since she has lain in chains.

Jägerstätter's witness is remarkable, but not unique. Over the centuries, thousands of other men and women have died for the same reason, refusing to bear arms or to submit to a government that demands allegiance in time of war. Such resistance is, however, a poorly publicized phenomenon, and the conclusion of Vietnam veteran and author Tim O'Brien ("I was a coward – I went to the war") seems shared only by a very brave few.

Jägerstätter was a civilian, but the consequences of resistance after one has been inducted into the armed forces are no less severe. Such acts of courage are no less meritorious either, even if they come late in the game. The young age of draftees and enlistees, coupled with deceptive advertising, ensures that many in the armed forces do not reach the stage of mature, sober conviction until they are on the battlefield. At that point, says Tim O'Brien, it is a palpable fear that drives soldiers to acquiesce: the fear of retribution for not doing so, and a greater nameless fear – the "fear of blushing." Speaking of Vietnam, he wrote, "Men killed, and died, because they were embarrassed not to…they were too frightened to be cowards."[3] Such is the cunning with which the military induces the blind sacrifice of a nation's young, and by which the timeworn facade of glory, duty, and honor is perpetuated.

What follows are the accounts of resistance among dissenters, some of whom were forced into military service against their will, or willingly joined to clarify their position in the eyes of the state and create a groundswell of protest from within. What shines through all their stories is not a turning back at the point of sacrifice, but rather a conviction made firm by fire and acted upon at great personal cost.

Conscientious objection to war was not afforded official recognition or sanction until after World War I. During the Civil War it was customary for conscientious objectors to be starved, driven on forced marches, hung by their thumbs, or whipped. Forced conscription met with widespread protest, including riots in New York in July 1863, during which 1200 were killed.[4] Soldiers who refused to fight on grounds of conscience or profound conviction were executed.

The tribulations of American COs during World War I were no less difficult, and more than one resister died under military persecution. The Selective Service Act of 1917 allowed members of recognized peace churches like Mennonites and Quakers to enter the military as noncombatants, but of the 65,000 men who applied for such status, 21,000 were still inducted as combatants.[5] It wasn't until 1918, the year the war ended, that Congress provided civilian service for those whose conscience would not allow them to accept even noncombatant duty.

■ ■ ■ ■ ■ ■ ■

When the First World War began, Howard Moore was working as an engineer for the New York Telephone Company. An aspiring young man with a keen mind and a vigorous social conscience, he stopped often in Madison Square Park to hear the soapbox orators holding forth on organized labor, Marxism, and socialism; he frequently visited the Socialist Party headquarters at the Rand School of Social Science as well. There he attended lectures by Charles and Mary Beard, Scott Nearing, H. W. L. Dana, Norman Thomas, and, of course, Eugene Debs – all of whom stimulated his growing abhorrence of the war and the capitalist exploitation that fueled it.

As Woodrow Wilson campaigned for reelection in 1916, Howard's antiwar convictions solidified. Wilson's campaign was, of course, a bitter deception, and with the passing of the Conscription Act in May 1917, Howard was faced with a crisis. Draft evasion was common, but he had no intention of joining the 125,000 "slackers" who had failed to register. Choosing vocal confrontation over silent evasion, he decided to oppose the war openly and take the consequences:

> The original will to peace was subverted by government propaganda, and all pretense of neutrality disappeared as soon as Wilson was reelected. Anyone who didn't go along with the tide was now called pro-German or downright treasonable…All these happenings made my antiwar feelings more intense. I had long regarded war as an ugly, bloody business, carried on in the name of patriotism and national security but actually for economic reasons and the profit of a few. I decided to take no part in it, whatever this might cost me.[6]

His first act of resistance took place in 1916, when he found a card on his desk at the telephone company informing him that he'd been automatically assigned to the Army Signal Corps and was to appear in Washington. Incensed, he took the card to the office of his department head, tore it in two, and laid it on his desk. He also drew up a declaration of protest which he sent to the local draft board, stating that "all war is morally wrong and its prosecution a crime…I hold life as a sacred thing and cannot bring myself to join in the slaughter of my fellowmen."[7]

Howard's fellow employees were aware of his stand, and their reaction was mixed. Some secretly agreed with him, but many others were hostile. Nearly all of them tried to distance themselves from his "seditious" behavior. Before long he was fired.

On April 20, 1918, he was ordered once again to report to the local draft board. Failure to comply, the notice said, would be considered a "grave military offense for which you may be court-martialed. Willful failure to report with an intent to evade military service constitutes desertion from the Army of the United States, which, in time of war, is a capital offense."[8] Once again, Howard stated his feelings clearly and unequivocally, notifying the board in writing that he would report in compliance with the law, but would refuse to accept either combatant or noncombatant service.

Nine days later, he reported to the draft board office at 2741 Broadway. Here, the hundreds of waiting men were reassured by a white-bearded speaker that "the government had already shipped thousands of coffins to Europe so that 'our boys' could have a decent Christian burial instead of being used for fertilizer as the Germans were (supposedly) doing with their dead."[9]

From New York, Howard was dispatched to Camp Upton on Long Island, where he was assigned to the First Casualty Battalion and issued a uniform. He refused to wear it, and from then on showed courageous endurance in the face of increasingly severe reprisal. In a letter dated May 11, 1918, he wrote to his family:

> We [have been] transferred to the Thirteenth Company, famed for its treatment of and reign of terror for the COs...One boy...was terrorized until he almost took his own life. In the middle of the night they poured pails of cold water through the window over his bunk until his clothes were soaked. Then they threw bricks and threatened to kill him, but his courage carried him through, and after three nights of such treatment he was transferred. I mention this merely to show that these men, standing firm for their ideals, are built of real stern qualities, and the war will produce no greater heroes.[10]

On his first day at Camp Upton, Howard was thrown out of a second-story window for refusing to line up for reveille; he was then transferred to a company of men with venereal diseases, where the petty officers threatened him with infection. Soldiers on the floor below would "accidentally" discharge their rifles at night, sending bullets through the floor near his bed. Along with fifty-six other COs, he was turned out into a tent field for the night, where the men were then raided by squads of soldiers who tipped them out of their cots, scattered their belongings, and pelted them with stones until they were cut and bruised. Not everyone survived this harassment, and the men heard only by rumor about the fate of Ernest Gellert, their comrade and the brother of a well-known artist.

> For no obvious reason, [Gellert] and another CO had been taken to the outskirts of the camp, where a squadron of soldiers ordered them to dig what they thought were to be their graves. They refused and were knocked unconscious. When they came to, they were made to stand in holes the soldiers had dug. If they leaned against the sides, they were prodded with bayonets. It was winter, and water collecting in the holes froze around their feet. At the end of the day the second man was returned to his barracks. The next morning, Gellert was found dead. According to the report, he had borrowed a rifle from his guard and shot himself, as a means of publicizing the CO problem.[11]

Once, when Howard himself refused to stand at attention, several guards beat him unconscious with their clubs. When he regained consciousness, his "head was in the lap of the regular guard on the wing. [The guard] was soaking up the blood from my hair and face with a handkerchief and saying as though to himself, 'Jesus, if he can stand that, he'll win.'"[12]

Over the years, many members of our Bruderhof communities had the privilege of meeting Howard and his wife Louise at their home in the village of Cherry Valley near Cooperstown, in upstate New York. An important friendship developed. More than once Howard met with our high school and college students to tell them of his experiences during the war. On one of these occasions, in 1978, he began: "Listen, my children, and you shall hear the opposite of Paul Revere!"

The government resorts to conscription when it is pretty sure it won't get enough volunteers to fight its wars. But war is essentially an evil, dirty business. It means killing, senseless killing on both sides, and generally they say that they have to fight the war for national security, self-defense, or for peace. But you can't divorce method from end. If you use bad methods to achieve a supposedly good end, it usually turns out pretty bad.

Young people who are called up have to decide for themselves whether they want to die for something that they believe in, or die for something they don't believe in. That is the choice, always. And my position was that I would prefer to die for something I believed in rather than die for something I didn't believe in. Fortunately, no objectors were shot in this country during the First World War, but in Germany there were thirty absolutists, those who refused to take part in the war in any way, who were shot. The rest, the great majority who objected, were discharged as "harmlessly insane." Thus it follows that everyone who went to the war was "harmfully sane" – and I think there is a great deal in this, that there is a kind of insanity about the business of war.

A conscientious objector is free of any self-condemnation. You do what you think is right. That's what conscientious objection is all about. It means that you conscientiously decide that you want to act as a free moral agent and refuse to kill your fellowman. They understand that, but they are afraid of it. They hate to face the challenge laid down by the objector who means it, who says no and means it. There is no gray area. Either they have got to shoot you or let you go eventually. That is why they put so much pressure on the so-called conscientious objector...

When I refused to go to war, in 1918, my townspeople wanted to tar and feather me. They did not understand it. Even some of my own relatives did not understand it, because the average American believes that you must stand for God *and* country. The two are inseparable for most people. And the people who really seemed to believe in God did not believe in the country enough to serve it. The people who thought they believed in God but were also willing to serve their country and shoot their fellow men, well, they were

superpatriots...People will corner a religious objector and bring out everything they can find in the Bible to justify their chicanery. A lot of young
people particularly are confused by this kind of thing. But fundamentally the
Ten Commandments are what you can stand on. "Thou shalt not kill" is
sound enough. You don't need anything more than that. And the Sermon on
the Mount...

Now, the government could understand an objection based on religion.
But it was very difficult for them to understand a political objector. I'm not a
professed Christian – I have always considered myself an agnostic. I was
brought up on Tom Paine, Ingersoll, Voltaire, Dostoyevsky, Kropotkin, and
people like that. I was reading Tom Paine when I was eleven. But I regarded
these people as essentially religious because everything they stood for was
decent.

People thought, as they said in my case, that I was stubborn and defiant.
Well, what difference does it make on what grounds you object, as long as
you take a stand? It doesn't make any difference as long as you refuse to be a
tool of someone else, to stick a bayonet through anybody. They'd say, "Well,
wouldn't you defend your mother if she were attacked?" What's that got to
do with war, with organized war? Nothing!

In July 1918, after his initial internment in Camp Upton on Long Island,
Howard was transferred to Fort Riley, Kansas.

We were supposed to carry raw food in open mess kits from the commissary,
about a mile away, and cook our food in this open field where there was no
wood, no way of making any fire. We all refused, and I went on a hunger
strike. I telegraphed Secretary of War Baker that I was on a permanent hunger strike. Three other men joined me: Harold Gray, Erling Lunde, and Evan
Thomas. After the first two or three days they came to the camp every morning and took our temperature and our pulse. Harold and Erling both gave up
the strike, feeling that they had no right to commit suicide; if the government
failed to feed them they would surely die. So they wired Secretary of War
Baker and apologized, and said they were giving up the strike. Evan and I
continued.

Evan was taken to the hospital on the thirteenth day; I was taken on the
eighteenth day. While I was in the hospital I had a guard sitting on each side
of my bed, all night. They would follow me into the washroom with fixed
bayonets. I was fed forcibly. A tube was put in my nose and down my throat
into my stomach and then they poured milk and eggs into me and kept me
alive. It felt like a brick hitting you, but I seemed to thrive on it to some extent. The captain of the section to which we had been assigned, and who had
asked that we be sent there, told me personally he regretted very much that

he couldn't put sandpaper on the end of those tubes when they'd yank them out. Thomas's mother came to him and pleaded with him to give up the strike. They ordered him to eat and he refused to eat. Later he was court-martialed on that order. It was finally decided that it was a false order; they had no right to order somebody to eat. And he got out on that technicality.

One of the captains by the name of Henry always came to visit me. I'd tell him how many hospitals could be built for the cost of a battleship, things like that. These people are really simpleminded sometimes. They know their own line but very little else...

I continued my hunger strike until a flu epidemic broke out and men died all around me in the hospital. I was the only one in the whole section that never got it. And the captain of that section said, "I won't have you exposing yourself. I want you to make yourself a bed in the linen closet." I said, "These people have to come in, and they are all getting exposed. I am no better than they are." Men were dying so fast they had them piled up like cordwood, rows of bodies hundreds of feet long covered with tarpaulin. And men who were assigned to watch them at night deserted their posts because rats would gnaw on the bodies during the night. They thought it was spirits or something.

One day the wife of the commandant, Colonel Rourdon, came into the prison and I got to talking with her. She came in primarily to help men either read letters from home or to help them write a letter. She said, "You know, you men are the talk wherever officers get together. You men are the subject of conversation." While we were speaking, the guard got impatient and pricked me with his bayonet in the back, motioning that I should go back to my bed. I turned and told him, "If you've got orders to run me through, you go ahead." Mrs. Rourdon fainted away and fell on the floor. I was helping to pick her up when Captain Henry came in. He was furious! He ordered the guard out of his hospital, called the prison officer and assumed personal responsibility for me.

Finally we were sent back to the prison. One night, twenty-one of us political prisoners were taken out and put in another guardhouse, in a basement, a cell about twenty feet in diameter with steel walls. We didn't know what this was all about. About twelve o'clock they came down with a three-inch regulation fire hose and began pouring water on us. This stream was so powerful it would pin you right up against the wall. Water rose in the cell, and we thought we were going to be drowned. The water rose to our knees. All our clothing and bedding and bunks were wet. They finally stopped and later came down in hip boots, opened the sluices, and the water went away. But we had to take our clothes off and huddle together to keep warm. Well, we got the story out. It got to Washington and they had an investigation. The Army's excuse for this was that we had used foul language. That was why we were doused with water.

Some of the other objectors were given the water cure. The water cure was famous in the Spanish-American War; it had been used in the Philippines. This water cure was administered by taking a rope and putting it over the balcony, then hanging the prisoner, once around the neck and once around the arm, alternately, until he collapsed. Then they'd lay you down and put a garden hose in your mouth, fill your stomach with water, and pound your stomach. Six men, one of whom was a graduate dentist, were taken to the guardhouse and given this "cure." I think all of them were socialists. A man by the name of Frank Burke, a socialist, had a ruptured stomach and died a few days later. Other men were held face down in a feces pit. Every two hours, day and night, for two solid weeks, they were raided by a company of soldiers who forced them outside in their underwear, and chased them around the barracks with drawn bayonets. This was done in the name of exercising the prisoners.

I was one of the first absolutists who notified the government that I would refuse to cooperate in any way in prison. So they told me that I would be free if I would only agree to work in the hospital where I had been taken as a result of my hunger strike, and when I refused, they said, "Well, we have methods of taking care of people like you."

So I was sent to Fort Leavenworth and put in solitary confinement on bread and water, shackled to the bars of the cell in standing position for nine hours each day, while the others worked. When everyone else stopped working, our hands were released from the bars of the cell and we were let down, but after standing all day you almost fell to the floor. You slept on the cement floor, and you learned to ignore the rats that jumped over you at night and gnawed on your hair.

At the end of fourteen days I was taken up to the executive office, and they asked me again if I wanted to work. And again I refused. So they sentenced me to two weeks on full diet, but still shackled to the wall nine hours a day. The full diet consisted of soupy beans in a tin plate that was shoved on the floor underneath the door of the cell. Very often the guard would spit into it, so you didn't eat it. But I ate the bread. And a colored man had concealed an onion in his shirt, which he tossed to me through the bars. He jeopardized his good time and endangered himself to do that. I hid that onion in the back of a book next to the toilet and peeled off a little each day and rubbed it on the bread to make it palatable. That is all I ate.

After fourteen days I was again asked if I would work, and I said no. To make a long story short, I remained in solitary confinement for sixty-five days.

I weighed ninety pounds when I came out. By that time the other prisoners had decided that if a conscientious objector could stand solitary confinement, they could too.

So the first strike that ever occurred in a military prison in America occurred at Leavenworth. And the prison officials were so frightened that they locked the gates, erected riot galleries, and ordered the trustees (inmates who were serving a life sentence for murder) to run the tiers with lead pipe and break the strike. Six men — not conscientious objectors but regular prisoners — were fired on by officers who took potshots at shadows from the prison walls.

In the end, we created such a furor among the liberals and radicals throughout the country that even the commandant said he would not be responsible for the prison unless we objectors were taken out. He called all the conscientious objectors to a meeting and read a telegram he was sending to Secretary of War Baker. The telegram read, as near as I can remember it, that Colonel Rice no longer would be responsible for the conduct of the prisoners at Leavenworth unless the conscientious objectors were removed.

Shortly after that, he called us together again and read a telegram from Secretary of War Baker, which said that solitary confinement and shackling to the bars of the cell had been used largely as a threat, that the longest such punishment on record was three days and that, since the influx of political prisoners and absolutist objectors, the treatment had proven ineffectual and therefore should be abolished.

And so we finally left Fort Leavenworth. We were taken out and transferred to Fort Douglas, in the Wasatch Mountains just outside of Salt Lake City in Utah.

Fort Douglas was an internment camp, used to intern Germans, and it covered several hundred acres. At every corner there were machine guns, and searchlights at night. And there were American citizens of German descent in that camp. Anybody could be interned if a complaint had been lodged against him. No trial, nothing. I talked with a former delicatessen owner from San Francisco, who later hung himself with a sheet the day before Christmas, 1919. He didn't even know why he was there. He'd had a prosperous little business and couldn't understand that somebody could just take it over by having him interned. But that is how many Americans got their shops and made money during that period — and it happened again with the Japanese who were interned during the Second World War.

Many of the men guarding us at Fort Douglas would come to us (as a matter of fact, the war was then over) and they would say, "Well, in the next war we'll be where you are." And we would say, "No, you won't. The next war will not be with the Germans. It will be with someone else, and there is no reason why you should have an objection to the next war if you didn't have any objection to this war."

Toward the end of his talk, Howard reflected on the difficulty faced by anyone who dares to follow a path that runs contrary to the spirit of war.

It's very difficult, very trying, and it's sometimes humiliating to disagree. There is a lot of hatred. But at the same time you feel an inner strength, and you know that you are doing exactly the right thing. People said, "Well, you must be a great egotist to think that you are right and everybody else is wrong. Everybody agrees with this war except for you." Well, I said, "If you feel any satisfaction about that, you're welcome to it."

I think it is going to be increasingly difficult for today's government to go to the extent that they did in the First and Second World Wars. I think there is going to be another war. We don't have universal military training yet, but that is in the works, because the voluntary system has not worked. It is too costly. They don't want to pay for these things, they want slavery. They can only conduct a war through that method. Conscription is slavery.

It isn't so difficult after all to say no if you really mean no. And there is no power on earth — there never has been a power on earth — that has been able to quell or completely do away with the people who said no. But each individual has to decide this for himself. Chances are, you'll get to feel that the love for your fellowman will induce you to say no and refuse to register.

Now we face the prospect of another war. Let nobody make a mistake. These wars — every one that I know anything about — are all economic. Even the First World War. When Woodrow Wilson addressed the American people, he said, "Is there a man or woman or even a child that doesn't know that this is an economic war?" Whenever the economy is bad, the easiest way to settle these things is to bring on a war, create an incident, which is very easy to do.

If there is any hope of survival for the human race, it is this: community, cooperation, working together. The spirit that's here tonight needs to survive, and it can't survive in the competitive world outside. Most people don't know what to do. There is no central idea to keep them together, to hold them together. I meet young people all the time who are alienated from the system and don't know what to do. They are moving out to the country, building little shacks to live in, taking down old barns and building places where they can stay and have a garden.

I can assure you that to do what you know you ought to do will be much more satisfactory than any other stand you could take. You may be called upon to go to prison. But I don't think that is comparable to the plight of men who find themselves in the trenches and find they can't do anything else. They're the people who suffer – the people who for some reason or other didn't take a stand in the beginning.

Looking back, I wasn't trying to get out of anything. I was trying to convince them that I had a right to say no and not be a soldier. Well, I made it tough for myself!

■ ■ ■ ■ ■ ■ ■

Of all the accounts of resistance during the First World War, there are few more harrowing than the story of the four Hutterites who were imprisoned in Fort Leavenworth in 1918. The Hutterites are descendants of a large group of Austrian peasants who broke away from the Catholic church in the sixteenth century, living in self-sufficient communities and vowing allegiance to God over man. As pacifists, they refused to fight in any war, to hold public office, or to take oaths. In the sixteenth and seventeenth centuries they were martyred by the thousands, but by the nineteenth century had emigrated to Russia, where they lived peacefully until the late 1800s. At that time, their special exemption from military duty was repealed, and they were given six years to tie up affairs and leave the country.[13] Howard Moore (who met the four men while imprisoned in Fort Leavenworth) writes:

> What could be more natural than that their leaders should look to America, the land of the free, a land that had been founded on the principle of individual liberty of conscience, a land settled by men who had fled from the four corners of the earth to escape religious persecution and, having settled, still welcomed all who wished to come to this continent to practice, free from persecution, their religious faith?[14]

By 1874, most of the Hutterites had moved to South Dakota and begun new communities, or "colonies." For forty-five years they lived in relative peace. But that peace was shattered by Wilson's Conscription Act, and by the summer of 1918, four Hutterites living in South Dakota had been drafted into the Army against their will.

Joseph, Michael, and David Hofer were blood-brothers. Together with a brother-in-law, Jacob Wipf, they were ordered to report to Camp Lewis, Washington, on May 25. Because they objected to military service on grounds of conscience, however, they refused to cooperate with even the basic induction procedures, and were thus considered to be military prisoners subject to military discipline.

Persecution began immediately. Already on the train ride to the camp, another group of young men on their way to induction had grabbed the four Hutterites and tried to cut off their hair and their beards. Upon arrival, they refused to promise obedience to military commands, to stand in formation, or to put on the uniforms given to them. For this, they were thrown into a "guardhouse," where they were kept for two months before being court-martialed and sentenced to thirty-seven years in military prison.

Following their court-martial they were transferred, with hands and feet shackled, to Alcatraz in San Francisco Bay. There they were forcibly stripped and commanded to dress in military uniforms. When they refused, they were taken to a dungeon where water trickled down the slimy walls and out over the bare rock floor. The darkness, cold, and stench were overpowering. Their uniforms were thrown down next to them, and they were told: "If you don't give in, you'll stay here till you die, like the four we dragged out of here yesterday!"[15]

Shivering in their underwear, the prisoners were forced to sleep on the cold, damp floor without blankets. During the first four-and-a-half days, they were given nothing to eat and received only a half glass of water every twenty-four hours. Then, for the next two days, their hands were chained to iron rods above their heads so that their feet barely touched the floor. They were beaten with sticks, and Michael passed out. All the same, they were separated from one another so as to prevent communication; David later heard Jacob crying out: "Oh, have mercy, almighty God!"[16]

When the men were brought up from the dungeon into a yard containing other prisoners, they had severe eczema and scurvy and had been badly bitten by insects; their arms were so swollen that they were unable to put on their coats. Altogether, they had not eaten for six days. They were finally fed but then were returned to their cells and locked in for twenty-four hours a day, apart from a single hour on Sundays when they were allowed to stand in the courtyard under heavy guard.

They endured this treatment for four months until they were chained once again for the four-day journey east to Fort Leavenworth, Kansas. They arrived in Kansas at eleven o'clock at night and were driven through the streets like pigs, prodded by shouting guards with open bayonets; they fumbled to retain the Bible, bag, and pair of shoes each had been given to hold in his manacled hands. After being forced to run uphill to the prison gates, they were made to undress in the raw winter air and kept waiting, soaked in sweat, for their prison garb to be brought out. For two hours they shivered naked in the wind; by the time their clothes arrived, around 1:30 A.M., they were chilled to the bone. At 5:00 A.M. they were brought outside again and forced to stand in the cold wind. Joseph and Michael collapsed in pain and were taken to the infirmary. Jacob and David stood fast but refused to join a work detail and so were put in solitary confinement. Their hands were stretched through iron bars and chained together, and they were forced to stand in this position for nine hours each day, with only bread and water for nourishment. After two weeks, they began to receive occasional meals.

Jacob Wipf managed to send a telegram to their wives, and they traveled immediately to Leavenworth. They started out from their homes at night, leaving their small children behind them. But a railroad agent mistakenly gave them tickets to the wrong station, causing a delay of an entire day, so that when the women finally arrived at Leavenworth around 11:00 P.M., they found their husbands close to death and barely able to speak. By the following morning, Joseph Hofer was dead.

His wife Maria was told his body had already been placed in the coffin and could no longer be viewed, but she was persistent and pushed past the guards to the commanding officer, pleading for permission to see her husband once more. Her request was granted, but she was not prepared for what she found: through her tears, she suddenly realized that the lifeless body of her beloved husband had been dressed in military uniform. Joseph had been faithful to the last, and now he was mocked in death.

Michael Hofer died only days later; at the insistence of his father he was allowed to lie in his own clothes. Immediately following Michael's death, David Hofer was brought back to his cell and chained to the bars, unable to wipe away the tears that streamed down his face for the whole day.

The next morning, with the help of a willing guard, David relayed a message to the commanding officer, requesting that he might be placed in a cell closer to Jacob Wipf. The guard returned an hour later and told David to pack up his things for immediate release. David was at first incredulous, but left a brief message for Jacob and prepared to go. It is not clear what prompted this unexpected and sudden release, but it is probable that rumors of his brothers' deaths were beginning to leak out, and the prison was worried that they would become martyrs in the public eye. Soon after, on December 6, 1918, the Secretary of War issued an order prohibiting handcuffing, chaining, and the otherwise brutal punishment of military prisoners — a token political gesture to counteract the case's growing negative publicity.

In reality, Jacob's battle continued. When two Hutterites visited him at Leavenworth five days later, they found him in solitary confinement, his hands still chained to the iron bars for nine hours a day. He was still receiving a diet of bread and water and sleeping on a concrete floor, although he had been given several blankets. In a message sent home to his family, he wrote:

Sometimes I envy the three who have already been delivered from their pain. Then I think: why is the hand of the Lord so heavy upon me? I have always tried to be faithful and hardworking and hardly ever made any trouble for the brotherhood. Why must only I continue to suffer? But then there is joy, too, so that I could weep for joy when I think that the Lord considers me worthy to suffer a little for his sake. And I have to confess that, compared with our previous experiences, the life here is like in a palace.[17]

Considering that the Armistice was signed on November 11, 1918, it is hard to believe that the chaining of military prisoners was only stopped on December 12. The prisoners were given planks on which to sleep, and conditions gradually improved as the War Department continued to receive petitions on the men's behalf. Jacob Wipf remained behind bars for four more months and was finally released on April 13, 1919, after being hospitalized for a brief illness. But the deaths of the two Hofer brothers could not be so easily forgotten, and by the end of the year, the great majority of Hutterite colonies had emigrated to Canada to escape further persecution — including vandalism by their neighbors because of their refusal to buy war bonds. So ended one of the most shameful episodes in American military history.

■ ■ ■ ■ ■ ■ ■

In October 1997, I traveled to New Haven, Connecticut, for an interview with George Edwards, veteran of the Air Force and a Black Panther. New Haven is a starkly segregated city: white upper-middle-class residential areas give way to poor black neighborhoods in the space of a few blocks, and racial tensions are quickly noticeable. But things felt a little different around George's house. When I asked passersby for directions, they pointed down the street to a turn-of-the-century wooden apartment building. They were kind, but I could see the hint of surprise in their eyes: "What is *he* doing here?"

I knocked on the old oaken door of George's apartment and then waited as I heard someone shuffling down the stairs. The knob turned, and there was George. He was small, thin as a rail, with a slightly graying afro parted severely down the middle, and a short goatee. His big brown eyes were warm and sparkled when he smiled with a wide, gap-toothed grin. Although he is sixty years old, he looked closer to forty, and with his red, slogan-bedecked T-shirt and faded jeans he looked the well-preserved hippie.

His third-floor apartment was fragrant with burning incense, and every wall, nook, and cranny was filled with memorabilia: posters featuring Mumia Abu-

Jamal hung next to photographs of Malcolm X, Billie Holliday, and Martin
Luther King; in the corner lay a huge pile of signs and banners, apparently
ready for the next rally.

We got down to business quickly, and the story that unfolded made me
ashamed at times to be white. I found it remarkable that this man could speak so
plainly of the racism that hounded his saga of resistance without attaching it to
me personally in the slightest way. As he spoke, there was no condemnation in
his eyes but only warmth and understanding; through my interest in his work, I
was a "brother of the cause."

George was born in Goldsboro, North Carolina, in the heart of the legally
segregated South, in 1937. His father died when he was young, and the family
lived in extreme poverty. A brilliant young man, he was fully conscious of the
"chattel slavery" which aggravated his family's already burdensome existence,
and with the Supreme Court's Brown vs. Board of Education decision in 1954,
George and his high school friends saw a sudden chance to escape the system
that had kept them "separate but equal." George knew that blacks weren't equal
at all, and he sought ways to exploit the shifting winds of domestic policy.

In the 1950s, many poor minorities went into the military to take advantage
of the GI Bill's educational opportunities. George and his friends also thought
they had finally found the ticket to equality. The deadline to apply was January
3, 1955, and they studied long hours in an attempt to graduate from high school
six months early. Their goal was to test the integration theory of Eisenhower
and Truman, who had publicly espoused the notion that the U.S. military forces
must be integrated.

In the years to follow, George experienced repeated discrimination. His technical abilities were ignored or suppressed, and though he rated consistently high
in terms of the criteria for promotion, he was not promoted even once in a four-
year period. At the same time, white counterparts with lower ratings enjoyed
continuing elevations of rank. When he was finally denied training because of
"inferior mental aptitude," despite the fact that his test scores were excellent, he
realized he'd made a terrible mistake. All his ambitions and dreams were dashed.

I was told I had to brown-nose, kiss-up, in order to be noticed. But I refused.
I said that if that was going to be the basis of promotion, then I would just
never be promoted. And I never was. But the night of my discharge they kept
me almost in isolation, trying to convince me to reenlist. But I wouldn't, and
so they discharged me one minute after midnight, with a check so I didn't
have any cash...

That was January 11, 1959, and I went back to North Carolina. But those
four years in the military had disoriented me, and I was indoctrinated in some
ways, of course. You can't escape that. But I didn't know what to do. My family

was poor. The Civil Rights struggles were reaching their height – marches, sit-ins – and you had to be careful because there were repercussions. White supremacists and racist organizations were attacking black people.

Now, I was very assertive. I was not about to take that kind of crap, and my family thought that with such an attitude they really didn't want me in North Carolina. If a black person was assertive in those days he was considered to be a little crazy. There were all these racial hostilities, all these threats and assaults, and my family said, "George, there's nothing here for you; why don't you go back into the military?" They all thought I should just go back – that with my clean record I could have a great career, with good benefits. I really didn't want to go back, but I didn't know where to go, and I was somewhat demoralized by not having a support system, and so I listened to them.

I went back and I became an instructor at Lowry Air Force Base in Denver, Colorado. That's where I'd gone to technical school, but now I was an instructor, and I was much more aware of racism and of my need to assert my dignity and my human rights. So I didn't fit in too well, and my superior officers let me know very soon that my "attitude" was going to cause me "problems." One day my commander came to me and said, "Look, if I could court-martial you and throw you in prison, I would. But since I can't discharge you, here's how we're gonna get rid of you. They're opening up a new missile school, and they need instructors. And that's where you're gonna go." They gave me twenty-four hours to travel from Denver, Colorado to Illinois, to Chanute Air Force Base, and it was a punitive measure: they told me that if I arrived there even one minute late I would be court-martialed under Article 15...

I got there within the specified time frame, and I walked into the worst racist situation I had ever encountered in the military. Out of four hundred instructors, only two were black. And we were all supposed to go to school in California for further training as instructors, but I was told that I was not intelligent enough to go. They singled me out because I didn't have a high school diploma – I had refused to march across the stage for that, to let the principal know how angry I was at having been ripped all those years. And I also refused to accept the GED they wanted to award me later. That was part of my protest.

Eventually I was asked to be an instructor, and that enraged the white instructors. They were still promoted ahead of me, but the very idea was galling to them: a nigger smarter than *us?*

Actually, I had seen it coming way back. And I remember asking myself, in 1959/1960, in the midst of all the racism and the struggle, "Why am I here? Why am I putting up with this business when I'm conscious and aware of what I'm being subjected to?" I was beginning to have a broader sense of my history as an African-American and a Native American, and the prejudice, the discrimination, was hitting me at every turn. People were waking up and fighting this, and I was watching it on television, listening to it on the radio, reading about it in the papers — and I'm sitting here going through this idiotic nonsense in the military.

It was during a trip home for Christmas that George reached a point of decision, one that was to spur him along a path of increasing resistance to the military establishment, but also toward eventual membership in the Black Panther Party. He recalls:

> In a bus station, I was challenged by a white gentleman who said he was a Klansman. He said he was gonna kill me, and he had a gun. And I'm wearing a U.S. military uniform. A white soldier is sitting there with his wife and child, but he doesn't do anything.
>
> So this guy is cursing me, calling me "nigger," threatening to kill me, and I'm thinking: "Now, I'm an American citizen, wearing a military uniform, sworn to uphold and to protect the United States, and this man is threatening to kill me."
>
> And then I say to myself, "I gotta be stupid sitting here, wearing this uniform, fighting to defend people like this, and the institutions of power that they represent." And I decided that I had to do something about it.

Back at Chanute Air Force Base, George was shaken by yet another military "accident": he learned that his fellow airmen had dropped a nuclear weapon onto his home county:

> The safety mechanism that controls detonation is a system of interlocks. They're complex interlocks, numerically, and seventeen of those interlocks went off inside that detonating system. That was awesome for me to realize. This was the very same missile system that I'd been teaching, and now one falls in Wayne County.*

---

* During this interview, George said that several hydrogen bombs had been accidentally dropped near his base in North Carolina in the early 1960s. I was initially tempted to dismiss this as colorful exaggeration, but I was stunned to read, months later, that the Reuters news agency had indeed obtained an internal DOD document admitting to what the Pentagon had for years denied: "On January 24, 1961, a crashing B-52 bomber jettisoned two nuclear bombs over Goldsboro, North Carolina, according to the document. A parachute deployed on one bomb, while the other broke apart on impact. The bomb with the parachute was jolted when the parachute caught in a tree and five of the six interlocking safety switches were released, said the former officials. Only one switch prevented the explosion of a 24 megaton bomb, 1800 times more powerful than the one dropped on Hiroshima in 1945…" (Zinn, *Declarations*, 284).

They recovered it; they always do. Accidents happen all the time; they are just never reported to the general public. But when I heard about this incident it really affected me. And I started thinking, "You know, George, all of these doubts, all of these thoughts you're having – what does it all mean? Where is all this going? Why am I here? What's all this about? And how is this affecting everybody else in the world?" I mean, what we were involved in is one day going to affect an awful lot of people.

Now all of this began to weigh on me very silently. I was very introspective. I didn't dare speak to anyone. I started to look for a way out of this madness, and I began to rebel and resist.

The first thing I did was to stop addressing noncommissioned officers as sergeants. I began to refuse to salute officers. I began to mix civilian clothes with my military uniform. I began to be late. I refused to participate in parades. I knew I wasn't going to make it through the four years, that I'd have to leave, sometime, somehow.

That was my state of mind at Chanute Air Force Base in 1961. I was on a head-on collision course with the U.S. military. And so it was in early spring that I went to a Nation of Islam meeting in Ohio with a weekend pass. That just did it for me. I heard Malcolm X and what he had to say about this racist society – "Christianity didn't deliver *me*" – and I began to challenge my religious beliefs.

So I went to two chaplains at the base. One was Catholic and one was Protestant, and I told them that I was having some conflicting ideas about the military, about weapons, and about destroying people. And they cursed me out – cursed me right out. They told me, "Don't come in here with that crap! Your first duty is to the military." And I said, "Yeah, but you're a man of Christ. You've got the cross, and you've got the Bible, and we come to chapel – I don't understand how you can justify..." And they sent me packing immediately: don't even come in here with that!

I remember thinking, "Ah, now I've unmasked something" – and then I knew for sure that I was on my way out of the military.

I began to envision massive destruction from nuclear weapons. I began to have nightmares. I was greatly bothered by the work I was doing and what it implied. My colleagues all said not to think about such things; they said that I should just stick to my job, and leave worrying about the other end to the higher command – the Pentagon, the President, and the Joint Chiefs of Staff. That was *their* business, and my job was to be a lowly technician.

The movement for national independence in Africa gave us a sense of pride, beginning in the early 1950s with the Mau Mau rebellion against British Kenya. Inside the U.S. military the whites called us Mau Maus; there was all kinds of graffiti, "Nigger Mau Maus," for example. And it made us realize that we were closer to the Africans than we had realized. Why were American whites identifying with the British?

All the military hype was very pro-American, us versus them, and *them* was always communist. But nobody explained who the communists were, and why they were so evil. Communism was bad, and these people were communist, and therefore they were the enemy. And then I started to wonder about imperialism – what is it, and isn't it pretty evil, too? And am I not a part of it?

At that time we heard bits and pieces about the Cuban revolution. That was close to home, and I thought, why are they rebelling? And why not? We had an American Revolution – and the French revolted, and so did the Haitians. Revolutions change things. They can't be all bad.

But after being cursed out by those two chaplains I thought I'd better be careful who I spoke to. People were beginning to say that I was crazy. They'd tell me, "George, you're acting kind of crazy. You're reading too much, and you can't solve everything anyway. Slow down – all this stuff is driving you crazy."

At any rate, I woke up one morning, checked in, walked to the missile building and signed out the teaching materials, walked into the classroom, and told my students, "Today's lesson will be the most important lesson of your life!" And I proceeded to review, in cursory fashion, everything I'd taught them all the previous weeks of instruction up to that point – an eighteen-week course in fifteen minutes. At the end I said, "Now, gentlemen, you got the super-mega accelerated course. I bid you goodbye." They were all just astounded, and sat there, stunned. Then I started to erase the boards, and they began to jump up and down: he's gone crazy, this is really it!

So I walked out, and the captain and the lieutenant escorted me over to the commanding officer and said I'd had a nervous breakdown, that I needed a three-day pass, a vacation.

In the end they called the military police and had me committed to the hospital. They locked me in the psych unit for about three weeks, and they had me see a psychiatrist, who turned out to be an intelligence officer as well. And he didn't waste any time. We got right into it. He cursed me out, and I cursed him out. And he threatened me with death.

So I ended up with more than one court-martial. They said, "You're on a bad conduct discharge, ninety days of hard labor, forfeit your whole pay, blah-blah-blah." I said, "Fine. I'll take it, I don't care. I'll take a dishonorable. I'll take anything to get out of here, because I am no longer under your control. I will not subscribe to doing anything for the U.S. military, ever again, period."

So I was sent to the stockade. That's where I began to pursue Buddhism, because you can practice it in any place. You don't have to go to a chapel; you don't have to go to a synagogue, a mosque, or a temple…

Anyway, while I was still locked up, they sent a priest in. He told me that I was not going to get out, and when I asked why, he said that the Pentagon could never let me go with the kind of inside knowledge and ability I had. He said they wanted to offer me something: a chance to become a covert intelligence officer, at the covert operations school on a secret base in the desert of Texas. I thought, "This is a death sentence." That's all I could see, skull and bones. And I said, "No, I can't accept this." He said, "It's to your advantage to accept this, you know." And I said, "I don't even know you. What are you, working as an advocate for me? Who are you?"

He kept playing with his cross, trying to hypnotize me, and I thought to myself, this is no man of God. They sent this guy in here. So I challenged him on his religious beliefs, and I basically stripped his facade away, and he got really upset. I said, "You're a man of God, and yet you have no shame coming in here, offering me a dirty deal like this? Get out of here." He was clearly an intelligence agent, and he was more than a little shaken, but he said, "Well, if you reject this, you're not going to get out."

To make a long story short, I finally threatened to go AWOL, and they ended up giving me an administrative discharge. Of course, as soon as I got home, the police showed up at my house with a warrant for my arrest, saying that I was AWOL. So I showed them my discharge, and after some discussion they said, "Well, we just want you to know that even if you have that discharge, you're not gonna get employed. So stay out of trouble." And I said, "Being black, I couldn't get employed in this city anyway. So get off my porch. Get off my property." And they left. That was plain old harassment.

Would you believe it, thirty days later I received a document from the Department of Defense saying that I'd been reclassified from 4F to 1A and was eligible for resumption of military duty. I thought, "What is this? What are they doing?" And the next week my bell rang, and there were three guys from the Navy. Recruiters. They were there to get me, and I was incredulous. They had obtained my Pentagon records and told me they had an offer I couldn't refuse: rank promotions if I signed up, with an enlistment bonus. Of course, each of them would have received a rank promotion, had they landed me. They wanted me for the nuclear submarine guidance system on the *Thresher*.

In the end I applied for conscientious objector status. After several weeks, the Department of Defense notified me that they'd received my application, but that I basically knew too much, and that, in the event of a national emergency, I was subject to be taken under military custody and held there in detention for two years. So I wrote back: "Be ready to send the best you have, because I'm not coming back." That was in 1961.

So I became an activist, a revolutionary, a member of the Black Panther Party. And I'm going to remain dedicated to the fight for justice to the day I die, on behalf of all the people in the world who are fighting against discrimination and prejudice, subjugation, suppression, oppression, human exploitation. I'm dedicated to a better place and a better world for all people. And I'm definitely against the nuclear war machine, totally, irreversibly. There is no place for nuclear weapons anywhere on this planet.

During the Vietnam War, I became involved with street protests in New Haven. I had begun to work for the phone company, and during my lunch break I would go out and join the demonstrators. That really enraged my coworkers. They got really very nasty toward me, and they said, "You should be defending your country." And I said, "Why don't you go? I mean, there are other Americans over there losing their lives unnecessarily. And there are plenty here profiting from the killing. Go ahead, sacrifice your lives for some Wall Street billionaire." And I asked them what gave us the right to go to Vietnam when people are being exploited right here in Alabama and Mississippi and Georgia and North Carolina and Virginia...And the answer was always, "Oh, Edwards, you've got an answer for everything. You talk just like a communist." So I said, "Well, what is a communist? From what I'm beginning to read they don't sound all that bad. I don't have problems with them."

I can foresee the time when nuclear war will engulf this planet. It's going to happen, sooner or later. And we're just sitting and biding our time, flailing away, when in fact we should go attack the Pentagon. They are really a minority of a minority of a minority. There are tens of millions of us, and yet we're at risk because of them. We think that they have all the power, and yet we do; we just don't realize it. But we don't dare to cross that threshold. We don't dare, but if we wanted to, we could shut down the Pentagon.

I've worked to get veterans into drug-and-alcohol-treatment programs. I talk to those who need counseling and advice and try to guide them to the resources they need. Some of them are homeless, and some live at the soup kitchens. But I try to build relationships with them, to get them engaged in meaningful and productive activity for their communities, to mentor young people, which is very difficult for a lot of them. I try to get them to talk against the military war machine, why there is no need for it, how they have been victimized.

One thing I just can't understand is how people will try to rationalize insanity. For example, when I speak out against this crazy Star Wars technology,

I am accused of being irresponsible. Now, who is being irresponsible? Everything, of course, depends on profits. If you can profit, nothing else matters. So what if 50 million people die – if you make 150 billion dollars, that's fine. People say I shouldn't speak out, that I'm putting myself at risk. And I tell them that I'm not afraid: I'm already at risk, and so I'll take the chance to be responsible, to pursue the truth.

Over the past thirty-six years George has been harassed again and again. Toward the end of our interview, he laughed and warned me that we were probably being recorded by the government – his apartment has been raided and searched countless times, and he is convinced that his phone is being tapped, his walls bugged. But then his voice softened, and he whispered, "Death, destruction, devastation...It's all such a lie! How wonderful the world could be without war and racism and greed!" It was time to leave, and we embraced. He followed me down the long flight of creaky stairs, past the smoldering incense, and out into the cool evening. His warm smile stayed with me for a long time.

■ ■ ■ ■ ■ ■ ■

During the Vietnam War, more than a thousand COs were imprisoned, while another 4200 received amnesty.[18] These objectors were joined by military men who turned against the war from within the ranks; many of these were AWOLs who converged in San Francisco's Haight-Ashbury section, the center of hippiedom and a refuge for all kinds of runaways from the establishment. The Army's Presidio Stockade, a World War I-era prison just a stone's throw from the Haight, was filled to bursting by the summer of 1968. Originally built to hold 56 prisoners, the Presidio was now jammed with 115 men – many of whom had arrived in Oakland but had refused to be shipped on to Vietnam.

The stockade was a den of chaos. There were frequent escape and suicide attempts, some made in the hope of obtaining a psychiatric discharge. None were granted, however, and suicide attempts were punished by time in the "box," a small, dark segregation cell.

On October 11, 1968, a guard shot and killed Richard (Rusty) Bunch, an AWOL from Ohio, when he broke into a run fleeing his work detail.* The next day, fearing a mutiny, the twenty-five-year-old officer in charge of the stockade read Article 94 of the Uniform Code of Military Justice to the assembled prison-

---

* The guard who shot Richard Bunch was court-martialed within an hour and fined a dollar (for wasting a shell) so that a second trial would result in double jeopardy. Then he was given a carton of cigarettes, a three-day pass, and a change of duty at the post of his choice (Gardner, 80).

ers: "Persons found guilty of mutiny may be punished by death." But the threat had little effect, and three days later the prisoners went on strike.

When the first name was called at morning roll call, twenty-seven men answered "here" in unison and sat down in protest. One of them, Walter Pawlowski, then stood up to read a list of grievances, including the killing of Rusty Bunch. The captain of the prison promptly ordered fire hoses, but the demonstration remained peaceful; the guards manning the hoses refused to obey orders and had to be forcibly removed by the military police, and before long the Presidio Twenty-Seven were singing "We Shall Overcome" and "America the Beautiful" as they flashed peace signs at Army Intelligence photographers.

Within a week, the twenty-seven were court-martialed for mutiny, and sentences of fourteen, fifteen, and sixteen years were imposed. The interest of the press and the public was of course aroused, and even those who were divided about the war found it hard to believe that a prisoner could be given a sixteen-year sentence for participating in a peaceful, sit-down demonstration. But Army officials were unmoved, believing they had acted with mercy and restraint; the military penal code, after all, called for the death penalty.

Many of the mutineers had been misled by recruiters. One had been promised technical training and ended up mowing grass; another was promised a high school equivalency program that never materialized. Ernest Trefethen had signed up as an auto mechanic but was denied because of color-blindness, and Ron Pulley had registered for fixed-wing aircraft maintenance, but was assigned as a helicopter door gunner. Not surprisingly, the media questioned their sincerity: these were no "Mao-quoting student radicals"; in fact, they all seemed to be members of the lower class. But as Fred Gardner writes, this was exactly the point:

> The Presidio Twenty-Seven came from that part of the white working class that has not profited from America's wealth: the transient, the insecure, the badly educated, the emotionally hurt, the poor. They, like their parents, would not share in the bounty of a war like the one in Vietnam. But unlike their parents, they sensed it.[19]

Looking back, Randy Rowland reflected: "[We] were working-class, and it was the very thing that made the GI movement in that period unusual and really dangerous, I think, to the establishment...These were guys who were disenfranchised and oppressed and they were taking it up. That's what made the GI movement such a threat."[20]

The Presidio Twenty-Seven was not an isolated incident. In fact, American GIs had been resisting the war on an individual basis ever since the troop buildup ordered by President Johnson in 1965. A lieutenant, Henry Howe, was sentenced to two years incarceration for toting an anti-Johnson sign at a demonstration in El Paso, Texas, in November 1965. Months later, Captain Sanford Wolfson, a surgeon at Bien Hoa, was court-martialed for informing General Westmoreland that the hospital was ill-equipped to handle the overwhelming number of civilian casualties being inflicted by the Army.[21]

Steve Spund enlisted in the Marine Corps in 1965, but soon went AWOL and refused to go to Vietnam. His father reported him twice; the second time he was taken to a Navy brig (military prison) and worked over by Marine guards:

> You'd be stripped of all your clothing, they take your unmentionables and put them through the bars and hit them or stretch them or choke you until you're white, or out of air. They usually tried to do things that would not leave bruises or blood...Two of these guards told me this was my last weekend, that they were going to kill me. I checked around with other prisoners and quite a few of them told me that the guards had hung a few Marines and made it look like suicide. I couldn't believe at first that anyone would do that to another American, or another Marine. But they assured me it was so, and at that point I wasn't going to take any chances...I was faced with another tough choice. One was going...to Vietnam, or take my own life. [After I threatened suicide] I received a general discharge with honorable conditions at the Brooklyn Navy Yard...The sergeant asked me — and he was serious — if I would like to enlist again. I don't remember the vulgarity I used, but I'm sure I let him know that I wasn't interested.[22]

Alan Klein enlisted in the Air Force the same day he got his draft notice in 1966. But on a trip home from training, before he left for Asia, he and his father saw a veteran at O'Hare Airport who was so badly burned that it was impossible to tell whether he was black or white. Only later, when his father exulted openly about the "killing" he'd made on a munitions company stock offering, did everything became crystal clear:

> It was a bolt of lightning. I said, *he's* the one who should have been in that young guy's place — he has a real reason to fight, he needs the war to make money. Those are the guys that ought to be fighting this war, not that kid. And certainly not me.[23]

From then on, Alan was actively opposed to the war and decided to engage in subtle forms of sabotage. He and his friends quietly destroyed the efficiency of their unit, and finally went AWOL with a group of others in the fall of 1966 — an act which landed him in jail.

There were thousands and thousands of guys who were doing time, costing
the military a lot of money. It's really interesting in retrospect to think that,
unbeknownst to me, I was part of something larger. I was operating in a
vacuum, but I wasn't alone. Rather than feeling anonymous, I found tremendous solace in subsequently knowing there were so many other people who
were as ill-informed as I, groping along trying to find their way, and reacting
to anger and fear, but all of us, in our own way coming to the same point.[24]

In February 1968, an Army doctor named Howard Levy refused to train Green
Beret medics after hearing about battlefield atrocities; he was sentenced to three
years at Fort Leavenworth. When a group of thirty soldiers at Fort Jackson,
South Carolina, gathered at a chapel meeting in a show of solidarity for his actions, they were attacked by twenty-five MPs with gas masks and clubs.

Women, too, protested the senseless slaughter in Asia. Susan Schnall, a Navy
nurse stationed in California, was court-martialed in October 1968 after she and
a pilot friend flew over Bay Area military installations, dropping leaflets to announce the GI-Veterans' Peace March. "I remembered hearing about B-52
bombers dropping leaflets on the Vietnamese, urging them to defect," she later
reflected. "I thought, if the United States can do that in Vietnam, then why can't
I do it here?" She attended a peace march in full uniform, in willful violation of
Navy regulations:

> I thought, if General Westmoreland can wear his uniform before Congress
> asking money for Vietnam, I can wear mine as a member of the Armed
> Forces speaking out against the war. I had as much right to freedom of speech
> as he...[25]

Susan was charged with disobeying an order and conduct unbecoming an officer. A prosecution witness from Naval Intelligence testified against her: "I
heard her say that young men are being trained as killers and the Vietnam war is
a dirty, filthy war. She said, 'End the war now. Bring the boys home. Bring the
boys home alive!'"[26] Schnall was found guilty on both counts and sentenced to
six months at hard labor.

Another draftee was arrested for passing out the Declaration of Independence at an air base in Washington State on the July 4, 1971. His crime was to
point out that he was fighting for "life and liberty"; his right to "alter or abolish"
a government that had clearly become "destructive to these ends" earned him
three years in Leavenworth. The charges were later dropped for lack of witnesses.

Then there is the remarkable story of Andy Stapp and his crusade to unionize
American GIs. After witnessing firsthand the ravages of British colonialism on
a trip to Egypt in 1964, the twenty-five-year-old student returned to Penn State

convinced that no nation had the right to impose its will upon another. He had serious misgivings about the escalating turmoil in Vietnam and soon formed an American Servicemen's Union to provide legal aid and moral support to GIs who were being abused by the military establishment. In his book, *Up Against the Brass*, Stapp relates his inspiration and struggle:

[In] August 1964, the Students for a Democratic Society at Penn State distributed a leaflet on which was a picture millions of Americans have since seen. The picture showed a National Liberation Front (NLF) prisoner being dragged behind a U.S. Army half-track. Seeing the United States employ this kind of torture was like being punched in the guts. I still remember the picture's caption: "The long slow slide into barbarism is quickening."

I began studying the background and the events of the war, and the more I read the more I discovered what a hypocritical role the government was playing. They placed puppets in power and preached democracy. They killed and said they abhorred violence. They burned and bombed and called it progress.

...We marched on the Capitol. The police warned us not to get closer than three blocks from the Capitol, but we kept marching. Police jumped in and clubbed us down. I was beaten unconscious. A friend of mine took pictures of the clubbings. One showed a policeman standing on my neck. Three hundred and sixty-one of us were herded into buses and paddy wagons, and I remember seeing a lot of blood. Blood was everywhere, on the ceiling and the wall and the seats, but mostly on people who had just wanted to show their displeasure with a war they had voted against nine months before.

My second stay in jail was different from the first. I refused to give my name or cooperate in any way until I was allowed to see an attorney. When I refused to let them take my fingerprints a policeman pulled out a steel whip and laced me across the arms until they went involuntarily limp. Then they fingerprinted me.

I continued to refuse to give my name, so they put me in a cell apart from the other prisoners. At one point four guards grabbed me and walked me into a wall. It knocked me unconscious and broke one of my teeth, Finally they put me back in with the rest...

But in spite of our efforts, massive draft resistance did not build up as we had hoped. Instead, some citizens seemed more outraged at draft card burners than at a government that burned women and children with napalm...

I reported for my induction physical in December 1965, believing I could be more effective if I joined the Army and organized from within. After all, it was the GIs who faced the immediate prospect of death in Vietnam. And it was the GIs who, if they refused to fight, could bring a sudden halt to the

war. I felt reasonably sure that Lyndon Johnson and Dean Rusk weren't so
convinced of the justness of the war that they would fight it themselves.

Months went by and I wasn't called. In April 1966 I went to the draft
board and asked why. "We can't take you. You don't have a draft card." "Get
me one. I want to serve my country the best way I know how." I was drafted
into the Army on Friday, May 13, 1966. It was to be an unlucky day for them,
not me. [27]

A year later, the Army broke into Stapp's locker with an ax. It took them two
hours to go through his belongings, which included socialist and revolutionary
books; among the literature confiscated was the *Harvard Crimson*, the *New Republic*, *Fact* magazine, and his American Civil Liberties Union membership card.

They were afraid that the organization I was helping to build was a threat to
their security. The brass were scared that a union of servicemen would un-
dermine everything they glory in – the privilege and power and position, the
right to unquestioned obedience, the smug satisfaction derived from a
snappy salute and, above all, the big pay differential and the thousand material advantages they enjoy in contrast to the wretched living conditions and
rotten pay GIs receive.[28]

The brass prefer to ignore...dissent, just as they publicly ignore the 190,000
desertions in 1967–68. But the dissent is not going to go away. More and
more young men...are beginning to turn away in revulsion from a system
that places their lives in forfeit to a policy that can and will change, depending
on the whims of the military engineers in the Pentagon..."The supreme sacrifice" is a noble-sounding phrase for a Fourth of July speech, but its reality
is mud and death and a military mortuary where they scrape the blood off
your dogtags so they can read your name, and parents, too old to bear any
more sons, and young wives suddenly become widows, and children orphans,
with nothing left of a young father but a few pieces of paper, a crumbling
uniform, and a couple of dusty medals.

So the battle is fought, the necessary hill is taken, or the necessary camp
defended...Then the decision is made that the hill wasn't that vital after all;
so the soldiers troop back down the winding path to the plain below...
Everything in that spot is now the same as it was before.

But not the same. Lives have been lost...Young men, their childhood
barely ended, are dead. Dead is a long time. Dead means no more college, no
medical school,...no high school sweetheart that you planned to marry, no
children to carry on your name...What epitaph shall we give all those young
dead? "I died, and then they changed their minds" – how about that?

How long must the young go on dying at the pleasure of others? How long must they pay with their blood for the ambitions of Generals and the greed of corporations? Or is the day coming when they will turn and say, "If you want this war, you go and fight it. If it means that much to you, you make that sacrifice you so grandly call 'supreme?'"[29]

Resistance in the ranks is a phenomenon that dries the throats of the brass, that makes their hearts pound in dismay. The rules require that there be men to obey and others to command. Without this logic the game of warfare will not work. So the brass strive mightily to instill in the common soldier the thought of obedience, at all times, without question.[30]

There are those who believe that young people who object to military service in time of war are simply chickening out; that they are avoiding personal cost and sacrifice for their own convenience. In reality, whether COs die for their beliefs or are ostracized by those close to them, their sacrifice can be as great as that made by those who willingly go to battle. Perhaps one of the most poignant examples is the story of John Douglas Marshall.

John's grandfather, S. L. A. "Slam" Marshall (1900–1977), was a brigadier general of the U.S. Army and served in both world wars. Later he became a famous American personality, appearing often on television, and he worked for the *Detroit News* as an editorial analyst. He also wrote *Pork Chop Hill*, which was made into the movie starring Gregory Peck. Well-known as one of the country's staunchest defenders of the intervention in Vietnam, he was a fierce critic of the press's performance there and called it the "most wretchedly reported war."[31]

In the summer of 1969, the day after the twenty-fifth anniversary of D-Day, "Slam" gave an ROTC commissioning speech at the University of Virginia as his grandson John sat in the crowd, one of a group of young men about to become officers. S. L. A. waxed metaphorical in words that would be prophetic of his relationship with his own grandson. "True decision-making," he said, "is the resolution of a dilemma, a leap into the dark where nothing is certain, but some action is requisite...Moreover, when the worst trials come along, one may have to decide altogether in solitude..."[32]

Certificates of commission were awarded on the stage after the speech, as each young man stood before S. L. A. with a crisp salute. John remembered: "There I was on the stage, this newly commissioned second lieutenant in the infantry, an Army branch assignment I had not sought, and I was just about to raise my right arm when my grandfather snapped, 'Don't you dare salute me!' And then he enveloped me in a hearty bear hug, while expressions of surprise rippled through the crowd, followed by applause. Little did I know then that this public embrace was destined to become one of the last close moments the two of us would ever share."[33]

Five months later, S. L. A. Marshall was the graduation speaker for John's officer class at Infantry School in Fort Benning, Georgia — the "famous general and his grandson, now the infantry lieutenant." But though John Marshall was dressed in Army green, he was not the gung-ho ROTC officer his family assumed him to be. "As the years of college passed, amid the tumult of the late 1960s and the war," the nagging doubts John harbored inside began to leak through. "People I knew were shocked when they saw me in my Army uniform for Tuesday afternoon ROTC drills," he wrote. "I would respond with what I hoped was a shrug that conveyed this was not the real me."

Finally, faced with the prospect of fighting in Vietnam, John took his "leap into the dark." And, as his grandfather had predicted, he took it "altogether in solitude." "For I had done something my grandfather could not abide," John wrote. "I had taken a stand against the Army."

> I had finally come to a point where I could no longer uphold family tradition when faced with all-but-certain assignment to Vietnam. I had become convinced the war was wrong, for both moral and political reasons...I had decided to seek discharge as a conscientious objector; I preferred taking a stand to taking flight...After much agonizing and months of study, I had completed a voluminous application for discharge as a CO. "My commitment to Unitarian Universalism is fixed and I can no longer deny the calling of my conscience," I wrote. "I must now submit this application — regardless of my family heritage or tradition. I can no longer hide my true beliefs beneath my uniform."

I had tried to explain this to my grandfather in a letter after my CO application was approved. I do not have a copy of that letter anymore, but I am certain it began with "Dear Poppy," as my letters to him always did. A letter from him came back soon afterward. It began: "Dear Mr. Marshall."

Even twenty years later, after all the times that I have read his letter, I take those two pages of paper into my hands and almost expect them to burst into flames, so incendiary is the language, so intense the emotions. It went well beyond the worst that I had imagined from him. I was staggered as I read:

> That the Army seemingly prefers to give you an honorable separation means nothing to this part of what was once your family, means nothing either that the Army will ship you back home free. You are not entitled to an honorable and you are simply playing the freeloader on the taxpayer. We know why you quit. It wasn't conscience. You simply chickened out. You didn't have the guts it takes. Vietnam or any point of danger was unacceptable to you. You may fool the Army but you cannot fool and fail

your Family at the same time. No male among us has ever been like that, and the women, too, thank heaven, are stronger. That means you don't belong. So go on the course that you have chosen for yourself, that of comfort and convenience, all sweetness, love and lollipops. I would not push the Army to change its course with you, nor would I counsel you to reconsider. Neither is worth doing. You will not be welcome here again and you are herewith constrained not to use our name as family in any connection. Truly, S. L. A. Marshall. Cate Marshall.

These words reverberate through my brain as I stand at my grandfather's grave...My grandfather and I were never reconciled. A few cautious letters passed between us, but no more. Which is why I did not attend his funeral. I figured I was not welcome there either...Our once-close relationship had become a casualty of the Vietnam War, never reported in any weekly body count, but a casualty of the war just the same...[34] I finally allow myself to notice that my chest is tied in knots, my breathing is halting, and I seem to be shivering despite the heat. I am, I suddenly recognize, close to tears. I did not know what to expect when I finally came to my grandfather's grave, but I did not expect this, certainly not anything this intense after all the years. My head spins, my heart aches as memories of my grandfather come flooding back, those I still treasure, and those I have tried to forget...[35]

I have long wondered about [my grandmother] Cate's role in the letter disowning me. She had been, after all, a cosigner. And I had discovered in the library that Cate, a Navy veteran, had actually written the dedication to S. L. A. Marshall's 1968 Vietnam book, *West to Cambodia*. The dedication shares the tone and emotions of that damning letter to me. "To all the good and gallant guys who fought for this country," the dedication goes, "and the back of my hand to the punks, professors, and preachers who ran around ranting that they were careless killers of women and children in a no-good war."[36]

■ ■ ■ ■ ■ ■ ■

During the Persian Gulf War, it is estimated that between 1500 and 2500 men and women already in the service applied for discharge as COs. But fewer than a thousand applications were processed by the Pentagon, and over a hundred objectors were incarcerated.[37]

In fact, a groundswell of resistance was steadily building already by the fall of 1990, months before the bombing began. The Chicano organization Raza, which had marched in Los Angeles against the Vietnam War twenty years earlier, mobilized thousands of people to protest the military buildup in the Persian Gulf.[38] Six hundred students marched through Missoula, Montana, shouting

"Hell no, we won't go!" and in Boston, a group of Veterans for Peace confronted a Veteran's Day parade with signs reading "No More Vietnams – Bring 'em Home Now!" and "Oil and Blood Do Not Mix, Wage Peace."[39]

Vietnam veteran Ron Kovic made a 30-second appeal on television, urging all citizens to stand up and speak against the war: "How many more Americans coming home in wheelchairs – like me – will it take before we learn?"[40] The protesters swelled in number as Bush's deadline for the war neared. In Santa Fe, New Mexico, 4000 people blocked a four-lane highway for an hour, and 6000 people marched through Ann Arbor, Michigan. In San Francisco 5000 people gathered to form a human chain around the Federal Building, and in Washington 75,000 people marched on the White House. Compared to the first months of the military escalation in Vietnam, this movement was one of extraordinary vigor.[41] Some acts of resistance were tragic: a Vietnam veteran in Los Angeles and a young man from Amherst, Massachusetts, immolated themselves in protest of the war, imitating the sacrifice of Buddhist monks in Vietnam some 27 years earlier.[42]

The Persian Gulf War was short, decisive, and well orchestrated. The Pentagon had apparently learned the lessons of Vietnam, and feared the inevitability of domestic dissent. Thus television sound bites were carefully rehearsed, and public opinion polls showing "overwhelming public support" were flaunted at every opportunity. A massive advertising campaign was launched, and yellow ribbons showing support of "our boys in the Gulf" soon adorned trees in neighborhoods all over the country. The tactics (which Bush's successor Clinton called "educating the American public" and later used himself) worked. A month after the vicious bombing of Baghdad in January of 1991, war fever was at its height, and the conflict was supported by 83 percent of Americans.*[43]

Undeterred by the polls, thousands of servicemen began to place themselves in opposition to the war, facing charges of desertion, court-martial, and military prison. Tod Ensign, director of Citizen Soldier, a New York-based soldiers' rights advocacy organization, recalled:

> Opposition to U.S. military intervention in the Gulf was widespread among active-duty GIs and reservists. Although the media tried to portray a nation that was united behind President Bush and his war plans, thousands of GIs facing deployment to the Gulf swamped the War Resisters League, the Central Committee for Conscientious Objectors, Citizen Soldier, and other counseling groups in search of information.[44]

---

* In June, the figure had dropped to 70 percent. After that, the war spirit evaporated, Bush's support dropped steeply, and he was defeated in the 1992 election.

By the time air strikes over Iraq commenced in January 1991, 2500 people had applied for conscientious objector status; 26 were charged with disloyalty and were adopted by Amnesty International as prisoners of conscience.[45]

Corporal Yolanda Huet-Vaughn, a physician and mother of three, was called to active duty in December of 1990. She refused to go, stating that she would not be "an accomplice in...an immoral, inhumane, and unconstitutional act." For her defiance, she was court-martialed, convicted of desertion, and sentenced to two-and-a-half years in prison.[46] Stephanie Atkinson had enlisted in the Army reserves in 1984 but failed to report for activation during the Gulf crisis in October 1990. She remained AWOL for two weeks to speak out publicly against the war, and so was charged with desertion and missing troop movement. She was imprisoned at Fort Knox, Kentucky, until released with an Other-than-honorable Discharge.[47]

As America bowed to the video-game-like carnage of the bombing of Baghdad in early 1991, I obtained from the War Resisters League a list of twenty-three GIs who had expressed publicly their opposition to war and were now facing courts-martial or the brig. The list of addresses was prefaced with the statement:

> The war George Bush launched against the Iraqi people killed an estimated 150,000 Iraqis in uniform and an additional 20,000 civilians. Thousands more will die in the coming months from wounds received from cluster bombs and "smart weapons," and by disease attributable to the intentional U.S.-caused destruction of Iraqi sewage and water facilities. If there is a bright spot in what has occurred in the last eight months, it is that thousands of U.S. troops refused to participate in this horrible killing. It is urgent that the voices of these military resisters be heard across the U.S.

I wrote to Warren Davis, who was facing court-martial in San Diego for desertion from the Navy, but got no reply. Correspondence with congressmen and military brass was similarly disappointing. When I wrote to Arizona Congressman Jon Kyl in March 1991, on behalf of another CO, Gary Galligan, I received the following response: "Thank you for your letter...I am sure Mr. Galligan is grateful for your support. If Mr. Galligan contacts me, I will certainly make an inquiry on his behalf with the Department of Defense...I am sure you join me in being grateful that the present hostilities have ceased and a complete cease-fire is near."

A woman I know had been corresponding with conscientious objector Sergeant Coil, and she drafted a letter to Brian Johansson, Coil's commanding officer, on his behalf. She received the following reply:

Johansson
S TRP 4/2 ACR
Op Desert Storm
APO NY 09759

February 18, [1991]

I received your letter concerning Sgt. Coil today. Normally receiving mail is the only joy we get in this heartless barren place. Your letter only served to remind me that, as usual, people only hear what they want to hear.

In fact, AR 600-43 states that until his case is decided upon, Sgt. Coil may be ordered to perform his normal duties. Those duties here require him to carry his weapon, which he refused to do. Based on this, I could have had him thrown in jail.

I completed all that I could within 5 days of Sgt. Coil notifying me of his desires. Since that time I have done my best to ensure that his beliefs are not infringed on. I am *not* required to do this until his case is decided upon. In fact, the recommendations from both an Army chaplain and a Navy psychiatrist were that he be returned to normal duty and, if he failed to do those tasks required, to punish him…

If you feel you have time to write, please do not waste this time in support of Sgt. Coil, but rather, write to "Any Service Member" and tell them you support them, too. Most of us need that reassurance as we are all frightened and unsure of our future. We do not, however, bail out on our country when the going gets tough. Sgt. Coil volunteered for the service and had no qualms about being paid to perform those tasks associated with his job. Those tasks included firing a machine gun at man-shaped targets as recently as August. He never mentioned any thoughts of his supposed beliefs until one day before we left Germany. I want you to think about that for a while and reconsider your support for him…

Brian K Johansson
CPJ AV
Commander, S Troop, H2 ACR

Such a response from within the military is to be expected. All the same, it is in direct opposition to the U.S. Armed Forces' own Department of Defense Directive 1300.6, which guarantees that "military personnel who develop conscientious objections to military service may seek reassignment to noncombatant duties or discharge from the Armed Forces." Clearly, bravery is measured not by the ability to withstand popular pressure but by one's willingness to fight other men's wars; listening to one's conscience still amounts to disobedience and cowardice.

One of the soldiers on the War Resisters League list was Darwin Airola. He had been charged with desertion to avoid hazardous duty and was sentenced to eight months in the brig at Camp Lejeune, North Carolina. I began corresponding with Darwin in early April and received two letters, after which I never heard from him again. Darwin was the first CO to be held at Camp Lejeune, and he suffered extremely harsh treatment because of this. The thirty or so other COs who joined him later on faired better; apparently, there was strength and protection in numbers.

On April 24, 1991, Darwin wrote:

Dear Dan,

Hello! It was really good to receive your letter!

Yes, my stand was very costly indeed! However, it was not nearly as costly as it could have been, had I gone along with this atrocity in the Middle East. Thank you very much for standing with me – it really means a lot to know that there are people who are on my side!

Well, unfortunately, my brig experience is more horrible than anyone but God knows. This is because I haven't told, am not allowed to tell (a violation of my First Amendment rights), and I don't think I even really want to tell, everything that goes on in here. I don't get depressed as often as I used to, but when I do get depressed, unfortunately, I get really depressed...

There are a few guards who really seem to resent what I did and do anything they can to cause me grief.

Thank God, though, that this place isn't as bad as the prisons of World War I. However, from what I've read of imprisoned COs in the Vietnam era, this brig is much worse than they were.

Yes, I agree that my peaceful stand represents the innate goodness that resides inside of each and every human being...However, many of the people in our military and our government have been blinded...I truly believe, after all this, that the military is a tool of the devil.

Thank God I am out! Finally, I am free, free from the lies, the intimidation, free from training to think hateful thoughts and from killing. Finally I am starting to take comfort in knowing that I finally said "enough is enough" and meant it!

Oh man, your community sounds so wonderful! After this, it is hard for me to believe that I will ever be able to find peace on earth. I often longed for but never found anywhere where people live in peace and unity...

Jesus' command was this: love each other! He also said, "Blessed are the peacemakers, for they will be called sons of God." My God has not called me to kill. He has called me to love and peace!

Once I wondered what God's purpose could have been for allowing me to be placed in here. Now, I think I understand. I have helped educate so many poor and uneducated in here. I know that, in some small way, I have made a difference! I might never have done this, had it not been for me being placed in here.

Also, I realize and really see that there is something more than my small little world, than struggling to obtain as much material wealth as I can. There is a greater good, a higher cause. (Actually, I have believed this for quite some time, but this experience has helped crystallize my beliefs.)

…I am really glad to hear that my stand means something to you! All along, I just thought that I was saving myself – keeping my conscience clean. It is good to know that my stand is also strengthening others!

You are absolutely correct! If we don't hold true to our beliefs, we are really empty and all we do is in vain! I hope that God will allow me to continue to remain strong and hold secure to my beliefs.

For me, this is truly a difficult test. Actually, probably the most difficult test I've yet had to endure. Sometimes it is difficult for me to see the light at the end of the tunnel.

Thanks again for your letter! I really appreciate your support!…

Take care,

Darwin

Several weeks later, Darwin wrote again:

Dear Dan,

Hello! I received your April 30, 1991, letter. It was great to hear from you again!

Sorry it has taken me so long to write you. Sometimes I get down…

There is not any real physical abuse here, it is all mental anguish…It is especially difficult for me here, since I used to receive (and sometimes still do) a lot of flak because of my beliefs and what I did…

They wouldn't allow me to do a phone interview that was longer than 10 minutes with a company that was thinking about hiring me, so I could have a job when I get out, for example…

I guess this doesn't really give you a good idea, but it is very hard for me. The new COs have it a lot better than I did in some ways, since they have the support of each other.

When I first came here I was all alone. (There was another CO here in special quarters, but I didn't find out about him until a couple of weeks before my court martial.) We didn't get put in the same dorm until almost the end of January (I turned myself in on December 15, 1990)…

Yes, knowing that you and others appreciate what I did really does help. Even if the whole world was against me, as it often seems it is in here, I would hope that I still wouldn't have killed anyone. However, it helps greatly to know that someone out there cares about me and supports what I did...

Well, I do see many of these people as sadistic people bent on brutality, whose main pleasure in life is to observe and cause others to suffer. That is just the path they are taking. Often it does sadden and upset me to see that they so willingly and eagerly increase the burdens of those poor, oppressed souls under them.

However, I realize that the punishment they receive is far greater than any pain they could ever hope to inflict upon us. This does make me sad, at times, too. I realize that, given the proper circumstances, I could very well have been one of those doing the oppressing, rather than being oppressed... Hopefully, it is not too late for those who do oppress...

There are dark powers behind the military...for those trapped within it. Unfortunately, I did not understand this until I joined.

Though it is often difficult for me, I forgive them...

I guess part of the reason that this whole experience is so hard is because I am a weak person. It is only by God's grace that I had the strength to refuse to kill, because I was extremely terrified not to do what the men at my unit wanted me to...

Thank you so very much for your support and for your prayers! I and all of those who are imprisoned here because of our beliefs can certainly use all the prayers we can get! I will pray for you as well!

Take care,

Your friend Darwin

This was my last communication with Darwin. For years I worried about what might have become of him. Letters I sent came back marked "return to sender," and at times I feared the worst, as ugly rumors circulated about the brigs. So when, in the summer of 1997, I heard about another CO who'd been among the group of Marine Corps reservists imprisoned at Camp Lejeune, I was eager to contact him, both to hear his story and to ask if he knew what had happened to Darwin. Erik Larsen now lives in California, and on an October morning in 1997 I spoke with him for an hour and a half. To my great relief, he had indeed known Darwin and assured me that he'd been released and was "out there somewhere." He did confirm, however, that Darwin had received especially harsh treatment as the first CO to be interned at Camp Lejeune.

■ ■ ■ ■ ■ ■ ■

Erik's own story of resistance is remarkable. He enlisted in the Marine Corps reserves in 1986 but declared himself a conscientious objector in August 1990 and decided he would refuse to go to Saudi Arabia if called. Erik was to become one of the most outspoken GI resisters of the Gulf War, spearheading a group of publicly active COs on the West Coast and traveling worldwide for speaking engagements. Erik was charged with "desertion in a time of war" and, upon reporting to a naval base in San Francisco, was handcuffed and taken to Camp Lejeune. He was threatened with the death penalty, later reduced to seven years in prison. In November of 1991, he was sentenced to six months in the brig. Erik remembers:

> I'm a first-generation American. My parents came here in 1958 from Denmark. Their farms were occupied by the Germans during World War II, and my parents came here in their early twenties with a seventh-grade education, looking to raise a family, looking for job opportunities, for a better life. They came here and worked in hotels and restaurants, and Dad eventually became a plumber. My mom raised four boys (I'm the third). During that time, the sixties and seventies, my parents wanted us to become good Americans and fit in with the rest of society and all that. So my parents got us involved in the Lutheran church. I was involved in Boy Scouts and sports, in soccer and cross-country. All during junior high and high school I was involved in different student government stuff. That was a turbulent time in the United States, during the Vietnam War. But my family sat out the whole thing – we were in survival mode. I remember my parents telling us that when they moved into their first apartment, all they had was sleeping bags and some mattresses. So they were just building our family, you know, trying to put food on the table.
>
> I wasn't always the best student. I was a C student and had a tough time with English and just learning – because my folks' first language was Danish. I didn't get much support in school, and I wasn't that disciplined anyway. By my junior year of high school I was getting Ds in my English classes. I think I even flunked a couple of classes.
>
> And in addition to that I just had conflicts with my parents. I guess that's something that any normal teen grows up with. So I was having a rough time in high school, and when my senior year comes around, I'm wondering, what am I going to do? I almost didn't graduate from high school because I had to double up in several classes and there was a lot of pressure for me to make sure I passed those classes. All my friends were getting accepted at these big-name universities, and their plans for the future were in place and geez, I didn't even know what I wanted to do.

So I started looking in the high school career center for different possibilities, and one day I met my old scout master there. He was a Marine Corps recruiter, and we spent months talking about my options. He suggested, "Why don't you join the Marine reserves and get some job training and discipline and get away from home, take a break, do something different?" I thought that was great. My family had some hesitation about it, but they thought it might be a good thing for me to get some discipline, to get some focus, and at the same time earn money for college.

So I signed up for the Marine reserves and went into active duty for a year. I went to boot camp and learned to prepare the radar for the Hawk missile system. After that year of active duty I went to my unit, which was in Hayward, California. Everyone signs an eight-year contract, and part of mine was to stay in the reserves for six years active and then two years inactive, during which I could be called up in case of war. During those six years of reserve duty, I'd go for one weekend each month, and for two weeks during each summer, for training. I had volunteered for extra training. Once you're with your unit, you can begin using your GI Bill benefits and go to school. And that's what I did. I decided to go back to community college and start taking classes. I think that was the beginning of a lot of questioning.

During boot camp I was a real gung-ho Marine recruit. I loved the training. It was hard, both physically and mentally. I was put in leadership positions. I was a squad leader and a fire team leader. I really enjoyed the combat training part of it. It was just exciting.

I had joined the Marines to defend freedom and democracy. I joined the Marines to pay back to this country what had been given to my parents and my family. I had no problem going along with the program. It involved bayonet training and throwing grenades and charging dummies with your M-16, charging up the hill with your M-16, shooting at human silhouettes. And I had no problem with that initially. During boot camp and later on in electronics school, we'd go out for five-mile runs every other day and sing chants like "Blood makes the grass grow!" "Devil Dog shock troops, blood-sucking war machines, ready to fight, ready to kill, ready to die but never will. Blood makes the grass grow! Marines make the blood flow! Ooh Rah! Marine Corps!" Or "Rape the town and kill the people! That's the thing we love to do! Rape the town and kill the people! That's the only thing to do! Throw some napalm on the schoolhouse, watch the kiddies scream and shout! Rape the town and kill the people! That's the thing we love to do!" Or "Hey we want some pussy, lick it, you can stick it, you can fuck it till it's raw! Ooh Rah! Marine Corps!"

The training was to get you hyped up about going to war and doing your job. And if that meant killing civilians, that's what war is about nowadays.

Collateral damage. That's a reality. Whether you're on bombing missions or artillery strikes, an assault on some city or town or whatever, the military and especially the Marine Corps wants to prepare young men and women for that eventuality. It was all part of the training for me and I didn't really question any of it. I just did it.

But back at the college one of the first classes I remember taking was a class on Central American history. That was around 1988, when all the Iran-Contra stuff was happening – Oliver North and Ronald Reagan and guns for drugs, all kinds of stuff going on in Central America, the war in Nicaragua and El Salvador. There were human rights abuses, and I was learning for the first time what American foreign policy really was and how it was being implemented. That was a big wake-up call…

I started a student group that began to address some of these issues and to organize discussion groups and demonstrations. I could see that something was very wrong with our country, that we weren't as worried about freedom and democracy as we were about training foreign armies and promoting campaigns in El Salvador to "kill a priest, be a patriot." Through the Lutheran church, I learned about liberation theology and Oscar Romero and El Salvador, and I read about Lutheran pastors being targeted by the death squads for preaching the Bible and acting on it. It was a shock. I could see that people were being persecuted for their religious and spiritual beliefs. And these were the very same beliefs that I had…

Pretty soon I was questioning my boot camp experience and my Marine Corps training – and even what I was doing in electronics school. I realized that the very same chants that we had sung in boot camp were actually being implemented in El Salvador, and I could see the correlation between what I had been trained for and what was going on down there. It suddenly clicked that, hey, there may be a point beyond which I cannot go, where I may have to refuse orders.

Already in 1989 I had started to think down these lines, and by 1990 I was actively looking for a way out of the military. I contacted the Central Committee for Conscientious Objectors in San Francisco, and then along came the Gulf War. I decided that I would have to take a stand.

Just before we sent troops to the Middle East that summer, we were sent for training out in the desert in Utah. It was to prepare us for the desert environment, to practice shooting missiles – and to deal with chemical exposure. There was actually some kind of chemical alert on when we arrived; somebody had exploded something, and there was some sort of exposure. This was an area where the U.S. does chemical and biological testing, and there was apparently unexploded ordnance lying around.

My friends were saying, "You know, Erik, you should speak out about this stuff. You have an obligation." Now at that point I wasn't ready to do anything like that, but a seed was planted. By then I had a certain experience that other people don't have. And because of our militarized culture, when a soldier says something, people listen. And I had read accounts of soldiers in Vietnam doing similar kinds of things. In 1990, when we began to send troops overseas, I reconnected with some of my friends and said, "What do you think about all of this?" And they said, "What do *you* think, Erik?" And I said, "This is wrong. We shouldn't be fighting over oil."

Then things started to escalate. I was at a church in San Francisco, and some of my friends had set up a press conference. I read a statement and got quite a bit of coverage, and the same day I spoke at a demonstration at the Chevron Oil building downtown. And it just kind of snowballed from there; I became involved in numerous demonstrations around the country. I was a very vocal critic of the war, and at this point I applied for discharge as a conscientious objector.

I found out later that the Pentagon was briefed weekly on my whereabouts and activities. In September of 1990, after my initial press statement, the Marine Corps had even considered discharging me for uttering disloyal statements. So when I arrived at drill the next weekend, they didn't know what to do with me. Certainly they didn't want me disrupting their activities or trying to influence other Marines. So I was separated from the rest of my unit. But there was another guy who was speaking out: Tahan Jones, an African-American Marine who happened to be in the same platoon as me. They definitely didn't want us to be noticed, so on drill weekends they gave us menial tasks such as cleaning, way off in some corner of the base.

My discharge was denied because I was apparently too "political" – my spiritual beliefs were supposedly grounded in political ideology and political action. The Marines just couldn't see the connection between "love your neighbor as yourself" and "thou shalt not kill." So I was denied CO status.

A couple of months later my unit was activated for the bombing strikes and the ground war, but I refused orders and went AWOL for thirty days. After thirty days I turned myself in to the authorities at Treasure Island, where I was put in handcuffs for twenty-one hours and flown from San Francisco to Camp Lejeune in North Carolina, where I was charged with desertion and summarily sentenced to death. Thus began a yearlong legal battle to reduce the sentence from death to seven years. Amnesty International and many other groups around the country came to my assistance and helped raise money for a legal team. In the end, I was offered a plea bargain, pled guilty to unauthorized absence, and did six months in military prison. There were nearly thirty other Marines who faced the same charges, and we all did time together...

Erik was dishonorably discharged in 1992. In time he returned to California, where he now heads a community organization, working for nonviolent change in a neighborhood devastated by drugs, racial tensions, and economic disparity. And he sees an obvious connection between his present-day work and his decision to become a CO:

We're spending millions of dollars for an enormous military while our cities crumble around us. The connections aren't being made, and I don't think people who are in positions of power, the industrial giants and actual policy makers, like General Dynamics and Martin Marietta, want us to be making our own decisions.

We have all these JROTC programs, and it seems as though now the military is the *only* job skills program. Everything is geared to getting young people to join the military. And it really does start at a young age. It's easier to get people while they're young, before they've formulated their value systems or thought about issues of conscience or started building families. You start a family and have children and you'll start thinking about things a little differently...

In the video documentary, *Blood Makes the Grass Grow,* Attorney Ron Kuby illustrates the absurdity of ostracizing young people who "bail out on their country when the going gets tough" and denying the right of conscientious objection to those who have a change of heart while in the military:

Certainly there's a lot of truth to the notion that these kids...did sign a contract. But these kids were seventeen, eighteen years old at the time. They went to school. They learned things, they changed, they matured. And they realized that the world was a lot more complicated than the way they thought it was when they were seventeen or eighteen years old. The amazing thing is that, in any other context, we would think this is fantastic. If you have an eighteen-year-old kid who basically is thoughtless and tough and believes that violence is the way to solve problems and the world is divided into good and evil, and you take that kid, you stick him in college for four years, and he comes out as an adult who's rational and thoughtful and realizes that the world is composed of shades of gray and that violence is not an appropriate solution to problems, you'd say, "Fantastic! This is wonderful. You have matured. You have done exactly what we want you to do in society." Why is it filled with suspicion by the military when it happens to a soldier? They go out and they recruit kids right out of high school and they put them into college…knowing that they're going to change and they're going to mature, and they're going to see things that they've never seen before and consider things that they never considered before. That's what happened with most of these young men and women. Fine. They changed. Society should allow for that, and in fact the military, in theory, does allow for that by allowing you to file for conscientious objection, based on the fact that your objection, your beliefs, formed or crystallized after you enlisted.

■ ■ ■ ■ ■ ■ ■

I never paid for my convictions with jail-time or persecution; in actual fact, my reasons for leaving the Navy had more to do with escaping the insanity of military life than moral conviction. But years later, I did give up a good job in the military industry, when I began to see that my work was no more defensible than that of a soldier on the firing line. My friends and family had a hard time understanding that, but that didn't surprise me. I had taken almost a decade to come to such a radical stance myself, and in the end it was something I simply had to do.

After I left the Navy, I grew my hair long and became a 1970s hippie – without conviction, but with a staggering diet of alcohol, pot, and psychedelic drugs – trying desperately to live and find out who I was supposed to be. The next two years led me nowhere – almost to nonexistence. I remember that time of confusion and revelation as if it were yesterday…

Time to pay the piper again. All this college stuff has to materialize into something concrete after all. The voice of pressure nags anew: "Get back on the track. You know you're nothing if you get off the train. Think. You know what comes next. Good job. Good money. Nice home. Nice wife. Two-car garage. Two kids. Picket fence…" I cave in. My bachelor's degree in Mechanical and Aerospace Engineering lands me a job with one of the leading designers and manufacturers of military helicopters. It's the early 1980s, and there's not much for engineers to do outside of the defense industry anyway, so I shrug off that insistent "other" little voice and go to work. I do a great deal of computer programming, simulating helicopters in flight. I work on projects involving artificial intelligence and other cutting-edge technologies. A number of fatal helicopter crashes happen while I work at "the company"; many take the lives of test pilots, and it's part of my job to run simulations to find out what went wrong. We're talking about human lives here, but it's hard to think like that among the long, neat rows of desks and darkened cubicles filled with computer consoles.

After two years at the company, the bottom drops out. I am a full-blown alcoholic, sometimes downing a case of beer with rum and whisky at night. I am still young, and at least present the illusion of a functioning, upwardly mobile engineering whiz, but inside I am self-destructing. My family has struggled hard to climb up out of the pit of my father's abandonment, but the scars are permanent and immeasurable. I have led my younger brothers and sisters into the world of drugs and alcohol, and my girlfriend of four years, now nineteen, leaves suddenly. We had planned to marry, but she is scared and repelled by what is happening. My words and promises mean nothing now, and she is gone. Perhaps it is good that she escapes, but what of me? Damn you for taking my heart and leaving! Damn me for taking yours!

There is no reason to live now, and these aren't just words anymore. There really isn't any reason to go on. Gradually, I try to kill myself. Drugs no longer affect me; they *are* me. One night, I snort far too much cocaine. My heart is pounding, fibrillating in my chest. The surging energy and fear drive me to my car. I do not know where I am going that night. I drive for many hours, fast, down dark back roads and along empty freeways, trying to have an accident. It never happens. I don't remember why, but I think I didn't have the guts to end my life. I call in sick the next day, my heart still fibrillating from the overdose of cocaine. When I come back to work, I tell no one, and nobody knows.

I see my friend Dan during a trip home to Long Island. He has enlisted in the Marines and is just back from boot camp; he got out on a psycho discharge. I laugh. He is one of the few people who could actually pull it off, actually fake being mentally deranged. We assume he faked it, at least, and congratulate him, but he is changed. He doesn't say much — only that they made him say prayers to his gun. He shakes his head a lot and says, "Those guys are crazy. I mean really crazy." Another friend of mine, Eddie, gets out on a psycho discharge, too. He is anything but crazy. He wanted to get out the minute he reported for duty. They put him on Thorazine, a drug for schizophrenia, for six months, and kept him bedded down in a naval hospital until he "turned around." He doesn't remember much of his time there. He tells me about some buddies that were put in the brig and never made it out. He doesn't even know how *he* got out, but he is glad, very shaken and very confused. I think to myself, "Man, there it goes again."

I sit in my room alone, like always. Something has happened to my mom, and I'm thinking about that. She has hope. I've seen it when I've come home to Long Island on the weekends, but I can't understand it. She tries to tell me about it, but I mock her and her new faith. It can't be anything real. But today — this hour, this moment — it is different. I feel something I have never felt before in my life.

Tears roll down my cheeks. It is silent, except for the muffled city noises outside. Someone is with me, has always been with me. I can see and feel for the first time that there is a God in heaven and that, wonder of wonders, he loves even *me*. Yes, there is a Love far greater than my depravity and despair. Slowly, I am awakened.

I've been five years at the company now, and I want out for the third time. It is not fear now, but a calm, new certainty. I remember my old wrestling coach and in my thoughts I speak to him: "You would be proud of me, coach, like you were when I spoke my mind like a man. I love you for it, but I wonder if you'd understand." Anyhow, coach's approval doesn't matter now. I see my "work" in an entirely new light: the Love that visited me is changing me, changing my view of the world, and I can no longer work for a corporation that designs machines of death.

I announce my resignation. The vice president, whom I've never seen before, summons me to his office and tries to size me up. He tries to get me to change my mind — I am supposedly very good at my job and will be difficult to replace. He tells me that I would make a good consultant, that I can work part-time, picking and choosing my hours, and be paid even more than I am now. But I don't buy in this time. He tries to convince me that helicopters do good things, not bad. I point to the calendar on his wall, which depicts a fast-attack helicopter with Tomahawk missiles mounted beneath the fuselage. "What do you think that thing does?" I ask. Our conversation ends, and I walk out of the company and come home to my beloved Long Island soil, trying to rediscover just what it is I've lost along the way.

As Vietnam veteran Steve Bentley once said to a group of high school students, bravery is much more than just following orders:

> In the last fifty years there have been over a hundred million people killed by their fellow human beings. Nobody's got a monopoly on it. Out of our fear and our paranoia and our inability to face the biggest lie of all — that other people are less human than we are — we live in a world where we spend billions of dollars annually on weapons systems…And while we spend billions of dollars a year on these weapons, thousands of children starve to death every day…
>
> My point is that if we are so good, if we care so much about justice in the world, maybe we need to start to address some of those problems. Why do we continue to build an average of two nuclear weapons a day when we already have a stockpile of 60,000 of them, and 100 million people in the world are homeless?

What I'm trying to say is that there are always going to be people who want to run off and be warriors, and there are always going to be people that buy into that. But I want to say what nobody said to me when I was in high school. And that is that some of the bravest people I know work for Green Peace or Amnesty International. There are many ways to be a warrior without picking up an M-16 or flying a jet. There are a lot of things worth fighting for, a lot of things worth having passion about and believing in. Maybe even things worth dying for.[48]

■ ■ ■ ■ ■ ■ ■

Never forget that the airplanes don't fly, the tanks don't run, the ships don't sail, the missiles don't fire unless the sons and daughters of America make them do it. It's just that simple.

General Norman Schwarzkopf,
West Point, 1991

CHAPTER 12

Against the Stream

Our apologies, good friends, for the fracture of good order,
the burning of paper instead of children.

Daniel Berrigan, in court for the burning of draft cards, 1968

I **remember watching** the old black-and-white TV screen in the semidarkness as the draft numbers scrolled by. My best friend, Brett, had a brother who had just been killed in a place called Vietnam. He didn't talk as much as he'd used to; he wasn't fun anymore, and he just sat in the cafeteria looking sad. I was nine, maybe ten years old, and I tried to understand why those numbers meant that my uncle, too, might have to go away for good. "Bub" had made his way to Notre Dame (a big thing then), and he had earned his very own VW bug by painting our old farmhouse in Aquebogue. I can't forget that color of green, nor how he slipped and fell off the roof. My mom was scared out of her wits, but Bub was okay. But now, because of those eerie numbers on the TV screen, he might not be okay in the end…

Somehow, things went on, but they were more and more confusing for a young kid like me. One of my earliest and most vivid memories – Mom holding my hand as we walked down the street on a brisk autumn day in 1963, kicking at leaves as she told me that the President had been shot – was played out again with many more tears and frustration as Robert Kennedy lay on the floor, bleeding, on the television set. Then there was Woodstock and Kent State.

Bub survived, spared by the lottery at a time when public anger at the war was already forcing Nixon to retreat. But there were others who did not – those who spoke out against the war so clearly and convincingly that it cost them their lives. One of those men, whom I didn't hear much about then, was Martin Luther King. We didn't cry when he died – not that I can remember anyway. It makes sense now, but it's a tragedy just the same; we didn't talk about "uppity niggers" around our farm. The only black men I knew lived in the ramshackle section of town or worked for us, and they always had ragged clothes covered with grease and dirt. They didn't seem to want much from life except cars and women, and I always thought they got that from us white folk, because all we wanted was cars and women, too. What a strange mixture of heartland and hot rods, pinups and potato fields!

Little did I know then that this assassinated man had held more promise for the future of our country than perhaps any other figure in modern history. While I was cutting out paper Santas and listening to Nat King Cole on our first living room stereo on Christmas Eve 1967, King was giving his historic Christmas Sermon on Peace from the pulpit of Ebenezer Church in Atlanta. Had I known then what I know now, I would have understood why he "had to go," why he posed such an enormous threat to the rising phoenix of the military-industrial complex and its orchestrators. On that Christmas Eve, less than four months before he fell to an assassin's bullet in Memphis, Tennessee, King challenged the nation with prophetic power, attacking the war in Vietnam "not only as a moral outrage but as an enemy of the poor." "Do to us what you will," King challenged.[1] And America did – to Martin Luther King, Jr., to the Kennedy brothers, to the four kids at Kent State, and to a whole generation of young men and women.

Those who managed to avoid the carnage were a diverse lot. Certainly, there were "draft dodgers" – those who by influence of power or money managed to stay home, or better, to seek temporary refuge in Canada or Europe. Others, however, were simply lucky. Andrew Rimes lived at our New Meadow Run Bruderhof in Pennsylvania back then and had to appear before the draft board in Uniontown to defend his stance as a conscientious objector. Andrew recalls:

> I had decided early on that all war was immoral, that it was about nothing more than money and power. And I was willing to go to jail; I was determined not to go to the war. Fortunately, though, our board in Uniontown was very lenient – I think because it was such an impoverished county and they had no problem making the month's quota of new conscripts.
>
> But by the end of the year I had to go to Pittsburgh for an Armed Forces medical examination. My friend John Trapnell had the same date and so, on the morning of January 2, 1968, we stood with a lot of other young men outside the West Peter Street Selective Service office to board a bus bound for the Pittsburgh headquarters. Many of these young men had already been inducted and were saying good-bye to their families. It still cuts to my heart as I remember them all on that sub-zero morning, weeping as they said their last farewells and boarded the bus. Obviously the mothers of these young men were hurting the most, and of course their wives or fiancées.

I still hurt for the veterans of Vietnam, and, rightly or wrongly, I still deal with feelings of guilt at times – guilt that they had to go through what they did. And they have to bear for the rest of their lives the enormous trauma and emotional harm done to them by this war, not to mention the thousands that died a horrible death over there.

A couple of years ago, while picking corn with Lee (a Vietnam veteran friend), I told him about these feelings of guilt. And he said to me, "No, you shouldn't feel like that. You did what you had to do."

Andrew did, in fact, have to perform alternative service; he ended up doing two years of community service in New York, 500 miles from home. But there were others who suffered considerably greater hardship, including time in jail. These men risked friends, families, and careers for the greater cause of peace.

■ ■ ■ ■ ■ ■ ■

I drove over to the Catholic Worker's Peter Maurin Farm in nearby Marlboro on a cold November day in 1997, hoping for an interview with renowned peace activist and Bruderhof friend Tom Cornell. Tom, garbed in a faded sweatshirt and barnyard boots, greeted me with characteristic warmth and humor. After the requisite tour of the rugged and somewhat swampy farmland, we headed for the Cornells' kitchen, where we pored over pictures and news clippings of by-gone arrests and demonstrations and talked peace and politics over ziti, coffee, and homemade bread.

When we finally retired to the living room by early afternoon, it was nearly dark outside, threatening snow. Tom looked out into the winter sky, and began:

I was much too young for World War II – I was eight years old when Congress declared war in 1941 – but that war was quite an experience, even for a kid, because everybody loved it in a way. It really bound the country together. We were just getting out of the Depression. People of my class and kind thought that Franklin Roosevelt was the fourth person in the Trinity. Irish-Italian Democrats, we all thought the world of FDR. We went to war with great enthusiasm, like most people. Maybe with more enthusiasm than many. But I saw how the older people worried. One of my uncles became a temporary alcoholic, just from worrying that his oldest boy, who was in the tank corps with Patton in North Africa, was going to get hit.

Well, our boys came home. I was still too young by a hair for the war in Korea, but for some reason the war in Korea never excited anybody that I knew. I was more excited about the Trojan War. I was learning Greek and reading the Iliad and the Odyssey. I was doing Virgil in Latin. So the wind-swept hills of Troy meant far more to me than anything in Asia.

I registered for the draft when I was eighteen. Everybody did; you just did it. So I registered and thought nothing about it. One of my buddies had applied for the Marine Corps officers training program, and they were offering to pay his way through college. Now it looked like I was going to have a hard time paying for college, and I thought, I'll give it a try. So I presented myself to the Marine Corps and they said, "You're a little too scrawny. Put on enough weight and we'll take you." I just ate and ate for a month, but I couldn't put on quite enough weight. They said that they'd take me as a recruit, but not as an officer. I told them I was born officer class – that would never do, I was just brought up that way. So I gave up that idea.

I always just assumed that a Catholic couldn't be a conscientious objector to war. At the pre-induction physical examination they ask, "Are you a conscientious objector?" I said, "No." There was a kid behind me, though, who couldn't speak English, only Italian, so they asked me to translate for him. I couldn't figure out how you say "conscientious objector" in Italian. Now I know how to say it, but then I didn't. So I said to him simply, "Are you Catholic?" And he said, "Yes, I'm Catholic." And I said, "No, he's not a conscientious objector" – because in my mind the two were mutually exclusive. Conscientious objectors were Jehovah's Witnesses and obscure Protestant sectarians, and it was very dangerous to be one.

Years and years later I remembered an episode from the third grade. This was right in the middle of World War II. Miss Coughlin – I had a crush on her – brought in the front page of the *Bridgeport Post*, and she showed it to the class. There was a photograph of a young Jehovah's Witness who had just gone to Danbury Prison. She said he'd gone to prison because he refused to kill, and that he was a conscientious objector to war because of his religious beliefs. Miss Coughlin was Catholic and I was Catholic, and I remember saying to myself, "Gee, I'm glad I'm Catholic and will never have to face a question like that." Years later I realized that yes, I did.

I spent quite a bit of time trying to figure out if I really was a conscientious objector. I wanted to look good, because I knew that very few Catholics had taken this stance, and that if I was able to make a convincing statement, then the Selective Service System would have to deal with me as an authentic Catholic and not just another eccentric.

The Selective Service System, of course, is not there to scrutinize Catholic doctrine. But they do have the responsibility to determine whether or not a person is sincere, and so they wanted to know if I was representing a movement that might become significant. If authentic Catholics were going to start claiming conscientious objection, and there were 26 million of them in the United States, this could be a problem. So they wanted to know if this was indeed an authentic expression of Catholic faith. The bishops they consulted said, "We never studied this. We don't know. They didn't teach us this in seminary." But they finally got a bishop in Chicago to get a bunch of theologians together, and they said, "Yes, this guy is right. This is an authentic Catholic position."

I struggled with the idea of conscientious objection. I didn't struggle with pacifism. Pacifism made a lot of sense, as soon as your eyes were opened. I remember reading the New Testament again and thinking, "Oh my God, that was there all the time and I never noticed it!" So the issue of pacifism was clear to me, but I didn't know what to do with it, practically. There were no other men my age at the Catholic Worker, nobody my age to talk to. I met one guy who had applied, but everybody else was either too old, or had been in World War II, or was 4-F because of flat feet or lunacy or some other debilitating condition.

I went for help to a theologian. He said, "You know, I have to agree with you that this is a legitimate Catholic position, but I don't think I could take it myself." I said, "Why, Father?" And he said, "Because I couldn't have taken it in the Irish War," which was the war against England. To him that was the "just war." Everybody has his "just war."

I got my first draft card shortly after I applied, right out of college, in 1956. In high school I was given a student deferment, 1-S; in college I had a 2-S. When I got out of college I lost the deferment and got a 1-A. I rejected the 1-A and told them I would not be available. (1-A means you're available for service as a combatant.) I wasn't going to accept that, and I insisted upon having a hearing as a conscientious objector. They said, "Okay, we'll make a compromise with you. We'll give you a 1-AO, which means that you're available for induction into the military as a noncombatant. You don't have to carry or transport weapons, and you can be a Christian witness all you like. But you're in the Army." I said, "No, I can't accept that. I won't be under military authority at all. And besides, if I put that uniform on, the uniform says something; it says something I don't believe in." They said they couldn't buy that, but then nothing happened for four years. The fighting in Korea had ended, and Vietnam was almost a decade away.

In 1960, they gave me a 1-O. I'm twenty-six, and I said, "Wow, this is great. I don't have to worry about going to prison anymore, and I don't even have to do alternative service, because I'm too old to be drafted." I kept the draft card in my wallet to prove that I was old enough to buy a beer. That's the only thing it was ever useful for.

That summer I went out with A. J. Muste, Dave Dellinger, Marge Swann, Bob Swann, and others – we all belonged to the Committee for Nonviolent

Action – to New London, Connecticut, where my great-grandfather John Cornell had helped to build the first operational submarine, the USS *Holland,* in 1911.

There we mounted a series of demonstrations. They started out as an informational protest. There wasn't any civil disobedience at first, no obstruction. We figured we'd test the waters and escalate step by step. A really wonderful campaign, wonderfully conceived, a great educational experience for a young man like me to be involved in, learning the principles of Gandhian nonviolence, not in a classroom but in a real-life laboratory. It was great. I was kind of scrawny, and I was in a rowboat with a large, middle-aged man and two large, middle-aged ladies. At one point they were all exhausted and they couldn't row any longer, so they gave me the oars. I had never rowed anything before, and it was really far too much weight. There are currents that I had no idea about. We were holding up placards that said, "Quit the ship of death," telling these boat workers that they should quit their $3.75-an-hour jobs, which was a nice wage then. What we were really asking them to do was pitch themselves back into the poverty they had left in West Virginia, because their ships were immoral. Of course, they really were ships of death, tools of death, weapons of death.

All of a sudden I realized I wasn't in control of the boat. We hadn't intended to be close to the ship; you couldn't come within so many yards of this ship or you'd be trespassing on federal property. It was a nuclear-powered submarine, the *George Washington,* the very first Polaris submarine. It would soon have sixteen nuclear missiles on it, each one something like twenty times more powerful than the bomb that fell on Hiroshima. And all of a sudden I'm crashing into this ship! I put my hand out to feel its hull, and it really was like cold electricity.

Well, we managed to get back to the shore, and we said, "Wasn't that a fine demonstration?" We were pretty pleased with ourselves, and my buddy Loren Miner and I decided we should go have a beer. So we went, and the bartender said to me, "Are you twenty-one years old?" And I said, "No, sir. I am twenty-six years old." "Can you prove it? Where's your draft card?" "Here's my draft card." And I handed it to him. He looked at it, he handed it back, and I said, "I don't want it." I realized that I really didn't want the card. So I had the beer, and then I said, "Loren, you know what I think I'm going to do? I'm not going to be part of this system anymore. I'm going to 'unregister.' And I'm going to burn this card right here and now." So I burned it in the ash tray on the bar at the Goldenrod on Bank Street, had another beer, and went home.

I had quite a few draft cards that I had kept, my 1-S, my 2-S, my 1-A, my 1-AO. And I still had my registration card. All in all, I had something like ten cards. And I'd pull them out at appropriate moments to burn them. I remember one of those occasions in particular, the Worldwide General Strike for Peace, which was the ultimate in pacifist hyperbole. Sixty-eight people showed up. We were gathered at Washington Square in Manhattan, and there was a camera aimed at me, so I took out a draft card and burned it. It was 1962, maybe '63.

Back then, nobody paid any attention. The law said you had to be in possession of a valid registration and classification certificate. But it didn't say, "Thou shalt not burn your draft card" or tear it up or otherwise destroy it.

In 1965 the antiwar movement began to heat up. Young people went to Washington that spring, 1500 or so, to a very conservative demonstration that was sponsored by the Students for a Democratic Society. A couple months later, from August 6 to 9 of 1965, there was another demonstration of 1500 people, 353 of whom were arrested. But the ante was being upped and it looked as if students might really be getting upset about the draft. On August 28, I think it was, *Life* magazine had a full-page color photograph of Dellinger, Staughton Lynd, and Robert Moses covered with red paint. It was a very dramatic photograph; I'm in it, too. In fact I remember digging the paint out of Dave Dellinger's eyes.

On the other side of the page was a full-size black-and-white of a young man burning a draft card at the Whitehall Induction Center. This young man happened to be the great-great-grandson of a signer of the Declaration of Independence, and he was a good-looking white boy with a blond crew cut, looking intently into a burning draft card. They had a copy of the magazine in the Senate barbershop, and when the senators went to get their hair cut and saw the picture they just went berserk, or, as they say today, they went ballistic. They said, "Look at these kids doing these things! This can't be tolerated! This is America, after all!" So they rushed through a law saying that you'd get five years and a $10,000 fine if you burned your draft card.

It was clear what they intended to do. They intended to use the law to stifle dissent. Do you remember your civics classes? Is that what American law is for? I think of myself as a patriotic American. I really do. I really love the democratic traditions of this country, and the one I love the most is the freedom to dissent. We have the freedom to question our government, to gather in association with others, to press for redress of grievances. This is the American tradition. The American tradition is not using the power of law and police and prisons and courts to stifle dissent. But that's what they were doing. It was perfectly and instantaneously clear.

Well, didn't we then have an obligation, those of us who had burned draft cards and suggested the idea to others, to defy this law? It was immediately clear to me that we did. I didn't have any draft cards left to burn, so I wrote to my draft board. I said, "Ladies and gentlemen of the draft board, I am not in possession of a registration or classification certificate. I burned them years ago. Would you please send me duplicates." And they did. And we had another ceremonial draft card burning.

Then we planned the first group act. David was the first one to do it as a single individual, but we wanted to have a group act of resistance to the Vietnam draft. We thought we would do it on the steps of the federal courthouse with A. J. Muste and Dorothy Day there to support us. But the crowd was so intense, a crowd of photographers and newspapermen, and they were acting in such an unruly manner, that we were afraid for the health of Dorothy and A. J. So we called the demonstration off. We went to our offices at 5 Beekman Street, where the War Resisters League and the Catholic Peace Fellowship and the Student Peace Union had their headquarters. These guys from the *Times* came over with us, and they said, "Look, you're supposed to be professional agitators. You don't even know your own business! This is a hot issue. Give us something that we can photograph. Give us something that's timed for the Sunday papers. Don't throw it away on a Thursday afternoon! Don't you know better than that? Spend some money, get yourself a good sound system. Make a stage."

So we did. We spent about $2500 of the Committee for Nonviolent Action's money, erected a stage at the north end of Union Square, hired a sound system, and timed it for the Sunday papers. We attracted 2500 people to an event that was staged with great dignity. We all wore suits and ties; we didn't look like hippies. Dorothy read something, A. J. read something. It was really beautiful. And we burned the cards. As the cards were burning, just before they ignited, a jet of fluid flew in an arc and landed right in our midst. We had no idea what it was. I thought, "Is this volatile? Are we going to go up in a puff of smoke?" It was water. Somebody had brought a pressurized container of water in past the police and just doused the cards. So there we were holding cards that were soaking wet and applying a zippo lighter to them. You know the story of Elijah and the sacrifice? Well, the cards were drenched, but they still burned! It was marvelous, just marvelous, that they burned.

Well, it was on the evening news. My stepfather and my mother were watching back home in Connecticut. He was so furious he almost broke the set. He managed to get to bed and get to sleep. The next morning he went to mass with my mother as usual. He came out of the church to the parking lot afterwards, and there were all the local papers and the New York papers for sale: the *New York Times*, the *New York News*, the *New York Mirror*, the *New York Post*, the *Herald Tribune*, the *Journal American*, the *Fairfield County Herald*, and the *Bridgeport Post* – and I'm on the front page of every single one! Me and the other four guys, Dorothy, and A. J., and the cards burning. He went berserk. For three years I couldn't go home. I couldn't see my mother unless she came to New York, and she was getting older and afraid of New York. So that was very, very painful. But our appeals were finally exhausted, and we had to surrender for imprisonment.

At the trial we had a wonderful defense team made up of top civil liberties lawyers. They understood what we wanted to do. We didn't want to get off the hook. That was not the point. We wanted to broadcast a moral principle. We didn't want a jury. We wanted to be tried by the court, convicted by the court, and overturn the law on appeal. In other words: First Amendment. The act of burning a draft card is an act of speech, symbolic speech. The new law serves no purpose other than to stifle dissent, and therefore it is invalid.

Well, the Supreme Court didn't want to hear this. Only one voted in our favor, but they didn't even hear it. It took three years for them to decide that they weren't going to hear it. The judge must have been impressed with the fact that we weren't trying to save our skins but that we were trying to make a constitutional case. He gave us a much more lenient sentence than we had anticipated. We thought we'd get what everybody else was getting under Selective Service, which was two to three years. But he gave us six months. I breathed an enormous sigh of relief. I mean, I could do six months. I *knew* I could do six months.

But it was hard. Maybe it's my own weakness of character, I don't know. But it was terrible, really awful. The food was execrable. After the first week I simply couldn't eat it anymore. I lived on ice cream and Fritos. This was 1968. I developed a little tire around my middle. I never had one before. Then it was a Schwinn. Now it's a Goodyear. I was incredibly bored. There was nothing to do. I was married, and I was the only guy in the whole prison who insisted on keeping his wedding ring on. That told the other prisoners that there was something special about me. They knew it immediately. They knew I had some kind of "juice," as they say. So I was protected by that. Then I let the Mafia guys know that I was Italian. It was foolish not to. I mean, I tell the Jewish kids, don't ever think you're not Jewish. Other people are not going to forget; Hitler didn't forget. If you're going to pay a price you might as well have the reward too. And the reward for me was Mafia protection.

I was sitting in Danbury prison, and who comes to see me but my mother and her husband. He said nothing about the silence that had been between us. Finally he opened his mouth and said, "I did time myself once. Thirty days. The numbers." Illegal gambling. The point was, I was doing time, so I'd won my manhood back. Now he could talk to me again. Now it was all right.

My daughter Deirdre took her first steps in the Danbury prison in the visiting room. She was about a year or thirteen months. Tommy was three. He was old enough to be affected by it. When I got out, he was fearful that I'd leave again. If I went to the grocery store or something like that, he was afraid I might never come back.

The other prisoners called us "fucking hippies." They lumped the very few draft resisters — and there were only six of us — with the druggies, because we were middle-class white. I remember watching the Democratic Convention of 1968, the one that erupted into a police riot in Chicago, with a bunch of Mafia guys. They were all doing time, all victims of the justice system, and they were rooting for the police: "Kill those fucking hippies! Kill 'em!" But they would steal meat for me. They would give me a steak, and I would cook it on the dishwasher, which would get sufficiently hot so that in about an hour-and-a-half's time the steak would actually cook. All because my mother's name is Caruso.

So I got out, and the *New York Times* did a story about my experience for the magazine, and they paid very generously. Now, the grand gesture is one thing. Take the burning of draft cards, for instance — you get famous for fifteen minutes, but it's hollow, it's not really you. It's somebody's image of you, a public thing, and it bears very little resemblance to the real you. We're addicted to grand gestures in the peace movement, flashy things that seem to have an effect, and then they're gone. A generation later, who remembers? But if you can institutionalize something, then it affects future generations. Isn't it more important to have a generalized widespread attitude than it is to have a few people with a very well articulated intellectualization of all these issues? Those people you'll always have. But they're not representative.

We're not really in control of events, and in the end it's by the grace of God that any good comes out of our protests. It's a gift. On the other hand, we weren't put here just to wait. We have the Scripture, the experience of our communities, and we need to take action. But there are so many surprises along the way. We can't really control things. We are mistaken if we think that we are in control. "Let go and let God" — it means a kind of ultimate detachment so that we just make room for God.

I don't know what's going to happen in the future. We may never have a draft again, because war has become so sophisticated, technologically, that you no longer need millions of men. Now we have missiles that can turn a 90-degree angle in midair. If we have a prolonged war, even without a draft, the public is going to be much less apt to write a blank check. People aren't going to buy it. They know better. At least I hope that there are enough people asking questions now, so that it'll be harder to wage a war that lasts for any length of time. Just to start asking those questions is the most important thing for young people.

■ ■ ■ ■ ■ ■ ■

Not all protesters were as peaceful as Tom and his friends at the Catholic Worker. Walter Hochstetler reacted to the war with a rage he now regrets. He grew up on a quiet Amish farm, but the sixties found him plunging headlong into the turbulence of the antiwar movement. Like many other students of his time, his quest for peace was marred by increasing anger and frustration at a system that seemed to be impervious to change. Now a member of our Bruderhof movement, he recently told me about his "awakening," and the hard-won wisdom he now shares willingly with others:

> My background is from the historic peace church: the Mennonites and the Amish. My parents were Old Order Amish, and none of my relatives were ever part of the military in any way or form as far as I know. "We do not kill others to save our own lives" — in a nutshell, that's my background, thoroughly rooted in pacifism, willing to suffer even the death of one's closest relatives rather than to inflict pain and suffering on anyone else.
>
> During the Vietnam War I was just appalled at our country's apparent indifference to such terrible violence, and my image of America as a "free land" was shattered. I'd experienced the benefits of living in this country and appreciated them in many respects. But I couldn't take part in this conflagration, and I became actively involved in the peace movement on campus, at Eastern Mennonite College.
>
> I think there was a genuine longing for peace in the hearts and minds of many thousands of young people in the late 1960s and early 1970s. I think there were many of us who said, "This materialistic society, which requires a strong military to support it and defend it, is all wrong." There was something positive, something fantastic, trying to be born — we really were part of a movement that might have been the embryo of a new society. And I'm convinced that God's revolution was being experienced by many people, that there was something coming alive in a genuine way. But so often it was incomplete, or smothered by our own egos.
>
> What really catapulted me into the center of the conflict was an event that happened in the summer of 1969. I was serving as a youth counselor in a Mennonite camp, and on July 19 I received the news that my nephew, who was only eighteen, had been killed in a car accident. He had been on his way to the draft board, even though he'd already been approved to do alternative service in some third world country — but there was an error in the files and they made him come in to clear it up. So he was killed in a car accident, in the prime of his life. That was the last straw for me.
>
> His death sent me spinning. I completely lost my footing. I had a real hatred toward anyone who was involved with the military. I resented that the military could just use all of our young men for their purposes, when they

could have been doing useful service elsewhere – construction, community service, teaching.

All we ever heard from Vietnam was that our American firepower was overwhelming the commies in a very devastating way. And I have to acknowledge now that in some ways I lost my faith in society, in God, and became quite agnostic. How can you believe there's a loving God when this kind of thing happens? I took it very personally.

From that point on I became much more active in what we called the draft resistance movement, especially with the Mennonites and Quakers and Church of the Brethren people. By that time I had moved to Indiana again and was attending seminary, 1968–71, and in the summer of 1968 we had many meetings of young draft resisters. We met mainly with young people who were considering the military and debating what they should do. I know there was at least one seminarian who had been to Vietnam, and the stories he told were enough to convince us. He'd been there in combat, and he knew firsthand. We were also influenced by the Berrigans, by Martin Luther King's 1967 speech against war – those kinds of leaders were the ones we trusted.

In 1969 our discussions focused on getting Agnew and Nixon out of office. The sooner the better. We talked in pretty radical terms. How could we tolerate Agnew's speeches any longer – those long, colorful adjectives with which he described folks like us? I had a vicious hatred toward Agnew and others, although I'd never met them personally. In my heart there was just a terrible hatred for everything he represented. And Nixon – he was a liar, a bone-faced liar. We had no respect for him whatsoever. He told us one thing on TV, and it was all bullshit. It was crazy! And we thought, how can the American people believe this rot? Our anger was directed toward the leaders in Washington who were betraying the American people by sending hundreds of thousands of young men to die for a senseless cause. They were just pawns in the hands of a chess king.

We categorized the police with the Army. They were all in the same game as far as we were concerned – look what happened at Kent State. So we categorized people, and it polarized people. We couldn't imagine having a rational conversation with the police...

I see now that even national leaders, in a way, are pawns. All politicians are somehow serving powers that are much greater, much more sinister and evil than they realize. I don't think most of them are even aware that their activities are on the side of death, that they are serving the god of death.

If I had to do it all over again, I would not focus my anger at the top echelons of power. I think I would rather seek forums for discussion. I would go and talk to veterans. That's what I would do – that's what I want to do, now – to try to understand what they experienced. I've never really talked at length with any veterans — it has always seemed a difficult subject to bring up, or one I didn't want to bring up, because of the way I've cut myself off from them.

If I had the opportunity to say something to a group of veterans, I'd say, "We love you." I recognize now that in many cases they were also doing what they felt they needed to do. They thought they were serving their country, and I respect anyone who honestly does what he feels is for the best of his country and his people. Perhaps we'd laugh about how we've stumbled along the way...

I would want to be more humble and apologize for our arrogance in the peace movement. I think we were far too arrogant — we thought we had all the answers — and we shouldn't have been arrogant at all. We had nothing to boast of. We were much too confrontational, in the wrong sense. We had no humility. We should have worked for reconciliation — worked to reduce the tensions, to build trust and understanding between Americans and between all nations.

A new society has to begin with us — with inner transformation. Things have to become concrete, have to be lived out. That's the fantastic thing about living on the Bruderhof now: to think that my friend Ed Baird was loading bombs in Thailand at the very same time I was demonstrating angrily in DC. It's sheer grace that we now sit at the same table, that we can be brothers and feel absolutely no resentment toward one another. Back then, we were worlds apart...

■ ■ ■ ■ ■ ■ ■

Walter does not stand alone in condemning the violence of many ostensibly nonviolent movements. His view is shared by many others, most notably the Buddhist monk and teacher Thich Nhat Hanh. Thây, as he is affectionately called, was born in 1926 in central Vietnam. He became a Zen Buddhist monk at the age of sixteen and later cofounded the most influential center of Buddhist studies in South Vietnam, the An Quang Pagoda. In 1964, he established the School of Youth for Social Service, an organization that started schools and health clinics, assisted refugees, and rebuilt villages destroyed by American bombs. During the war, five of his students were abducted in the middle of the night and shot on the banks of the Saigon River. Only one survived. All were dear friends, and he suffered greatly over their deaths.

In the 1960s, Thây became the natural leader of the nonviolent protest against the "American War," as it was called in Vietnam, and was soon sent to the United States to seek the support of the American peace movement.

His work was not appreciated by Saigon, and in 1966 he was exiled from Vietnam. Still today he is barred from returning to his home. He has thus spent much of the past thirty years traveling around the globe to spread the message of non-violent protest as a way of life; to date he has written eighty-two books. In 1982 he founded Plum Village, a retreat center and community in southern France, where he lives with a hundred monks, nuns, and laypeople and welcomes thousands of visitors each year.

I found myself deeply moved by the writings of this gentle man. Though I had come of age in the 1970s, I had never heard of the Buddhist peace movement in Vietnam. I could recall the smoldering figures of burning monks on TV, immolating themselves in protest of the rising insanity, but I was unaware of the extent to which these monks worked, tirelessly and under severe persecution, for peace. In that time of chaos, it was the Vietnamese Buddhists, far more than most American Christians, who lived and taught the essence of nonviolence and love.

The story is told best by Thây:

> The Buddhist struggle for peace in Vietnam in the 1960s and 1970s arose from the great suffering inflicted on our nation by international forces. Blood and fire ravaged the countryside, and people everywhere were uprooted. The Vietnam War was, first and foremost, an ideological struggle...The Buddhists only wanted to create a vehicle for the people to be heard – and the people only wanted peace, not a "victory" by either side. During our struggle, many scenes of love arose spontaneously – a monk sitting calmly before an advancing tank...hunger strikes held silently and patiently; monks and nuns burning themselves to death to try to be heard above the raging noise of the war. And all these efforts bore some fruit.[2]

In a play Thây wrote to memorialize the five young students who were shot at night, he shows that even their murderers were pawns, pushed around by the forces of death and destruction. But these forces could be overcome by a genuine attempt for mutual understanding:

> *Mai:* You do not understand, Tho. The ones who killed you were only obeying the orders of their superiors. And those superiors were also victims. Yet, those who shot you did show their human qualities. They hesitated, not wanting to kill you, fighting against themselves. They had to carry out their orders because they were crushed between the hammer and the anvil – the orders and their families, their jobs, even their lives. Their consciences and perceptions had been greatly obscured.

> *Hy:* One man even exclaimed, "God, you are all so young!" It was not just an expression of pity for us, but also a protest against his own fate.

> *Mai:* Men kill because, on the one hand, they do not know their real enemy, and on the other hand, they are pushed into a position where they must

kill...The soldier only wanted to kill Vietcong. He could hate the VC only
because he did not really know what the VC were. He imagined that they
were wild, cruel monsters that had to be hunted down. In his country the
people are fed so much of this that they keep letting their government send
men over here to kill and be killed. So, men kill unjustly and in turn are killed
unjustly, and it is their own countrymen who kill them...Who is really killing
us? It is fear, hatred, prejudice.

Lanh: The world of the living is shrouded in fog. All I feel now is compassion for the destiny of mankind. It is like walking in a moonless, starless
night...3

Nearly three decades later, Thây was still speaking out against war – this time,
the war in the Persian Gulf:

Immediately after ordering the ground attack on Iraq, in February 1991,
President Bush addressed his nation, saying, "Whatever you are doing at this
moment, please stop and pray for our soldiers in the Gulf. God Bless the
United States of America." I suspect that at the same moment many Moslems
were also praying to their God to protect Iraq and the Iraqi soldiers. How
could God know which nation to support? Many people pray to God because
they want God to fulfill some of their needs. If they want to have a picnic,
they may ask God for a clear, sunny day. At the same time, farmers who need
more rain might pray for the opposite. If the weather is clear, the picnickers
may say, "God is on our side; he answered our prayers." But if it rains, the
farmers will say that God heard their prayers. This is the way we usually
pray...4

If we divide reality into two camps – the violent and the nonviolent – and
stand in one camp while attacking the other, the world will never have peace.
We will always blame and condemn those we feel are responsible for wars and
social injustice, without recognizing the degree of violence in ourselves...5

We may think of peace as the absence of war, that if the great powers
would reduce their weapons arsenals, we could have peace. But if we look
deeply into the weapons, we will see our own minds – our own prejudices,
fears, and ignorance. Even if we transport all the bombs to the moon, the
roots of war and the roots of the bombs are still here – in our hearts and
minds – and, sooner or later, we will make new bombs. To work for peace is
to uproot war from ourselves and from the hearts of men and women...

If President Bush had had more understanding of the mind of President
Hussein, peace might have been obtained. President Gorbachev made a number of proposals that could have been acceptable to the allies, and many lives
could have been spared. But because anger was there, Mr. Bush rejected Mr.

Gorbachev's proposals, and Mr. Hussein gave the order to burn Kuwaiti oil wells. If President Bush had seen clearly the suffering of the Iraqi people, he would not have allowed his anger to be expressed by starting a war. He asked the American people to pray for the allied soldiers. He asked God to bless the United States of America. He did not say that we should pray for the civilians in Iraq or even the people of Kuwait. He wanted God to be on the side of America.

Eighty percent of the American people called the Persian Gulf War a victory — only a few hundred American soldiers were killed. But every human life is precious, and the loss of the 100,000 or more Iraqi people was a great tragedy! You may identify yourself as an American, but that is only partially true. You are more than that. You may have lost just a few hundred American lives, but you also suffered from the Gulf War in many other ways. The deaths of so many Iraqi soldiers and civilians are also casualties that America suffered, because their death was your country's work. When President Bush said, "God bless the United States of America," he was not paying enough attention to the lives of non-Americans. To those of us who are not American, this was not a good image of America. It was selfish and arrogant, and this was also a casualty that America suffered — not just by guns and bombs, but by your President's statement. If the President had said, "God bless us so that the war will end soon and that Americans as well as Iraqis will suffer as little as possible," he could have won a lot more sympathy from people around the world. But he did not say that.

Who is President Bush? President Bush is us. We are responsible for the way he feels, for everything he does. Eighty percent of the people in America supported him in this just war. Why blame him? Our capacity of loving and understanding was so limited. We were not peaceful enough in our own hearts, and we were not able to bring peace to the hearts of other people. When I saw how we prepared for war and practiced killing day and night in our hearts and minds, I felt overwhelmed.

After the parades ended and the yellow ribbons were no longer there, what did we have? What did the wives, husbands, children, brothers, and sisters of the soldiers receive when their loved ones returned from the Gulf after so much fear, hatred, and killing — in reality and in their daily practice? We cannot imagine the long-term effects of watering so many seeds of war...

Sit still, breathe, and look deeply, and you will see the real losses, the real casualties that America suffered and continues to suffer from the Gulf War. Visualize 500,000 allied soldiers stationed in Saudi Arabia, waiting for the order to invade Iraq, jumping and screaming as they plunge their bayonets into sandbags that represent Iraqi soldiers. You cannot plunge a bayonet into a person without first transforming yourself into a beast. On the other side, one million Iraqi soldiers were practicing the same. One and a half million soldiers were practicing violence, hatred, and fear, and the American public supported them to do so. They thought that this war was somehow clean, quick, and moral. They saw only bridges and buildings being destroyed, but the real casualties were the souls of the men and women who came home after practicing violence for so many months...

If we are able to share the truth concerning the Gulf War, we will be able to avoid starting another war like it in the future. We have to see how deep the wounds of war are. How could anyone call the Gulf War a victory? A victory for whom?[6]

Through such writings, Thich Nhat Hanh has challenged my own faith and conviction. And though I believe that there is no example of nonviolence more powerful than that given by Jesus, I must agree with Thây that a supposedly Christian America has twisted his message beyond recognition.

■ ■ ■ ■ ■ ■ ■

While Thich Nhat Hanh worked for peace in Vietnam, Daniel and Philip Berrigan were working for peace in the United States. Among "God's troublemakers," few of their contemporaries are better known. Daniel, a Jesuit, and Philip, a World War II veteran and former Josephite priest, have been fighting the military-industrial complex since the early 1960s. They've poured their own blood on the steps of the Pentagon and lain down on its grounds in poses of mock massacre, hammered on the metallic nose cones of nuclear missiles in the bowels of a General Electric plant, and wreaked havoc in the control rooms of Navy destroyers. Odd exploits for members of Catholic orders, perhaps, but then the Berrigans have never been ones to entertain the status quo.

When I visited Dan at his apartment in the small Jesuit community on 98th Street in New York City, I marveled to think that this 76-year-old "soldier" had caused perhaps the biggest embarrassment of FBI director J. Edgar Hoover's career, evading capture for four months after burning draft files with homemade napalm at the Selective Service office in Catonsville, Maryland. His brother Philip has likened him to the "proverbial fox," dodging the well-laid trap of undercover FBI agents during an antiwar rally at Cornell University. I came to Cornell eight years too late to experience his organized student protests against the war – but then, had I been born eight years earlier, I might have ended up in Vietnam...

The Berrigans' actions have always been controversial, and even among peacemakers their protests have more often than not been condemned as vandalism, a stain on the witness of pure nonviolence. But after a closer look at their writings, and meeting them both in person, I am convinced that they see the state of our nation more clearly than almost all of their critics. To dismiss their actions, often undertaken at great personal cost, is to tragically misunderstand their lives and their message. All the same, the brothers shrug off the sniping and affirm that alienation is a part of their lot. Dan fully understands the risks of swimming so vigorously against the tide and says that "if you are serious about resistance, you better look good on wood." Phil reassures himself similarly with the words of Dorothy Day: the important thing is to be faithful, not effective.

Dan entertains an endless stream of visitors, writes tirelessly, and still teaches part-time at Fordham, but he agreed to sit with me for several hours to reflect on his decades-long battle with the war machine. For all his notoriety he is humble, disarming, and gentle. Looking back, he does not consider his acts of resistance to be courageous at all, but rather a natural expression of his faith and his calling: something he simply had to do.

Dan firmly believes that without the organization of resistance against the Vietnam War, Johnson and Nixon would have used nuclear weapons. When I talked, only months later, to a veteran weapons crew chief who had been disciplined for refusing to load nerve gas bombs and claimed to have witnessed an aborted nuclear strike, I remembered Dan's words.* He minces no words for the "mythmakers" who held the power of life and death in their hands: McNamara, Nixon, Johnson, Eisenhower, and MacArthur; and yet his heart overflows for the generation of young men who were used and deceived, ushered to their deaths in the heat of Vietnam. His journey is the story of a man every bit a veteran as they:

> I feel that we did what we did for the soldiers and veterans as well as for ourselves. This war was doing nothing for anyone, other than killing people, and yet who was going to stop it? Who was going to put his body in the way of it?

---

* Gabe Bass, Air Force Combat Support, '70–'71, told me the following harrowing tale in October 1997. He enlisted as an illustrator to "stay out of the Army," but he was assigned to artillery and spent the war loading 500-lb. napalm bombs. His crew had top-secret security clearance and inspected the weapons being loaded onto their planes; during one such inspection, he lifted up a nose assembly to find an ATM12C nerve gas bomb. He recalls: "I stood there with my hand on it, and I really felt confronted. It was real. I thought about my grandmother, a Lithuanian lady who survived the Nazi death camps, and pretty quickly I realized that I didn't want to be part of this. The three other crew members were standing there with this belt containing four shots of atropine — just in case something went wrong. I looked at the guys, and I asked them what they thought. Denis, who is from West Virginia, looked at me and said, "Gabe, this is the kind of thing you go to hell for." That helped. I went back to the load officer and said, 'I won't be able to do this.' All hell broke loose after that. I was charged with failure to obey a lawful order of the commander in chief, and they put me in a tractor for discipline. But I don't think they knew what to do with me at that point."

God knows how much worse it would have been if we hadn't gone to jail. I was in Vietnam in '68, and the conventional wisdom was that Johnson had ordered nuclear weapons to Vietnam and that they were there, already in Southeast Asia, just waiting. I was present at the Paris peace talks and it was quite clear that Kissinger and Nixon had threatened, were still threatening the Vietnamese with nuclear weapons repeatedly. So it was very close. The only reason that Vietnam was not actually obliterated was because of the heroism there and the people on the streets here. The war became unwageable and then unwinnable, and it removed two Presidents from office. We could have done worse...

But to speak of courage, I don't know; I always kind of wince at the word, because it seemed to me and to Philip and to our friends that we were doing very simple things we really couldn't avoid. And we had one another — most of these young men didn't have anyone. They had the very lonely horrors of combat to deal with, and silence from their churches and families, while we had a very close community and a very close family. We had the sacraments and we had prayer together. We had years of this kind of discipline. And it would have been horrible if it hadn't come to something. But I don't know whether it was courage or not. We were just a small part of the common life of the church, doing what good people ought to do...

There were some hilarious aspects, though. It was very nice for the ego to be evading [FBI Director] J. Edgar Hoover and his minions for months, hiding out with a few friends. It was great. We saw the papers. He was absolutely furious because he couldn't pick me up. In recent years we've been able to see internal documents with his writing, scrawled in red across the top: "Get him! Top priority, get him!" When Phil went on trial in Harrisburg in '72, Hoover was still living. He was determined to send us away for life. Those conspiracy trials were very heavy. He gave orders, we learned later, to be awakened any hour of the night or called away from any meeting during the day, when the jury reached its verdict. He wanted us. Then there was no verdict, and he died. He died the same week. He lived just to see us put away...

I was teaching at Cornell while all of this was going on. We had the son of Secretary of State Dean Rusk up there, the son of the man who was running the war. He was a very silent kid, sort of on the edge of the students who were most active against the war. I didn't really get to know him until all of a sudden everything exploded around Christmas 1967. The president of Cornell invited Rusk up to speak on the war, and the place just went berserk, and this boy — this poor, poor kid — just broke like a melon under it all. I got a call informing me that he had been hospitalized and that he wanted to see me. So I went down, and I spent a lot of hours with him in that hospital as he tried to

unravel his hatred of his father, his hatred of the war, his sense of being one
of its victims. But then his mother and father came up, a couple of days later,
and they took the boy off. I was there, and I remember thinking, "There goes
another victim of the war, right from the top." I never saw him again.

Our most significant act of resistance to the war? Oh, my. I don't know.
There wasn't any. We never used that kind of language – what is going to be
successful, or what is going to do it "big," or anything like that. Our acts
were always very modest, and we were drawn toward them, sometimes even
unwillingly. Certainly we were never very lighthearted about anything. But
these things had to be done because of an inner voice that beckoned us. And
we were never alone; we always prayed together with others, gave everything a lot of time. Every one of our actions was preceded by months and
months of preparation – not tactically, but rather: are we ready, knowing
that it could be very difficult? It was much more about the spirit of the thing
than developing a tactic, or dwelling on the outcome, whether people would
understand us or not. We hoped they would, obviously, and as it turned out,
they usually did, and people were turned around. But we were never motivated by outcomes. That didn't appeal to us as being biblically correct, because the great acts of faith in the Bible were always done without respect to
their success. Abraham just went; Mary just said yes. Then great things happened, things they hadn't expected…

On February 12, 1997, Ash Wednesday, Philip Berrigan and fellow members of
the activist Prince of Peace Plowshares boarded the USS *The Sullivans*, a Navy
guided-missile destroyer, at the Bath Iron Works in Maine. Armed with hammers and bottles of blood, their goal was to penetrate the ship's control room
and "disarm" the main console. One of the men quickly ran past the gathering
security personnel and managed, somehow, to find the control room. For several minutes, he hammered away at the key pads and controls, finally pouring
his blood over the cracked display panels. When he was finally apprehended, he
knelt down on the deck in front of his captors to say a short prayer for them.

   Meanwhile, Philip Berrigan had been stopped on the topside deck. A frantic
young security officer brandished a beretta at him, cursing and screaming.
Philip, trying to calm him, said, "Son, put that thing away. That thing you've got
in your hand is the source of all that's wrong with this country." The young man
continued to threaten Philip. "You gonna shoot me, huh?" Philip asked softly.
"That's what the Navy's all about. Don't you get dragged into it too." "Na, I
wouldn't shoot ya," the young man retorted, glaring. "I'd come upside your
head and knock you out."

I visited Phil and three other members of the Plowshares group at the Cumberland County Jail in Portland, Maine, eight months later. Shortly afterward, he was sentenced to two years in prison, followed by two years of probation, and a fine of $4,703.89 for the damage incurred to the warship. The federal district judge made a point of saying that he was not passing judgment on the morality, propriety, or sincerity of Phil's actions, but that his views on nuclear weapons could not justify violation of the law.

Little did I imagine that I would ever sit with Phil face to face. A warm, hearty man, he was soft-spoken and meek, dressed in bright orange prison pajamas and with a smile that defied that overheated and harshly lit cubicle where we met.

His personal journey is remarkable. As a young man, he marched into battle in World War II with the patriotic fervor of a trained killer. As a member of a field artillery outfit, he served first in Normandy and later fired on German submarine emplacements at Lorient and Brittany, moving across Northern France into the Low Countries and then on toward Germany. He came home a "victory boy," restless but idle, basking in the fading light of glory. The fifties found him in the Deep South, a Josephite priest teaching black children and learning from them, firsthand, their oppression and struggle to survive. Such experiences fueled a growing discontent with the status quo and revealed to him the very deep connections between racism and war. By 1967, he joined his brother in burning draft files in Catonsville, Maryland – the first link in a ponderous chain of actions taken to arouse the American mind and to protest the manufacture of weapons of death. Since 1967, Philip has been arrested for civil disobedience more than one hundred times, and has spent a total of more than seven years in prison.

The Irish twinkle in his eye warms the heart but belies the deadly seriousness of his convictions. There is an air of craziness about him, too, but one calculated, it seems, to counteract the craziness of a society gone mad. He spoke of the Plowshare group's discouragement, during a recent action, when they found they couldn't even dent the missile hatches with their hammers. "The only thing we could do was take off a few flakes of paint," he said. "But it's a symbol. You cause even a little damage and the action becomes symbolic."

Phil has been dubbed a "disturber of sleep," and I cannot think of a more appropriate epithet. In him is nothing of the easy peace of the world, nothing of false contentment. His dedication has made me face my own apathy. Though I'd been through the mill in Navy-Marines ROTC in college, and knew full well the destructive power of modern weaponry, I had done nothing about it after I "escaped." For years, I had taken the New London ferry home across the sound to Long Island on weekends, passing only a few hundred feet in front of the nuclear submarines under construction at the Groton Electric Boat shipyard. Why was I not affected? Why was I unable (unwilling?) to take in the fact that weapons capable of destroying entire countries were being manufactured right under my nose, and do something about it?

It is bitterly ironic that Plowshare's actions are so quickly condemned as violent. We hear of the hammers and the blood in the inner sanctums of nuclear submarines and Navy destroyers, and our sensibilities are violated. Yet we consent to the existence and the continued production of these weapons of mass annihilation without the slightest twinge of apprehension or guilt. For now, these weapons may lie dormant, but they were made to be used; they stand ready to unleash their death and destruction at a moment's notice. They sleep, and we sleep with them. Thus Plowshares members hammer at the gleaming controls to disturb our slumber and – they hope – to avert the massacre of millions. They spill their blood to decry the preparation of the world for death.

Phil cannot conceive of a peace that coexists comfortably with the institutionalized violence of the world. For him, an isolated peace is no peace at all – it must come to the whole world or to none.

I was a very good killer. I was a superior marksman – I knew how to handle a bayonet, an automatic rifle, a BAR (Browning automatic rifle), and on and on and on. I mastered those weapons and was eager for combat simply because my brothers and so many of my friends were in combat, too. But God had his hand in it, somehow, because I came home unscathed. Actually, I got an assignment to return to the States very, very quickly, to prepare for the invasion of Japan. The Bomb had not been dropped yet...

So I went back to the States and was on thirty-day relief, and while I was on leave I went to see my brother in Baltimore. During my stay with him the Bomb was dropped on Hiroshima and Nagasaki, and we had a victory celebration, if you can feature such a thing.

But through all of the years, through the Civil Rights struggle, I was led to reflect on my war experiences and to come, slowly, to a position against war. That took the form of opposition to the Vietnam War. It all started in the early sixties – I was teaching at a black Catholic high school in New Orleans, and then we had the Cuban missile crisis. That was a turning point for me. Kennedy and Krushchev were threatening the very people I was trying to serve. They were playing God with my life and with the lives of people all over the South. That was a real crisis. We came very close to a catastrophe there; all of the southern Gulf ports were targeted by those intermediate-range ballistic missiles, and millions of Americans could have died. Of course, we would have slaughtered the Soviet Union in retaliation. It almost happened; Robert Kennedy wrote about it later on. We've come to the brink with tactical nuclear weapons twenty-five times since, but nothing was more close than the Cuban missile crisis...

When I was in New Orleans I came to the realization that we were one of the most racist nations in the world. Hitler actually had read about American racism when he was developing his sick philosophies. Then the Vietnam War came and I noticed that a disproportionate number of the troops going to Vietnam were black. And later on, after 1965, when I was stationed at a black parish on Baltimore's west side, I had to bury them when they came home in tin boxes. They accounted for a third of the combat troops in Vietnam but only one-tenth of the general population. These guys were mercenaries, fighting the empire's wars, and they had no rights as citizens back home...

It seems to me that when you live under the Bomb for fifty-five years, and contribute your silence to the whole sick enterprise, you open yourself to very destructive influences on your spirit and on your mind and on your will. Our national denial starts with the Bomb. All other violence becomes possible because of the intention to use the Bomb. We wouldn't have built it if we didn't plan to use it. So it's the intention that wreaks havoc. The gospel says, well, maybe the act never really happened, but the intention was there. And our predilection toward denial and myth and unreality and Disney-like behavior — a lot of it is traceable to that...

Making the weapon is robbery from God and from creation. It's as simple as that. God made us. And when you trace the origin of a weapon, it means that you have to take certain materiality in order to build it; you have to use the genius of a laboratory and all the rest, and you have to use skills and training that really belong to God. These metallurgists, the physicists, chemists, whoever would work at Los Alamos, or Lawrence Livermore Laboratories or the Applied Physics lab between Baltimore and Washington — all those professionals — their skills and talents and all belong to God, because that's where they came from. God didn't give us the matter of creation to do these things against one another.

Now, what can we do about all of this violence, this injustice? During the Vietnam War there were legions of Americans who would work with these questions for six months but then drop them, because they weren't realizing what they wanted to achieve, they weren't getting results. The Fellowship of Reconciliation did a study of this and found that the Americans who opposed the war were involved, on the average, for only six months. They were just wiped out because they didn't see any results. But you learn very quickly what you're responsible for, what you can effect, as opposed to that which is simply beyond you. And there's an awful lot that can't be done. Take the media, for example. If we do a protest, will the *Boston Globe* send a guy up here? Probably not. Is the *New York Times* going to show interest? Probably not. The main media stations, CBS, ABC, NBC? Probably not. And you can't effect that. If they do show up, it's not because of you. In the end, after we confronted them at the Bath Iron Works, we got coverage from CBS and the *Boston Globe* and the *Washington Post* and the *New York Times*. We never expected that. So it's all in the hands of God. You do things for the honor and glory of God and for the Kingdom, and you do it because it's right and just. That's enough. If nothing else happens, that's enough. That attitude has to be cultivated, though, because we're a very pragmatical-minded people. We want results. We want to be effective. And Dorothy Day always said that trying to be effective was missing the point. The point is simply to be faithful.

The silence is deafening; you choke on the silence. And if you just believe but don't act, you cannot be at peace. Nonviolence requires that you pursue truth in the way you live personally, right to the last figment. Why else does Isaiah say that swords will be beaten back into plowshares? That swords will be turned back into tools that nourish? That's what we try to do. It's not vandalism, it's conversion...

I can sleep at night and I can live with myself. Not that I've made any great achievements, but I know that I've tried. I know that I've tried...

■ ■ ■ ■ ■ ■ ■

I'll never forget the first time I really met Kevin Bruce, who now lives at the Bruderhof in Pennsylvania. We were twelve, crammed into a van for a twenty-six-hour drive to Canada. There was room enough for one person at a time to lie down on the back seat, so we took turns dozing through the seemingly endless night. But in the long hours that I sat staring out at the bleak, darkened prairie, Kevin started asking me about my background. (I was new to the Bruderhof then.)

I told Kevin about myself, but it wasn't long before I was asking him questions, too. Tired eyes lifted around us as he spun a tale of a Yogi in the mountains of Micronesia, shaved head, sandals, saffron robes and all, who'd been converted by Bob Dylan. I thought, "You gotta be kidding – in this crowd of beards, suspenders, and black trousers?" But it was true. Years later, over cups of tea with Kevin and his wife Barbara, I heard the full story, a saga of resistance to more than just the Vietnam War.

I grew up a devout Roman Catholic in Worcester, Massachusetts. I attended mass and took Communion every Sunday at the Immaculate Conception parish. Our pastor was Father Edward Connors, who later married us; he'd been a chaplain for the 9th Infantry Division, which was stationed in North Africa, during World War II. I was an ardent American boy...

After high school I was accepted at Brown University. I still remember November 22, 1963 – standing in the student lounge and asking someone,

"What is that enormous crowd in front of the television?" They said, "The President has been shot."

I was nineteen, and I really struggled to deal with that. Here was a Roman Catholic President, Irish like me, charismatic to the core...I felt certain, at some level, that he had been killed because of his attitude toward peace and his attitude against war. He had somehow saved us from nuclear conflict with the Russians, and we heard rumors that he'd made a deal with Krushchev behind closed doors. But we knew very little; the public had very little idea of what Kennedy was up to. I've since read his speech of June 10, 1963, at the American University graduation ceremonies, where he laid out his plan for peace, and he clearly would have become an architect of world peace for all time. He really wanted to end the Cold War. This man brought something totally new to his office.

So Kennedy was, for me, a kind of hope, and I felt that something inside of me was shattered on November 22, 1963. I had to change my attitudes, wake up, and realize that I was becoming a man. To some extent I did, but it was very, very difficult.

I fell in love with Barbara in 1965. I still had a year at Brown; she still had a year at the Rhode Island School of Design. We were an odd pair: she was Jewish, from Brooklyn, from a great family but not religious, and I was from this very orthodox and conventional Catholic family. We didn't know if we wanted to stay together, but in the end we both applied to the Peace Corps.

I had lined up a job at my hometown newspaper after graduation, and though I didn't think I could survive the draft with a newspaper job, I hoped that the war would end in time. Of course, I didn't realize then that the war was intentional and wasn't planned to end; it was planned to go on.

I ended up in the Peace Corps, and my brother ended up as a Green Beret in Vietnam. We were both in Asia at the very same time, but we were miles apart in attitude...

The two years in the Peace Corps changed Barbara and me for good, because we began meeting people who were for peace — not just against war, but for peace. We were sent to a reef island in the South Pacific, in Micronesia, and we had a very good experience on that island. The people loved us, and we loved the people. To us they seemed just one big extended family, yet there were three clans, and they basically lived a kind of communal existence. We had no idea that such things still existed on the face of the earth. It was a real eye-opener; culture-shock is putting it mildly for two very shallow middle-class dreamers. Again, we were taken out of the American culture and shown something totally other, totally new.

Both Martin Luther King and Robert Kennedy were assassinated while we were away, killed by the same conspirators and for the same reasons that John

Kennedy was killed. And the war was going to grind on – that was clear. It was clear from the riots at the Democratic Convention in Chicago. Clear from what we read between the lines in *Time* magazine or heard on the radio. And we became more and more disenchanted with America.

When we got back to New York I was twenty-three and still had three more years of draft eligibility. So we had to make some quick decisions. We were advised by the Peace Corps in Washington that we could get an annual deferment if we would teach in inner-city New York. The turnover of teachers there was terrific, because the problems were so enormous. So Barbara and I both got provisional New York City teaching licenses, which allowed us to teach school in Brooklyn.

The bodies were coming home fast and furious. My brother came back. I managed to establish a connection with him again, but he was changed for the worse. We knew then that even after I was no longer eligible for the draft, we would have to make some life-changing decisions for the future. The school in Brooklyn wanted me to stay: I had a way with the kids, I was able to reach their hearts and motivate them. At least I knew some of the reality their parents had emerged from...So there was every inclination on my part to stay there, to make something out of my life for the good of the next generation in America.

But what did we have to offer these kids anyway, apart from an entry-level place in a system that had already rejected them? And our existence in New York was so fragmented. The teachers who had survived were wrecks, hulks, former humans. And we would soon look the same.

America was so committed to that war that very soon we just could not go along with it anymore. And the culture at large wanted business as usual. We were fed up. So we went to Woodstock Peace and Music Fair and took part in it wholeheartedly – for the first day at least. Halfway through the second day we decided this was not really for us, and we left. We saved ourselves for further battles.

So we moved to Spain. We got rid of all our belongings, including the car. We felt that this was the point at which we could take up full battle against the war. Until then, we had just "bled inside each other's wounds" in Joni Mitchell's words. Now I had a chance to strike a blow against the machine itself by telling my family that, in conscience, I could no longer live in America. My father was now Nixon's campaign manager for Central Massachusetts. We were fed up and getting furious...

We felt that rejecting the benefits of America, physically going away from it and turning our backs on it, was all we could do to retain our freedom and maintain some semblance of a fight for the freedom of the Vietnamese people. We all knew that 58,000 Americans had died, but who mentioned the

2½ million Vietnamese who had died as well? And the Vietnamese people who were being slaughtered were not only men, but women and children, and because they had a different culture, they were completely overlooked. It was an evil attitude of mind and heart which we couldn't argue against any more.

That was 1971. We got rid of all our belongings, including the car. We sold everything we could and gave away what we couldn't. I handed out all my neckties at a farewell party at the school. We told our friends that we were leaving the country as a protest against the war. We felt like we were holding ourselves hostage against the liberation of the Vietnamese people. That's how intensely we felt it.

Now we joined a battalion of freedom fighters who were using the weapons of the spirit to fight the war, which went on within and without us. We became vegetarian. We found something in Buddhism, and later in Yoga, which is truly ancient and goes back 3000 years in the Hindu tradition. We read all the books, like *Siddhartha*, by Hermann Hesse, *Be Here Now*, by Ram Dass. We read *The Tibetan Book of the Dead* by Timothy Leary. We read books on Hatha Yoga. We were very active in fasting, but prayer for us meant meditation. Personally I fasted down from 205 pounds to 129. My clothes no longer fit. It was ludicrous. We had to change, and we saw quickly that other people would be blessed by changing too. But we often grew shrill and they couldn't hear us!

Before we got into Yoga, I almost became an alcoholic myself. I was a meat-eating, 205-pound American misfit. I lived in bitterness, fear, anxiety. A group of friends and acquaintances took me out of all that into another world where there wasn't any war, any hatred, any power trips. Those experiences convinced me that I had to oppose the U.S. culture in order to help stop this war. Only if Americans were willing to do what Dan Berrigan had done – to go underground and hold himself hostage against the government of the USA, against the system that was killing "our boys" – would it be stopped.

We were fighters, but we were shell-shocked. We had wounds. We had hurt each other, wounded each other, broken with other couples we had been close to. We had run out of purpose, and we hadn't found a new purpose to live for. We were tired and weak from living against everything, and we grew desperate for something whole. We had reached a low point in our lives.

This led us to India, where we spent six months with a guru called Dr. Swami Gitananda and dabbled in Tantric Yoga. Yet it was only in Kriya Yoga, a system of mental (and of course physical) exercise that helped us to liberate the psyche from past programming by our native culture. We felt we'd found a new freedom.

You know, Gandhi actually had brought out most of the answers. We saw something in India of nonviolence that had just never penetrated the American psyche. There were only a few Americans – those listening to Alan Watts telling of Zen in Japan or those who were reading the poetry of Allen Ginsburg – who would dare to gaze beyond the American military logic of might and right, the insidious corporate world of Secretary MacNamara's double-breasted goon squad. The greatest world power in history was totally in the wrong; we were way over our heads in an immoral, illegal war. In fact, it had never been declared. It was totally illegal, and it broke international law. And it's been going on ever since, in the Persian Gulf and everywhere else, in spite of showy treaties and travesties of human justice.

I came back to the United States in 1978, and it wasn't easy. I had been away for more than seven years, and things had really changed. By then, the Vietnam War was supposedly over. But it's not really over yet – it has only changed battlefields, only changed countries. The war is still going on. The war hasn't stopped. And I'm not going to be able to stop it – Barbara and I together cannot stop it. But we have our sanity back, and we have four charming daughters, full of life and rebellion and nerve...may God help them to grow into flowers for his garden.

Finally, we have found something to live for, something beyond ourselves, something that filled the hollow places that cried out for love.

My brother came back from the Green Berets, but he was changed beyond my heart's ability to cope. I can't heal him. God can, and he somehow will, I trust. God heals. And the only hope for me, and him, is that we turn to God and pray and ask and receive.

I was told, somewhere along my journey, to take a step in faith, a leap in faith. And once you test that faith, you can take another step in the same direction.

■ ■ ■ ■ ■ ■ ■

Few people know the extent of deception permeating the Vietnam War better than Daniel Ellsberg. A brilliant student at Harvard in the late 1940s, he trained as a Marine in the early fifties and then joined the Rand Corporation, a private think tank which advised the Pentagon on strategies and policies of war, particularly the retaliatory strategies of potential nuclear war. His rise at Rand was meteoric, but in the early 1960s he surprised his colleagues by volunteering to go to Vietnam to observe firsthand the implementation of the U.S. "pacification" program. Remarkably, he ended up in live combat more than once; he has kept a handful of shell casings, which he picked up while still hot and doused in the water of a rice paddy.

A high-level military advisor by the late 1960s, Ellsberg's moment of truth came in 1969, at an antiwar rally in Philadelphia. Thousands of young men were dying for what he knew was a lie, and he had the ability — and the influence — to put an end to it all. His actions would certainly be regarded as treasonous, but if draft resistors were willing to go to prison, so was he.

In his position at Rand, Ellsberg was privy to a top-secret study of America's Cold War involvement in Southeast Asia, commissioned by Secretary of Defense Robert McNamara, which he knew revealed rampant "miscalculation, bureaucratic arrogance, and deception" by U.S. policy makers. The document patterned a history of death and deception, greed and power — in short, it stunningly exposed American imperialism at its worst. With the help of his young children and his friend Anthony Russo, a former Rand employee who'd been fired for exposing torture and other American war crimes in Vietnam, Ellsberg began to duplicate the 7000-page document. He sent copies to antiwar Congressmen and then leaked a copy to the *New York Times*, which printed selections of the Pentagon Papers in June 1971.

In the national furor that ensued, Nixon ordered the *Times* to stop publishing the classified papers, and Ellsberg was charged with conspiracy, theft, and violations of the Espionage Act. Nixon secretly directed his henchmen to "incapacitate" Ellsberg, but the plot was revealed by John Dean during the Watergate hearings, and the trial was called off. Ellsberg was free, but Nixon's credibility was seriously damaged. The revelation of Nixon's crimes made it impossible for him to renew the bombing in Vietnam, and they figured crucially in his impeachment proceedings, which led to his resignation and made the war endable.

I tried to piece together all this history as I waited in my car, in the pouring rain, outside Ellsberg's apartment in Washington. Here was a Pentagon insider who had risked family, friends, and career — in fact, his very life — to stop the war. Remarkably, thankfully, he was successful.

Ellsberg gave me a warm reception. He is a man of intense energy, and though he is slightly graying, he gives the image of one still young and vital. His modest apartment is crammed with books: volume after volume on foreign policy, Vietnam, the Kennedys, the Cold War. But these are more than just reading material — in a very real way, they are the chronicle of his life and his work. One senses keenly the presence of history, the fact that here is a man who has seen it all and turned his back on what others embraced. I settled into a comfortable chair next to Ellsberg, eager to hear his story.

What unfolded that afternoon went far beyond my expectations. Ellsberg moved quickly from bouts of passionate reflection to moments of speechless tears, and he apologized more than once for his emotion, noting that his memory is especially acute just now, as he is writing his own memoirs. But the experience was clearly cathartic for him, and I was later to reflect on the fact that he is still paying dearly for his actions, having lost a lifetime of friends and colleagues in this city that he once tried so desperately to awaken.

In the course of nearly three hours, he told his story – the story of a war, four Presidents, and a very sick nation.

At the Rand Corporation, I worked on what seemed like the most important problem in the world: to deter a nuclear attack by the Soviets. We based our strategies on top-secret estimates of the Soviets' capabilities, and at the time it was believed that they were in a crash program, building up the capability to wipe us out, to wipe out our retaliatory forces, all of our strategic air command bases in one big surprise attack. That was the so-called missile gap – they were believed to be far ahead of us in the number and destructive capability of nuclear weapons, and of course they had put up their first satellite before us.

Everyone I worked with at Rand really believed that this surprise attack would come anytime, not so much in 1958 when I started, but definitely by '59 or '60. It was regarded as a real danger. And I worked night and day, seventy hours a week, to figure out ways to retaliate, but also to deter, to prevent that attack from ever taking place. I should say that my attitude toward nuclear weapons was as abhorrent back then as it is now; that was true ever since Hiroshima. So I was in effect working on nuclear retaliatory capability, and ultimately nuclear retaliatory plans, which might seem a total irony or reversal, but for me it wasn't. The whole point was to prevent any such war from ever taking place. It just seemed that the only possible way to prevent nuclear war, which we thought would come only as a result of a Soviet attack, was to ensure a prohibitive threat of retaliation.

Rand is a private, not-for-profit research corporation that uses foundation money (to start with, Ford Foundation money) to do research in the public interest. In those days we worked almost entirely for the Air Force, and then later for the secretary of defense. I was one of the first people at Rand to work directly for the secretary of defense, but my work was obviously and essentially for the President, initially Eisenhower and then Kennedy. I was a Democrat, a Cold War Democrat, but my initial work was for Eisenhower.

That's a long story, how I tried to change the Eisenhower plans, which I thought were very dangerous. The important thing is that in September of '61 I learned that the Soviet's "crash program" was an illusion. There simply was no such effort and no such force.

When I visited the Strategic Air Command headquarters in Omaha in August 1961 it was estimated that the Soviets had 1000 missiles. We had only 40

ICBMs and perhaps 120 submarine-launched weapons, and 60 or so intermediate-range missiles in Turkey and England that were within range of Russia. Not to mention 600 B-52s, 1400 B-47s, and a thousand tactical bombers on bases like Okinawa or Korea or on carriers, or in Europe, largely in England. So, 3000 bombers and roughly 200 missile warheads, about 40 of which were ICBMs.

But in September of '61 we learned that the Soviets had not 1000 missiles, which was the SAC estimate, and not even the 120 to 160 that was the national estimate. What they had was 4, compared to our 40 or 200 or 3000, depending on how you figured it. But at a minimum we had a ten-to-one advantage in ICBMs alone, not counting everything else we had. And the 4 the Soviets had were 4 missiles on one pad. They could have hit Washington, let's say, or even Omaha, but that wouldn't have done them any good. They had no capability to speak of at all, and the only force that existed as a first-strike force in the whole world, a force that could disarm any opponent, was clearly ours. So it was a total delusion, and it took me years to realize, on the basis of a good deal of evidence, that our Joint Chiefs had known it all along.

Now the Army and Navy had been questioning those numbers for some years, but those of us working for the Air Force were told that these were treasonous, wishful estimates to keep us from buying the number of missiles we really needed. The Army and the Navy said that the Soviets had only a very few at best, and they were right. The Air Force had lied, and it was a wishful delusion.

I tried to understand how we'd gotten into that situation, how that delusion had arisen, and then I found myself in the middle of the Cuban missile crisis the following year, which really did come very close to blowing the world up, and which again involved a great deal of illusion, on both sides, as to what the risks really were. Obviously, there had been great misunderstanding on both sides, but that's another story...

Anyway, I was offered a job at the Pentagon. I was actually working in the Pentagon already, as a consultant and a researcher, but I was then offered a post on the GS-18 – which is the highest civil service rating. I started at the top, in other words. The only position higher is a presidential appointee, the deputy assistant secretary. So I had the highest civil service super-grade, equivalent to lieutenant general. And I thought that from the inside I'd be able to understand things better and identify these risks so as to reduce them. I was assigned right away to work on Vietnam.

The very day that I started work in the Pentagon was the day on which an attack was supposedly going on, twelve hours away across the globe, in the Tonkin Gulf. An attack was supposedly taking place at that very moment against our destroyers, for the second time, there having been a daylight attack two days earlier. It's not clear to this day whether even that was an attack, although there had been boats in the vicinity of our destroyers two days earlier. Now on August 4, 1964, they seemed to be doing it again: firing on us with their torpedoes.

There were supposedly a lot of torpedoes in the water this time, unlike the first time. But the commodore of the two-destroyer American squadron wanted to wait until daylight before responding; it wasn't clear that there were any torpedoes, and he wanted to check for wreckage. Already by then they realized that most of their reports, in fact all but one – and it later turned out that that one, too, was false – had been mistaken: the sonar man had somehow mistaken the beat of the ship's propeller against the curving wake for torpedoes. So the torpedoes didn't exist.

But President Johnson was unwilling to wait until morning, unwilling, really, to miss the chance of launching an attack against North Vietnam and showing the world, the public, that he was as tough as his opponent, Major General Goldwater. Goldwater was a senator, an Air Force major general in the reserves, who was calling for the bombing of North Vietnam. And, of course, he was Johnson's opponent in the presidential race, and Election Day was only months away. Johnson wanted to show the public that he could be just as tough as Goldwater – just as tough, but at the same time restrained and precise. He would reply just once, with sixty-four planes. He certainly wouldn't undertake an unlimited bombing campaign until after the election.

He knew full well that the circumstances were very uncertain, but he announced that the attack on our ships had been "unequivocal and unprovoked." Even then it was clear that it was not unprovoked, because that very night we were attacking North Vietnam in covert operations. But we went ahead with the attacks, and that was the beginning of the bombing. And then it was all over, until after the election. The President thought the public had seen enough bombing for that period.

Like Wilson and FDR before him, Johnson ran on the notion that he would keep us out of the war. He promised that he would not expand the war, in contrast to Goldwater, who was calling for an immediate widening of the war, the bombing of North Vietnam, and the possible use of nuclear weapons. In fact, Goldwater had called for the delegation of the authority to use nuclear weapons to field commanders, and Johnson turned this into the number-one issue of the campaign, even greater than Vietnam – that this was an irresponsible suggestion, and that as President he had not delegated and never would delegate his most serious responsibility. He ran as someone to be trusted, someone far more responsible than his opponent. Actually I knew that Johnson had delegated that authority, and General Goldwater also knew, but he didn't announce it because it was a secret.

I was in the Pentagon, and we were making plans to widen the war as soon as the election was over. At the time, I believed this to be a very wrong judgment, also wrong practically. It would not succeed, and it was immoral. Illegal and immoral. I thought it was totally wrong, but it was my job, and so I did it. It's hard for me to explain now why I didn't just quit or expose it. I should have exposed it, definitely, but it didn't occur to me to do it at that time.

So we were now at war. The bombing started early in 1965. And at that point, being a former Marine, I thought, well, now we can't turn back. We can't afford to lose this. At the very least, we've got to fuzz things up if we are defeated. We just can't afford a blatant defeat, for international purposes.

I didn't think the bombing would accomplish anything, but with troops we could definitely avoid losing the whole country. I was not opposed to the idea of putting troops in, now that we were there. So we put troops in.

By then I felt we were getting misled a great deal by Washington, and I didn't want to watch the war from Washington. I wanted to go see things for myself. So I volunteered to go to Vietnam, and I said I would go at any level, any salary that would pay my alimony (by then I was divorced and had two children). But they transferred me at the same level I was at, which was FSR-1, foreign service reserve officer-1. So I got a bonus for going to the combat zone...

I remember asking a radio operator there if he didn't feel like one of the Redcoats. He said, "I've been thinking that all day." It was impossible for anybody who'd been through American grade school to miss the imagery of it. Here we were walking tree lines in somebody else's neighborhood, 10,000 miles from home, big guys weighed down by web gear and helmets and packs and heavy equipment, being fired at by militia, guerrillas – just like the minutemen at Concord. There was the unspoken realization that we didn't have any business being there...

I got hepatitis in the field. I came back, went back to the Rand Corporation, and worked on a study of the war that later came to be known as the Pentagon Papers. The study had been commissioned by Secretary of Defense McNamara, and it examined the history of U.S. decision-making in Vietnam from 1945 to 1968. The reason it ended then, in 1968, was because many people believed the war was really over. The Tet Offensive had shaken public confidence; Johnson had announced his plans to retire, and the bombing had been stopped, at least ostensibly. But the war wasn't over. It had seven years to go. By 1969 it was clear that Nixon intended to carry on the war until he was successful, pretending all the while that he was going to get us out. In other words, the country was being misled in the same way that it had been five years earlier, in 1964. And I started to wonder what responsibility I had, now that I was convinced we were going in a very bad direction.

I should say that by then, by 1968, nearly everyone who had been to Vietnam was disillusioned with the war. They realized that what we were doing could not succeed. Many of them believed that there were other ways in which we might succeed – perhaps by sending more troops or something – but if they had been there long enough, they had also realized that we weren't going to change what we were doing. Therefore there was no chance for success, and that meant that the people who were dying or being killed were doing so without any useful effect of any kind. Nobody was being benefited by it. It was wasting lives, and it was wrongful.

That was especially true of the bombing. It was obvious that the bombing was doing no good at all. My friend Mort Halperin was in the Pentagon then, and in March 1968 he said to me, "You know, there's only three people in Washington who believe in what we're doing." He was speaking about the bombing in particular, before the bombing. We counted: Johnson; Rusk, the secretary of state; and Rostow, Johnson's special assistant. We tried to think, is that really all? We tried to think of anyone else who believed that it was worth bombing, but we couldn't. And Johnson kept bombing North Vietnam until just before the election, even though everybody understood that it wasn't achieving anything.

At that point the bombing had five years to go (Congress stopped the bombing in '73), but we'd already dropped one-and-a-half million tons. And there were six million to go. Four times as many! We dropped two million in all of World War II, including the Pacific. After 1969 there were still three World War IIs ahead, at a point when everybody understood that the war was totally pointless, totally useless – especially the bombing.

Now, two things affected my life at that point. I'd been reading Gandhi since the spring of '68, when I happened to meet people from the Quaker Action group at a conference in Princeton. I had gone there to study counterrevolution, and they were there as nonviolent revolutionaries. So I started reading Martin Luther King, *Stride Toward Freedom*, and Barbara Deming, who wrote an essay called "Revolution and Equilibrium." I read and reread many times a book by Joan Bondurant called *The Conquest of Violence*, on Gandhian thought, which converted me very strongly, very impressively.

Then in late August 1969 I went to a conference of the War Resisters League (they were founded by World War I COs; Einstein was once their honorary president), and in the course of this conference I was induced to go to a vigil for somebody who was going to prison for draft resistance, which was a very unusual thing for me to be doing. There I was, standing in the street outside the Philadelphia post office, passing out leaflets. This was not the sort of thing a GS-18 did. It seemed, you know, rather undignified – giving away your influence and your access in such a ridiculous way, just handing out leaflets like a bum.

Then at the end of this conference I met another young man, Randy Kehler, a Harvard College graduate who had gone on to Stanford but then stopped his studies to work for the War Resisters League. He gave a talk, and at the end he announced that he was on his way to prison for refusal to cooperate with the draft. And this came to me as a total shock. It just hit me that it was a terrible thing for my country that the best he and so many others could do was go to prison. I went to the men's room and just sat on the floor and cried for about an hour and thought, "My country has come to this? We're eating our young. We're relying on them, to end the war and to fight the war?" And I felt it was up to me. I was older, I was thirty-eight. It was up to us older people to stop the war.

So the question was, what could I do to help end the war if I were willing to go to prison? Once I thought about it, it wasn't that hard to decide. As for my readiness to go to prison, I'd already risked my life *for* the war when I had gone to Vietnam. And if I could do that, I could now go to prison if necessary, as the price of opposing it.

I realized that one thing I could do was to copy the study I had on the origins of the war. Now it wasn't immediately obvious that this was a useful thing to do, because the study had ended with 1968. We had a new President, and the study was now history. And it wasn't clear that pointing out the history of the war would help Nixon end it. If I'd had documents to prove what I'd been told about Nixon's plans to expand the war, I would have put those out instead; that would have been much more relevant. But I didn't have such material. I had a study that I had done for Kissinger and Nixon earlier that year, suggesting their interest in expanding the war, but it didn't really prove anything. So that wasn't going to do it, either.

I knew that no President would pull out of the war if he felt that it was his to lose, if it was in any way associated with him. If he did, he'd be the first President to lose a war, and no one wanted to live with that distinction. He'd rather keep going, no matter how many people died, to save face. But if Nixon could be induced to get out before he was too strongly associated with the war, he might be willing to do it. And I thought the only way he would do this was to get the Democrats to share the responsibility with him, to say, "Mr. Nixon, this isn't your war. This is our war. We got ourselves in. But don't make the same mistakes. Get us out, and we'll stand with you. We'll take the responsibility." I actually called up several key Democrats: Paul Warnke, who had been assistant secretary of defense, and Harry McPherson, who had been the assistant to President Johnson. Both of them were in a high-level policy group called the Democratic Policy Advisory Group. But they weren't willing even to try.

Ellsberg's voice choked with emotion as he related this plan to approach President Nixon. His eyes filled with tears, and as he remembered the profound struggle of conscience he had gone through – a struggle that culminated in a bold move to place his own life at risk – his voice was barely audible.

> The Democrats weren't willing to do any such thing. They said the Democratic Party would suffer, they'd be accused of stabbing Nixon in the back. To lose a war after getting us into it in the first place would have been disastrous for the Democratic Party. One of them said there would be a bloodbath "such as you and I have never seen" – meaning a political bloodbath, of course, like McCarthyism. He said, "And that means you and me, Daniel. We'd get it." I said, "Well, you might be right. That might very well happen. But I'm not willing to see the real bloodbath go on in Vietnam, to see more Americans being killed in order to save the Democratic Party or to save myself politically." So they couldn't rise to that, and I began to realize that if anyone was going to say anything, it would have to be me.
>
> I had already been helping draft a letter from Rand to the *New York Times*, which identified ourselves as being at Rand and said, "We should get out of Vietnam in one year." Six of us at Rand were involved in that, and it was a very controversial thing to do. Later they clung to their jobs by their nails – their bosses tried to fire them for writing this very unusual letter. I had also written to other people, trying to get us out, and it all looked more promising than the Pentagon Papers – which, as I said, was just past history.
>
> But then something else occurred, which led to my final decision. On September 30, 1969, while I was in the midst of all this activity, I was on the beach in Malibu. I was reading the paper, and the story that day was about a special-forces murder trial that had ended and had been dropped. Eight men associated with the special forces in Vietnam, including the commander of the special forces in Vietnam, a colonel, were on trial for having killed a Vietnamese agent, one of their own, whom they suspected had also been working for the Vietcong. They had taken him out over the South China Sea and shot him with a .22, with a silencer, and then dumped him over the side, weighed down with chains. His body was never found.
>
> Well, it was a very controversial case. Most Americans complained, "Why are we persecuting our special forces for killing a Vietnamese agent? What the hell! This is war. And why are we putting these brave men on trial for doing what they thought was right, after their bosses decided that it was the right thing to do?" That was the main feeling about it. It had been a very

unpopular trial, as was Calley's trial for My Lai later: the most popular single act that Nixon ever took was to shorten Calley's sentence and put him under house arrest, out of the stockade. Anyway, these men were then taken out of confinement because there was such a popular outcry. That had all happened before September 30, but it had all been going forward to trial.

Now the trial had been dropped, and the newspaper stories on it had a peculiar form which I'll just summarize this way: "The secretary of the Army has dropped charges, saying that it's his decision to do so." Clearly, this was a lie. It was very clearly a White House decision. The White House was saying that it had not taken part in the decision, but that was obviously a lie. And the secretary of the Army was saying that he did this because the CIA wouldn't testify, but that was obviously a lie, too, because the CIA could have been ordered to testify by the President. In fact, Haldeman's diary later revealed that indeed the White House had ordered the CIA to say that they could not testify.

But the lies didn't end there. Abrams said that he had no choice but to bring charges, and now he was being overruled by the secretary; it was a straightforward murder case, he had to bring charges — he had no choice. But that was obviously a lie. There were murders every day in Vietnam, on a massive scale and on a small scale. They didn't have to bring charges. They had never brought charges before. Contrary to what was said, Abrams had brought charges because he'd been lied to by the colonel in charge of the special forces — lied to about the circumstances under which this agent had been killed. And the colonel had ordered all of the people under him to lie, too. So Abrams was very angry at being lied to by all of these captains, majors, sergeants, and warrant officers, but especially by the colonel, who was a West Point man. That is why he had brought charges of murder against them.

I lay there and I thought: this is the system I've been part of for fifteen years, including the Marine Corps. It's a system that lies automatically at every level of command, from the sergeant to the commander in chief, up through the captains, the majors, the colonels, and the generals. And the secretary of the Army. To conceal a murder. And I said, I'm not going to be part of this system any more. I'm not going to be part of this lying and this murder and this war.

At that moment, I had 7000 pages of top-secret documents in my safe, evidence of a quarter century of lying and murder, aggression, broken treaties, deceptions, stolen elections — I had proof of it all. It wasn't clear how much good it would do to bring it all out. It might not help, but it couldn't hurt. And at any rate, I was going to get out of this system of lying.

The lying didn't bother me so much as what we were lying about. After all, if lying bothers you too much, you can't be in the government for a month, and I'd been in for fifteen years. The Marines didn't involve me in too much lying that I can remember, but every month in the executive branch did. It was what the lying was about: lying about mass murder. To continue the war with no hope of any benefit to any American interest was murder; it was unjustified homicide. Even if you could justify some killing, you couldn't justify *this* killing.

I figured that what I was going to do would put me in prison for life. They would send me to prison forever, and I would not have done that just to set a lie straight. But the point was that there were many more murders coming; it was the future prospect of more lying and more murder that concerned me.

So I decided to phone a friend of mine who had been fired from Rand for exposing serious crimes in Vietnam. His name was Tony Russo; he had become an embarrassment for Rand, and so they had chosen to get rid of him. And I asked him if he knew where there was a Xerox machine. He said he had a girlfriend who ran an ad agency. She had a Xerox machine, and we could use it if we paid for it. So we started that night, copying the Pentagon Papers.

Even before I went, as I was getting dressed that night, I thought of two principles in the light of what I'd now decided to do. One was that no one would ever again tell me that I had to lie. I could imagine lying again in my life, but I said, "I will take the responsibility for it. I won't tell myself or anybody else that I'm doing it because I was ordered to lie. I'll be responsible if I feel it's necessary."

And the other principle concerned the question of violence. I was wrestling then, as I have been ever since – thirty years, almost – with the question of whether it's ever justifiable to kill someone. I had even talked to Pastor Niemöller at the War Resisters League conference. He'd been a decorated U-boat commander in World War I but was later imprisoned, as the bishop and pastor of Berlin, when he opposed Hitler's treatment of the Jews.

So I thought, "No one will ever again tell me that I have to go to war to kill someone." Now they always say that in war killing is justified – you share the responsibility, and they say, "It's our responsibility. It's not your responsibility." But none of that made any sense. You cannot delegate such a responsibility to anybody else. You can't delegate your conscience to somebody else who says it's all right to kill somebody. If you kill somebody, you have to take full responsibility. So that answered the question about the draft. As Dan Berrigan once said, "To register for the draft is to announce your availability to kill on command."

I came to believe that the draft represents a system based on violence, on the legitimacy of organized violence, that gives far too much power to national leaders and to national policy. It really is worthy and important to announce, if you're capable of doing it, that you're not available, that you don't accept the authority of such commands. I know it used to be true, and I suspect it still is, that the constitutionality of the draft as involuntary servitude has never been tested in the Supreme Court. And there's a very good reason for that: the constitutional basis for it would be very, very suspect.

At any rate, the bombing continued. And the bombs did not drop themselves. They were dropped by humans who planned the missions, who loaded the bombs, who flew the airplanes, and who knew just as well as everybody else in the world that they had no justifiable purpose whatever. But it went on – for five more years.

Of course, my own experience had shown me that it was very foolish to think that these higher-ups, with their "better information" and their "higher responsibility," their "judgment" and their "knowledge" and their "values," could ever be believed. Look at the examples: the missile gap, which didn't exist; and going back earlier, the Manhattan Project, which recruited people to deter a German risk that didn't exist.

You could delegate the responsibility for this killing to a national leader only if you had managed to remain ignorant of all this history. To say that these people should be given the benefit of the doubt implied either that you were too young to know better, or that you were some kind of an idiot who was not aware of what had been going on for the last twenty years. And how often these people had made terrible and stupid judgments in the face of all the information! People, men in power, are the last people in the world whose judgment you should trust with these decisions. You're much better off trusting their wives or their daughters, but unfortunately they never get near the decision.

The Pentagon Papers came out in 1971. I had given them to the Senate in '69, but the Senate didn't hold hearings. They were afraid of the consequences. So two more invasions took place, Cambodia and Laos. My son turned eighteen, and the war was still going on. I was put on trial, facing 115 years in prison (my feeling that they would try to put me away forever was not off the mark). Twelve felony counts. The trial ended; Nixon was kicked out of office. And the war was still going on in Vietnam. U.S. troops were no longer directly involved, but we were still paying the entire cost of the bombs; it was still our war. We were still paying the Army, paying for the bombs and the planes. We had equipped South Vietnam with the third-largest Air Force in the world, after Russia. So it was not exactly their war. It was still very much ours.

Well, I didn't pay the price that they had in mind for me. Nixon was much more interested in destroying me outside of a trial than inside. The newly released transcripts of the Nixon tapes are very funny, actually, on the importance of getting Ellsberg and destroying him, not in the courtroom but in the press, by reputation, smearing me, and so forth. They broke into my former psychoanalyst's office in Los Angeles, not so much to smear me as to blackmail me, to get information which they hoped would buy my silence. Well, none of that happened. They didn't find too much, and what they found they couldn't use. They didn't manage to hurt me very much. They wanted to, but they failed.

The actual price I paid, which was quite significant, was that they made me into a kind of Typhoid Mary – a contagious, dangerous person from the point of view of my professional life. All my friends had clearances, and their clearance status and their access to office and to information would be jeopardized if they dealt with me at all. Seymour Hersh, the newspaper man, is one of my oldest friends, because he goes back to the period when I was on trial. But I don't have very many friends that go back before him, because I lost them all. I essentially lost all of my friends. Of course I had some relatives and a few old school friends that I see once in a while, but by and large the people from my adult working life have all vanished. It was as if I'd emigrated, and it was a very stiff price to pay. But I don't regret what I did.

Looking back, my decision to put out those documents had no immediate effect. It affected people's minds, but the war went on. And I hadn't risked my life just to affect people's minds. I wanted to end the war, and the war didn't end for another four years. But still it seemed very worthwhile at the time, and in the end it did turn out to be very effective.

The reason for this was not apparent back then. Nixon was carrying on his secret policy of expanding the war, which would have been very unpopular if known. And I was a threat to those secret plans. He feared that others who knew of his secret policies might imitate me, but even more he feared that I had documents proving his actual policy. I didn't. I had a couple, but not enough; he thought I had far more evidence than I ever had. So he had very strong reasons to try to shut me up, and that's what he tried to do. He ordered a bunch of people to "incapacitate" me, to kill me or at least to beat me up, at a critical moment in 1972. He tried to blackmail me so that I wouldn't put out the documents he feared I had. Blackmail, of course, is a crime. And so it had to be covered up.

The people who broke into my doctor's office and who later tried to beat me up on the steps of the Capitol were, by an error of Nixon's, the very same people he sent into the Watergate Hotel. If they hadn't been, if it had been a different set of people, the war might have gone for several more years. But the moment these people were caught in the Watergate, Nixon worried that they would tell about their earlier crimes against me. And so he bribed them into silence. That was another crime, and it, too, had to be kept silent. More and more people knew; they all had to be paid off, and sooner or later some of them began to talk.

To this day, the actual break-in at the Watergate Hotel cannot be traced to Nixon. In fact, Nixon says throughout the tape transcripts, "I didn't know they were going into the Watergate." That's probably a lie, but we don't have any proof. So he would never have been forced to resign because of Watergate alone, or because of the campaign contributions or the other dirty tricks. The only things that could be traced to him were the things he did against me and other antiwar activists, the cover-up of his direct and personal involvement in trying to destroy me. If it had just been Hunt and Libby and those guys in the Watergate, he wouldn't have had to cover things up. Let them go to jail. The cover-up was to protect himself.

In the end he got caught and he had to resign from office, which allowed Congress to end the war. Congress could have cut off the money when he was still in office, but he would have defied them, which Ford wasn't willing to do. So Ford, facing a congressional cutoff of money, had to let the war end. But the bombing could have gone on many more years. It might have gone on another ten years.

In principle we could be bombing still. It's hard to believe that President after President would bomb and bomb forever. But they'd been doing it for a long time. I think Carter would have kept the bombing going if it hadn't stopped before he got in. So we could have bombed a hell of a long time. We'd really have bombed until the North Vietnamese managed to take Saigon in the face of the bombing. They might have been able to do that, or they might never have been able to do that. We could still be bombing...

As my meeting with Ellsberg came to a close, he received a phone call from his friend Seymour Hersh, to whom he began quoting, rather excitedly, excerpts from a book containing transcripts of the newly released Nixon tapes. After hanging up he was still absorbed in the book and continued reciting selections to me, with obvious relish, in a gravelly voice full of drama:

Here's a good one...

Nixon: What in the name of *God* have we come to? Well, I'd put out stuff on the Democrats. We'll put out all these documents. We're going to expose them. If we do this correctly they'll never recover. But we need a sonofabitch to do it. Who would you put in charge, Bob?

Haldeman: That's what I'm trying to figure. Because —

Nixon: You've got Colson doing too much, but he's the best. It's the Colson type of man that you need. You don't want an Ehrlichman or a

Mitchell; they're too concerned about the law. It'll be very good to have somebody who knows the subject. I mean, what you really need is an Ellsberg; an Ellsberg who's on our side, in other words, an intellectual who knows the history of the times, who knows what he's looking for.

That was from '71. Here's one from two years later when my trial ends:

Nixon: Don't worry about Ellsberg's trial. Just get everything out. Try him in the press. Try him in the press. Everything, John, that there is on the investigation, get it out! Leak it out!

He's all against leaks:

Leak it out. We want to destroy him in the press. Is that clear?

He's so worried, you know, that we'd stolen everything — we were thieves, and they were stolen documents. You have to go after the *Times* for dealing in stolen documents...But there are documents that *he* wants from the Democratic administration in the Brookings Institute. And here's his response to that:

They (the Brookings Institute) have a lot of material. I want Brookings. I want them just to break in and take it out. Do you understand?

Haldeman: Yeah, but you have to have somebody to do it.

Nixon: That's what I'm talking about. Don't discuss it here.

They're all on tape.

You talk to Hunt. I want the break-in. Hell, they'll do that. You're to break into the place, rifle the files, and bring them in.

To do what? To give them to the *Times,* you know, because they're dealers of stolen documents!

Haldeman: I don't have any problem with breaking in. It's a defense-department approved security place.

Nixon: Just go in and take it. Go in around eight or nine o'clock.

Haldeman: Make an inspection of the safe.

Nixon: That's right. You go in to inspect the safe. I mean, clean it up.

He was taping everything himself for later use in his memoirs...he taped every word!

Nixon: We're going to use any means. Is that clear?...Did they get the Brookings Institution raided last night? No? Get it done. I want it done. I want the Brookings Institute safe cleaned out and have it cleaned out in a way that makes somebody else responsible!

It was somehow heartwarming to see the comic relief these quotes provided, after the obvious trauma our earlier discussions had inflicted. Though I was now even more keenly aware of the tremendous toll taken by the Vietnam War, the absurdity of such statements, by men in positions of enormous power, made me laugh along with him. It was a sane, tired, all-encompassing laugh at the silliness of this race we call human.

I asked, on a whim, if the Watergate boys had managed to pull off the break-in of the Brookings Institute. A smile played on Ellsberg's lips and his eyes twinkled again. "No," he said, "but they got pretty far. They were going to rent a fire truck, and have somebody go in and start a fire; have fake firemen go in to tear the place apart, break open the safe, take the papers. But they couldn't get enough money out to hire the fire truck. It turned out to be very expensive, and they didn't have enough petty cash."

■ ■ ■ ■ ■ ■ ■

Maryknoll priest and former Navy officer Roy Bourgeois has spent nearly two decades working to close the School of Americas in Fort Benning, Georgia. Established in 1946 in Panama but later moved to Georgia under the terms of the 1977 Canal Treaty, the school's reputation for turning out assassins and despots has earned it the nickname *Escuela de Golpes* or "School of the Coups"; among its 60,000 graduates are some of the most feared names in Latin America, including Bolivia's Hugo Banzer, Panama's Manuel Noriega, and Robert D'Aubuisson, leader of El Salvador's infamous death squads.

In 1996, the Pentagon released documents showing that from 1982 to 1991 the school had used training manuals that taught torture, executions, and blackmail; the story received front page coverage in the *Washington Post,* and a *New York Times* editorial called for the closing of the "School of the Dictators." But despite a mass protest outside its gates in the fall of 1997, the school remains open and continues to train anywhere from 800 to 2000 Latin American soldiers a year in combat skills, commando operations, psychological warfare, and military intelligence – on U.S. soil.[7]

At a conference in Norfolk, Connecticut, in 1997, Roy shared something of his personal saga:

> We are not born peacemakers – we need others to show us the way. And in my childhood in a small Louisiana town along the Mississippi River, we didn't talk much about peace and justice that I can remember. I went on to college and studied geology, hoping to get rich in the oil fields of South America. Then I became a naval officer and went to Vietnam, where I met the missionary friend who helped me to see healing as a vocation. He was one of the biggest influences on my life. He and his small staff of orphanage

workers stood out in the midst of all the despair and violence. They were trying to heal the suffering of the people, and when I went out to do volunteer work with them I began, for the first time, to see the war through the eyes of its victims — especially innocent children. That started me on the road to peacemaking and to healing, and it helped me to put behind my life as a soldier and all that meant.

Still, it took me three or four years after coming back before I could speak out against the war, before the day I was arrested for demonstrating in front of the White House. That was a sacred moment, because change — at least in my life — didn't come easily. At that first demonstration I had this sign that said "Peace," and I was terribly embarrassed — I just prayed that no one I knew would see me there. But then something very important happened: I met kindred spirits who helped me realize there was nothing to be ashamed about. They were ordinary people like me, but they hungered for peace and justice, and they wanted to make changes in our country's policies. And working for change brings about changes in our own lives.

After Vietnam I joined the Maryknoll religious community and became a priest. I wanted to be a missionary in Latin America, so when my studies were completed I went to Bolivia to work with the poor. There I got my real education, from sisters and brothers who taught me about U.S. foreign policy, about the CIA, and about the large corporations that exploit South America's natural resources and cheap labor.

After five years I was forced to leave by Bolivia's brutal dictator, General Hugo Banzer. I came home to the United States and did educational work, but my heart was in Latin America, and after the deaths of Archbishop Oscar Romero and the four American nuns — murdered in El Salvador because of their defense of the poor — I became an outspoken critic of our foreign policy there.

On November 16, 1989, there was another massacre in El Salvador. This time the victims were six Jesuit priests, a young mother, and her teenage daughter, Celina. A U.S. Congressional task force reported that those responsible had been trained at the U.S. Army School of the Americas at Fort Benning, Georgia.

At the time, I was living in Minneapolis, educating people about El Salvador and the nuclear arms race. But after this massacre I couldn't remain silent, and together with some of my friends, I moved to Georgia to research the School of Americas.

At first, Fort Benning was an open base, and I could go in and ask questions. I talked to soldiers waiting for the bus that took them to the firing range. We only spoke for about a minute, but I was very nervous. I was just a civilian, and I wasn't in uniform, but they thought I was military personnel. The soldiers were Salvadoran, so I spoke to them in Spanish. I followed the two busses out to the firing range and found out that they were learning how to use M-16 rifles. It was then that I decided I had to stay and find out more about this "school."

I wanted to find a place nearby, and there were some very cheap apartments right outside the main gate of the fort. Apartment Number 1 was vacant, and the rent was only $175 a month, so it became our "watch house" — *Casa Romero*, we called it, after the slain archbishop.

In time, we learned that the school taught soldiers the art of killing and how to repress the poor. It was a school that trained soldiers to protect a socio-economic system which keeps the rich rich, and the poor poor.

In March of 1993, the United Nations Truth Commission made public a report concerning the massacres that had occurred during El Salvador's long civil war. Nearly all of the killers cited in that report — 73 percent — had been trained at the SOA. Many of the soldiers at Fort Benning were there to escape prosecution, to escape investigations going on in their countries. Many of them had already been implicated in massacres, but they were in the United States for a cooling-off period.

So we began a very serious water-only fast at the gates of Fort Benning to try to call attention to what was happening there. Our fast lasted for thirty-seven days. Our bodies grew weak, but our spirits were very strong. And we gradually built a little movement of solidarity among people from the local community and elsewhere...

After three months of talking in churches, in colleges, and in other groups in Columbus, Georgia (the home of Fort Benning, and where 25,000 active-duty personnel are stationed), three of us from the solidarity community decided to take the message to the Salvadoran trainees themselves. We went to an Army surplus store called Ranger Joe's, down the road, and we bought those fatigue uniforms that everyone wears. We dressed as high-ranking officers, and we put the names of victims on our name tags — I was Oscar Romero. You buy the rank with the uniform, and because the prices for lieutenant and colonel were the same, we figured we'd go in as a colonels.

That night we went onto the base, dressed as officers. We carried with us a very powerful boom box and a tape of Romero's last sermon, in Spanish, given in the cathedral the day before he was assassinated — the sermon where he pleads with the men in the military to stop the killing and to lay down their arms. We wanted those soldiers to hear his message one more time.

Dressed as officers we were able to penetrate the high-security area; we even got saluted. We went past the barracks, scaled a tall pine with tree climbers, and we waited. When the last lights had gone out in the barracks, we said,

"Bishop Romero, this is for you, brother." And his voice boomed out into the darkness. It was another one of those sacred moments. Those soldiers heard it, came out in the middle of the night, and looked up into the sky. They couldn't see or hear us, but they heard the voice of their martyr loud and clear: "Stop the repression! Stop the bloodshed! Disobey your superiors and obey a higher law, the law of God, that says 'thou shalt not kill'!"

They were frightened, of course, and we wondered: what are they thinking? Of course the MPs heard it, too, and they came running with their dogs and guns and after several minutes threatened to shoot us down. They were very upset, and we came down pretty quickly. They cuffed us and brought us in for questioning, put us in separate rooms in the MP headquarters. We had no identification with us other than the name tags on the fatigues. So when they asked us who we were and what we were all about, we simply said, "You should know. You are responsible for our deaths." They got the message.

They took us to the county jail and then to trial. We planned to be very eloquent in the courtroom. My friends were there; my parents came from Louisiana, my brother and sister were there. And we wanted to explain what we had done and why we had done it. We wanted our loved ones to understand, because at that point they didn't. But it was a bad day in court — we were cut off, unable to speak. In the end, though, the best statement is not made with words.

So we went to prison. I went to the hole, to solitary confinement for a month, for disobeying an order I felt I couldn't obey. That was the hardest part of prison. I was cut off from my support group, my friends. And in the solitude and the loneliness of the cell, the question kept coming: how effective are you? What did you prove? What did you accomplish? We hadn't stopped one M-16 from going to El Salvador. But something very important happened, and it happened through the words of Dorothy Day: "Let us not worry so much about being effective, but let us concentrate on being faithful – faithful to what we know in our conscience." I started to feel free, and I cannot think of another time that I felt so free.

Well, we got through in good shape. We went back to work, and there is still a lot of work to be done to stop this madness, this violence, this death, this military aid. Our government has given six *billion* dollars of military aid to El Salvador, one of the biggest shows of weapons and training ever, all to keep that system going, to protect the landowners, the wealthy, the elite.

The school is still open, still teaching murder and violence, and we want it to be closed. We're not going to stop until it is closed, because it is causing a lot of needless death and suffering. We can't do anything about much of the world's suffering, really, but this is the kind of suffering we can do something about. Closing this school would be a giant step toward bringing about democracy in Latin America. It could help bring about justice. It could help bring about peace. And we're not going to stop until this school shuts down.

Romero said it best: "We who have a voice, let us speak for the voiceless." We are not expected to be miracle workers, but we have to speak up wherever we are. And we can speak with more clarity, with more boldness. At the same time, though, we have to have peace in our hearts if we want to work for peace in the world. That is a challenge, to hold on to our joy and our hope, not to be stripped of that in the struggle. We must take care of ourselves and of each other on this road to peace.

The people I lived with in Latin America had so little and yet shared so much. They had something called solidarity, and it gave a deeper meaning to their lives and sustained their hope. They taught me that if we come together and live in community and work for peace, wonderful things can happen...

■ ■ ■ ■ ■ ■ ■

David Hibbs, a friend who worked for a military contractor in England, notes how small the distance between the high-tech manufacture of weapons and their murderous use really is. It is a connection that is rarely made, one that we prefer not to think much about – after all, those well-paying jobs at Lockheed and Rockwell and Martin Marietta are a mainstay of our economy. But a comment made by his former employer sent chills up my spine. Coming in to work the day after watching the nightly TV news, which included footage of a riot in Mecca being brutally squashed by Saudi Arabian security forces, David's boss had greeted him with a broad smile: "Did you see that, Dave? They were using our equipment, and I bet a lot got broken." Not long afterward, the company received a large order for batons, CS gas, and shields.

Dave says it's still hard for him to talk about his time in the company.

I usually gloss over it when asked because much of the equipment that I sold was extremely harmful. I cannot be sure that I did not kill people by "remote control." But when I brought this up in the office one day, my boss told me that if we did not sell it to them, somebody else would. He was right in that respect, as we were always being chased by other countries just as anxious as ourselves to sell arms – the French, Israelis, South Africa, Russia, and of course the United States.

In my desk drawer I kept a number of catalogues and one of them advertised a small jeep-mounted mine delivery unit. It operated rather like a road gritter: the mines were dropped into a hopper and spewed liberally all over the ground behind the vehicle. The mines themselves were plastic, colored brown and green or sandy, "to use on the beach," and did not even need to be buried. Almost impossible to discover because of their high plastic content, they were designed to blow the foot or leg off a soldier but would probably have killed a small child.

Where do I go from here, I wonder? I recently read a report of the trial of an elderly Frenchman accused of aiding the Nazis' genocidal activities. He stoutly denied the charge that he helped to deport Jews until presented with a report on the evacuation of Jewish children with his name signed to it.

I wonder on which document my own name lies, and when I will be shown it again?

■ ■ ■ ■ ■ ■ ■

Brian Willson was wounded in the fight for justice in Latin America. He lost both legs, his left ear, and a chunk of his skull. It happened on Tuesday, September 1, 1987, on a naval base in northern California.

I read about it ten years later and decided then and there that I had to meet him in person. I finally did, in November 1997, and as I drove up to his house in Wendell Depot, Massachusetts, I was surprised to see him walk out onto the back porch to greet me. If I hadn't seen the dark wood grain of the prostheses above his sneakers, I might never have known about his legs. They had done a good job with his head and ear, too – he grabbed his left ear and wiggled it as proof. He was tall, with gray hair hanging down in locks to his shoulders, a red bandanna over his forehead. He smiled from time to time as he told his story.

That day in 1987 began like so many others. Brian's small vigil group had notified U.S. Navy personnel at the Concord Naval Weapons Station weeks in advance, and again on the day of the protest, about their forty-day fast on the railroad tracks. Duncan Murphy, David Duncombe, and Brian were all veterans of war, and they planned to stop the trains carrying U.S. arms to repressive forces in Central America.

They thought they knew what was coming. The train would stop, and they would be arrested and hauled off to jail; business would suffer a delay before resuming as usual. As Brian saw it, however, the action could also result in saved lives in Central America. He was accustomed, quite literally, to putting his body on the line. But today would be different.

The train did not stop. Duncan and David managed to escape with minor injuries, but Brian, seated in the middle of the tracks, was run over. The train operators had received orders to drive through the crowd to prevent anyone from boarding, and they increased the train's speed to three times the legal limit. The Navy meant to make their point, brutally and unambiguously. As Brian lay there bleeding to death – both legs severed and a hole in his head gushing – Navy personnel stood by, denying medical assistance and transportation to a hospital. Brian was not on Navy property, they said.

It was only thanks to the medical knowledge of his wife, a lay midwife, and Duncan, a World War II medic, that Brian was kept alive for twenty-three minutes until an ambulance arrived. His ear was sewn back on and his skull patched up, but it took him days to realize that his legs were gone.

Later, as Brian was fitted for prostheses, he felt a strange sense of belonging: he had become part of a special "peer group" of those who had suffered under U.S. imperialism. Now he could understand them and feel what they felt. The day after he was released from the hospital, he returned to the tracks, with walker and artificial limbs, to resume the demonstration and make a point now more closely his own. Looking down at the plastic pylons that now replaced his own legs, he remembered a visit to a Nicaraguan hospital filled with amputees, among them children injured by American-made landmines. "Damn it!" he had cried. "Their arms and legs are worth just as much as mine!"

As we sat together, Brian reached back to his childhood.

I was born in Geneva, New York, in the Finger Lakes region, and grew up in a pretty traditional working-class family. It was a small town, conservative, racist; my parents, like everyone else, were very religious and very Republican. This was right after World War II, and America was everything, it was paradise.

I went to a one-room school house and was valedictorian of the eighth grade. At commencement I had to give a speech, and it was on sportsmanship. And one of the features of a good sportsman, I said, was that he never gives up, even when physically handicapped. So that was kind of prophetic...

By the time I had finished high school I was contemplating being a professional baseball player. I even had a contract offer from St. Louis, but I wound up going to college instead. Then, shortly after I got into college, I thought I wanted to be an FBI agent. I was very anticommunist, and back then, during the Cold War, it was just understood that the single most serious threat to humanity, to society, was the communists.

Next I became a born-again Christian. I'm not a Christian now, but it was part of my journey. I ended up at Eastern Baptist College near Philadelphia, but by the time I graduated from college I didn't want to be a minister anymore, so I went on to law school. But I still remember getting up at chapel in my senior year – we had a chapel presentation about U.S. foreign policy – and saying that we should just bomb the Vietnamese into oblivion and end the spread of this godless communism once and for all. I got lots of cheers. I even campaigned around campus for Barry Goldwater in 1964...

In January of 1966, during my second year of law school, I was drafted. I had never been militarily oriented, but I was totally for the war. I really believed in that war. So I ended up in the Air Force for four years, from 1966 to 1970.

I was still very straight-laced, and I taught Sunday school while I was assigned at the Washington, DC headquarters as a second lieutenant. I was a big white male, and I used to talk with my friends about going out to beat up hippies. Hippies, of course, were the scourge of the earth, the downfall of our great nation. But even then my feelings about race were beginning to change — I noticed that I was a little more empathetic for anybody that wasn't white…

I got my orders to go to Vietnam in 1968, but I was sent first for twelve more weeks of training at Fort Campbell, Kentucky. I was ordered to an assignment at an army base, and we trained in patrols, ambushes, and other kinds of intelligence work. I had six six-man fire teams and two three-man mortar units under my command. Then I had to go for bayonet training. The trainers, who were sergeants, put bayonets on our M-16s; we were to shout "Kill" as loud as we could, one hundred times, and plunge the bayonet into the dummy. I was pretty athletic, and I didn't want to be identified as weak or unable to do anything. But I had a pretty hard time of it, and when the twenty other guys screamed "Kill!" I hesitated just slightly. The sergeant was on me right away, shouting into my ear: "Did you hear that order?" I was sure I could get myself psyched up to do it, but I couldn't, and the next thing I knew the sergeant had kicked me in the calf so hard that my legs buckled. That was an early sign that there was another dimension to my being.

I wound up going through that entire twelve-week training without ever having to use a bayonet again, and I was sent to Vietnam as scheduled. I was sent to Binh Thuy, ninety miles south of Saigon in the Mekong Delta, and as soon as I arrived I had to help set up base-perimeter security. We had machine guns and mortars, and I had three jeeps under my command. Our job was to fortify security at the base, and we were specially trained, with extra weapons and higher firepower, antipersonnel radar, and starlight scopes that allowed us to see at night.

So there I was, in March of 1969, working around the clock in the 117-degree heat, sleeping when I could. We were attacked fairly often. Then I was assigned to go into villages that had been bombed by the South Vietnamese. They wanted a "gringo" to go around with one of the Vietnamese commanders, because they suspected that the bombers weren't following orders. I was only a rookie, what the hell did I know? But I went along. I thought it would be an interesting thing to do.

I'll never forget the first village we went into, just fifteen minutes after it had been bombed. We went in my jeep. What we saw was a lot of dead people, mostly mothers and children, and water buffalo. At least half of the villagers were dead; the others were wounded, moaning and groaning. The water buffalo that were still alive were roaring in pain. I came upon a woman lying on the ground with two children in one arm and one in the other. Her eyes were wide open, and it seemed that she was looking right at me. I bent over. It looked like she was dead. She was bleeding heavily, and then I saw that her eyelids were burned off because of napalm. The skin had just melted off her face.

In that moment – and it only took a second – I got it. I thought, is this what it all comes down to? Is this what my arrogance comes down to? I started crying. I stood up, and the Vietnamese lieutenant was looking at me: "Why are you crying?" I thought it was very obvious. I said something like, "Well, she could be my sister, and these kids could be my kids." He laughed – they were just communists. And then I knew I had moved on to something completely different. It seemed as though I now had a new soul.

(It's hard for me to talk about it, twenty-eight years later. It's really hard. Just recently I was at the VA hospital, screaming at the shrink, because I *had* to talk about it. I just sat there saying, "Fuck you, fuck you, fuck you!" Why do I have to bare my soul to *you?* There are a lot of feelings in there, and sometimes they just pour out like a flood...)

It took over an hour to get back to the base. We had to cross the Ba Sac River on a ferry, and I didn't say a word the whole time. I drove, and the Vietnamese lieutenant sat next to me. I went on one other such mission, and then I quit. I just refused to go into another village. I started speaking out against the war, and I had a pretty important position at the base. I stayed in the command bunker at Binh Thuy and tried to educate everyone about the senselessness of this bombing – how it was alienating us from the Vietnamese and needlessly killing thousands of civilians. I started studying the history of the war by going to the little base library, and I started, for the first time, to delve into history, genuine history. And it all started making sense to me.

Then one day I had to review a 7th Air Force report about the bombing of a village one month earlier. I suddenly realized that this was the same village I had gone into, and I was horrified. The summary said "130 VC killed." I knew that was not true – there hadn't been a soldier in the village. It had all been young mothers and children, and I was just outraged. Of course I was no longer an asset to the U.S. military, and I was sent home after only 120 days.

When I came back to the States, I still had a year left to do. Already in Vietnam I was told that I faced twenty years in prison for sedition, which was just short of treason. But I was assigned to a base in Louisiana, and the first thing I did was to sell my Corvette and buy a little Volkswagen beetle and put flower decals all over it. Big flowers. And when I drove up to the base to report for assignment, they stopped me at the main gate and said that flowers were considered political paraphernalia and were not acceptable. In fact they were supposed to be saluting me – I still had my blue officer's sticker on the bumper, and they were supposed to salute officers when they drove through. But I didn't give a shit about that. In the end, they wanted me to scrape the decals off, but I couldn't have done that without scraping off all the paint. So the chief of security said, "Well, we're just not going to salute when you come through the gate." And of course that was just fine with me, too. Already in Vietnam we had dispensed with saluting in my unit.

So I got through that whole year. I did a lot of antiwar speaking on the weekends, though not in uniform. I joined a Unitarian fellowship, and I gave a series of talks on the history of U.S. involvement in Vietnam, which lasted for five Sundays. A lot of people in the community came to that. The Air Force was also very interested in my talks, and they sent people there to monitor me. I'd see them in the audience and wave, and say, "Hey, I'm just exercising my First Amendment rights." I thought that if I had to do twenty years in prison anyway, I might as well keep on talking. What did I have to lose? My wife was concerned, but she was a lawyer, and by that time she was also against the war.

I finished my four years in the Air Force and they didn't court-martial me. So I went back to law school and passed the bar in DC in '72. I had become very radical, politically. I could now see that Vietnam was more than just a mistake, an aberration. It was part of our national ethos of arrogance, a predictable result of a long history of imperialism.

At this time I was ready to start my own practice. I had a master's degree in criminology. But I couldn't stand up with everyone else when the judge walked into the court room. It was like with the bayonet. I wanted to stand up, because I knew it was what I was supposed to do, but I couldn't. I also hadn't realized how much the flag hanging there affected me. As a boy I had carried that flag in my hometown parades – I had been so proud to carry that flag, but now it represented something very hypocritical. I remember thinking how I could ever explain these dilemmas to my wife. "It's a little, trivial thing, Brian – it's not a big deal. As an adult you have to adjust, adapt. You have to do these things if you want to be a lawyer..." But for me it *was* a big deal, and I decided that I wasn't going to subject myself to it.

I was almost ashamed of myself, but these things were emotionally loaded. In the end I didn't practice law. I couldn't handle the protocol, and I wasn't interested in business law or estates or wills or trusts or domestic law. So for four years I directed a program for the Unitarians called the National Moratorium on Prison Construction. I organized communities all over the United States to educate the public as to why more prisons were not going to be helpful for the future of our society; that we needed to look at alternatives to prison and at the basic socioeconomic reasons for crime. I lobbied Congress a lot, advocating against the Federal Bureau of Prisons budget started by Nixon. He wanted to build eighty new federal prisons. I ended up in DC for ten years altogether...

In the eighties, I lived in Boston working as a legislative aide for a state senator. One of the things I did was to investigate inmates' complaints at a notorious prison in Massachusetts. In the course of thirteen months I investigated over four hundred brutality complaints and six homicides. Then, near the end of the investigation, I witnessed the beating of a prisoner in a cell block by two guards, and I had a flashback to the woman on the ground with the three kids, whom I hadn't thought about for more than ten years. He was screaming and they were stomping on him. At that point I had to get out of the prison. I couldn't even begin to address what I had seen happening. I just had to leave, to get out – I was totally shaken. I had thought Vietnam was behind me.

That was in June of '81, and that's when I became a Vietnam veteran. Before then I hadn't thought of myself as a veteran. I was ex-military, but I wasn't a "veteran." I had been to Vietnam, but it was behind me. But that was a myth, and I realized at that point that I *was* a Vietnam veteran, and there was nothing I could do to change it.

That was when I took a leave of absence from my job. I had already been getting death threats at my apartment in Cambridge, telephone calls in the middle of the night: "If you know what's good for you, you'll lay off this investigation."

So I became the director of a Vietnam Veterans Outreach Center here in Massachusetts, filing claims with the VA, working with vets who were struggling with homelessness, drug addiction, alcoholism. Twelve Vietnam veterans committed suicide while I was there. That was no small thing to deal with. Fifteen, twenty years later, this war is more than a war, really. It is profound. It has pierced the bubble, destroyed the myth of the American way of life. There was something so fundamentally sick about Vietnam...

Then I started hearing accounts about what was happening in El Salvador and Nicaragua and Guatemala in the early 1980s. I heard things from people who had been there, and as I heard and read more in the regular news media,

I started to get really upset in my chest and in my stomach. Whenever I read the words Marxist-Leninist, or Marxist-Leninist Sandinista, or Marxist-Leninist guerrilla, I saw the pattern. "Marxist-Leninist" was a code word that meant, send down money, send down arms, and kill 'em. And that brought up incredible feelings of outrage, grief, sadness, and anger. We were going to kill mothers and children again. But who gave a shit? We went on with our jobs, living our lives, buying newspapers that say whatever the government tells them to say. I started to feel the pain of the people, and once again I began thinking of that mother and her three children. It was happening again. I was hurting. And I couldn't remove myself from that connection.

By then I think I had a basic understanding of U.S. foreign policy, which was perhaps simplistic but ultimately true. I knew that the United States has less than 5 percent of the world's population and yet consumes anywhere from one-third to two-thirds of its resources. And to live like that you have to steal resources from around the world. We are imperialistic because we insist on living at a certain level of consumption, a level that is impossible to support unless we steal, collectively. That was a difficult reality to contend with. I didn't know how to deal with it myself. I knew that this realization pointed toward community, but I'm kind of dysfunctional myself, and I don't know if I could live communally. But I wanted at least to address this issue directly, even if I didn't know how to solve it or correct it. I wanted to be part of a discussion about it.

I started going to Nicaragua and El Salvador and Guatemala, and I became immediately aware of our policies by virtue of visits to many villages. I went to Nicaragua twenty times, as well as to El Salvador, Honduras, Guatemala, Panama, and Costa Rica. I spent a lot of time with the *campesinos*, the rural poor, and I just let them know that I was an American but that I could never support my government. The devastation was unbelievable. Our government's policy was torture, assassination, wiping out entire villages, destroying schools, blowing up bridges. Who can possibly support that kind of behavior? It doesn't take any intelligence at all to realize that this is not acceptable behavior. And it was my country against these people.

There were many other people, many other Americans who were also concerned, who were working in the Solidarity Movement. And in 1986 I joined with three other vets in a water-only fast on the steps of the Capitol in Washington, DC. We called it the Veterans' Fast for Life, and our goal was to change U.S. policy in El Salvador and Nicaragua. We wanted to encourage the American people to resist this murder, this destruction, and we wanted to make it clear that we were willing to die for this cause, if necessary. We had been part of the killing, and we were sick of it. We felt our country was in a state of emergency, inwardly, and we wanted to address the nation as war veterans and put our lives on the line. We had been challenged to put our lives on the line for war, and now we were putting our lives on the line for peace.

People were very upset with us because we said we were willing to die. That to them was a terrible thing. But we said, "Well, if you feel that strongly, why don't you show some concern for all the people being killed down in Latin America. They are dying, too, even if you can't see their bodies." We wanted people to make the connection between their concern for us, on the steps of the Capitol, and the women and children dying every day in Central America.

We sat there. We made wills. We knew where we wanted our ashes sprinkled. I wanted mine to be sprinkled in Nicaragua, in a little town up in the mountains. We had no money. We had no assets. But we were going to sit there indefinitely, until something happened or until we died. It turned out that after forty-seven days we were able to stop fasting. By that time we had received 30,000 letters, and 25,000 people had walked by us at the steps. We had been visited by 2000 people in a single day, and we had basically taken over the whole east side of the Capitol. That was a very important experience for me, because I learned then that I could not have any fear of dying. I had nothing, but I felt very free. I didn't have a job; I didn't have money; I didn't have life or health insurance; I didn't have a house; I had nothing to maintain. I was just there.

After that, I wound up organizing something called the Veterans Peace Action Teams. We went to the war zones of Nicaragua, and we rebuilt what the U.S.-backed contras had destroyed. During the Reagan years we had a motto: "What the U.S.-financed contras destroy, U.S. veterans will rebuild." So we went into these villages and rebuilt health clinics and schools. It was an atonement, a sign that we were no longer part of the violence. We could not be silent; we had to be active in some way, in a personal way. And we ended up sending eight teams to Nicaragua.

While all of that was going on, I got involved with the Nuremberg Actions in California. These were a series of actions aimed at blocking the munitions transports then being sent from the Concord Naval Weapons Station to El Salvador and Nicaragua. That's where I got hit by the train. Actually, it was all very well rehearsed – we were in many ways a fairly conservative group of people. At least, we never did anything rashly. We thought about everything we were going to do very carefully; we even notified the government about our planned actions. Being a lawyer, I studied the history of train blockades – I prepared myself for two months before blocking that train. I knew it was going to be a hard experience, a fast of forty days, just on water, sitting in front of the death trains. And I figured that the worst that could happen would be jail. I figured I would be hauled off to jail once the fast had weakened me.

The rest is history. I don't even know how I survived. I lost both legs below the knees, lost a big piece of my skull – a piece of bone from my cranium went in and destroyed my right frontal lobe. Most of my ribs were broken, my arm was broken, my shoulder was broken, my ear was cut off completely. My right kidney was basically destroyed. Hey, I have been given the gift of a second life!

I still don't remember being hit by the train. And they say it took another five days before I was really conscious. I remember waking up, looking around the room, and then noticing all these green plants. I thought, what an interesting jail cell – I assumed that I was in a prison. My wife was there, and she said, "Well, Honey, the train ran over you. It didn't stop." I thought she was kidding. And then I started to get mail. The day I was hit on the tracks I had no money, no health insurance. But I got thousands of letters every day, and within two weeks 3000 people had contributed $200,000 to help with the hospital bills – totally unsolicited.

For the first week or so I was just happy to be alive, like, "Wow! How could I have survived?" And then I remember feeling that I was now somehow part of a new peer group. In the spring of 1987, just months before this all happened, I had been in Nicaragua. I had been at the bedsides of more than four hundred amputees, all victims of our American mines. After shaking each man's hand I had told them how much they motivated me to do even more work back home.

I thought about hating the train crew, the people who'd run me over. But I knew that hatred would destroy me – I've seen what it does to people. It destroys their bodies, their minds, their spirits. So I had to work on being liberated from hatred.

I also thought about my parents. They were crushed. Here I was, the only kid in my town to get a real education. The son who was supposed to be a success, make lots of money. A military officer and a lawyer with a master's degree and a Ph.D., sitting on the railroad tracks like a bum. Fasting on the steps of the Capitol and flying off to Nicaragua. With no money and no health insurance. They were devastated. It was very, very hard for them to comprehend, and I could understand why.

Already many years earlier, my father had disinherited me to Jerry Falwell. In his will, he wrote "Jerry Falwell" in lieu of me. He was a big contributor to Falwell, to the Moral Majority. And Falwell contributed a lot of big money to the contras. My father got this newsletter from Falwell describing how Reagan's freedom fighters, the contras, were liberating Nicaragua from the Marxist-Leninist Sandinistas. And he would tell me: "Falwell has a Ph.D. He's a man of God. And you have renounced Christianity, and you are supporting the communists." I would argue that I really wasn't supporting communism but rather condemning imperialism, and that I had a Ph.D. too, and that I was also his son. But my father just couldn't make it out. That was really painful for me.

I had hated my father already, for years. That's one of the reasons I know hate is so damaging, because I hated my old man. And he really was a mean, cruel father. I know from the men's groups I've been in that this is not atypical. In fact, it's almost universal. It's fairly rare among men in my generation to have had fathers that were emotionally or even physically present enough for us to know that they really loved us. Hardly any of us have had fathers who showed anything that could have been interpreted as love. Of course, they were simply imparting to us what they knew; I don't think they ever intended to screw us up. So it was pretty hard, but I made peace with my father in 1983, and by the time my father died, in 1989, I actually loved my father. Before he died he even changed his will – took Falwell out and put me back in. And I had nothing to do with it.

I made peace with my father by realizing that I didn't have to like him to love him. What a concept: unconditional love. Doesn't have anything to do with liking a person. It's nice if you like him, but it's not necessary. I had to find a whole different attitude toward my father, because he wasn't going to change for me to love him. I had to change. I had to learn to love somebody that I didn't like. That was a big help to me later, with the train crew. Obviously I was devastated by what they did to me, but I can still have a sort of *agape*-love for them.

I guess some people can go and do acts of civil disobedience without even thinking about it, but I have to think about it, because I don't want to think of the police as pigs. I have to prepare myself, and I'll only do it when I feel that I can present a model of love. I have to spend time talking about it with people, get very centered, do a lot of breathing. When I went out to confront the military on September 1, 1987, I wanted to be loving. I had anticipated that to be loving would be very difficult: we were going to be pulled off the tracks, probably gruffly. And having been a right-winger myself, I could imagine what I would feel like if I had to deal with the "goddamn stupid-ass people sitting on the goddamn tracks, what the hell do they think they're do-ing" demonstrators. I understood that way of thinking.

So I never went through a period of hatred. I went through a period of grieving, but not until seven years after the accident. That was in '94, and I went through months when I cried every day. I was crying for more than my

legs: the loss of my veteran buddies, my parents' death, my second divorce —
I was suddenly dealing with all these losses at once. It went on so long that I
began to think I'd never get over it, but it turned out to be very cathartic. I
became much more deeply grounded after that.

I do a lot of men's work now, trying to get men to give up their definition
of manhood as machismo — to start being emotionally honest, to leave the
competitive world, to get in touch with their feelings, to stop pretending that
they're tough and disinterested and always in charge. I'm after a transformation of some kind. I don't care how you define the meaning of life spiritually
or religiously, but I am concerned about becoming aware of what is sacred.
In fact, everything in life is sacred, but the concept of sacredness has been
lost in our post-agricultural era. We've been seduced by technology and ma-
terialism and science, but if we are to find meaning in life again, we have to
search for what is sacred.

We vets were simply the right age at the wrong time. And our personal
identities have been shattered, our loyalty to the nation-state has been shattered; our religion, our psyches and egos have all been shattered. We came
back to a society that couldn't deal with us. The war was much more than a
lie — it was demonic, diabolical. And I am convinced, after working with
vets, that we need to find new souls, a new meaning for our lives, which is
completely different from what we have believed in before. And how do you
do that? Who do we talk to about it? Who do we share that process with? All
these guys are blowing their heads off with shotguns. Their pain is that intense.

Who am I? What is the meaning of life? We have experienced all these
terrible things, and now we're back in a society where everybody is running
around buying each other Christmas presents, where life is "normal," and we
can't even talk to them…What are we doing? What is all this about? *What
the fuck are we doing?*

I don't think people grasp how profound the Vietnam War is for the
United States of America — not only for vets, but for the whole society. To
understand the Vietnam War, you first have to try to understand our society.
And you begin to wonder, "Gee, maybe our whole society needs to go
through a healing, and no empire has ever done that." We vets, of course,
have no alternative. We have to choose a journey of healing and transformation or else check out. And even if society doesn't seek this healing with us,
as individuals we have to find healing if we want to survive. We have to get
really clear about our own personal lives if we are going to navigate ourselves successfully through this culture, which, in many ways, is a very sick
culture.

CHAPTER 13

The Healing of the Sangha

We have to listen in a way that we understand the suffering of others...Just by listening deeply, we already alleviate a great deal of...pain. This is an important practice of peace...We have to listen to everyone, especially those we consider our enemies. When we show our capacity of listening and understanding, the other person will also listen to us, and we will have a chance to tell him of our pain. This is the beginning of healing.

Thich Nhat Hanh, Love in Action

In September of 1997 I met with Jim Savage from Pennsylvania. He went to Vietnam at age eighteen, in April 1965; five months into his tour he was hospitalized for a severe infection and then malaria. After losing sixty-three pounds, he was transferred, still feverish and delirious, to a hospital in Japan. There he spent five weeks in isolation, during which time he learned that his wife had given birth to a premature child, which died.

Jim made it back, but many of his friends didn't. As we sat together, he reflected on his own journey to healing, one that could not start until he could begin to talk about what he had seen and done in Vietnam:

A lot of things stay with you for years and years — things you don't want to talk about, things you can't even discuss with your own wife. I used to wake up at night with hallucinations, with dreams and nightmares, for years after coming home...

During my tour of duty there was an incident — our perimeter was broken through, and we had a firefight. It's very hard, very difficult, to have to take someone's life. But it's even harder when you have to do it in a close situation. The memory stayed with me, very vividly, for years. The eyes, the facial expression — everything stays with you for a long, long time. It's something I don't think I can ever forget.

When I first came home I drank heavily and secluded myself, put myself in a shell that nobody could penetrate. I had trouble dealing with other people, and at work I insisted on being alone. I didn't want people around me. I had a lot of anger, a lot of hate, a lot of prejudice inside me. I also had a lot of fear, which people can't understand if they haven't been through it themselves.

I was looking for forgiveness, from people or from God, trying to convince myself that there could be healing. I knew I had to face these things. I couldn't pretend they weren't there, because just then they would always raise their heads. Certain things would bring them out. You get overworked or overtaxed or overtired, and the next thing you know, your dreams are very vivid again.

It's like taking out the garbage. You can put your garbage in the can, but if you don't remove it, get it cleaned up, it stays right there. That's what I did. And I tried to ignore it, pretend it wasn't there, wish it away.

Over the past twenty years, Jim has slowly begun to find healing. It was through a newfound belief in Jesus that he realized forgiveness was possible, for himself, his family, the people around him who "couldn't understand," and the war-makers who had indirectly caused him so much pain and suffering. His most important realization, however, was the recognition that he would have to confront the monsters in his own closet before he could ever hope to break free from the nightmares of his past. "There were things I was still keeping way down inside, but that needed to be brought out," he said. "They weren't easy to look at, and I didn't want to do it, but little by little the walls came down. And I found I was able to be around other people, too." Our conversation ended with words of wisdom: "We used to say that some people came home, but never got off the boat. That period of your life has to be dealt with — it has to be talked about. And very often it's other veterans that can best help you to go on from there, because all of us have scars…"

■ ■ ■ ■ ■ ■ ■

Jim's assertion that veterans cannot find healing without first sharing their pain was the focus of a weeklong Buddhist retreat I attended in October 1997. There forty-five of us — veterans, spouses, and friends — met together at the Omega Institute in New York's scenic Hudson Valley, in a common search for healing and understanding. There were tears as well as joy, and beautiful living pictures of reconciliation between Vietnam veterans and the Buddhist monks and nuns led by Thich Nhat Hanh, who guided the retreat. Many veterans shared their stories by writing them down and then reading them aloud to the whole group. This process of opening one's pain and burden to the *sangha*, or gathered community, was powerful and cathartic.

I was amazed to find that registration for the main retreat, of which the veterans' retreat was only a small part, had filled to capacity (850 people) only weeks after being announced in the spring. Clearly, Buddhism offers something that cannot be found in institutional Christianity. But then why should veterans embrace a religion that has blessed the wars which ruined their souls? It is no wonder they turn to a gentle Buddhist monk to hear what are, in large part, the truths of Christ.

Through Thich Nhat Hanh and his fellow monks and nuns, Vietnam veterans saw the goodness of a country they were sent to destroy. They saw the beauty of a people they had dehumanized and called the "enemy." Peace and compassion reached above the war like a rainbow. Hate and fear dissolved as people listened deeply to one another. There was great healing to be found in the Sangha, if you could only open your heart to share pain, suffering, wisdom, and love. Notes from my diary explain it best:

Our retreat is being held on the campus of Omega Institute in a single-roomed building called "Cabin by the Field." It is a beautiful place. The lake across from the dining hall mirrors the perfect quiet, disturbed only by the occasional cry of waterbirds. No sound distracts us — no highway or train, crowd and activity, none of the noisy bustle to which we are so accustomed.

It was a gorgeous autumn day when we arrived three days ago. I felt at home with the other "boys" right away. Bruce Cole is handsome, with long, gray hair pulled back into a ponytail, and penetrating eyes. Billy is almost impossible to describe — the original's original, part Native American, face carved from stone, bronzed and pensive — a serious clown. In the rigors of Buddhist "mindfulness" that we've endured over the past few days, he has kept it all in perspective, making fun of it one moment and pointing out its wisdom at the next. But there is seriousness beneath the surface of his antics, a result of the tremendous burden he has borne these thirty-odd years. As a Navy gunner, he loaded shells in a "friendly fire" incident in Vietnam that killed nine American GIs. For years afterward he lived on the streets, homeless, cheating and stealing to feed his dope habit, and eating out of dumpsters.

The veterans gathered here have come to Omega because they feel safe. The retreat is a space where dark secrets can be shared with others who understand, who will not judge or seek retribution. The stories I have heard in just three days are mind-boggling; in many cases it is the first time they have ever been told. And the atmosphere of reverence and listening in which these stories have been told is deeply challenging. One can feel and see the pain being taken into each heart, shared, and so divided.

Part of the Buddhist mindfulness practice involves bowing, with hands clasped, before speaking, and again when one is finished. In this way, there is no fear of interruption, no need to speak forcefully lest someone else jumps in to interrupt one's train of thought. If the speaker pauses for a minute, the listeners pause too, taking time to collect their thoughts and process what they have heard. Another Buddhist practice is the ringing of a small bell, sounded at random during a meeting or other activity. When the bell sounds, all become quiet for several moments, breathing in and out deeply and "mindfully." The practice is intended to "return us to the present moment," to free us from being caught in the past or future, distracted by fears or anxieties unrelated to the here and now. Mindfulness is a practice which extends into every area of daily life: not only in talking and listening, but in eating, working, walking.

I sat with Bruce Cole at our first meal in the communal dining hall. Cole saw Vietnam in its full, bloody horror. He enlisted after getting his master's degree and ended up in the infantry, a stupidity that overwhelms him now. This isn't his first retreat; he's been to several before and is slated to lead the beginning of this one.

Cole described his feelings as we prepared for the first gathering: "When things are going good, I get scared. One, because I feel I don't deserve good things to happen to me. And two, because that's when ambushes happen — when things are going good. In Vietnam, I got away with murder...I keep waiting for some kind of revenge or retribution."

That evening, we sat together in a circle at "Cabin by the Field," our *sento*, or safe haven, for the week. A few of us are noncombat vets, but the majority of the group saw combat in Vietnam. Heidi Baruch, a nurse, was there for two years. She doesn't look old in body, but her eyes say that she's seen it all, that she was long ago stripped of all her innocence. She has spent the last six years treating veterans with severe PTSD (post-traumatic stress disorder) at a VA hospital and will join a group cycling from Hanoi to Saigon in the coming months. She said she used to think that she was helping veterans, but now she realizes it is they who are helping her to heal. Others, too, said the same thing. They find that working with the retarded or the mentally ill helps them to find healing: their hurt melts away as they lose themselves in caring for other hurting people.

Tom is quiet, scared, and depressed. He stepped on a landmine in Vietnam and wears an artificial leg. Jane lost her brother in Vietnam and sits pensively in the darkness at the edge of the circle. Chuck, a veteran of the 1st Air Cavalry, lost his best friends in the war, saw their bodies being loaded onto the plane for that last ride home. Jeff, from Connecticut, did two tours in '65 and '68; he tried to go back again in '74, but found he couldn't fire a rifle anymore.

It was the next day that Bruce Cole shared his poem with the group, and it broke open a floodgate of stories and tears. He began:

> I've been thinking about Francis Scott Key: "The rocket's red glare, the bombs bursting in air." That's our national anthem, and it's a fucking bloody one. But here's my poem. I'll just call it "American Warrior":

> Our father played the piano while we sang the Navy hymn.
> (Don't wave your fucking flag at me –
> that's why boys are killed in wars,
> or after wars, when warriors find no peace...)
> I am the arrow, I am the sword – I lie in bed all soaked in sweat.
> I choke and retch, I scream and cry; I'll grieve until the day I die.
> Forgive me, Lord, I didn't know. Forgive me, Lord, it wasn't me.
> Please tell me, Lord, it wasn't me.

We were silent for a moment, and then Billy, the loving, hurting, compassionate clown, walked across the circle and embraced Cole, who sobbed gently on his shoulder. They stayed in one another's arms for a long time.

It is hard to describe what we experienced in "Cabin by the Field." We were opening wounds, purging them of their old filth, letting them bleed so they could finally close. It was painful, but it had to be – and more than one vet expressed the feeling that this was the place to do it, a safe place where fears could be brought to the light.

Cole told us about his first retreat. He had tried to write down his experiences in Vietnam but had gotten stuck trying to explain how he had lost his first man. Until then, he couldn't remember just how it had happened, but the writing process triggered memories suppressed for decades by shock. Frightened, he told his wife, "I'm going to need your help. I think I know how it happened. O God, I remember now!" He wrote it down and showed it to her. They held one another and cried together under the trees. When they returned to the group, Cole wanted to share his story to be free, but he didn't have the courage to read it aloud. Finally, with Billy holding one arm and his wife holding the other, he told his story, fully, for the first time.

Call it what you will – group therapy, cathartic release, getting in touch with your tears – it is very close to what we Christians call remorse, confession, and repentance. There is great healing in sharing the darkest secrets of our lives with others. As the Buddhists say, "Releasing what is deep inside you will save you; keeping it to yourself will destroy you."

We immerse ourselves, at intervals, in small writing groups. We've written a lot, but we also talk a lot — when we don't feel like writing and need others to listen, or need to listen to others. Marshall, a middle-aged man, has a story which seems too horrible to tell. He goes to the brink and turns back. He worked for the CIA in Operation Evergreen. "I thought I was doing the right thing at the time," he says, choking. "But I remember this six-year-old girl…" He can't say anymore. He has to leave us often. But yesterday he left a note near his pillow on the floor that said simply, "God bless. I love you all. Have to go process." Later, he tells us that he dreams about meeting the people whose lives he has taken. In the dream, they are alive; he says he is sorry, and they embrace and laugh. But then he stops short: "I don't deserve forgiveness."

Nikko has wept rivers of tears. As a young man, he tried to resist the war, refused the draft, and joined antiwar protests at school. But he was inducted only months later and was sent to Vietnam as an Army medic. He was there at "Hamburger Hill" — one of eleven men to survive from a company of 155 GIs. His company was sent up that hill twice a day for twelve days. His comrades recommended him for the Medal of Honor, but the government didn't even give him that small satisfaction. They told him that a conscientious objector who is still alive doesn't get the Medal of Honor. Nikko came back an old man, his hair turned white from the stress of fear and death.

We were touched, too, by Phâp Úng, a Vietnamese monk, who came in unannounced and left a short note with the retreat's facilitator, asking how he might nurture the veterans gathered. He wanted to share our pain and help to alleviate our suffering. Bob, a Hispanic vet, said he felt resentment at the presence of the Vietnamese — they forced him to bring to the surface things he thought he'd put behind. Ron Orem, dark-haired and boyish-faced, echoed this sentiment, but acknowledged that such confrontation was a necessary step to reconciliation:

When I first saw your group of monks and nuns coming toward me down the path, I thought, "Oh, shit! It's the little people again!" I didn't know if I was supposed to jump into the bushes or open up or what.

Every time I see you, I am reminded…I want to go back to your country one day without fear, to sleep in your jungles without claymores and trip-wires. I have to deal with you because you are here. And I know I have to meet you face to face much more.

We broke up into smaller writing groups shortly afterward, but I witnessed a remarkable happening. Ron and the young Vietnamese monk were kneeling face to face, completely absorbed in listening to each other. Ron spoke softly to the monk — I couldn't make out the words, but I didn't need to — over his shoulder

I could see the tears rolling down Phâp Úng's face, his eyes locked on Ron's. I was trying to concentrate on writing but looked up when I heard what I thought were the sobs of a child. Phâp Úng and Ron were embracing one another. The upturned face of Phâp Úng was filled with understanding and compassion. They held one another for what seemed an eternity. The circle was completed. Ron held the "little people" and the monk held the soldier. There was forgiveness and peace.

At last they let go and wiped away the tears. The smile on the face of Phâp Úng was radiant. Together with Ron, he joined the small writing circle. Everyone felt their joy. It was a beautiful island of reconciliation in an unforgiving world. Later, Ron read something about this encounter to the group: "I used to hunt people like you; now you hand me a flower. I am confused..."

Yesterday, Heidi spoke of her special pain as a nurse. The presence of the young monk had touched something deep inside her, too, and she related the guilt she still feels toward the Vietnamese people. She couldn't hold back the tears, either.

> I went as a girl of twenty-one, but I came back an old woman. I wanted to help, but I wasn't prepared to see what I saw. When you live in an environment of hate and anger, you become hate and anger...
>
> In triage, I was told to keep Americans alive but let the Vietnamese die. Nobody should have to make such choices.
>
> I went back a second time because it was the only place I fit in. I was a machine. Vietnam stripped me of all emotions...

She ended with what I felt were her most important words: "You have to forgive in order to heal. A lot of Vietnam vets go around feeling victimized, but you have to turn it around to begin to heal. You have to start taking responsibility for what you did." Her words are quiet and yet authoritative, and she has a remarkable effect on the veterans. It is as though she is still caring for their hurts and wounds, and they respect her deeply, knowing that if anyone shares the agony they have been through, it is she.

There came a point when the veterans comforted Heidi much as she had once comforted them. I was sitting by her then, when in the middle of writing, she suddenly covered her face with her hands and began to sob gently. Many of the veterans were instantly at her side, a silent presence as she cried out her pain. Marshall, his face clear and radiant for the first time, whispered, "You did what you could – hold on to that. The ones who died...it really was their time to go. I've been able to tell my pain for the first time because of you. You've given me the courage to face it, and I feel better now than I've ever felt in all my life. Thank you, Heidi." She smiled and wiped her tears away.

Not every minute is filled with mindfulness or tears. The intensity must be balanced with comic relief, which gushes out at unexpected moments. Heart-wrenching stories are followed by absurd gestures and silly comments, and the silence of the bell is broken by an occasional wisecrack.

On the second day of the retreat, our whole group had a "walking meditation" from "Cabin by the Field" down to the lake. Ordinarily, it would take perhaps five minutes to stroll the distance, but the painfully slow, pensive steps of the meditation turned it into a twenty-minute affair. When we finally reached the lake, we stood at the shore, looking out on the sheet of clear, still glass. All of us remained silent, perhaps taking ourselves and the moment too seriously. It was then that we saw Billy. He had gotten himself a canoe and was paddling across the lake in front of us, really plowing into each stroke. The stillness was abruptly broken by his cry of "Go Navy!" Billy, dear Billy. He keeps us human.

There was another such incident at the lake when, in what seemed to be an especially holy moment, a monk bent down to flick a handful of water into his companion's face. And throughout the week there were songs, drama, and ceremonies with flowers and incense.

Most of the time, however, the discussions were pretty heavy. Ron noted how the war had made it harder for him to interact with women. In Vietnam they had been objects of desire for him, but on his return many women hated him. He recalled how an attractive young woman had approached him shortly after his arrival home. Flipping the bronze medal on his chest, she had taunted, "Hey, motherfucker, how many babies did you kill to get that one?"

Marty told about a buddy in Vietnam, "Cherry Bunny" (all new soldiers were called "cherry boys"), who arrived as a virgin. The fellows had joked about it, and Marty arranged for him to meet with a prostitute; Cherry Bunny soon lost his innocence in a clump of brush. The next day, his jeep hit a mine. Cherry Bunny was the gunner and was wounded the worst – he was castrated by the shrapnel. Marty told us what had brought this all back: that morning, at the retreat, he had met a young Buddhist nun to whom he bowed. When he looked up, their eyes had met; to his shock, she looked for a brief moment like that young Vietnamese prostitute. "When the seeds of violence are watered, the young women of a country become prostitutes," he reflected. "But when the seeds of love are watered, they become beautiful young nuns."

One afternoon there were tensions stemming from confusion about schedule changes, and some of the men began to get pretty uptight. I thought it a bit overdone until I heard Heidi's explanation: in Vietnam, when things didn't go down according to schedule, men died. A late medevac, a poorly timed helicopter insertion or extraction, a fumbled ambush – these could mean the difference between life or death. Heidi also noted that the men most traumatized by the war were the ones who had to live through life-or-death situations without weapons. A guy with an M-16 had an outlet for his fear; he could shoot at people or things to make them go away. Corpsmen and other noncombatant personnel had no such outlets.

Later that evening we met again to continue reading aloud our written reflections. Jack Meagher said that Tom's story about stepping on a landmine gave him courage to tell his own. He had gone back to Vietnam as a member of the "PeaceTrees" project, in which American veterans and Vietnamese plant new trees together. "I found peace in the place where I lost it," Jack said.

At the close of the evening, a Vietnamese monk named Pháp Trú spoke of his appreciation for the retreat in a marvelous, child-like way:

> I felt very moved when I met you three days ago. I feel very close to you...I appreciate all of you very deeply. I was moved by the story of Jack, who came to help the Vietnamese people. We can learn to forgive, to transform our suffering and our deep wounds. This is the meaning of the sangha: to forgive, and to relieve suffering. I became a monk to bring peace and harmony to my people and to my society, but now I would like to work with you, too. It is cold outside, but I feel warm with all of you...Do not hold on to your suffering forever – look at the blue sky, the leaves, and sing! Let us hold hands and work together.

Then, Pháp Trú and Pháp Úng performed an incense-lighting ceremony, with beautiful, reverent chanting. At the end they bowed deeply, and Úng smiled, walked over to Tom, who had removed his prosthesis, and embraced him. "We all have the capacity to love," he said in farewell. "We want to look with the eye of compassion, of brotherhood and sisterhood, to practice deep listening with one another." We stood, silently, and there was great love and understanding in the room, a spirit of peace and reconciliation.

On the last morning of the retreat, at 6:30 A.M., we attended a final talk by Thich Nhat Hanh. Thây focused on the "five mindfulness trainings," which convey a powerful sense of the heart of true Zen Buddhism:

> The five mindfulness trainings help us to create peace and joy among our families and society. They keep us from creating suffering, pain, and despair...

We renounce all fanaticism and intolerance through compassionate dialogue…We reject the way of wealth, fame, and sensual pleasure…We are committed to share with those in need…We must look with compassion into the eyes of those who are the cause of our anger…

We cannot utter words of division, which cause the community to break, but must only use words that inspire hope and confidence. We must never speak to impress people or cause hate or division…We vow to speak out against all injustice, even when it may compromise our safety…

The sangha cannot be political or used for personal gain, but must struggle against injustice…Our livelihood cannot deprive others of their chance to live, and we reject all profit from the suffering of others…We vow to cultivate nonviolence, compassion, and understanding among our communities and nations. We vow to protect life and prevent war, to cultivate loving-kindness…

These words stayed with me as I left the retreat. The Buddhist practices of mindfulness, deep listening, and compassion had been a wake-up call, and I realized how much more I, a professed Christian, needed to rediscover these same teachings in the life of Christ.

Just weeks after the retreat, I received a letter from Nikko, the survivor of "Hamburger Hill." His reflections exemplify the type of healing that veterans of all wars must — and can — find:

The impact of our time together has led me to a whole new world of insight and healing. Since leaving Omega, I have celebrated Veteran's Day — a first — by being with other vets, and reading some of my writings with the local Buddhist group in the San Francisco area. The result has been a sense of peace around my Vietnam experience that I've never known before. It is as if I am finally beginning to put that part of my life into its proper place in my own personal history, and I no longer feel like I am toting around a huge bag of smelly garbage that I am incapable of letting go of or dealing with…

I am even sensing a need to become involved in socially conscious programs again. That's a huge step for me, as I haven't had the energy for that in twenty-five years. I am still in pain, but thanks to our being together I have begun to move on from the place in which I have found myself stuck for so many years. It seems to me that if, in the course of our stay on this earth, we can impact even one other person in a significant way — then that is a powerful reason for "being."

Clearly, one of the most effective catalysts for healing involves creating "spaces" in which veterans can speak about their experiences and emotions in a group setting. Again and again I have heard statements like "nobody else knew I was a Vietnam vet," or "for twenty years I never told anyone." But just as often I have heard veterans say that until they could talk openly about their experiences, the road to healing was blocked. However, they stress the need for an audience that listens without judging, that seeks to share pain rather than to point fingers.

Such opportunities demand time, care, and a willingness to listen. Perhaps this sharing and listening is what our national leaders fear most of all – that by listening to veterans we will never forget, and that by opening our hearts and minds to their ongoing suffering we will never want to have another war.

The benefits of simply having others to talk to cannot be underestimated. But therapy groups can become ends in themselves and may cause more harm than good. In an atmosphere of such overwhelming need and suffering there is the danger of seeing oneself either as a victim, hurt beyond forgiving, or as an inhuman monster destined to wallow forever in his guilt. The two may seem far apart; in reality they are close twins. In the intensity of the struggle, the pull to either side is so strong that the survivor is left teetering on the brink.

Much of my pain was to see men unburden themselves of their tremendous weight, uncovering wounds not yet healed, only to leave the load at the threshold and walk away without opening the door. The deeper one's recognition of guilt and sin, the deeper one's despair, unless the door is opened so that the light of forgiveness can stream in. I have tried unsuccessfully to encourage those in my writing group by reminding them that we are all the same, that they have not "crossed the line" into some unreachable darkness, that you don't have to shoot someone to kill him, because the anger of the heart can be just as murderous. And you don't have to rape someone to rob her of innocence. We *are* all the same. There is a door for each of us to open, and on the other side there is life, there is hope. There *is* a Love which has the power to change the whole world. We don't have an inkling of the restoration to come.

■ ■ ■ ■ ■ ■ ■

Lee, whose story opens this book, is still looking for that part of his soul that was stolen away by the war. When I arranged for a group of veterans to get together to share their stories last summer, he was reluctant to come. He finally did, but he hid himself at the back of the audience, and at one point motioned for me to come over to him. When I did, he whispered, "Don't mention my name." I assured him that I would not, but I kept my eye on him for the rest of the evening, the glow of his cigarette shifting through the gathering darkness. I wasn't at all sure what was happening inside, and I hoped that the stories and discussion weren't going to make him too upset. But the next day his buddy

Marcus came up to me and said, "Lee didn't say much, but last night meant a lot to him. He said it was the closest to heaven that he'll ever get."

What exactly did Lee mean? I am certain that it was the open and honest discussion in a safe, supportive environment — the healing of the sangha — that had touched his heart. Lee writes:

> When I was first arrested I was put on suicide watch, but I did go to a meeting with some Amish-looking people who had a religious service at the jail. I didn't listen much to what they said, but after the meeting was over, one of them came over to talk to me. I don't remember what we talked about, or even his name, but he gave me a good cup of coffee and a doughnut. At Christmas they showed up again. They walked through the jail singing Christmas carols, and before they went, they left us stockings full of fruit and cookies and candies. Mine had a card in it, signed by Dorothy, age ten, grade five. I've always tried to be a courteous person, so I wrote her a thank-you note.
>
> To my surprise, she wrote back, sending along a little pamphlet which told about her church and their way of life. I couldn't believe it. Here I was, at the lowest point of my life, ready to die — and a ten-year-old girl writes me a letter. I answered that letter, too, and then her dad wrote, and then her grandmother.
>
> Something happened when I read that Christmas card. I don't know why, but we kept on writing. Finally I got out of jail, and in February 1990 I visited Dorothy and her family. My life was a still a mess, but I was alive, and for some reason I felt I had to thank in person the people who had written me when I needed it the most. It's now been seven years, and I know that they are seven years I wouldn't have had without that card.
>
> On my first trip to the Woodcrest Bruderhof, I met Dorothy's grandmother. Dorothy herself wasn't there, so I decided to leave. But my van wouldn't start, so I started walking. I'd gone at least a mile when a car pulled up behind me, and a man got out and asked if I was Lee. I told him I was, and he said he was Dorothy's father. He drove me home and we talked a little. Then he offered me a job, tearing some old trailers apart. I took it, and very soon I was working steadily at Woodcrest. I've been working there five years now, and it's by far the longest I've ever worked at one job.
>
> Life is also better for me because of their horses. When I found out that Dorothy and her friends wanted to learn how to ride, I arranged horse-care and riding lessons for them. That was in the summer of 1992. Since then I have arranged riding lessons for more than thirty kids. I take them to horse shows, and I pay for their lessons. I think I have made a small difference in this world, and when I die, more people will think good of me than not...

It was a long time before I could mow the grass in the middle of their property – there were just too many people around. I also had a hard time going to their dining hall, because most of their meals were eaten communally, with more than two hundred people present. When I did, I had to sit by the door so I could get out if necessary.

I still don't go to most of their community meals or meetings, even though I am invited all the time. But I am changing. The people here have welcomed me with open arms. I can now walk into a room full of people and not think anything of it. I feel more comfortable around people now. For the first time in my life, I feel like I am home.

■ ■ ■ ■ ■ ■ ■

When I asked Daniel Berrigan what he thought was the ultimate answer for hurting veterans, he spoke first of the need for ongoing connections with other vets, for caring friendships, and for someone to listen. But then he added that healing has to be actively "dramatized." Drama – that seemed to be the word I'd been searching for, but what exactly did it mean? Over many months I had noted, almost without exception, that those veterans who were working to rebuild what had been torn down, who were reconciling face to face and relieving the suffering of others despite their own massive suffering, were the ones who were most at peace. You could see it and feel it when you talked with them: a sense of renewed purpose, a sense of fulfillment in what had been a dark void.

Dan explained:

A year ago in June I was invited by a Vietnam vet and his wife to conduct a retreat for Vietnam veterans in the mountains north of Albany. We met for just one day with these very afflicted men. Some of them couldn't even stay in a strange place overnight, so we limited it to one day. But it was a great experience for me to hear those men unwind – and to hear their wives speak about what it had been like to see these very young men go off, after just starting a family, and then to see a stranger come back. There was a lot of weeping that day, a lot of emotions.

I was asked to tell my story, how I had developed in a different direction, but how in the end we were all together in the aftermath of that horror, having gone through a great deal – whether in court or in prison or in combat – and all having survived and having come to a better understanding of what it is to be human and, in many cases, what it is to have faith. Toward the end of the day they wanted to have some kind of a ritual. I said that would be wonderful, and then one of them suddenly went off to his car and brought out his guitar. Another was a very accomplished artist, and he had brought this big portfolio along but was too shy to open it. I finally said to him, "Can't we all see your art?" Anyway, we got out a table and all began to look at this marvelous work, which he had done in Vietnam – photographs of children, women, villagers, soldiers, the dying. He had gone back home after the war and had done these very fine paintings from the photographs. So we were all gathered around the table, around the paintings, and with the guitar. And these guys got singing, and they didn't want to go home. They wanted to stay and sing and talk, and we stayed there for hours...

I think above all other kinds of help for veterans who are suffering is just some kind of intelligent friendship. For many of them, of course, it has to involve a return to some kind of religious faith, which was just bombed out, too, by the war, by the scandal. There are other opportunities that bring slow, slow healing. Many veterans are rebuilding, building dispensaries, making friends. You know, in a sense the healing has to be dramatized. The talking is important, but it seems to me that's not the whole story...

Dan's words brought to mind a talk I'd had with Steve Bentley, who mentioned a program called "Veterans Initiative," sponsored by the Vietnam Veterans of America. According to Steve, there are two basic factions among Vietnam veterans today: those still "stuck" in the war, and those who have moved on. The difference? Steve thinks it has a lot do with whether or not a vet has actively sought opportunities for reconciliation.

Such an active search for healing and reconciliation has changed the life of Philip Salois, whom I met in May 1998 at New York City's Hunter College for a conference on the emotional wounds of veterans. Phil is the national chaplain for the Vietnam Veterans of America; he went to Vietnam in 1969 and served with the 199th Light Infantry Brigade. His baptism of fire came on March 1, 1970. During a search-and-destroy mission, his men had found a battalion of NVA, backed off, and camped the night, waiting till morning to attack. The next day the company commander foolishly ordered them back down the same trail, where they walked right into a U-shaped ambush. Six men were immediately separated from the rest of the group, and a long firefight ensued. Phil finally volunteered, along with two other men, to try and rescue those six men.

One of the volunteers took a round in his shoulder and was immediately incapacitated, but Phil and his buddy Herbert Klug made it out to an open clearing, where they laid down enough diversionary fire to allow four of the six men to escape. It was then that Phil realized Herb was no longer with him. He was lying face down in the grass, a bullet hole in his chin.

Phil had a "foxhole conversion" in Vietnam. "I told God that if he'd get me out of that mess without a scratch, I'd do anything he wanted," he says. But it wasn't until 1974, while in the second year of seminary in Los Angeles, that he remembered the vow he had made. Almost ten years later, in 1983, he decided to attend a conference called "Healing the Vietnam Veteran," thinking he had something to contribute. But by the time the conference was over, he realized that he himself had not yet dealt with his time in Vietnam. There were ghosts from his own past that needed to be confronted before he could help others.

He enrolled in a six-month program for vets with PTSD, hoping to deal with the tremendous guilt that he felt over his friend Herbert's death. Why had Herb died while he lived? The rescue had been his idea, and this added to his torment.

He also realized that he still had negative feelings about the Vietnamese people, that he harbored mistrust and contempt for them. Finally, in 1990, he was able to return to Vietnam, to the battlefields where he had once fought. He went to a cathedral in Saigon and confessed to the congregation that he was a former American soldier who had once fired on their relatives. He asked their forgiveness, and he found healing and reconciliation in their presence. But it was the children of Vietnam who reached out to him and touched his heart, and it was through them that he began to look beyond himself and toward his fellow veterans.

His mother, friends, and colleagues all had opposed his returning to Vietnam. They thought he was crazy – that he could not "let go" – and thus he was denied support from those he loved and trusted most. Unable to share his private pain, he succumbed to alcoholism; he finally entered a treatment program late in 1991. But this low point in his life also brought forth a positive result: the National Conference of Viet Nam Veteran Ministers, which he founded, in part, as his own support group.

In 1991, Phil came to the realization that his healing had to include visiting the family of his dead buddy Herb Klug. He tracked them down and spoke with Herb's father. Then he wrote Mr. and Mrs. Klug a long letter, explaining who he was and what he wanted to do. In July of 1991, the Klugs picked Phil up at the airport and took him into their home in Dayton, Ohio. The day after he arrived, Mr. Klug took him to Herb's grave. Phil wanted to "talk" with Herb alone, but Mr. Klug wanted to stay, so Phil began his conversation with Mr. Klug at his side:

Herb, I'm finally here. And I'm sorry it took twenty-one years to get here, but you can be assured that I have never once forgotten you or the sacrifice you made on March 1st. I have always included you in my work with other vets, and I believe that we're doing this work together. Hardly a day goes by when you are not included in my thoughts and prayers...Be at peace, brother, and stay with me!

When Phil stood up, Mr. Klug was sobbing. Phil apologized for opening old wounds, but Mr. Klug said, "No, it's not that at all. I listened to what you said, and it made me think that I never once took the time to tell Herb that I loved him. And I never talked to my wife about his death. I always felt I had to be strong for her."

Around the supper table that evening, Phil told the Klugs how their son died, and related the events leading up to his death. He told them how guilty he felt that Herb died while he himself lived, and that the rescue had been his idea. Herb's mother, Beulah, grabbed Phil in both arms and said, "Never say or think that again! We never held you responsible for the death of my son. It was meant to be."

Phil's honesty allowed Beulah to speak of her own pain. She remembered how her Baptist minister had come up to her during the funeral and said, "Oh, Beulah, if you'd only come to church every Sunday, maybe God would have let you keep your son." She never set foot in church again.

On the twenty-fifth anniversary of Herb's death, Phil called the Klugs again. He wanted to organize a reunion for his platoon, which would include a cookout at the Klug's house and a ceremony at the cemetery. The Klugs thankfully agreed, and a sizable number of men gathered in Dayton at the Klug's home. One of them was among those whom Phil and Herb had rescued from the ambush, and he expressed deep gratitude to the Klugs for Herb's life, which had been spent to save others. Beulah was overcome with emotion. She could hardly believe that so many people still cared about her son after so many years.

Phil's story is wonderful, but he points out that the healing didn't just drop into his lap. "Healing is very hard work," he says. "In order to heal, you need to *do* something. You need to move. You need to be creative and find healing for the whole community." He also maintains that spirituality is an essential part of healing — that talk therapy and medication can only do so much. "We need to get in touch with the mystery of ourselves," he says. "I certainly couldn't face the demons, the ghosts of my past, without the Christ-person inside of me."

■ ■ ■ ■ ■ ■ ■

In collecting stories of how veterans are "dramatizing" the healing process, I have been amazed at the number of ongoing projects Vietnam veterans are involved in. Jack Meagher has dedicated himself to "PeaceTrees," a group that plants trees and creates parks, not only in the inner cities of Washington, Los Angeles, and New York, but also in the minefields of Southeast Asia. In

Vietnam, they first had to clear the land of unexploded ordnance and landmines, and in the summer of 1996, they removed 300 landmines and 1500 pieces of mortar, bombs, and shrapnel to turn an 18-acre battlefield into a park.[1]

Nurse Heidi Baruch recently joined Vietnam Challenge, a 1200-mile bike trek from Hanoi to Ho Chi Minh City (formerly Saigon) undertaken by eighty American and Vietnamese military veterans in January 1998. The Challenge was not a race or competition, but a chance for the participants, who once fought against each other, to find emotional healing and a sense of closure. Many of the cyclists had physical disabilities, among them a young man born blind due to Agent Orange exposure who rode tandem with his veteran father. And at the end of the ride the U.S. contingent gave Vietnamese officials a check for $250,000 to help rebuild Bach Mai — once Southeast Asia's biggest teaching hospital, but never fully rebuilt after it was leveled by a B-52 strike in 1972.[2]

After returning to the United States, Heidi wrote:

> I am at peace with Vietnam after thirty years. I spent twenty years pretending that Vietnam had no impact on my life, but I always knew that it had — my life *was* atypical, although perhaps no different from those others who experienced the war...
>
> I have now received treatment for PTSD, and have been fortunate to return to Vietnam. I was able to visit three of the four places where I served as a very young nurse, and instead of the intense emotions I expected, I felt a wave of release and then peace. Something changed inside of me when I saw those places — when I saw cows grazing quietly where field hospitals once stood. I was just amazed at how green everything was. I'd always remembered Vietnam in "dark" colors — the colors of fear, hate, anxiety, and helplessness — but now I'll think of Vietnam as a beautiful, colorful place of peace. Every vet should return to Vietnam!

■ ■ ■ ■ ■ ■ ■

Jim Murphy, the teacher at West Side High School in Manhattan, agrees that "drama" is important. He saw his friend Dayl start to fall apart at the beginning of the Gulf War, and he is sure that it is only because of drama that Dayl was able to pull through. But before he could act, Dayl had to learn to speak about the war.

> Dayl never said anything to anybody after he came home wounded from Vietnam. Even the people he worked with for fifteen years didn't know he was a veteran. But then the Persian Gulf War broke out. He was driving

home on the Taconic State Parkway, and the news of the first air strikes comes over the radio. Just at the same time, somebody cut him off in the traffic. And he wanted to kill that guy. He just started coming apart...

Dayl was in the Army's 1st Air Cav in Vietnam, wounded after six months in-country, and spent thirteen months recovering in a Naval hospital in Queens:

When I came back, I kind of retreated. I had several months to think about things in the hospital before I reentered society, and I did what I did to protect myself. I thought it was the easiest way for me to move on – mistakenly so – but, as my family said, I wanted to just bite the bullet: to draw a line in the sand, and then move on. So that's what I did.

I got out of the hospital after a year, but I was still wearing a brace and using crutches. I went to college, and when people would say, "What happened?" I would say, "I was in a horrible car accident." When they asked me if I was a veteran I always said, "No, no. I was 4-F; I never served." That's how I dealt with it.

My son is now twenty-one years old. When he was ten, he had a school project for which he had to interview someone, and when he asked if he could interview me, I thought, "Wow! This is going to be great." So we set up a table and got our stuff ready, and he asked, "You were in Vietnam, right?" and I said, "Yes, I was" – and then he asked me, "What branch of the service were you in?" I was taken aback, but he said, "You know, you've never told me." So there it is. I've been against the war and I have never even talked about it with my own son. I guess that's because it was too difficult to do. That's why I've come out now. And I am moving on, but first I had to stop and look back, because I'd buried so many things.

Now Dayl is active in Project Hearts and Minds. This organization, which enables veterans to return to Vietnam on missions of help and assistance, has changed his life.

In a sense, I always had trouble moving beyond Vietnam. Vietnam was always with me – it was with me daily. I'd never had a chance, really, to deal with my involvement there as an infantryman in 1970. But Project Hearts and Minds allowed me to return to Vietnam.

I went back for the first time in '93 and then again in '95. That first trip was the result of a project, started in 1991, to collect medical supplies. It was very symbolic, and it enabled me to let go of a lot of things. It also allowed me to deal with my sense of loss – *our* loss – not only of comrades, but also of youth and of innocence. Then I was able to talk to a Vietnamese veteran about *his* sense of loss, and I found that he had moved much further ahead from the war than I had...

The trip helped me to get rid of some of the anger that I had toward my government. And, on a very simplistic level, it relieved a lot of the guilt that I had. I went there as a teenager, you know – nineteen years old, carrying a rifle, calling in mortar fire, inflicting casualties on people, on civilians. And now I'm handing out medical supplies. There's something that's very spiritual about that.

Vietnam's medical situation now varies from area to area, but back in '93 there was a shortage of practically everything. Under the American embargo there was very little ability to import things, and so a lot of the equipment they had was old or broken down. One thing that really struck me was a hospital in Hue. It had electrical power, which is still unusual in Vietnam, but they were still using Coke bottles to hold IV solutions. And they reuse everything, recycle everything – even surgical gloves, which cost next to nothing. They wash them and put them out to dry on little wooden hooks in the operating room. It's amazing...

Then there's the problem of bombs still going off, not only in Vietnam, but also in Laos and Cambodia. During the monsoon season, the heavy rains bring mines to the surface; on our trip this last May, a farmer and two other people were killed just a week before we arrived. In some areas the percentage of farmers who are also amputees is very high. So in a sense the war is continuing.

There are many other personal experiences that stand out in my mind. I met a doctor in Hue who had been with the 33rd North Vietnamese Regiment, and we were the same age. He asked me what unit I was with, and I said the 1st Cav. That really got him going; he knew all about the 1st Cav, and it turned out that we had both fought in Cambodia at the same time, on opposite sides. Just think: in 1970 he was plopping mortars onto my firebase (we even pinpointed one night in particular) – and now we're here, a surgeon and a civil engineer, drinking terrible espresso and eating French bread together in Hue. We were talking about our kids: his son didn't know what he wanted to do, and neither did mine. All he wanted to do was to practice his English. It was beautiful!

Then on my last trip I went to Hanoi, a beautiful, sleepy town of over a million. They have these two big lakes, and every morning around 5:00 A.M. everybody goes down to the lakes to bathe and practice Tai Chi. They're heavily into badminton, and you see these little birdies flying all over the place. I rented a bike and went down there early in the morning, and a family invited me to breakfast. It was very intimate. They were obviously poor, but they served me breakfast and shared what they had. I was very touched, and I tried to give them some money – 5000 Dong, which is like 5 cents – but they wouldn't accept it at all. Those are the things that stand out.

I was always amazed at the love with which I was received by the Vietnamese people. We dropped bombs on them and shot them and laid mines for them. We left children behind us, children for whom we did nothing. And yet I was received lovingly wherever I went. People just invited me into their homes. It was absolutely amazing.

It was very important for me to go back; it's given me the ability to move on beyond Vietnam. Now I can think of Vietnam as a country – it's no longer just a war. I will always be involved in the project, and I plan to go back and spend more time there.

We veterans are afraid to open up the "box" because we're afraid that we might not be able to close the lid. But I've done it, and though the box is still there, I'm now able to close it and move on. Doing something, anything, is an important part of the healing process. It's just essential that it be *done*.

■ ■ ■ ■ ■ ■ ■

Before becoming a teacher, Jim Murphy helped to found Vietnam Veterans Against the War (VVAW) and was active in the Winter Soldier demonstrations, including a staged take-over of the Statue of Liberty and a gathering at the Lincoln Memorial to protest American military policy in Vietnam. Jim says that if it hadn't been for his early involvement in the antiwar movement, he would have ended up on the street, debilitated and stewing in his own anger, pain, and frustration. "The VVAW movement was the world's largest therapeutic collective," he added. "The important thing was that we got together and cried together and talked with one another and worked on each other. I'm sure that the guys who were involved in the early 1970s antiwar movement have better mental health today than the guys who just buried their experiences." But what drama inherent in the VVAW movement impacted him the most?

I remember being very angry and very restless. I was drinking a liter of Scotch a day. I had no self-control, and I didn't understand why, but I knew I was angry. At the University of Maryland I ran into a Vietnam vet buddy of mine who'd been a radioman like me. He had been really, really angry over his entire final tour in Vietnam. There was a protest being organized in DC, and we decided to go down and see what these guys were doing. We went to the All Souls Unitarian Church, and their minister was very active in the antiwar movement, involved with other vets, so we just hooked in.

All of a sudden I had a mission. I was surrounded by guys who knew how screwed up Vietnam really was, and we had a goal. The war was wrong, and we were going to end it through this demonstration. This was in 1971, and the demonstration was to take place in April, eight days before the May Day demonstration. So I went back to the University of Maryland and I just started putting up signs. Another guy who had been organizing with Vietnam Vets Against the War was there, and we started a chapter; fifty vets came to our first meeting. All of a sudden I went from being angry and restless and drunk to being focused, with a mission, and surrounded by people who could support me. It was just incredible.

Then Dewey Canyon happened. The famous media picture shows all the guys standing in line, waiting to throw their medals down on the Capitol steps. Guys were throwing back Silver Stars and Gold Stars and Bronze Stars and Purple Hearts and you name it. The steps were covered. I mean, there was a pile of decorations. The federal government didn't have a clue as to who we were or what we were doing, so naturally we were "confused communist Vietnam veterans, drunk and drug-crazed." There were 2000 of us at that demonstration. It was no longer fifty or a hundred; it was 2000 Vietnam veterans in jungle fatigues. The California contingent had M-60 machine guns and bandoleers of ammunition, which was one way to keep the park police away. They didn't mess with us once the California vets got there. And guys just kept coming in all night long, people in jungle fatigues and guys with antiwar sentiments scrawled all over the same boony hats they'd worn in Nam. It was just incredible. It was wonderful.

The park police wouldn't let us camp out on the Mall without a permit. They wanted us over in West Potomac Park, which is as far away from the Capitol as you can get in Washington, DC. But we camped out on the Mall anyhow, and they didn't dare confront us, because by the next morning we were up to 5000 Vietnam veterans. We had demonstrated to ourselves that we were not alone, and that what we felt about our government and the war in Vietnam was right: the war was wrong; bring our brothers home! That was it. That was the glue.

I got my "fifteen minutes of fame" at the next demonstration, Christmas 1971, when I joined a group of fifteen vets who took over the Statue of Liberty. It was symbolic: this is what you're taking away from the Vietnamese people – their liberty. We made some grandstand statements like, "We won't give up this statue until you bring our brothers home from Vietnam!"

The Park Service had a goon squad, a SWAT team. But they couldn't really storm us, because that would have looked bad – the majority of us were disabled Vietnam veterans.

Our initial plan was to rent boats out on Long Island and make an amphibious landing with five hundred or a thousand vets. But given the amount of undercover agents, provocateurs, and FBI throughout the antiwar movement, we realized that was a little grandiose, and that maybe something small and quiet with good media follow-up would serve the same purpose.

We went in on Christmas Eve. We'd just come up from Valley Forge, where there were about 1000 vets camping out as part of the Winter Soldier demonstration, and we had set up eight or nine simultaneous demonstrations. We painted Honeywell's driveway with blood, and they refused to drive across it. We shut down Caroll MacIntire, the "victory in Vietnam" minister in New Jersey — we just went in and joined the congregation, didn't do anything nasty, but evidently he felt uncomfortable with all of us vets there. We painted the Liberty Bell with blood, and we held a major demonstration at the Lincoln Monument, which was a major bust.

We entered the Statue in threes and fours — I'm sure it's much more secure now than it was then — and hid in the arm until after the last boat had left at 5:00 P.M. We had our jungle fatigues on underneath normal clothes, and we all wore our decorations. Anyway, they went after us with a court order, a cease-and-desist order for trespassing, but we were able to hold that up based on the fact that they couldn't get a hold of the secretary of the interior. He was hunting in Alaska, which we actually knew, so they had to go on down through the chain of jurisdiction, and by the time they got down to the New York City level we'd been in the statue for twenty-four hours. By then the Park Service had called a SWAT team in and had surrounded us, but we were barricaded in so well that they couldn't have stormed us without some pretty major property destruction.

The international media was three-deep at all the doors, and there are a lot of doors. The park police couldn't do anything privately; the whole world was watching. So the park police backed off. They didn't want to look bad. So we had control, and we used it. Every one of us was well qualified to speak against the war in Vietnam, and we got a lot of airtime. We were from all over the Northeast: from Boston, from New York, from Philadelphia and from DC, but we made sure that our message was consistent — we didn't go off on any tangents.

In the end, the government dropped it. They didn't charge us with anything. Nothing. They wanted it out of the public view. If there'd been a trial, it would have dragged on forever and we would have been able to make our point over and over and over. We would have loved a trial...We didn't do any damage. We drank all the coffee in the employees' area and ate some of their food, but we left them money for it.

Much later, though, I met Sherman, a guy who was on the desk for NBC News over Christmas 1971, and he told me that they were just getting ready to break the story for the 11:00 news when they got a call from the White House telling them to kill it. Sherman had said, "We can't kill this story," but the White House was adamant and demanded to speak to his supervisor. So the supervisor took the call, and the story was killed. Just like that. By

Richard Nixon. And I'm sure that every President does this. It's amazing how much information people never get. How many people know the real deal about Cuba? Or anywhere?

We're still getting revisionist history about Vietnam now, and I think one of the important functions VVAW serves is to make it difficult for the government to lie and change the history of Vietnam. We make sure people don't forget what the real facts were.

Jim is convinced that his activism helped to end the war, but even more important, he feels that it allowed him to connect with other veterans and gave purpose and meaning to a life that was on the brink of ruin. After the 1971 actions he returned to the University of Maryland to study education – believing that if he'd been taught to "think instead of follow," his life might have turned out differently.

Today, he is dean of West Side High School in Manhattan, an alternative school that serves students whose social and economic backgrounds have robbed them of a decent start in life. Jim and his wife Susan, also a teacher, try hard to foster a sense of community at West Side and have visited our Woodcrest Bruderhof several times with their students. When I asked them about their work and its connection to the antiwar movement in which Jim played such an active part, he replied:

It's amazing how many of us in the antiwar movement became teachers or other members of the helping professions – special ed teachers, therapists, and social workers. It's been our way to healing.

The kids I work with tend to come from the poorest neighborhoods in the city. So they're the easiest targets for recruiters. I try to help them see what their options are; to help them understand that you don't have to sign up for four years and $40,000, that you don't have to give away four years of your life.

I had a young man, Muslim, who was in the Persian Gulf War. He joined to get money for college, and he was sent to a Muslim country to kill Muslims. He says that they just blew people away. The Iraqis tried to give themselves up, but we just ran them down; there was no time to take prisoners on the front. So we killed them, ran them down, bulldozed them, buried them alive. That's his "be all you can be" story.

The system that educates our kids to accept the military also educates kids to accept all the other things that are wrong with our society. Inherent in having a strong military is racism, and the need for economic separation. If you don't have poor people you can't have privates first class.

I still remember the targets in basic training. The stand-ups we had were "Ruben the Cuban" and "Luke the Gook." Could Vietnam have occurred if people had understood cultural differences? It was a war of cultures and economics.

Our kids love to come up to Woodcrest because it demonstrates a sense of community that is totally outside of their experience. To create community really brings out the most that you can be. That's where you can "be all that you can be" – in a community that works for public change, for equality. I realize it's a minimal experience, but the important thing is that hope is there…

■ ■ ■ ■ ■ ■ ■

That drama is an important part of healing is made clear by the hurt that results when it is denied. Richard Lutrell was haunted for three decades by a photograph of a little girl standing next to a man – the Vietnamese soldier he had killed – and when in 1997 he finally received a letter from the man's son, confirming his identity, he was ecstatic. His goal was one day to find the girl and apologize for what he had done. When her brother's letter arrived, it seemed that this wish might soon become reality.[3]

I decided I had to contact Richard and learn the whole story, and we talked several times on the phone over the next summer. Though busy, he was eager to help with my project and willingly shared his journey with me:

I joined the Army in 1966 and was assigned as an infantryman. Then I went through jump school in Fort Benning, Georgia, and from there I was assigned to the 82nd Airborne Division at Fort Bragg, North Carolina. I was there about a year before going to Vietnam, where I served with the 101st Airborne Division.

I was pretty much a naïve adolescent when it happened. We were on a mountain ridge, and we were staggered on the trail facing opposite directions, about fifteen yards apart, as a safety measure. The point man was teaching me to walk point, so I was walking slack. Then they held the column up – I think they wanted to get a radioman up close or something – and as we were standing there resting and taking a break, I lit up a cigarette. As I did, I saw, out of the corner of my right eye, an NVA soldier squatting and pointing a weapon at me on the trail just thirty feet away. We stared at each other for what seemed like an eternity, and then I fired and killed him.

There was return fire from both sides, and when it was all over, we moved up and found three dead NVA. We didn't have any casualties. I remember the guys going through the NVAs' personal belongings, taking belt buckles and belts – souvenirs, so to speak. One of the troopers offered me the belt buckle of the guy I had killed, and I said, "I don't want it." I was just sick. It was surreal. I couldn't believe it had really happened – that I'd actually taken a life. I'd never seen anybody shot before, so it was pretty traumatic.

One of the guys went through the wallet of the soldier I had shot and threw it to the ground. I was still standing there in shock when the command came, "Okay, let's move out." We just left them lying there, but as we started down the trail I looked down at the wallet. A picture had fallen out of it. I bent down and picked it up. I looked at the picture and looked at the soldier. It was obviously his picture; he was in uniform, and there was a little girl in the photo, too. Her hair was braided in pigtails. It looked like she was about eight or nine years old. I don't know why, but I took that photo, and I carried it in my wallet for the next twenty-two years.

I'll never forget the look in his eyes. I'm sure he could see it in my eyes, too. I was scared to death, although he looked more solemn and sober. I found out later that he had been twenty-seven years old. For whatever reason – he hesitated, chose not to fire, and I've asked myself many times, "Why?" Then I ask, "But do I carry any regret or guilt for my actions?" And the answer is, "Yes."

I suffered survival guilt for years, not just because of that picture, but because of all the troopers I served with for a whole year. As time went on the fights got more and more serious, and pretty soon I was the only guy of my original unit still alive. I dreaded each day – I was just tired of it, sick of it. Sick of the killing, just sick. I think this particular incident had so much impact on me because it was the first time I'd ever seen an enemy soldier and then it was the first life I ever took. But as time went on, it got easier. I hate to say that, but it did. It became a defense mechanism for me. They were just targets after that. The line between sanity and insanity is real fine, especially in combat. Most of us just tried to block it out, like it wasn't really happening.

Anyway, I carried that picture for years, and my wife would say, "You really should get rid of that, it just upsets you so much." At one point she even asked me about it, so I shared it with her. I knew she was right, but to get rid of the photo, to throw it in the trash or burn it, was just too disrespectful. If I ever got rid of it, it would have to be done with some kind of respect and honor to the people in the picture.

Then, in 1989, I made my first pilgrimage to the Wall. I remember sitting in a hotel room in Fairfax, Virginia, and I knew I was going to leave the picture at the Wall the next morning. I tried to think: if I could say something to that soldier, what would I say? So I wrote a letter. I took the letter and the photograph and put them in a sandwich bag I had with me. The next morning my wife and I went to the Wall, and we left it there and placed a rock on it. Perhaps it was the first time that somebody left something for the enemy at the Wall, but it was catharsis, closure, and I felt good about it.

Richard's story wasn't over. In 1996 a friend walked into his office and said, "Hey, I want to show you this new book. It's called *Offerings at the Wall*. Turn to page 52." When he did, there was the photograph and his letter. It had been collected, like most other memorabilia, by the National Park Service. Once again, Richard was thrown into inner turmoil:

> It just — I mean, I'd been at peace with myself, I'd found some closure, and then here it all comes back. It took up two full pages. I just really lost it, was torn up immediately. It felt like it was my fate that no matter what I did, this would keep coming back.
>
> From that day on, I decided I was on a mission to find that family. I knew the odds were against me. I knew it probably wasn't very realistic, but I took the mission on.

Over the next months, he published articles in American and Vietnamese newspapers and contacted ambassadors and veterans' groups in both countries. In time, he received a letter from a man who said he was the son of the soldier he had killed, but when he tried to arrange a personal meeting with the man's family, government agencies on both sides began to stonewall. According to Richard, even U.S. Ambassador Peterson in Vietnam, himself a Vietnam veteran, has turned his back on the matter. "They're just totally ignoring the issue. It's taboo; nobody wants to touch it," he lamented. "They're trying to hold reconciliation beyond my grasp."

I expressed my hope to Richard that the year 1998 might see a resolution to his long search for healing and closure, and that he might, at long last, find the peace he has been seeking these past thirty years. But his response showed me more deeply than ever how essential drama can be to the process of healing, and how consumed with thirst a human soul can be when it is denied:

> I wake up at night with cold sweats. You know, my platoon was overrun twice, and I dream about that again and again. And I dream about the little girl. She keeps coming back to haunt me, in my dreams — this little girl in pigtails. If I ever met her, I'd just ask her to forgive me. I don't know what more I could say.
>
> You know, my dad died at forty-eight of cirrhosis of the liver. He was an alcoholic. He was an abusive father, very abusive. With time I was able to forgive him. But try and forgive yourself — that's the hardest part. You can forgive people for transgressions of all types, but just to try to cut yourself some slack...That's the ultimate. It's hard to do. Really hard.

Richard's words made me think of Thich Nhat Hanh, who maintains that such inner suffering can lead to compassion and forgiveness, to a wonderful freedom of the soul. He reminds us that we must focus on the "present moment" – the here and now – if we are ever to move beyond the pain and evil of the past. And we can live in the present moment in very simple, practical ways, as he illustrates in the following piece of advice given to the veterans at Omega:

> I talked with a soldier who saw many of his friends die in an ambush, and who then set up an ambush in revenge. Five children stepped into it and died. From that day on, he has suffered terribly. Every time he finds himself in a room with children, he cannot bear it and has to run out of the room. The image of the five dead children follows him day and night. I told him that there are many children dying this very moment all over the world – children who die because they lack just one tablet of medicine. Now, if you can bring that medicine to just one child and save his life, and then you do the same for four other children, you have saved five children.
>
> We must live and work in the present moment. Forty thousand children die every day because they lack food and medicine. So why cling to the past, to the five who are now dead, who have already died? There are more children dying now, and we have the power to change this by touching the present moment. [4]

■ ■ ■ ■ ■ ■ ■

We can go to great lengths to announce God's mercy and forgiveness for a person, but then he has to make a response. And the grace to make that response is always there. It's always there. God does not give up, as the poor veteran or I will. In the end, it depends on us. And veterans should be aware of that – they should be told that they need to respond. They can't welter in self-pity and brooding and guilt for the rest of their lives. They've got better things to do. They've got a unique position from which to work against war, to announce to the people of our country that war can't be our number-one business. These guys all have a role. They have a mission, and it's a very definite one...

Philip Berrigan

CHAPTER 14

An American Story

I pledged my allegiance
To the Flag.
Oh, so brave...
Makes me gag.
Her American dream.
Yeah, she loved me the best
Bring a few home
Bury the rest.

We danced the Red,
White, and Blue Rag
Yeah, all dressed in green
Oh, what a scream.

Ron Landsel

The story of Ron Landsel, like the stories of all veterans of war, is not the story of an isolated individual. It is the story of an entire family, and, ultimately, the story of a nation: a father who died in an army accident before he was born, a mother who aged many years when she thought her only son was killed in Southeast Asia, a wife who kept vigil over the long, anguished silence of his "coming home"; a son ridden with the odd mix of guilty curiosity and reverence, wanting to know his father's heart...All were affected, and all suffered the legacy of war.

Unlike the stories of many veterans, however, Ron's is also a story of light and hope. When work on this book began, and Ron appointed himself as my "veteran advisor," I said a silent prayer of thanks. I had met Ron and his family soon after I came to the Bruderhof, and they'd made me feel very much at home. It wasn't long before I felt as if I'd known this fellow Long-Islander all my life.

But there was something in Ron that never yielded in friendly conversation. His year in Vietnam was untouchable, unmentionable, well guarded. I couldn't understand why, and neither could his family. But there was something that made me want to know, and it was more than just curiosity. Perhaps it was that I'd learned, from my own life, that private pain is the worst pain of all.

Ron was encouraging whenever I talked to him about my ideas for a book, but he never offered to contribute his own story. Only when the project was officially kicked off did the shrapnel begin to surface, piece by piece, as we traded newspaper clippings and swapped addresses. But by the time he accompanied me to a Buddhist retreat for veterans, I noticed that he was beginning to open up. It was there, in the presence of other Vietnam vets, that I watched as he began to make himself vulnerable by degrees, slowly peeling back the barbed wire that fenced off a whole year of adolescent dread and horror, to find healing in the presence of Vietnamese monks and nuns and fellow survivors.

He came to two other events as well: public forums in which veterans of many wars were invited to share their wisdom and experience with a new and naïve generation.

Altogether, these opportunities for open and honest discussion – in the presence of a supportive and respectful audience – had a profound effect. Ron's wounds were deep, but their pain could now be shared, lightened, and divided. His relationship to his wife and three children deepened, and he began to reach out to younger veterans with compassion and understanding. And though his journey to full healing may not be over, he feels that he is well on the way: in February 1998, he was able to commemorate the thirtieth anniversary of the Tet Offensive with Vietnamese brothers and sisters at the Plum Village Buddhist community in France. For him, it was the link that closed the circle – Vietnam was no longer just a terrible war, but a beautiful country and a loving people. "There is great hunger and need for veterans to find peace and a whole life again," Ron recently said. "And the message I can bring to them, out of my own experience, is one of repentance, acceptance, and forgiveness."

How many families have suffered like the Landsels? Many, perhaps, have suffered even more, but the story that follows ought to give them hope: hope in forgiveness, hope in reconciliation, hope for a new future.

Jason Landsel

I have dreamed of the day you'll come home
and finally be my dad.

From a letter left at the Vietnam Veterans Memorial in Washington, DC

I can't recall the first time I realized my father was a Vietnam veteran. When I was little we would visit his mom in Bayside, New York, and under the coffee table in her apartment there was always a collection of battered photo albums. One was labeled "Vietnam." It held few photographs, but empty photo holders told of a once-larger collection. The photos left showed little of Vietnam, but rather a young man posturing in military attire. Beneath a few, my grandmother had written things like "Ronnie in San Diego," and in a few other American cities. Other pages had more exotic headings, like "Australia" or "Puerto Rico," but they offered little more for my inquisitive mind.

I had a childish fascination and ignorance about it all – I knew only that my dad had done something unusual, something the other kids' dads hadn't. This was an obvious source of pride and one-upmanship at school: "Well, *my* dad went to Vietnam!"

Maybe Mother had warned us not to, but I can't ever recall asking Dad about Vietnam when I was a kid. There were the little anecdotes he would tell now and then, the light stuff, the stories we came almost to memorize over the years. There was the night a huge rat had crawled over his chest as he slept in a field, the time he was served gin in a teacup and saucer at an Australian bar, the speedboat rides in Sydney Harbor, the nights in a hurricane off the coast of Puerto Rico, and the fact that he almost died of malaria. This is what I knew.

We moved to the Bruderhof when I was in the first grade, and I count myself lucky to have had such a safe and privileged childhood. During those carefree years I was removed from most of the pain and difficulty so many other kids face, and Dad's time in Vietnam all but disappeared.

It was only when I was older that I began to wonder about his experience in a serious manner. He still never said a thing, but my mother would spill a few details now and then, mostly from the time when he first came home: the silence; the nightmares; the late-night promise, made to God on his knees, that none of his sons would ever fight in a war…I was deeply impressed, and I wanted to know more, but I knew I would never, ever, dare to ask.

Over the years I schemed to get his story, feeling that it was important to document his life – if for nothing but for his family. I wrote him lists of questions and even hinted at taped "interviews," but nothing happened. And

I felt guilty planning such projects, fearful that he might "lose it" — that my questioning might bring back something from the past to trigger a very negative reaction. I even discussed my plans with my minister, hoping to get his support, but was told that "it wouldn't be helpful to bring up the past."

Then, last summer, after we had worked together on an event presenting the truths of war to a group of young people, he spoke to me about Nam for the first time. We had watched *Platoon*, and it had been a long evening. We went outside to get some fresh air, and I hesitantly asked him whether or not the film was authentic. His answer was to tell me of his own experiences — general information at first, but it was something: the sound of the bullets, the food, the missions. I probed on carefully, not wanting to stop him, aware that I was being entrusted with something that was very deep, very personal. Never before had I felt that close to my father. Then our walk was over, but our relationship had been forever changed.

The details of his trip home stand out in particular. The ride from jungle combat to suburban Long Island took less than forty-eight hours, and after Vietnam, life in New York was more than he could bear. He remembers sitting in his hometown mall, watching the hurried and self-absorbed shoppers, wishing he could just "blow them all away." I told my mother about our talk late that night, and she agreed that it was a very special moment.

There were other times that summer when he told more — unexpectedly, to be sure, and with obvious difficulty. But I saw in his stories a man changed, and in spite of the strong emotions and unusual profanity, I gained new trust and new respect. I had been given a glimpse of untold pain.

That summer I read all I could about Vietnam. Reading the accounts of other veterans, I realized how lucky our family had been. Dad had started out no differently than the men I was reading about, but by some twist of fate we had been spared the ongoing misery that is the lot of so many veterans and their families. And when I considered the statistics of divorce, abuse, suicide, and alcoholism, I knew it was nothing other than a merciful God that had steered us to where we were now.

Without God's help, and the help of a committed and supportive community, there's no way my father could have overcome the violence of the war. And I pray that many others might be granted the same mercy.

Pat Landsel

Women did not go to Vietnam in great numbers, but great numbers have been scarred by the war. One by one, without the awareness of danger that strikes those who put on uniforms, we met and fell in love with men whose combat experience would change our lives...The men of our generation were called to Vietnam: some went off to war, some of them came home. We thanked God it was over. And wearing frilly-nightgown smiles, we slept snuggled next to walking time bombs.[1]

Wife of a Vietnam veteran

Ron and I met when he was already in the Marine Corps. In those days, Marines were admired. To be in the military was normal and expected of a young man growing up.

My father was wounded in the Second World War and received a Purple Heart. He came home to a very young wife, and for the rest of his short, hard life, he suffered a serious drinking problem. He died very suddenly at the age of thirty-two, leaving behind three young children. I was seven.

My mother married again. My second dad had served in the Navy; later, my brother Joe served in Korea. I grew up on movies that gloried in the fight for Democracy – the fight against the evil communists. And as a Catholic, I learned early what a privilege it was to fight for one's country.

Ron stopped at our house on his way to Vietnam, and over a Scotch-and-water, he asked me to marry him when he came home. I said yes, and together with his mother and a friend we headed for the airport. Neither of us saw the incredible step that he took at that moment.

Then he was gone, and I wrote him faithfully, sitting in his car which he had left in our driveway. I sent pictures and tapes, and went often to the parish church to light candles for his safety. My walls were covered with his letters and pictures, but I never asked once what the war was all about. And I never questioned my country, or the President. Even after Kent State, after the cries to "bring our boys home," I didn't see what was happening.

Ron served a year in Nam, and I went with my dad and his mom to the airport. All of a sudden, there he was, holding me, kissing me, but not saying very much at all. Over the next weeks we spent as much time together as we could, but he slept and slept and slept. I didn't know what to say – I didn't know how to help or support him. I never asked him about Vietnam, either, and he never said anything. He was tough, he was the all-American Marine, and he could handle it.

I had made a large poster from a picture he had sent from Vietnam. He was sitting on sandbags, holding a machine gun – a really tough picture. But when he saw it, he made me take it down right away. I did, but I never asked him why it bothered him so much.

We saved up and had a dream wedding, but we were nothing special. We were selfish young adults, and there was nothing in particular that held us together. Then he came home drunk one night – he had damaged the car a little – and I remember sitting on the stairs and looking at him as he said, over and over, "I'm crying, I'm crying, and I haven't been able to cry since the war." I felt real sorrow for him, but again I didn't know what to do or say. I wish I could relive that moment now…

Another time he was yelling, and he said, "If we have sons, I'll never let them go to war." I was scared when he said that, because it might mean we would have to leave the country. But he still said nothing about the war…

Let me make one thing clear: we would never have stayed together if Jesus hadn't come into our lives. Both our lives had been wounded from early on, and neither of us knew what it would take to make it through, to keep our vows to each other. But then we had a life-changing conversion; we opened our hearts to Jesus' words, and we became radically serious about following him in our everyday lives.

At that time, our son Jason was born, and things started to change fast. We renewed our marriage vows and dedicated our lives to God. But the pain was still there, and Ron said nothing about the war.

After twelve years in a Catholic community attempt on Long Island, we joined the Bruderhof movement and we were confronted right away with the nonviolence of Jesus' teaching. It struck us immediately – "Oh my God, of course!" – and we embraced this new calling for the rest of our lives. Here was a life of love, lived by people who were seriously committed to what Jesus had demanded for the whole world.

Still no sharing about the war…

Even within a supportive community, our marriage and our lives as individuals were in need of continuous renewal and recommitment. We continued to hurt each other, our three children, and those around us. We had tough years, but because of our clear commitment to God, we made it through. And we came to see that this was so only through God's help, through our willingness to work out any problem between us, however painful.

Only recently have we become involved with other Vietnam veterans. God has opened up this area of our life again, through the work on this book, and we have been put in touch with the incredible casualties of the young men and women who are fighting new wars, the casualties of their families, and the utter ruin of their lives.

But Ron *still* said nothing about the war, and it wasn't until he wrote his account for this book that the whole story came out. He labored over it for months, and it took much prompting and many prayers. But there was a purpose to it all, and I pray now that many more veterans can be granted the healing and new life he has found. His story is about the horror of war, but it also points to a God who cares.

Ron Landsel

"Back Azimuth"

War's unreality
Is horrible
Inseparable
Languishing
Silently
In faded rooms
On the other side of a latch
Just outside a window
Imminent
It will lift
One of many mask-faces
In terror's hoary remembrance
Knowing your deepest emotions
Your limits
Never needing to speak
You sigh

Ron Landsel

The first date on my tombstone was recorded on August 16, 1946, just a few blocks from the star shows of Hayden's Planetarium, uptown, Big Apple. Shadows of World War II nightmares remained a secret for millions, but not to Mildred H. Landsel or to the tens of millions who suffered in the world's new killing fields.

Little-known brush fires in a remote area called Indochina were already flickering on the newsreels, fed to us growing boys at the 25-cent Saturday matinee between the cartoons and heroes that mustered us out into games of "playing guns." We divvied up into good guys and bad guys in the empty lots of working-class Queens. Fellow players considered my mock deaths a great contribution to the game. My cold-war MOS (military occupational specialty) in Catholic grade school was "window-shade monitor" during air raid drills. As the widow's son went to hide under his desk after "protecting us from the bomb-shattered glass," Sister Mary Ronald, my heroine and the consoler of my insecurities, knelt and prayed with us for the conversion of Russia. I loved her kindness and hoped her prayers, and the benignant Dwight David Eisenhower, would make us safe from "the enemy."

After school, Sir Baden-Powell's followers, Scout merit-badge courses in hand, prepared us for the field disciplines of tracking, communications, first aid, compass, and topographical map skills. Our weapons: the war-surplus store's sheath knife, entrenching tool, compass, semaphore flags, combat pack — and ignorance, the lethal seed of war.

Except for pointing out a neighborhood man as a World War II flying ace, and rare comments like "it was good to have a general for President," Mom never talked about the war or politics. Her love, Earl, "died in an Army accident just before you were born." A Cornell-graduate and a lithographer, he and Mom, a physician's adopted daughter, hailed from the lake region of Syracuse and Buffalo. (I learned later that over 10,000 deaths in Vietnam were due to accidents...)

Mom never remarried, and we were a lonely pair, comforted for the next nineteen struggling years by precious little of Dad's artwork or his life story. We talked little about our pain, and never about his death. Nor did we talk, years later, about the terrible day — the shock and then the relief — when two Marines in dress-blue uniform rang the doorbell to Mom's second-floor Queens apartment. Did she somehow already "know"? Did she think, at that moment, about my father and another war? The news was not as terrible as the setting: I'd been nearly a month in the hospital in Da Nang, but "the nice young fellows" assured her I was recovering well.

I wonder sometimes if I didn't nearly die in that hospital, if some power didn't reach down and push me back into life just as they were speaking to my mother. Vietnam presented me with several experiences of what I now know as eternity.

We were working-class poor, with nothing much beyond the basic necessities to speak of. I was never the best-dressed kid, and I vividly recall the long discussion that Mom had with Father Terence Sharkey, the retired businessman-turned-priest, about first-grade "tuition" — whatever that was. She told me nothing, but in September I found myself in the first grade at Sacred Heart School in Bayside, New York.

In the eighth grade, I went to work as delivery boy for an Italian butcher and grocer. I worked every day after school, and eight hours on Saturdays. I earned eight dollars a day, lunch on Saturday, and tips to boost the ninety dollars Mom made as a secretary at the air conditioner factory. As I sorted smelly beer and soda bottles in the dingy store basement on those long Saturdays, I quietly perfected my broken English-Italian accent, considered the life of the martyrs, of runaways, and whether the hottest thing in town, old man Doyle's basement fallout shelter, was motivated by his World War II experiences. He had the whole deal: lead-lined walls and ceiling, canned water, and shelves full of food. His son secreted us neighborhood boys in for a peek; we were buddies and "on the list."

The neighbors offered painting, snow-shoveling, and mowing, but we were still pretty poor. I remember stealing a crisp five-dollar bill from a friend, and needing lots of help to face it. Just around Easter, a neighbor hanged himself one Saturday night in the back of his hardware store. Man, that rocked my life. He'd had a good job and was always around. We'd always admired his family; his son was just a little younger than me. But he stopped coming to our school, and I felt terrible. I didn't want him to be without a dad. Mom told me that he had fought in the war...

I was crushed when my first love left me after I told her I wanted to be a priest. She was also upset because I never kissed her. My feelings of inferiority had not brought me to such achievement; carrying her schoolbooks and sharing dreams on the long walks home from school were wonder enough for this latch-key kid.

A basketball scholarship came along by the time I was ready to enter Holy Cross High School in 1960. My Catholic Youth coach, Mr. Miller, was a great encouragement. But high school moved too fast; and although I loved art and music, the pressures of basketball, football, beer parties, girls, and fraternity life came rushing at me in those short years of getting an education. My independence cost me my virginity by the end of the tenth grade.

One day, as I stood in front of our favorite after-school luncheonette, a young black guy was shot right across the street by a chasing cop. Other cops kicked and beat him as they waited for an ambulance; I wanted to shout out and stop them because he was obviously hurt. But I was already learning the moral "freeze," and though I was stunned and angered by this violence, I did nothing.

I was sixteen when a very tough neighborhood kid lost his legs in some place called Vietnam. It was all over town: "A booby trap – blew his fucking legs off." I was sickened and wondered why we never saw Tom again. And though it seemed that the prayers of Sister Ronald and Cardinal Spellman were keeping the Russians away, what about the commies in Vietnam?

Mom was always there, quiet but supportive. She pointed me toward the church, though she rarely went herself, and there was the copy of Kahlil Gibran's *Prophet* that I was supposed to read when I got older. She gave herself tirelessly, coming home from work, shopping, cleaning, making supper, and sleeping on the couches of our one-bedroom apartments — all her life. And only rarely did her calm, which hid a deep well of pain, erupt in bitter outbursts — usually when someone had hurt her.

Only days out of the combat zone, I came home to my second-floor apartment in Queens and lay down for three solid weeks of sickly sleep. I also conversed with the ghosts that had accompanied me home, which try as I might would not relax their grip on my soul.

I was looking down at my shoes when Mom, Pat, and her dad came to Kennedy Airport to pick me up. That was weird; I felt like a movie actor who'd forgotten his lines. I just stood there grinning, mumbling innocuous "hi's" and "how are ya's," hugging, hoping everything was going to be okay. I was freezing, and Pat's dad covered my tropical uniform with his coat. Then we walked to the car for a very difficult hour-and-a-half ride home. What do you say after the clichés and the standard explanations? I lied, because I no longer believed them to be true. I was supposed to be a hero, but I felt like I was riding in an open coffin. My family stared at the corpse, occasionally stuttering, but afraid to break the silence. The DJ on the radio sounded like an empty suit. Every sense was assaulted. Sounds, sights, and smells. It was all wrong. This was not what I had fought for.

By that time, though, I was morally compromised by the values I lived for. Selfish interests, the easy life, women, drinking — all my posturing in Catholic-American loyalty denied the response of my own heart, which knew it was all wrong. And it seemed that the Marine recruiter who'd gotten me into this hadn't listened to his heart, either. He never told me that I could easily and legally have avoided the conflagration as a sole surviving son...

Pat was my constant in this lost world of my peers. She was the "back azimuth" that I could follow to safe haven. She didn't ask the stupid questions: "Did you kill anybody?" "What is war like?" She knew I would never be the same again, that there was no point in telling me that it was okay. It wasn't. Something in me was gone. Dead, but not yet buried, and wandering, like the *mat tich*, the hundred thousand wandering souls of the missing Vietnamese war dead.

I was worried. I couldn't concentrate very well anymore, and the things I had been through in Nam were breaking into glimpses like the pieces of a broken mirror. The days and months there no longer fit together. I was easily exhausted. Malaria had taken my stamina, and still keeps it. I ignited in rages over things insignificant, and I kept everything inside. I desperately wanted the war to be over, but it was everywhere, and still in my own sickened spirit.

The Vietnamese find peace through a rootedness to their ancestors. They revere their forefathers and keep little altars of remembrance for deceased loved ones in their homes. But there were no altars of reverence in our society — not for the dead, and certainly not for returning veterans. We were ignored in the job market and on the street. We were spat upon, beaten, and denied our promised benefits. There was no incense for us. We symbolized an America shocked into awareness of our lifestyle's horrible effect on the rest of the world. We fought for its corrupt system and were hated for it.

"Ask not what your country can do for you…" That call had been an appeal to survival, to community, to a brave new future. But the America I fought for in 1969 was more interested in watching the N.Y. Jets-Baltimore Colts Super Bowl, and standing in long lines at malls returning unwanted Christmas presents. And worried about the upholstery in their cars.

I wanted to draw from under my cloak the bloody, heavy pieces that my soul had become. I wanted to hold out the dead, the POWs and the captured VCs — to stand with them in front of the 21-inch color TV sets, sit with them in the shiny new cars, hold them up in the department-store windows for everyone to see: stumbling, tagged, and blindfolded, as their "liberators" led them to the punishing winds of the huge CH-53 choppers that would take them away to refugee camps in the South…

When the bartender asked me what time the game started and who was going to win, I wanted to scream out: "When I was on duty, not one capture was shot or raped!" And it was true — I had refused orders to call in fire on a group of women. I dumbed the barman's stupid questions, stirring scotch and ice with my trigger finger, thinking that a tour in the Nam might do this guy some good.

I came home from a war very few Americans cared about or understood. It was the TV war: "Oh yeah, I saw that Tet thing on TV — nasty business." It was, but they hadn't drawn its pain down into their lungs, holding the hit as long as they could. Their noses, throats, and eyes hadn't been seared by the heat of terror, grief, anxiety, and rage. They hadn't heard the sucking sighs of the dying, hadn't seen the pink bubbles and the flapping gauze. They had just turned the channel while I rock-and-rolled* ten magazines into an early morning ambush that took out a quiet new kid from Wisconsin. He was hit only inches from me, and his life and hope and love gushed thick from his mouth and nose as we followed each other's eyes all the way down to the jungle floor. He never said a word, and neither did I. Why wasn't it me? In a way, it was.

---

* Full automatic fire from an M-16: about 750–900 rounds per minute.

I'd already seen a KIA (killed in action) in boot camp. We diagnosed his death as terminal fear, but rumor had it he died of pneumonia. He'd been sick for a while but was terrified of the harassment you could get for going to sick bay. It all came back now: "Kill a commie for Christ!" "I can't hear you ladies! Are you my ladies?" "Sir, yes, Sir!" "Who you gonna kill, ladies?" "Sir, commies, Sir!" "Who for, ladies?" "Sir, for Christ, Sir." "Bullshit – I don't believe you – bends and thrusts forever. Reaaady – begin!"

I came off battalion OP (observation point) too sick to go out on patrol. I'd had a wicked fever and no strength for over a week. Our sick bay couldn't come up with anything, but I couldn't walk or eat anymore. I just shook and burned. Then the high-pitched whine of rocket-propelled grenades came into base camp, and I had to be dragged to a bunker. Next morning I was medevaced to a unit near Freedom Hill. I had a temperature of 106.8. Malaria. I was going to die lying there in the ER. A dustoff brought in three grunts and a child. The child was like a skinned animal; he had been dragged behind a Six-By, and died on his litter. One of the grunts had been hit in the abdomen and was screaming; they were catheterizing him when his heart stopped. I remember his body lifting up off the cart, again and again, as they defibrillated him. He died, too. How did the medics keep this up all the time? Then I was strapped across the back of a jeep and taken to China Beach.

At the Da Nang Naval Hospital, I was thrown into crushed ice baths, blasted with floor fans, and pumped with medication. The one rocket attack I remember during my stay wasn't as scary as the ice treatments and the allergic reactions I had from the medications. A doctor told me I was going home, but the big boys had other ideas. I had recently been promoted to sergeant, and they reassigned me as 1st recon communications chief for Delta Company.

After boot camp, I had trained in combat and radio-telegraph operations on the East and West Coasts. Then, at the kind invitation of General William Westmoreland, who asked for 206,000 more troops in 1968, I had gotten orders for Vietnam. Martin Luther King and Robert Kennedy were both slain that year. History was screaming at us, but nobody listened. I still remember the flight to California when reality first hit. I sat there and began to cry, silently. No one said anything, but the well-dressed Asian businessman next to me got up from his seat and moved.

But I was in denial right up to the moment I stepped out of the air-conditioned commercial airliner that landed in Da Nang. No one from training was with me, and my own countrymen didn't know me, nor I them. Like the Vietnamese workers, they were callous and careworn – we had little in common beyond our births on the same huge continent. Their slang, indifference, and even threatened violence were a painful destabilization. And the terrific heat was like a beast drawing me into its den. I was convinced that I had come here to die, and assured of my premonitions when I got assigned to my new unit.

The touted life-expectancy of a Marine radio operator in a firefight was about eleven seconds. Entire reconnaissance teams were given half that. There were always three dead men in a recon team: the point man, the patrol leader, and the man with the antenna. But like the men around me, I kept my fears to myself. No one voluntarily exposed his fears. From the grunt to the North Vietnamese regular, from the Vietcong sapper to the boys in Hanoi, all the way to the State Department — we were very courageous warriors. There was plenty to bitch about, but we hung tough in our fear. And so the wars of our minds lasted longer, and were as destructive as the exploding shells and the bullets.

In-country recon meant training on a battalion OP, in a so-called free-fire zone southwest of Da Nang. Our position commanded a full view of the river and valley below, and we ran constant patrols off the hill as well — the Vietcong and NVA were constantly moving into the area. I got plenty of experience calling in air and artillery strikes, including *Puff the Magic Dragon*, a slow-flying transport plane equipped with Vulcan machine guns that could saturate every square inch of a football field in minutes. We would watch the lights of its tracers in dumb amazement as it flew up and down the valley for twenty minutes at a time, spitting red fire...

It was Christmas 1968, and it was the pits. Bare, dusty, blown-up red soil, stony rubble, trash waving in the concertina wire fences. This place was hell. Brown rats crawled over our chests as we feigned a night's sleep in the bunkers. They reminded me that there were brown men all around us who could easily do the same. Our platoon was not overrun, but we were randomly mortared — sometimes heavily. Our bunkers were no match for their shells. But their ammunition was precious, and unless they locked in on us quickly, they didn't stick around to wait for the artillery support we would call in as retaliation. All the same, the silence between explosions was infuriating. They seemed to be right on top of us, and then — nothing. Just our heartbeats. It was torture.

One side of the OP was often subject to sniper fire. I was standing in a trench one very hot afternoon with two other guys when rifle shots came in. The first round hit a hand's width in front of my chest. Years later I could see that nightmare round, going through my head, spinning me around as I took two dead steps away...

2:00 A.M.: a repeated radio message from an OP across the valley saves us from being overrun. They didn't know our call sign but still managed to get our attention. They had seen beaucoup lights ascending the steepest escarpment of our hill, but to call in artillery was useless; these guys were doing some serious rock climbing. We set out extra claymores and impatiently tore open cases of hand grenades. As we lobbed them over the edge, the lights fell and went out. We called in Willie Peter (white phosphorus) at the base of the hill and stayed on 100 percent alert the rest of the night – our silence spoke the memories of being overrun before. I radioed in a schedule of the sickly-white illumination rounds until dawn. We didn't speculate too much about what could have happened, but we knew they had to be sappers, climbing a ledge like that. If it weren't for the radio call and the clear night…The little parachutes of spent illumination rounds hung lifeless in the dead trees, like symbolic ghosts.

Reconners hated OP. We were stealth, silence, jungle – the cat. We never used trails, streams, or low ground. But patrols off this hill offered little safe cover. Ambushes and mines were not infrequent encounters on the worn trails up and down the slopes. My first patrol was a total screwup. We got down to the valley floor beautifully. I was quiet and alert, the only new man; it felt right. But then we had movement in the thickly vined brush ahead. The team leader signaled, and we nudged our M-16s off safety. My heart was pounding as we crept forward. BLAM! Everyone was on their bellies in a circle, in a split second. I'd had an accidental discharge, and "Country," the team leader, was ready to blow me away. His rifle muzzle shook an inch away from my nose as my round echoed along the valley floor. I could never do that again to him and live.

Afterward, we did several successful patrols together. He was good, and I learned a lot from him. We became buddies but partied separately: he liked country music and cold beer; I did Hendrix and pot. It was hard to say goodbye when Country rotated. I wrote him once, but I never got in touch with him stateside. I was reluctant to reach any of the guys, for that matter. I didn't want to go through it all again.

Recon patrols were dangerous, frustrating work. Insertions and extractions by helicopter were occasions for ambush by the Vietcong, and I lived through three of them. One correctly placed bullet could bring a helicopter down, and even if you lived through the insert and made it to high ground, each hour was still pregnant with death. There were mines, and even bad weather could get you killed. One of our force teams was totally wasted – wiped out – by lightning. Heavy fog and rains prolonged our patrols beyond coordinated extraction, and more than once we were forced to move on to an alternate LZ (landing zone). On occasion, we had to use a precious claymore to blow an area open ourselves. This was the nastiest way out, risking an invitation to the bad guys to see us off.

We only carried M-16 rifles and one M-79. No mortar, and no M-60 machine gun. We did not wear the normal flak jacket and helmet, and there were no ponchos or blanket-liners to soften the cold night-rains. We took no extra food and went hungry if socked in; once, we humped three days on stream water. We slept on razorback slopes, up against rocks or trees. Our stealth and our face paint were our only security, and as night surrounded our tiny, eight- or nine-man team, we would eat our cold rations or tinned fruit, assign watches, and commit our grid position to memory — just in case we needed to call in artillery around us. It was a farewell ritual. Only "Situation Report," the voiceless keying of the radio handset on the quarter hour, told the relay on Monkey Mountain that we were still a part of creation.

Exhaustion numbed the day's fears but magnified the images and sounds of night. One night, on watch near the border of Laos, I woke the team to hear the horrible sound of hundreds of troops in the underbrush. We listened, frozen, as we double-checked our memories for the grid coordinates. They came closer and then stopped. Now they were walking around in circles. Then they stopped. Were they going to spend the night this close? We dared not make a move. They were too close, too many, to do anything but make deals with God. Then, after what seemed like an hour, we heard them again. Elephants! A herd of freaking pachyderms!

It was late in the afternoon of June 21, 1969, when we got a red alert that a recon team was compromised and being chased and fired on by a large enemy force. We pulled an emergency reaction team together from Delta Company; they were ready to go within minutes. Second Lieutenant Bill Schenck of New Jersey and Lance-Corporal Joe Bosco of Providence, Rhode Island, headed up the patrol.

Two hours later, we received the crushing news that our Delta team, along with their CH-46 crew, had been ambushed on insertion. All were killed. A third team had been unable to insert in the vicinity because of heavy ground fire, and our chopper was in flames. Secondary explosions from the craft meant that the mines and grenades they carried on their backs and belts were being set off by the inferno. It was getting dark and S2 lost radio contact with the first team. It was a long, painful night. I was just back from Da Nang, recovering from malaria, and I nearly made this trip. It would have been my fourth and last time in ambush.

At home, a Gallup poll revealed that 55 percent of Americans opposed the war. On October 15, 1969, more than 10 million Americans across the country demonstrated their opposition to the war. In November, 200,000 people marched in San Francisco, and half a million more converged on Washington's Mall...

We have a .50-caliber machine gun on our OP. It's a horrible thing to use against men: it takes two hands to fire, and it rips off chunks of flesh and bone. Its recoil travels through my upper body and sets me to rocking with every round fired. If they wear black pajamas, I open fire. Conical straw hats fly as they dive for cover. They're pinned down now, behind a huge fallen tree near the base of our hill. This is madness. Free-fire zone? What am I doing? I'm going insane.

We are tunneling down through the canopy into view of the early-morning jungle floor. The *Sea Knight* drops her dragonfly tail only five feet from the wind-flattened grass. We jump as one – like young from the belly of a dragonfly. Our canvas gear dances into a hasty perimeter. Seconds pass. Prone. Silent terror. Then the CH-46 lifts her tail, and as she turns, the brittle snapping of rounds sounds overhead. She opens with withering M-60 fire – 550 high-velocity rounds per minute – and we unleash our M-16s into the same direction. The chopper lowers once again, firing into the ambush. We crawl backwards, shouting our names, dragging, pulling one another back on board. A thud, and our chopper is hit. But we are covered by a swarm of Huey gunships, strafing and destroying their position, and as we lift off, I radio in: Two Oranges, Zero Apples."* Actually, we all died a little more that day.

Nearly five thousand helicopters went down during the war, and all but a few of them had crews on board. I have reconciled with the war. I respect and love the Vietnamese people. But there are certain things I still cannot stand, and one of them is the sound, sight, or smell of a military helicopter.

Even before I ever saw action in Vietnam, I was assigned to a burial detail in North Carolina. The funeral ceremony for James was held in his poor-as-dirt Pentecostal church. There we were, five crackers and one black, sitting right in front of the pulpit, where hope was spoken to the inhabitants of little more than tin and board homes: "Oh, yes, brothers and sisters! Jamie's life was poured out for freedom! Hallelujah!" shouted the black pastor. The worship and song was highly emotional. It had to be. The open casket held no warrior – he was such a small, young boy. Church attendants fanned those passed out in heat or ecstasy – the pain of poverty, repression, and now the pain of death. It was more than I had realized up till now.

We took James's casket out into a field of his family's small farm. The heat of the day was broken by a strong, steady rain, and I remember the weight of the rain-soaked flag as I extended it to James's mother in proper ceremony. Her eyes did not meet mine; her pain was too tangible. Was she thinking of her boy working in this very field just last spring? And then we

---

* Two wounded; none dead.

realized that a terrible mistake had occurred: as if to salt the wound, the casket did not fit into the marble-lined grave site. Even today I ask myself, would it have helped if I had gone back on my own and dug the grave larger? Would they have believed that the government really cared?

There are other stories: the rocket attacks, the wretched night-ambush missions. But the hardest ones, the daydreams that are still a part of me — those are my real war stories, because they are obscene and evil.

The battalion sergeant and I are out on the town. Top knows the older woman — the young girl's mother? Their sunlit room rings with giggling and laughter, as I and the child-woman (she couldn't have been more than sixteen) were thrown together, trembling with the horrible business of war… Hate for myself, and the incessant memory of this young girl, left the house with me. She was the victim I took as a hostage to my loneliness and selfish lust.

Many tales of violent fighting, bloodshed, and terror could still be told. But they pale in comparison to that quiet, sunny Sunday in residential Da Nang, that brief, wordless moment when the screams of two souls echoed in eternity.

In a large part, the Vietnamese have forgiven us. They love their roots, their people, and their country too much to hold on to hatred. They have born many more wounds than we, but their suffering has brought them understanding. And we can learn from them, because we understand, in part, the same suffering. We can rebuild our lives in the same way that they fill the bomb craters in their villages: one basket of soil at a time. They don't dig much from outside the crater, because they have learned that the soil is deeply compacted from the force of the explosion. So they loosen it, and basket by basket they level the earth from within. We can heal, too, by gently loosening the clay of our own hearts. We can fill the craters of our souls, basket by basket.

When I returned from Vietnam, I was angry and confused. I had no understanding of how to become free of my burden, so I turned to the alcohol and marijuana that I had learned to depend on in the military. I had no peace, and I sowed the seeds for more war. I became more angry, more guilty, and more confused. One night, in a drunken argument over the war, I found my hands clenched around the throat of a very good friend. My burdens were destroying friendships, our marriage, and slowly killing me.

Now I am at peace. I can say this only after a long journey into the awareness of Jesus and his living truth. War is not the beginning of evil in our society; it's the result of evil. And I've been a part of it — I have to look at my own responsibility. So I've been given the wisdom of repentance, seeing my complicity in the pain of war. And I've learned to trust in the power of for-

giveness that Jesus speaks of in the Lord's Prayer: "Forgive us our tres-
passes, as we forgive those who trespass against us."

I believe that my fellow survivors can learn to know Jesus just as fully —
can follow after him in their own lives and identify themselves with his own
historical concern for peace and justice. But I'd say that you have to live for
something else, something bigger than yourself, bigger than your own problems. There have to be deeds motivated by the spirit of his love. Giving my
life to something more meaningful, to working for peace and justice in a life
of nonviolent brotherhood, is the only way I can deal with it.

■ ■ ■ ■ ■ ■ ■ ■ ■ ■ ■ ■

As long as there is no communication, there is no insight or compassion, and you will continue to suffer. Non-veterans do not
understand veterans, and they refuse to listen to you. You know
the truth about war, but you have not been able to share your
insight with them. You have suffered so much, but you have not
been able to find ways to tell people about it, and they have not
been ready to listen.

You continue to suffer, because you feel guilty about your
actions…Shame, guilt, and regret can be helpful or harmful; it
depends on how you use them. When you realize that you have
caused a lot of damage, if you vow not to do it again, that regret
is wholesome and beneficial. But if your guilt persists for too
long and becomes a complex, it blocks the way to joy and
peace…

When you went to war, you went for the whole nation. The
whole nation was responsible for what happened there, not you
alone. Your hand was the hand of the whole nation. If you made
mistakes, the whole nation made mistakes. If you went to war
believing you were doing something important – trying to save a
people, fighting evil – it was not your thinking alone; it was the
thinking of the whole nation. You were sent there to fight, destroy, kill, and die. You were not the only one responsible. We
cannot just shout at you and say, "You did that!" We all did it
collectively.[2]   *Thich Nhat Hanh*

CHAPTER 15

The Road to Peace

If only there were evil people somewhere, insidiously committing evil deeds, and it were necessary only to separate them from
the rest of us and destroy them. But the line dividing good and
evil cuts through the heart of every human being. And who is
willing to destroy a piece of his own heart?

Alexander Solzhenitsyn

I, myself, am heaven and hell. Both the animal and the divine.
Capable of cruelty and compassion, mercy and murder. There are
no good guys. There are no bad guys. There are only us guys.

Steve Bentley, Vietnam veteran

Though the very insanity of war suggests forces and powers at work beyond the realm of human influence, it is not something thrust upon an
innocent humankind. We are its co-makers; we allow it to take root within us.
No one is free of its guilt, and this is a fact we must face if war is ever to be
banished from the earth.

The blame cannot be placed solely on national and military leaders who demand the lives of young men and women. Acquiescence to war is war, too. And
when a person enters the "machine," however reluctantly, he or she soon becomes co-guilty of crimes which place a tremendous burden on the soul. In a
recent letter, Phil Berrigan described how relief from this weight can be found.

> We are all in need of healing, but we will not find healing by focusing on
> healing itself. Rather, we will find it through nonviolent resistance.
> There will be no healing for spectators, for those who sit watching from a
> safe place. And there will be no healing for veterans, myself included, until
> we disavow war completely, until we disarm the Bomb and the killing ma-
> chine and ourselves.

Why did God spare us in war except to expose its horrors for others? Why are we alive except to unmask the Big Lie of war?

The jails teem with Vietnam veterans, but virtually all are imprisoned for the wrong reasons. Where are veterans from all the empire's wars in the struggle for disarmament, for justice and peace? They should ask themselves: can I remedy my violence, can I heal myself, until I try to heal the body of humankind from the curse of war?

George Zabelka is one veteran who sought the healing Berrigan prescribes. As a Catholic military chaplain stationed on Tinian Island in August of 1945, he gave his blessing to the two atomic bombing crews under his care. But he deeply regretted this years later, and on the fortieth anniversary of the bombing of Hiroshima, he reflected:

> I painted a machine gun in the loving hands of the nonviolent Jesus, and then handed this perverse picture to the world as truth. I sang "praise the Lord" and passed the ammunition...All I can say today is that I was wrong. Christ would not be the instrument to unleash such horror on his people...I say with my whole heart and soul I am sorry.
>
> I asked forgiveness from the Hibakushas (the Japanese survivors of the atomic bombings) in Japan last year, 1984, in a pilgrimage that I made with a group from Tokyo to Hiroshima...I fell on my face there at the peace shrine after offering flowers, and I prayed for forgiveness – for myself, for my country, for my church. Both Nagasaki and Hiroshima. This year at Amarillo...and also at Toronto, I again asked forgiveness from the Hibakushas present...I asked forgiveness, and they asked forgiveness for Pearl Harbor and some of the horrible deeds of the Japanese military, and there were some, and I knew of them. We embraced. We cried. Tears flowed. That is the first step of reconciliation – admission of guilt and forgiveness.[1]

In a quiet moment on a pilgrimage to Japan, five years before his death, George Zabelka's quest to look ever more deeply into his part in the atomic bombings seemed concentrated into a single, powerful realization. On the morning of August 6, 1987, Father Zabelka was making the Stations of the Cross, when at 8:13 (the hour of the destruction of Hiroshima) he and all those with him stopped on the side of the mountain for a moment of quiet remembrance. A deep and vast wound was laid bare at that instant: Father Zabelka was overcome with remorse, and tears flowed between gasping breaths. "How could I have missed it?" he asked – of himself, of God, of his Japanese brothers and sisters. "How could I have missed it?"[2]

■ ■ ■ ■ ■ ■ ■

Paul Pappas served with the U.S. Marines during World War II. He was among the American troops who occupied Nagasaki only weeks after it had been bombed, at the end of August 1945. Paul had been taught to hate in boot camp, and after the war he rebelled inwardly at what had been done to him – and at what he himself had seen and done. He struggled for years to break free from the burdens of his military life, but it wasn't until he faced his own guilt – and stopped pointing fingers at others – that he was able to begin the slow road to full healing. He writes:

Mary and I married while I was still in the Marine Corps, and after the war we settled down to start a family. It should have been a happy time. I had a good job, a nice family, two young children. But as I look back, it is clear that I lived, or rather existed, in a constant state of depression. Outwardly, the future looked good. Inwardly, there was no hope, only bitterness and rebellion.

In 1952 we met members of the Bruderhof community in Paraguay, South America, who were traveling in this country. Mary immediately responded to the idea of community living, but I did not, having no hope that life could be any different. Mary was so convinced that we finally decided that the only way to resolve our differences was to go and see for ourselves. Actually, our marriage was already on the rocks, and our disagreement about the Bruderhof only made our situation more obvious.

Our visit did not solve anything. Mary was completely convinced, but I didn't want anyone telling me what to do, when to do it, or how to do it. I'm sure I developed this strong negative reaction to being told to do anything as a result of years in the Marine Corps. But thinking of it now, it is amazing how tenaciously I held on to the life and the society I knew, even though I was very unhappy and completely disillusioned by it. There is a strong binding power in the military that opposes new ideas, new life, and I was in its grip – so much so that after seven months I temporarily left the Bruderhof and returned to the United States. Mary and our two children stayed in Paraguay seven more months.

For me there were two stumbling blocks – my fierce independence and my hidden sins. There was also a feeling in me that all religion was hypocritical. But through the experiences of daily, practical living in the community and sharing with others who were seeking wholeness together, my resistance had already started to melt. Slowly, a purpose for life began to be revealed.

There was one person in particular whom I learned to love and trust – I, who had trusted no one. This trust led to a life-changing experience which opened the door and allowed me to share the things that bound me. From the moment I was able to tell him about them, I was completely free. There was no flash of light, no outward sign, but I felt the reality of the words of Martin Luther King: "Thank God Almighty, free at last!"

In spite of the freeing and healing given to me, there was still a lot of self-will and independence I had to let go of. To believe that I could become a new and different person was very difficult to accept. Ultimately, it boiled down to accepting Jesus for who he is, and trusting him.

Every person on earth has the desire to be free. But our concepts of freedom can be very diverse. I thought I was free when I refused to allow anyone to tell me what to do, how to do it, or where to do it. This attitude was both blind and arrogant. Now, at seventy-two, I am certain that freedom and inner health depend on just one thing: a clear conscience before God. And this can be attained by repentance for personal sin and by forgiveness.

Jay Wenk also served in World War II. Like Paul, he has come to recognize his guilt in being a part of what so many Americans still regard as a "good" war. And though he doesn't use the word, his emphasis on tears is very much what Paul's "repentance" is all about.

When I was a little boy of five or six, we would catch butterflies and moths and flies and pull the wings off. I don't look back on that with any pride. I had no sense that I was causing horrible pain to those creatures. Fortunately, I learned somehow, somewhere, that "we don't do that." But a lot of people, I guess, just continue tearing the wings off. Then they end up tearing the arms off people. We graduate from one species to another.

You know, we talk about the horrible Japanese and their internment camps and the horrible Nazis and their slaughtering of people. But there were guys in my platoon and in my infantry company who killed prisoners. And what's the difference between that and My Lai? So they killed women and children as well as men – what's the difference? Taking life is taking life.

I remember our platoon medic. Whenever he had a chance, he would inject enough morphine into wounded German prisoners to kill them. There was another guy, Red, who was told by the lieutenant to take twelve prisoners back to company headquarters for interrogation. It turned out that there was one more than had been requested – the lieutenant had wanted twelve, not thirteen. So he shot one. It didn't just happen. There were Nazis in our own Army during World War II. And I venture to say they were there any place you cared to look.

What about me? I was a witness to some of that killing, and I never said anything about it, because I thought they would blow me away. Isn't that a war crime? That's a piece of my guilt. I was afraid to say anything then.

We need to get in touch with our tears somehow, some way. And then to continue, somehow, some way. What I'm suggesting is that it can't be done on an intellectual basis. It's got to be done on an emotional basis. I suggest that it starts and continues with tears. Because the pain that I and others have felt about our lives, wartime or not, can lead others to better places. But it takes a lot of time and a lot of work.

As Jay spoke, I had to think of Lee, the Vietnam vet who says that he can never forgive himself – that he has no energy to love, and often not even enough to live. Lee contends that he is trying, and acknowledges that his problems are not the only problems in the world, or even the worst – but he feels as though a part of his soul is missing, and he wonders if he'll ever get it back. What would Jay say to a man like him?

> I know enough about forgiveness to know that it's exactly like peace, and peace begins at home. Forgiveness begins at home. You've got to forgive yourself, and tears are really the only key I know. If you haven't forgiven yourself yet, that doesn't mean that you can't. But if the tears are still there, let them come. As long as they need to come, let them come.

And if the tears don't come, how do you start them flowing again? Paul Sullivan, a veteran of the Persian Gulf, says there is no magic formula. But there are times and places in which we can get back in touch with ourselves, with our deepest emotions.

> It takes years to deprogram the intensive weeks of military training. It doesn't happen overnight. I would argue strenuously that there is no golden moment…But I could tell you that one milestone was when my daughter was born, and I sat there crying about how beautiful life was, and how on earth could anybody possibly kill anybody.
>
> I could argue that my moment of truth came as I looked at pieces of dead body and blood on my uniform, when I realized that the Pentagon had lied about massive chemical exposures. I could say that it was when a student asked me, "Would you do all this again?" or when someone put me on the spot and asked me to state publicly where I stood on all of this. I could also say it was when I watched slides of the suffering of the Iraqi children and learned that there have been one million Iraqi deaths due to American sanctions. Or was it when I learned that the Gulf War never really ended, that it's still going on? It's all these different things…
>
> There was a gentleman in the Gulf who did a job similar to mine. He was in the infantry; I was in the armor. He was also a Bradley driver and a Bradley gunner. He came home, just like me, and went to the VA in 1992 and was turned away, just like me. This gentleman said, "That's bullshit." So he started hanging out with a militia group. Then, when he saw what the government did at Waco, which was terrible and truly indefensible, he said,

"Look, we have to take out this government." So he went and bought some fertilizer, rented a truck, and drove it to Oklahoma City and blew up the federal building. Timothy McVeigh is a decorated Gulf War veteran who went to the VA in 1992 saying that he was sick, and he was turned away. Isn't it obvious that the lies of the Gulf War have fostered poison for generations to come – death, destruction, lies, hatred, mistrust…

So what do you do? After you've been through an event like that, what do you do? One thing is very clear: you have to start with yourself. We have to recognize, each of us, one at a time, that we have participated in something horrific. And this recognition is the first step toward recovery. Perhaps that makes it sound like I'm an alcoholic, but violence really is an addiction. And as with all addictions, recognizing this is the first step. The next is facing up to what has happened: the deaths and the destruction, the illness and its causes. And then we need to give veterans ways to atone, opportunities that bring about or at least allow for reconciliation. That's not going to be easy, but it's the only way…

■ ■ ■ ■ ■ ■ ■

David Harvey and his wife heard of our Beech Grove Bruderhof in England in the late 1990s and were soon visiting us regularly. Now a good friend, this British Special-Ops veteran once carried out England's policies of colonialist repression with military force.

David was brought to Beech Grove by the same yearning for camaraderie that had led him to the military as a 16-year-old orphan. At the Bruderhof, he found himself moved by a life of dedication to the service of others, whereas in the military he ultimately found only regret and sorrow. His search for peace and reconciliation shows that although the journey is long and difficult, it is in the end worth every effort. On a recent telephone interview from England, he said:

> The time I spent in the military was very much a waste of time, a waste of my life. Most of the places in which I served were places which had been colonized. We weren't there by invitation; we were there by force. And all of the things I was ordered to do, and did willingly, were against what the people of those particular countries wanted or expected of us.
>
> It was called "colonialism," but the military was there to suppress the local people – to see that big business got what it wanted and to ensure that nothing interfered with the British way of life.

His nightmares about his time in the service weren't only about brutalities committed against indigenous peoples. While in Kenya, David was shaken by a friendly fire incident, in which he accidentally shot his own platoon commander during an ambush of "terrorists." The man survived, but David didn't see him again for decades.

> There was a military court of inquiry, and I was exonerated of all blame. But my conscience gave me no peace. Four years later, my term of service in the Army ended and I returned to civilian life. But I couldn't forget what had happened. Questions stuck in my mind: if he was alive, where was he? How was he?
>
> After a number of years, I started to make my own inquiries. But all the avenues I tried drew a blank. I met ex-comrades, each of whom had a different story as to what had become of him. Then in 1996 my wife Marion found a book which mentioned the very incident. I telephoned the author, who admitted that he hadn't seen him recently but heard that he was living in London.
>
> I decided to enlist the services of a local newspaper. They published my story and photograph in a weekly edition of their paper, and within 48 hours I received a call from the person I had been seeking for years.
>
> It was a difficult experience. After a number of telephone conversations, we arranged to meet at my house. And he came bearing gifts to the man who had shot him! Because of me, he was paralyzed down one side and had difficulty walking and moving his arm.
>
> I didn't quite know what to expect. I didn't know how he would feel about this, but he was just so full of forgiveness. It wasn't just a question of being wounded; it was a serious head wound, and it's left a scar on him even to this day. But the guy was just so full of forgiveness it was unbelievable. I asked if he could forgive me, and he said, "There's nothing to forgive. What you did was done in the line of duty."
>
> After all that, I still found it difficult to accept that he was able to forgive so readily. I should have been overwhelmed, overjoyed, but it wasn't that easy, strangely enough. I thought he would show at least a little resentment, but there was nothing like that at all. It was just immediate forgiveness.

When I asked David what advice he might give to others who find themselves in similar circumstances, he emphasized the need to believe that everyone can be forgiven – and that accepting this forgiveness is a choice that everyone can make.

> I can't undo what I've done; I can only regret it. I've wasted my life, and the life God gives us is the most valuable thing that we'll ever have. I've wasted quite a lot of mine, and I can't get that piece back. But to say that you can't be forgiven or you won't be forgiven? If you dig deep enough, people who say that often don't *want* to be forgiven. They feel so badly about what they've

done that they want to punish themselves mentally. But I do want to be forgiven, and that's made a big difference.

■ ■ ■ ■ ■ ■ ■

Carroll King, a Bruderhof member since 1957, only experienced this freedom
many years after World War II. He enlisted in the U.S. Air Force two months
before his eighteenth birthday in 1942, and by June 1944 he was flying a B-24
bomber in the 15th Air Force Division in southern Italy. His crew continued its
bombing raids till the end of the war, striking cities, factories, transport facili-
ties, and enemy troops. Planes all around him were shot down, but Carroll survived, though inwardly he was falling apart.

"I hated the Nazis, and I expressed my hatred from the nose of a B-24, raining down death and destruction on Germany and German-occupied towns and
cities," Carroll recalled. Once, his crew even dropped bombs left over from an
aborted run onto a manor house in the Austrian countryside, indifferent to the
pain and suffering of the innocent people below.

After the war ended in Europe, Carroll was sent back to the States for retrain-
ing in a B-29, for the continuing air war in the Pacific. On the ship home, he
came face to face with the human wreckage of the war: men without eyes, missing limbs, or disfigured by burns and scars. He was shocked and tried to reach
out to them, but was met with bitter silence.

The bombing of Hiroshima and Nagasaki brought a sudden end to the Pacific
War, and he came home, went to college, and married. He tried to get on with his
life, but the horrors of the war wouldn't leave him. It wasn't until much later,
when he and his wife, Doris, joined the Bruderhof, that he was struck by the violence in which he had taken such an active part. His actions and experiences came
to him again with blinding clarity, and he recalled the famous painting of the cruci-
fixion by Rembrandt, which depicts the artist himself as one of the executioners.
When he first had seen it, the notion seemed ridiculous, but now he understood.
The war was in *him*, not in the past, not in the world at large...

He went to a minister and poured out the memories and feelings of guilt from
the dark recesses of his heart. Suddenly he felt a peace he never had before.
Somehow, in the presence of people he could trust, Carroll experienced the forgiveness of God as a power that cleansed his life.

I had souvenirs, pictures of the bombs, the targets – everybody had them.
Pictures of me in uniform. I tore them all up. I trashed everything that had
anything to do with the military. I got rid of my uniforms and those medals.
In that way, I expressed my determination never again to fight in a war...

I wish I could bring back the people I know I killed, but I can't. You can't undo it; it's just there. And I imagine every murderer feels the same way. I visit men in prison now, and when I hear their stories, I tell them, "You know, in a way I'm just like you, I've done the same things." And I remind them that without God's forgiveness I'm no different than any other murderer. We wish we could bring our victims back to life and ask their forgiveness. But we're not in that position, and so we simply have to accept God's forgiveness.

I trust in the forgiveness I have found – and I really have found peace, by looking into my own heart and confessing the things that burdened me. I've never been tormented by the past again, and I feel that there has been real closure. Of course I still regret the past, and I will always feel the pain of it, but it has lost its power over me.

Carroll's freedom has not stilled his desire to continue setting things right, however. On February 25, 1998, just as America prepared for new confrontations in the Gulf, Carroll and Doris flew to Baghdad. They went, they said, not out of high-minded idealism but simply to stand in solidarity with the Iraqi people. On their return, the Kings wrote to the President:

Beloved Mr. Clinton:
We have spent the last two weeks in Iraq and have seen firsthand the consequences of Operation Desert Storm and the seven years of economic sanctions that followed it. Several weeks ago, when the threat of renewed bombing still loomed large, we heard of an international group that planned to go to Iraq, offering to share in that country's suffering and to act as human shields for its people. We were inspired to join them, and though we had no illusions about our effectiveness as a deterrent, we felt that our offer to stand with the Iraqi people, even to the point of death, might assure them of a genuine love.

Even as we traveled, political negotiations seemed to be bearing fruit, and the threat of war diminished. But we continued on our way all the same, eager to see for ourselves the conditions about which we had read, and to express our love regardless of seemingly wide political and religious differences.

What we saw was devastating. Hospitals were trying frantically to respond to a sea of need, with very little medicine, equipment damaged beyond repair, and wages for skilled surgeons so low that they were forced to work as elevator bellhops. We saw severe and widespread malnutrition and an epidemic of birth defects and rare diseases that were virtually unknown before the Gulf War. Schools were in shambles and lacked the most basic supply of paper and pencils, and indoor plumbing – for potable water and for sewage – did not exist at all. There is much more that we could share with you and we would welcome any opportunity offered...

We were especially touched by one very personal experience – our visit to the Al-Amariyah Shelter in Baghdad. This massive, Swedish-designed shelter was built especially for children, using reinforced concrete. It was penetrated by two American "smart bombs" during the Gulf War, which in a moment incinerated more than 400 children and many of their mothers.

The walls of this shelter are now adorned with photos or drawings of the murdered children – beautiful children of all ages. As we toured it, I could not help being reminded of the five hours I once spent in the Holocaust Museum in Washington, DC...

As we left the shelter we happened to meet a woman who lost all nine of her children in this shelter. She had gone off to do her washing, and when she returned, they, like hundreds of other children, were gone. We talked, and before leaving we asked her forgiveness – for the deaths of all those children – on behalf of the American people. This she readily granted, but with one exception: she said she could never forgive President Bush.

What would I suggest as an alternative to our present policy in Iraq? After the First World War, the "victorious" Allies wanted to teach Germany a lesson. Territory was ceded and huge reparation payments demanded. The German economy was in shambles and inflation was rampant. When Germany could not meet reparation payments, a blockade was imposed. Like in Iraq today, the poorest and the youngest suffered most. The response of the German people was understandable and predictable, and within a decade, the people's resentment and despair provided a perfect seedbed for the rise of National Socialism. By contrast, after World War II our country flooded Germany with billions of dollars to rebuild a shattered economy and infrastructure. History did not repeat itself.

I have a dream: that President Bush and the Joint Chiefs of Staff might visit Iraq and observe the results of their Desert Storm and its sanctions, and then humble themselves and ask for forgiveness. This apology could be followed by a program of assistance toward a recovery of the economy, and massive medical and nutritional aid. While I'm still dreaming, I can see Saddam being moved to repentance.

Ridiculous? Perhaps. But I would rather live with such a dream than face the nightmare of hatred and violence that our present policy inescapably is leading to.

Sincerely,

Carroll and Doris King

■ ■ ■ ■ ■ ■ ■

Siegfried Ellwanger, whose story as a soldier on the Russian front I recounted earlier, was born the same year as Carroll, in 1924. Once enemies in Hitler's Europe, Siegfried and Carroll met again as friends and brothers almost half a century later. Siegfried and his wife Renate joined the Bruderhof in 1986, disillusioned with the prosperous silence of post-war Germany. They and the Kings met that same year, and were astounded to discover that Siegfried and Carroll had once fought against each other. They asked each other's forgiveness, embraced, and marveled that they had both ended up in the same church, now committed to God, to one another – and to world peace – for the rest of their days.

Siegfried and Carroll are not the only former enemies who met and reconciled at the Bruderhof. Adolf Braun, whose enthusiasm to defend his German fatherland had been quenched in the trenches of Russia and France, was unable to settle down after the war and found himself increasingly frustrated by the injustices of society. He and his wife heard a representative from the Bruderhof speak at a town meeting in Nordhausen, Germany, in 1924, and they joined the fledgling movement soon afterward. Englishman Victor Crawley was only fifteen years old when the war began; he, too, fought in the trenches but was a convinced pacifist by the time he was discharged in 1921. With war on the horizon once again in the late 1930s, he and his wife Hilda joined the British Peace Pledge Union and then came to the Bruderhof in 1940.

When Victor and Adolf met shortly thereafter, they made a remarkable discovery: at Marne and again at Verdun, they had both been in the trenches, separated by only a few hundred yards as their shells and artillery mowed down an entire generation. A staggering 500,000 soldiers on each side had been killed in the first Battle of the Marne; the Allies alone lost 600,000 men to the Germans at Verdun.[3] The loss of lives had been cataclysmic, and yet somehow these two men had survived to become brothers in a common cause. Discovering this, the two were overwhelmed with emotion and went on to become good friends. It was no longer war that bound them, but a life lived for peace, love, and community.

Though these two brothers have since passed on, the witness of their lives, and of their first meeting together, stands as a beacon pointing the way to the true reality, that reality which breaks through all the death and falsehood of war, the demonization of peoples we do not know, the hidden economic agendas of the all-powerful, the lies scantily cloaked in mantles of "glory" and "duty" and "sacrifice." When death and destruction have held their sway and the smoke lifts from the field of battle, veterans of war find that, inside, they are all the same. And they will search, as do the rest of us, until they have found the simple but elusive truth: war, under any other name, is still a crime, and bears no fruit but lying and torment and death. All men are brothers. That is the "true reality." Jesus came to unite men as brothers. To me, the miracle of our communal life is that veterans of all wars, and from all backgrounds, can now work together for peace and justice and live together in love and harmony.

John Risser is one more example. John served in the Navy during the Vietnam War. But today he is dedicated to a way of life that, in the words of early Quaker George Fox, seeks to "take away the occasion for war."

John grew up near an Army base in southern Arizona and followed a long family tradition by joining the Navy. He enlisted in 1970, while the Vietnam War was still in full swing; when he finally left, eight years later, his soul was damaged, and he yearned for purpose and peace.

> The military totally messed up everything I was as a human being. It completely destroyed me and then rebuilt something else that hadn't been there before. I just laughed in the face of religion. It was the furthest thing from my heart. Yet there was something drawing me; something I wanted to believe.

While still in the military, John and his wife and six others started a small community just off their base in Spain. They lived together and began searching for that elusive "something" in the writings of Dietrich Bonhoeffer and the New Testament Book of Acts.

> We got together and began studying the Bible. We had finally decided that whatever it might cost, whatever it took, we had to do it – community just seemed to be a natural outgrowth of the gospel.
>
> Even now, it's kind of tough to understand, yet something new was trying to break into our hearts. And for the first time we started to look critically at the military, how it was shaping people, what was really going on. It was only a beginning, but it was enough, I think, to open up a small hole, big enough for even a little light to start filtering in.
>
> Life started to take on a new meaning. Before that, the only things that had made any sense were getting drunk, doing dope, carousing with my pals, and making sure that I got to watch on time. But now, where I was, what I was doing, and who was around me started coming together in a cohesive whole. It wasn't anything solid. But it offered me a future, and I hung onto it as best I could.
>
> Then there was a turning point. Our "community" fell apart, overnight. I don't get along with a lot of people anyway, but it was devastating all the same. And it put more salt on the wound, so to speak. I thought that my world had disappeared, but it turned out to be only the beginning of something completely new. Through that experience, I suddenly realized that the

answer to my problems was not seeking after happiness as much as it was seeking after the happiness of other people – looking out for the needs of others. I didn't know how to do that, and maybe I still don't. Because that is the very last thing that the military wants you to do.

In a way, it's where the world stops and where God's kingdom has to begin. The question is, how can I live for my brother? Selfishness is the basis for how we think in this country. The reason why nobody wants to believe that there is anything wrong with things like the Gulf War is that they all live in their own little houses on their own little streets; they've all got their own little neighborhood watches. Yes, there's crime all around them, but nothing is happening to them. They get in their cars every morning, and they go to work. They're chasing retirement, and they're moving forward.

It scared me when I saw that I was doing that, too. I was on the outside looking in, and I was accepting the same lies that everybody else was.

It's not that I'm a totally different man today, but I'm changing. Life is precious to me now, and I see that it's more than just the absence of violence. It's the way you act toward your brother...

John has a lot of friends who came back from Vietnam, and though he hesitates to hand out advice, he says that healing is there for everyone:

I don't have any wisdom. All I can say is, hold onto life. Embrace it – embrace life! It's the children that you meet, the poor and the handicapped, that need to affect you. Reach out to them, and something will start to heal in your heart. Children – they're the ones who will heal you.

John and his wife found new life – and a purpose for living – when they found community with like-minded people. And their community is there for all men, for veterans and for their wives, for anyone who has been ravaged by the curse of war, and who longs for a life of peace and brotherhood. Such a life does not come without sacrifice: it demands personal transformation and a commitment to the truth, to the fight between good and evil. But as Eberhard Arnold wrote in 1920, the struggle for truth must lead us to action. Recognition is never enough.

Jesus' way is a practical one: he has shown us a way of life which is more than a way of concern for the soul. It is a way that says very simply, "If you have two coats, give one to him who has none – treat men as you would be treated by them..."[4]

Unless you become so totally different that you begin life all over again, like a newborn baby, you will never be a part of the new order that is coming.

Then you will never again kill, never again serve killing. And this means not only that you will never take another's life under any circumstances, including war or revolution, but also that you will make no resistance, will not fight for your "rights," especially when people harass you or try to rob you of your goods and even your life. It means that you will despise no one and degrade no one; that you will know no anger, revenge, or ill will toward anybody.

The character of the people of the future is that they make peace and have fellowship in all things...[5]

■ ■ ■ ■ ■ ■ ■

Ron and Pat Landsel and their daughter Hannah traveled to France in the winter of 1998 to live and work with the monks and nuns of Plum Village, a Buddhist community gathered around the teachings of Thich Nhat Hanh. The Landsels stayed at Plum Village for a month, and I was privileged to join them there for the lunar New Year – a celebration which for Ron stirred up awful memories, but also brought healing and reconciliation. Ron writes:

I was invited to spend a week with the monks during Tet, the Vietnamese New Year, in January 1998. It was time spent in joy and brotherhood, and it strengthened my friendship with two young monks I'd met at a veteran's retreat in the United States, Phâp Úng and Phâp Trú. We talked often during that week of the lunar New Year, and I could not forget the fact that it was thirty years ago – 1968 – when I had arrived in Da Nang as a young Marine with the 1st Reconnaissance Battalion.

After supper one evening, Phâp Úng told me how the war had affected his relationship with his father, Lap, who served nine years in the South Vietnamese Army and was then was interned by the victorious communists in a "reeducation camp" – really a prison – for another seven years after the war ended. Dear God, I thought to myself, what these brothers and sisters suffered!

There were long spaces of quiet as we sat in the monastery's empty dining room and reflected on how the war had influenced my relationships, emotions, and perceptions. As Phâp Úng shared memories of his childhood, he recognized these same effects in his own father. Together, and through my own pain, we could project how his father must have felt. War creates a deep love among comrades, but with it comes a fear that they will be torn away in an instant. I realized that, out of the same fear of losing them, I had been unable to let my own children get too close to me, and I assured Phâp Úng that anger and distance was not what his father had wanted. He surely loved his children more than he may have felt "safe" to express – perhaps more than fathers who have never experienced the hell he did. There were tears and more silence. Then Phâp Úng said softly, "I am a monk, and a suffering soldier." My heart went out to his dear deceased father, and I wept for our suffering world.

Thây Giac Thanh was born during the revolution and lived through the French and American wars. I never heard French bombs back in Queens, New York. But I certainly took part in sowing the seeds of many wars in my youth, and lived to hear more bombs falling as I joined the "American War" years later.

Born in the Year of the Dog, we were both twenty-one in 1968. The most he would offer about his youth was that it had been unhappy. I had to think about mine; I couldn't really label it as all happy, either, though I didn't have to duck bombs or bury my family. But there were things that damaged my soul in other ways. Giac Thanh and I shared a great deal at his hillside hermitage, and I learned much from his gentle wisdom. "The war is only one small part of your entire consciousness, one sad part amid so many other joyful and wholesome aspects of life," he said. "When you searched for the soldiers of the North, you were only doing what you thought was expected of you…" Such was the magnanimity I encountered many times in my Vietnamese brothers and sisters…

The scream of two French fighter-bombers flying low over Plum Village tears open red-hot memories. At their sound I squeeze my eyes tightly closed, lean forward, hands over my ears, nearly dropping to the ground in anticipation of the roaring heat of napalm. I am sickened at the thought of a Tet thirty years earlier: a North Vietnamese offensive thrust that continued through 1971, with catastrophic loss of civilian and military lives – and hopes for peace torn to shreds – on both sides. At home, the silence of mainstream churches, the rioting, the murders of college student protesters, Civil Rights workers, Martin Luther King, Jr. and the Kennedys, all symbolized the moral and political cost of satisfying the war machine…

No one seems to sense the intent of those French fighter pilots but me. I look around me at the survivors of piracy and refugee camps: Ti, a beautiful child spun out of her world by a war she didn't know; Chi Tinh Thuy and Anh Hoang, who abandoned his medical practice; Chi Doan and Anh Duc, who left behind his engineering career; Dieu Hanh; her parents, Bac To and Ba Suong; and so many others I have come to love…"Gooks." My God! I am overwhelmed by the shameful mockery of the word.

Memories crush my heart as I try to swallow the ache in my throat.

■ ■ ■ ■ ■ ■ ■

Josef Ben-Eliezer is a pastor at one of our Bruderhof communities. The son of Orthodox Jewish parents, he fought in the Israeli Army in the turbulent days of national liberation; later, he became an avowed pacifist and sought to reconcile with the Palestinian people he had once sought to destroy. Like many other veterans, his turning point came quite unexpectedly: a survivor of severe persecution himself, he suddenly felt compassion for the civilians who inevitably suffer in war.

Josef was born in Frankfurt, Germany, in 1929, into a time of intense hatred and persecution of his people by the rising Third Reich. His first memories are not pleasant. At age three, he watched a formation of the Hitler Youth marching past the window on the Ostendstrasse, singing a song that even a young child could understand: *Wenn Judenblut vom Messer spritzt* – "When Jewish blood spurts from the knife." His parents were silent, but the horror on their tight-lipped faces was obvious.

In 1934, the family fled the country and returned to their native Poland. They settled in the small town of Rozwadów, on the River San. Most of the inhabitants were Jews: artisans, tailors, carpenters, and merchants. There was a great deal of poverty, although Josef's family was considered middle-class. But their peaceful existence was short-lived, and by 1939 it was clear that more fear and upheaval lay ahead. Josef remembers:

> I was ten when the Germans entered our town. A great fear could be felt all around. My father and my older brother hid in the attic. Whenever someone knocked at our door and asked for them, we said they were not at home. Then we heard a public announcement: all Jews were to gather in the little town square. We were given only a few hours. We took whatever we could carry, just tied things in a bundle to carry on our backs. There the *Schutzstaffel,* Himmler's SS troops, gave orders for us to walk toward the River San, a couple of miles from the village. We started walking, herded like cattle. Uniformed men rode alongside on motorcycles. One of them stopped his motorcycle and shouted at us to hurry up; then he walked up to my father and hit him. That left an unforgettable feeling in me.
>
> At the bank of the River San, more uniformed men were waiting for us. They searched us for valuables: money, jewels, gold, and silver. But they did not find the sum of money my parents had hidden in my little sister's clothing, which was later to be of great help to us. Then they ordered us to cross the river to "no-man's-land," an area still being contested by both the Russians and the Germans. We found lodging in a village across the river.
>
> Only a few days later, we heard that the Germans were coming again. We panicked. With the little money we had hidden, my parents, together with

two or three other families, bought a horse and wagon. It carried what little we had managed to bring along on our backs and some of the young children.

The day turned to evening as we tried to reach the Russian border. We came to a large forest at nightfall. Suddenly out of the forest came two robbers with guns. They demanded that we hand over everything we had. It was a frightening moment, but there were a few men in our group who had the courage to say, "No, we will not give you anything. Kill us, but we won't give it. We will fight for it." I remember that they took a bicycle and a few other items from someone else but then decided to leave us alone.

When we realized that we would have to make our way through the forest in the dark of night, we turned back to wait for the dawn. We arrived at a village with an inn, where we met several Jewish people in the same predicament as ourselves. Suddenly, a whole mob of villagers came and began to mock and molest us. We were very frightened; I was afraid they were going to lynch us. I don't know what would have happened, had not one of them climbed up on a wagon and shouted: "Aren't you ashamed of yourselves? Today these unfortunate people are in need. Who knows what will happen to us tomorrow? If you touch one of these people, it will be over my body. My son and I are going to stand watch over them; you go home!" This courageous act had its effect, and the mob dispersed; we were left in peace for the rest of the night. The next day we started on our long journey and eventually reached the Russian border.

After three years of exile in Russia, Josef traveled to Palestine in 1943 and entered an agricultural school. The war ended in 1945, and survivors of Bergen-Belsen and Buchenwald began to arrive at the school. Josef was shaken to hear what they had gone through. Though only twelve or thirteen years old, to him they looked like old men. Inwardly, he was devastated, and he lost the faith of his childhood. He began to call himself an atheist – out of rebellion more than conviction – and he began to hate.

The years from 1945 to 1948 were years of struggle for our country's liberation from the British. Jews in Israel, and all over the world, felt that they could never again go like sheep to slaughter – at least not without putting up a fight. And we hated the British especially, because they had prevented those few Jews who had survived the Holocaust to resettle in Palestine. We were living in a world of wild beasts, and we could no longer be the docile lambs. I volunteered for the Israeli Army precisely for that reason: we could no longer allow ourselves to be trampled on.

I was eighteen when I enlisted, and I was determined to fight to the very last. I wanted to be at the front, and so I volunteered for the elite corps. We encircled the towns of Lod and Ramla, and we ordered the people to leave, just as we had been ordered to leave in Europe nine years before. "Go to Jordan!" we yelled. We searched them for valuables just as we had been searched by the Germans.

Suddenly, it came to me that we were doing exactly the same things that the Germans had done to us. We were now the ones in power. We were cruel to the Palestinians out of sheer malice, and the interrogations and beatings I witnessed were frightening. We had not been ordered to do these things, but we did them anyway, on our own initiative. I witnessed atrocities, and innocent people were deliberately killed. The lower instincts of man had been released. I was present for some of it, and I heard of even worse things happening elsewhere. I was very confused, and I thought, What has happened to us? What are we doing? Where is humanity? At the same time, I rationalized: we are fighting for our very existence. There were many things going through my mind…

Josef's turmoil gradually gave way to a firm conviction: he could not, and would not, be part of the repression any longer. "I realized that there would always be strife between Palestinians and Jews in Israel and unless I left the country, I would always be involved, whether I wanted it or not." He left his beloved Israel in 1953 and began looking elsewhere for answers. It would take years of often very painful searching, but his struggle was rewarded.

I turned away from Judaism, from all religion, and tried to work out everything with my mind. It seemed insane to me that what was done to my people had been done in the name of Christ; just hearing the word made me shudder in horror. For me, this name was connected to the Inquisition, to persecution, hypocrisy, and idolatry.

Then I stumbled across the brothers and sisters of the Bruderhof and experienced something which overwhelmed me. At Easter time in Poland we had always locked our doors, because when the Christians came out of church they would often start pogroms. But at the Bruderhof I experienced for the first time the real meaning of Easter, that Jesus has nothing to do with what so often is done in his name, that in reality he comes, not to separate people, but to gather them and unite them from all the nations.

This reality was visible throughout history, even though the official churches chose to ignore it. For me, it was an overwhelming realization. It turned my life upside down. I found that Jesus could bring people together, and that he could heal hatred and forgive sins — *my* hatred, *my* sins. And then I had to ask myself, how can I not forgive others when I need so much forgiveness myself? I was filled with the hope that one day all people might live in that spirit of forgiveness.

In 1960, I visited the crematorium at Dachau. I was deeply shaken. I saw the signs on the wall reminding people of the terror that had occurred there, and my heart bled and wept. But I felt that Christ wept with me; his heart bled with me and with every weeping, suffering heart. I felt that I had been placed in the middle of a struggle against the powers of darkness, which are a tangible reality. And I could not survive this struggle in my own strength. Only in faith and trust in the reality of God and Christ could I hope for a new future.

I look back now and wonder that I could have been so blind. God's love is so great, and we are such miserable creatures! I experienced shame and great thankfulness and joy at the same time. Shame, because I had repeatedly pushed Jesus Christ away from me. Joy, because he was still alive...

More than thirty years later, Josef began to correspond with Salim Munayer, a Palestinian whose father had endured the Israeli oppression in Lod in 1948. When Salim heard Josef's story, he wrote: "It excites me to hear from you, because my family was at that time on the other side of the fence...What you are describing is true." And Josef wrote back: "Ever since you first wrote to me, I have wanted to tell you that the memory of that time, now fifty years ago, has been a great burden for me. Now I ask your forgiveness for my part in the terror you experienced."

Josef was overwhelmed by Salim's reply: "I understand. I respect your apology, and I receive it in reverence." In the winter of 1997, Josef was able to return to Israel and meet with Salim and his father Yakoub, face to face. That journey moved Josef very deeply, and he found peace in humbling himself before the Palestinians who had once been the objects of his wrath.

The most moving moment of my trip came when we arrived in Lod and I met Yakoub. He took me around to the church where he and his family had hidden from the Army. Apparently some of the people hiding there had been deported in trucks, and of the 1500 who were unable to escape, many were murdered.

Yakoub spoke Hebrew, so we understood one another right away. We embraced, and I asked for his forgiveness.

We even found the place where I had been stationed, on the edge of town, and I recalled how deeply affected I had been to see the Palestinian women and children being hurt. I had tried to stop my comrades, but I was not decisive enough, and now I felt a great guilt.

It was very painful to remember these things, but it was also redeeming to be able to recount them with Yakoub. And in the end, it's not only the Israelis and Palestinians or Germans and Jews who are the issue. All men have done these things to one another, and all wars are terrible.

We were silent for awhile, and then we went back to Yakoub's home. As we walked along, he held my hand — a sign of love and forgiveness.

■ ■ ■ ■ ■ ■ ■

They shall beat their swords into plowshares,
and their spears into pruning hooks;
nation shall not lift up sword against nation,
neither shall they learn war anymore.

Isaiah 2:4

True Future

And I heard a loud voice from the throne saying, "Now the dwelling of God is with men, and he will live with them. They will be his people, and God himself will be with them and be their God. He will wipe every tear from their eyes. There will be no more death or mourning or crying or pain, for the old order of things has passed away." He who was seated on the throne said, "I am making everything new!...To him who is thirsty I will give to drink without cost from the spring of the water of life. He who overcomes will inherit all this, and I will be his God and he will be my son."

Revelation 21:3–7

I 'll never know what I would have done had I found myself in the middle of combat. I was very fortunate to have entered the Reserve Officers Training Corps between wars. Had I become a second lieutenant during the escalation of Vietnam, I might well have been shipped off to die in Southeast Asia. And the Gulf War drew heavily on military reserves. Yet war was the furthest thing from my mind back then, as it is for the vast majority of young men and women who join ROTC.

I still have nightmares, though, about my drill sergeants — that by some terrible bureaucratic mistake I have been sent back to train under them once again...I wake, sweating, and shudder to think of what might have been. I managed to get out with most of myself intact. All the same, it's hard to measure the damage done.

Somehow, I was led through the wreckage of pain and confusion to a community of brothers and sisters who love and care for one another. My work designing machines of death for the military has been replaced by designing children's playthings and equipment for disabled youth. In the life that I now live, I find the true fulfillment of all the good things the military pretends to

offer. Here is true fellowship, true sacrifice; here is order and discipline and respect to the highest degree.

The military can only pretend to offer what is good, because its foundation is
isolation and fear. It does violence to bodies and souls and is part of a darkness
far greater than any single human being's power to resist. It demands absolute
allegiance, forcing young men and women to sign over their persons to the
property of the United States government, and encouraging them to break
every one of the Ten Commandments and all other precepts of moral behavior,
whether Buddhist, Muslim, or Native American. It mocks God through forced
prayer to guns and other military paraphernalia, and uses his name in vain. It
teaches the art of killing, and proclaims that this sin of murder is necessary. It
steals lands and villages from the poor, devastates economies, and perverts the
ideal of "manhood" by idolizing murder and promiscuity.

How can men be comrades, how can they serve God and country, when they
are driven by fear and ambition, by the "glory" of beating an enemy into sub-
mission? Make no mistake: the final goal of military training is to break down
the will and conscience of soldiers to the degree that they are capable of anything. The military does not want people, but machines that will execute orders
without questioning them. Men in uniform must work smoothly like well-oiled
cogs. If they try to look for meaning and purpose beyond their immediate
duties, they bog down the machine and make very poor soldiers.

After all I've been through, it's my gunnery sergeant's last, desperate question that stays with me most forcefully: "Son, you know there's a rhyme and a
reason to all of this, don't you?" His plea is the stifled cry of a man deeply
bound and yet longing in his inmost heart to be set free.

■ ■ ■ ■ ■ ■ ■

The stories of anguish in this book must point us to something far beyond the
immediate horror of war. Knowledge alone does not lead to truth. Films like
Apocalypse Now and *Platoon* offer no answers, no matter how powerful and convincing their drama may be. They have become ends in themselves, and the fact
that such graphic depictions of war have become entertainment is an indictment
of our unfeeling culture. We watch, like appeased addicts, as the needle is inserted and the plunger depressed, numbing soul and conscience, heightening the
deadly bliss.

How, then, can we find the truth? Perhaps veterans can show us the way. But
the remorse, forgiveness, and healing they testify to in these pages is dearly
bought. Confronting guilt and facing war's memories head-on – and striving to

set things right – is a wrenching process, never to be sought for its own sake. Yet there is tremendous power in the "ought" of the human conscience. All men know that they *ought* to do good things; that they *ought* to be at peace; that they *ought* to be free of dark, haunting memories; that they *ought* not to kill. Without the power of that "ought," the anguish of so many veterans would be incomprehensible; we would wonder why they couldn't just buckle down and enjoy the rest of their lives until they passed into nonexistence.

But the fact is that men are not destined for nonexistence. The conscience – an insistent voice in some, and a hellish torment for others – is the hand of eternity upon each human soul. It demands that the truth be faced here and now, and it begs for recognition and action. If there is one thing that veterans have taught me, it is this: the *real* battle takes place in the heart. And because our lives will not end with physical death, it is a battle that all men must eventually face.

What *is* the truth? That question has never been more important than it is now, in this century of unprecedented blood and destruction. Our willing consent to the deaths of millions is beyond the power of human reason. It is time to awake, time to acknowledge that we have all become willing agents in a plan for self-annihilation. It is the hour of reckoning, the time to see that we are at war against ourselves.

It is impossible to win any war between men. As the stories in this book have shown, the human cost of war far outweighs any perceived gain in "freedom" or "way of life." A generation ruined by war has spoken; if we ignore the wounds and fail to listen and learn, we will orchestrate our own defeat. The powers now working for mankind's annihilation – and they are very real, and very active – count on the human tendency to resist the truth.

The veterans in this book point the way to true victory. Although the world is quick to condemn, there is no sin so great that it cannot be forgiven, no deed or memory so sordid that it cannot be wiped away. I have been witness to this miracle many, many times. God can redeem everyone, and for this reason we cannot ignore the anguished pleas of veterans like Lee and Doug, who doubt that they can ever be forgiven.

Michael, a man who wrote to me from Connecticut's death row, said that he had all but given up on himself when he suddenly felt the reality of God:

> I couldn't see beyond my bloodstained hands. But I suddenly felt God's love as a reality. God is love. And God loves me…
>
> There is no instant victory over sin. It is a long, ugly, and painful process. And it only happens because God has the patience and love to give us time, time to allow the transformation to take place.

The specter of death hangs over me daily, and yet I know that I will meet Christ soon; I know this every morning when I wake up. But I try hard not to count on tomorrow, for there are only a few tomorrows left...

Don't count on tomorrow. Cherish and live each day as if it were your last. Live each day for God, for his glory, and seek to forgive – and to be forgiven. Not tomorrow. Today!

I believe that God is nearer to this death-row inmate than he is to most of us. He has experienced Christ, not as the founder of a dead religion, but as a person and a friend – a living, transforming reality in the midst of pain and need. For Michael, Christ is power. He is love. He is freedom and forgiveness, sanity and security. When he opens the door, light comes streaming through.

When I think of the pain so many veterans suffer – the suicides and the homelessness, the mental illness and the drug abuse – I think of Jesus: Jesus, who was mocked and whipped, scourged and spat upon, and nailed to a cross – by *soldiers*. Most of all, though, I think about his words as he hung dying: "Father, forgive them, for they know not what they do..." And I cannot forget that it was also a soldier who gazed up at him in awe and cried, in sudden realization: "Truly, this man was the Son of God!"

"What is truth?" Pilate asked. Jesus' answer perplexed him, but it need not trouble us: "My kingdom is not of this world...I will draw all men to myself... Be of good cheer, for I have overcome the world!" These are no hollow statements. If he has truly overcome the sin and death of man through his own death and resurrection, then he has overcome the horror of My Lai, too. He has overcome Hiroshima and Nagasaki, the Holocaust, the bombing of the Al-Amariyah Shelter, and the blood of Omaha Beach. The pain of these horrors may not yet be removed, but the cross promises a future when all things will be restored and reconciled. The real war – the only holy war – has already been fought and won. And it is up to us to take hold of its victory.

In my many encounters with veterans and their families, conscientious objectors, resisters, and dedicated activists, I have thought often of a passage in J. R. R. Tolkien's tale *The Lord of the Rings* – a powerful metaphor of humankind's battle for the light of the future. This fairy tale might seem an inappropriate ending to such a serious journey, yet it gives a glimpse of the future, a dream that will come true – an answer to the deepest longings of the human heart.

When Sam awoke, he found that he was lying on some soft bed, but over him gently swayed wide beechen boughs, and through their young leaves sunlight glimmered, green and gold. All the air was full of a sweet mingled scent... Full memory flooded back, and Sam cried aloud: "It wasn't a dream! Then where are we?"

And a voice spoke softly behind him: "In the land of Ithilien, and in the keeping of the King; and he awaits you." With that Gandalf stood before him, robed in white, his beard now gleaming like pure snow in the twinkling of the leafy sunlight. "Well, Master Samwise, how do you feel?" he said.

But Sam lay back and stared with open mouth, and for a moment, between bewilderment and great joy, he could not answer. At last he gasped: "Gandalf! I thought you were dead! But then I thought I was dead myself. Is everything sad going to come untrue? What's happened to the world?"

"A great Shadow has departed," said Gandalf, and then he laughed, and the sound was like music, or like water in a parched land; and as he listened the thought came to Sam that he had not heard laughter, the pure sound of merriment, for days upon days without count. It fell upon his ears like the echo of all the joys he had ever known. But he himself burst into tears. Then, as a sweet rain will pass down a wind of spring and the sun will shine out the clearer, his tears ceased, and his laughter welled up, and laughing he sprang from his bed.

"How do I feel?" he cried. "Well, I don't know how to say it. I feel, I feel" — he waved his arms in the air — "I feel like spring after winter, and sun on the leaves; and like trumpets and harps and all the songs I have ever heard!"...

"The King...has tended you, and now he awaits you. You shall eat and drink with him. When you are ready I will lead you to him..." And when Sam heard that he laughed aloud for sheer delight, and he stood up and cried: "O great glory and splendour! And all my wishes have come true!" And then he wept.

And all the host laughed and wept, and in the midst of their merriment and tears the clear voice of the minstrel rose like silver and gold, and all men were hushed. And he sang to them...until their hearts overflowed, and their joy was like swords, and they passed in thought out to regions where pain and delight flow together and tears are the very wine of blessedness.[1]

Appendix A

Resources for Veterans, Dissenters, and Conscientious Objectors

Information on the military

Center for Defense Information ■ 1500 Massachusetts Ave NW
Washington DC 20005 ■ Tel: (202) 862-0700; 1-800-234-3334
Website: www.cdi.org

> The Center for Defense Information (CDI) is a clearinghouse for inside information on the Pentagon and on military issues worldwide. The Center is staffed by former military careerists and publishes a selection of pamphlets and informational brochures. It also arranges lectures for student groups at its Washington, DC, location.

Organizations for conscientious objectors and dissenters

CCCO ■ 655 Sutter St #514 ■ San Francisco CA 94102 ■ Tel: (415) 474-3002
Website: www.libertynet.org/ccco ■ E-mail: cccowr@peacenet.org

CCCO ■ 1515 Cherry St ■ Philadelphia PA 19102 ■ Tel: (215) 563-8787
E-mail: ccco@libertynet.org

> The Central Committee for Conscientious Objectors (CCCO) was founded in 1948 to protect and promote the rights of conscientious objectors to war. The group's long-term goals include demilitarizing schools and communities, improving conditions for military personnel who come to realize their objections to war, and eliminating the Selective Service System. In 1994, CCCO helped launch a new, toll-free, nationwide hotline, which either directly counsels GIs or refers them to a growing network of volunteer counselors. The number is especially designed for military personnel who want to resist being deployed, wish to be discharged, are being abused or discriminated against, are AWOL, or believe they may be conscientious objectors. CCCO also publishes a journal, the *Objector;* and recently opened a new hotline to resist increasing JROTC presence in high schools and to provide accurate information on JROTC.

GI Rights Hotline: 1-800-FYI-95GI (1-800-394-9544)
JROTC Hotline: 1-800-NO-JROTC

NISBCO ■ 1830 Connecticut Ave NW ■ Washington DC 20009-5732
Tel: (202) 483-2220 ■ Website: www.nonviolence.org//nisbco
E-mail: nisbco@igc.apc.org

The National Inter-religious Service Board for Conscientious Objectors (NISBCO) is committed to supporting all those who conscientiously question participation in war. NISBCO provides information on how to document one's convictions as a conscientious objector, and provides help for COs in the armed forces who seek discharge or transfer to noncombat status. NISBCO also trains draft counselors and advocates for CO rights before the Selective Service System, the White House, the courts, Congress, and international bodies. The group alerts concerned persons to changes that take place or are under consideration regarding military conscription and coercive national service proposals, as well as changes in regulations regarding conscientious objection within the military. It maintains a referral service to local counseling agencies and attorneys who can aid those in need of legal counsel, and acts as a national resource center for documents relating to the draft and conscientious objection, as well as the religious response to those issues. Finally, it advises religious and other agencies with regard to educational curricula on war, peace, and conscience, and educates citizens through articles, speaking engagements, and publications. The group also maintains a website, Global Internet Resources for Conscientious Objectors.

War Resisters League ■ 339 Lafayette Street ■ New York NY 10012
Tel: (212) 228-0450 ■ Website: www.nonviolence.org/wrl
E-mail: wrl@igc.apc.org

Founded in 1921, the War Resisters League (WRL) affirms that all war is a crime against humanity. The League strives nonviolently for the removal of all causes of international and civil war. WRL centers its work on education and action, organizing demonstrations, cooperating with other peace and justice groups, and opposing conscription and all forms of militarism, including ROTC. The group supports men and women who resist the military at all levels, and cosponsors the Fund for Education and Training (FEAT), which assists young men who, for reasons of conscience, do not comply with laws requiring registration for the draft. WRL's primary program is YouthPeace, a campaign promoting nonviolence, justice, and an end to the militarization of youth. YouthPeace strives to develop a culture of nonviolence from childhood on, working against war toys and military recruiting. WRL has strong international ties through membership in War Resisters International (warresisters@gn.apc.org) and affiliation to the International Peace Bureau (ipb@gn.apc.org). WRL offers a video with facts about joining the military, *It's Not Just A Job,* designed for high school programs.

Veterans Organizations

National Association of Atomic Veterans ■ Pat Broudy
35492 Periwinkle Dr ■ Monarch Beach CA 92629 ■ Tel: (714) 661-0172

National Association of Black Veterans ■ Tom Wynn, Jr.
PO Box 11432 ■ Milwaukee WI 53211 ■ Tel: (800) 842-4597;
Fax: (414) 342-0840

National Gulf War Resource Center ■ 1224 M Street NW
Washington DC 20005 ■ Tel: (202) 628-2700 ext 162; Fax: (202) 628-6997
Website: www.gulfwar.org/resource_center/ ■ E-mail: charles@gulfwar.org

Veterans for Peace ■ 100 Maryland Ave NE ■ Suite 106
Washington DC 20002 ■ Tel: (202)488-9225

Vietnam Veterans Against the War, Inc. ■ PO Box 408594
Chicago IL 60640

Vietnam Veterans of America Foundation ■ 2100 M Street NW Suite 407
Washington DC 20037 ■ Tel: (202) 828-2630

Resistance and Community Groups

Black Veterans for Social Justice, Inc. ■ 686 Fulton St ■ Brooklyn NY 11217
Tel: (718) 935-1116; Fax: (718) 935-1629

Citizen Soldier ■ Tod Ensign ■ 175 Fifth Avenue #2135 ■ New York NY 10010
Tel: (212) 679-2250; Fax: (212) 679-2252

Coalition to Oppose the Arms Trade (COAT) ■ 489 Metcalfe Street ■ Ottawa
ON K1S 3N7 Canada ■ Tel: (613) 231-3076; Fax: (613) 231-2614
E-mail: ad207@freenet.carleton.ca

Iraq Action Coalition ■ Rania Masri, Coordinator ■ 7309 Haymarket Lane
Raleigh NC 27615 ■ Tel: (919) 846-8264; Fax: (919) 846-7422
Website: leb.net/IAC ■ E-mail: rmasri@ncsu.edu

Leonard Dietz ■ DU Citizen's Network Technical Advisor
1124 Mohegan Road ■ Niskayuna NY 12309-1315 ■ Tel: (518) 377-8202

Military Out of Schools Hotline: 1-800-NO-JROTC

Dolores Lymburner, Military Toxins Project ■ 471 Main Street 2nd Floor,
Lewiston ME 04240 ■ Tel: (207) 783-5091; Fax: (207) 783-5096
E-mail: mtp@igc.apc.org

National Association of Radioactive Survivors ■ Coy Overstreet, Desert Storm
Coordinator ■ PO Box 2815 ■ Weaverville CA 96093-2815
Tel: (800) 798-5102; Fax: (916) 623-2027
E-mail: falling229@aol.comnars1@tcoe.trinity.k12.ca.us

The National Gulf War Resource Center, Inc. ■ 1224 M Street NW ■ Washington DC 20005 ■ Tel: (202) 628-2700 ext. 162; Fax: (202) 628-6997 Website: www.gulfweb.org/ngwrc ■ E-mail: charles@gulfwar.org

Patriots for Peace ■ Chris Larson ■ PO Box 1092 ■ Shalimar FL 32579 Tel: (904) 651-0392

SOA Watch ■ PO Box 3330 ■ Columbus GA 31903 ■ Website: www.soaw.org

Swords to Plowshares ■ Dan Fahey ■ 995 Market 3rd Floor ■ San Francisco CA 94103 ■ Tel: (415) 247-8777; Fax: (415) 227-0848

William Joiner Center for the Study of War and Social Consequences Dr. Paul Camacho ■ University of Massachusetts ■ 100 Morrissey Blvd Boston MA 02125-3393 ■ Tel: (617) 287-5850, Fax: (617) 287-5855 Website: www.umb.edu/COMMUNITY_CONNECTIONS/Centers&Institutes/ William-Joiner/William-Joiner.html

Woodcrest Bruderhof ■ Attn Dan Hallock ■ PO Box 903 ■ Rifton NY 12471 Tel: (914) 658-8351; Fax: (914) 658-3317 ■ Website: www.bruderhof.com www.plough.com ■ E-mail: dhallock@bruderhof.com

Veterans for Peace ■ 100 Maryland Ave NE ■ Suite 106 Washington DC 20002 ■ Tel: (202)488-9225

Vietnam Veterans Against the War, Inc. ■ PO Box 408594 Chicago IL 60640

Women Strike for Peace ■ Edith Villastrigo ■ 110 Maryland Ave NE Washington DC 20002 ■ Tel: (202) 543-2660; Fax: (202) 544-1187

Appendix B

The Bruderhof

Basis The basis of our communal life is Christ's teaching, especially his words on brotherly love and love of enemies, nonviolence and the refusal to bear arms, and faithfulness in marriage.

Our members own no private property but share everything in common, the way the early Christians did, as recorded in the Book of Acts. Each member gives his or her talents, time, and efforts wherever they are needed, and all are provided for and cared for.

Lunch and dinner are eaten together, and meetings for fellowship, singing, prayer, or decision-making are held several evenings a week.

Vision Though we come from many cultures, countries, and walks of life, we are all brothers and sisters. We are conscious of our shortcomings as individuals and as a community, yet we are certain that it is possible to live out the teachings of Jesus – not only on Sundays, but from day to day.

We believe that God is working to transform the world, and that our task is to participate in this work for a completely new social order, a new life of unity, joy, and peace throughout mankind. We believe this vision to be at the core of Christ's message, which is especially urgent today.

Family Life Though many of our members are single adults, family life is the foundation of our community. Babies and small children receive daily care in our Children's House while their parents are at work; preschool, kindergarten, and elementary grades are educated in our own schools.

From the ninth grade on, teens attend public high school and may move on for further education or technical/vocational training. Young adults are encouraged to leave the community for at least a year – to stand on their own feet – before deciding whether or not to become a community member.

Work We earn our living by manufacturing Community Playthings (play equipment and furniture for children) and Rifton Equipment for People with Disabilities. Our work is far more than a business venture; we feel it is – and must be – consistent with our vision for a transformed world.

Roots The roots of the Bruderhof go back to the time of the Reformation of early 16th-century Europe, when the Bible was first translated into the common language of the people, and thousands of so-called Anabaptists left the institutional church to seek a life more consistent with Christ's teachings. One branch of this dissident movement, known as Hutterites after their leader Jakob Hutter, settled in communal villages or Bruderhofs – "place of brothers" – in Moravia (in what is now the Czech Republic).

Recent History In 1920, Eberhard Arnold, a well-known lecturer and writer, left the security of his Berlin career and moved with his family to Sannerz, a tiny German village, to found a small community based on the practices of the early Christian church.

Despite persecution by the Nazis and the turmoil of World War II, the community survived, but was expelled from Germany in 1937. New Bruderhofs were founded in England in the late 1930s. In 1940 a second migration was necessary, this time to Paraguay, the only country willing to accept our multinational group.

During the 1950s branch communities were started in the US and Europe. In 1960–61 the South American communities were closed, and members moved to Europe and the United States. Today there are Bruderhofs in New York, Pennsylvania, and southeastern England.

Outreach We involve ourselves locally in a variety of voluntary service projects, including jail and prison ministry. On a broader scale, our contacts with other movements and individuals have taken us to many places around the globe. As with the early Christians, mission is the focus of our activity – to share the vision of God's new order, to connect with others who seek brotherhood, and to help in building up a new society. We welcome anyone searching for tangible ways to live out this vision. Come join us for a weekend!

For further information, or to arrange a visit, give us a call.
US: 1-800-521-8011, or 724-329-1100
UK: 0800 269 048, or +44 (0) 1580 88 33 44

Endnotes

Chapter 1
1 O'Brien, 63.

Chapter 2
1 Conrad.
2 O'Brien, 21.
3 Muller.
4 Kovic, 16–17.
5 Sharples.
6 "Military Training Mandatory."
7 Sandy.
8 Carroll.

Chapter 3
1 Simons.
2 Interview with U.S. Marine Corps conscientious objector Erik Larsen, October 13, 1997.
3 Winerip.
4 Chang.

Chapter 4
1 Trumbo, "Introduction."
2 *Chronicle of America*, 584.
3 *Chronicle of America*, 587.
4 Zinn, *History*, 265.
5 Zinn, *History*, 263.
6 Gordon.
7 Bilton & Sim, 8–9.
8 *Chronicle of America*, 603.
9 *Chronicle of America*, 589.
10 Zinn, *History*, 267.
11 *Chronicle of America*, 603.
12 *Chronicle of America*, 599.
13 Trager, 758.
14 Trumbo, 228–232, 240–242.
15 *Life Magazine*, May 1950.
16 L. A. Dietz, "Veterans Day Service at Fusa," Nov. 11, 1990.
17 Spock, 38.
18 Spock, 38.
19 Spock, 8.
20 See Robert Sherrill's *The Accidental President* (New York: Pryamid Books, 1968), quoted in Dowd, 350, note 31.
21 Shesol, 127.
22 Shesol, 465–466.
23 Spock, 12.
24 Zinn, *History*, 356.
25 Berry, *Community*, 70–71.
26 Printed in the *Congressional Record*, June 16, 1934.

Chapter 5
1 *Trauma and the Vietnam War Generation.*
2 "Vietnam Combat Stress."
3 Goodwin.
4 Bilton & Sim, 24.
5 Bilton & Sim, 5–8.
6 Personal communication, September 8, 1997.
7 David Grossman, 50.
8 Bentley, "Vets Still Haunted."
9 Bentley, "Remember the Vets."
10 Bentley, "These Wounded Veterans."
11 Bentley, "VA Budget Cuts."
12 Thich Nhat Hanh, 87.

Chapter 6
1 Holm, 9.
2 Holm, 10.
3 Jobst.
4 Zinn, *Declarations*, 88.
5 Palmer, xvi. See also: Terry, xiv.
6 King, *Trumpet*, 23.
7 Holm, 9.
8 Berrigan, 81.
9 Loewen, 241.
10 Terry, 11–12.
11 Terry, 146, 147, 150–151, 152.
12 Terry, 203.
13 K. Marshall, 6.
14 Freedman & Rhoads, 13.
15 Freedman & Rhoads, 39–40.
16 K. Marshall, 10, 11–12.
17 K. Marshall, 143–144.
18 K. Marshall, 60.
19 Palmer, 125–129.
20 Trujillo, I, II.
21 Trujillo, 32.
22 Trujillo, 126.
23 Trujillo, 50.
24 Trujillo, 83–84.
25 Trujillo, 153.
26 Trujillo, 96–103.
27 Holm, 10–11.
28 Matthiessen, 532.

Chapter 7

1 CDI, "Landmines."
2 Lewis.
3 CDI, *1997 Almanac,* 26, 27.
4 Z. Grossman, 1990.
5 Chang.
6 Gilbert, 746.
7 Gilbert, 746.
8 Chang.
9 Trager, 982.
10 Gilbert, 746.
11 Trager, 982.
12 Trager, 983.
13 Gilbert, 746.
14 Gilbert, 745.
15 Le.
16 Z. Grossman, 1990.
17 Z. Grossman, 1995.
18 Catalinotto.
19 Matawi.
20 CDI, "Invisible Soldiers."
21 O'Brien, 76, 84.
22 Hayslip, xiv–xv.
23 Hayslip, 326, 215, 70, 195–196, 200.
24 CDI, "Landmines."
25 CDI, "Landmines."
26 CDI, "Landmines."
27 CDI, "Invisible Soldiers."

Chapter 8

1 Stokes.
2 "Exhibit Blunders," 23.
3 Gerson, 44.
4 Gerson, 38.
5 Anders, 80.
6 Gilbert, 712.
7 *U.S. News and World Report,* July 31, 1995.
8 *U.S. News and World Report,* July 31, 1995.
9 Hersey, 68.
10 *Chronicle of the Second World War,* 652.
11 Dugger, 115.
12 *Burning Conscience,* ix.
13 *Chronicle of the Second World War,* 648.
14 Gilbert, 707.
15 Gilbert, 708.
16 *Burning Conscience,* 99.
17 *Burning Conscience,* 36.
18 Dugger, 174.
19 Dugger, 175.
20 *Burning Conscience,* 25–26.
21 *Burning Conscience,* 78.
22 *Burning Conscience,* 82.
23 Joseph B. Treaster, "Claude Eatherly, Hiroshima Spotter," *The New York Times,* Friday, July 7, 1978.

24 Bentley, "Agent Orange."
25 Bentley, "In the Name of Freedom."
26 Viereck, 37.
27 Chomsky, 9–10.
28 CDI, "Military and Society."
29 CDI, "Military and Society."
30 "Murder."
31 Loewen, 221.
32 Loewen, 223.
33 Loewen, 265–266.
34 Bilton & Sim, 256.
35 Bilton & Sim, 258.
36 Bilton & Sim, 44.
37 Bilton & Sim, 181.
38 Bilton & Sim, 310.
39 Bilton & Sim, 319.
40 Bilton & Sim, 315.
41 Bilton & Sim, 321.
42 Bilton & Sim, 320.
43 Bilton & Sim, 364.
44 Bilton & Sim, 204.
45 Vistica.
46 Chang.
47 Marks.
48 "The Chance for Peace," address, April 16, 1953.
49 Yant, 209.
50 Yant, 208–209.
51 *House Report,* 105–388.
52 Clark, 55.
53 Report of the World Federation of KSIMC, September 1996.
54 Robert Burns, "Bush says he misjudged Iraq's stability," Associated Press, Washington, January 15, 1996.
55 "Bush defends Gulf War decision not to oust Saddam," Reuter Information Service, London, January 21, 1996.
56 Radosh.
57 Berry, *Community,* 85.

Chapter 9

1 1 Chronicles 22:8
2 Zinn, *History,* 427.
3 NACLA Report on the Americas, 1980.
4 Zinn, *History,* 429.
5 Zinn, *History,* 430.
6 "Interview," *Sojourners.*
7 Zabelka, Pax Christi 1985.
8 Arnold, "Love."
9 Arnold, "Longing."
10 Arnold, "Influence."
11 Arnold, *Seeking,* 236, 237.
12 Arnold, *Inner Land,* 270.
13 Adolf Braun to Emil Becker, March 11, 1947.

[14] *Congressional Record,* June 16, 1934.
[15] Emerson, 210, (italics added).

Chapter 10

[1] Hauptman and Wherry, 73, 76.
[2] Loewen, 110.
[3] Alden T. Vaughan, ed., *The Puritan Tradition in America,* 1620–1730, 66, quoted in Loewen, 76.
[4] Zinn, *History,* 3.
[5] Loewen, 56.
[6] Loewen, 52.
[7] Zinn, *History,* 6–7.
[8] *Cheyenne* (Wyoming) *Daily Leader,* March 3, 1870, quoted in Brown, 189.
[9] Horsman, 291.
[10] Custer.
[11] Conrad.
[12] Bilton & Sim, 3.
[13] Bilton & Sim, 23.
[14] Bilton & Sim, 367.
[15] Bilton & Sim, 366.
[16] Mosley.
[17] Gleick.
[18] *The New York Times,* August 4, 1995.

Chapter 11

[1] All quotations from Zahn, *Solitary Witness,* 47–119, passim.
[2] Putz.
[3] O'Brien, 21.
[4] CCCO, "Beginnings."
[5] CCCO, "Beginnings."
[6] Howard Moore, *Plowing,* 93.
[7] Howard Moore, *Plowing,* 95.
[8] Howard Moore, *Plowing,* 96–97.
[9] Howard Moore, *Plowing,* 98.
[10] Howard Moore, *Plowing,* 100.
[11] Howard Moore, *Plowing,* 103.
[12] Howard Moore, *Plowing,* 131.
[13] For more information about the Hutterites, see *The Chronicle of the Hutterian Brethren, Volume I,* Rifton, NY: Plough Publishing House, 1987.
[14] Howard Moore, "Persecution."
[15] Ewert.
[16] Hofer.
[17] Zieglschmid.
[18] Yolton.
[19] Gardner, 46.
[20] Seidenberg & Short, 56.
[21] Gardner, 3.
[22] Seidenberg & Short, 14.
[23] Seidenberg & Short, 28.
[24] Seidenberg & Short, 28.
[25] Seidenberg & Short, 12.

[26] Gardner, 13.
[27] Stapp, 13–16.
[28] Stapp, 99.
[29] Stapp, 118–119.
[30] Stapp, 146.
[31] J. Marshall, 14–15.
[32] J. Marshall, 4–5.
[33] J. Marshall, 6.
[34] J. Marshall, 7–8.
[35] J. Marshall, 3–4.
[36] J. Marshall, 85.
[37] Yolton.
[38] Zinn, *History,* 453–454.
[39] Zinn, *History,* 456.
[40] Zinn, *History,* 457.
[41] Zinn, *History,* 458.
[42] Zinn, *History,* 460.
[43] Zinn, *History,* 461.
[44] Ensign, "Gulf Cover-up."
[45] Seidenberg & Short, 69.
[46] Zinn, *History,* 460–461.
[47] Seidenberg & Short, 75.
[48] Bentley, "Beyond Vietnam."

Chapter 12

[1] King, *Trumpet,* 23, 74.
[2] Thich Nhat Hanh, 39–40.
[3] Thich Nhat Hanh, 31–32.
[4] Thich Nhat Hanh, 73.
[5] Thich Nhat Hanh, 65.
[6] Thich Nhat Hanh, 75–80.
[7] Bourgeois, "Going to Jail."

Chapter 13

[1] Earthstewards Network.
[2] Cowles.
[3] "Vietnam vet gets letter."
[4] "Peace is Every Step."

Chapter 14

[1] Quoted in Matsakis, *Vietnam Wives,* 3.
[2] Thich Nhat Hanh, 88–89.

Chapter 15

[1] Zabelka, Pax Christi 1985.
[2] McCarthy.
[3] Gordon.
[4] Arnold, *Seeking,* 237.
[5] Arnold, *Salt and Light,* 254–255.

Chapter 16

[1] Tolkien, III, 229–230, 232.

Bibliography

Abu-Jamal, Mumia. *Death Blossoms: Reflections from a Prisoner of Conscience*. Farmington, PA: Plough, 1997.

Arms for the Poor (video). Maryknoll World Productions, 1998.

Arnold, Eberhard. "The Influence of the World of the Spirits on Our Time," 1917. Bruderhof Archives, EA 17/18.

——. *Inner Land: A Guide into the Heart and Soul of the Bible*. Rifton, NY: Plough, 1976.

——. "The Longing for Peace," 1915. Bruderhof Archives, EA 15/22.

——. "Love and Hatred in War Time," 1915. Bruderhof Archives, EA 15/16.

——. *Salt and Light: Talks and Writings on the Sermon on the Mount*. Rifton, NY: Plough, 1967.

Arnold, Eberhard and Emmy. *Seeking for the Kingdom of God: Origins of the Bruderhof Communities*. Rifton, NY: Plough, 1974.

Bao Ninh. *The Sorrow of War: A Novel of North Vietnam*. Translated by Phan Thanh Hao, edited by Frank Palmos. New York: Riverhead, 1996.

Bentley, Steven. "Agent Orange Still a Vital Concern to Vietnam Vets." *Perspective*, Lewiston, ME, March 5, 1989.

——. "In the Name of Freedom." *Bangor Daily News*, July 9, 1991.

——. "The Lessons of Vietnam." *The Maine Progressive*, November, 1987.

——. "Remember the Vets Who Suffer." *Bangor Daily News*, May 28, 1989.

——. "These Wounded Veterans Need Better Health Care, Not More Parades." *Journal Tribune*, March 21, 1991.

——. "VA Budget Cuts Add Insult to Injury." *Bangor Daily News*, April 4–5, 1992.

——. "Vets Still Haunted by War in Vietnam." *The Sunday Telegram*, Portland, ME, June 1984.

Berrigan, Philip, with Wilcox, Fred A. *Fighting the Lamb's War: Skirmishes with the American Empire*. Monroe, ME: Common Courage, 1996.

Berry, Wendell. *Sex, Economy, Freedom and Community*. New York: Pantheon, 1993.

——. *The Unsettling of America: Culture and Agriculture*. San Francisco: Sierra Club, 1977.

Beyond Vietnam: Lessons Unlearned (video). Steven Bentley, producer. Tom Keane, director. n.d.

Bilton, Michael, and Sim, Kevin. *Four Hours in My Lai*. New York: Penguin, 1992.

Blood Makes the Grass Grow: Conscientious Objectors and the Gulf War (video). Producer and distributor: The Video Project, Media for a Safe & Sustainable Planet. 1970.

Bould, Geoffrey, ed. *Conscience Be My Guide: An Anthology of Prison Writings*. Atlantic Highlands, NJ: Zed Books Ltd., 1991.

Bourgeois, Roy. "Going to Jail for Justice: A Priest Writes from Prison." *Catholic Digest*, April 1997.

——. *School of the Americas* (video). Talk given at WESPAC (Westchester Peace Action Coalition), November 2, 1995.

Brown, Dee. *Bury My Heart at Wounded Knee: An Indian History of the American West.* New York: Holt, Rinehart & Winston, 1971.

Burning Conscience: The case of the Hiroshima pilot, Claude Eatherly, told in his letters to Günther Anders. New York: Monthly Review Press, 1962.

Carroll, Eugene J., Jr. "Junior R.O.T.C.? Who Needs It?" *The New York Times,* June 26, 1993.

Catalinotto, John. "VA Medical Expert Exposes Pentagon Cover-Up." *Workers World Newspaper,* August 14, 1997.

CCCO (Central Committee for Conscientious Objectors). "1658-1948: The Beginnings." *Standing with Those Who Say No.* n.d.

CDI (Center for Defense Information). *1997 CDI Military Almanac.* Washington, DC, 1997.

CDI. "The Invisible Soldiers: Child Combatants." *The Defense Monitor,* vol. 26, no. 4, (July 1997).

CDI. "Landmines: The Real Weapons of Mass Destruction." *The Defense Monitor,* vol. 25, no. 5 (July 1996).

CDI. "The Military and American Society: A Clash of Values." *The Defense Monitor,* vol. 22, no. 8, 1993.

Chang, Iris. "Exposing the Rape of Nanking." Book excerpt in *Newsweek,* December 1, 1997.

Chomsky, Noam. *What Uncle Sam Really Wants.* Tucson, AZ: Odonian Press, 1996.

Chronicle of America. Jacques Legrand, publisher; Clifton Daniel, editorial director. Chronicle Publications, 1989.

Chronicle of the Second World War. Jacques Legrand, coordinator; Derrik Mercer, editor. London: Chronicle Communications Ltd., 1990.

Clark, Ramsey. *The Fire This Time: U.S. War Crimes in the Gulf.* New York: Thunder's Mouth Press, 1992.

Conrad, Joseph C. "Environmental Considerations in Army Operational Doctrine." White Paper, CR-9421, January 1995.

Cowles, Chris. "Vets Set for Hecaling: Vietnam Bike Trek." Reuters, Hartford, CT, December 26, 1997.

Custer, George A. *Wild Life on the Plains and Horrors of Indian Warfare.* North Stratford, NH: Ayer Company, 1980.

Daly, James A., and Bergman, Lee. *A Hero's Welcome: The Conscience of Sergeant James Daly Versus the United States Army.* New York: Bobbs-Merrill, 1975.

Dear America – Letters Home from Vietnam (video). HBO. Bill Courturié, director. TV 1987.

De Mott, Stephen T. "Patriot, Priest and Prophet: Faith Journey of Roy Bourgeois." *Maryknoll,* October 1995.

Dowd, Douglas. *Blues for America: A Critique, a Lament, and Some Memories.* New York: Monthly Review Press, 1997.

Dugger, Ronnie. *Dark Star: Hiroshima Reconsidered in the Life of Claude Eatherly of Lincoln Park, Texas.* Cleveland: The World Publishing Company, 1967.

Earthstewards Network, "PeaceTrees Vietnam: The Miracle Unfolds." Bainbridge Island, WA, n.d.

Ehrhart, W.D. *Vietnam-Perkasie: A Combat Marine Memoir.* Amherst, MA: University of Massachusetts Press, 1995.

Emerson, Gloria. *Winners & Losers: Battles, Retreats, Gains, Losses, and Ruins from the Vietnam War.* New York: W. W. Norton, 1992.

Ensign, Tod. "Gulf Coverup Radicalizes Vets." *The Nonviolent Activist,* March-April 1997.

"Exhibit Blunders Force Smithsonian Probe." *Air Force Magazine,* July 1995.

Ewert, J. Georg. "Christ or Country." *The Plough,* no. 4 (May 1984).

Freedman, Dan, and Rhoads, Jacqueline, eds. *Nurses in Vietnam: The Forgotten Veterans.* Austin, TX: Texas Monthly Press, 1987.

Gardner, Fred. *The Unlawful Concert: An Account of the Presidio Mutiny Case.* New York: Viking, 1970.

Gerson, Joseph. *With Hiroshima Eyes: Atomic War, Nuclear Extortion and Moral Imagination.* Philadelphia, PA: New Society Publishers, 1995.

Gilbert, Martin. *The Second World War: A Complete History.* New York: Henry Holt, 1989.

Gleick, Elizabeth. "The Oklahoma blast reveals the paranoid life and times of accused bomber Timothy McVeigh and his right-wing associates." *Time Domestic,* vol. 145, no. 18 (May 1, 1995).

Goodwin, Jim. "Continuing Readjustment Problems Among Vietnam Veterans: The Etiology of Combat-Related Post-Traumatic Stress Disorders." Published by Disabled American Veterans, n.d.

Gordon, John Steele. "What We Lost in the Great War." *American Heritage,* July/August 1992.

Graham, John W. *Conscription and Conscience: A History 1916–1919.* New York: Augustus M. Kelley Publishers, 1969.

Grossman, Dave. *On Killing: The Psychological Cost of Learning to Kill in War and Society.* Boston: Little, Brown & Co., 1996.

Grossman, Zoltán. "One Hundred Years of Intervention." Committee Against Registration and the Draft, 1990.

Grossman, Zoltán. "Update to 'One Hundred Years of Intervention,'" Committee Against Registration and the Draft, 1995.

Grün, Max von der. *Howl Like the Wolves: Growing up in Nazi Germany.* Translation from the German by Jan van Heurck. New York: William Morrow, 1980.

Hamilton-Merritt, Jane. *Tragic Mountains: The Hmong, the Americans, and the Secret Wars for Laos, 1942-1992.* Bloomington, IN: Indiana University Press, 1993.

Harris, David. *Our War: What We Did in Vietnam and What It Did to Us.* New York: Times Books, 1996.

Hauptman, Laurence M., and Wherry, James D., eds. *The Pequots in Southern New England: The Fall and Rise of an American Indian Nation.* Norman, OK: University of Oklahoma Press, 1993.

Hayslip, Le Ly, with Wurts, Jay. *When Heaven and Earth Changed Places: A Vietnamese Woman's Journey from War to Peace.* New York: Plume, 1990.

Heinemann, Larry. *Paco's Story.* New York: Penguin, 1989.

Hersey, John. *Hiroshima.* New York: Alfred A. Knopf, 1993.

Hofer, David. "Desecration of the Dead by American 'Huns.'" Chicago: American Industrial Company, February 1919.

Holm, Tom. *Strong Hearts Wounded Souls: Native American Veterans of the Vietnam War.* Austin, TX: University of Texas Press, 1996.

Horsman, Reginald. *Race and Manifest Destiny: The Origins of American Racial Anglo-Saxonism.* Cambridge, MS: Harvard University Press, 1981.

In the King of Prussia (video). Interview with Daniel and Philip Berrigan. Emile De, director. n.d.

"An Interview with a Military Chaplain Who Served the Hiroshima and Nagasaki Bomb Squadrons." *Sojourners,* August 1980.

Jensen-Stevenson, Monika. *Spite House: The Last Secret of the War in Vietnam.* New York: W.W. Norton, 1997.

Jobst, Marc, producer. "Chocolate Soldier from the USA." BBC Radio, March 13, 1997.

King, Martin Luther, Jr. *The Trumpet of Conscience.* New York: Harper & Row, 1968.

Kovic, Ron. *Born on the Fourth of July.* New York: Pocket Books, 1976.

Le, Nhu T. "Screaming Souls." *The Nation*, November 3, 1997.

Lee, Larry. *American Eagle: The Story of a Navajo Vietnam Veteran.* Madrid, NM: Packrat Press, 1977.

Lewis, Anthony. "Suffer the Children." *The New York Times*, November 29, 1996.

Loewen, James W. *Lies My Teacher Told Me: Everything Your American History Textbook Got Wrong.* New York: The New Press, 1995.

Marks, John. "Swiss Cupidity, but German Evil." *U.S. News & World Report*, December 15, 1997.

Marshall, John Douglas. *Reconciliation Road: A Family Odyssey.* Saint Paul, MN: Hungry Mind Press, 1993.

Marshall, Kathryn. *In the Combat Zone: An Oral History of American Women in Vietnam, 1966–1975.* Boston: Little, Brown & Co., 1987.

Matawi, Abdullah. "UN Sanctions on Iraq Lead to Deaths of 500,000 Children." *OneWorld News Service*, London, May 17, 1996.

Matsakis, Aphrodite. *Vietnam Wives: Facing the Challenges of Life with Veterans Suffering Post-Traumatic Stress.* Lutherville, MD: The Sidran Press, 1996.

Matthiessen, Peter. *In the Spirit of Crazy Horse.* New York: Penguin, 1992.

McCarthy, Emmanuel Charles. "Homily for George Zabelka, April 11, 1992." *The Jesus Journal*, n.d.

Metal of Dishonor: The Pentagon's Secret Radioactive Weapon (Video). People's Video Network. n.d.

"Military Training Mandatory for Youth." *The Reporter for Conscience' Sake,* Winter 1997.

Moore, Harold G., and Galloway, Joseph. *We Were Soldiers Once...and Young: Ia Drang: The Battle That Changed the War in Vietnam.* HarperPerennial, 1993.

Moore, Howard W. *Plowing My Own Furrow.* New York: W. W. Norton, 1985.

———. "Religious Persecution in America – A Communication." *The World Tomorrow,* May 1919.

Mosley, Don. "Jubilee Partners Report," Comer, GA, May 1991.

Muller, Bob. "A Veteran Speaks – Against the War," *The Fight for the Right to Know the Truth: A Study of the War in S.E. Asia Through the Pentagon Papers and Other Sources* (monograph). New York: The Student Assembly of Columbia University, 1971.

"Murder: Another CIA Manual Surfaces." *CounterPunch*, June 1–15, 1997.

Nhat Hanh, Thich. *Love in Action: Writings on Nonviolent Social Change.* Berkeley, CA: Parallax Press, 1993.

No Longer Enemies: Healing Wounds in Vietnam (video). A Citizen Soldier & Green Valley Media Production, 1996.

O'Brien, Tim. *The Things They Carried.* New York: Penguin Books, 1990.

The Panama Deception (video). Barbara Trent, director. 1992.

Peace is Every Step: Meditation in Action: The Life and Work of Thich Nhat Hanh (Video). Mystic Fire Video, April 1998.

Pentagon Papers, The: As Published by The New York Times. The New York Times, 1971.

Putz, Erna. *Against the Stream: Franz Jägerstätter, The Man who Refused to Fight for Hitler.* Translated by Michael Duggan. London: Pax Christi, n.d.

Radosh, Ronald. "Historian in the Service of Power." *The Nation,* August 6, 1977.

Reed, Paul, and Schwarz, Ted. *Kontum Diary: Captured Writings Bring Peace to a Vietnam Veteran.* Arlington, TX: The Summit Publishing Group, 1996.

The Reluctant Prophet (video). Spark Productions, Bart Gavigan, Director. n.d.

Sandy, Leo R. "JROTC: The Antithesis of Education," *The VFP Journal,* Spring 1997.

Seidenberg, Willa, and Short, William. *A Matter of Conscience: GI Resistance During the Vietnam War.* Andover, MA: Phillips Academy, Addison Gallery of American Art, 1991.

Sharples, Vivien. "Working Against Military Recruitment in High School." *Nonviolent Action,* no. 53 (Spring 1996).

Shesol, Jeff. *Mutual Contempt: Lyndon Johnson, Robert Kennedy, and the Feud That Defined a Decade.* New York: W.W. Norton, 1997.

Simons, Anna. Review of *Making the Corps* by Thomas E. Ricks. *The Christian Science Monitor,* December 15, 1997.

Signing Up: It's Your Choice (video). Tod Ensign, Citizen Soldier. n.d.

Spock, Benjamin, and Zimmerman, Mitchell. *Dr. Spock on Vietnam.* New York: Dell Publishing Co., 1968.

Stapp, Andy. *Up Against the Brass.* New York: Simon & Schuster, 1970.

Stokes, Anson Phelps. *Church and State in the United States, Vol. III.* New York: Harper & Brothers, 1950.

Terry, Wallace. *Bloods: An Oral History of the Vietnam War by Black Veterans.* New York: Ballantine Books, 1984.

Tolkien, J. R. R. *The Lord of the Rings.* Boston: Houghton Mifflin Co., 1965.

Trager, James, ed. *The People's Chronology: A Year-by-Year Record of Human Events from Prehistory to the Present.* New York: Holt, Rinehart & Winston, 1979.

Trauma and the Vietnam War Generation: Report of Findings from the National Vietnam Veterans Readjustment Study. New York: Brunner/Mazel, 1990.

Trujillo, Charley. *Soldados: Chicanos in Viet Nam.* San José, CA: Chusma House Publications, 1996.

Trumbo, Dalton. *Johnny Got His Gun.* New York: Bantam Books, 1988.

U.S. Congress. House. *Gulf War Veterans' Illnesses: VA, DOD Continue to Resist Strong Evidence Linking Toxic Causes to Chronic Health Effects.* 105th Congress, 1st Session, House Report 105–388, November 7, 1997.

Viereck, Jennifer, ed. *The Oil War Primer.* Nuremberg Actions, n.d.

"Vietnam Combat Stress: Linked to Many Diseases 20 Years Later," *Advance for Occupational Therapists,* November 24, 1997.

"Vietnam Veteran Gets Letter from Son of Soldier He Killed." AP, Rochester, IL, *Kingston Sunday Freeman*, August 10, 1997.

Vistica, Gregory L. "A Quiet War Over the Past: The Brass Battles Over Giving a Hero of My Lai a Medal." *Newsweek,* November 24, 1997.

Voices of Veterans (video). Veterans for Peace, Washington, DC. n.d.

Whitmore, Terry, as told to Richard Weber. *Memphis – Nam – Sweden: The Story of a Black Deserter.* Jackson, MS: University of Mississippi Press, 1997.

Winerip, Michael. "The Beauty of Beast Barracks." *The New York Times Magazine*, October 12, 1997, 46–53.

Worth the Price? (Video) Bruderhof Video Productions 1998. n.d.

Yant, Martin. *Desert Mirage: The True Story of the Gulf War.* Buffalo, New York: Prometheus Books, 1991.

Yolton, L. William (executive director, NISBCO, Washington, DC). Letter to Roy L. Piepenburg, July 24, 1995.

Zabelka, George. "Peace of Jesus Christ: Our Only Hope." Pax Christi 1985 (tape of speech obtained from Notre Dame University Archives, AO541).

Zahn, Gordon. *German Catholics and Hitler's Wars: A Study in Social Control.* Notre Dame, IN: University of Notre Dame Press, 1989.

———. *In Solitary Witness: The Life and Death of Franz Jägerstätter.* New York: Holt, Rinehart & Winston, 1964.

Zieglschmid, A. J. F. "The Martyrdom of Joseph and Michael Hofer" from *Das Klein-Geschichtsbuch der Hutterischen Brüder.* Translated by Franz Wiebe in *The Mennonite*, August 5, 1975, 454–455.

Zinn, Howard. *Declarations of Independence: Cross-Examining American Ideology.* New York: HarperPerennial, 1991.

———. *A People's History of the United States.* New York: The New Press, 1997.

Index

Other Titles from Plough

Seeking Peace
Notes and Conversations along the Way
Johann Christoph Arnold
Preface by Thich Nhat Hanh

Seeking Peace explores many facets of humankind's age-less search for peace. It plumbs a wealth of spiritual traditions and draws on the wisdom of some exceptional (and some very ordinary) people who have found peace in surprising places. **$20.00/£13.00**

Death Blossoms
Reflections from a Prisoner of Conscience
Mumia Abu-Jamal
Foreword by Cornel West

Short essays on nature and religion, politics, culture, and race from a celebrated journalist behind bars.
$12.00/£8.00

Seventy Times Seven
The Power of Forgiveness
Johann Christoph Arnold
Foreword by J. I. Packer

No matter how heavy the weight of our bitterness or despair, forgiveness is always possible. Indeed, Arnold writes, it is the only way out from under these burdens.
$13.00/£9.00

Salt and Light
Living the Sermon on the Mount
Eberhard Arnold
Foreword by Jürgen Moltmann

Arnold lays before us the most important choice of our lives – to live for Christ and his kingdom, or to live for ourselves. **$15.00/£10.00**